JAMES:
THANKS SO MUCH FOR YOUR
CONTRIBUTIONS TO THIS BOOK.
ENJOY!
BEST,
TOM

TIME IS MONEY!
THE CENTURY, RAINBOW,
AND STERN BROTHERS COMEDIES
OF JULIUS AND ABE STERN

Thomas J. Reeder

By Thomas Reeder
Foreword by Richard M Roberts
Afterword by Gilbert Sherman

BearManor
Media

Orlando, Florida

Published in the USA by
BearManor Media
1317 Edgewater Dr. #110
Orlando, FL 32804
www.BearManorMedia.com

Softcover Edition
ISBN: 978-1-62933-798-2

Printed in the United States of America

Table of Contents

Dedication   vii

Foreword by Richard M Roberts   ix

Acknowledgements   xv

Introduction   xix

Chapter 1 The Origins of L-Ko   1

Chapter 2 The Brothers Stern   11

Chapter 3 The Birth of Century Comedies   35

Chapter 4 Regrouping   61

Chapter 5 The Serials and Other Distractions   77

Chapter 6 Competing With Oneself (The 1919-1920 Season)   87

Chapter 7 A Girl and Her Dog (The 1920-1921 Season)   119

Chapter 8 The Return of Henry Lehrman, Albeit a Brief One   135
           (The 1921-1922 Season)

Chapter 9 Julius Stern, Carl Laemmle, and the Ties That Bind   159

Chapter 10 From Filler to Focus (The 1922-1923 Season)   175

Chapter 11 Too Many Cooks in the Kitchen (The 1923-1924 Season)   215

Chapter 12 The Star Series Plan Redux (The 1924-1925 Season)   243

Chapter 13 The Planting of a Seed (The 1925-1926 Season)   269

Chapter 14 Like a Phoenix Rising.... (The 1926-1927 Season)   297

Chapter 15 The Ascendancy of Snookums (The 1927-1928 Season)   335

Chapter 16 Decided Make Our Own Comedies   353
            (The 1928-1929 Season)

Chapter 17 From Here to Eternity   379

Chapter 18 C'est La Vie   397

Afterword by Gilbert Sherman   401

Filmography   403

Endnotes   523

Bibliography   543

Index   547

Dedication:

For Gil, who trusted me with his family's story

and

Susan, who made me laugh

"What is put on film must be as right as it can be the first time it is put on film. What one can do, of course, is retakes on the spot. And more retakes. And still more. Retakes use up film quickly, to be sure, but film stock is one of the negligible costs of film production. What retakes really use is time, which, as everyone knows (and no one better than movie people), is money."

Steven Bach
Final Cut (1985)

FOREWORD: WHY SHOULD WE CARE ABOUT THE STERN BROTHERS?
by Richard M Roberts

Hello There,

What you hold in your hands is another of those page-thick tomes with dusty old pictures and text about dusty old long gone people who once made funny films for other dusty old long gone people.

Now, it is unlikely that you've found this in one of the few still-existing book store shelves where you are perusing it with the potential perspicacity to perpetrate a possible purchase. If you are even looking at a printed copy (how some of you read those Kindle thingys is beyond my comprehension), it has likely arrived fresh out of the padded envelope pulled from the mailbox and your charge-card has been billed which means you are interested enough in books about long gone funny dead people to have made the effort.

Good for you, unless of course you are peering at this as you stand in front of an author's table at some film conventions' dealers room and Tom Reeder is sitting behind it looking up at you with a slightly nervous smile on his face hoping to make a sale so he doesn't have to lug all those heavy boxes of extra copies home again, in which case BUY THE DAMN BOOK FOR HEAVEN'S SAKE! People who write these things do not do it for the money, mainly because they get so little for it if they do, but they have mostly done it because they themselves wanted to see a book about these subjects and it looked like no one else was going to write one so what's a film historian to do? If you're not going to buy the book, put it down carefully now, don't bend the cover or crinkle or crumple any pages, give Tom a nice smile, and move away quickly so someone who is going to actually put their money down has a chance!

In any event, and however you are scanning these words, paper or kindling, my extrasensory perception can feel through your fingers holding the book or device that you are experiencing a two-fold trepidation. First, I hear you cry, "Is this a good book?".

Of course it is, I don't write forewords to lousy books! Next question!

Secondly, and this brings us to the title of this foreword: "Why should we care about the Stern Brothers?"

Ahhh----now you ask a fair question, and one that is being asked more and more about anyone who made films more than a hundred years ago, from Charlie Chaplin on down, and to many walking and talking on the planet today it is harder and harder to make that explanation, even when you have enough of their work around to *show* them why they should care.

It is unfortunately an absolute fact that much of the tastes and attitudes of film history buffery is shaped by what actually survives and is available to be seen, thus with only a frankly fraction of the large output of Silent Film actually coming down to us, obviously some names, even very important ones, have remained in obscurity because their work today has not been able to be reassessed or rediscovered. At-the-time well-known Directors like George Loane Tucker or George Melford would probably be more and better thought of if more of their films actually existed and could be seen by the general populace, even that equally small fraction that care about Silent Film at all.

In Silent Film Comedy History it is no different; for years the cinematic cognoscenti knew or acknowledged few if any comedians or comic filmmakers beyond the "Big Three" and perhaps a few other names officially certified as worth viewing by James Agee, but even among that select list, the likes of Harold Lloyd or Harry Langdon were less paid attention to simply because their output, though it had mostly survived, was not generally available for viewing, especially in the pre-home video days, so even those major names were not discussed so much indeed.

And below that haughty short list, the literally hundreds of funsters working in the Comedy Film Industry during the Movies' Golden Age were neither mentioned, revered, or even known by what was passing for film expertise in the following decades. Reasons were many: myopic snobbery was one aspect, yet another bare truth was that so much of the work was not available to be seen, much or even whole filmographies of some comics, heck, even some comedy producers, were wiped off the table by the many varying vagaries of time that demolish such things: The Fox Sunshine Comedies, the early Vitagraph Comedies of John Bunny, Mr. And Mrs. Sidney Drew, Lloyd Hamilton's prime work as a comedy star, all were indeed vagaries, even to the more expert experts, represented more by stills and contemporary reviews than picture that moved. How could their worth be assessed, deemed important or dismissed, without the proper proof, even if they had much press and review at the time?

So, the canon was compiled on what could be seen, with occasional marvels and over-hopeful praising of some missing titles in the known filmographies, and it meant that even these later-compiled histories, no matter how thoroughly researched at the time, were not complete, were not that foolish word used by the seriously OCD----*definitive.*

The Fox Sunshines were major studio comedy shorts, starring known comedy talent and made by craftsmen who went on and made quality work elsewhere that did survive and earned their place in the histories and hearts of the fans. Lloyd Hamilton remained a shadowy figure, despite being a major comedy star and praised by the likes of Buster Keaton, but the actual quality of his work could only be judged on his earliest and later work that had survived destruction. The early Vitagraph comedies went in an entirely different direction from the slapstick of Keystone and its imitators, more situational and character-driven comedy, and its influence spread over to those who later wanted to move away from surreal grotesquery to the more humane humor of everyday living, but who could really realize that when only little scattered bits of it seemed to be around?

And so, with little or no footage to see and study on these films, the proclamations were passed down on what was worthwhile and valuable, and with little or no footage they got little or no mention. Yet gradually, over just the last few decades, a new group of film historians, ones who found it more fun and interesting to watch old funny films by old funny dead people than to ruminate over depressing never-ending pretensions from the likes of Carl Dreyer or Abel Gance, began to venture out into the uncharted territory, and discover more and more about a large and much untapped genré. This led to the formation of strange collectives with odd names like the Silent Comedy Mafia or the Al Joy Fan Club, and the creation of annual get-togethers like the Slapsticon where rare goodies were unearthed, viewed, and rediscovered.

Then these Festivals spun off more research, more digging, and the recovery and release of many fabulous funnies from the past for all to see. Light was finally being shined on those forgotten and-----to use another unfortunate and greatly abused buzzword of the fans: "lost" little areas of silent comedy film history. Gradually, some of these shadowy figures on the mountaintop started to come back down to ground and solidify their substance, their long forgotten laughs mined, dusted, polished, and put out to display again to tickle funnybones anew. Once again---they *existed,* and slowly began to elbow their way back amidst and among their contemporaries.

Thomas Reeder is one of those Silent Comedy Mafiosi, and he has done well in illuminating several dark and dingy corners of film and film comedy history, with excellent and recommended volumes on Henry "Pathe" (aka Suicide) Lehrman and Ben Pivar, names that resonate not with many film aficionados for various reasons, not that they necessarily should, but Lehrman was indeed another unsung figure in silent film comedy with too few movies available (a lot of those Fox Sunshines were his) to show us the real talent for truly wild and surreal silent comedy that he possessed. Tom gave both Mr. Lehrman and Mr. Pivar the bios and credit they deserve, and now it is Abe and Julius Stern's turn to have their memory updated among us.

It's Tom Reeder's job to give you their life histories, but my ESP is still vibrating with the remnants of your second question, all fine and dandy that these guys are getting a mention, but is what they actually created actually any good and worthy? Well, one thing one has learned from screening many silent and early sound comedies for actual audiences (truly an endangered species these days, even before it was life threatening to converge in groups), is that whatever the nonsensical distinctions there are in so many internerd film fan arguments in the "my comedian can beat up your comedian!" chat threads, the endless and pointless attempts to list and classify a "hierarchy" of comedians (Fatty Arbuckle should be Number Four of the Big Three, not Harry Langdon! Is Billy Franey the 2,647[th] comedy genius, or should he be 2,649?), if a comedy gets the laughs, it has basically succeeded in what it has set out to do. When a Clyde Cook comedy gets the same number or more laughs than the Keaton comedy shown just before it, can it really be considered the lesser of the two? Realistically, one does have to consider that Charlie Chaplin and Soupy Sales were essentially in the same line of work.

In 2005, at a special Slapsticon screening at the National Gallery of Art in Washington D. C., the Century Comedy TELEVISION GEORGE (1928) starring Syd Saylor was shown to an audience of around 500, the majority being the standard tourists and patrons of the Museum who probably had as much idea who Syd Saylor was as Harold Lloyd: it killed. Just happy to rest their feet for a spell and catch a free movie, this audience let the two-reeler work its magic, nearly eighty years after its release, not caring in the slightest what position Syd Saylor held in anyone's hierarchy. In 2008, Slapsticon screened BUSTER'S PICNIC (1927) starring Arthur Trimble as Buster Brown, Doreen Turner, and Pete the Pup, once again, the audience loved it, if perhaps appreciating the fine pit bull performance of Petey over the somewhat anemic Mr. Trimble, but no matter, the laughs were loudly there, the film succeeded.

So yeah, they're not bad, like anyone's comedy short series, they have their ups and downs, but these were solid performers doing good work. The actors who worked in the Comedy Film Industry were not only seasoned professionals, they worked in a genré that entailed a bit more risky workday than showing up for your average six-reel teacup society melodrama. When I introduce a program of silent comedies, I frequently say to that endangered audience, "These people risked their lives on a pretty much daily basis for your entertainment, so you damn well better appreciate it." I doubt Elliot Dexter or Marie Doro, or even their stand-ins, ever had to hang by wires, off buildings, or were forced to work with adult chimpanzees, or orangutans------or lions.

The comedies of the Stern Brothers are important because a lot of well-known members of the Comedy Film Industry parked their cars at the L-KO/Century lot over the years, many familiar faces we would know from other studios' films: Alice Howell, Hughey Mack, Bert Roach, James Finlayson, Neal Burns, Jimmie Adams, Cliff Bowes, Bud Jamison, Harry Sweet, Blanche Payson, Jack Cooper, Tiny Sandford, Max Asher, Arthur Lake, Pete the Pup, Charles King, Syd Saylor, names that any reasonably immersed film comedy fan will recognize from other places, other films. The Sterns even created a few important stars of their own, especially Baby Peggy, aka the amazing Diana Serra Cary, whose own personal wisdom and stamina allowed her to win the tontine and become our final link to that era until she just recently left us at the age of 101, a woman who had lived a life well-lived, even if she had become a has-been before the age of puberty, she was literally the last person on Earth one could ask for personal reminiscence of working with Alf Goulding or Blue Washington. Diana Serra Cary was the amazing exception (along with---perhaps unfortunately, Mickey Rooney) of the general child-star rule in lacking life-longevity, something frequently shared by many movie moppets (realize the sobering thought that Hal Roach outlived more than half of the Our Gang casts), including the Stern Brothers' other child-stars Arthur Trimble and Sunny McKeen.

So once again, yeah, Abe and Julius Stern are worthy of remembrance, and their films are still important simply because they *are funny*, and the people like Tom Reeder, myself, and others in the Silent Comedy Mafia will continue to do what we can to promote and present these funny films because we understand that laughter is precious, these days, *very precious*. In these damn unfunny times, every giggle needs to saved, spread, shared, and savored, no one seems to be creating much new comedy that is indeed worthy these days, it makes the large gift this generation of laugh makers gave us in the first half of the Twentieth Century all that more meaningful. If you have this book, that's a good sign that this sort of work may be all that is needed to send you out to look for, learn, laugh and love these films, if you can find them (look in your attics, basements, and barns. You never know, and that's where they seem to turn up, and call me if you find any, I'm generous.), they really do make the World a bit more tolerable.

That's it-----that's all I can tell you----go and read your book then---this is a foreword so, Forward and Onward!

RICHARD M ROBERTS

Somewhere in Arizona

November 2020

Acknowledgements

My original goal for this book was quite modest. As initially intended, this was to be a detailed chronological checklist of the two-reel shorts of the Stern brothers—Julius and Abe—and their Century, Rainbow, and Stern Brothers Comedies, 1917-1929. This checklist was to be accompanied by a monograph about those studios and their histories, to place the films in proper perspective.

Fate and good fortune quickly altered those plans. While searching for an image of the White Front Theatre—future Universal owner Carl Laemmle's original exhibition outlet in Chicago, circa 1906—this led me to the Chicagology web site hosted by Terry Gregory. At the bottom of a piece about Laemmle, I found a posted comment by a fellow named Gilbert Sherman, who said he was Julius Stern's grandson. Needless to say, this caught my attention. Attempts to contact both Gregory and Sherman hit a dead end, so I contacted a Chicago-based friend named Steve Zalusky to see if he, by some remote chance, knew Terry.

"I'm a member of the Chicagology group," responded Steve, "Terry and I and a number of group members met at Manny's Deli years ago to share photos and other memorabilia about Chicago in the 19th Century."

Bingo! To make a long story just a bit less long, Steve contacted Terry in Hawaii, obtained Gilbert Sherman's email address, and forwarded same to me. This opened the door to what would soon become a wonderful friendship with Gil.

Gil is the Stern family historian, and graciously shared family history, remembrances, and personal photos over the course of the following year. This wealth of new information resulted in an expansion of my book from a straight-forward history of the studios and their films, to a more personal, in-depth look at the life of Julius Stern and, to a lesser extent, his brother Abe. Armed with whatever information Gil was able to provide (which was voluminous), I expanded my personal research to fill in the gaps and, in many instances, connect the dots. Without Gil's considerable contributions, the book otherwise would have been a mere skeleton of its current self.

Other Stern descendants chipped in as well, with additional tidbits of information and still photographs. These descendants included Abe's grandson Andrew Stern, Abe's great-granddaughter Rachael Rose-Stern, and one of Julius's daughters, Miriam Marie Stern Ariel. Julius's other daughter, the late Susan Stern Sherman, was the source of many detailed stories about life with her dad in her unpublished memoir, *Remembering*, written shortly after Julius's death in 1977. Susan, it should be noted, was Gil's mother.

Numerous others contributed, in ways both large and modest. Along with Gil, film historians Steve Massa and Richard M. Roberts read through the manuscript, and offered suggestions and corrections that were readily and gratefully embraced.

Susan Wiley Forbes-Eppler, great-niece of Century comedienne Wanda Wiley, provided heretofore unknown detailed biographical information about Wanda's life during the years before and after her brief period of fame working for the Sterns. Mark Jungheim provided filmed interviews with Bartine Burkett, a once popular comedienne during the 1920s at Century and elsewhere, along with a number of photographs from his personal collection.

Marc Wanamaker, of Bison Archives, contributed as well, but in a rather roundabout fashion. His detailed notes and photographs involving the Sterns and their studios eventually ended up in Gil's hands, so it's difficult at this time to discern what actually came from Gil's family's holdings, or originated with Marc. Since everything came to me through Gil, I have used my best judgment in assigning credit based on the contents of each image. I apologize in advance for any image that has been incorrectly credited.

Special thanks to Richard M. Roberts and Gilbert Sherman for efforts beyond the call of duty. Richard provided this book's thoughtful, generous, and oft-times witty Foreword, while Gil provided his heartfelt remembrances of his grandfather in the book's Afterword. I can't thank them both enough for interrupting their otherwise busy schedules to take time out to provide words and thoughts for this book.

I attempted to view as many Century, Rainbow, and Stern Brothers Comedies as possible in preparation for this book, but the COVID-19 pandemic of 2020-2021 impacted those attempts. In spite of that rather daunting impediment, I was able to view nearly fifty of those that survive via some early visits to film archives, supplemented by showings at the annual Mostly Lost workshop at the Library of Congress's Culpeper facility, and the earlier Slapsticon conventions in Arlington, Virginia. Additional viewing opportunities were a result of the generous efforts of others to provide digitized copies of films, along with the occasional Sterns film that has made it into commercial release on DVD. I want to thank Rob Stone, Rachel Del Gaudio, and George Willeman of the Library of Congress's Moving Image Section of the Motion Picture, Broadcasting and Recorded Sound Division. Additional thanks to Zoran Sinobad of the Library of Congress's Moving Image Research Center, as well as Ashley Swinnerton at the Museum of Modern Art's Film Study Center. Other sources for Sterns' shorts include Dino Everett at the USC School of Cinematic Arts Hugh M. Hefner Moving Image Archive, Ben Model and his Undercrank Productions, Dave Stevenson and his Looser Than Loose Productions, and videos provided by Bill Sprague, Dave Glass, and Mark Johnson.

A book about films—especially films that are rarely seen, inaccessible to the public at large, or are believed to be "lost"—demands the inclusion of as many images from those films as feasible, to provide readers with a glimpse of the actors, settings, and situations taking place in the films mentioned in the text. Images for use as illustration were graciously provided from a large number of individuals. Dr. Robert James Kiss, Mark Johnson, Richard M. Roberts, and Jim Kerkhoff opened up their vaults and were all extremely generous in sharing their holdings. Additional images were provided by Steve Massa and Sam Gill, along with Michael G. Ankerich, Rob Arkus, the late Robert Birchard, Ralph Celentano, James L. Freedman, Diana R. Garcia (Heritage Auctions), Paul E. Gierucki, Michael Hayde, Tommie Hicks, Nelson Hughes, Elif Rongen-Kaynakci (Netherlands's EYE Filmmuseum), Deborah and Christina Lane, Drina Mohacsi (YoungHollywoodHoF. com), Lisa Robins, Steve Rydzewski, Kay Shackleton (SilentHollywood.com), Marguerite Sheffler, and, as before, the anonymous individual who prefers to remain as such. Additional thanks to Bruce Calvert, David Denton, Jason Engle, Rob Farr, Ed Hulse, Peter Minton, Frank Thompson, and the always-reliable Ned Comstock at USC's Cinematic Arts Library.

And as always, a big tip of the hat to Ben Ohmart and his BearManor Media publishing company, my go-to publisher for books of this sort. For the past two decades, Ben has provided a much needed outlet for writers and researchers to commit our findings to the printed page, for the interested casual reader's enjoyment and, just as important, for future study and reference by historians. Ben's catalog is staggering in its breadth, and I sincerely hope that he and his company prosper for decades to come. Additional thanks to this book's editor at BearManor Media, prolific author and editor Stone Wallace. Stone and I hit it off immediately, and I knew I was in good hands with him from day one.

Lastly, many thanks to my wife Barbara, whose patience and quiet support of a husband who spends countless hours hunched over his laptop, mumbling to himself, is truly humbling. I wish I could promise her that it will get better once this book is published, but who am I fooling? She deserves some sort of award.

If I've failed to acknowledge anyone else who contributed in any fashion whatsoever, I offer up my sincerest apologies; feel free to give me hell next time our paths cross.

Introduction

Century Comedies: Only the most dogged of silent comedy enthusiasts have seen any of the films from this studio, or are even aware of their existence. Ditto for Rainbow Comedies and Stern Brothers Comedies.

Unlike Mack Sennett's Keystone Comedies, which practically everyone of a certain age has heard of, these three brand names are probably meaningless to most, aside from the ever-shrinking coterie of silent short comedy devotees. And that's not surprising, given the lack of name performers populating their ever-changing roster of so-called "stars," and the dearth of published information about them.

Numerous volumes have been written about Sennett and his studios and, to a lesser extent, competitor Hal Roach and his studios. Throw in the biographies and/ or autobiographies of Charles Chaplin, Harold Lloyd, Buster Keaton, Harry Langdon, Roscoe Arbuckle, Laurel and Hardy, and a handful of other comedy greats and you could easily fill a couple of bookcases. And that's all fine and well deserved, but what about so many other second tier comedy studios and comedians? Shouldn't someone research and write about Al Christie and his lengthy career, or that of Jack White and his comedies for Educational? Or, for that matter, any number of other smaller, short-lived studios and brands that popped up and disappeared shortly thereafter, like a filmland game of Whack-a-Mole. As for the comedians, most of the familiar names have been covered, but what about the other, lesser known inhabitants of the comedy industry, fellows like Hank Mann, Jack Cooper, and Jimmie Adams, or comediennes like Gale Henry and Dot Farley. Noted film historian Steve Massa has gone a long way towards bringing the members of this unheralded group to light in biographical sketches in his two volumes, *Lame Brains and Lunatics* (BearManor Media, 2013) and *Slapstick Divas* (BearManor Media, 2017), and perhaps that's all the more recognition that some of them deserve.

Call me a champion of the underdog, but I've always been fascinated by the individuals and companies that populate this cinematic netherworld, which led me to research and write my previous biography, *Mr. Suicide: Henry "Pathé" Lehrman and the Birth of Silent Comedy* (BearManor Media, 2017). Lehrman's partner in his L-Ko Komedy Kompany, which launched back in 1914, was a fellow named Abe Stern, and by 1916, Lehrman had sold his interest in the studio to Abe and Abe's older brother, Julius. The Sterns continued that company until 1919, creating a sister company—Century Comedies—in 1917 that eventually replaced L-Ko. What little I learned about the Sterns while researching Lehrman percolated in the dark recesses of my mind, and with the completion of that book I couldn't resist the siren call compelling me to look further into their lives and comedy brands. Hence, the book you are now holding in your hands.

There were, arguably, four phases to the Stern brothers' output via these three brands. Phase One consisted solely of the comedies of Alice Howell, who was the primary reason for the creation of the Century brand in the first place.

Phase Two followed Howell's departure from Century, a hodge-podge of comedies featuring children and animals and, on occasion, a comedian freed up from having to share the limelight with either of the former. Slapstick abounded during this phase, but with only a few exceptions the human actors of voting age went almost as quickly as they had come; the turnover at Century was considerable.

Phase Three was a transitional period, more focused, with a shift to situational comedy. A return to the Sterns' so-called "Star System," it featured a comparatively consistent stable of stars (or the Sterns' version of "stars"), including the likes of Wanda Wiley, Al Alt, Edna Marian, and Eddie Gordon.[1]

And then there was Phase Four, with the studio—now reinvented as Stern Brothers Comedies—making the wholesale shift and commitment to comedy series based on popular comic strips and their characters.

So why aren't the Stern brothers and their films better known? L-Ko, initially under Abe's oversight and later with Julius's contributions, released two hundred eighty-four comedies over the six years of its existence, while the combined total of Century, Rainbow, and Stern Brothers comedies totaled five hundred eighty releases from 1917 to 1929. That's a combined total of eight hundred sixty-four comedies over a fifteen year period; one would think that that sort of prodigious output would be remembered, or at least acknowledged, in some of the numerous film histories that have appeared over the intervening years—but they haven't. There are several reasons for their comparative obscurity.

First of all, their films were populated by a grab-bag of actors and actresses, only a few of whom had any sort of name recognition back in the day, and almost none a century later. The L-Ko's had a few participants whose popularity flowed and ebbed, like Billie Ritchie, Mack Swain, and Gale Henry, but hardly anyone today remembers these comedians. The Century Comedies' biggest name was Baby Peggy Montgomery, with Alice Howell a close second, but they too have been relegated to the footnotes of history. As for the Stern Brothers Comedies, there was practically no one of any sort of note aside from Syd Saylor, who had a lengthy career thereafter as a western sidekick, remembered today more as a face than a name, if remembered at all. And, of course, Lawrence "Snookums" McKeen, whose overnight fame evaporated almost as quickly as it had appeared—and we should be thankful for that. The Sterns' cost-effective approach was to populate their films with individuals who they thought had some potential, be it from vaudeville, the stage, or with prior limited film experience and exposure. They were hired and turned over to the studios' directors and gag men, then given the chance to either swim, or sink. Many of them sank.

Another reason is the lack of survival of these comedies. This can be attributed to a large degree to the loss of most of the films, through intentional studio house-cleaning for silver reclamation, outright disposal, unintentional nitrate decomposition, or "Act-of-God" vault fires. A few that survive were those released in smaller gauge format for home use, but a perusal of the film catalogues of Mogull's, Eastin-Phelan, and its Blackhawk offspring reveals an almost total absence of Stern entries, the few offered paling in comparison to the dozens of films from Sennett, Roach, and other, even smaller companies. (The *Kodascope Library of Motion Pictures* in 16mm, it should be noted, was an exception, with more than two dozen of the Sterns' comedies included.) Lack of star power and name recognition was likely a contributor to this imbalance. A few of the Sterns' other films survived in foreign archives, some of which have been repatriated to stateside archives. Only a subset of these films is accessible to researchers and the public at large, the latter group in all likelihood unaware of the archives' existence.

Some of the early books by noted historian Kalton C. Lahue provided readers with a lot of forgotten information about silent comedies and their stars, and were instrumental in sparking interest in these among a new generation born long after the films had faded from view. Unfortunately, the Sterns and their various brands barely warranted a mention. In his *World of Laughter* (University of Oklahoma Press, 1966), Lahue provides some cursory background on L-Ko, but even less on Century, focusing primarily, and briefly, on the later comic strip series of the Stern Brothers Comedies. In *Clown Princes and Court Jesters* (A.S. Barnes and Company, 1970), co-authored with Sam Gill, Alice Howell's chapter mentions L-Ko, with Century named as little more than an afterthought. Other entries on Lee Moran, Max Asher, and Jimmy Finlayson—the latter two very briefly and only sporadically affiliated with Century—fail to mention the brand at all. As for Walter Kerr's lovingly written *The Silent Clowns* (Alfred A. Knopf, 1975), neither the Sterns nor their brands receive any mention whatsoever. As a result, awareness of the Sterns and their studios was put on a back shelf and left to gather dust. Perhaps the best account of Century was provided by Glenn Mitchell in his *A-Z of Silent Film Comedy* (BT Batsford, 1998), although only a brief single paragraph in length. Even Neal Gabler's excellent *An Empire of Their Own* (Anchor Books/Doubleday, 1988), which included lengthy and detailed pieces on Carl Laemmle, lumped an unnamed Julius among "other family members." Which isn't surprising, since Laemmle's authorized biography of 1931, John Drinkwater's *The Life and Adventures of Carl Laemmle*, had nary a mention of Julius Stern's considerable contributions to the Imp and Universal studios from their inception into the early 1920s.

Some of the blame for the Sterns' quick fade from memory can be attributed to the Sterns themselves. Julius was a tireless self-promoter, but with only a few exceptions his interviews, articles, and promotional pieces were consigned primarily to the trades, away from the eyes of the public at large. And while a portion of the filmgoing public of the 1920s recognized the Century and Stern Brothers brand names, these individuals tended to reside in rural areas where Universal's output predominated. Universal relied on smaller, independent venues to show their films since they did not have the luxury of a chain of theatres of their own; exhibition in urban areas was the rarer exception. The Century and Stern Brothers brands' output aside, Julius and Abe were essentially non-entities in the minds of filmgoers. With the coming of sound and the brothers' retreat from filmmaking, those promotional releases to the trades disappeared just as quickly as the films had from the screens. From that time on, Julius shunned any sort of film-related public appearances, and never gave any more interviews about his years in the industry. As for Abe, he always took a back seat to Julius, allowing his older brother to be the face and voice of the studio. Comments from Abe in the trades were few and far between, and from the 1930s up until his death Abe effectively disappeared from the public scene.

Lastly, and perhaps the most critical reason for the lack of awareness of Julius Stern and, to a lesser extent, his brother Abe, falls at the feet of Carl Laemmle himself. From the sound era on, Laemmle adopted a tight-lipped policy about any sort of acknowledgment regarding Julius Stern's considerable contributions to the development and growth of Imp and Universal. These contributions, and Laemmle's ongoing reliance on Julius, will be detailed in the chapters that follow, along with the causes of their eventual estrangement in the late 1920s. You'll find nary a word about any of this, or about Stern himself in

Laemmle's authorized biography of 1931, John Drinkwater's *The Life and Adventures of Carl Laemmle*. Had Laemmle been magnanimous enough to give credit where credit was due, Stern's place in early film history would have been documented and available to future researchers and historians. As it stands now, however, one has to dig deep for this stuff, and take many of Laemmle's long accepted claims and assertions with the proverbial grain of salt.

This book is a humble attempt to redress that historical imbalance. I hope to provide an impartial and objective account of the Sterns' various studios and their numerous films, as well as their lives before, during, and after their impressive run as purveyors of lower budget, but frequently inventive and wildly entertaining cinematic fare. I now present the Stern Brothers.

The original Keystone and Broncho studio, 1912. Courtesy of Sam Gill.

Chapter 1: The Origins of L-Ko

The Century Comedies of Julius and Abe Stern weren't created out of thin air. They were instead an offshoot of the L-Ko Komedy Kompany, which had been in business since 1914. And while Julius Stern would later attempt some revisionist history by claiming that upon relocating from the East to West Coast "he formed his own company called the L-Ko,"[1] nothing could be further from the truth. Rather, the L-Ko was the brainchild of silent comedy pioneer Henry Lehrman and, if either of the Stern brothers should have made such a claim, the honor would have gone to Abe, one of Lehrman's original partners.

Born in 1881 in the town of Sambor, then part of the Austro-Hungarian Empire, twenty-five-year old Lehrman emigrated to the U.S. in December 1906. Within three years he had landed an on-again, off-again position with New York's Biograph company, appearing primarily in small supporting parts and assisting his new friend Mack Sennett in developing filmable scenarios. During some breaks with Biograph, Lehrman also held positions with the Kinemacolor Company of America, as well as the Independent Moving Picture Company (aka Imp) where he would serve as a scenario editor and, fortuitously, direct a short comedy.

At the end of 1912, Lehrman headed out to the West Coast to join up with his buddy Sennett and the latter's newly-formed Keystone Film Company. Here Lehrman would frequently appear before the camera and, more importantly, be put to work as a director, guiding such individuals as Ford Sterling, Mabel Normand, Charles Chaplin, and Roscoe Arbuckle through their comedic paces.

In early 1914, Lehrman and Sterling left Keystone to helm their own Sterling Comedies in partnership with Fred Balshofer, for release through Universal. This relationship didn't last long. Having a taste of "freedom" and now finally receiving recognition for his filmic

1

contributions, Lehrman approached Universal head Carl Laemmle about creating his own comedy brand independent of Sterling, with whom he was frequently at odds. Laemmle agreed, and the result was the L-Ko Motion Picture Company, the "L-Ko" for "Lehrman Knock-Out."

Incorporated in Los Angeles on July 22, 1914, Lehrman had four fellow stockholders in this venture, likely there at Laemmle's insistence to keep an eye on things, and to provide a quick cash infusion to get the studio up and running. They were Isadore Bernstein, Sam Behrendt, Alfred P. Hamberg, and Laemmle's brother-in-law Abe Stern.

Isadore Bernstein was the general manager of Universal's West Coast studios. Sam Behrendt was a wealthy former real estate tycoon who had made his fortune selling studio insurance policies, considered a big risk in those early days of the industry. Alfred P. Hamberg was a former newspaperman, theatrical manager, and most recently the manager of a New York movie theatre. And Abe Stern, the younger of Carl Laemmle's two brothers-in-law with whom he would have business relations, was the manager of several film distribution exchanges. Only Stern, with "considerable experience in the business end of the motion picture business,"[2] would take an active part in the new studio's operations, serving as business manager.

Henry Lehrman, circa 1914. Courtesy of Museum of Modern Art/Film Stills Archive.

L-Ko's base of operations would be the former home of Universal. Located at 6100 Sunset Boulevard on the southwest corner of Gower Street and Sunset, the premises was in the process of being vacated as part of Laemmle's consolidation of operations in the newly-built Universal City. Bernstein had a hundred foot square stage hastily erected so that filming could commence upon the arrival of Lehrman and his new employees.

Lehrman assembled a stock company to star in his initial comedies, with former British music hall comedian Billie Ritchie as its star. Ritchie was supported by heavyweight Henry Bergman, Gertrude Selby, and Eva Nelson in the initial releases, with Louise Orth brought on shortly thereafter. Former Keystone comic Hank Mann was part of this early group as well, along with Peggy Pearce, formerly with Keystone and Sterling. It wasn't long before Alice Howell, Frank "Fatty" Voss, Gene Rogers, and Harry Gribbon came on board, and by 1916 Raymond Griffith, Lucille Hutton, Billy Bevan, Reggie Morris, Phil Dunham, Billy Armstrong, Dave Morris, and Charles Winninger were all added to the payroll, if only in some instances for short periods of time.

Lehrman directed the company's first few films, including the premiere release *Love and Surgery* (released October 25, 1914) and its follow-up *Partners in Crime* (November 1, 1914), but he quickly beefed up the directorial ranks with the addition of Harry Edwards, Rube Miller, and John G. Blystone.

L-Ko's first release, *Love and Surgery* (October 25, 1914), directed by Henry Lehrman.
Billie Ritchie wields a really big mallet. Courtesy of Library of Congress.

Over the next two years directors David Kirkland, Craig Hutchinson, and Noel Smith were engaged as well. New comedies were released each Sunday, but it wasn't long before the enthusiastic acceptance of the L-Ko's by exhibitors and patrons alike prompted a twice-a-week release. 1915 opened with the arrival of the additional Wednesday offering, and seventy-five films would be released that same year. Along with running the place and micro-managing all of his directors' output, Lehrman would occasionally step behind the camera for his three-reel "Specials," which included *After Her Millions*, *Silk Hose and High Pressure* (both 1915), and *For the Love of Mike and Rosie* (1916). He would act in each of these films as well as direct.

For the Love of Mike and Rosie (1916), a Lehrman-directed three-reel "Special." Left-to-right: Bert Roach, Eva Nelson (background), Louise Orth, Harry Russell sans hair, and Charles Inslee with top hat. The fellow in the window unidentified. Courtesy of Steve Massa.

By mid-1915 three of Lehrman's fellow trustees were no longer a part of L-Ko. Alfred Hamberg had left to direct for Dallas, Texas's Southern Feature Film Association soon after L-Ko's incorporation. Isadore Bernstein had severed ties with Universal to set up his short-lived Bernstein Film Productions, notable primarily for introducing Stan Laurel to filmgoers in *Nuts in May* (1917). As for Sam Behrendt, the whole endeavor seemed to have been a mere lark for him, opening some additional doors to fraternize with the industry's elite.[3] Only Abe Stern remained in the seemingly thankless job of business manager, struggling to keep the company financially afloat by ensuring the release schedules were adhered to.

Production still from *Cupid in a Hospital* (1915), featuring cast, crew, and visiting executives. Left-to-right seated: Gertrude Selby, Abe Stern, Carl Laemmle, Louise Orth, unknown. Standing: Hank Mann on crutches, Billie Ritchie with bandaged head, Alice Howell behind Stern, Eva Nelson behind Laemmle, director Henry Lehrman with bowtie, and Rube Miller at right with goatee. Courtesy of Marc Wanamaker and Bison Archives.

Victor Heerman, who joined L-Ko shortly after it opened as Lehrman's assistant, had this to say about Abe's stress level during a period where Lehrman was physically incapacitated:

> Abe is saying to me, "What are we going to do? What are we going to do? We need to get these pictures off." He was upset because if your picture didn't leave for New York Tuesday night, there would be no payroll in Los Angeles Saturday morning. Those on the East Coast would look at the thing, wire the money to the bank, and the checks on the West Coast would be okayed. "We can get them out," I said. Just to keep him quiet.[4]

To that end, Abe would reward—or should I say *bribe*—Heerman to get the product out the door:

> Abe would give me twenty-five dollars a reel for every picture I made. He says, "Don't ever tell Henry. Don't ever tell Henry."[5]

It wasn't all studio-bound work for Abe, however, and he was still able to make the occasional business trip back to New York. His new-found wealth called to him, and he took an understandable interest in material things. "Abe Stern, manager of the L-Ko films," wrote the *Los Angeles Times*, "blew in from New York a few days ago, bringing with him a whole repertoire of new clothes, which promise to make him the Beau Brummell of filmland. He moved in and out of several suits yesterday, but dwelt for the most part in his white linen, garnished with a tasty Panama."[6] And it didn't end there: "Abe Stern will be in Bradstreet's before long if he keeps on buying automobiles," wrote *Variety* a year or so later.[7] The fruits of his labors.

Abe Stern seated in rear of his chauffeur-driven limousine. Courtesy of Rachael Rose-Stern.

L-Ko's star comedian, of course, was Billie Ritchie, but Hank Mann offered some stiff competition, appearing in more than two dozen comedies by the end of 1915. Of the studio's female performers, Alice Howell was the standout. A rough-and-tumble comedian who would do most anything for a laugh, her filmic characters stood in stark contrast to those of Selby, who tended to play the love interest, to those of the more elegant and fashionable Orth, and to the fiery-tempered housewives played by Nelson. Howell made the rounds of the studio's numerous directors, but by mid-1916 had settled in with director John Blystone, who helmed all but two of her films from *A Busted Honeymoon* on through the end of the year. So popular were Howell's films that three of them—*The Great Smash*, *Tillie's Terrible Tumble*, and *Alice in Society* (all 1916)—were released in three reels, a length heretofore reserved for the Lehrman-directed "Specials."

L-Ko's *Under the Table* (1915), directed by John G. Blystone. Hank Mann, victorious, Eva Nelson, crying, and Reggie Morris with arm around Gertrude Selby, seated at right. Courtesy of Steve Massa.

Lehrman had a great success on his hands with the L-Ko brand, and by April 1916 had leased the balance of the old Universal studio at Gower and Sunset. Offices were moved to those formerly occupied by the Universal executives, and four directors were at work.[8] While the bulk of the studio's output was of one- and two-reel lengths, with the very occasional three-reeler thrown into the mix, Lehrman boldly announced in June 1916 his plans to film a five-reel comedy. This was, perhaps, in response to the success of Mack Sennett's Keystone feature-length *Tillie's Punctured Romance* from late 1914. To be titled *The Mirth of a Nation*, a title for which he had just paid the unheard of sum of $500 to author H.H. Van Loan, it appeared that Lehrman was ready to take his studio to the next level.[9] And then, seemingly out of nowhere, it was announced that on July 8, 1916 Lehrman had sold all of his shares in L-Ko.[10]

Billie Ritchie and Henry Lehrman on their return from New York, January 1916.
Courtesy of Lisa Robins.

This came as a surprise to the rest of the industry, but it is likely that Lehrman's departure had been agreed upon months earlier. Back at the end of 1915 it was reported that Lehrman was returning to Hollywood from a trip to New York where he was "arranging details in his contract with the Universal Film Mfg. Company."[11] If mutually agreeable terms had not been arrived at, the split may have been decided at that time with a handshake. Lehrman's departure, after all, was almost two years to the date of the company's incorporation, and the announcement of that five-reel feature may have been a separate agreement reached in the interim.

There are several possible explanations that would explain this parting of ways in spite of the company's success. Lehrman's personality may have had something to do with it, alienating Laemmle and his ongoing support of L-Ko with its current leadership. Then again, Laemmle was notoriously tight with a buck, and Lehrman may have rankled at the continuous penny-pinching. Or perhaps, with the apparent success of L-Ko under his belt, Lehrman's talents may have become a more valuable commodity, and the prospect of a new comedy brand with a company having deeper pockets than Universal's—like Fox—may have played into it.

Hank Mann and Billie Ritchie ready to do battle in the Lehrman-directed *The Death of Simon LeGree* (1915) That's Eva Nelson holding the baby, and Harry Russell in blackface. Courtesy of Sam Gill.

A more likely explanation would be that Laemmle's reputation for nepotism led him to a decision to push Lehrman out and replace him with another brother-in-law, Abe's brother Julius. Julius by now could well afford to acquire the bulk of Lehrman's stock, either alone or in conjunction with Abe. And what became of the stock of those other three original incorporators? Perhaps it had already been acquired by one or both of the Sterns, who by this time now had a controlling interest.

Whatever the explanation, this would be the end of Lehrman's tenure, and the ascension of the Sterns to full control of L-Ko.

But before we continue our story, some background on the brothers Stern.

The L-Ko Motion Picture Company, posed for a group photo on April 22, 1916.
Left-to-right, front row seated: Editor Charles Hochberg second from left, Jack White,
Billy Bevan (straw boater), Lucille Hutton, director John G. Blystone, and Billie Ritchie
(tie and flat cap) after the two women seated to the right of Blystone. Dan Russell seated
on ground in front of Ritchie, and Bert Roach seated on ground at far right. Fatty Voss in
back row with dark hat and bow tie, dwarfing the others. Might that be Lehrman in the
far back with the flat cap and bow tie? Courtesy of Marc Wanamaker and Bison Archives

Chapter 2: The Brothers Stern

Had it not been for the encouragement of Carl Laemmle, the future owner of Universal, Abe and Julius Stern might never have left their homeland of Germany.

Carl Laemmle was born on January 17, 1867, in the town of Laupheim, located in what was then the South German kingdom of Württemberg. The tenth of thirteen children born to Julius Baruch Laemmle and wife Rebekka, Laemmle spent his early teens as apprentice and errand boy to a business selling stationary goods and novelties, eventually working his way up to bookkeeper and office manager. Enticed by letters received from older brother Joseph, who had emigrated to the U.S. some years earlier, Laemmle packed his bags and followed, his father having purchased a ticket on the S.S. *Neckar* as a seventeenth birthday present. He arrived in New York on February 14, 1884.

A varied assortment of menial jobs followed, in locations that included New York, Chicago, and South Dakota before Laemmle ended up in Oshkosh, Wisconsin in 1894. There he took a job with the Continental Clothing Company, a branch of the Chicago-based business owned by a fellow named Sam Stern. Laemmle was appointed manager of the Oshkosh branch four years later, now receiving a commission on the branch's profits.

Here's where Julius Stern enters the picture. A visit by Laemmle to the main office in Chicago happened to coincide with that of Stern's niece, Recha Stern, visiting from her home in Flieden, a municipality in the district of Fulda, Germany. Laemmle and Recha fell in love and married in 1898, moving into a home on Church Street. Laemmle was a busy man, however, and the newlyweds would not have time to take a honeymoon for another five years, when they returned to Germany in mid-1903 to visit their respective homes. It is likely that the couple's belated honeymoon trip was the occasion where Laemmle finally met Recha's siblings, her two sisters Anna and Frieda, and her brothers Abe, Julius, Herman, and Joseph Stern.

Carl Laemmle in 1884, age seventeen. Courtesy of James L. Freedman.

The second youngest of the male Stern siblings, Julius Stern was born in Flieden on March 22, 1886 to Loeb Stern and Malchen Herzberger Stern. He had five older siblings: Recha (1875), Anna (1877), Joseph (1879), Frieda (1882), and Herman (1884). Julius emigrated to the U.S. in 1903, accompanying Carl and Recha on the return trip from their honeymoon; they arrived on September 15 aboard the S.S. *Kaiser Wilhelm II*. Julius "had twenty-five American dollars sewn in his pants," or that was his claim later in life, echoed here by his daughter, Susan Stern Sherman.

The Stern family and brother-in-law Carl Laemmle, circa 1906. Standing, left-to-right: Abe Stern, Julius Stern, Frieda Stern, Joseph Stern, and Herman Stern. Seated, left-to-right: mother Malchen Herzberger Stern and father Loeb Stern. To the right of them: Recha Stern Laemmle, her husband Carl Laemmle (with mustache!), and seated on Recha's lap daughter Rosabelle Laemmle. Courtesy of Gilbert Sherman.

Flieden, Germany, a district in the municipality of Fulda; the Stern family's birthplace.

Julius's emigration to the U.S. was at the behest of his uncle, the stores' owner Sam Stern, and his brother-in-law Carl, to join Carl in his store in Oshkosh. Good timing, for as Julius put it years later: "The reason I left there, I didn't want to go in the army." He was put to work as a salesman for the princely sum of five dollars a week, Stern the youngest of eleven salesmen. He later said that he was the sole Jewish boy among the other ten gentiles, but they all got along. "I had a lot of good friends there, lots of nice boys."

It would appear, however, that relations between Julius and his uncle, Sam Stern, weren't as congenial. Many decades later, daughter Susan recounted the ritualistic back-and-forth that took place between Julius and his children at the dinner table, regarding his earliest days in America working for an unnamed "Uncle," Sam Stern:

> Dad had not come to the Land of Golden Opportunity for five bucks a
> week, so he discovered spifs and p.m.'s. Neither term was ever explained to us
> precisely; we knew only that they were both promotional gimmicks, and by
> selling them one earned a commission over and above one's salary. Overnight,
> to hear dad tell it, he was making not five, but twenty dollars a week. "And do
> you know what I did to save money?" he'd ask us. "You'd walk both ways to
> save the nickel carfare!" we'd chorus. "That sonofabitch, what do you think he
> tried to pay me for a whole week's work?" he'd ask us. "Five dollars!" was the
> only reply accepted. "But was I letting that miser—that sonofabitch—get away
> with that? To pay a relative only five dollars a week—do you know what I did
> then?" he'd thunder. "You sold spifs and p.m.'s" we'd say and then, the ritual
> complete, he was satisfied. Except of course to finish smugly, "And then the
> sonofabitch was paying me twenty dollars, and I was still walking to save the
> nickel carfare."

Within a year or so of Laemmle's return from his honeymoon trip to Oshkosh, however, a disagreement with Sam Stern over profits led to Laemmle's return to the legions of the unemployed, as well as a return to Chicago. Or at least that's how Laemmle told it to his biographer a number of years later; Julius offered a different explanation. According to Julius, Sam Stern wanted both Laemmle and Julius to switch over to the store's children's department, and the two of them refused to do so and quit.

Laemmle teamed up with Robert H. Cochrane, the ad agent behind the Oshkosh store's ready-made advertising. The two decided that the future lay in the marketing of large quantities of cheap goods, and to that end they pondered the idea of opening a chain of five and ten cent stores. That plan fell by the wayside, however, when Laemmle realized that a more lucrative future might instead lie with moving pictures. So, in February 1906, Laemmle opened "The White Front" nickelodeon in a vacancy on Milwaukee Avenue. Its immediate success was such that Laemmle opened a sister theatre, "The Family Theatre," a mere two months later.

Robert H. Cochrane, circa 1920.

Julius claimed in later years that he was a part of this decision-making process, and that they had flipped a coin to decide between the chain of stores or the motion picture business. He also said that there was a theatre in Oshkosh that preceded The White Front in Chicago, but his memory may have been faulty about this. Regardless, Julius lent Laemmle some money to open the theatre. "I think eventually he paid it back," he said, ruminating about this transaction. Julius managed the Milwaukee Avenue Theatre.

During those earliest days, the theatre got by "using two reels of film a week, showing one on three days and the other on four days." It wasn't always easy, and one needed to be a Jack-of-all-trades to keep it going, but the theatres did well. Julius recalled that when the projectionist would fail to show, he would have to fill in, cranking the projector with one hand while eating a sandwich with the other. And during those simpler times, Julius would carry each day's take home with him, on foot and unescorted. This led to at least one attempt to rob him when the assailant threw a rock at Julius's head but only managed to knock off his hat; Julius beat a hasty retreat.

All that risk to save a nickel carfare.

The White Front Theatre. Young Julius Stern is seen standing directly on the left side of the ticket booth. Courtesy of Gilbert Sherman.

Julius related several amusing anecdotes about his years managing the theatre. "When we ran the nickelodeon in Chicago we also had entertainers," recalled Julius. "A girl, she was very good, but she wasn't with us anymore. Then we got another one, and a fellow, and I was going to let her go; she wasn't very good. The fellow hits me, here," he said, pointing to his nose, "and he breaks my nose. See it? I had him arrested, put him in jail. That's what happened to me here."

Another story involved his ongoing issues with the help. "We had a cashier there, and a manager.... He had one of those folding beds down in the basement, and we found out, and he played around with the girl down there, downstairs; we fired them!"

Laemmle's efforts to secure more film for his theatres sparked his interest in the film exchange business. This led to the formation of the Laemmle Film Service in October 1906, to distribute films to theatre owners. That venture proved to be a considerable success, quickly outearning his theatres for revenue. Robert Cochrane bought a piece of the business a year later, and within two years they had branch offices in Minneapolis, Des Moines, Omaha, Memphis, Salt Lake City, Portland, Winnipeg, and Montreal. By 1909 Laemmle's Film Service was the largest in the country with its nine branch offices.

Carl Laemmle poses with one of his theatres' projectors. Courtesy of James L. Freedman.

In 1907, Julius joined the Laemmle Film Service. He was appointed assistant manager and placed in charge of the Booking Department. In those pre-Imp days he obtained films primarily from Italy's Itala and Ambrosia film companies. "I would have been glad to have had Imps, if I could have got them," said Julius in 1912, by which time he was part of Imp. "Neither did we have any posters, lithographs or synopses in those days; things were very different in the business."

"Julius Stern," wrote *Billboard*

...is directly responsible for the wonderful success and growth of this concern.... Julius is particularly well qualified for his position, and has a peculiar faculty of studying each customer's wants. He does not throw a program together in "helter skelter" style, but gives his patrons just what they demand with a view of pleasing the different and varied tastes of large audiences. No wonder Julius is the most popular young man in the Laemmle establishment. He is always pleasant and accommodating, and it is no surprise that the exhibitors stick to him like glue.

Julius served as purchasing agent and booker as well at the small quarters on Dearborn Street. The Film Service's manager was a fellow named Maurice Fleckles, who would go on to marry the Sterns' sister Anna. Anna had emigrated to the U.S. a few years earlier, where she was put to work as a ticket taker in one of Laemmle's theatres. And no wonder, since some other cashiers had caused problems. "They would take the ticket, and they wouldn't tear it up," remembered Julius. "I was cheated...they were resellers."

In 1908, the Motion Picture Patents Company—unaffectionately known as The Trust—had been formed. This was a pooling of sixteen patents that related to the production and projection of motion pictures. In so doing, The Trust felt that it now had an ironclad stranglehold on the industry, with motion picture cameras, projectors, and film stock all falling under these patents. Production companies were now licensed by The Trust to use the affected equipment and film. Distributors were licensed to handle films made solely by The Trust's licensee companies, and exhibitors to use projectors manufactured by Edison. And, of course, they all had to pay ongoing fees for the privilege. The fallout was the elimination of the remaining independent producers and the approximately one thousand independent film exchanges and exhibitors operating at the time.

Laemmle rankled at the ultimatum delivered by The Trust, but as the nation's largest distributor was understandably concerned about having a lack of product to distribute if he failed to acquiesce to their demands. And so he decided to make his own films.

Laemmle went independent in April of 1909, pooling whatever financial resources he had with those of his brother-in-law Julius. As Julius later put it during some of those ritualistic, back-and-forth dinner conversations:

"When Laemmle wanted to start Universal Pictures, who do you think gave him the money?" "You did." "I did. And there was a time we could have sold out for fourteen million dollars, but..." That one always left us wistful.

By June 1909 Laemmle's Independent Motion Picture Company—commonly known as the Imp—was cranking out low budget fare in its New York-based studio at 111 East 14th Street. A dozen films were released during the remainder of that year, another one hundred films in 1910, and one hundred twenty films in 1911. According to one of his many ads placed in the trades, "My motto will be: The best films that man's ingenuity can devise, and the best films man's skill can execute." Needless to say, a bar set unrealistically high.

The Imp studio on Dyckman Street in the Bronx, New York, 1909.
Courtesy of Marc Wanamaker and Bison Archives.

By late 1910, Julius had added the management of Laemmle's Colonial Theatre in Oshkosh to his other duties. "A year ago the Independent films were unknown in this town," wrote *Moving Picture News* in early 1911. "When the Colonial opened with Independent service the other managers all laughed and said it would not last long, but to-day out of four picture houses three are using first run Independent pictures...." By 1914, Stern had a circuit of theatres that included the one in Oshkosh as well as in Burling, Iowa, Beloit, Wisconsin, and Chicago.

Imp was doing so well by this time that in April 1911 Julius relocated to New York to serve as the company's business manager, and within a half year was appointed general manager of the company. The studio had relocated to 102 West 101st Street by this time, and Stern would eventually take up residence at 417 Riverside Drive.

Part of Stern's job was to acquire the necessary talent to appear before the cameras in the unending stream of fare cranked out on an ongoing basis. Not as easy as it may sound, since many stage actors and actresses were hesitant to sully their good names and reputations by lowering their standards to accept roles in this "disreputable" new medium. And so Stern had to think outside the box, and occasionally hire individuals without any prior training, both for before- and behind-the-camera positions. He later spoke of his approach to finding new talent:

> I am always watching for fresh talent, and if I think I see promise in a person, absence of past reputation doesn't count an iota. Not only that, but having given a man a chance I will not discard him if his first effort is not what I expected of it. Under this system I have given many of the "big lights" of the business help in their early picture days that I know have been fruitful of results.

Henry Lehrman, Imp's first scenario editor, was cited by Stern as a successful example of this approach.

An ad in *Variety* titled "Wanted: Attractive Ingenue and Leading Lady" provides an example of Stern's approach to acquire talent in these early days: "Must have appearance that will photograph well. Moving picture experience not essential. Communications treated confidentially. Address JULIUS STERN, Mgr., Imp Studio."

Stern's name would surface in the press sporadically during this period. In September of 1911, a blaze broke out in the ladies' underwear factory that occupied the floor below the Imp offices and factory. Several Imp employees tried to extinguish the blaze while Stern and the others ushered their fifty-five employees to safety, their arms full of negatives and the bookkeeper's books.

Two months later, Stern's engagement to a Miss Minnie Dienstag of Chicago was announced. Dienstag, it was said, "is a very popular member of the Chicago young society set, and will, undoubtedly, bring Mr. Stern into the social limelight." Dienstag was a friend of Julius's sister Anna and her husband Maurice Fleckles, but after the two women took a trip to New York to visit Anna's sister Recha and other friends over the holidays, nothing more made it into the press about Minnie. It would appear that this marriage never actually took place.

Full-page ad for the Imp comedy *Squnk City Fire Company*, Harry Pollard in the lead, from *The Implet* (March 23, 1912).

A year earlier, The Motion Picture Distributing and Sales Company had been formed, to distribute the product of the majority of the country's independent film producers. Imp was the principle unit of this concern, which would go on to be reorganized and renamed The Universal Film Manufacturing Company in 1912. By this time the product of the independents accounted for half of the market. Laemmle would serve as Universal's president, and became a major stockholder in the company. Stern became an investor in the studio at this time as well, and while maintaining a low profile as far as publicity was concerned, was effectively "the man behind the man." Stern was second only to Laemmle in the decision making process and ongoing success of Imp and, for that matter, Universal's growth.

Carl Laemmle, circa 1912.

Stern's importance to Laemmle is underscored in a telegram sent to Universal's vice president, William H. Swanson, dated December 12, 1912. This was during a period when Laemmle was embroiled in a power struggle for control of the company, and at one point had threatened to resign. "My resignation was not to be acted upon except my say so or Julius Stern," wrote Laemmle. He continued:

> I already have withdrawn it and have had it returned to me by our company attorney Waldo G. Morse. Give it me without a moments hesitation. Morse at the same time told me that Stern was legally elected. Consult him right off with Julius Stern and ask his advice and wire fully what he says. If necessary will leave tomorrow night for Chicago arriving Monday morning on the Century. Do not think it is necessary to hold directors meeting in conjunction with stockholders meeting. Be sure wire fully today and under no consideration at end a meeting without Julius Stern."

The "Implet"

THE MOVING PICTURE NEWSPAPER

Edited by THOMAS BEDDING

Published at 102 West 101st Street, New York

SUBSCRIPTION PRICE, $1.00 PER YEAR
SINGLE COPY, 5 CENTS

Mr. Julius Stern, the General Manager of The Imp Films Company, although only 26 years of age, has had a remarkably varied experience in the film business. In 1906 he managed a theatre on Milwaukee Avenue, Chicago, using two reels of film a week, showing one on three days and the other on four days. In 1907 he joined the Laemmle Film Service in Chicago, being appointed Assistant Manager and placed in charge of the Booking Department. In 1909 he bought Itala and Ambrosia pictures, "but," says Mr. Stern, "I would have been glad to have had Imps, if I could have got them. Neither did we have any posters, lithographs or synopses in those days; things were very different in the business."

With his valuable experience in the exhibiting and exchange ends of the business, Mr. Stern came to New York in April, 1911, being appointed business manager of the Imp Films Company. On Mr. Laemmle's return from Europe in October 1911, he was appointed General Manager of the Company.

In the summer of 1911 he undertook a European trip, visiting London, Paris, Berlin and Munich, making a close study of the business in those great centres.

Mr. Stern's aims are progressive. It is his object to constantly improve the quality of the Imp pictures in respect to story, acting and photography, so that the Exchange may be able to handle Imp films which cannot fail to please his customers.

JULIUS STERN
General Manager of The Imp Films Company

"Julius Stern, General Manager of The Imp Films Company" promotional piece, from the January 27, 1912 issue of *The Implet*.

In April 1912, Stern headed out to Los Angeles, to check up on the progress of the Imp's new West Coast studio, located at the southwest corner of Gower Street and Sunset Boulevard. "Mr. Stern's work was chiefly directed towards the proper organization of the West Coast Company," wrote *Moving Picture World*, "which is now in full going order." The studio was directly across the street from the former Blondeau Tavern, acquired a year earlier by the Nestor Film Company and retrofitted into a studio; Nestor was by now one of Universal's brands. A second West Coast studio—the Universal Oak Crest Ranch—was opened shortly thereafter in 1913, on two hundred fifty leased acres in the San Fernando Valley on what had formerly been the Taylor Ranch.

A less flattering picture of Stern and the other Universal directors made headlines in early 1913. Minority stockholder Charles V. Henkel alleged that Laemmle, Cochrane, Stern, Charles S. Swanson, Joseph Engel, Patrick Powers, David Horsley, and Mark Dintenfass had created their own film exchanges, cutting off the others and undercutting the corporation on the per-foot cost. More than $200,000 of the corporation's money, it was claimed, had been diverted into their pockets. It is unknown whether or not Stern was actually an active participant in the organization of these exchanges, or simply included in a net cast wide.

Stern spent the summer of 1913 in Europe overseeing the Imp Company's various

Universal's Hollywood studio at Gower and Sunset, 1913.
Courtesy of Marc Wanamaker and Bison Archive.

productions, filming there to take advantage of numerous English, French, and German locations. The biggest of these was director Herbert Brenon's lavish *Ivanhoe* (1913), Brenon's fluency in French a decided plus when he was assigned the job. Other productions filmed in Europe during this time included *The Child Stealers of Paris*, *Absinthe*, *Love and the Lottery Ticket*, *Love or a Throne*, and *Time is Money*, all directed by Brenon as well and released in late 1913 into early 1914. While in France, Stern took the opportunity to visit the nation's various studios, with a particular interest in photography. "He thinks that European photography has heretofore been a little better than ours on this side," wrote *Moving Picture World*, "but he is determined that the disadvantage shall not long exist."

Upon Stern's return to the U.S., Laemmle had the studios "decorated with flowers and fitted up in a gala array." Stern was presented with a pair of beautiful cuff links by an Imp director named Bob Daly, but within a month Daly would leave the studio in a huff, enraged by an order from Stern.

Last Monday afternoon, Stern, who in combination with the Exchange Building's agent for film supers, E. Fealy, introduced the $3 per day scale in filmdom, plumped a stranger under Dailey's [sic] wing while the latter was posing some people. "Bob, I want you to teach my friend all about the directing business," said Stern. Dailey, preoccupied, and tense with his own troubles, didn't "get" the Stern suggestion readily. The Laemmle relative repeated it. Still Dailey was obtuse. Stern then forced the request across. Dailey at last understood, stopped the posing, grabbed his hat, and made for an exit. Stern interrupted him. "I only want you to show my friend how everything is done. I just wish him to stand beside you for a week." "Not for a minute," said Dailey, torridly. "I had to learn this business by hanging on to the game with both hands and feet and all my bicuspids, getting up at 6 in the A.M., to get to a studio that maybe sent me home in the snow unengaged for the day at $3 or $5 per.... I'll stay up all night to teach any friend of mine anything I know, but I'm blanked if I'm going to be any correspondence school for turning out directors by the week for any boss or near boss of mine!"

And with that, Daly and Universal were history, or at least for a year or so. "Dear Julius," wrote Laemmle in February of 1915, "Bob Daly wants to come back to New York. He is a much better director than he used to be and I really think he would make good with you. However, you can do as you please about it. I simply want to make good my promise to Daly to write to you." Stern ultimately relented, and both Daly and his wife Fritzi Brunette returned to the fold.

Disaster struck once again in May 1914 when fire broke out in the company's new fourth floor facilities at Columbus Avenue and 101st Street in New York, destroying thousands of feet of footage. The building's damage was estimated at $20,000, but a quick inspection by Stern and Laemmle placed the value of the destroyed footage at $300,000 or more.

Julius's younger brother Abe's early years are more difficult to track. Only two years his elder sibling's junior, Abe doesn't seem to have had the same level of breaks as Julius, be that due to a comparative lack of motivation or capabilities, or more likely just another example of the elder receiving the most attention. "Elder," that is, among the Sterns within Laemmle's sphere of influence.

Born Abraham Stern on March 8, 1888, Abe first visited the U.S. in September 1910. Arriving on the S.S. *Kaiser Wilhelm*, Abe stayed with brother-in-law Carl Laemmle at his Lake Drive home, his occupation listed on the ship's manifest as "merchant." By 1911 Abe was acting as manager of the Crusaders Exhibiting Company, as well as the Illinois

Exhibiting Company a year later, purchasing films for State Rights distribution. It is reasonably safe to assume that both of these ventures and Abe's managerial position in same were courtesy of his brother-in-law Carl Laemmle.

Young Abe Stern, circa 1904. Courtesy of Gilbert Sherman.

Abe remained as a guest at Laemmle's Lake Drive residence during this period. Little more was heard about Abe in the two years that followed, so he likely continued plugging away in his various distribution companies. All of that changed in 1914, however, when he received his first substantial break as one of the partners in Henry Lehrman's L-Ko Komedy Kompany, as detailed in the previous chapter. Releasing through Universal, this was yet another opportunity one can lay at Laemmle's doorstep.

Laemmle, or "Uncle Carl" as he came to be known (although he preferred that others call him "Lemmy"), would soon acquire a reputation for unbridled nepotism, and its roots can be found early on with the plum positions doled out to his two brothers-in-law.

During the L-Ko's first two years of operation, Julius continued serving the Universal at its East Coast studios. A trio of Lubin players—Harry Myers, Rosemary Theby, and Brinsley Sheridan Shaw—were lured away from Lubin and put to work in the Imp studios under Julius's supervision, the Imp by now one of Universal's brands. A month later, Julius added supervision of the productions of the Victor brand to his responsibilities as well.

The Universal Film Manufacturing Company's first annual "Harmony and Happiness" ball, January 3, 1914. Front row, seated, left-to-right: King Baggot, Robert H, Cochrane, Cochrane's wife, Recha Laemmle, Carl Laemmle, William H. Swanson, Patrick Powers, Mark Dintenfass, Julius Stern, J.C. Graham, and Phillips Smalley.

Shortly thereafter Stern moved the entire scenario staff from their headquarters at the executive offices at 1600 Broadway to the Imp studio. The move was suggested by Stern and ultimately implemented so that "co-operation may be developed between the directors and the Scenario Department," wrote *Moving Picture World*. "It is essential that these two departments work in unison and the move is considered a great thing in the way of saving time. It also enables the Scenario Department to judge what is necessary in the way of photoplays for the various companies under Stern's supervision."

In 1946, distinguished critic and industry veteran Norbert Lusk looked back on his dealings with Julius sometime during that early period, when Lusk was looking to secure a position as a scenario writer:

All one had to do was see Julius Stern, if one could. He held forth in his company's metropolitan studio, otherwise a rookery on Tenth Avenue near Forty-second Street, a dark maze of wooden stairs and halls and shabby cubbyholes.

Mr. Stern was young, impetuous and too busy to question or converse. He simply said he would pay me $75 a week for six months, forgetting, or not caring to bother with telling his scenario editor he was taking on a new man. It is pleasant to recall that Raymond Schrock, who held that post, received me cordially when I bounced in with news that might have given me another sort of reception. Pleasant, too, was Mr. Stern, whose reputation was not that of a Chesterfield in dealing with men nor a Galahad when women came to his office. But he put a fine point on the meaning of honor in keeping a promise to me and, more than all else, discerned my fitness for a very special assignment.

Lusk was so taken with his first assignment and collaborator, Alice Muriel Williamson, that he made sure to say one final positive thing about Stern:

> That is how I charted the duties ahead of me, and that is how the often ridiculed intelligence of Julius Stern sent me to Elysian Fields hand in hand with an amazing character, a rapturously charming woman and a divine friend if ever there was one.

Meanwhile, Carl Laemmle's dream of a huge central location to consolidate all production was realized on March 15, 1915, with the gala opening of Universal City. More than ten thousand people were in attendance for the event, along with members of the Universal rosters, some of whom put on performances for the assemblage of star-crazed filmgoers. "Southern California will always be the center of the motion picture industry of the world," said Laemmle four months later while scouting Riverside, California for potential location shooting.

> You have every advantage over every other section of the globe. In the summer you have the perfect weather and the perfect light, and light and weather are the two greatest features of motion picture photography.
>
> Then you have so many beautiful resorts and private homes, parks and other settings that fit right into a picture and the producers are put to less

expense than in other sections. Even in the winter, when the companies back east are doing interior pictures, the directors are very seldom handicapped with weather conditions.

All compelling reasons to relocate production during these early days of filmmaking, which renders another of Laemmle's decisions all the more questionable, or at least in hindsight. Concurrent with this was the building of a new Eastern plant in the Leonia Heights section of Fort Lee, New Jersey, scheduled to open in September. The $500,000 undertaking would result in an administration building, studio, and laboratory, with Julius Stern the studio's manager upon its completion. The new space was deemed a necessity, since the East Coast employees couldn't all fit in the current space at Forty-third street and Eleventh Avenue, requiring a day shift and a night shift. By the end of the year, the staff of Universal's Coytesville studio had moved into the new space as well.

Carl Laemmle and Robert H. Cochrane breaking ground for the new East Coast Universal studio in the Leonia Heights section of Fort Lee, New Jersey, 1914. Courtesy of Marc Wanamaker and Bison Archives.

The letter from Laemmle to Julius in March suggests the strain that both of them were under at opposite sides of the country. "You will have to have patience until I return and then I will tell you everything of interest," wrote Laemmle, then overseeing the official opening of Universal City.

> Above all things a man in this place here [Universal City] needs system and organization. A first class general manager can save this company at the very least two thousand dollars a week but I would not be surprised if he could make it four thousand, not in money but for the same amount that we are spending here I venture to say that we can get four thousand dollars more in footage, and what is more, we will get it.... We are all well and hope the same of you.... With love, Yours, Carl.

It would appear that Laemmle was, in his own less-than-subtle fashion, "suggesting" that Stern do some similar belt-tightening. Stern was learning well from his mentor, and ran a tight ship. He wrote at this time of how a film studio should function, leaving little doubt that there was no room for slack:

> [M]y plan of giving aspiring persons a hearing and an opportunity has netted me as fine results as it has those persons. It has brought new, forceful ideas into the production end, and new, popular faces into the acting end. I do believe, however, in strict discipline at a studio—to which the biggest star and director should adhere. A film producing studio, in my eyes, is just like a big business office, and while there are certain conditions that make office rules useless in a studio, I do believe in a firm and rigorous general system. You can operate a studio more economically under it.

There was a policy in place at the time that allowed cast and crew alike access to passes permitting the holder to "stand by when the cameras were clicking scenes they were not in." The studio's directors claimed there were too many distractions and too much interference from the side lines. Julius, sticking to his belief in "strict discipline at [the] studio," put an abrupt end to this policy. The "players and first-aides," wrote *Variety*, were shocked.

As it turned out, the East Coast expansion was not a well thought out endeavor, resulting in what appeared to be unnecessary expenditure. Within less than a year the entire production staff was relocated to Universal City, leaving only the East Coast studio's laboratory functioning. As for Julius, it was announced that he was no longer connected with the Universal Company, although he remained a major stockholder in the firm. Instead, he was relocating to the West Coast where he would become part of the L-Ko Komedy Kompany. "I regret that I am leaving the Universal," said Stern. "But there comes a time in every young man's life when he wants to spread out and go into business for himself. I have that desire now, and it is this ambition which is causing me to leave this great organization." Well, not exactly, as his importance to Laemmle and the day-to-day operations of the studio would soon suck Stern back into its orbit.

Universal picnic, 1915. Julius Stern seated front row center, necktie and white hat in lap. Carl Laemmle and wife Recha seated second and third to the left of Julius. Courtesy of Marc Wanamaker and Bison Archives.

And with this move, Abe would in effect become to Julius what Julius had heretofore been to Laemmle, the quiet fellow in the background getting the work done.

There were some hints during the past six months that a change was to take place. Publicity for L-Ko and Lehrman citing the latter's considerable contributions had been the norm since the company's inception, but there had been a dearth of it issued in the final months. The press for Abe and Julius, on the other hand, was increasing proportionately. It was reported in mid-May that the brothers had teamed with a fellow named Louis Jacobs to form a new $50,000 production company, but more on this in a later chapter.

Abe's marriage in May to Jessie Jacobs, a native of Milwaukee, garnered a lot of press as well, centering primarily on his splashy return to Los Angeles. Abe sent a telegram requesting that a few cameras be set up for their arrival at the station.

> Five automobile loads of employees of the company accompanied by two automobiles filled with flowers and a moving picture camera met Mr. and Mrs. Stearn [sic].... After a parade through the business district the party returned to the studios of the company at Hollywood, where a reception was held.

Clearly the employees of L-Ko knew who signed their paychecks, and if Lehrman was a part of this grand greeting party, it wasn't reported.

Not to be outdone, Julius's arrival in Los Angeles two months later was similarly acknowledged in the press, minus the carloads of employees and flowers:

> All members of the four Universal L-Ko comedy companies...assembled in front of the studio recently to greet the new general manager, Julius Stern, upon his arrival.... At the head of the receiving line was Abe Stern, brother of Julius, who presented him with a gigantic key to the film world's production center. Stanley C. Kingsbury, who was formerly the New York representative of the L-Ko Company, and is now at the studio as business manager, was at Mr. Stern's elbow, and beside him were the directors, players, cameramen and others.

This, a mere week after Lehrman's departure from the studio.

And what became of that five-reel feature that Lehrman was supposed to direct, presumably a parting "gift" on Laemmle's part, its details still to be worked out? Julius quietly deep-sixed that one, by telegram to Laemmle in New York a mere week-and-a-half after his arrival:

> Don't go through with Lehrman deal. Leaving Sunday wait my arrival. Deal not satisfactory to me.

It would appear that Stern wanted nothing further to do with Lehrman, and that Lehrman's name would no longer be associated with either Universal or L-Ko.

Abe (left) and Julius Stern at the L-Ko studio, circa 1917.
Courtesy of Marc Wanamaker and Bison Archives.

Abe Stern with sisters Recha (left) and Anna, circa 1918. Courtesy of Gilbert Sherman.

Dan Russell, wife Marjorie Ray, and Phil Dunham ham it up for the camera.
Courtesy of Steve Massa.

Chapter 3: The Birth of Century Comedies

It didn't take long for Julius to make his presence felt, and to exert his considerable influence on the company's future. All of Lehrman's original stock company—Billie Ritchie, Henry Bergman, Gertrude Selby, Gene Rogers, Louise Orth, and Eva Nelson—were gone by now. Only a handful of the more prominent players who'd been with the company for any length of time remained with the Sterns—Dan Russell, Marjorie Ray, and Vin Moore among them—with newcomers Phil Dunham and Billy Armstrong kept on as well.

Alice Howell, the company's darling, was quickly signed to a new two-year contract. She would work exclusively under Jack Blystone's direction,[1] who by now had been promoted to director general of the studio as well. Of the other studio directors, Craig Hutchinson, Harry Edwards, and Victor Heerman had all departed by this time, although Hutchinson would return in short order. Noel Smith stayed on, as did Dave Kirkland, but the latter only for a short while due to a falling out of favor with Julius: "Kirkland picture rotten a tragedy. Let him out immediately" wrote Julius to Abe, adding "How can we have heart to ask Universal for more money with rotten stuff coming along and Exchanges kicking." And while he was at it, "Vin Moore unpopular let him go."[2] Instead of dumping Moore, however, Abe moved him behind the camera, joining the ranks of other new directors culled from the acting ranks, Jay "Kitty" Howe, Dick Smith, and Frank "Fatty" Voss among them.

Julius made his plans for the studio known in no uncertain terms, in an article appearing that November:

> The old adage, "A new broom sweeps clean," seems to have unusual realization in the recent reorganization of the L-Ko Komedy Co.'s forces at

Hollywood, California. Since the advent of Julius Stern at the L-KO studios things have been happening thick and fast. Now that Mr. Stern has been elected to the office of President and General Manager he has swept aside all the old time methods of comedy productions, surrounded himself with the most capable comedy people in the business and is headed on the straight road to a huge success. Associated with Mr. Stern at the L-KO studios in Hollywood are his brother, Abe Stern, as Secretary and Treasurer, and J.G. Blystone as Director General, plus a combination of other clever minds not found in the comedy field in this or any other country. The old regime has been entirely discarded. Entirely new and cleverer methods have been instituted throughout the entire plant. The vulgar slap stick has been "canned." The old time thread bare "love in the park—brick throwing["] picture has also been sent to the scrap heap. L-KO'S from Mr. Stern's advent have taken on a new dress. Newer in idea—newer in props, newer in every detail of production and no expense being spared now to make L-KO the topnotchers in the entire comedy producing field. Mr. Stern can feel complimented by the associates who have surrounded him and thru whose loyalty and brains, plus Mr. Stern's own initiative, augur a huge success for L-KO films and for all Exhibitors who are now showing them or who will show them.[3]

Alice Howell and her tumbleweed of hair. Courtesy of Robert James Kiss.

During this transitional period, the remaining backlog of Lehrman's productions was exhausted, and it wouldn't be until the end of the year when the Sterns' own productions took over. The Wednesday and Sunday, two-per-week release schedule remained in effect, or at least in theory, since nearly as many Sunday releases were missed as were made. The wholly unreliable availability of product resulted in the occasional switching-off with other companies' release slots, and by the end of 1916 L-Ko retreated to a once-a-week Wednesday release only. Abe Stern and Louis Jacobs, the company's business manager, plugged away handling the day-to-day executive and business affairs of the studio, while Julius made his headquarters on the opposite coast in New York's Mecca building at 48th Street and Broadway, right alongside of the corporate offices of Universal.

Hughie Mack holds Eva Novak's dress in L-Ko's *Pearls and Girls* (February 13, 1918), while Merta Sterling looks on in shock, far left. To the right of Novak: Harry Lorraine and Eddie Barry. Courtesy of Deborah and Christina Lane.

As the company struggled to right itself, the upheaval at L-Ko led to some amusement elsewhere in the film community. One satirical set of lyrics made the rounds, sung to the tune of Tony Jackson's recently published song "Pretty Baby":

If you want to join the movies,
Go and see the L.K.O,

Little Abey, Little Abey.

They have leading Men and Women

There for fifteen a week,

Work for Abey, Little Abey.

He will put you in the Movies

And try to break your neck,

An Alibi on Saturday

And Want to Keep your check.

So if you want to join the Movies

And Get into the game,

See Abey and Julius Stern.[4]

There were quotes attributed to Abe as well, possibly accurate and just as likely apocryphal. Most famous of these was in response to some gentle ribbing about the quality of the L-Ko comedies, as reported and paraphrased by *Photoplay*: "Boys, our comedies are no laughing matter!" When that failed to quell the merriment, Abe quickly added "Say— now quit it, will you! I tell you again, our comedies are not to be laughed at!"[5]

Almost as famous was Abe's supposed response to a director's request to shoot at a remote location: "A rock is a rock, and a tree is a tree. Shoot it in Griffith Park!"[6]

By 1917, however, L-Ko had regained its footing, successfully meeting its one-per-week release schedule and, in some instances, additionally able to provide a short on other days when another Universal brand couldn't meet its deadline. Phil Dunham appeared to be the company's lead performer, starring in fourteen comedies during the first seven months, with Lucille Hutton his co-star in all of them. The unit was beefed up, and in more than one way, with the addition of newcomer Merta Sterling, who would soon take over as the unit's lead comedian with Dunham's eventual move behind the camera. Dan Russell was another of the studio's workhorses, with eleven comedies to his credit by mid-August; his wife, Marjorie Ray, appearing with him in a handful of these films. By mid-1917 L-Ko's stock company included Charles Inslee, Harry Lorraine, Bert Roach, Chester Ryckman, Robert McKenzie, Russell Powell, Dick Smith, Walter Stephens, Eva Novak, Gladys Varden (formerly Gladys Roach, Bert's sister), and a number of even lesser names.[7] But not for long.

Universal was undergoing some internal strife at this time. J.D. Spreckels, of Spreckels Sugar, had acquired a large amount of Universal stock in late 1915 or early 1916, and part of the deal was H.O. Davis's insertion into the staff to represent Spreckels's holdings.

As efficiency engineer—and one earning an eye-opening $100,000 a year at that—Davis initiated some rather Draconian policy changes that proved to be unpopular with casts and crews alike. "One of the first reforms inaugurated by Mr. Davis after accepting the managership was the issuance of an order calling for the entire roster of camera men, players and directors on the salary roll to report for duty at the hitherto unheard of hour of eight A.M.," wrote the *New York Clipper* of one of his lesser changes. More impactful was the decision to reduce the studio's roster of players. "Whether the aforementioned artists quit in a huff or were discharged has been a topic of those curiously inclined...."[8] Regardless, both Dunham and Russell were no longer part of L-Ko. Both, however, would be back at the studio in less than two years. Billy Armstrong, who had joined the studio in 1916, was another casualty, but he too would return within a year.

Harry Mann in top hat, Rosa Gore in striped dress, and Eddie Barry with Bartine Burkett at right, in L-Ko's *It's a Bird* (1919). Joe Martin seems to be the center of attention. Courtesy of Mark Jungheim.

By year's end, Julius had announced the studio's adoption of the so-called "star system," with a separate production unit for each star and his or her dedicated director. The idea, of course, was to attract even more customers to the box office to see films by names they actually recognized. "The players we begin with have all established an individual reputation for fun-making with theatregoers," said Stern, "that cannot fail in adding to the attractiveness of L-Kos in their representation of clean, wholesome and inoffensive comedies of the strenuous type."⁹ As part of this policy, Stern hired Hughie Mack, Gale Henry, and Mack Swain, and rehired Dave Morris to head up their own units. All were hired in late 1917, but both Henry and Swain were gone after a mere half dozen films each; Morris lasted a bit longer, but only Mack would stay on until L-Ko's demise in 1919.

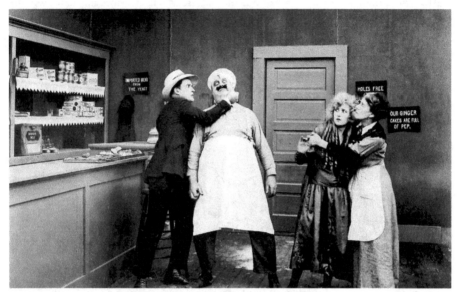

Defenseless Mack Swain in L-Ko's *Home Run Ambrose* (January 16, 1918). Rae Godfrey and Mai Wells to the right of Mack. Courtesy of Sam Gill.

While all of this was going on and comedians were coming and going through the Sterns' revolving door, the company's one constant and all-around workhorse was Alice Howell, whose tenure with L-Ko reached all the way back to its first year of existence and her appearance in *Father Was a Loafer* (1915). Howell starred in a total of thirty-five comedies during 1915 and 1916, that latter year including the aforementioned *A Busted Honeymoon*, *The Great Smash*, *Tillie's Terrible Tumble*, and *Alice in Society*, as well as *Flirtation a La Carte*, *Saving Susie from the Sea*, *Her Naughty Eyes*, *Dad's Dollars and Dirty Doings*, *The Double's Trouble*, *The Bankruptcy of Boggs and Schultz*, *How Stars Are Made*, *Pirates of the Air*, *Lizzie's Lingering Love*, *Where is My Husband?*, *Unhand Me, Villain*, *His Temper-Mental Mother-In-Law*, and *Tattle-Tale Alice*. So successful were these comedies that Julius decided that Howell deserved a studio of her own and the success that would go with it, rather than continue on churning out comedies for L-Ko where she was only one cog in the larger wheel.

Full-page ad for Alice Howell's L-Ko comedy *Pirates of the Air* (1916),
directed by John G. Blystone; from the June 10, 1916 issue of *Motion Picture News*.

"Alice Howell and her work in L-KO Komedies under the personal direction of Mr. Blystone have made both herself and L-KO Komedies famous throughout the entire world," read a promotional piece in *Moving Picture Weekly.* "LOOK FOR THE BIG ANNOUNCEMENT IN THE TRADE PAPERS"[10]

Lehrman had lured the thirty year old Howell away from Keystone back in 1915, one of several acquisitions from the Keystone studios around that time. Born on May 20, 1886[11] in New York City, and a former vaudevillian, the five foot two inch, one hundred thirty pound Howell had been forced to seek work when her second husband and fellow performer Richard "Dick" Smith contracted tuberculosis, bringing their act to an end. Bit parts at Keystone followed in 1914, and her comedic talents and rough-and-tumble willingness were quickly noted. Having the appearance of a disheveled, overworked cherub, Howell soon came to be known as "the scrub woman" due to the number of characters of that sort that she was assigned to portray, always sporting that massive tangled knot of hair atop her head. Journalist Marjorie Howard described Howell in a piece published in 1917:

> Alice Howell scores deeply by her ability to combine pathos and humor. As a down-trodden, put-upon, abused slavey, which she portrays so often, she is absolutely pathetic, while at the same time she is immensely funny.... There are very few women comedians, and especially few in slapstick comedy. Most of them could not stand the strain.... [Howell] is as indifferent to bruises and battering as if she were a British tank in action. And yet she possesses one of the prettiest white skins you ever saw, and a complexion that does not need a grain of powder—it is so smooth and creamy. But she'll stop a pie in mid-career with her face, and she'll let herself be dragged all over the set by the beautiful blond hair of her head, if J.G. Blystone, her director, thinks that the picture requires it.[12]

With the move to L-Ko, Howell was rewarded with more prominent roles in both a supporting and starring capacity.

Howell's director and her films' creative force, John G. "Jack" Blystone, had been hired by L-Ko at the end of 1914. Born on December 2, 1892 in Rice Lake, Wisconsin, Blystone had worked for Universal for three years prior to this, as a prop boy and actor in a handful of films for Nestor. He also had at least one credit to his name as director, the single-reel comedy *On Again, Off Again Finnegan* (1914) for Joker. At L-Ko, Blystone would direct the Hank Mann unit in *Their Last Haul, Rough But Romantic* (with Howell co-starring), *A Change in Lovers, Under the Table, Shaved in Mexico, The Child Needs a Mother, Gertie's Joy Ride* (all 1915), and a number others before taking over the direction of Alice Howell's comedies. Not exclusively, however; Blystone managed to juggle several other films along with Howell's, fitting in *Gertie's Gasoline Glide,* the Billie Ritchie comedies *Cold Hearts and Hot Flames* and *Where is My Wife?* (all 1916), and a trio of Dan Russell vehicles. Blystone took time out in July 1915 to get married as well.[13]

Stern and Blystone's "big announcement" didn't come for another half year. In the meantime Blystone was working furiously around the clock with Howell to create three really big comedies, ones that could be previewed to exhibitors to generate interest and excitement in the new brand once its existence was made public. Blystone would be the sole creative source for these new Howell two-reelers: "Mr. Blystone writes the scenarios, arranges all the details of production, passes on the locations, edits the completed product, and sees that it is shipped in good order to President Julius Stern…in New York," wrote *Motography* a month later.[14] This, a chore he had to juggle while continuing to oversee the operations at L-Ko, and the four directors then churning out that studio's films. According to contemporary reports, those four were Craig Hutchinson, Jay Howe, Dick Smith, and, curiously, Sammy Burns, although whether or not Burns actually ever directed a film for L-Ko is unknown, and highly suspect.[15] The birth of Blystone's first child in late February probably didn't help to lighten his load,[16] nor would Abe's later incapacitation in August while recovering from an appendectomy.[17] With the country's entry into the war, the threat of the draft loomed large over Hollywood's citizens, Blystone included. He lucked out, failing to pass the physical examination in August.[18]

Alice Howell in an unidentified film. Bert Roach at far right, and James Finlayson playing the cop. Courtesy of Robert James Kiss.

The new studio's existence was finally announced in May 1917, adopting a variation of Howell's name for the brand: Howl Comedies. "Having determined that Alice Howell, under the direction of J.G. Blystone, has established herself as a general favorite with exhibitors and their public through the merry medium of L-Ko Comedies," wrote *Motography*, "Julius Stern, president, and Mr. Blystone, have decided to recognize her talents and reward her energy by establishing her as a star of a new series of comedies, separated entirely from L-Ko's."[19]

"There is no reason why a woman cannot be just as funny as a man. In three years service with L-Ko's Miss Howell has abundantly proved that she is good for as many hearty laughs in a given number of reels as almost any man who ever appeared before the camera," wrote Julius.

> On the stage women have advanced scores of individual instances where their abilities to make mirth have won them boundless public favor. Some of the women in musical comedy, vaudeville, burlesque and farce are a great deal funnier than a large majority of the men who work in the same branches of stage entertainment. We believe that women on the screen deserve to have their chance and we believe that Miss Howell, in particular, has earned the right to be a star in her own series.[20]

Howell hated the name Howl Comedies.

In a not-so-thinly-veiled threat expressed in a Western Union telegram sent to New York, it was reported that "she would cease in her endeavor to extract howls of laughter from the populace," wrote *New York Morning Telegraph*, "if the company did not change the name of her productions from Howl Comedies to something more dignified." Within a week the brand was rechristened as Century Comedies.[21]

The Century studio, circa 1918. Courtesy of Rachael Rose-Stern.

These new Century Comedies were to be released through state rights channels, the first three announced as *Balloonatics, Automaniacs,* and *Neptune's Naughty Daughter.*[22] The latter film was shipped to New York's Strand Theatre for pre-release showings and to drum up interest, proving "an endorsement valuable both to the exhibitor and to the manufacturer in the process of publicity."[23] The timing seemed fortuitous. With the U.S.'s entry into the war, local exhibitors were reporting an increased demand for comedies, many of them expressing the hope that films of "the morbid and depressing type be tabooed." The comedy companies of Keystone, Rolin, and Fox took note, as did Universal with its L-Ko and new Century brands.[24]

The reasons behind Stern's decision to distribute the Century Comedies on a state rights basis are unclear. It was soon announced that "Julius Stern disposed of the distribution rights,"[25] and that the Longacre Distributing Company had "purchased the selling rights to the Century Comedies."[26] Longacre's offices were on the seventh floor of the Mecca building, one of the same floors occupied by Universal. It would appear that Carl Laemmle had a stake in Longacre, since all of the Centuries released through Longacre were heavily promoted and advertised in the pages of Universal's weekly trade publication, *Moving Picture Weekly.* What is not clear is whether or not Stern had a stake in Longacre as well, but while all of the press releases would suggest not, Stern's long and close relationship with Laemmle would suggest otherwise. The *New York Dramatic Mirror* had a strong hunch that there was:

> Wonder if I had it right last week about the "tremendous sale—complete negative output," the Century Comedies admitted they had made to the Longacre Distributing Company, newly formed, and at the same address as the Century Company. Well, I knew that some Universal stockholders were Century stockholders. And to make it easy Universal, Century and Longacre are all at 1600 Broadway. I think my last week's item intimated that Century closed their "tremendous sale" close at home. Well, page 721 of a trade paper that comes out Saturday confirms it. An innocent item says: "The Longacre Distributing Company has taken office space in Universal Film Company headquarters, 1600 Broadway, New York." Universal to Century to Longacre to Universal—bat 'er *out!*[27]

Whatever the case, Longacre issued invitations to a trade showing of the first three Century Comedies, to be held on July 27 at the Broadway Theatre.[28]

The Longacre plan calls for the division of the territory into districts. The "district rights" will be sold in each of these divisions. The Century Comedies will be furnished to exhibitors regardless of any other service which he may be receiving, for Longacre has no connection whatever with any other film service. For the benefit of those purchasing district rights, Longacre designates a "district" as a town, or in the case of a large city, a section of the town, in which there is either one theatre which draws from the entire populace, or two or more theatres, which run in direct competition to each other, and to which only one of the so-called "first-run" of a picture can be sold.[29]

By August, Longacre exchanges had been established in more than thirty U.S. cities, with plans for distribution in Canada as well.

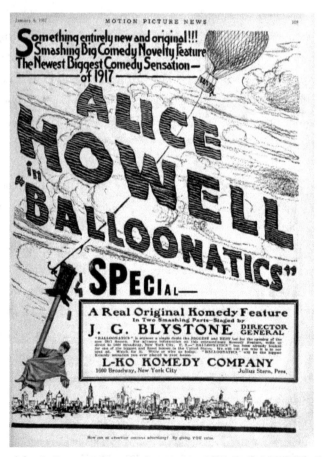

Full-page ad for *Balloonatics*, from the January 6, 1917 issue of *Motion Picture News*. The film was still being promoted as an L-Ko Komedy at this time.

The Century Comedies were scheduled to go into release on the first of each month, beginning with *Balloonatics* on September 1, 1917. Tentatively titled *The Balloon Bandits* while still in production,[30] in this one Howell, playing a maid, elopes with her employer's son, played by Joe Moore. Fatty Voss's cook is in love with Howell as well, and pursues the two lovers in a hot air balloon, its dangling anchor creating much havoc before picking up the bungalow with Howell and her groom inside. They go for a long ride before crashing to the trees below.

If promotional pieces were to be believed, production was interrupted when Howell's balloon broke away from its moorings and took the actress for a five mile joy ride before being rescued.[31] "If every Century Comedy offered state rights purchasers is as good as 'Balloonatics,' the first two-reel number shown for review," wrote Ben H. Grimm for *Moving Picture World*, "independent exchanges soon will be busy handling bookings for them."[32] Dick Smith and Joe Moore co-starred.

Alice Howell hangs onto fellow auto mechanic Fatty Voss, in Century's *Automaniacs*. Courtesy of Robert James Kiss.

Automaniacs followed on October 1, with Howell and Voss auto mechanics in a small town garage. "Some of the incidents, which are of a knockabout type, are funny and others are too vulgar," wrote *Moving Picture World*'s reviewer. "Both of these comedians get better effects when they perform with more restraint than is shown here."[33] That same publication's Ben H. Grimm said "The comedy is of the rapid-fire, hurry-up action sort, and is a thoroughly acceptable number."[34]   Decorah, Iowa exhibitor R.J. Relf was less enthusiastic about the results, reporting that it "Contains a few new stunts but is only fair on the whole."[35] We'll have to take these fellows' word for it, since neither film is known to survive.

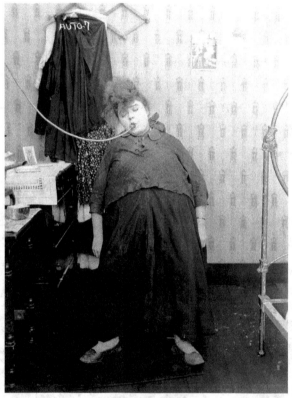

Human balloon Alice Howell in Century's *Automaniacs*. Courtesy of Robert James Kiss.

Neptune's Naughty Daughter followed on November 1, and we are on firmer ground here since this film survives and was recently made commercially available on Undercrank Productions' DVD *The Alice Howell Collection*. In this one Howell is a fisherman's daughter who is shanghaied by ship's captain Fatty Voss, but eventually rescued by her sailor boyfriend, played by Joe Moore.[36] As the two lovers sail away, Voss and his cohorts, now atop a lighthouse, attempt to stop the vessel but instead end up riding the lighthouse down as it topples into the sea.

The tearing down of a lighthouse was as sensational a piece of work as has been accomplished by the L-Ko in many a day. It was necessary to employ one hundred and fifty men and two steam dredges to get the lighthouse to move, and then in order to get it to fall they employed a tug whose tow line was fastened about the building.[37]

"It was necessary to employ one hundred and fifty men and two steam dredges to get the lighthouse to move, and then in order to get it to fall they employed a tug whose tow line was fastened about the building." The lighthouse's demise in *Neptune's Naughty Daughter*. Courtesy of Library of Congress.

Tentatively titled *The Worshippers of the Cuckoo Clock* before its release, the film co-starred Robert McKenzie, his wife Eva, and their young daughter Ida Mae, as well as Howell's pet dog Coo-Coo. This energetic early effort by Century Comedies makes for pleasurable viewing, and Howell gives it her all. There are some great gags here, among them a carriage ride where Howell first gets caught on a wheel and spun silly as it makes its way down the road. Regaining her seat, she accidentally kicks through the flooring and needs to run furiously to keep up with the carriage surrounding her. Later on while working at a diner, Howell resists an amorous patron's advances and knocks him out cold, then quickly assembles a makeshift sail, sticks it in his mouth, and starts a fan which blows his body sliding out of the diner.

Sailor Joe Moore and his girl Alice Howell living it up at a local tavern, in *Neptune's Naughty Daughter*. Courtesy of Library of Congress.

Two more films finished out the year, the circus-based yarn *Her Bareback Career* (December 1; production title *Alice of the Sawdust*), and *She Did Her Bit* (December 30; production title *The Village Blacksmith*), wherein Howell plays the daughter of—you guessed it—the village blacksmith. Neither film is known to have survived. Meanwhile, Howell, exhausted from Blystone's unrelenting production schedule, managed to take a couple of weeks off to go hunting and fishing,[38] while Abe Stern was laid up for a short while, convalescing from his operation for appendicitis.[39]

Full-page ad for Century's *She Did Her Bit* starring Alice Howell, from the January 26, 1918 issue of *Moving Picture Weekly*.

Eleven more Howell Centuries were released in 1918. The first, *Oh, Baby!* (February 14; working title *School Days*), stars Howell as a former prisoner who impersonates a Salvation Army girl. *What's the Matter with Father?* (April 1) followed, with Howell "an aspirant for [heavyweight boxer] Jess Willard's crown." *Her Unmarried Life* (May 29) came next, with Howell's father attempting to marry her off to a teacher he thinks in line for an inheritance.

Alice Howell's *Oh, Baby!* featured on the cover of the February 23, 1918 issue
of *Moving Picture Weekly*.

In Dutch (June 26) features Howell as a wooden-clogged stowaway who ends up
marrying one of her shipboard protectors, later landing a dancing gig at the night club
where he serves as a waiter. Howell has plenty of opportunity to shine in this film, her
various attempts to steal food from two below-deck sailors—one of them an uncredited
Jimmy Finlayson—while stowed away in a crate is an extended delight, as are her charming
little dances in the night club, one of them sped up to such a degree by under-cranking
that her moves become a visual blur. Her co-stars, Hughie Mack as her waiter husband

and Neal Burns as a persistent suitor, take part in another sequence that is one of the film's highlights. When Howell spurns Burns after his repeated attempts to woo her, he decides to kill himself. Mack, eager to have this nuisance out of the way, impatiently waits outside for him to do so, barring both the owner and a waiter from entering until the deed is done. Burns's attempts all fail. First, his pistol jams and then the hammer slams on his finger, so he tosses it away. Mack quickly replaces it with his own pistol, but it turns out he forgot to load it, so then Mack sneaks in a large knife. It bends when Burns attempts to plunge it into his chest. Frustrated, Mack enters and tries to club Burns with a coat tree, but Burns exits while the tree is hung up in a drape. The sequence is a hoot!

Alice Howell, *In Dutch*. Courtesy of Library of Congress.

Choo Choo Love (July 17) was another of those seaside comedies, this one with Howell falling for traveling salesman Billy Armstrong. *Hey Doctor!* (July 31) features Howell as a doctor's assistant attempting to drum up new patients. *Bawled Out* (August 14) has Howell assist in her sweetheart Hughie Mack's escape from prison, and *Hoot Toot* (August 28) follows Howell's frustrated attempts to join the Red Cross and the army. Howell is forced into servitude at a sanitarium in exchange for mortgage forgiveness in *Cupid vs. Art* (September 11), and *Untamed Ladies* (October 9) has gypsy Howell falling for an artist. The year's final release, *The Cabbage Queen* (December 18), follows German spies Phil Dunham and William Irving and their attempts to steal Howell's secret recipe for sauerkraut. Only *In Dutch* and *Hey Doctor!* are known to have survived, the former available on that same aforementioned Undercrank DVD set, and the latter in a copy held by the Library of Congress's film archives.

Two more Howell comedies were released in early 1919. In *Behind the Front* (February 12), Howell falls for a milkman when her overweight hubby, played by Hughie Mack, is drafted into the army; and *Society Stuff* (March 12), with maid Howell impersonating her employer at a swank ball.

Publicity shot of Alice Howell taken by photographer Julius Estep for *Neptune's Naughty Daughter*, 1917. Courtesy of Robert James Kiss.

As for Longacre, its life was short lived. In January 1918, Emanuel H. Goldstein was appointed to take charge of the merging of Universal's various New York City exchanges into one large unit, to occupy the entire seventh floor of the Mecca Building. These exchanges included Longacre and Bluebird—another corporation separate from the

Universal—along with Universal's various exchanges.[40] Four months later, effective May 20, 1918, Universal Film Exchanges, Inc. then took over the business of the numerous, nation-wide branch exchanges that had been distributing Universal films in the U.S. Once the change was in place, not only would all Universal productions be handled by the Universal Film Exchange, but the output of Century Comedies, Lyons and Moran Comedies, Jewel Productions, Lois Weber Productions, and Bluebird Photoplays as well. "It is in combining the numerous interests that the economy in distribution will be practiced," wrote *Moving Picture Weekly*.[41] As a result of this new policy, *Her Unmarried Life*, released on May 29 and originally advertised to be distributed by Longacre, was instead distributed by Universal, with its predecessor, *What's the Matter with Father?*, the final Century Comedy to be distributed by Longacre.

With the new policy in effect, the Howell releases would appear every fourth week, taking the place of an L-Ko comedy which had by this time become a weekly release. Universal informed exhibitors who had contracted for weekly L-Ko comedies of this new policy, "guaranteeing" them that "the Howell comedies will have a drawing power equal to that of the L-Ko."[42] Not that exhibitors had any say in the matter.

But then it really didn't matter, since aside from the brand name accompanying each release—be it Century or L-Ko—the differences were negligible, and the on-screen results essentially a throwback to the earlier Howell comedies of L-Ko. Howell's co-stars in these films were all appearing in L-Ko productions as well during this period, and were shuttled back and forth between the two brands as needed. A simple task, needless to say, since the films of both brands were all made on the same studio lot. Familiar faces abounded, and along with those already mentioned—Hughie Mack, Fatty Voss, Robert and Eva Mckenzie, Joe Moore, Neal Burns, Billy Armstrong, Phil Dunham, and William Irving—other of L-Ko's performers appearing in the Centuries whose faces would be recognizable to viewers included Bert Roach, Russell Powell, Eddie Barry, Vin Moore, and Bartine Burkett.

Frank Voss was Howell's lead of sorts in the first three releases. A heavyweight comedian with former stage experience, Voss had been hired by L-Ko back in 1915 to be the studio's resident fat man. Born Franklin H. Voss in Chicago in either 1888 or 1890—sources vary—Voss was dubbed "Fatty" for his screen appearances. Fat and stocky but with the appearance of muscle under the girth, Voss was an imposing fellow, nearly matching Roscoe Arbuckle for size but lacking any of his grace or impish attractiveness. Voss's roles for L-Ko were a varied lot, ranging from the trumpet-playing rube of *Love and Sour Notes* (1915) to one of Paul Jacobs's youthful classmates in *Little Billy's School Days* (1916). Perhaps his most outrageous—and funniest—turn was as the three-hundred pound, sixteen year old Gwendolyn in *The Child Needs a Mother* (1915). Voss's antics as the overweight teen are the funniest thing in that particular film, and aside from the ridiculous visual of a grown man in a "little" girl's clothing, the film's high point occurs early on when "she" throws a hissy-fit, slowly demolishing a sturdy chair with bare hands. Voss had appeared in three comedies for L-Ko during the first four months of 1917—*Brave Little Waldo*, *Fatty's Feature Fillum*, and *Crooks and Crocodiles*—all of which predated the release of the three Centuries.

Voss's roles in the Centuries are seemingly of a less mirthful nature, first as the jealous cook in *Balloonatics*, followed by the garage owner in *Automaniacs*. Given that neither film survives, however, we'll need to rely on the scant reviews for our tentative assessment of these. In *Neptune's Naughty Daughter*, however, Voss gets to come on as a full-blown heavy as the cruel captain who has Howell shanghaied and later threatens her in her small cabin; his menace is palpable. It's not known whether Blystone had intended to use Voss as a regular in the upcoming Howell comedies, but the decision was made for him. Voss's career was unexpectedly cut short when the twenty-eight year old comedian died in his apartment of heart failure on April 22, 1917.[43] Filming of *Neptune's Naughty Daughter* had finished a mere week or two earlier.

Frank "Fatty" Voss in *Neptune's Naughty Daughter*. Courtesy of Library of Congress.

After a few more of Howell's films were produced, Hughie Mack was brought in as a replacement of sorts for Voss, co-starring in at least seven of these. Another plus-sized comedian, Brooklyn-born comedian Hughie Mack arrived in this world in 1884. Mack was hired in a supporting capacity by Vitagraph back in 1913, but over his four year stint and more than one hundred forty films with that studio had worked his way up to headliner status. Mack signed his contract to appear in L-Ko comedies on August 2, 1917, and worked under directors Noel Smith, James Davis, and Robert Kerr over the following year. His first for the studio was, *Hula Hula Hughie* (1917), one of a dozen comedies released before his first for Century—the aforementioned *In Dutch*—made it to the screen. After his roles with Howell, Mack would star in only one more film for the Sterns, L-Ko's *Charlie the Hero* (August 20, 1919), a Chai Hong vehicle that was likely a rebranded Century.

Hughie Mack hides under a table, from *In Dutch*. Courtesy of Library of Congress.

Neal Burns stood in stark contrast to Voss and Mack, a more youthful and physically attractive actor with leading man good looks. Born in 1891 in Bristol, Pennsylvania, Burns headed west where he began appearing in juvenile roles on the stage in 1910, and would bounce back and forth between the coasts for roles through 1914. He entered the film industry in 1915 in shorts for Al Christie's Nestor, following Christie to his Christie Film Company a year later. After dozens of shorts for that studio, Burns moved over to Piedmont Pictures where he co-starred with Gertrude Selby in a series of short romantic comedies before engaging with the Sterns to act in their Century and L-Ko comedies. *Oh, Baby!* was the first released of these, followed by *What's the Matter with Father?*, *In Dutch*, *Choo Choo Love*, and *Hey, Doctor!* before he was moved elsewhere at Universal.

Neal Burns unsuccessfully attempts suicide, from *In Dutch*.
Courtesy of Library of Congress.

Eddie Barry, Burns's older brother, had entered the industry in 1916 with Christie as well, after a short stint spent as the American sales manager for Italy's Ambrosia film company. He would appear in four of Howell's films, but it was with the L-Ko's that he most frequently appeared during this period.

Billy Armstrong (1891-1924), a Brit with Fred Karno experience, had spent a year at Essanay, most notably with roles in some of Chaplin's early films, including *The Bank* (1915) where he played a rival janitor. A few starring roles in Cub Comedies preceded his hiring by L-Ko, his first for L-Ko Lehrman's *For the Love of Mike and Rosie*. Armstrong had roles in three of Howell's films, which tended to be smaller character parts, such as *In Dutch*'s drunken heckler, and his traveling salesman in *Choo Choo Love*. Aside from *Hey, Doctor!*, Armstrong would only appear in two other films for Century, *Trouble Bubbles* (December 22, 1920), which he directed as well—his only credit as such—and *Tee Time* (January 12,

1921), after which he would move on to greater success, primarily with Sennett, before his untimely death in 1924 from tuberculosis.

Billy Armstrong, soused, from *In Dutch*. Courtesy of Library of Congress.

The "every fourth week" release schedule of the Howell comedies didn't last very long, and by mid-July they were being released every other Wednesday. That only lasted into mid-September, with only two more Howell releases that year. L-Ko comedies plugged in the rest of the Wednesday gaps, with the exception of five weeks in later October into mid-November when there were no releases due to the Spanish Influenza epidemic then plaguing the nation, which had shut down all production.[44]

Blystone had continued as director of the first six of the 1918 releases, after which he broke from the studio and the reins were turned over to Jim Davis and Vin Moore for the remainder of Howell's comedies. By the end of 1918 Blystone had reunited with Henry Lehrman at his Fox Sunshine Comedies.[45] Alice Howell would depart somewhere around this time as well, ending up with Emerald in 1919 making comedies for release through Reelcraft. It's unclear whether she had followed Blystone out the door, or whether her departure prompted Blystone's. Regardless, with both Howell and Blystone's departure, the original reason for Century's existence had evaporated.

"It's a Century"

Chapter 4: Regrouping

So why had Howell left Century?

A rather baffling article appeared in May 1918 in the midst of those popular Alice Howell releases: "Carl Laemmle has cast out his lines for a female Charlie Chaplin," wrote *Motion Picture News*:

> Instructions have been issued by Universal's president to the directors of the L-KO, Nestor and Century comedies that their main effort in life henceforth is to find, rope and keep a female who will be known as the "funny woman of the screen" for some years to come. "With the women working in your companies," President Laemmle informed Abe and Julius Stern, who are responsible for the three [sic] comedy brands, "you certainly should have some woman capable of development.[1]

What about Howell? Howell had signed a two-year contract back in mid- to later-1916, so perhaps she was refusing to sign another, or demands for more money had been turned down. Nearly a dozen more of her comedies were yet to be released at the time this article was published, so it would appear that she remained with Century for more months to come, as it is unlikely that a backlog of finished films of that amount would already be sitting on the shelf. But with no mention in this article of Howell and her considerable popularity and filmic achievements, it would appear that she had been written off by this time.

Perhaps it had something to do with the elimination of Longacre. If Julius had a major piece of Longacre, the added revenue from that venture may have gone a long way towards covering the salaries of both Howell and Blystone, and the comparatively lavish schedules and budgets afforded them. With Longacre's elimination and distribution now handled by Universal, belt-tightening may have been required, resulting in a seismic shift in the production schedules and budgets allotted to Century's films.

There was one other film produced by the Sterns in 1918, this one the slightly more ambitious three-reeler *The Geezer of Berlin* (August 15, 1918), directed by Arthur Hotaling. Intended as a burlesque on Universal Jewel's propagandistic wartime drama, *The Kaiser, the Beast of Berlin* (March 9, 1918), lead Ray Hanford was supported by L-Ko's stars Hughie Mack, Bartine Burkett, Monty Banks, and Bert Roach. Julius Stern touted the film as "the most ambitious undertaking ever attempted by the Century Company and without doubt one of the most expensive comedies produced."[2] *Motography* chimed in: "Any audience will enjoy 'The Geezer of Berlin,' but it will probably meet with greater success in theatres that have shown 'The Kaiser.'"[3]

Monty Banks and Bartine Burkett in the feature *The Geezer of Berlin*.
Courtesy of Mark Jungheim.

1919 opened on a sad note, or at least for the Sterns and Carl Laemmle, when Laemmle's wife Recha—sister to Julius and Abe—died on January 13. Forty-three year old Recha had contracted influenza at the beginning of the month, with pneumonia developing and the eventual cause of her death. As a tribute of respect to her memory, employees of Universal exchanges worldwide suspended work for five minutes.[4]

Century's output in 1919 was meager at best. Aside from the final two Howell releases in February and March, there was only the occasional release through the summer until the studio was on more solid footing. These were, with only a few exceptions, "lions on the loose" comedies, featuring animal trainer Charles Gay's menagerie of trained lions. It seems apparent that the Sterns were riding on the coattails of the success of Henry Lehrman's Fox Sunshine lion comedies of 1917 and 1918. Lehrman's string of comedies included *Roaring Lions and Wedding Bells* (1917), *Hungry Lions in a Hospital, Wild Women and Tame Lions*, and *Roaring Lions on the Midnight Express* (all 1918). But while Lehrman's comedies were interspersed with a number of other, non-lion comedies, the Sterns produced and released theirs in a continuous, once-a-month stream over the course of six months, with director Fred Fishback overseeing the films (or at least for a short while) and Gay's "Century Lions" cavorting before the cameras. The budgets and filming schedules for these, it would seem, must have paled in comparison to the more lavish Sunshines.

Director Fred Fishback toasts Edith Roberts and an unidentified cameraman.
Courtesy of Robert James Kiss.

Fred Fishback (1894-1925), late of Lehrman's Sunshine unit, was a surprising choice in that he had not been responsible for any of that company's lion comedies. Lehrman had been unceremoniously canned by Fox on January 18, and the bulk of Sunshine's personnel were fired along with him. Fishback was one of the casualties, but the Sterns were quick to snap him up.

Romanian-born Fishback had come to the U.S. around the turn of the century and, after a short stay at Thomas Ince's Broncho, was hired by Keystone in 1914 as a bit player, prop man, and on-call stunt man. After a short stint as assistant director later that same year, Fishback was promoted to full-fledged director in 1916. He was prolific and proficient in this capacity, overseeing comedies primarily starring Mack Swain, including *A Movie Star*, *His Bitter Pill*, and *Madcap Ambrose* (all 1916); and Polly Moran, with titles such as *Cactus Nell* and *Roping Her Romeo* (both 1917).

Lehrman had hired Fishback towards the end of that year to direct comedies for his pre-Sunshine studio, L-Ko, but that didn't pan out. Fishback's attempts to avoid the draft fell on deaf ears, in spite of his claiming an exemption due to being a Rumanian. His draft registration was produced, and it claimed New York as his birthplace, so that's all the proof the draft board needed. Fishback was shipped up to American Lake, Washington, for training late in 1917.[5] Lehrman did successfully lure him over to his later Fox Sunshine studio in 1919, where Fishback directed the delightful spoof *Oh, What a Knight!* and *Money Talks* before they were both let go and Century snapped him up.

Julius recalled his hiring of Fishback years after the fact, but his memory was faulty on at least one of the details, claiming that he hired him away from Keystone. "It was all dollars and cents. He came to us because we gave him more money. I paid him a thousand dollars a week." Why such an exorbitant salary? "Because he was making them quicker," said Stern, "the two reelers, he made them quicker than the other fellows."[6] Then again, Julius may have been thinking about another director rather than Fishback.

Frenchman Charles Gay (1886-1950), for years the right-hand man to "The Animal King" Frank Bostock[7] (1866-1912), would oversee the antics of his lions and, on occasion, appear before the camera as well when face-to-muzzle interaction was required. These one-on-one occasions would in some instances result in bodily injury, as in 1916 when Gay was nearly killed by "Nero" while filming a battle scene for Horsley.[8] A later incident occurred at Century in 1920 on a set enclosed by wire netting, when one of the lions broke through and attacked Gay as he tried to stop him. Gay's right leg was badly lacerated, resulting in several weeks of recuperation.[9] Gay housed his lions at Century's premises until May 1921, when they were relocated to Universal City[10] on the insistence of the studio's insurers. Gay eventually shipped them all to his appropriately named Gay's Lion Farm in El Monte, California in the mid-1920s.

Wild animal trainer Charles Gay and friend at his Gay's Lion Farm.

The Sterns' lion comedies of this period were numerous. *Looney Lions and Monkey Business* (April 23, 1919) and *Frisky Lions and Wicked Husbands* (May 28, 1919) both co-starred Dot Farley, late of Sunshine, and Charles Dorety. Of the former of these, one reviewer wrote that "The subject is one that will please lovers of knockabout, slapstick situations, with no particular dependence on plot structure."[11] Others included *Howling Lions and Circus Queens* (June 25, 1919) with Farley and Billy Bevan as her co-star, and *A Lion Special* (July 30, 1919) with Chai Hong, recently signed to a long term contract due to favorable exhibitor feedback.[12] *Lonesome Hearts and Loose Lions* (August 27, 1919) co-starred Dan Russell with his wife Marjorie Ray, supported by newcomer Harry Sweet; and *A Lion in the House* (September 17, 1919) with Zip Monberg, Cliff Bowes, and Merta Sterling.

CENTURY ANIMAL COMEDY
LOOSE LIONS

A trio of lovelies and their actress friends, in director William Watson's Century comedy *Loose Lions*. Courtesy of Jim Kerkhoff.

Vin Moore had taken over the unit sometime in 1919 so that Fishback could focus his attention on other shorts. Moore's unit would include the stars Dot Farley and Billy Bevan, with Billy Joseph and Billy Garcia supporting; Walter Stevens served as assistant director and Ted Stevens master of props.[13] Fishback's new unit consisted of the stars Jimmie Adams, Edith Roberts, Bud Jamison, and Charles Dorety, with Bob Doran his cameraman, Earl Olin his technical director, and Al Alt his assistant director.[14] Or at least that's how the units were advertised, but the Sterns would move personnel wherever needed, and frequently so, rendering these lineups fleeting at best.

Fishback's *A Jungle Gentleman* (April 9, 1919) was one of the non-lion comedies of this period, co-starring Jimmie Adams, Esther Wood, and new-to-the screen Mrs. Joe Martin. In this one, Adams's doctor has Mrs. Joe scatter banana peels outside his office in an attempt to drum up new patients. This was another instance of the Sterns riding on the coattails of an earlier screen "star," the orang-outan Joe Martin. Joe Martin, brought over from Singapore back in 1911,[15] had appeared in a handful of comedies and dramas from as early as 1915 in Universal's Victor brand, the first of these titled *Joe Martin Turns 'Em Loose* (September 15, 1915).

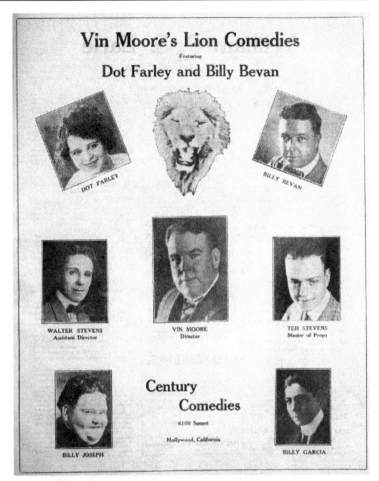

Full-page ad for "Vin Moore's Lion Comedies" unit, from the *1919 Camera! Yearbook*.

Mrs. Joe Martin was introduced to the public through her "marriage" to Joe, her pre-marital name given as Miss Topsy Tree. Joe didn't seem to care that his bride was actually a female impersonator known on the vaudeville stage as "Milton,"[16] or at least as far as this ridiculous staged marriage was concerned; one can only hope that this "marriage" was not consummated.

The Missus would appear in a brief series of four Stern comedies, apparently none-too-popular with viewing audiences. The other three films were *The Good Ship Rock 'n' Rye* (December 17, 1919), with the missus impersonating a sailor boy on a pirate ship; *A Baby Doll Bandit* (January 12, 1920) as a teacher in a small western town whose bank is robbed; and *Over the Transom* (February 9, 1920), with hotel bellhop Martin assisting Jimmie Adams in his pursuit of a count who has stolen the hotel's cash. All four of the Mrs. Joe Martin entries were directed by Fishback, and starred Jimmie Adams.

Joe Martin, screen star.

Mrs. Joe Martin in director Fred Fishback's *A Baby Doll Bandit*.

Mrs. Joe Martin peeks at Jimmie Adams in Century's *The Good Ship Rock 'n' Rye.*
Courtesy of Robert James Kiss.

Joe Martin was a bit more successful, or at least up to a point, starring in a series of Universal Jewel two-reelers from 1919 to 1922. The initial entries were *Monkey Stuff* (July 7, 1919) and *The Jazz Monkey* (July 21, 1919), with Joe foiling a kidnap attempt in the former, and a bank robbery in the latter; both were directed by William S. Campbell. Campbell's base of operations was at Universal's back ranch, a 1,299 acre property at the lower part of Universal City. Campbell soon jumped ship and formed his own production company with $100,000 backing. Shooting out at the E and R Jungle studios in Lincoln Park, Campbell's new comedies were made for Chester Comedies and released through Educational Film Exchange. The featured performer was Snooky the "Humanzee," a female chimpanzee pawned off on viewers as a male, resulting in a series that was quite popular with audiences. Campbell left Chester within a year or so to create his own Campbell Comedies, also released through Educational.

Before Campbell had left Universal, however, he had directed a third five-reel feature starring Joe Martin. Titled *Wild Lions and Loose Bandits*, the completed film was to be given a private showing in August 1919 to critics at Universal City's Theatre de Luxe.[17] It was never released as such, however, and with Campbell's departure a month later was temporarily shelved.

Joe Martin feeds an infant in the Universal Jewel *Monkey Stuff*.
Courtesy of Richard M. Roberts.

But not for long. A year later, three more Joe Martin comedies would surface: *A Prohibition Monkey* (September 13, 1920) was the first, followed by *A Wild Night* (October 11, 1920) and *No Monkey Business* (February 28, 1921). Campbell was credited with the first of these, and director Al Santell connected to the second, but the third was released without credit attribution. It's likely that Campbell's five-reeler was torn apart and cannibalized, new connecting footage shot, and resurfaced as the above three films. A wise decision, it would seem, since who in their right mind would want to sit through a five-reel Joe Martin comedy?

Campbell's assistant director on his three Universal Joe Martin comedies was a fellow named Harry Burns (1885-1948).[18] Burns had followed Campbell over to Chester Comedies, at first assisting and, according to contemporary reports, eventually taking over direction of four of the Snooky comedies. Burns left Campbell and Chester in late 1920, and was signed by Universal to take the helm of the revived Joe Martin comedies.[19] Universal's general manager, Irving Thalberg (more on him later), instructed Burns to churn out these comedies quickly, with the goal of one per month. Within two weeks Burns had knocked out scripts for four comedies, and went to work directing them,[20] the first of which was *A Monkey Hero* (April 19, 1921). Joe Martin's trainer, Curley Stecker, assisted with direction, and camera work was handled by Lee Garmes, who had followed Burns over from Chester.

The goal of one each month turned out to be an unrealistic pipe dream, however, with an interval of two-to-four months between the releases of each. Burns's three other comedies were *A Monkey Movie Star* (July 4, 1921), *A Monkey Bell Hop* (November 28, 1921), and *A Monkey Schoolmaster* (January 2, 1922). Joe showed off his pearly whites and was fully anthropomorphized in each of them, the titles providing a sense of the hook on which the meager plotlines were based.

Joe Martin in Harry Burns's Universal Jewel *A Monkey Movie Star*. The fellow in the striped coat may be Hap Ward. Courtesy of Heritage Auctions, Ha.com.

The Joe Martin comedies were generally well reviewed, but by the time Burns's *A Monkey Bell Hop* was released the series was wearing thin. "Just about as poor a comedy as it is possible to make," wrote one angry exhibitor from Bellaire, Ohio. "Not funny and at times disgusting. Martin is poorest of the monkey actors."[21] An exhibitor in Mississippi agreed, having this to say about *A Monkey Bell Hop* and *A Monkey Movie Star*: "Take a tip and lay off these two comedies. The first Joe Martin comedies were great, but for some cause these are silly and nothing to them."[22] William Campbell's contributions, it would appear, were sorely missed.

While Martin had earlier been described as "the most tractable of actors and as gentle as a kitten,"[23] by later 1919 Martin had made an about-turn, now under surveillance after a three day rampage in which he wrecked his trainer's quarters. "[The] uncanny animal tore the door from its hinges, unlocked the wolves' cage, freed the elephant and created general havoc at the world's film capital," wrote *Moving Picture Weekly*.[24] Martin's mood change likely precipitated William Campbell's departure from the studio. "I was terrified of Joe," wrote Diana Serra Cary, the name that child star Baby Peggy would come to be known by in later years. "My skin crawled whenever the chimp put his hairy arm around my shoulders or flashed an entire keyboard of yellow ivories in a grimace known the world over as 'Joe Martin's Smile'."[25]

Things went from bad to worse by 1922, when Martin, on loan-out for Rex Ingram's production of *Trifling Women*, got a bit over-enthusiastic while filming a scene with Edward Connelly and "crushed" him in his arms. "The actor is at present confined to his home in Hollywood suffering from severe nervous shock as well as from injuries about the body and a bite in the hand."[26] Martin was placed in solitary confinement.

Full-page ad for the pieced-together final Joe Martin single reelers, *A White Wing Monkey* and *Down in Jungle Town*. From the February 9, 1924 issue of *Universal Weekly*.

There were a final two Joe Martin comedies, both of them single-reelers attributed to Harry Burns: *A White Wing Monkey* (January 7, 1924) starred Joe as Jungle Town's street cleaner, and *Down in Jungle Town* (January 28, 1924) had Joe riding to the rescue atop an elephant. These were both quickie productions slapped together with footage from earlier Joe Martin productions, intended for one last quick buck to capitalize on the Joe Martin name. The reason? That very same month it was announced that Martin had been sold to the Al. G. Barnes Circus for $25,000 where he would be a headliner...behind bars.[27] His place before the cameras was taken by "Jiggs," ballyhooed as a "remarkable chimpanzee."[28]

While the Joe Martin comedies have occasionally been connected to the Sterns in one account or another, the Sterns had no direct involvement with any of them. The Burns-directed comedies were all filmed at the Universal City studios and the Universal zoo, and not at the Sterns' studio. Diana Serra Cary's comments about Joe Martin in her various memoirs suggest that Joe was either borrowed from Universal to appear in one or more of her Baby Peggy shorts, or she may have misremembered *Mrs.* Joe Martin as Joe.

Curley Stecker, Joe Martin's trainer, didn't fare much better with Universal. As Universal's animal trainer and custodian of the Universal Zoo since 1914, Stecker was in charge of training a number of the zoo's members, one of whom was Charlie the elephant. Not as pliable an actor as Joe, Charley had a temper that would frequently cause issues at the studio, as in 1915 when he snapped his restraining chain and went on a destructive stampede before ending up bathing in the Los Angeles River.[29]

"He gets his signals with this stick," said Stecker in an interview with *Photoplay*, hefting the long stick with the heavy iron prong at the end. "Of course I give him his orders too, but for some of his stunts it is easier to make him understand with this."[30] Charlie finally had enough of Stecker's not-so-gentle prodding and went berserk while taking part in one of director Maurice Tourneur's features. *Motion Picture News* described the incident in graphic terms:

> Stecker, in his efforts to quiet the animal, was seized and lifted high in the air. So tightly was he held in the elephant's trunk that two ribs were fractured. The climax came when the screaming beast drew Stecker's head in its mouth. Carl Stecker, a brother of the trainer, probably saved a life by remaining on the scene and beating the animal with a heavy stick. Studio workmen and extras arrived with spears and the trainer was dropped to the ground suffering from concussion of the brain, in addition to the fractured ribs.[31]

According to *Picture-Play Magazine*, "a crack marksman came and fired the shot that killed [Charlie],"[32] and Diana Serra Cary recounted a similar fate for Charlie in one of her memoirs. Columnist and screenwriter Jimmy Starr tells another story, however. He claims that Charlie was allowed to live for a short while, but demands for his death from the press and S.P.C.A.—for the "safety of civilization"—resulted in Universal's decision to put the aged creature down. As "evidence," Starr offered up a poem written at the time by a fellow newspaperman named Ted Taylor:

"What are the p.a.'s howlin' for?" asked Charge-to-Overhead.

"To make you stop and think and look," the Camera Grinder said.

"What makes you so white, so white?" said Charge-to-Overhead.

"I'm dreadin' what I've got to film!" the Camera Grinder said.

"For they're hangin' Curley's Charlie;

You can hear Carl Laemmle choke.

The Crowds are surgin' out the Pass—

For Charlie has to croak.

They will hoist him with a derrick

Till his bloomin' neck is broke!

Oh, they're hangin' Charlie out at Univer-sal!"

"I've fed him hay a score of times," said Charge-to-Overhead.

"He's munchin' bitter hay alone!" the Camera Grinder said.

"His actin' for the screen was fine," said Charge-to-Overhead.

"They'll sell his tusks for ivory now," the Camera Grinder said.

"Yes, they're hangin' Curley's Charlie;

Order is to execute.

For he kneeled on Curley Stecker

You admit that wasn't cute.

Then S.P.C.A. said 'Kill him'

And his hide's too tough to shoot,

So they're hangin' Charlie out at Universal!"[33]

If accurate, one can see why the PR people offered the press a "tamer" version of Charlie's demise, but I personally kind of hope he was shot rather than hung.

As for Stecker, Universal filed a suit against the ailing trainer, who had earlier convinced the studio to sell its two camels, "Prince" and "Babe," for a pittance based on Stecker's claim they were both suffering from tuberculosis. It turns out that both were in good health, so the suits at Universal were understandably unhappy.[34] It's not known what became of this lawsuit, but within a half year Stecker would die at his home in Lankershim as a result of those pachyderm-induced injuries.[35]

By the time the 1919-1920 season rolled around, Century was back on solid footing, and a new brand of comedies was announced. This was to replace the former L-Ko comedies, the last of which—director Alf Goulding's *Charlie the Hero* starring Chai Hong—was released on August 20. Bearing the brand name of Rainbow, the new comedies would alternate on a week-by-week basis with the Century comedies. Rainbow, it was reported, would release "high-class two-reel slapstick comedies," while Century would stick with "animal comedies with lions, bears, monkeys and snakes."[36] Or so it was reported.

For the record, the name Rainbow Comedies was not a new one. There was a United States Motion Picture Corporation operating out of studios in Wilkes-Barre, Pennsylvania that had released a series of single-reel Black Diamond Comedies through Paramount in 1916-1917.[37] They created a new brand in 1918—Rainbow Comedies—to co-star Lillian Vera and Eddie Bouldon, for release through the General Film Company. Seven of these were released into early 1919, after which nothing more was heard about them.[38] The Sterns appropriated the name a few months later, but whether their choice of the Rainbow name was sheer coincidence or, less likely, to ride in on the coattails of another previously established brand with some name recognition, is anyone's guess. IMDb.com erroneously has United States Motion Picture Corporation affiliated with the Sterns' Rainbow comedies.

The L-Ko studios were promptly renamed the Century Studios in July.[39] Within a year the board of directors, as represented by president Julius Stern and new vice president Louis Jacobs, voted to increase the capital stock of L-Ko from its original one hundred shares with the par value of one hundred dollars per share, to seven hundred fifty shares.[40] In the meantime, Abe had been appointed treasurer of the Universal Film Manufacturing Company, succeeding the departing Patrick Powers in that position; Abe would continue as L-Ko's secretary and treasurer.[41] The company's name would officially be changed two months later from L-Ko Motion Picture Kompany (as it was called in the petition) to Century Film Corporation, the application approved by Superior Court judge Grant Jackson on October 26, 1920.[42]

And with that approval, L-Ko as an entity was effectively shelved, and Henry Lehrman's earlier involvement quietly swept under the carpet. Not completely, however;

diehards would continue to refer to the studios as the L-Ko Studios, or at least up until those studios were destroyed by fire six years later.

(For a detailed history of the L-Ko Komedy Kompany, 1914-1919, see *Mr. Suicide: Henry "Pathé" Lehrman and the Birth of Silent Comedy* by Thomas Reeder, published by BearManor Media, 2017.)

Chapter 5: The Serials and Other Distractions

Julius's announced breaking of ties with Universal back in 1916 and his teaming with younger sibling Abe at L-Ko was not the only business venture the two now had in the works. "It is my intention of starting a producing company on the Coast," Stern had said, "where I will make my own pictures which may be released on the Universal program."[1] (Note Julius's use of "my" and "I" in this quote, a tendency to dominate the limelight that would carry on through the rest of the silent era.) This was a decided change of plans for Stern, who had as recently as a month earlier announced his intention to start a feature organization to produce films in New York for the open market. "Several stars have been tentatively approached for the new Stern feature company," wrote the *New York Clipper*, "with varying degrees of success."[2]

Anyway, Julius's claim took shape when it was further announced that the brothers had teamed up with mid-western theatre manager Louis Jacobs to form a new $50,000 production company. Within days it was also announced that Abe had recently married Jessie Jacobs of Milwaukee.[3] Jessie, as it turned out, was the daughter of Louis Jacobs, their new production company partner, demonstrating that Laemmle did not have a lock on nepotism.[4]

Contracts had been secured with popular film stars Francis Ford—older brother to John Ford, then in his earliest days as a director—and Grace Cunard, the duo having recently left Universal after filming five episodes of the serial *Peg O' the Ring*; Ruth Stonehouse had assumed the lead role.[5] Ford and Cunard had, as *Photoplay* put it, "clashed with the new efficiency system"—presumably H.O. Davis's doing—resulting in a "severance of diplomatic and business relations" with Universal."[6] This split proved to be short-lived, and the couple returned to filming under even more grueling circumstances than before, necessitating the completion of three episodes—or six reels—every two weeks due to the interruption of their filming.[7] Stonehouse, it was reported, had been injured when she fell from a trapeze and was out of commission for the better part of a month,[8] perhaps the reason for luring Ford and Cunard back to the serial. Stonehouse was reassigned to a new film upon her return to work, and her footage dropped from the serial when it was finally released.

Francis Ford.

Grace Cunard.

While it is clear that the Sterns had involvement with a number of other serials over the better part of the decade that followed, only a few of these received any sort of publicity that connected the Sterns to the production. As a result it is impossible to document the entirety of their output, but we'll touch on some of those that we know of. The earliest was the Ford-Cunard twenty part serial *The Purple Mask*, released on the last day of 1916.[9] This one's episodes were written by Cunard, who co-directed with Ford.

The serials receiving the most hype, however, were those produced by Julius Stern's Great Western Producing Company, operating out of the Sterns' studios at 6100 Sunset Boulevard. The earliest of the Great Westerns, *Elmo the Mighty* (working titles *The Modern Hercules* and *The Phantom Raider*), co-starred Elmo Lincoln and Grace Cunard, and was released to theatres beginning in June 1919. Lincoln, who had just made a name for himself as star of the recent First National features *Tarzan of the Apes* and *The Romance of*

Tarzan (both 1918), was signed to a two-year contract by Great Western,[10] and as "Elmo (Armstrong) the Mighty" portrayed a forest ranger seeking to frustrate the unlawful designs of a syndicate out to defraud the government. Henry McRae, former manager of production at Universal, was chosen to helm the production.[11]

Elmo Lincoln. Courtesy of Heritage Auctions, Ha.com.

Lincoln's next for Great Western, announced as *Fighting Through*[12] but released in 1920 as *Elmo the Fearless*, had direction by J.P. McGowan[13] and co-starred newcomer Louise Lorraine. Other Lincoln vehicles for Great Western from that same year included Robert Hill's serial *The Flaming Disc* and the Rex Ingram feature *Under Crimson Skies* (working title *The Beach Combers*), all released through Universal.

There was some level of involvement with other of Universal's serials as well, but exactly what form that involvement took is unclear. Julius was connected to the studio's "Thrills-in-History" series when Eddie Polo, slated to star in the upcoming third entry *The Adventures of Robinson Crusoe*, abruptly departed from the studio. This may have been only in an as-needed advisory capacity, but it was Stern to the rescue, or at least according to Universal press releases: "One of the objects of [Stern's] recent trip to 1600 Broadway was the selection of a serial star.... This search culminated in the engagement of Jack O'Brien, who has all of the physical characteristics required and who has had enough experience in the serial 'Bride 13' to weather the arduous role mapped out for him."[14] Perhaps this was the sole extent of the Sterns' involvement with that series.[15]

Elmo Lincoln makes a "death-defying" leap in this poster for episode one of the serial
Elmo the Fearless, produced by Great Western for Universal release.
Courtesy of Heritage Auctions, Ha.com.

In April 1918, a telegram from Julius, now in Hollywood, to Abe on the East Coast indicates that Universal's auditors were keeping close tabs on the expenditures for the Sterns' serials. "Universal auditor will finish tomorrow checking Elmo Mighty," wrote Julius

will take him at least two weeks more-so far found everything correct if
C.L. [Carl Laemmle] insists checking everything might take too long-will
share advise soon as he gets through with first one....[16]

Was this business as usual? The relationship between Julius and Laemmle had suffered some stress a mere month earlier (see Chapter 9), so the timing of this audit—if not a regular, on-going procedure—seems oddly coincidental.

Eddie Polo.

In 1921, Great Western entered into an arrangement with Numa Pictures Corporation to film the fifteen part serial *The Adventures of Tarzan*. A new organization was formed for purposes of exploitation and marketing of the serial, bearing the unwieldy name "The Adventures of Tarzan Serial Sales Corporation." The principals included Great Western's president Julius Stern, along with Louis Jacobs and Louis's brother Oscar Jacobs, who served as Great Western's Eastern representative. Other principals included Adolph Weiss, Numa's president; Louis Weiss, Numa's vice president; and Max Weiss. *The Adventures of Tarzan* would be distributed on the state rights market through independent exchanges rather than through Universal. Elmo Lincoln would again appear in the lead role,[17] and

Robert F. Hill directed a cast that would include other Stern regulars, Louise Lorraine, Percy Pembroke, George "Zip" Monberg, Charles Inslee, and Lillian Worth among them. And, of course, Joe Martin,[18] with an assist from Numa the lion and Tantor the elephant.

UNIVERSAL'S SUPREME CHAPTER PLAY
The Adventures of
ROBINSON CRUSOE
Chapter 11 = NO GREATER LOVE
FEATURING
HARRY MYERS   *Morgan*
with GERTRUDE OLMSTED *and* NOBLE JOHNSON
DIRECTED BY ROBERT HILL

Universal went ahead and made *The Adventures of Robinson Crusoe* without Eddie Polo. Julius Stern had chosen Jack O'Brien as Polo's replacement, but Harry Myers ended up in the lead. Courtesy of Heritage Auctions, Ha.com.

Director Hill was particularly effusive about his work on this serial: "I have specialized in the direction of chapter film plays for many years and I believe that in [this] serial I have finally achieved my dream of what should really constitute this peculiar form of screen entertainment." Hill went on to describe the menagerie required for the film's production:

> The remarkable numbers of wild animals used throughout the entire production necessitated the most difficult kind of handling on the part of Charles Gay, wild animal trainer who was called upon at different times for

apes, lions, tigers, leopards, hyenas, elephants, crocodiles, jaguars, etc. Only a single accident for which the animals were responsible marred the making of the thirty-one reels.[19]

These are the five men responsible for the serial "The Adventures of Tarzan," for distribution by Numa Pictures Corporation. Left to right they are: Julius Stern, president Great Western Producing Company; Oscar Jacobs, Eastern representative; Adolph Weiss, president Numa Pictures; Louis Weiss, vice president, and Max Weiss, of the board of directors of Numa Pictures Corporation.

"These are the five men responsible for the serial 'The Adventures of Tarzan'." Left-to-right: Julius Stern, Oscar Jacobs, Adolph Weiss, Louis Weiss, and Max Weiss. From the June 25, 1921 issue of *Exhibitors Herald*.

One would think that Curley Stecker must have had a part in all this as well, but Gay gets all the credit.

One amusing result of this filming was a suit brought by Lincoln against both Abe and Julius Stern, seeking $4,000 plus interest. Lincoln alleged that he was compelled to shave his entire body to play the part of Tarzan, which he considered an unusual demand. The Sterns, he claimed, promised him an extra $5,000 to do so, but only paid him an up-front $1,000, while the Sterns claimed the latter figure was all they had promised.[20] The result of this suit is unknown, but at least Elmo's hair would grow back.

Another production company was formed back in 1919 named the Pacific (Coast) Producing Co., to film the serial promoted as *The Radium Mystery* but eventually released as *The Great Radium Mystery*. Early episodes were shot at Universal City, but production soon relocated to the Sterns' lot where it was completed. Directed by Robert Broadwell and starring Cleo Madison, Eileen Sedgwick, and Bob Reeves,[21] it is unclear whether the Sterns had a financial stake in this company, or if they were merely leasing a portion of their lot—advertised as the Pacific Coast Studios—for filming. A blurb appearing in *Wid's Daily* stating that The Pacific Producing Co. was the same company engaging "J.P. McGowan … to direct Elmo Lincoln in a new serial" would suggest that this was yet another Stern endeavor.[22] Pacific Producing Co. would go on to advertise for "Two Reel Western Comedy Dramas for Male and Female Lead" stories, further suggesting the Sterns' involvement in western shorts for Universal, but that's just speculation.[23] Yet another article stated that Julius was president of the Pacific Film Co.,[24] which sounds like a simple misreporting of the Pacific Producing Co.'s name.

Elmo Lincoln and Louise Lorraine administer aide while Joe Martin looks on, in *The Adventures of Tarzan*, produced by Great Western for Weiss Brothers' Numa Pictures Corp. and release through the state rights market.

A more curious involvement on the Sterns' part was with a film written and directed by Capt. Leslie T. Peacock for the Democracy Film Co., a "film concern organized by colored business men of Los Angeles." The six reel feature film, released as *Injustice* in 1919, was touted as "a fitting tribute to the loyal negro citizens of the United States, as many scenes in the picture depict the sterling part played by the colored race in the late war."[25] The Sterns were engaged to distribute the film which, according to the *AFI Catalog of Feature Films*, they cut "to five reels, added titles in dialect, possibly added additional footage, and advertised the result as a comedy." Released as *Loyal Hearts*, Democracy brought suit against L-Ko.[26] Not one of the Sterns' finest hours, it would seem.

Poster for the fifteenth episode of *The Great Radium Mystery*, produced by Pacific Producing Co. for release through Universal. Courtesy of Heritage Auctions, Ha.com.

Julius also had his hands in some other lucrative business ventures during this period as well, theatre ownership among them. Along with partners Maurice Fleckles and Louis Jacobs, they owned the Rex and Strand Theatres in Michigan, and in 1917 had secured an option at Beloit, Wisconsin where they contemplated the erection of a third theatre that would seat 1,200 patrons.[27] The partnership had Rex and Strand Theatres in Beloit as well, which they eventually sold to the Orpheum Picture Company in 1921.[28]

What we currently know is likely only a subset of the actual involvement of Julius and his brother in other projects outside of those for L-Ko and Century. That said, it's still evident that Julius was a very busy man, and we haven't yet touched on the other demands placed on him by Laemmle during this period; these will be detailed in chapter nine.

What's not clear, however, was the extent of brother Abe's involvement in these various other projects. Given that Julius's ongoing releases to the trades usually placed himself at the center of the story, and frequently to the exclusion of other contributors, awareness of Abe's participation may well have been an unfortunate casualty. Perhaps Abe was content to stay in the background. Or perhaps not, and it may have been a bone of contention between the brothers; we'll never know for certain.

Chapter 6: Competing With Oneself
(The 1919-1920 Season)

Both Century and Rainbow were up and running by the time the 1919-1920 season opened, a given season defined as running from the first of September through August of the following year. Century's *A Village Venus* (September 3, 1919) and *A Lion in the House* were released on the first and third Wednesdays of September—both directed by Fred Fishback—while Rainbow's *A Roof Garden Rough House* (September 10) and *An Oriental Romeo* (September 24) were released on the second and fourth Wednesday. James Davis and Jess Robbins directed the two Rainbows, respectively. This alternating schedule was adhered to through the year with only a couple of hiccups in October and December, when two of a given brand's films were released successively.

Both Julius and Abe had spent the summer on the West Coast overseeing the ramped up production of the two brands,[1] but with the new season's opening it was Abe's turn to head back to the East Coast to take charge of the Eastern office.[2]

In spite of the Rainbow brand's buildup in the trades, it turned out to be a short-lived affair lasting only the one season and its two dozen-plus releases. The primary male "stars" of the series were the trio of Chai Hong, Billy Engle, and Zip Monberg, with Phil Dunham and newcomer Harry Sweet secondary. Their female co-stars were a more varied bunch, with Lois Neilson, Consuela (aka Connie) Henley, Lillian Biron, Bartine Burkett, and Virginia Warwick present in a handful each. Many of these comedians had an earlier start with L-Ko, and would be used in Rainbow (and Century) productions as needed. Hong had appeared regularly in L-Ko comedies since mid-1918, and Dunham since the beginning of 1916. Burkett had appeared in eight L-Ko's since early 1918, but Sweet had only a single L-Ko to his credit. Neilson, who was featured in a trio of L-Ko's from early 1919, would now appear only in the Rainbows.

There were three primary directors of the Rainbow Comedies: Jay A. "Kitty" Howe, a former actor with L-Ko since mid-1915, and directing for that brand since 1917; William H. Watson, new to L-Ko and with three films for that brand under his belt; and Jess Robbins. A few other directors would step in to helm a single comedy each or, in the case of James Davis, two comedies.

Director Jay A. "Kitty" Howe.

The Sterns weren't bashful in promoting the new Rainbows, as an ad in *Moving Picture Weekly* targeted at exhibitors modestly stated:

> In the big new RAINBOW COMEDIES for the coming Fall and Winter season of 1919 and 1920 there will be released 26 pictures in all; 14 of these will be high-speed straight comedies packed full of new ideas and laughs; 12 of these will be roaring animal comedies that will bring home the profits to exhibitors.
>
> 14 of the gosh-darnedest, craziest comedies you've ever run. 14 roar fests. 14 side splitters. 14 knock 'em dead winners that you can boost hard. That's

what you're going to get in these 14 new RAINBOW COMEDIES. Watch for them. Speak to your Exchange.

12 of the thrilliest, hair-breathiest, most blood-curdlingest, terrifyingest wild animal comedies you've ever run. Wild animal comedies, fast and furious. A riot of joy and oodles of fun. 12 of 'em to give you 12 big houses. Speak NOW to your Exchange.[3]

Sheer puffery, of course, since several of the initial offerings were re-branded L-Ko Comedies and the remainder basically the same stuff they'd been releasing for several years. As for those animal comedies, most of them were released as Centuries. Not that it really mattered to exhibitors, since they would have signed on for the whole Rainbow-Century package.

Zip Monberg's about to administer a spanking to Johnny Fox, while Jackie Morgan, Ena Gregory, and Pal look on, in Alf Goulding's *Live Wires*. Courtesy of Marguerite Sheffler.

Rainbow's first release was the aforementioned *A Roof Garden Rough House*, which had earlier been advertised in full-page ads as an upcoming L-Ko release. The film co-starred Zip Monberg and Lois Neilson, with direction by James Davis. "The plot has to do with the downfall of a motor cop whose persistence in winning the affections of another man's wife leads to all sorts of complications, which carry through the dance on the roof garden, to the skating rink and also the top of the building" wrote *Motion Picture News*'s reviewer.[4]

The film's "star," Chicago-born Zip Monberg (1890-1925; born George Williams), had been hired by the Sterns after he had appeared in a handful of comedies for Vogue in 1917 and a single entry for Bull's Eye in 1919. Rechristened Zip Monberg (and occasionally billed as Zip Monty), Monberg appeared in a total of eight Rainbows, interspersed with the occasional appearance in a Century release. Monberg would continue with Century into 1923, with the occasional side gig in the serial *The Adventures of Tarzan* and a couple of Hall Room Boys Comedies for CBC. An underrated and forgotten talent, Monberg's life was cut short with his death in 1925 at the comparatively young age of thirty-four.

Monberg's co-star, Lois Neilson (1895-1990), was a blonde ingénue with a few earlier films for Rolin and Vitagraph to her credit, along with those three L-Ko Comedies before she was reassigned to Rainbow. Neilson only appeared in two other Rainbows, *Dainty Damsels and Bogus Counts* (October 8, 1919), and *Oh! You East Lynn* (November 26, 1919). In this latter film, Neilson appeared as a member of a traveling troupe scrambling to replace its star performer, who has failed to show. Neilson would appear in an additional four films for Century as well before moving on. Neilson became the first Mrs. Stan Laurel in 1926.[5]

Actress Lois Neilson.

James D. Davis (1889-1944), the film's director, had a handful of previous efforts for Vogue in 1917 before L-Ko hired him later that same year to direct films such as Hughie Mack's *Hula Hula Hughie* (1917) and *Barbarous Plots* (1918). He was prolific, if uninspired (his extant L-Ko *The Belles of Liberty* is almost unwatchable, or at least in its surviving, truncated form), cranking out seventeen films for L-Ko—eighteen if you count *A Roof Garden Rough House*—before switching primarily to Century Comedies, with only this and one other Rainbow—*An Oil Can Romeo* (August 11, 1920)—to his credit. Outside of Century, Davis would direct numerous other comedies for CBC's "Hallroom Boys" series, Hal Roach, and Weiss Brothers-Artclass before his directorial career met the same fate as the silent film.

Director James Davis.

The second Rainbow release, *An Oriental Romeo*, starred Chai Hong as a beachside restaurant's waiter, mixing it up with some beachgoers. Hong, frequently billed as Charlie of the Orient, was a diminutive comedian who may or may not have been born in China; his origins remain clouded in mystery. Purported to have been on the speaking stage in China, he had come to America and, finding no immediate openings here, took a job as bellhop at the Hotel Alexandria. Later discovered there by Julius,[6] Hong had ten comedies to his credit for L-Ko before switching over to the Rainbow brand. There he starred in a total of seven Rainbows along with two others for Century, the final for that brand *Brownie, the Peacemaker* (August 25, 1920), supporting Phil Dunham and Merta Sterling, who believes that Brownie is her reincarnated husband! Hong then parted ways with the Sterns and made a few more random appearances for other producers through 1922 before his career fizzled. By mid-1925 he was found working as actor Lew Cody's valet and houseman, reportedly with a "contract for life."[7]

Billy Engle (left) and Chai Hong (right) in Rainbow's *A Barnyard Romance*, directed by Jess Robbins. Courtesy of Mark Johnson.

An Oriental Romeo's director, Jess Robbins (1888-1973), had a long career with Essanay before hooking up with the Sterns. A cameraman for that studio from 1908 to 1912, Robbins made the switch to direction for Essanay for the two years following, after which he worked for Chaplin on his comedies. With Chaplin's departure and the closing of Essanay's studio in Niles, California, Robbins followed Gilbert M. Anderson, who had sold his share of the company to his former partner, George Spoor. Robbins served as business manager at Anderson's new Golden West Photoplay Company for a short while before being lured over to L-Ko in 1919. His first film for L-Ko as director was *An Oriental Romeo*, eventually re-branded as a Rainbow release. Robbins directed Hong in three more for Rainbow, *A Barnyard Romance* (December 3, 1919), *Charlie Gets a Job* (December 31, 1919), and *Over the Ocean*

Wave (February 4, 1920), in which Hong appeared as a tramp, a butler, and a boat's chef, respectively. Robbins's *Adam and Eve a la Mode* (January 7, 1920) starred William Franey, and *A Roaring Love Affair* (March 17, 1902) featured Monberg and Harry Sweet. Robbins would depart but return in 1925 and remain with Century for another two years, after which he moved over to Fox to direct a number of short comedies. Robbins's career appears to have met the same fate as Davis's, tanking with the coming of sound.

Director Jess Robbins.

Another Rainbow release was *The Jail Breaker* (September 2, 1919; date unconfirmed). This was the sole Rainbow release directed by Charles Parrott, more commonly known by his before-the-camera alias Charley Chase. *The Jail Breaker* was likely another older, rebranded L-Ko, since Parrott had had five previous credits for that studio during the previous year and had by this time been directing for Bulls-Eye. One of *The Jail Breaker*'s stars was Austrian-born Billy Engle (1889-1966), who had only a couple of comedies for Triangle before the Sterns hired him. Engle starred in at least nine for Rainbow, one of these *He Loved Like He Lied* (May 19, 1920), where he played a fellow impersonating a soldier with hopes of separating a war widow from her insurance money; this was director Mal St. Clair's sole film for any of the Sterns' brands. Engle's *Moonshines and Jailbirds* (June 9, 1920) was a prohibition yarn wherein turtles are used to smuggle liquor from Mexico into the U.S.; and *Off His Trolley* (July 21, 1920) followed the increasingly heated competition between the owners of a rural jitney and a trolley car. Engle appeared in a number of Century comedies as well into 1921, and would be rehired by the Sterns for future work in 1923 and 1925.

Billy Engle (left) and William Irving in Rainbow's *He Loved Like He Lied*, director Mal St. Clair's sole effort for the Sterns. Courtesy of Jim Kerkhoff.

Billy Engel's trolley has had a slight accident in director Jay. A. "Kitty" Howe's *Off His Trolley*, a Rainbow release. Courtesy of Jim Kerkhoff.

All for the Dough Bag (January 21, 1920) was one of only three Rainbows that London-born Phil Dunham (1885-1972) appeared in. Hired by L-Ko back in 1915, Dunham's early years of stage experience in England and Ireland were followed by some work in vaudeville here in the states. Dunham then entered the film industry in 1913 with roles in productions for Nestor, Joker, Powers, and Kalem. At five feet six and one hundred forty pounds, the compact comedian would appear in nearly three dozen comedies before expanding into direction as well. Dunham would remain with L-Ko—starring roles included *Dad's Dollars and Dirty Doings* (1916), *On the Trail of the Lonesome Pill*, and *The Joy Riders* (both 1917)—until its rebranding as Century. In addition to his handful of films for Century—*The Cabbage Queen*, *Brownie's Doggone Tricks* (November 5, 1919), and *Brownie, the Peacemaker*—Dunham's Rainbows included *Oh! You East Lynn*, *All for the Dough Bag*, and *The Bull Thrower* (February 18, 1920). In this latter film Dunham is forced to perform as a matador to win the hand of co-star Edna Gregory. Evidently director "Kitty" Howe's handling of this sequence left something to be desired, or at least according to *Film Daily*'s reviewer:

> And this is where the direction slipped up, for the manner in which it has been screened is not effective. The scenes where the characters jump out of the enclosure wherein is supposed to stamp about the wild bull gives no one pause to imagine that what is supposed to happen, really occurs. Some of the stuff included in the piece is really clever, but it has several faults that are a handicap.[8]

With his departure from the Sterns, Dunham would appear in a couple of comedies for Reelcraft before rejoining Henry Lehrman for a trio of films for his short-lived Henry Lehrman Comedies, *The Kick in High Life* and *Punch of the Irish* (both 1920) among them. Nearly sixty films—most of them comedy shorts—would follow into 1928, the bulk for Educational. By the 1930s Dunham was reduced to taking bit parts in more than a hundred shorts and features, as well as serving as screenwriter for a number of others in a career that would last until the early 1950s.

All for the Dough Bag, which survives in a print held by the Museum of Modern Art, is a wild little chase comedy wherein a number of look-alike valises—one of them stuffed with stolen cash and jewels—get switched repeatedly among a number of participants. Dunham plays dance instructor Prof. A. Natomy, in love with his pupil and neighbor Bartine Burkett, and she with him, much to the annoyance of her modiste mother, Mme Iva Fit. Zip Monberg plays the crook of the piece, his face whitened and shoulders continually hunched, and outfitted in too-tight and too-short clothes. Hoping to retrieve his ill-gotten gains, his pursuit occupies the better part of the film, ending up with a rooftop chase sequence. Zip is now the pursued, crawling along inside a barrel with both Dunham and a cop close behind, in barrels as well and with guns blazing. There's a lot of teetering on the edge before Zip's barrel plummets to the street far below, where he is arrested. Burkett's mother gives her blessing to a marriage, lovebirds Dunham and Burkett now skipping off merrily and into a lake.

"Expert Butcher" Phil Dunham at work with an assist from Jessie Fox, in the Century comedy *Brownie the Peacemaker*. Courtesy of Sam Gill.

Brown-eyed, brown-haired Bartine Burkett (1898-1994) was another talent who made repeat appearances at the Century studios. A native of Shreveport, Louisiana, petite Burkett had one of the longer film careers on record, spanning the years 1917 to 1984 (albeit with a gap in performances of close to fifty years). With a handful of shorts for Nestor, Triangle, and Universal before hooking up with L-Ko in 1919, Bartine was used by the Sterns in their spoof *The Geezer of Berlin* before appearing in her two Rainbows, *All for the Dough Bag* and *Over the Ocean Wave*. Burkett would then part ways with the Sterns for a year where she would co-star in Buster Keaton's *The High Sign* (1921) among many others, returning in 1921 for another dozen shorts for Century, and yet again in 1924 for another series. One of her cutest moments in *All for the Dough Bag* occurs when she's been banished to her room by her mother. Now alone, Burkett proceeds to silently "tell off" her mother in extreme close-up, a throw-away shot that would have been wasted by an actress of lesser talent.

Burkett had an amusing story to tell about her early interactions with one of the Stern brothers, although she couldn't recall which one when she was interviewed some sixty years afterwards.

Cute-as-a-button actress Bartine Burkett.

I'll always remember one morning, I was standing out front. And one of the Stern brothers came along and said "Good morning Miss Burkett."

And I just looked away and said nothing.

"I said 'Good morning.'"

I said "Yes, I've been out here several mornings and I've said 'Good morning' to you, and you didn't answer me."

He said "Well that has nothing to do with it. When I say good morning to you, you say good morning to me."

And I said "No, sir, I won't do it."

He says "I'll fire you."

I said "Okay, go ahead."

He called me in the office and we had a little argument.

I said "Why should I say 'Good morning' to you, when it's the first time you've said it to me? I stood out there and said 'Good morning' to you, and you would just look at me and pass on. I'm not used to being treated that way, and I won't take it."

Well, I was in a couple of pictures already by then, and so he couldn't fire me, you know; it would have been too expensive.

So he said "You better watch your manners from now on."

I said "I will if you will."[9]

Feisty!

Grandson Gilbert Sherman favors Julius as the Stern in question, but isn't certain. "I never knew Abe, but I would say that this could be accurately attributed to either of them, as I feel as though they shared a number of personality traits. Brusqueness and expectation of recognition among them. While I don't remember Julius being at all polite, he was generally not overtly impolite—when I was with him…. He was a hard man in many respects and didn't tolerate disrespect—I do remember that personally."[10]

Both Burkett and Diana Serra Cary have placed Abe at the studio's front door on frequent occasions, impatiently awaiting the arrival of cast and crew members alike. He would stand there, stone-faced, tapping his wristwatch and continuously uttering "Time is money! Time is money!"[11] This would suggest that the individual in Burkett's other remembrance was Abe. Suggest, but not prove.

All for the Dough Bag's director, Jay A. "Kitty" Howe (1889-1962), was a native of Kansas. He was hired in 1915 by Henry Lehrman to act in his L-Ko Comedies, but with the Sterns' takeover was promoted to director in 1917, handling such comedies as the Phil Dunham vehicles *A Limburger Cyclone*, *Nabbing a Noble*, and *Tom's Tramping Troupe* (all 1917). After a break during which he directed comedies for Fox and Vitagraph, Howe returned in 1919 to direct all of Dunham's Rainbows, which included *A Popular Villain* (October 29, 1919), *A Restaurant Riot* (May 5, 1920), *Moonshines and Jailbirds*, *A Villain's Broken Heart* (June 30, 1920), and *Off His Trolley*. A single Century, *Brownie's Busy Day* (January 28, 1920) was Howe's sole remaining credit for the Sterns before departing to direct primarily for Hal Roach, Will Rogers's *The Cowboy Sheik*, *The Cake Eater*, and *Gee Whiz, Genevieve* (all 1924) among them. By the end of 1928, Howe's career as director had come to an end.

As you can see, the Sterns' roster of comedians was anything but powerhouse, more a schizophrenic mishmash of second- and third-tier comics with a few newcomers thrown into the mix. Phil Dunham was among their bigger names at this time, but the likes of Alice Howell were noticeably absent. Admittedly they would loosen their purse strings on occasion when they would hire a Mack Swain or a Gale Henry to head up one of their "Star Series," but these were always short-lived associations. They would, however, in short time develop some new talents who would rise above the others, but these were few and far between. Julius, the voice of Century, would usually take credit for tracking down the new hires who proved to have some legs, but it was Abe who had the most experience in the realm of comedy, observing and learning at the side of Henry Lehrman during his leadership of L-Ko. That, and Abe was for the most part the ongoing presence at the studio, while Julius would reside in New York with only the occasional trip to the West Coast. Still, it was a collaborative relationship.

Billy Engle displays the day's take in Rainbow's *Off His Trolley*, directed by Jay A. "Kitty" Howe. Courtesy of Robert James Kiss.

One of the Sterns' new hires who would click with the filmgoing public was a young man named Harry Sweet. Hailing from Colorado, Sweet (1901-1933) was a former acrobat and "rapid fire jazz" musician.[12] He had joined L-Ko in 1919, his only credit under that banner the brand's final release, *Charlie the Hero* (August 20, 1919). Born Harry Swett and originally billed under that name, Sweet would continue to star in both Century and Rainbow Comedies into mid-1920, and in Centuries into 1924, after which he left to direct for Sennett, Fox, and F.B.O. Sweet's Rainbows included *A Champion Loser* (April 7, 1920) and *A He-Male Vamp* (June 23, 1920), while his Centuries included *Lonesome Hearts and Loose Lions, Loose Lions and Fast Lovers* (February 25, 1920), and *Lions' Jaws and Kittens' Paws* (June 16, 1920).

Century comedian Harry Sweet, making a mess of some footage.
Courtesy of Robert James Kiss.

Harry Sweet, Dan Russell, and Marjorie Ray recoil from one of the Century Lions in
director Fred Fishback's *Loose Lions and Fast Lovers*. Courtesy of Richard M. Roberts.

Lions' Jaws and Kittens' Paws is another lucky survivor of the ravages of time, the print held by the Museum of Modern Art a showcase for Sweet's considerable talents and comic timing. Sweet and wife Edna Gregory live in an apartment building upstairs from "Ladies Tailor" Zip Monberg and his wife, played by Merta Sterling. Zip takes measurements of Edna for a fitting, and proceeds to flirt with her. Merta observes this and brings it to Sweet's attention. Sweet arrives, pistol in hand, and after some verbal threats a chase ensues, Sweet's pistol spewing forth what seems like dozens, if not hundreds, of bullets. Sweet eventually tires of the chase, but follows up by unloading a truckload of caged lions into the apartment house. The beasts bound up and down staircases, crash through doors, and leap through open transoms, terrorizing every one of the building's occupants. Zip and Merta eventually flee to their bed and cover themselves, a bunch of lions quickly joining them. There's a dissolve from the lions to a bunch of kittens on the bed, the whole film—or at least the lion portion of it—turning out to have been a bad dinner-induced dream.

Tailor Zip Monberg "measures" Edna Gregory for size. Zip's jealous wife Merta Sterling, and Edna's vengeance-filled husband Harry Sweet, look on, in director William Watson's *Lions' Jaws and Kittens' Paws*. Courtesy of Mark Johnson.

Sweet, who gained a lot of weight within a few years of these early comedies, is pleasantly slim in this one. His single-minded determination to kill Monberg is surprisingly bloodthirsty, especially given the latter's essentially non-threatening flirtation with Sweet's wife. It is, in effect, a 1920 version of an over-the-top #MeToo quest for justice, silent slapstick comedy style. Monberg plays his role as the tailor comparatively straight in this one, a far cry from his ruthless thug in *All for the Dough Bag*. Edna Gregory is an attractive presence, but sadly given little to do here. And then there are the two black janitors, on board here for the obligatory—for the era, at least—sequence where they are scared out of their wits by the marauding lions. One of them jumps into a furnace to escape the lions, while the other garners some good laughs with a close-up of his terrorized face, going through all sorts of eye-bugging, cheek-puffing contortions before the closing shot where he shrinks and un-shrinks multiple times in a clumsily, not-so-special effect shot. As for those lions, director William Watson's handling of them is competently executed, or reasonably so, with lions seemingly everywhere making numerous breath-taking leaps. These sequences are occasionally marred by some poorly executed double exposures, the lions "crossing" that dividing line into the other half with the actors, their snouts and heads momentarily "disappearing" as they cross the matted line.

Zip Monberg displays a kitten for Merta Sterling's inspection in *Lions' Jaws and Kittens' Paws*, one of the later comedies to feature The Century Lions. William Watson directed. Courtesy of Jim Kerkhoff.

As Monberg's jealous wife, Merta Sterling was another transplant from L-Ko, having appeared in nearly two dozen comedies for that company before switching brands. Wisconsin-born Sterling (1892-1944) had been a stenographer in the office of Klaw and Erlanger, supposedly managing to convince producers to let her take part in a revival of *The Prince of Pilsen*.[13] Success in this role led to some work in vaudeville, after which she joined up with Kalem in 1915 and appeared in films for that company (as Myrtle Sterling) before moving over to L-Ko and Phil Dunham's unit in films such as *A Limburger Cyclone* and *The Fat Little Rascal* (both 1917), and later in Vin Moore's *Cannibals and Carnivals* (1918). Her first for Century was *A Lion in the House*, followed by a handful more which included *Romeo and Jolly Juliets* (October 22, 1919), *Good Little Brownie* (February 11, 1920), and *Lions' Jaws and Kittens' Paws*, all directed by William Watson. *Film Daily's* reviewer paid more attention to Sterling's younger, prettier co-actresses in *Good Little Brownie*, commenting that Sterling was forced to share the screen with "Bathing damsels in tight-fitting one-piece apparel, that permits a considerable limb display." It would appear that the L-Ko Beauties soldiered on in some of the early Centuries.

Sterling would star in no fewer than fifteen films before moving on, one of which, *A Restaurant Riot*, was for Rainbow. Sterling's career had peaked with her comedies for the Sterns, later appearing in random shorts in 1923 and 1924 with the likes of Stan Laurel, Monty Banks, and Slim Summerville, as well as several features before retiring from the business in the late 1920s.

Born in Montreal, William H. Watson's (1896-1967) family relocated to Los Angeles where he joined his older brother Coy at Keystone in 1912. Eventually graduating to supervising editor, Watson departed in 1918 to assist Jack White, who was directing for Henry Lehrman at his Fox Sunshine Comedies. Watson was lured over to L-Ko by the Sterns in 1919 where he directed three comedies—*In Bad All Around*, *All Jazzed Up*, and *Sirens of the Suds* (all 1919)—before the brand was terminated, after which he was reassigned to Century to assist Fred Fishback with his lion comedies. Quickly promoted to full director, several more Centuries followed before tackling the Rainbows. Watson's four Rainbows included *A Red Hot Finish* (March 3, 1920), *Light Hearts and Leaking Pipes* (March 31, 1920), *A Jazzy Janitor*, and *A He-Male Vamp*, along with another five for Century by the season's end. An additional thirteen shorts would follow during the 1920-1921 season, the last of these the Charles Dorety vehicle *Hold Your Breath* (August 31, 1921). *Hold Your Breath's* climax featured Dorety and co-star Bert Roach flirting with death twenty-two stories above the street, teetering on the building's ledge. "Director Watson with his cameraman were perched most of the time on the water tank," wrote *Moving*

Picture World, "and a special observation tower had to be made to get the action"[14] which included "a few hair-raising stunts that will give nervous ones in your audience a jolt."[15] With the completion of this film, Watson moved over to Universal's Star Comedies to direct. He would return to the Century family in mid-1924.

Director William H. Watson.

One of Watson's recurring female stars, or at least for a mere four films in 1920, was Virginia Warwick, an actress about whom little is known. She was a star athlete in boarding school, where she was captain of the basketball team and a proficient swimmer. Warwick was later plucked from a fashionable Los Angeles finishing school by Mack Sennett to serve as one of his bathing beauties,[16] but whether she ever actually appeared in any of his comedies is questionable. Warwick was soon snapped up by the Sterns, making a single film for Century and a trio for Rainbow before moving on to hoped-for better things. A plum role in Metro's *The Four Horsemen of the Apocalypse* (1921) was a promising start, but after a few minor films for Fox and a string of independent productions, her career petered out in 1926. Warwick married comedian Jimmie Adams in 1924, and was with him up until his death in 1933.

Charles Dorety (1898-1957), the star of Century's lion comedies *Looney Lions and Monkey Business, Frisky Lions and Wicked Husbands*, and *My Salomy Lions* (May 12, 1920), was a competent performer whose career in comedy lasted into the sound era. Sadly, Dorety failed to catch on with the public in any sort of meaningful way. This may have had to do with the fact that he never established a single recognizable on-screen character, morphing from a bushy-mustached grotesque to a clean-shaven, unassuming character. Dorety's dapper baron in Fox Sunshine's *His Musical Sneeze*, and his Keatonesque character in the Henry Lehrman Comedy *A Twilight Baby* (both 1919), are two contrasting examples, but he would soon acquire a large brush mustache for some of his later films. At least one exhibitor was dismissive of Dorety's "Keaton," in his brief assessment of *The Nervy Dentist* (November 2, 1921): "Charles Dorety tries to mimic Buster Keaton and makes a dismal failure."[17] A valid observation, since any attempt to compare Dorety's comedic abilities and creativity to those of Keaton would be a fool's errand; Dorety was a different kind of comedian.

Comedian Charles Dorety and his brush mustache.

Born in San Francisco, Dorety had experience on both the stage and in vaudeville where he was a dancer and comic. Moving into film comedy, he had appeared in a number of those Fox Sunshine comedies, which included *Hungry Lions in a Hospital* and *The Son of a Hun* (both 1918), before hooking up with the Sterns later that year. A trio of L-Ko's— *Rough on Husbands* (1918), *A Skate at Sea*, and *In Bad All Around* (both 1919)—preceded his move over to the Century Comedies where he would appear in at least three during the remainder of the 1919-1920 season. These included the Brownie comedy *Dog-Gone Clever* (April 14, 1920), *A Birthday Tangle* (July 28, 1920), and the aforementioned *My Salomy Lions*, as well as a pair of Rainbows. Reviewer Laurence Reid was quite taken with Dorety's comic abilities, which provides a sense of how Dorety was regarded during this period: "Dorety is funny without stressing his points. He doesn't work hard. There is no mugging. He has as keen a sense of burlesque as any comedian before the camera."[18]

Charles Dorety sans mustache, in Century's *Hold Your Breath*, William Watson director. Courtesy of Mark Johnson.

At one hundred twenty-six pounds and five foot four in height, Dorety may sound on the shortish side, but he would have towered over his new boss and, for that matter, over the owner of Universal—or at least according to one article: "Curiously enough, it is the little men who accomplish the big things in that organization," wrote *Motion Picture News* in 1915.

"First comes President Laemmle. He is a man who stands just under five feet.... Julius Stern, manager of all the Universal studios in the East, is another who can hardly touch the five-foot measure."[19] Not really, since Julius's height was actually five feet six inches.[20]

Pretty Consuela "Connie" Henley, in a photo inscribed to fellow actor Phil Dunham.

Dorety's female co-stars in the early Stern comedies were Connie Henley and Lillian Biron. Little is known about Consuela "Connie" Henley, aside from the fact that her onscreen debut was with Rainbow in *A Roaring Love Affair*. Henley would appear in three more for Rainbow, the last of these *Won By a Nose* (August 4, 1920), along with an additional three for Century; Zip Monberg and Bud Jamison were her other frequent co-stars. She "graduated" to the Hoot Gibson short *The Cactus Kid* (1921) for Universal before disappearing from the filmic scene. It was reported much later in 1942 that Henley, along with Chester Conklin, Heinie Conklin, Neal Burns, Charlie Nimbo, and George Ovey were all being used by Republic in some of that studio's current pictures, but this hasn't been confirmed.[21]

Connie Henley looks on with admiration after Charles Dorety has won the horse race! From the Rainbow comedy *Won By a Nose*. Courtesy of Robert James Kiss.

Actress Lillian Biron. Courtesy of Heritage Auctions, Ha.com.

Lillian Biron (1898-1957), who was occasionally billed with her last name spelled as "Byron," had a comparatively lengthy career before moving in with the Sterns in 1920. With nearly three dozen shorts to her credit since 1917 for studios such as Triangle and Christie, Biron's two for Rainbow teamed her with Charles Dorety and Brownie, the wonder dog. There were an additional eight films for Century into 1922 before she would depart to co-star with Little Napoleon the chimpanzee for director Harry Burns. A final short for Roach in 1928 signaled the end of her film career.

Dorety would appear in his "Keaton" guise in William Watson's *Third Class Male* (June 20, 1921), a fragment of which survives. Dorety had a new feminine lead for this film, a pretty ingénue named Florence Lee (1902-1993)[22] whose film career appears to have begun with the Sterns at Century, appearing in a handful of films released in early-to-mid 1921. Lee's co-star in the first three was Percy Pembroke, after which she was bounced around with leads as varied as Harry Sweet, Brownie, Baby Peggy, Zip Monberg, Lige Conley (his sole appearance in a Century), and Dorety. With her departure from Century, Lee would appear with Sid Smith in at least one "Hall Room Boys" comedy, and go on to co-star with boxer Jack Dempsey in the *Fight and Win* series (1924) as well as a number of other shorts for Universal. Lee wrapped up her film career with a couple of western features before retiring from the industry in 1926.

Dorety is backed up by a very cute Baby Peggy in *Third Class Male*, the toddler having an unfortunate encounter with a badling of ducks before becoming the heroine of the piece when she cleverly extinguishes the fire engulfing Dorety's general store. Co-star Lee doesn't have that much to do, or at least in this fragment, except fret over the spreading fire. For that matter neither does Dorety, aside from getting soaked while conducting an orchestra of hayseeds, ineffectually attempt to put out the raging fire, and—well, that's pretty much it.

Comic Jimmie Adams relayed a story about Dorety that took place during one of Dorety's earlier breaks from the Sterns for outside work at Henry Lehrman Comedies, Bull's Eye, and Comique. Dorety's departure was noted by one of his four-legged friends, a small burro he had befriended, likely during the filming of L-Ko's *A Skate at Sea* (February 2, 1919). According to Adams, who had taken over Dorety's old dressing room, the burro would show up at the dressing room and, as he put it, "cry," or whatever it is that a burro does that sounds like crying. Adams placed an old pair of Dorety's shoes outside the door, after which the burro curled up alongside the shoes and went to sleep, contented. Or so we were told.[23]

Dorety would appear in nearly two dozen more Centuries into 1922 before departing the studio. His only known credits after that were the two-reel comedy *The Dry Agent*

(1925) for Verity Film Co., which he also directed, and several Two Star Comedies—which were anything but—with Gene "Fatty" Layman in 1926. Dorety returned to Century in 1927.

Jimmie Adams (1888-1933) was yet another comedian with potential, whose career spanned the twenties and into the thirties without pause. Initially brought into film by Henry Lehrman for his Fox Sunshine comedies, Adams appeared in *Roaring Lions and Wedding Bells* (1917), *Hungry Lions in a Hospital*, and *A Waiter's Wasted Life* (both 1918). Adams moved on, joining Century in 1919 where he first appeared in the Mrs. Joe Martin comedy *A Jungle Gentleman*. Adams's sole director for this and the other dozen or so comedies that he starred in through the 1919-1920 season was Fred Fishback. These included *A Village Venus*, *Chasing Her Future* (October 1, 1919), *The Good Ship Rock 'n' Rye*, and *A Baby Doll Bandit*.

Cowboy Jimmie Adams doesn't trust that puppy, possibly from director Fred Fishback's *A Movie Hero*. Courtesy of Robert James Kiss.

All of the Adams/Fishback comedies co-starred Edith Roberts (born Edith Josephine Kohn; 1901-1935), a pretty brunette and former child actor on stage who had starred in dozens of shorts for other Universal brands dating back to 1915. "[It] is something quite different from anything she has done before," wrote one reporter after speaking with Roberts about *A Village Venus*, "in fact something quite novel in the comedy line, a slapstick-comedy-drama, all in one, minus the pie, ink and milk throwing."[24]

Edith Roberts on the set of an unidentified Fred Fishback-directed comedy.
Courtesy of Kay Shackleton.

Adams's other films included *Daring Lions and Dizzy Lovers* (October 15, 1919), *African Lions and American Beauties* (November 19, 1919), and *Over the Transom*, all of these with co-star Esther Wood.

His stint with Century complete, Adams moved on to star in films for Jack White's Mermaid Comedies, and as "Ferdie," one of CBC's Hallroom Boys. Adams was re-hired by Century in 1922 to direct young Johnny Fox and Herbert Jenkins in *Ginger Face* (November 1, 1922), for which Adams also wrote the script.[25] In spite of some favorable reviews ("The comedy will provide a good measure of amusement and is well worth looking over" wrote *Exhibitors Trade Review*[26]) it would end up being Adams's sole effort behind the camera. Century and Adams parted ways, but he would soon find himself teamed once again with Fishback at Educational.

Fred Fishback was Century's workhorse during these earliest years, and was in no small part responsible for the success of the brand during this transitional period and the year or so that followed. As director of at least twenty-one comedies from his first in April 1919 through the 1919-1920 season, Fishback would direct another sixteen comedies the following season and yet another eighteen comedies in the 1921-1922 season. Fishback got along well with the Sterns, and seemed unfrazzled by the working conditions at Century, in terms of schedules, tight budgets, and the capricious temperaments of his bosses. An immigrant himself who had worked hard in the burgeoning film industry for the success he now enjoyed, Fishback appreciated what the Sterns had carved out for themselves. Diana Serra Cary put it this way:

> A self-made man like Fred Fishbach (himself a Romanian Jew from Bucharest) understood this immigrant-film connection well. It not only explained but justified the cost-cutting methods of producers like Julius Stern, and made working for this fiscal tyrant far less stressful for Fishbach than it was for Century's American-born employees.[27]

The Sterns must have been given a scare when it was announced that Fishback had signed a long-term contract with Select Pictures for a salary "far in excess of that ordinarily paid for high-class dramatic directors in the business,"[28] but either the report was erroneous or the Sterns managed to quietly lure Fishback back. Regardless, he remained with Century and his Fred Fishback Productions for another two years. But more on Fishback in a later chapter.

William Edward "Bud" Jamison (1894-1944) was one of the Sterns' better catches, a prolific six foot, two hundred seventy pound heavyweight with years of experience already under his belt. Born in Vallejo, California, Jamison (originally spelled "Jameison") spent his formative show biz years touring with stock companies and appearing in vaudeville before going to work in January 1915 for Essanay as part of Chaplin's unit, appearing in films such as *A Night Out*, *The Champion*, and *The Tramp* (all 1915). A four-year stint with Hal Roach's Rolin Comedies, where he supported Harold Lloyd's "Lonesome Luke" character and others, ended in 1919 when Jamison was lured over to Century, his first appearance for the Sterns in Fishback's *Daring Lions and Dizzy Lovers*. For the first year, Jamison was most often seen in comedies featuring the Century Lions, such as *A Lion's Alliance* (March 24, 1920), but there were others, which included *My Dog Pal* (March 10, 1920), *A Birthday Tangle*, and *A One Cylinder Love Riot*. Jamison's tenure with Century would last through the 1921-1922 season, nearly three dozen credits to his name.

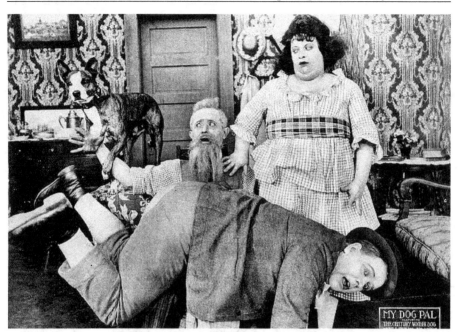

Bud Jamison's about to get spanked by Billy Engle, while Merta Sterling and Brownie,
"The Century Wonder Dog," try to prevent it. From Century's Fred Fishback-directed
My Dog Pal. Courtesy of Richard M. Roberts.

We are fortunate that reel one of *A Lion's Alliance* survives in a copy held by the Library
of Congress, since the survival rate of the Sterns' comedies is dismal. Jamison's co-stars in
this one were Merta Sterling, Billy Engle, and, of course, the Century Lions. Mert and
Bud play young, overweight lovers, with Engle her beleaguered father whose wife is played
by an uncredited little person. Mert flirts with a cop, saying "Chase me, I want to reduce"
before she runs off.

She encounters a physically fit young man who hands them a business card for the
Uglee Beauty Parlor, run by Prof. Mussel: "Faces Patched and Bodies Revarnished." Switch
to the beauty parlor where a negro trainer, Blue,[29] works out with his young son, the latter
toppling over each time a medicine ball is tossed his way. Meanwhile, Engle has waited
for their attractive young nursemaid to arrive, removing the infant from its carriage and
taking its place. His shameless flirting with her succeeds, but only up to the point where
Bud smacks a fly on her back and she responds by walloping Engle, whom she believes to
have delivered the blow. Sadly, we never get to see the lions, since all of their footage was
in the missing reel two. A surviving synopsis fills in the gap, however: "Mert and Bud go to
the circus and chase each other about, accidentally letting loose some lions. The lions find

their way to a beauty parlor/athletic club where Blue, the black masseuse and his young son both work. The son is chased about until Blue returns, the lions falling into parlor's water tank." According to one contemporary reviewer, "Hokum of the sort offered herein has not yet lost its mirth-provoking powers, and in spite of the fact that much of this does not rise above the mediocre, a worthwhile latter portion will make it pay."[30] Which only makes one miss that second reel even more.

Lillian Biron struggles to keep Bud Jamison from dragging Billy Engle off a ladder, in Century's *A One Cylinder Love Riot*, Tom Buckingham director. Courtesy of Heritage Auctions, Ha.com.

Overweight lovers Bud Jamison and Merta Sterling in Century's *A Lion's Alliance*. Fred Fishback directed. Courtesy of Library of Congress.

The Sterns also peppered their films with actors hired for only a single film or two, moving on with the completion of their given project. Among these were Cliff Bowes (1894-1929), Harry Mann (1893-1965), George Ovey (1870-1951), and William Franey (1889-1940). Edna Gregory (1905-1965) was another, appearing in only four known films for the Sterns and with a subsequent career that was anything but stellar. Similarly named Ena Gregory (1906-1993), an Australian-born actress who had a few previous credits for Universal, didn't come to Century until 1922 with her debut in Jess Robbins's *A Dark Horse* (April 12, 1922), co-starring with Charles Dorety. Due to the similarity with Edna and Ena's first names, their respective credits frequently get jumbled. They do not look at all alike, however, so if one is lucky enough to see a film starring Edna there will be no mistake about it being her rather than Ena.

The Sterns' creative decisions would, on occasion, backfire on them. It was reported that one of their "girly" comedies was deemed sub-par, so they sold it to a rival studio for $25,000. Its new owners went to work on it, and over the course of five days hired a cutter, made some tweaks to the film, inserted new intertitles, and then resold the "new" film to Select for $50,000. The film's original cost? $12,000.[31]

Bud Jamison's about to strangle Charles Dorety in this unidentified still, possibly from Century's *An Oil Can Romeo*, directed by James Davis. Courtesy of Robert James Kiss.

It wasn't all business for the Sterns, however, with lengthy, battery-recharging vacations becoming part of the norm, and always promoted as "working vacations." Over the past few years Julius had been reported at various times as vacationing in the White Mountains[32] and spending Easter in Atlantic City along with Laemmle (both in 1917);[33] and spending the summer of 1918 at his vacation home on Long Island.[34] Abe and Laemmle vacationed in Coronado at the Hotel del Coronado outside of San Diego in 1916, where Abe took advantage of the location to send Gertrude Selby and her unit down to the Tijuana race track to film some scenes.[35] Abe and his brother-in-law would vacation in Lake Tahoe[36] and later in French Lick Springs, Indiana in 1919;[37] and sailed together in summer of 1920 to Europe for a three month vacation, accompanied by a bevy of others, Abe's wife Jessie included; Julius would soon follow.

Laemmle was feted the night before their departure at a surprise bon voyage dinner and dance attended by family, friends, and a select number of Universal employees. Planned by the so-called "U" Girls, Laemmle was entertained by the singing of a song written expressly for this gathering:

Far, far away across the sea
Friends watch and wait for you
Old friends of bygone boyhood days,
Still faithful, ever true.
The little town where you were born
May have changed with passing years,
But not the hearts of those who'll greet
You, smiling through their tears.

I won't bother with the chorus; you get the idea.[38]

At any rate, this was the first of the summer-long excursions to Europe that would become the norm over the next few years, in most instances with both Julius and Abe setting sail along with Laemmle and various family members, but not always on the same ship or on the same day.

The Sterns decided in May 1920 to pull the plug on the Rainbow brand and concentrate solely on Century Comedies for the coming 1920-1921 season.[39] There had been twenty-eight comedies released as Rainbows by the season's end, *An Oil Can Romeo* the final offering, co-starring Jamison, Dorety, Biron, and Brownie. Given that its director was James Davis, the brand likely limped to a close.

The new policy was announced to exhibitors, and sugar-coated to make it sound like an improvement: Universal would release only one brand of two-reel comedies: "They will be called Century Comedies, and the Century bathing girls will figure largely and pleasingly in most of them. A certain number will have lions, and some will have both," wrote *Moving Picture Weekly*. "With Lillian Byron, Edna Gregory, Emily [Gerdes] and Fay Holderness as the nucleus, a bevy of beauties is being picked for the new Century Comedies that will open the eyes of the most sophisticated film-fan."[40]

It wasn't reported which of the Sterns would be the one to select those new beauties.

"Brownie, The Never-Failing Wonder of the Screen" Full-page ad appearing in the March 11, 1922 issue of *Exhibitors Trade Review*.

Chapter 7: A Girl and Her Dog
(The 1920-1921 Season)

Upon their return from Europe in early November 1920, Julius greeted reporters and gave his thoughts about the current state of the post-war European film industries:

> Despite reports I have seen and heard to the contrary, the film producers in Europe are far behind the status of the industry in the United States. I would not want to say that that they ever will catch up to us. I have been in six European countries recently, and nowhere did I find the general opinion in favor of the home-production compared to American photoplays.[1]

The German cinema of the mid- to late-1920s would turn that prediction on its head. One of Century's more successful acquisitions had taken place at the end of 1918 when they added Brownie, soon to be billed as the "Century Wonder Dog," to their stock company. Brownie first appeared in a small role in the Alice Howell comedy *Behind the Front* in early 1919, but would soon find his name in the many of the titles of his films that followed. These included *Brownie's Doggone Tricks*, *Brownie's Busy Day*, *Good Little Brownie*, and *Brownie, the Peacemaker*, a testament of sorts to the dog's immediate popularity with the filmgoing public and reviewers alike. *Film Daily* commented on Brownie's second appearance in a Century comedy: "A dog of average size figures most prominently in a two-reeler in which all of the incidents are built about the stunts of the educated canine.... It is the antics of the dog...that hold the eye, for the plot of the picture could be dealt with in a fraction of the footage making up this offering. Many of the incidents have been added just to enable the hound to do his work, which is good for numerous laughs."[2]

119

Brownie, a mixture of Bull Terrier and Fox Terrier, was born in California back in 1916 or 1917.[3] If the press of the time is to be believed, Brownie's new owner and trainer, Charles Gee, rescued him from a disgruntled former owner on his way to the dog pound. Described as standing "4 ½ feet high on his hind legs and weighs about 60 pounds" and with a coat of "a beautiful brown, with spots of white here and there,"[4] Gee put the receptive mutt through some intensive training, after which Brownie was ready for his debut on the big screen. An appearance in Chaplin's *A Dog's Life* (1918) was one of several that included Smiling Billy Parson's *Pink Pajamas* (1918) for Capitol Comedies, Bert Lytell's *Blind Men's Eyes* (1919) for Metro, and several Universal Westerns and serials.[5] Now with Century, Brownie was earning—okay, Charles Gee was earning—a cool $300 a week.[6] This in comparison to the Louis Burston studio's Queenie who was earning $150 per week, or Sennett's Teddy at $250 per week.[7]

Curiously, while Brownie was touted as liking most people and having a "great affection for children," the one person he didn't take a shining to was actor Chai Hong, one of his co-stars in *Brownie, the Peacemaker*: "Brownie not only took away the seat of his trousers but a good-sized hunk of his Celestial flesh."[8]

As popular as Brownie was in the films that starred him, it was his teaming with a tiny little moppet billed as Baby Peggy that took things to the next level. Born in San Diego on October 29, 1918, Peggy-Jean Montgomery (1918-2020) wasn't even two years old when she later said that she was discovered by Fred Fishback, who needed a tyke to star opposite Brownie in the film later released as *Playmates* (May 18, 1921).[9]

Playmates survives, and it is immediately apparent upon viewing it why the teaming of toddler and dog was a hit with audiences. In one lengthy sequence, Brownie assists Peggy with her bath. He leads her by her arm to the staging area, and while she begins to undress, Brownie drags a large basin over to the outside spigot, turns it on, and proceeds to fill the basin. Concerned for her modesty, Brownie then grabs a large piece of cardboard and sets it up so that Peggy can complete her disrobing in comparative privacy. He then leaps through the bathroom window where he retrieves a long-handled brush and a bar of soap. Dragging the basin over to his make-shift dressing room allows Peggy to climb in with privacy, and commence to suds herself and scrub with the brush. Brownie attaches a hose to the spigot, turns it on, and rinses the suds from the little girl. A return trip to the bathroom provides Peggy with a towel with which to dry herself. "[Brownie] is ably assisted in this piece by a very cute youngster, Peggy Montgomery by name," wrote *Film Daily*, "and the child and the dog work together in a manner calculated to excite admiration and get numerous laughs."[10]

Baby Peggy and Brownie in director Fred Fishback's *Playmates*.

Fishback was not solely responsible for the on-screen results. "On this set there were actually three directors," wrote Diana Serra Cary of *Playmates*, "Brownie's trainer and Peggy's father, who each guided his own puppetlike creature with hand signals and spoken commands." The Sterns, evidently pleased with her performance and un-childlike demeanor, immediately hired her at $75 per six-day work week.[11]

While Peggy would occasionally appear in films with others (as would Brownie), it was Brownie who would become her most frequent co-star in monthly releases, such as *Pals* (June 15, 1921), *Golfing* (August 24, 1921), *Brownie's Little Venus* (September 14, 1921), *Brownie's Baby Doll* (October 5, 1921), *A Muddy Bride* (November 16, 1921), *Chums* (December 28, 1921), and *Circus Clowns* (January 25, 1922). Brownie shines in this last film, which also survives. The story involves circus performer Baby Peggy, who was kidnapped and forced to work by the circus's ringmaster (William Irving). Peggy's despondent parents hire a detective (Earl Montgomery, former Vitagraph star as half of the Montgomery and Rock team), who successfully tracks her down and spirits her back to her family. Brownie, Peggy's assistant in her act, follows, thinking his friend is being kidnapped, with Irving close behind. Needless to say, all ends well.

Detective Earl Montgomery returns Baby Peggy to her parents, in *Circus Clowns*,
Fred Fishback (as Fred Hibbard) director. Courtesy of Library of Congress.

This is one of Century's better comedies, courtesy of writer/director Fred Fishback,
now working under his "Hibbard" alias, a "nom de film" that will be explained shortly.
Baby Peggy is as cute as usual, in spite of her frequent mugging and glances off-screen
for direction. Brownie gets to strut his stuff, not only in the act he performs with Peggy,
but at various times helping her to dress and undress, as well as performing his own horse
bareback ride. Brownie is at his energetic best during an extended pursuit of a mouse. He
trashes the kitchen by knocking down shelves and spilling the contents of sugar bowls
and bags of flour, followed by the beneath-the-carpet pursuit through the living room,
culminating with a standoff at the mouse hole. It's a delightful sequence.

For the record, Baby Peggy did not appear in the earlier Brownie comedy *The Kid's
Pal* (April 27, 1921), despite what a number of sources claim. Century was emphatic about
this, stating that "Baby Peggy is not the same youngster that played with 'Brownie' in his

previous Century comedy, 'The Kid's Pal,' which is to be released April 25. 'The Kid's Pal' cast included a youngster several years older than Baby Peggy."[12] She did, however, appear in a trio of films teamed with other dogs, two of these interspersed with her monthly releases with Brownie: *Seashore Shapes* (October 19, 1921) and *Teddy's Goat* (November 30, 1921) both teamed her with Teddy, while *The Little Rascal* (May 24, 1922) had a mutt named Nip as her co-star. *Teddy's Goat* was the first Century to star trainer Joe Simpkin's Teddy, on a break from his work for Mack Sennett. It would appear that Teddy's contract with Century was a brief one, his four films released in a span of less than two months. Perhaps the breaking of Teddy's leg in filming *Teddy's Goat* had something to do with it.[13]

Brownie, Lillian Biron, and Baby Peggy preparing for breakfast in *Circus Clowns*.
Courtesy of Robert James Kiss.

As for Brownie, he too appeared alone in some films with nary a human counterpart, or at least on the "good guy" side. One of these, *Around Corners* (November 9, 1921), is merely an excuse for Brownie's antics to shine. There are several paper-thin plots at work here, one involving Brownie's "theft" of another dog's bone, and its owner's dogged pursuit of Brownie that follows. Another thread involves a dog catcher, here portrayed by an uncredited Larry Semon look-alike, and his frustrated attempts to capture Brownie. The third involves Brownie's aid being enlisted by cop Bud Jamison to help track down a burglar. Brownie does so, and successfully, but emerges with the burglar's lit bomb that was intended to blow up a safe. After first pursuing the fleeing burglar with bomb in mouth, and then terrorizing everyone in the police station, Brownie then buries the bomb. The dog catcher arrives just in time to be blown sky-high by the explosion, and upon falling back to earth lands in the crater created by the explosion. Brownie proceeds to bury him! A print survives in the archives of the Museum of Modern Art.

Director Fred Fishback's *Teddy's Goat* for Century, Fishback credited under his Fred Hibbard alias. Left-to-right: Viola Dolan, Bud Jamison, Jackie Morgan, Jackie's sister Dorothy Morgan, and Teddy. Courtesy of Marguerite Sheffler.

Cop Charles Dorety is about to clobber Bud Jamison in *Teddy's Goat*.
Courtesy of Mark Johnson.

Fred Fishback, directing under his Hibbard alias, provides the pleasantly diverting results, highlighted by two nicely executed tracking shots. The first takes place as the other dog pursues Brownie with the stolen bone, tracking parallel to the sidewalk as filmed from the adjacent street. The two dogs saunter at first, then slowly pick up the pace, eventually resulting in a full speed chase. The second, similarly filmed tracking shot, occurs as the bomb-carrying Brownie pursues the fleeing burglar. While nothing particularly special, it was the little visual touches such as these that helped set Fishback's films apart from those of some of the less inspired directors. One exhibitor's comments about the film, a W.P. Perry of Cheyenne Wells, Colorado's Rialto Theatre, are worth repeating here. While at face value they may seem rather dismissive of the film, they are rather humorous and, ultimately, spot on regarding the Brownie series:

> Actually heard some one laugh while this was being shown, and was very much surprised. However, the next day the mystery was explained when I learned that a newly-married couple in the audience were furnishing the entertainment. This dog is clever, we have to admit that; but most of his two-reelers are like a circus. When you see one, you've seen 'em all.[14]

View the film, which survives, and you'll see Brownie do the same spigot and pail trick that he performed in *Playmates*, released a mere six months earlier.

Brownie bites the ear of an unidentified Century comedian.
Courtesy of Robert James Kiss.

So popular was the teaming of Baby Peggy and Brownie that the Sterns arranged to have their four-legged star tour the Middle West in the fall of 1922, making a series of personal appearances at all first run houses where his films were booked. "Brownie will at his director's command show how he can emote on the spur of the moment," wrote *Exhibitors Trade Review.*[15]

Director Charles Reisner's *A Blue Ribbon Mutt* for Century. Left-to-right: Bud Jamison, Charles Dorety, Lillian Biron, and Brownie. Courtesy of Heritage Auctions, Ha.com.

In her autobiography *What Ever Happened to Baby Peggy?*, Diana Serra Cary claimed that Brownie died in his sleep, which brought their teaming to an abrupt end. This was not the case. Brownie would continue to star in his own monthly comedies for another year or so, culminating with the release of *The Imperfect Lover* (June 13, 1923). Alas, not only humans are susceptible to illness, as Brownie discovered soon after the completion of *A Howling Success* (February 28, 1923). A vet was called in and pronounced it a bad case of distemper, and said that it would be several weeks before Brownie could return to the studio.[16] Two months later, however, Gee was advertising in the trades that he had purchased Brownie's release from Century, the dog "now available for further engagements."[17] The details of Gee's parting from Century remain a mystery, but the Sterns quickly replaced their former canine star with a new one, ex-service trainer Harry Lucenay's dog Pal.[18] Brownie would appear in a few more films for Educational and Christie over the following year before disappearing from the scene and, most likely, to shuffle off this canine coil.

By late 1920 Century was promoting "Bud Jamison, the fat man, and Charles Dorety, the thin man" as their lead comics, along with Fishback, Watson, Chuck Reisner, and Jim Davis as their directors.[19] Two months later, the Sterns were promoting "the general excellency" of its comedians and comediennes, now listing Sweet, Jamison, Dorety, Louise Lorraine, and Dixie Lamont, while adding Thomas Buckingham's name to the roster of directors.[20] Dorety, who appeared in the early Centuries sporting a full brush mustache, would soon abandon that "character" and strive for a more normal appearance. *Moving Picture Weekly* noted that Dorety had "shaved off his little mustache and is greatly improved thereby."[21] To each his own.

Director Charles "Chuck" Reisner.

Minneapolis-born Charles "Chuck" Reisner (1887-1962; born Riesner) was in his mid-thirties when hired by Century, with a wealth of experience already under his belt by that time. Having spent ten years in vaudeville on the Keith and Orpheum circuit, as well as a stint in 1915 on Broadway in the Irving Berlin musical *Stop, Look and Listen*, Reisner had joined Keystone's scenario department in 1916, with appearances before the camera as needed. He spent several years as assistant director on some of Chaplin's First National comedies before joining Century in 1920, where he was made a full director. His first film for the Sterns was the Rainbow *A Champion Loser*, followed by Century's Brownie vehicle *Dog-Gone Clever*, co-starring Charles Dorety. Another five efforts would follow, interspersed with stints for Universal's Star Comedies, his final the Century Lions-on-the-loose comedy *Stuffed Lions* (March 16, 1921). And then he said goodbye to the Sterns and moved on to Jack White's Mermaid Comedies and elsewhere at Universal where he would direct—and frequently act—in his comedies. Reisner graduated to features in the mid-1920s, with such notable films as Syd Chaplin's *The Better 'Ole* (1926) and Buster Keaton's *Steamboat Bill, Jr.* (1928) to his credit, his career lasting well into the sound era.

Director Tom Buckingham.

Thomas Buckingham (1895-1934) signed in early 1920, primarily to oversee the films starring any combination of Bud Jamison, Charles Dorety, and Brownie, with titles such as *The Tale of a Dog* (May 26, 1920), *Should Waiters Marry?* (July 7, 1920), and *Should Tailors*

Trifle? (October 20, 1920). Born in Chicago, Buckingham had made his way west and landed a job assisting Karl Brown in the studio lab where both toiled for D.W. Griffith. By 1917 Buckingham had graduated to full-fledged cinematographer, assigned to film John Francis Dillon's feature for Triangle, *Indiscreet Corrine*. For the rest of that year and the one that followed, Buckingham was assigned to Gilbert Hamilton's unit at Triangle where he lensed several more features. With that behind him, Buckingham moved over to Mack Swain's Poppy Comedies for The Frohman Amusement Corp. where over the course of two years he filmed numerous entries of Swain's popular "Ambrose" shorts. Then he was snapped up by the Sterns, who gave him the opportunity to move into direction. His post-Century career would see him bouncing between shorts and lower budget features for Fox, Robertson-Cole, and Liberty Pictures, effectively coming to an end by the late 1920s. He switched to screenwriting, which he plugged away at up until his death.

Jimmy Finlayson has demonstrated his knife-throwing skills to reluctant subject Harry Sweet. From Century's *A One Horse Town*, Tom Buckingham director. Courtesy of Mark Johnson.

The Sterns, impressed with Harry Sweet's talents, decided to give the young actor a promotional push. "Mr. [Julius] Stern has been in New York for several months planning a campaign by which he hopes to establish Harry Sweet, the leading Century comedian, as one of the most popular funmakers of the screen," wrote *Moving Picture World*.[22] As a result, Buckingham was reassigned as his director, their first collaborative effort *Fresh from the Farm* (February 9, 1921). In this one Sweet appeared as a country rube who heads to the city, loses his money, falls for a female tenant, and incurs the jealous wrath of Bud Jamison's chef. Other Sweet films directed by Buckingham included *The Smart Alec* (July 13, 1921), *The Dumb Bell* (December 21, 1921), *A One Horse Town* (March 8, 1922), *Two of a Kind* (March 29, 1922), and *Off His Beat* (May 17, 1922). This latter film, as revealed at its end, was actually a film-within-a-film, with Sweet jumping out of character and dragging his director before the audience, calling him down for ruining his picture; Buckingham appeared here as the director, surrounded by the film's co-stars, Lois Scott, Bert Roach, and Ena Gregory.

Sweet and Buckingham's final collaboration was *The Kickin' Fool* (September 27, 1922), Sweet sharing the screen in this last film with Century's celebrated mule, Maude. Buckingham would also step in during this later period to direct Baby Peggy and Brownie in *Pals*. As for Sweet, he would star in more than three dozen comedies by mid-1924 before jumping ship to star and/or direct for Sennett, Fox, and several others. He landed at RKO in 1931 where he was in charge of their shorts up until his untimely death two years later in a plane crash.

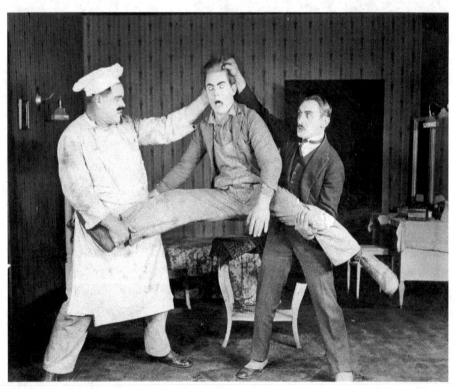

Bud Jamison and Zip Monberg have Harry Sweet at a disadvantage, possibly from Century's *Fresh from the Farm*, directed by Tom Buckingham. Courtesy of Mark Johnson.

Bud Jamison gives inebriated Harry Sweet some support, while Jack Henderson looks on with disapproval, in director Tom Buckingham's *Two of a Kind*.
Courtesy of Robert James Kiss.

For the most part, exhibitors seemed to like Sweet's comedies for Century. One of them wrote in to *Exhibitors Herald* with some telling comments regarding Sweet's *The Dumb Bell*, where the comedian once again played his familiar rube character: "Good Sweet picture. Gets the laughs, but do not show too many close together. Too much sameness in all. But they are good."[23]

Exhibitors in general, or at least the ones that wrote to Century and had something positive to say, appeared to be happy with the films they were receiving. "Allow me to congratulate you on the merit and laughing quality of your two-reel Century comedies," wrote one Brooklyn-based exhibitor. "I have been running same at my theatres for the past three years and find they are the best on the market. I cannot recommend them too highly to every exhibitor." A Texas-based exhibitor concurred: "I have been showing your two-reel Century comedies for the past two or three years and I have always been well pleased with them; in fact they are much better than most of the comedies now being produced."[24]

A twist of fate has put Harry Sweet (second from right, with monocle) on the wrong side of the law—and about to be clobbered by Bert Roach—in director Tom Buckingham's *Off His Beat*. Courtesy of Robert James Kiss.

Julius felt strongly that he and his brother were in tune with the exhibitors' needs and wants. "Abe Stern and myself have been exhibitors," wrote Julius. "We know the exhibitor's trials and tribulations, and that is why we know how to help them for the showmen."[25] They may have known those needs, but they didn't always meet them. The exhibitors writing in to *Exhibitors Herald* had more realistic responses to the films Century was turning out, providing feedback that ran the gamut from praise to dismissal. For *Table Stakes* with Brownie: "Can't see much to this two reel comedy. Got one or two laughs. Don't see how it did that." Brownie and his co-star Baby Peggy fared better with *Brownie's Little Venus*: "The Century comedies fill the bill and are improving.... My patrons like these." *Short Weight*, another Brownie vehicle, elicited the following ho-hum comments: "Just a fair comedy. Worth the price paid. It had little to boost, and about that much to knock."[26]

Audiences loved the antics of Brownie, however, and in April 1921 both Fishback and Brownie extended their respective contracts, renewing for an additional two years.[27]

Elsewhere at Universal, the popular team of Eddie Lyons and Lee Moran continued churning out their comedies, more than two hundred of which had been released since 1915. A native of Chicago, Lee Moran (1888-1961) had graduated from vaudeville and musical comedy, joining David Horsley's Nestor Comedies in 1912. Numerous supporting roles followed, frequently co-starring him with future teammate Eddie Lyons (1886-1926) in films such as the *Sophie of the Films* series (1914) and *Mrs. Plum's Pudding* (1915). Al Christie finally placed them together as an official team in 1915, and the two remained as such, first for Christie's Nestor—*Detective Dan Cupid* (1914) and *Pruning the Movies* (1915) among them—and later for Universal's Star Comedies, in films such as *Waiting at the Church* and *Taking Things Easy* (both 1919). Or at least until May 1921, when the industry was stunned to hear of their split:

> Hot stuff at Universal City. Eddie Lyons, well known comedian, is responsible for a small sized sensation at this film city. Officials of the corporation cut a comedy he and his partner, Lee Moran, had recently completed. The funmaker threw a temperamental fit and told the officials, "just what he thought of them" and walked off the lot declaring that "he was through." Lee Moran remained, and unless someone brings about a truce, he will probably continue without his old time foil. These two comedians have been making pictures together for many years. Their association has been of the Damon and Pythias variety.[28]

A truce never took place. Lyons defected to Arrow to make his own Eddie Lyons Comedies for the next three years, followed by a handful of smaller roles in features before his death in 1926. Moran continued to star in Universal-Jewel two-reelers.

Lee Moran (left) and Eddie Lyons in the Universal comedy *A Shocking Night* (1921).
Courtesy of Mark Johnson.

In June, Julius embarked on his annual trip to Europe for a planned three month stay,[29] Abe following soon after. Construction commenced during their absence on the enlargement of the studio, which by now could barely keep up with the ongoing needs of production. These enhancements and new additions included "additional dressing rooms, property rooms, and several new stages.... Great strides are being made to enlarge Century's studio to such a point that each director will have his own stage, with three stages ready for emergencies."[30]

Julius reported back from Europe that "Some of the largest countries in Europe in their great fight to reestablish normalcy have an unsatiating hunger for clean comedies." He went on to report that "The most popular comedies...are Sennett, Fox and Century Comedies, and the educational that show the wonders of America...."[31]

It was Julius's goal to continue to provide more of the same.

Brownie at the ironing board giving an assist to Eddie Barry in *Cheerful Credit*, Fred Fishback (as Fred Hibbard) director. Courtesy of Robert James Kiss.

Chapter 8: The Return of Henry Lehrman, Albeit a Brief One (The 1921-1922 Season)

By summer's end, Julius and Abe had boarded the S.S. *Olympic* and sailed back to the U.S, announcing plans for six producing units upon their return. This would double the studio's capacity, since at this time only three directors were employed: Alf Goulding, Fred Fishback, and Tom Buckingham. And to make matters worse, Buckingham was out of commission, stricken with influenza and not expected to return for another month or so, leaving the other two to shoulder all of the company's direction.[1] This reliance on only three directors to handle the studio's output is borne out by the upcoming 1921-1922 season's releases, where Buckingham was responsible for over a third of them, and Fishback nearly as many, the two directors having overseen thirty-eight of the season's fifty-two releases.

One of Julius's first "official" acts was his announcement of plans to elevate Baby Peggy to stardom:

> It is my intention to advance to stardom every deserving actor or actress working for me, who shows merit necessary in the producing of comedies. The day of just the handsome or pretty face, devoid of any talent, is over. I have starred Brownie our wonder dog only because of his merit. The same of Harry Sweet, my twenty-one year old star; he advanced unaided, winning only through his merits. Charles Dorety advanced from the ranks—and now comes Baby Peggy. Any actor or actress who proves to me that he or she can act, advances, and as to age—Baby Peggy my newest star is but two years and two months old.[2]

To that end Julius signed his little star to a new three-year contract,[3] and while he was at it he renewed Sweet's contract for an additional two years.[4] Dorety was not so lucky: his contract expired in October and wasn't renewed, a fate shared by ailing director Buckingham.[5] Buckingham would be replaced as Sweet's director in short order with the hiring of Arvid Gillstrom.[6]

Baby Peggy's popularity was such that Marshall Neilan approached the Sterns about a loan-out to appear in his upcoming feature *Penrod* (1922), and with the financial inducement accompanying that request, the Sterns happily agreed. Neilan was so pleased with her work on that film that he borrowed her again for his next feature, *Fools First* (1922), holding off shooting of her scenes until she was finished filming *Peggy Behave* (March 15, 1922) for Century.[7] Upon her return to Century, Baby Peggy went to work for Gillstrom on *The Little Rascal*, in which the tiny little thirty-six pound actress was surrounded by a cast of (by comparison) heavyweights: Blanch Payson at two hundred ten pounds, Fred Spencer at two hundred forty pounds, and Dick Smith at one hundred ninety pounds.[8] As big as her co-stars were, they all would be dwarfed by a young newcomer who would be teamed with her later in the year. But more on that big fellow in a future chapter.

Director Arvid E. Gillstrom.

Born in Gotenberg, Sweden, Arvid E. Gillstrom (1889-1935) emigrated to Chicago when he was still an infant. Educated in Chicago's Armour Institute and Colorado's Golden State School of Mines, early years spent as a mining engineer and prospector preceded his joining Kalem, and later Sterling, where he served as an assistant director. Gillstrom moved over to Keystone in 1915, with an eventual promotion to director. By 1917 he was directing Billy West in his King Bee Comedies—*Cupid's Rival, The Chief Cook* (both 1917), and *The Messenger* (1918) among them—ending up at Arrow where he directed Muriel Ostriche in a series of "Betty" comedies such as *Betty Sets the Pace* and *Betty's Green-Eyed Monster* (both 1920). Now at Century, Gillstrom's first with Sweet was *An Idle Roomer* (January 18, 1922), but he would soon direct Baby Peggy as well in films such as *Little Miss Mischief* (February 15, 1922), *Peggy, Behave!* (March 15, 1922), and *The Little Rascal*. Gillstrom would remain with Century well into 1924, his last for the studio the Buddy Messinger comedy *Don't Fall* (November 19, 1924). Gillstrom spent the remainder of his career directing for Jack White and Educational, Weiss Brothers-Artclass, Al Christie, and several others, effortlessly transitioning into the sound era where he ended up producing and directing shorts for Harry Langdon—released through Educational and later through Paramount—as well as directing some other shorts, including *Please* and *Just an Echo* (both 1934) starring Bing Crosby for Mack Sennett.

Roomer Harry Sweet sits on landlord Jimmy Finlayson's gout-ridden foot, while Bud Jamison—his rival for the hand of Finlayson's daughter, Thelma Dillerman—tugs at his hair. From director Arvid Gillstrom's *An Idle Roomer*. Courtesy of Mark Johnson.

If Diana Serra Cary's figures are accurate, both the Sterns and Universal made out like bandits on the Baby Peggy comedies. "On each Baby Peggy comedy the Stern brothers expended no more than $5000, including salaries," wrote Cary in her memoir *Hollywood's Children*. "It was then sold to Uncle Carl for $50,000, who distributed it worldwide for a gross return of between $300,000 and $500,000."[9] In her later autobiography *What Ever Happened to Baby Peggy?*, Cary added that "due to both the business and blood relationship between [the Sterns and Laemmle], the Stern brothers were given a generous share of Laemmle's final take."[10]

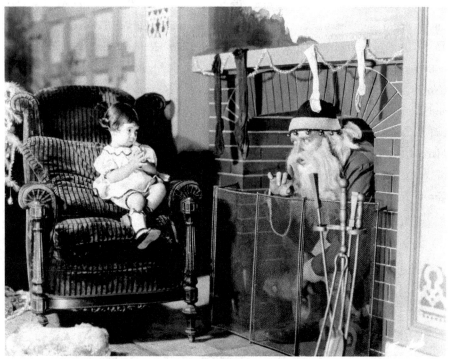

Baby Peggy and Santa Claus pose for Universal photographer Roman Freulich's lens.
Courtesy of Robert James Kiss.

Louise Lorraine (1902-1981; born Louise Escovar) made a return of sorts to Century in September. The five feet two inch tall, hundred pound Lorraine had appeared in a handful of comedies for Century released in late 1920 and early 1921, initially at a salary of $50 per week but soon upped to $100.[11] The first of these was Fred Fishback's *A Movie Hero* (September 1, 1920), where she went by the name Louise Fortune and played the western girl fought over by the new sheriff and his predecessor. Despite her petite build and comparative inexperience, the Sterns starred Lorraine in several serials where she displayed a gung-ho willingness to perform physical stunts, garnering favorable attention in *Elmo the Fearless* and *The Adventures of Tarzan*. This resulted in a new three picture deal, commencing with Goulding's *Seashore Shapes*.[12] Lorraine would star in an additional five comedies released sporadically through November 1925, the final of these the much delayed Baby Peggy's *Red Riding Hood* (November 21, 1925). When she finally left the Universal family, Lorraine was earning an impressive $500 per week.[13] Lorraine would finish out the silent era in numerous Western features and shorts, with an occasional return to the serial format. With the advent of sound, she would star in a few more films before retiring to care for her first child.

Versatile actress Louise Lorraine.

Australian-born Alfred J. Goulding (1896-1972) was rehired by the Sterns as well in mid-1921, to direct Harry Sweet and Charles Dorety. With stage work in both his homeland and in England, Goulding had come to the U.S. where he continued with live performances. He broke into film in 1916 with Fox, adding direction of two-reelers to his credits along with his acting chores. Joining Hal Roach at his Rolin studios, Goulding served as both Harold Lloyd's and Snub Pollard's director for a number of shorts, including *Step Lively* (1917), *Two-Gun Gussie*, and *Fireman Save My Child* (both 1918). Goulding remained with Roach until his hiring by Century in 1921.

Director Alf Goulding.

During his stint with Roach, Goulding had taken a short break in 1919 to direct a single film for Century, the Chai Hong Rainbow *A Tight Fix* (November 12, 1919). Evidently happy with his work on that earlier film, the Sterns decided to lure him back.

Goulding's initial films for Century included *Stealin' Home* (September 7, 1921) and *High Life* (September 21, 1921), both with Sweet and Bartine Burkett. The former of these exists in a fragment held by the Library of Congress, wherein Burkett and her boyfriend fool Sweet into believing that chunks of "Electric Spark" soap are actually fudge. Sweet's consumption of same results in bubble-producing burps, a sequence that at least one reviewer singled out for its cleverness. These two films were followed by *Mama's Cowpuncher* (October 12, 1921) with Harry Sweet, and the Baby Peggy-Brownie vehicle *Brownie's Baby Doll*. One of Goulding's stranger films was *Hello, Mars* (July 26, 1922), with Sweet and Johnny Fox crash landing on Mars. There they encounter several of the planet's more attractive inhabitants, as portrayed by Ena Gregory and Alberta Vaughn, before the film resorts to the old standby where they awaken from a plane crash and realize that it was all a dream. Goulding would remain as one of Century's writer-director powerhouses through 1924, by which time he had become Baby Peggy's exclusive director. Goulding was assisted on most, if not all, of these by his long-time assistant director David Smith.[14]

Harry Sweet attempts to protect his bride Claire Alexander from Chai Hong. From director Alf Goulding's Rainbow comedy *A Tight Fix*. Courtesy of Richard M. Roberts.

With the Eddie Lyons-Lee Moran team now consigned to history, Moran made the best of it and continued on as a solo act. Over the following five months, Moran starred in a couple of two-reel comedies for Universal-Jewel. These were *Robinson's Trousseau* and *P.D.Q.* (both 1921), after which he made the lateral switch over to Century. The two Universal-Jewels "were of such excellence," wrote *Motion Picture News*, "that Mr. [Julius] Stern was moved to enter into negotiations with [Moran] to make super-comedy two-reelers...." Moran, it was declared, was "much stronger than he was as part of a team." Alf Goulding was to be his director,[15] although those duties were split with Fishback and, in several instances, other directors.

The first of these, *The Straphanger* (January 11, 1922), was well received by *Exhibitors Trade Review*, which said that the film "will be sure to whet the appetite of film fans for future releases of this sort." *Film Daily's* review gives a fair idea of what the film, now believed to be lost, was all about:

> Lee Moran is the henpecked husband and straphanger in this fairly amusing two-reel comedy. Blanche Payson plays the "heavy" wife. Funny mechanical devices for heating baby's bottle form the opening shots of this comedy on suburban life. A hurried breakfast, a rush for the train and a long wait for another, make up the action of the first reel. The second reel deals with the home coming. Lots of bundles and a jam in the subway take up a good deal of footage. Friends arrive for supper, and the straphanger's wife is certainly not happy to see them. This ends a perfect day for the straphanger. The gags have all been done before and the comedy work is mild but full of sure fire laughs. If your people like to laugh at the same thing many times they will like "The Straphanger," which is the first of Lee Moran's Comedies for Century.[16]

Joe Murphy's atop the heap of human flesh crushing Harry Sweet, in Alf Goulding's *Mama's Cowpuncher.* That's James T. Kelley on top of Sweet having his hair pulled by Bob O'Connor, while Bartine Burkett tries to put a stop to the tussle. Courtesy of Robert James Kiss.

Blanche Payson, circa 1916-1918.

The Straphanger was followed by *The Touchdown* (February 1, 1922)—"as snappy a line of rural hokum as has been flashed on the screen in some time" wrote *Motion Picture News*[17]—and *Upper and Lower* (March 1, 1922.) In this latter film Moran appears as a strike breaker disguised in blackface and posing as a Pullman porter. "Exhibitors whose houses are below the Mason and Dixon's line would do well to examine this picture before booking it," advised *Exhibitors Trade Review*,

Lee Moran in *The Straphanger*, featured on the cover of the January 14, 1922 issue of *Moving Picture Weekly*. Fred Fishback (as Fred Hibbard) directed.

> ...as in one or two instances the star's blackface seems so genuine to a young wench that she is eager to make love to the porter, and in one case so far succeeds as to lay her head on his shoulder. It is hardly necessary to explain that the regard is unreciprocated...[18]

These were the first of seventeen shorts Moran would star in over the next eighteen months. Many of Moran's films would feature six foot four Blanche Payson, a former policeman at the San Francisco Exposition, as his towering co-star. Moran's comedies were described as "caricatures of real life," which he would plan and write, "his ambition for years."[19]

Farm boy Lee Moran says goodbye to his mama (is that Merta Sterling?) and dad (Joe Murphy) before heading off to college. From Alf Goulding's *The Touchdown*. Courtesy of Mark Johnson.

Lee Moran, confused quarterback, in *The Touchdown*. Courtesy of Robert James Kiss.

Scandal had a way of dogging Fred Fishback, and in a headline-hogging fashion. Fishback, along with actor Lowell Sherman, had accompanied Roscoe "Fatty" Arbuckle back in 1921 to San Francisco to spend the Labor Day weekend relaxing and partying at the Hotel St. Francis. Unluckily for Fishback, this was the event where sometime actress Virginia Rappe would lose her life, and Arbuckle would be accused of causing her death. Luckily for Fishback was the fact that he was off scouting locations when the actual incident—whatever it was exactly—took place, but he returned to the hotel and was privy to the events that followed. The result was that Fishback was called to testify at Arbuckle's trial and the two retrials that followed due to hung juries. By the time the third trial took place in early 1922, Fishback's memory of the events that took place was fading, much to the amusement—or should I say *stunned disbelief*—of those reporting on the trial. Arbuckle was eventually acquitted in April, and Fishback managed to emerge from the whole scandal with his reputation intact.

Lee Moran, not overly convincing in blackface, posing as a Pullman porter.
From Alf Goulding's *Upper and Lower*.

Fishback had an assistant director working with him at Century at the beginning of October, a fellow named Al Stein who'd been with him for several months. Twenty-six year old Stein didn't make it into November, however, expiring from a suspicious death on October 9. A half-empty bottle of "moonshine" was found in the kitchen, and the two young actresses who shared lodging with him were arrested, suspected of murder by poisoning due to the conflicting accounts they provided. "I have known Al Stein for several months," stated Fishback when interviewed, "and in all my dealings with him he has been sober and industrious. I did not know that he was a drinking man."[20] As it turned out, the two girls were soon released when the coroner judged Stein's death the result of acute alcoholism.[21] Much ado about nothing, as it turned out, aside from the impact it had on Fishback. The preponderance of newspaper articles that appeared covering Stein's death always seemed to take pains to remind readers of Fishback's part in the whole Arbuckle-Rappe scandal.[22] This proved to be too much for Fishback, or perhaps for the Sterns, with the result that the final Century comedy credited to Fred Fishback was *A Week Off* (September 28, 1921), after which *Seashore Shapes, Tin Cans* (October 26, 1921), and all subsequent films directed by Fishback were now credited to "Fred Hibbard." It would appear that this renaming was solely to avert any negative reaction to Fishback that overly moralistic viewers might have, since "Hibbard"'s identity was no mystery to industry insiders; trade magazines still advertised "Fred Hibbard Productions…under the direction of Fred Fishback."[23]

Century claimed that it had to double the number of prints of its comedies for the 1921-1922 season in order to supply the increased number of first-run accounts. An additional promotional stunt was put into effect in December, where the period from December 25 to January 1 would be called Century Week. The press release, if it was to be believed, claimed that "As a tribute to Julius Stern…salesmen handling the Century product have pledged themselves to put a Century comedy in every theatre in the United States and Canada during Christmas week."[24] Sales Manager Art Schmidt, it was reported, originated the slogan "A Century a Day Keeps the Blues Away" as the keynote of the drive.[25] Carl Laemmle, who was said to be "so impressed with the rapidly growing excellence of Century Comedies," had this to say:

> No time could be more fitting for Century Comedies than Christmas week. It is the happiest week of the year and people want to forget their troubles and enjoy themselves laughing at something funny. Christmas week is a family holiday and Century Comedies are the sort a man likes to take his folks to see. There is nothing in them that will offend the most fastidious taste and there is a laugh for every member of the family."[26]

Or at least we were told that's what Laemmle said. Century Week was to become an annual affair. At any rate, the bulk of the films re-released during this week were from the Brownie and Baby Peggy series, and were met with surprising success: sales from the different exchanges more than doubled their previous record highs.[27]

1922 ushered in the end of Century's seemingly ubiquitous lion comedies. Charles Gay severed his connections with Century,[28] and one of the last releases to feature lions in any sort of significant role was Harry Sweet's Goulding-directed *Shipwrecked Among Animals* (January 4, 1922), a spoof on Universal's popular pseudo-documentary *Shipwrecked Among Cannibals* of 1920. Sweet portrays the survivor of a shipwreck stranded on a South Sea island, and the film follows his attempts to win the heart of fur-clothed native Alberta Vaughn. These attempts are repeatedly interrupted by wild animals, lions prominent among them. *Film Daily* rated it "far above the average comedy production and will be enjoyed by all."[29]

"Ah, come out and play!" Harry Sweet, *Shipwrecked Among Animals*, director
Alf Goulding's spoof of Universal's popular *Shipwrecked Among Cannibals* (1920).
Courtesy of Robert James Kiss.

With the departure of the lions, however, the Sterns were quick to find some friendlier replacements. One of these was the "educated horse" named Sally, owned by trainer and Western star Pete Morrison. Sally was promptly renamed Queenie,[30] and would star in eight comedies released over the next twelve months. The first of these was *Horse Sense* (February 8, 1922) with co-star Harry Sweet, followed by *Horse Tears* (June 28, 1922). The first four were directed by Fishback (now billed as Hibbard), after which the mini-series was taken over by Al Herman. Queenie was joined in some of these later comedies by two additional entrants to the Stern menagerie, Rosie the monkey and Maude the mule, also a student of trainer Morrison. One of Herman's films, *Cured* (September 6, 1922), had a particularly large cast of nearly fifty non-humans, and took an atypical eight weeks to film. "The task of directing such a film is said to have called for rare patience on the part of the director," wrote *Universal Weekly*,[31] which went on to say:

> Rosie, the new Century monkey, is said to be unusually temperamental and on three occasions broke away from her master. It took a whole forenoon to catch her. Further difficulties developed through the aversion of Stripes, the zebra, for goats, a number of which were called for in the various scenes. Camie [aka Camisole, aka Cameo], the Century dog, gets sulky streaks every once in a while, and Maudie, the mule, packs a wicked pair of heels.[32]

Harry Sweet and his girl, played by Margaret Cloud, in *Horse Sense*, Fred Fishback (as Fred Hibbard) director. Courtesy of Mark Johnson.

Motion Picture News's reviewer rather liked the results, albeit with some back-handed comments: "It's a tremendous relief sometimes to see a comedy blessed not only by the absence of frankly vulgar slapstick but by a mercifully small number of human beings in the cast.... An unusual feature of the film is the fact that the creatures unfold the plot with an ease that makes it not at all apparent that their moves are directed from off-scene."[33] Apparently Herman was the right man for the job!

Jackie Morgan, second from left, atop Queenie in *Horse Tears*, Fred Fishback (as Fred Hibbard) director. That's Queenie's trainer and Western star Pete Morrison on the right. Courtesy of Heritage Auctions, Ha.com.

Another of Herman's all-animal comedies was *Just Dogs* (November 8, 1922) which, with the exception of male lead Joe the monkey, had a cast solely of the canine variety. The film was rushed into production soon after the success of Fred Fishback's earlier *Mutts* (March 22, 1922) had become apparent. "The cast of 'Just Dogs'," wrote *Exhibitors Herald*, "contains Joe as the leading man; Pal as the 'aerial police,' Camisole as 'the slicker,' Peaches as 'the father,' and Mary as 'the flapper.'"[34] And this seven years before Jules White's and Zion Meyers's "Dogville" series for M-G-M! Blake Wagner was the cameraman for many of Herman's animal comedies.

Albert Herman (1894-1958; born Adam Herman Foelker) got his early start as a prop man and actor at Essanay in 1913, departing for Liberty Films a year later only to return to Essanay in 1915. Accompanying the Chaplin unit to Los Angeles, he eventually landed with Henry Lehrman at Fox Sunshine where he served as a gagman and assistant director and, as William Beaudine once put it, Lehrman's "hatchet man." Herman was an imposing fellow, described by director Jack White as a former "prize fighter," adding that "his muscles bulged like two giant-sized salamis."[35] With Lehrman's termination from Fox in early 1919, Herman was promoted to director and helmed a few comedies before being lured over to Lehrman's ambitious but ill-fated new venture, Henry Lehrman Comedies. He served as general manager of the plant, and assisted director Al Ray on *The Kick in High Life* (1920), but soon found himself out of a job as Lehrman's financing evaporated and the studio folded. Herman made a brief return to Fox as director before being hired by the Sterns in late 1921 or early 1922.

Brownie, no doubt embarrassed being in the presence of all these wimpy dogs, in *Mutts* (working title *Putting On the Dog*), Fred Fishback (as Fred Hibbard) director. Courtesy of Robert James Kiss.

Herman's initial effort for Century was Lee Moran's *Hickville's Romeo* (August 30, 1922), the first of more than fifty comedies he would direct for the Sterns before his departure in 1925. And in spite of the constant pressure and unyielding deadlines that the Century directors were subject to, Herman could occasionally inject some visual creativity into his films, such as the half-reel opening to *True Blue* (November 22, 1922). *Universal Weekly* commented: "This picture opens up with about five hundred feet of nothing but hands playing cards, hands knocking at doors; hands [that] were playing cards clear the table of cards, in all a very funny situation."[36] Creative, or at least by comparison to so much of the competition.

Universal Weekly commented on one of Herman's many animal films, presumably with tongue firmly planted in cheek: "Al Herman...has dismissed each one of his assistant directors and their helpers for his present picture and has engaged in their stead a score of veterinaries, mule skinners and kindred animal trainers. Al is directing Queenie, the wonder horse, with a supporting cast consisting in part of 'Camie,' the dog; Jack, the parrot, a goat and her kid, a ram, an ostrich, a pelican, cats and kittens."[37]

Director (and, according to Jack White, former prize fighter) Al Herman.

An announcement in February 1922 must have caught a number of industry insiders by surprise: Julius had hired Henry Lehrman to direct "twelve super-comedies" over the next year.[38] Stern had taken great pains to distance himself from the mercurial director after L-Ko had changed ownership, but now appeared to have had a change of heart. Lehrman was now the studio's fifth director, along with Fred Fishback, Alf Goulding, Tom Buckingham, and Arvid Gillstrom. It was rumored that a new star would be engaged for Lehrman to direct, but by April he was reported directing one the Lee Moran comedies.[39] Lehrman's association with Century and the Sterns was short lived, however, and his tenure with the studio had ended by early June.

Baseball player Lee Moran woos his girl Betty May while Blanche Payson listens in, in director Al Herman's *The Home Plate*. Courtesy of Mark Johnson.

Lehrman wasn't alone in what appeared to be somewhat of a mass exodus, however. Tom Buckingham, it was reported, "and the Century studios had a parting of the ways the other day. They agreed to disagree."[40] Ditto for Harry Sweet: "He was giving some of the comedy producers the once-over the other day and seemed to be talking very earnestly."[41] Zip Monberg as well, heading over to Fox's comedy department.

Perhaps a source of their discontent can be found in an admittedly clumsily worded statement Stern made to the press back in March, regarding his aims for the company and its ongoing success:

While production in my Hollywood studio will be pressed forward at a rate I have never before attempted and while I am prepared to spend both men and money to double my present program and corner all the original ideas and the out of the ordinary stars both human and animal that can be obtained yet my policy of good films at the lowest possible rental will remain the same. This is what has brought Century so many friends and exhibitors who book with us for an entire series.... The success of Century is built on the success of the exhibitor which includes the small exhibitor as well as the big one. The big problem today is to produce good comedies so economically that they can be sold to the theatre owner at a price which guarantees him an absence of worry and an equitable profit.[42]

One way to produce comedies economically, of course, is to keep salaries in check. And that, perhaps, may in no small part been the reason for the ongoing turnover among cast and crew that affected all but the company's most valuable and prolific individuals.

Children and animals seemed safe at the studio, however. Baby Peggy, Brownie, and the current residents of the Century menagerie had recently been joined by two other youths, Jackie Morgan and freckle-faced Johnny Fox. "I am convinced," wrote Abe Stern in one of his infrequent utterances in the trades, "that in animals and children comedies lie some of the biggest possibilities in the short subject field.... Not only the youngsters like to watch [Baby Peggy], but mothers and fathers will telephone the theatre to find out her bookings, and the biggest houses advertise her in electric lights of the same size as their feature film, showing that in their eyes she is at least an equal drawing card." And regarding his upcoming return trip to Europe, Abe promised that "I shall be on the lookout for the best animal acts over there. It is quite within my plans that I may purchase some additional domestic animals to add to our already extensive collections."[43]

Lee Moran was still a considerable asset to Century, however, and Julius tinkered with the idea of taking Moran with him to Europe come summer to make some comedies in England "embodying the English ideas of humor."[44] These plans were soon expanded to take Moran to "Paris, Berlin and other large European cities" as well, to film comedies with these cities as backgrounds.[45] This may have been a result of the upheaval in Moran's personal life, and to get him as far away from Hollywood and his vengeful wife Esther as possible. In July, Esther had filed for divorce, charging him with excessive cruelty and claiming that he had been intoxicated for the last four years! "Bootleggers played an important part in the domestic affairs of the Morans," wrote New York's *Evening Telegram*.

"Mrs. Moran's philosophy was that she had a right to spend a dollar for every dollar he spent for 'booze'." Stating that Moran earned $2,250 a week, Esther went on to list that he complained about the food bill, about her cooking, about the way she raised the baby, and that he kicked her out of bed. A bunch of other complaints as well, all of which must have proved to be rather embarrassing for the comedian.[46]

Lee Moran's rube character goes sightseeing with his uncle Jack Duffy, in Alf Goulding's *The Rubberneck*. Courtesy of Mark Johnson.

Anyway, Moran's European plans were further ballyhooed in August as he began a cross-continent auto trip en route for New York, with personal appearances planned at various first-run houses showing his films. Accompanied by director Arvid Gillstrom and gagman "Brick" Enright, their first stop was in Denver, with New York and a departure for Europe their ultimate goal.[47] Alas, it was all puffery, and Moran remained stateside; within a month he was in the hills back of Los Angeles filming exteriors for a short about camping, tentatively titled *Camping Out*.[48] Released as *The Game Hunter* (February 21, 1923), director Al Herman's film proved to be Moran's last for the studio.

Century's comedies had gained a significant foothold among exhibitors by now, as reported by Julius:

> By careful examination of sales records, I have found that more than 90 per cent of new Century comedy users have continued to book our product.

We find that our comedies featuring Baby Peggy, Lee Moran, Harry Sweet and Brownie the Century Wonder Dog are replacing many comedy products which heretofore are supposed to have a monopoly in first run houses."[49]

One of Julius's last reported acts in early June was to entertain a group of Rotarians hailing primarily from Chicago and New York. He gave them a personal tour of the studio, providing a running explanation of the various goings on. The lucky fellows got to see Goulding, Gillstrom, and Al Herman at work, and the antics of Baby Peggy, Brownie, and Rosie the monkey in their various productions.[50]

Village fire chief Lee Moran and sheriff Jimmie Adams, rivals in love, while lunch wagon chef Bud Jamison looks on. From *Red Hot Rivals*, Fred Fishback (as Fred Hibbard) director. Courtesy of Mark Johnson.

Later that same month, Julius was once again making arrangements for his annual return trip to Europe. Abe was already over there arranging for European bookings of the Century output, his departure delayed by two weeks but finally having set sail back on May 13.[51] Abe, it was reported, would return to the U.S. "as soon as his brother's accomodations [sic] are completely taken care of."[52]

Julius, as usual, was there not only for some relaxation, but ostensibly to investigate filmmaking conditions in Europe and, more specifically, the comedy scene and the current and future market for Century's comedies. And as far as relaxation was concerned, it was much needed, given the events of earlier in the year that surely must have taken some sort of toll on Julius. These events, which will be detailed in the following chapter, may have left Julius wracked with self-doubt over his professional judgment and decisions or, more likely, convinced that his judgment was sound and with the deep-set conviction that he was his own best boss, and would remain so from that time forward. Whatever the case, the one major long-term distraction from the pursuit of his personal business affairs was now behind him, allowing both he and his brother to focus their combined efforts and concentration on their own business concerns.

Their own, and not those of Carl Laemmle.

Chapter 9: Julius Stern, Carl Laemmle, and the Ties That Bind

Perhaps the biggest distraction for Julius and Abe during these early years with Century was Carl Laemmle's continuous need for their assistance and counsel. Laemmle had come to rely on the Sterns—Julius in particular—and if they wanted to add the day-to-day management of their personal film businesses into the mix, that was okay with Laemmle. Okay, but just so long as they added to Universal's coffers and didn't detract from the ongoing attention Laemmle expected of his brothers-in-law. This reliance is reflected in the numerous telegrams and letters that passed between them, documents that clearly illustrate just how close the three brothers-in-law were, and the trust and confidence they shared.

Laemmle frequently asked Julius to deal with the studio's various stars during salary negotiations. One example is when Laemmle asked Julius in 1919 to speak with Eddie Polo (1875-1961), a former trapezist and star of nearly three dozen Universal shorts and serials since 1915. Julius's response is eyebrow-raising:

> Had long talk with Polo. Doesn't want to stay with Universal after expiration contract. Had proposition from [former Universal executive Joe] Brandt and Harry [Cohn, both of CBC Film Sales Corporation, later renamed Columbia Pictures Corporation] to draw thousand weekly and fifty percent profits. Personally can make following arrangements with him. He to draw seven hundred fifty weekly twenty five percent profits. Can sign him for three years. Can make serial with your money and sell it to you at whatever

price I see fit. You understand me. Believe if don't do this you apt lose him by next Fall. If you want me make him offer for second years salary let me have your best proposition as way it now looks he doesn't want work on salary any more.[1]

Polo accepted Julius's final offer of a four-year contract, to expire in 1924, reported as the highest salary on Universal's payroll.[2] Polo didn't make it to 1924, but more on Polo's departure later in this chapter.

Lobby card for *The Vanishing Dagger* (1920), one of Eddie Polo's many serials for Universal. Courtesy of Heritage Auctions, Ha.com.

This relationship between brothers-in-law could at times grow testy, as evidenced in that same 1919 letter from Julius to Laemmle:

> Very much hurt your criticizing me for interfering Superba [Theatre, Los Angeles] management. [Universal's Publicity department and theatre manager Arthur S.] Wenzel wiring you untruths. In fact he has been working entirely different since I went after him and threatened take matters up with you. Your criticizing my interference simply discourages me to mix up in any Universal business whatsoever.[3]

Abe was the beneficiary of Laemmle's largesse as well. When Universal's treasurer Pat Powers resigned from Universal in early 1920 after selling his interests in the company to Laemmle and Robert Cochrane, Abe was appointed treasurer. This was a position he would hold while continuing on as Century's secretary and treasurer.[4] Within a month it was announced that Abe, along with Emanuel H. Goldstein—Laemmle's secretary and Universal's general sales manager—as well as Harry M. Berman, general manager of exchanges, would be the three-man commission that would direct Universal activities. "Their word will be final in most of the general affairs of the film concern," wrote *Motion Picture News*.

> By the formation of this commission, Mr. Laemmle hopes to unburden himself and his chief aid, R.H. Cochrane, vice-president of Universal, of much of the routine details of the business.... Mr. Laemmle believes that the commission form of management is the only efficient way for handling the affairs of an organization of the magnitude of the Universal Film Manufacturing Company.[5]

Former Universal treasurer Patrick A. Powers.

Goldstein was important to Laemmle, not only for his considerable capabilities but for the fact that he followed orders and toed the company line. Laemmle encouraged—or should I say *ordered*—Julius to put him to good use, as evidenced in this letter from late 1921:

> Goldstein should be a wonderful help to you. In the first place he is a fine executive; he hardly ever loses his head and he can work twenty hours a day, if necessary, and – what is most important – he is a good soldier and knows how to take orders and carry them out; very few men can do that. Goldstein, once in a while…gives me an argument – but very rarely, but the moment I tell him to go ahead and do what I want – that ends it.
>
> Goldstein, as I said, will be of tremendous help to you if you will only let him go ahead and do things; in fact, that is the very thing I want you to do, and I am making it a demand to you. That is why he is out there. He doesn't care for any glory and neither do I; you can have all the glory if you want it. Goldstein is your First Lieutenant and you should take him into your confidence and consult with him just as I would if I were there. The more work you give him the better he likes it.[6]

Abe Stern would remain as Universal's treasurer until early 1922 when Laemmle replaced him Goldstein.

In 1920, Brooklyn-born Irving Thalberg (1899-1936) was made general manager of Universal City. Thalberg had first started with Universal back in 1918, serving as Laemmle's New York-based personal secretary. His critical comments regarding the Universal product he screened along with Laemmle soon grabbed his boss's attention, and he was taken along with Laemmle to the West Coast studios in 1920. Thalberg's wardrobe needed some work, however, and for that trip, Julius was assigned the task: "I bought him his clothing"[7] remarked Julius.

Surprising almost everyone, Thalberg was made the West Coast's general manager when Laemmle returned to New York. "During the last fifteen months," *Exhibitors Herald* reported in November 1921, "Thalberg's feat in bringing order out of chaos at the world's largest studio and in putting Universal's manufacturing plant on the same basis of expert management and respectability enjoyed by the best operated plants in the business has been the sensation of filmdom."[8] Arguable, perhaps, but Thalberg had managed to make a considerable name for himself in the industry.

Julius's strong ties to Laemmle reared their head once again, as rumors swirled that

Julius would "relieve his youthful general manager of some of the burdensome business routine so that he could give more time to production activities."[9] Laemmle denied having considered any management changes, or at least in a roundabout fashion, but within a week it was announced that Stern was the company's new general manager, and that Thalberg had become production manager,[10] all part of a greater shakeup within the company. In addition, Stern was named second vice-president of Universal, and had been transferred to the Western offices in late September or early October to serve in an advisory capacity.[11] This, in addition to continuing to serve as president of Century, Pacific Film Co., and the Great Western, and the ongoing attention they all demanded.[12]

Both Stern and Thalberg denied rumors that the latter was considering leaving Universal.[13] "The lot is said to be divided into two factions," wrote *Los Angeles Herald*, "those who are currying favor with the new administration, and those who remain loyal to Thalberg."[14]

Laemmle wrote to Julius that same month with his expectations, which offers some not-so-subtle hints as to his growing dissatisfaction with Thalberg and his performance:

> I will never be satisfied until you can reduce our pay-roll to at least $50,000.00 and, maybe, less.... You will have to go through every department with a fine-tooth and weed out every single solitary man that is not absolutely needed. You will have to get your heads of departments to do some work themselves, instead of playing the gentleman and sitting in the easy chair. You will be fought at every inch of the way by the politicians. They won't want you to make a showing. Therefore, it is my advice to you that every single one of these heads who is not working with you heart and soul should be weeded out, even if you can't get someone equally as good right now.
>
> Irving told me at the station yesterday that time alone would tell whether the men discharged would stay discharged. He let me infer that it will only be a question of a short time when they will all be back on the job. Naturally, that is what Irving would like to see, in order to clear himself so he could come to me and say "Yes, they discharged a lot of people but they took them all back after you were gone," which, of course, would be a feather in his cap; it would prove that after all he was the Manager and knew his business. Maybe he is right—maybe he did know his business, but he will have to go some to convince me. Do you get what I am trying to tell you?

…Irving, for instance, always argues with me and he would argue all day long and not do anything else if I were willing to listen.[15]

After detailing a lot of other Universal business that Julius should attend to—a lot of it of a cost- and employee-cutting nature—Laemmle concluded with two closing instructions:

These are all matters, of course, that you will have to take up with Irving, but please don't show him this letter because it is confidential to you…. Kindly let Abe read this letter.[16]

Laemmle followed up three weeks later with a telegram:

Fully appreciate you have enormous work to do—you may be sure I doing equal as much here—may be more……..all must be fully share if intend weathering storm successfully.[17]

Stern took Laemmle's advice to heart. *Exhibitors Herald* stated that "A decided cut in salaries is reported under the Julius Stern regime."[18]

Universal general manager Irving Thalberg.

Stern's arrival and the changes he was implementing were met with anything but open arms, or at least by the studio's employees. *Variety* reported on the unrest in an article titled "New General Manager Upsets Universal City:"

> Things are rather topsy turvey at Universal City with the realignment of the general managership there. Young Irving Thalberg has been replaced by Julius Stearn [sic] on the U. lot at the head of the works and the rank and file at the studio are up in arms since the change took place.
>
> Eddie Polo and Eileen Sedgewick [sic] have quit the company and Harry Carey is on strike, refusing to work under the new G.M.[19]

I'll elaborate about Stern's strained relationship with Eddie Polo and Harry Carey in a few pages.

Stern tried his best to keep Thalberg happy in his diminished position, and it would appear that Thalberg was reinstated as general manager after Julius had spent two months bringing "efficiency" to the studio's operations. When Julius headed back to New York a month later, he wrote a letter to Thalberg while en route on the California Limited:

> I certainly hated to leave, but at the same time I think that for the good of the organization it was the only thing for me to do. However, I feel that I have left things at Universal City in pretty good shape, and I feel satisfied that you will take care of things.
>
> Now, don't be afraid to talk matters over with my brother Abe, in fact, I want you to take things up with him just as if I were out there myself.
>
> I personally feel that we have accomplished a lot since I have been out there, but I think that we should feel that there is still an awful lot of progress to be made yet, and then set out and do it. You certainly have put your shoulders to the wheel and come to the front like a good soldier. At the same time I feel that I have helped you and the organization a whole lot, so I feel that they both have benefitted by it.[20]

And, to add a touch of levity, Julius finished by saying "Last but not least, don't put out such good comedies that my Century business will be ruined," and, as a capper, "Also when are they going to perform a briss [sic] on Joe Martin."[21] The *New York Morning Telegraph* had a more cynical explanation for Stern's return to New York:

Julius Stern, Universal executive, has departed for New York to confer with Eastern officials about the upheaval at Universal City, following the slaughter of the salary list. Irving Thalberg is holding the reins alone as of old.[22]

By the beginning of 1923, however, Thalberg had resigned from Universal to go to work for Louis B. Mayer.[23] Years later Stern would simply acknowledge that Thalberg "was a very bright boy" and leave it at that.[24]

One of Julius's additional tasks after returning to the East Coast was to tackle further editing of Erich von Stroheim's third film for Universal, *Foolish Wives*, and to oversee its presentation. Von Stroheim's unwieldy thirty-reel rough cut, which Stern called "the most perfect and smooth picture I ever saw or ever hope to see,"[25] had been reassigned to Arthur Ripley for further editing. Laemmle wired Julius in early December about the progress—or perceived lack thereof—that Ripley was making in reducing von Stroheim's cut to a more manageable length. Laemmle had a lot of money tied up in this film, and was justifiably concerned that it recoup his investment upon its release.

Haven't seen Foolish Wives. Ripley says seven eight reels ready Monday. Is afraid picture wont be ready new Years. Ripley very slow. Hardly believe will be in California before January. Absolutely essential remain East for opening Foolish Wives New York Chicago Philadelphia Boston. May be one or more cities essential. I watch prices. Have too much at stake.[26]

In spite of Laemmle's concerns, Ripley rose to the occasion and managed to cut it down to fourteen reels for its January 11, 1922 New York premiere.[27] Von Stroheim, asked of his reaction to Ripley's version, lamented that it was "only the skeleton of my dead child."[28] Laemmle wanted to knock a few more bones off that "skeleton," however, so he dumped the task on Stern.

"To this task Julius Stern brought the keen judgment, the patience and the efficiency for which he is noted," wrote *Moving Picture World*.

Over and over again he had scenes run before him in the projection room, while he went over titles with the title writer and ordered the cutter to take out or put back certain detail, even changing sequences when necessary to add suspense. In his spare moments and in the evenings he worked with the musicians, giving his ideas on the type of melody to fit various tempos.[29]

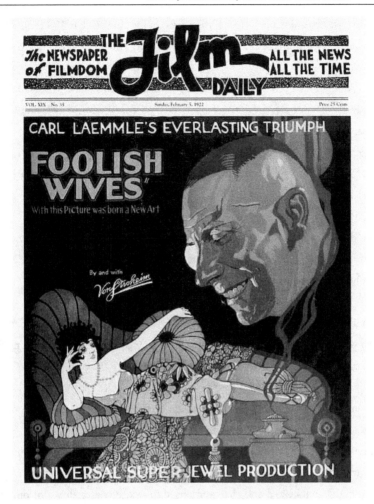

Erich von Stroheim leers in this stylish artwork for *Foolish Wives*, featured on the front cover of the February 5, 1922 issue of *Film Daily*.

It sounds like a reprint of some studio-generated promotional piece, but provides a sense of what he was up against. Stern's final cut was ten reels, a length he said "is in consequence of the earnest request of more than twenty exhibitors who will play the picture on any terms we suggest.... This will enable them to play two night shows instead of one...."[30] A pragmatic decision, made with the needs and desires of exhibitors foremost in mind. The film went into general release with Stern's cuts, and would remain as such for several years.[31]

Perhaps one of the reasons Laemmle trusted Stern with the task of reediting *Foolish Wives* was the degree of trust Stern had presumably established three years earlier when von Stroheim was finishing up his first film as director for Universal, 1919's *Blind Husbands*. The following telegram was sent from Laemmle to Stern, then out at the L-Ko studios:

Want you to become manager for Stroheim on my behalf. Of course have [Universal lawyer and Los Angeles law firm partner] Edwin Loeb draw up papers and see Stroheim sometime next week and fix it up. Let him know under your managership he will have better protection and that you will look out for him. Tie him up for at least three years. Once this is done you can hold him in line for me. Give this your prompt attention. Have fully made up my mind if Blind Husbands turns out big success and money maker will give Stroheim twenty five hundred or five thousand. Have told him nothing of this but will let you get credit for getting it for him to get on right side of Stroheim. Of course make no positive promise.[32]

Stern liked von Stroheim—"He was a good man" he once said—and it would appear that Stern was successful in wooing von Stroheim. Von Stroheim would remain with the studio for the next three years, following *Blind Husbands* (1919) with *The Devil's Pass Key* (1920) and *Foolish Wives* (1922). Von Stroheim's dealings with Universal would come to an abrupt end with his next film, however, when he was pulled from direction of *Merry-Go-Round* (1923) and replaced by Rupert Julian.

Laemmle's ongoing demands of Julius weren't the only distractions during this period, as marital woes plagued not only Julius but Abe as well. Abe's first shot at marriage came to a bitter, highly-publicized end that must have proved embarrassing, not only to Abe but to Julius and sister Anna as well. On September 16, 1921, Abe was made defendant in an action brought by his wife Jessie, for divorce on the grounds of cruelty; the couple had separated in May of the previous year. Her complaint sheds some light on Abe's income during the previous year, stating that he made $200 per week from Universal and $25,000 a year from Century. Add to that the additional $75,000 he received in the past twelve months for his half-interest in the "Tarzan" series, plus some other unstated revenue, placing his annual income in the area of $107,000. Or, in current 2020 dollars, roughly $1,550,000. Jessie hoped for alimony of $2,500 per month plus an equal division of Abe's motion picture holdings, and of $100,000 worth of property made up of real estate and bonds. She also petitioned for an injunction and restraining order, claiming that Abe had threatened to convert all property into cash and head back to Germany to establish a permanent home there.

Poster for "Stroheim's Wonder-Play" *Blind Husbands*.
Courtesy of Heritage Auctions, Ha.com.

Abe's sister Anna and Julius were dragged into the complaint as well. Anna, it was claimed, was allowed to live in the Sterns' home for months on end, and during those stays "continuously treated the plaintiff with disdain, criticized the wearing apparel of the plaintiff, and that the defendant countenanced all the acts of his sister." As for Julius, in addition to the "grievous mental distress" he caused her, also threatened to shoot her![33] The suit was settled and divorce granted in November, when Jessie was awarded "$55,000 in cash, securities, and furniture." Abe's "theatrical and partnership enterprises and royalties on photoplays in which he had an interest" were spared, Jessie relinquishing all claims.[34] As for Jessie's brother Louis Jacobs, his relationship with the Sterns appears to have evaporated shortly thereafter.

With this failed marriage behind him, Abe finally found happiness with a woman he had known for years. In early 1923, Abe married Hortense Westheimer in New York, a woman well known in New York society circles. Hortense agreed to relocate to California—not that it probably took too much coaxing—where the newlyweds honeymooned in Coronado. With the honeymoon done with, the couple moved into Los Angeles's recently-built Ambassador Hotel while their new home was being constructed,[35] and Abe returned to his daily grind. The Sterns would have an only child in 1927, Barbara Westheimer Stern, and would choose Laemmle's daughter Rosabelle as Barbara's godmother.[36]

Julius's first confirmed marriage didn't fare much better. He married a woman named Sylvia Born sometime around 1920, and she filed for divorce from him in March 1921 on grounds of adultery. Julius and Sylvia agreed on "the amount that should be paid by the defendant to the plaintiff in lieu of permanent alimony" along with Sylvia's counsel fees. Further wording of the interlocutory judgment of March 26 is somewhat interesting, stating that the judgment permits "the plaintiff to remarry again in the same manner as if the defendant were dead, but forbidding the defendant remarrying any other person during the lifetime of the plaintiff except by express permission of the court."[37] Given that the complaint for divorce was filed in New York state, and that in 1921 the sole grounds for divorce in New York was adultery,[38] it's possible that Julius and Sylvia had quietly agreed to use "adultery" as a means to dissolve an otherwise unhappy marriage, an approach then known as collusive divorce. That, or Julius had actually committed adultery; we'll never know for certain.

made and provided, doth

8

ORDER, ADJUDGE AND DECREE, that the plaintiff is entitled to a judgment dissolving the bonds
of matrimony heretofore existing between the plaintiff
and defendant, and freeing the plaintiff from the obli-
gations thereof, and permitting the plaintiff to remarry
again in the same manner as if the defendant were dead,
but forbidding the defendant remarrying any other person during the lifetime of the plaintiff except by express permission of the Court, and it is further

The rather curious wording disallowing Julius Stern to remarry anytime soon, as found in *Interlocutory Judgment: Sylvia B. Stern, Plaintiff, against Julius Stern, Defendant,* dated March 26, 1921. Courtesy of Gilbert Sherman.

Julius did, however, have an eye for good looking women, so an extra-marital tryst is certainly possible. According to his daughter Susan, "Dad liked nothing better than a good-looking woman. He assumed a woman to be attractive unless he knew otherwise, and so he verbally flirted with telephone operators whenever he had the chance. If a woman was really a knock-out, he'd tell her she was pretty enough to be in pictures, that being the highest compliment he could think of." When it came to his two daughters, however, "he wanted to make sure his daughters didn't get any bright ideas about becoming actresses. As far as he was concerned, there was only one way for an actress to become a star, and he preferred the women in his family to remain vertical."[39] It's that last comment about the "one way for an actress to become a star" that suggests that possibly—*just possibly*—Julius had some first-hand experience in that regard.

If Julius had committed adultery, however, perhaps one explanation for the judgment's seemingly odd stipulation regarding remarriage was that Julius was being "punished." New York Supreme Court Justice Joseph Morschauser later stated that more women seek divorces than men because they have:

> always had more cause for being plaintiffs than men. They are more sinned against than sinning. But bear this in mind—women generally do not seek to break up the home unless they are hard pushed…. The new rich are restless and seek extreme pleasures, they get away from a normal life, and then the mischief begins.[40]

Regardless, Julius was bound by the terms of the judgment, which became final three months later, forbidden to ever remarry until either Sylvia passed on or he obtained permission from the court.

With his failed marriage now well behind him, Julius made another move at Universal in January 1922 that may have raised some eyebrows and, perhaps, got the hopes up of some lower-level employees. Stern appointed Zion Meyers, his personal secretary and brother of actress Carmel Myers, to personnel adjutant of Universal City. Myers, it was reported, was commissioned "to compile an accurate service record of every employee."

> The information will be used for the individual advancement of workers at Universal City and for reassigning men, who, by reason of experience and aptitude, are fitted for positions of more importance. Myers will handle it much as it was practiced in the United States Army, where the personnel

adjutants discovered that the work being done at the moment by a man is no indication of what he can do. Preliminary forms have been prepared which will give a brief outline of the individual's experience and education. Then, in cases of particular interest personal interviews will follow.[41]

It's doubtful that anything ever came of Stern's newly-appointed personnel adjutant. By March, Stern and Laemmle were at odds with each other, resulting in Stern's tendering his resignation that same month shortly before returning to New York; it was accepted. The primary factor in this rift was reported by *Variety*:

> In the case of [Harry] Carey, Stern is reported when taking charge of Universal City to have informed the star his salary was to be cut 50 per cent. The star and his wife then kidded Stern to the extent he didn't have the authority, and that they would take the matter up with Carl Laemmle. This so incensed Stern, it is said, that to show his authority he gave Carey a release in writing. That was just what Carey wanted. He immediately started negotiations with [Robertson-Cole], which have concluded in a contract with that organization. In New York Laemmle raised the roof, it is said, when he heard the star had been released from the contract.

Poster art for Harry Carey's *Man to Man*, a Universal Jewel release of 1922.
Courtesy of Heritage Auctions, Ha.com.

And a lucrative move it was for Carey, his $2,500 weekly salary at Universal now upped to $5,000 at R-C.[42] What's even more surprising about this parting of ways is that several months earlier Carey had:

> ...offered U a five figure bonus to release him. They refused, though last week they agreed to cancel the contract without ado.[43]

Small wonder that Laemmle was "unhappy."

Lobby card for Eddie Polo's serial *Cap'n Kidd*, directed by Burton King and made in a huff after departing from Universal. Courtesy of Heritage Auctions, Ha.com.

Eddie Polo's departure was another factor behind Laemmle's roof raising. While still employed by Universal, Polo had started working on his own script for a film based on Robinson Crusoe, which he planned on making if contract renewal negotiations with Universal didn't pan out. When Stern heard of this he immediately had his writers churn out their own Robinson Crusoe script, "with the intention of practically giving it to exhibitors in the event that Polo went ahead with his production." This was the proverbial straw that broke Polo's back, prompting his departure from Universal and re-setting his sights on a production of *Cap'n Kidd*.[44] That film failed to click with the public, and Polo returned to his native Germany.

Stern, of course, denied that there were any problems or ruffled feathers, and attempted to put a positive spin on things. "The stars have left, but without the 'upheaval'," said Stern. "Mr. Carey was released from his contract and will probably give wide exploitation to 'Man to Man,' his forthcoming Universal-Jewel super-feature, through a personal-appearance tour." Note the word "probably." "Eddie Polo has gone to Europe to regain his pep," he went on to say. "When he returns he may perhaps be offered another contract."[45] Note the words "he may perhaps."

The souring of Julius's relationship with Laemmle may have been slowly evolving, but would eventually dissolve altogether as a result of events that took place in the late 1920s; these will be detailed in a later chapter. Still, business was business; as long as the two needed each other, their business relationship would continue throughout the decade, strengthened by the familial ties that would ensure the Sterns were included in all relevant social functions.

Chapter 10: From Filler to Focus
(The 1922-1923 Season)

The next three seasons showed a maturing of the operations at Century. A number of innovations were introduced with the goal of improving the studio's product, while producing each new film as efficiently and cost-effectively as possible. There was now a deliberate focus on, and promotion of, a handful of series and their stars, as opposed to previous seasons' unreliable mix of several series and isolated, one-off comedies.

Along with the ongoing weekly press releases to the trades, Century now placed a full page collection of promo pieces appearing monthly in the pages of *Universal Weekly* under the banner "Under the Spreading Century Plant." This replaced the earlier "The Century Limited" which had failed to click two years earlier.

Additionally, even though Julius regularly promoted that just about everything going on at Century took place under his "personal supervision," there was a greater reliance on the delegation of authority, allowing both Sterns to focus on the "big picture" rather than get bogged down with the little stuff. It didn't hurt that one of these individuals was another relative, a keep-it-in-the-family approach that had benefitted them so well in their relationship with Laemmle.

Despite Julius's resignation from Universal, he and brother-in-law Laemmle remained on amicable terms. Business was one thing, after all, and family another, but the lines between the two were definitely blurred in this particular relationship. The Century comedies were filling a comfortable niche in Universal's release schedule and making money for everyone concerned. To that end, Century's contract with Universal was renewed on April 29, 1922, for fifty-two two-reel comedies during the upcoming 1922-1923 season. "The demand for Century Comedies by the first-run houses all over the country has more than doubled," said Laemmle.

We receive daily letters from our exchanges and from the theatre owners themselves asking for more and more of this product and can only commend the business acumen and knowledge of human nature displayed by the Stern brothers when they specialize to such an extent on children and animal pictures which appeal to the heart as well as the sense of humor of the average theatregoer. The day for rough slapstick comedy is fast disappearing and human interest playlets with a strong comedy vein is taking its place.[1]

There was the usual turnover at the studio during this period. Julius had wired from Europe that he had signed a celebrated pair of French clowns known as the Renault Brothers, who returned with him to Hollywood. "A special committee met them in New York and took care of their passage to California, where they will begin work on a story vice-president Abe Stern is having written for them." As impressed as Julius must have been when he saw their "brilliant pantomime" over in Europe,[2] evidently it didn't translate well to film. Nothing further was heard about the Renault Brothers, who presumably returned to France, their collective tails tucked between their legs.

Julius also returned with a police dog whose name was Americanized to "Cap." Cap was assigned to trainer Thomas Wade, and it was anticipated that he would be a natural since he was the offspring of "Rolf," who had "an international reputation on the other side of the pond."[3] If Cap ever made it before the Century cameras, however, it was anonymously as one of the "Century Dogs." Not to be outdone, Abe went ahead and purchased a pair of trained ring-tailed monkeys from the Singer Midgets vaudeville act. Baby Peggy, it was reported, was to be the lucky beneficiary of Abe's simian generosity.[4]

Julius reported on the impact of his trip to Europe, and the observance of the comedies then being made there:

While the foreign comedies which I saw in Germany and Italy have none of the sparkle and quick laugh producers found in our gags and demanded by American audiences, yet I was impressed by their carefully thought out plots, and I intend to follow out some of their ideas while sacrificing in no way our rapid fire American humor.[5]

And he added this for lion-weary viewers nationwide: "I believe the day of the comedy lion is past." Did this signal a more mature approach for Century's product in the years to come? Not so fast, as Julius also said that:

> I find that we have received many demands for a new series of Century
> beauties, and we are going to produce comedies which have scenes that are
> easy to look at. Pretty girls are natural adjuncts to two-reelers and we intend
> to procure, in addition to those we have already, some of California's choicest
> examples of good looks which would by no means disgrace a Ziegfeld chorus.[6]

From lions to beauties: at least he'd be putting some humans back on the payroll. Abe took this to heart and scheduled a film of college life to feature these so-called Century Beauties. He sent a cameraman out to a sorority's annual conclave in Los Angeles to persuade and film some of the girls there "to add to the realism of the scenes." Tentatively titled *The Freshman*, Alf Goulding was to direct and Joe Bonner to star, with former lion tamer Zack Williams also in the cast, but it doesn't appear to have been filmed and released, or at least not released by Century.[7]

The success of the previous year's Century Week was such that Laemmle decided that the last week of 1922 would be rechristened Universal Joy Week. "All the best of the Universal and Century releases are being gathered together," wrote *Universal Weekly*, "and fresh prints made so all exchanges will be able to care for bookings, and made releases that are not scheduled for months are being pre-released for the occasion."[8] Concurrent with this was the additional announcement that Universal's name was undergoing a change, from Universal Film Manufacturing Company to Universal Pictures Corporation.[9]

Production had been ramped up by this time so that completed releases were being shipped to exchanges six to eight weeks in advance. Plans for a series of Baby Peggy fairy tales were announced, with potential titles such as *Little Red Riding Hood*, *Snow White*, *The Three Bears*, and *Alice in Wonderland* thrown out as enticement. "This will be the first time in history," wrote *Moving Picture Weekly*, "that as young a child as 3-year old Peggy will be able to carry through such parts, as they have always been played by older folk made up to look like children."[10] This was part of what was referred to as "a radical change in the manner of booking their product," where instead of selling fifty-two comedies for the season Century now offered series. These were listed as the Brownie series, the Lee Moran series, the Queenie series, the Johnny Fox series, the Baby Peggy series, and the previously mentioned Fairy Tale series. With the exception of the Baby Peggy films, these would be offered in blocks of twelve. In addition, a series of novelty pictures would be released, featuring casts of all dogs, all animals, and all children.[11] As with a lot of plans and announcements of this sort, it didn't always work out as intended.

To facilitate increased production, the Sterns were now hiring several more directors, many of them for only a film or two. This was necessary to alleviate some of the pressure on the studio's new workhorse, Al Herman, who directed seventeen of the new season's releases. Aside from seven comedies that had been directed by Gillstrom and another six by Goulding, the rest of the 1922-1923 season's shorts were handled by others, most of them either new to the studio or the random re-hire. Archie Mayo (1891-1968), who was given his start as a director by the Sterns back at L-Ko in 1917, was responsible for five shorts. Harry Edwards (1888-1952), a comparatively seasoned vet having directed comedies from 1914 for Universal, L-Ko, Nestor, Keystone, Kalem, Fox, CBC, and others, handled another five. Herman Raymaker (1893-1944), who got his start with Sennett and was signed in November 1922, directed another three, and Noel Smith (1893-1955), who similarly got his start as a director back at L-Ko in 1917, another two. Norman Taurog, Jimmie Adams, Jim Davis, and several non-entities helped fill a small portion of the release schedule with a single film each.

Director Archie Mayo.

Director Harry Edwards.

Director Herman Raymaker.

Director Noel Smith.

The remaining few spots were filled as the shelves were cleared of Tom Buckingham's and Fred Fishback's final efforts. Fishback was gone by now, his Fred Hibbard Productions having moved on to Educational where he would direct three dozen Cameo, Mermaid, and Lloyd Hamilton Comedies before his untimely death from cancer in January 1925; he was only thirty years old. Buckingham too was gone, heading to Fox where he continued to direct comedies through 1926 before switching to features, with only a handful of unremarkable Westerns and dramas to his credit. He died in 1934.

Director Norman Taurog.

The hiring of Norman Taurog (1899-1981) was touted in the press as somewhat of a coup, his former association as Larry Semon's director and co-author given prominent mention on films such as *The Bakery* (1921) and *The Sawmill* (1922), a "badge of honor" of sorts. With him as assistant director was Gil Pratt (1891-1954), formerly a Star Comedy director and gag man. Taurog's first, *The Fresh Kid* (October 11, 1922) starred Johnny Fox, after which Taurog was supposed to direct Lee Moran.[12] "Four new stages, a new large garage and a new fire protection are only a part of the visible growth of Century studios," wrote *Exhibitors Trade Review*, "which will also include larger and improved quarters for the recent added animal stars." These enhancements to the studio, it was said, were needed to accommodate the hiring of Taurog, Pratt, and Al Herman.[13] It didn't turn out quite that way, since Taurog's employment with Century was one-and-done, after which Taurog went freelance to direct comedies for Joe Rock, Fox, Jack White's Juvenile, Mermaid, and Cameo Comedies, Universal's "Andy Gump" series, Lupino Lane, and Lloyd Hamilton among others before eventually—and successfully—moving into features with the coming of sound.

Director Norman Taurog's *The Fresh Kid*, starring Ena Gregory (far left), Glen Cavender with straw boater, Johnny Fox, and shop owner James T. Kelley.
Courtesy of Robert James Kiss.

The films featuring younger children and/or animals continued to dominate, with Baby Peggy leading the pack. Maude the mule starred in a half dozen films with titles like *The Kickin' Fool*, *A Small Town Derby* (December 13, 1922), *Me and My Mule* (December 20, 1922), and *Hee! Haw!* (January 17, 1923).

Me and My Mule, which was filmed in the summer of 1922 by Al Herman, had a future director of note on its payroll. Mark Sandrich, who would go on to direct such films as the musicals *Top Hat* (1935), *Shall We Dance* (1937), and *Holiday Inn* (1942), was then a twenty-one year old vacationing in California during his summer break between junior and senior years at Columbia University. Hired as a $22 a week prop man on the Herman comedy, he got the job ostensibly due to his facility in higher mathematics, and "showed his knowledge of the engineering principles of stress and strain in solving a problem incident to the films." We'll take his word for it. Two weeks on the job and he was promoted to assistant director, and along with a $5 a week raise became a gag man as well. By 1924 he had moved on to Educational, and would specialize in shorts until graduating to feature production in the early 1930s.[14] Sandrich's career came to an abrupt end when he died in 1945 from a heart attack at the comparatively young age of forty-four.

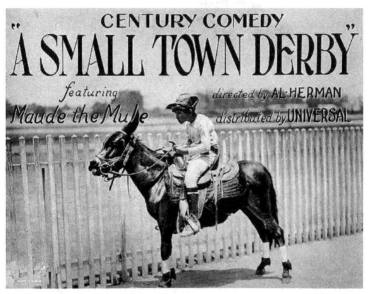

Johnny Fox atop Maude the mule in Al Herman's *A Small Town Derby*.

The Kickin' Fool, which survives in a print held by the Museum of Modern Art, is an excellent showcase for Maude's "talents." In this one Harry Sweet, erroneously blamed for ownership of the destructive mule, spends a good portion of the film attempting to get rid of her, first with dynamite and later by drowning. As grim as it sounds, it's actually a very funny film, and Maude gets to display her impressive kicking abilities by rendering the boards fed by wood yard owner Fred Spencer into kindling. One of the film's high points occurs when Sweet and Spencer, rivals for the hand of Lillian Biron, share a table at the local eatery. Maude, standing outside the window, continues to steal Spencer's pancakes when he isn't looking. The topper, however, is when she downs his bottle of beer, standing at the window with one hoof up on a rail as if drinking in a saloon. The consumption of alcohol leads to her town-wide rampage, thus confirming the worst fears of any prohibitionists viewing the film.

Queenie appeared in another four films, *True Blue* and *The Game Hunter* among them, but it was Brownie who came out on top with ten films to his credit, with titles such as *The*

Radio Hound (September 20, 1922), *A Howling Success*, and *Why Dogs Leave Home* (May 9, 1923). In *The Tattle Tail* (December 27, 1922), Brownie assists detectives while garbed in Sherlock Holmesian attire. By season's end, however, the novelty of four-legged stars had worn out, and there would be no more films from these particular animals.

Billy Engle and Brownie in Archie Mayo's *Why Dogs Leave Home*.

As for the kids, Jackie Morgan (1916-1981) and Johnny Fox (1909-1997) headed the list, or at least the list that didn't include Baby Peggy. Morgan, who had joined the company the previous season and was probably hired based on the mischievously destructive brat he portrayed in Harold Lloyd's comedy *I Do* a year earlier, frequently supported Brownie in films such as *Sic 'Em Brownie* (May 10, 1922), *The Radio Hound*, and *Wedding Pumps* (October 18, 1922). Morgan's mischievousness carried into the Centuries, a point of contention with at least one reviewer in his comments about *Sic 'Em Brownie*:

> What Jackie is made to do in the way of juvenile mischief hardly will meet the approbation of grown-ups. He proves to be more of a pest than cute. At least, that is the impression he created in the mind of one observer who can hardly be said to be any longer young.[15]

His mischievousness aside, reviewers were impressed by the young actor's talents. Comments about his performance in *Wedding Pumps* include "Jackie Morgan, a fine-looking chap and one that shows wonderful possibilities if properly directed"[16] and "Jackie does well—plays his part with understanding and with vim."[17] After his contract with the Sterns expired, Morgan would continue on in short comedies through 1926, primarily in Universal's "The Gumps" series, before retiring from the industry.

Street urchins Jackie Morgan and his big sister Alberta Vaughn, about to duke it out, in Alf Goulding's *Sic'Em Brownie*. Courtesy of Jim Kerkhoff.

Jackie Morgan. Courtesy of Marguerite Sheffler.

The older Fox had come on board the previous season as well, with *Three Weeks Off* (May 31, 1922), *Speed 'Em Up* (June 14, 1922), *The Fresh Kid*, *Ginger Face*, and others to his credit. The two of them appeared together in one or more of the above, as well as in *A Small Town Derby* and *Live Wires* (July 5, 1922). "This number of the Century is far below the average and will hardly entertain the simplest audience," sniffed *Film Daily* with reference to this latter film.[18] The reviewers for *Exhibitors Trade Review* were outright dismissive of Fox's talents or, as their comments would indicate, lack thereof. Regarding *Three Weeks Off*, "…there seems to be nothing about his work to stamp him as being any different from any other boy." Fox's efforts in *Speed 'Em Up* fared no better: "…aside from his freckles there seems to be nothing about him that is out of the usual or even up to the average of juvenile requirement for screen performance." The reviewer of *Hello, Mars* took pity on star Harry Sweet, stating that Sweet "is handicapped by the boy who is cast with him, whose chief if not sole title to consideration are swiftly moving, gum-chewing jaws and an unvarying silly grin."[19] Faint praise, indeed.

Farm hand Harry Sweet gets a drink of water from his girl Alberta Vaughn, in Arvid Gillstrom's *Speed 'Em Up*. Courtesy of Robert James Kiss.

Ena Gregory (left) and Alberta Vaughn (right) play Tug-o-war with Harry Sweet as Johnny Fox looks on from below. From *Hello, Mars*, directed by Alf Goulding. Courtesy of Jim Kerkhoff.

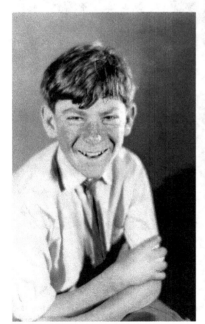

Freckle-faced Johnny Fox. Courtesy of Drina Mohacsi.

Ena Gregory has caught Johnny Fox in the act, in Alf Goulding's *Live Wires*. Courtesy of Heritage Auctions, Ha.com.

Baby Peggy, of course, was by now Century's biggest star. In addition to loaning her out for occasional parts in features, the Sterns had decided to satisfy demand by starring her in a series of six "super Century Comedies" to be known as Baby Peggy Special Universal Century Comedies.[20] This didn't pan out, and her eventual return from an extended illness and absence from the screen prompted the decision to put her films back on the regular program. Bookings would now be in blocks of six films, "and under no circumstances will the subjects be sold individually."[21] The new Baby Peggy offerings landed on the final Wednesday of each month, with *Peg o' the Movies* (March 28, 1923), *Sweetie* (April 25, 1923), *The Kid Reporter* (May 30, 1923), *Taking Orders* (June 27, 1923), *Tips* (July 25, 1923), and *Carmen, Jr.* (August 29, 1923) the first block of six, and continued well into 1924.

Baby Peggy, disguised, in Alf Goulding's *The Kid Reporter*.

The first four of these were well reviewed at the time, and we are fortunate that both *Sweetie* and *The Kid Reporter* survive. *Carmen, Jr.*, which also survives, was a different story, however. Directed by Alf Goulding, filming took place in part at the eighteenth century San Fernando Mission in the Mission Hills section of Los Angeles.[22] Peggy took ill with pneumonia midway through production, with the resultant reported loss to the Goulding unit—including overhead, salaries, and incidental expenditures—roughly seven thousand dollars.[23] It was claimed at the time that all of her scenes had been shot before she took ill, but that wouldn't account for the reported production delays. What it *would* account for is the disjointed look of the finished film, more a rough assemblage of disconnected scenes lacking any sort of coherent storyline. The result is not very good, although in fairness there are two scenes that provide comparative highlights of sorts, the first an impromptu tango where Baby Peggy clumsily attempts to keep pace with the smooth movements of six year old Tommy Wonder, another Gus Edwards protégé hired specifically for his dancing abilities. The other sequence involves an extended bull fight, with Peggy taking the place of the missing toreador. The bull, a ludicrous man-in-a-shabby-bull-costume, actually adds to the humor of the scene. It chases Peggy around the ring, Peggy temporarily hiding between its legs. Ready to dispatch the bull, her sword bends on his tough hide. She pokes him in the butt with a pin, shakes salt on its tail, then hangs on for dear life as the bull twirls in fast circles. She loses her grip on its tail, and crashes into the wall. Peggy finally perseveres, sitting atop the bull, on its back on the bullring's floor.

Matador Baby Peggy in the bullfight ring, in Alf Goulding's *Carmen, Jr.*
Courtesy of Robert James Kiss.

It probably goes without saying that the Sterns charged a premium for these popular two-reelers, but for that added charge exhibitors expected them to deliver, and consistently. "Wow! This is terrible," wrote an incensed exhibitor in Michigan about *Carmen, Jr.* "They charge me more for these Baby Peggys than for the other Centuries, but they're worth-less, and that goes both ways. The kid is clever, but you can let your voice fall right there."[24] Sour grapes? Perhaps, but reviewers, while not nearly as vitriolic in their assessment of *Carmen, Jr.*, were similarly unimpressed. "Not up to the standard set by former Baby Peggy comedies," wrote a reviewer for *Exhibitors Herald.*

> It lacks spontaneity and logic which every two-reeler to make any great appeal, should have. In this one Baby Peggy's talents are wasted. The story is weak and aside from the bull fight, in which a man dressed up in burlesque of a bull, jumps around, with Baby Peggy following him with a tin sword, it has little to recommend it. There are a host of youngsters in it and it is a pity something could not have been made of the material at hand.[25]

As for those earlier announced Baby Peggy fairy tales, *Little Red Riding Hood* had been filmed and *Jack and the Beanstalk* was under way, with *Hansel and Gretel* to follow, all of them helmed by Alf Goulding. Other possible titles bandied about included *The Little Match Girl, Little Bo Peep, Alice in Wonderland* (alternately announced as *Alice in Blunderland*), *Little Boy Blue*,[26] and *The Little Mermaid*.[27] Ambitious plans, but as it turned out only the first three would make it onto film, although casting had gotten underway for *Little Bo Peep* before it was deep-sixed.[28]

Johnny Fox watches Buddy Williams plant one on Baby Peggy in *Hansel and Gretel.*
Courtesy of Mark Johnson.

Perhaps it had something to do with the inflated budgets that accompanied their production. For *Jack and the Beanstalk*, technical director Tom O'Neill constructed "six enormous sets...for the giant's castle and other over-sized scenes." More than two hundred extras were used in scenes set in the city of the giant and the village where Jack [Albert "Buddy" Williams] spent his early youth. "Julius Stern has given out the word that no expense is to be spared in making these fairy tale productions worthy of the best moving picture houses in the country," wrote *Universal Weekly.* "Certain scenes have been taken over and over again to obtain the right illusion and atmosphere."[29] Not your typical Century five-day shoot! For *Hansel and Gretel*, O'Neill was said to have built some of the finest sets of his career. "The furniture in one set [was] entirely composed of little pebbles and consumed two and a half weeks to make."[30] Small wonder that the Sterns may have had second thoughts about producing these fairy tales.

Baby Peggy tries to find her way in Alf Goulding's *Red Riding Hood.*
Courtesy of Robert James Kiss.

Jack Earle, born Jake Erlich.

Then again it may have been the fate that befell *Little Red Riding Hood* that was the straw that broke the Sterns' back. Originally scheduled for release on November 6, 1922 as a Century Special, "Owing to a series of misfortunes—fire, sickness, and others—Century announces that 'Little Red Riding Hood' has been taken definitely off the schedule," wrote *Exhibitors Herald*.[31] Evidently the second reel of what had by then grown to feature length was destroyed in a fire. Additionally, Baby Peggy's pneumonia caused a delay that resulted in the unavailability of some of her fellow actors upon her recovery for necessary retakes.[32] The film was eventually salvaged and cut down to two reels, with some hand-colored scenes highlighting her little red outfit, and released on November 21, 1925. Now titled *Red Riding Hood*, it was noted that "a number of fill-in sequences have been built up that add greatly to the picture value of this offering."[33] The film was well reviewed, and exhibitors seemed pleased with the results:

I have waited three years to show this and am more than pleased. It is done beautifully and Little Peggy was never more cute and pleasing. Coloring is beautiful, wonderful for children and all the grownups were delighted with it. Will please any crowd.[34]

Whatever the case, the Sterns never made any more of their fairy tale shorts. Baby Peggy was long gone from the studio by this time, having signed with producer Sol Lesser to make features for a whopping $1,500,000 per year.[35]

Jack and the Beanstalk (July 6, 1924) would feature one of Century's unlikeliest breakout stars, a fellow billed as Jack Earle. Born Jacob Reuben Erlich on June 20, 1906 in Denver, Colorado,[36] the tiny little three and a half pound newborn would eventually be diagnosed as suffering from acromegaly. By adulthood Erlich had grown to gargantuan proportions, a reported seven feet three inches when hired by Century,[37] and was the perfect choice to star as the film's giant. Sixteen year old Earle was "discovered" after a day of fishing on the Santa Monica pier by then-Century gag man Zion Meyers and cameraman Jerry Ash.[38] Spotting a very unusual type they felt could be useful in the Century comedies, they convinced him to come to the studio for a screen test. He was hired, and his first released film for Century was 1923's opener *Sting 'Em Sweet*. "There is good comedy," wrote one reviewer, "where a very tall man has difficulty in getting into a flivver with an undersized body."[39]

Trolley conductor Jack Earle seems impatient with Jack Cooper in Al Herman's *Fare Enough*. Emily Gerdes observes with amusement from the trolley's window, third from left. Courtesy of Heritage Auctions, Ha.com.

Sting 'Em Sweet, along with five additional comedies, co-starred Earle with Jack Cooper (1891-1959), an accomplished British comedian with former music hall experience. Cooper had come to the U.S. and moved into film for Sennett and Lehrman's Fox Sunshine—*Oh! What a Knight!* and *Money Talks* (both 1919), among others—before moving on to Century. Some of the other Earle-Cooper comedies included *Farm Follies* (January 24, 1923), *A Howling Success*, and *A Spooky Romance* (March 7, 1923). Earle and Cooper had to share screen time with Brownie in *A Howling Success*, the dog as usual stealing the show. While one reviewer acknowledged the two human leads by name, "Jack Cooper as the professor and Jack Earl [sic], the human giraffe, as the house detective," he went on to state that "The center of interest throughout is the pup, and he commands it."[40] Cooper would only appear in a dozen films for Century during the 1922-1923 season before moving on to Mack Sennett Comedies.

A new team was in the offing when Earle—referred to by one reviewer as "the Century beanpole"—was placed with Austrian Billy Engle (born Maurice Braun), a former burlesque comedian. Engle had only a few films for Triangle to his credit before first joining Century in 1919, and more recently with Fox, Christie, Sennett, and Educational before his return to the studio.[41] The first release of the "two reliable funsters," as *Exhibitors Trade Review* called them, was *Vamped* (April 4, 1923), followed by *Hold On* (July 4, 1923), *Back to Earth* (September 5, 1923), *Golf-mania* (November 7, 1923), and several others. "Bille [sic] Engle and Jack Earl [sic] dish the dirt in this comedy,"[42] wrote reviewer Roger Ferri of *Golf-mania*, while another declared that the link-based film "should be particularly appealing to some, and the treatment is entertaining, on the whole."[43]

Philadelphia-born Harry McCoy (1889-1937) was Earle's third team-mate in 1924. A former vaudevillian who had worked for Gus Edwards, McCoy got his start in film with Universal's Joker brand where he was frequently teamed with Max Asher in a series of "Mike and Jake" shorts—*Mike and Jake Among the Cannibals*, *Mike and Jake Go Fishing* (both 1913), and *Mike and Jake Join the Army* (1914), for example—as well as roles for both American Film's Flying "A" brand and Selig. There was also a lengthy stint with Keystone—*Mabel and Fatty's Wash Day* and *Those Bitter Sweets* (both 1915) among them—followed by work for Fox Sunshine and others. Earle and McCoy's teaming resulted in *Obey the Law* (January 2, 1924), "with the physical contrast of Mutt and Jeff" wrote one reviewer; *Keep Going* (February 6, 1924); and several others, after which McCoy was signed to a long term contract.[44] "This is a more than usually entertaining comedy," wrote one reviewer of *Keep Going*. "There isn't much to the action, but the gags are funny."[45] It's probable that the young, inexperienced Earle was teamed with other more experienced performers as a sort of safety net, but contemporary reviews suggest that he was able to hold his own in the resultant comedies.

Billy Engle (sitting) holds the dancer's hand, Jack Earle towering to the right of her, and Joe Moore between and behind the two of them. From *One Exciting Day*, Al Herman director. Courtesy of Richard M. Roberts.

It looks like conductor Harry McCoy has caught Jack Earle attempting to smuggle some kids onto the trolley, while Hilliard Karr bellows from the trolley's steps. From director Noel Smith's *Lost Control*. Courtesy of Robert James Kiss.

It was Earle's teaming with Baby Peggy that brought him the most attention, with roles as Peggy's father in *Hansel and Gretel* (December 26, 1923), as the giant in the aforementioned *Jack and the Beanstalk*, and as a moonshiner in the extant *Peg o' the Mounted* (February 27, 1924). The latter, filmed in part on location at Yosemite, stands out among the other Century Comedies due to its beautiful location photography by cameraman Jerry Ash.[46] We're fortunate that it survives since it gives us a fair idea of Earle's talents (and limitations) as a comedian. Alf Goulding's direction is solid, filled with numerous cute close-ups of Baby Peggy's expression-filled reactions. In this one Peggy attends to a wounded Mountie, and then dons her little Mountie outfit and vows to track down the moonshiners responsible for his injuries. As could only happen in a silent comedy with Peggy in the lead, she succeeds.

Peggy's attempts to revive the injured Mountie garner a lot of laughs, first feeding him a spoonful of Sloan's Liniment, his mouth smoking after his first dose. Unsuccessful with that, she then grabs a bottle of Castor Oil and first rubs it on his face, then takes it a step further and dumps its contents over his head. This latter move brings him to! One of the film's funniest moments—or at least I thought it was funny—occurs when huge Earle mounts "his trusty steed," the horse so small and Earle's legs so long that he merely walks along as the horse walks beneath him. The horse was played by Peggy's own jet-black midget Mexican horse Tim, although it is unknown whether the Sterns paid for its use.

Canadian Mountie wannabe, Baby Peggy, in Alf Goulding's *Peg O' the Mounted*.
Courtesy of EYE Filmmuseum.

Peg 'o the Mounties' cameraman, Jerry Ash, related an amusing story about Abe in a 1942 issue of *American Cinematographer*. According to Ash, who was with Century in 1920, Abe and Julius were concerned about the films that former L-Ko owner Henry Lehrman was making for his studio, Henry Lehrman Comedies:

> Seems the Stern brothers, pioneer comedy producers, were deeply concerned over a competitor, Henry (Pathé) Lehrman, and sent a scout to catch the latter's first picture. The scout reported there was nothing to worry about—that Stern's comedies were every bit as good. "Don't tell me," erupted Abe Stern, "that they're as bad as all that!"[47]

This may, of course, have been yet another fanciful anecdote embellished over the years or, as likely, simply made up without any basis in truth.

As for Earle, his short career in film came to an abrupt halt due to an accident that occurred while shooting the film that would turn out to be his industry swansong. Earle's nephew Andrew Erlich described the incident in his book *The Long Shadows: The Story of Jake Erlich*:

> During the filming…he fell fourteen feet from a speeding funny car. After he had crashed into the asphalt, a piece of wood attached to a camera boom on the same automobile broke loose and hit him in the back of the head. When he regained consciousness Jake had a fractured nose and blurred vision. Within a few days he went totally blind.[48]

Curiously, x-ray treatments for the pituitary tumor pressing on his optic nerve not only cured him of his blindness, but brought a halt to his heretofore continuous growth as well. The Sterns attempted to lure the now-cured Earle back to Century, but he decided to move on to safer ventures, including a lengthy stint as the Ringling Brothers' new giant as well as sidelines as a painter, sculptor, and poet before dying in 1952 of kidney failure.

This year was no different than Century's previous in so far as the ongoing departure and replacement of the studio's various actors and actresses was concerned. Louise Lorraine had left for better opportunities with Universal and was replaced by Betty May (1904-1949), a pretty eighteen year old who would play opposite Lee Moran and others. May's introduction to Century's brand of filmmaking may have given her second thoughts about her move, when both she and Zip Monberg were thrown from a Ford when it tipped over, landing in a ditch full of stones. Bruised and with both arms bandaged, May was out of commission for several weeks.[49]

Another prominent departure was that of Lee Moran, who went on to obtain the rights to Ring Lardner's "You Know Me Al" stories. Intended as the basis of fifteen two-reel shorts,[50] the first of these was the Educational-Mermaid production *The Busher* (1923) which featured the exploits of Lardner's hick baseball player. Big league player Mike Donlin was induced to make a guest appearance, and additional scenes were shot at the training camps of the Chicago Cubs and the New York Giants. Jack White supervised.[51]

Australian Ena Gregory. Courtesy of Kay Shackleton.

One actress who was re-signed was Australian Ena Gregory (1906-1993), who had considerable prior dramatic experience playing juveniles in English companies touring her country. A beauty contest's first prize winner before coming to America,[52] Gregory was hired by the Sterns in late 1921, her first for Century *A Dark Horse* opposite Charles Dorety. Gregory eventually landed as Lee Moran's leading lady in a handful of films, *Apartment Wanted* (July 12, 1922), *Foolish Lives* (September 13, 1922; the title a spoof on Universal's lavish von Stroheim epic *Foolish Wives*), *Some Family* (October 4, 1922), and *Hello, Judge!* (November 15, 1922) among them.

Fred Spencer and his wife, Ena Gregory (both left), share an apartment with Lee Moran and his wife, Blanche Payson. As you can see, everything is evenly divided. From Arvid Gillstrom's *Foolish Lives*. Courtesy of Mark Johnson.

Even the car gets divided, 50-50, in *Foolish Lives*. Courtesy of Robert James Kiss.

Gregory would finish out the season before moving over to the Roach studios, with some Monty Banks shorts and a few features thrown into the mix. Gregory made a brief return in 1927 to star in several additional Stern Brothers comedies. As mentioned in an earlier chapter, Gregory had the professional misfortune of having a name far too similar to that of Edna Gregory, who had preceded Ena in several films for both Rainbow and Century, and the source of some credit confusion years after the fact. Gregory would make the switch to features in the later 1920s, and change her name to Marian Douglas as well to give her flagging career a boost. Her new name was purported to be a mash-up of the first names of Mary Pickford and Douglas Fairbanks.[53] Her career as such petered out in the early 1930s.

Lee Moran snuggles with Ena Gregory in Arvid Gillstrom's *Some Family*.
Courtesy of Mark Johnson.

Another recent hire was two hundred forty pound heavyweight Fred Spencer (1901-1952; born Fred Bretherton). After appearing in a small role in Jimmy Aubrey's *The Riot* (1921) for Vitagraph,[54] Spencer had roles in a handful of comedies for Century as the "heavy" in films starring Jack Cooper, Brownie, Baby Peggy, and Buddy Messinger, some of which— *Peggy, Behave!*, for instance—still billed him as Fred Bretherton. Impressed with his work, the Sterns signed him to a contract to head his own unit.

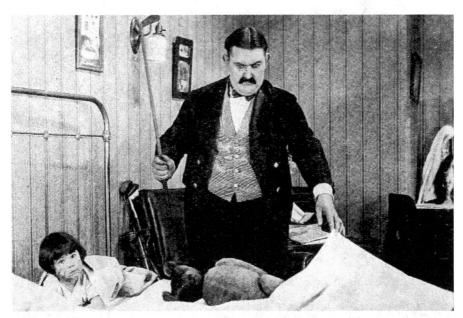

Snuggles lead to kisses in *Some Family*. Fred Spencer (top) looks shocked, Blanche Payson below and to the right of him, young Jackie Morgan hanging over the back of the car, and possibly Lige Conley with neck tie and mustache. Courtesy of Mark Johnson.

Fred Spencer ready to do battle with the Teddy Bear hiding under Baby Peggy's covers, in Arvid Gillstrom's *The Little Rascal*.

Spencer's first post-signing was the Archie Mayo-directed *Speed Bugs* (July 11, 1923), supported by Ernie Adams, Glen Cavender, and a newcomer by the name of Fay Wray.[55] Reviews were tepid: "Average entertainment is afforded in this Century comedy, chiefly concerning an automobile race. Fred Spencer plays the portly sweetheart of a garage owner's daughter and proves his right to her by winning the race.... A number of laughs but nothing especially new."[56] According to Wray's autobiography, novice Wray attempted to put on an amusing performance, but was brought up short when Mayo, not at all amused by her antics, screamed at her to "just look pretty!"[57]

Most of Spencer's output, with titles such as *Don't Scream* (October 17, 1923), *My Pal* (December 12, 1923), and *Quit Kiddin'* (February 20, 1924), was released the following season, but in spite of his supposed promotion to unit head he was, more often than not, in roles supporting other comedians. Spencer's final for Century under this contract was *Mind the Baby* (September 10, 1924), sharing the lead with Pal the dog. The fact that Spencer's name rarely, if ever, appeared in the reviews of his films probably didn't help his standing with the Sterns, and his contract was not renewed. The remainder of Spencer's brief career before the camera was spent on shorts for Sennett, Larry Semon, Lloyd Hamilton, Jack White, and Fox before disappearing from the screen.

Alice Day gets smooched by Roscoe Karns while guarded by Pal, in Al Herman's *My Pal*.

Far more successful was a youngster named Melvin Joseph "Buddy" Messinger (1909-1965). After a very early start at the tender young age of twenty-five weeks—he played the part of a neglected baby in a carriage[58]—Messinger's film career got its official start in 1916. Messinger appeared as the "heavy" in a number of Fox's Kid Series fairy tales and adventure features, as well as in Goldwyn Picture's "Edgar Series" shorts based on Booth Tarkington's stories. More recently Lon Chaney's 1922 vehicle *Shadows* provided Messinger with a meatier role, as did that same year's Universal-Jewel *The Flirt*, in which he played the part of the small brother.[59] This latter film brought him to the Sterns' attention, who signed him to star in a series of "small-town boy stories."[60] According to *Universal Weekly*:

> For a long time the Stern brothers have been looking for a boy about Buddy's age—twelve—to do regular boys' stories. Several youngsters were tried out, but they lacked the screen personality and the winning smile of Buddy, who has a large following of his own due to his natural and unaffected acting in the recent films in which he has appeared.[61]

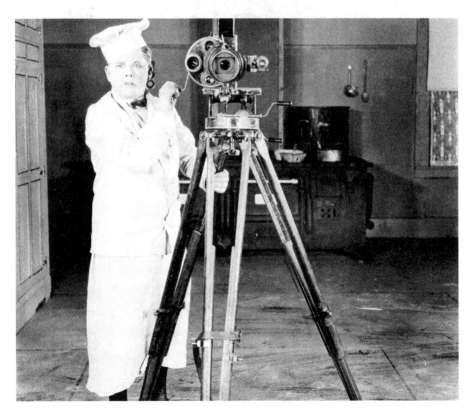

Buddy Messinger "manning" a motion picture camera. Courtesy of Robert James Kiss.

Harry Edwards was assigned to direct Messinger, assisted by Zion Meyers.[62] Messinger's first was *Boyhood Days* (February 7, 1923) co-starring newcomer Marjorie Marcel (dates unknown), a slightly older English beauty likely chosen to appear opposite him due to her appearance, as described by *Universal Weekly*: "She is very petite in build and has frequently taken child parts."[63] Which was a good pairing, since chubby hundred pound Messinger was only four feet one inch in height. This age imbalance didn't get past reviewers: "Buddy portrays a boy of eleven years, but the girl cast opposite him easily has seen several more birthdays than have fallen to Buddy,"[64] sniffed *Exhibitors Trade Review*.

Buddy Messinger's drive didn't go so well in this unidentified film—possibly Al Herman's *Buckin' the Line*—Sadie Campbell seated to the left of him, and Donald Hughes behind with glasses. Courtesy of Mark Johnson.

Messinger's subsequent films would use him wherever needed, occasionally placing him with other, more age-appropriate actresses such as Ida Mae McKenzie (1911-1986) and her cousin Ella McKenzie (1911-1987). It was with Sadie Campbell (1912-?), "a little pig-tailed towhead of Scotch descent"[65] and former protégé of Gus Edwards[66] that Messinger was most often teamed, appearing in numerous films like *Smarty* (March 21, 1923), *Don't Get Fresh* (June 20, 1923), *Buddy At the Bat* (July 18, 1923), *Bringing Up Buddy* (September 19, 1923), and *The Young Tenderfoot* (March 19, 1924).

When Campbell departed Century to appear in features, she was replaced by Martha

Sleeper[67] who, along with Spec O'Donnell, Arthur Trimble, James "Bubbles" Berry, Tommy Hicks, and others would form a loose assemblage of youths dubbed the Century Comedy Kids. One such film was *Budding Youth* (July 16, 1924), whose second reel survives and has supporting appearances by Sleeper, Berry, Hicks, and Pete the pup. There isn't much plot to this one, or at least in the reel that survives, focusing on Messinger and the rest of his gang's attempts to get even with (as an intertitle describes) "A mean attorney—whose disposition would make a Jersey cow give buttermilk." Actor L.J. O'Connor is all bluster as the target of their antics, finally softening when a street cop forces Messinger to apologize, only to have a hole blown in the seat of his pants by a stick of dynamite delivered by Pete. It's all harmless, if unexceptional, viewing.

Sadie Campbell and Buddy Messinger in Archie Mayo's *All Over Twist*.
Courtesy of Heritage Auctions, Ha.com.

Another behind-the-scenes fellow was moving up the Century ladder by the end of 1922. Bronx-born Sigmund Neufeld (1896-1979) had gone to work in 1914 at Universal's New York offices as a gofer, runner, and general all-around help, quickly advancing to the cutting room. By the late teens Neufeld was an experienced editor, and was asked to relocate to California to serve as an editor at the Sterns' Century studios, a position he held for four years. According to Wheeler Dixon in his *Cinema at the Margins*, and based on interviews with Neufeld's two sons:

> Sigmund saw that there was considerable wastage in the shooting of the comedies and impressed his bosses when he managed to put together a "new" two-reel film from outtakes and unused scenes of two or three comedies, creating more product and profit for his employers. For each "extra" comedy Sigmund manufactured for the Stern Brothers, he would get a modest bonus; on one occasion he got a diamond ring for his efforts.... But the young Sigmund Neufeld noticed that, while he might get a little something extra for his efforts, his bosses pocketed a cool $10,000 for each "instant" comedy Sigmund stitched together.[68]

This was the deciding factor in his goal to move into production, and in November 1922 Neufeld was promoted to the position of Century's production manager.[69] Part of Neufeld's additional duties was to supervise the large group of workmen—sixty carpenters and twelve painters—who were renovating the studios while Julius and Abe were in New York. With production on hiatus during these renovations, the goal was to resume production at the beginning of 1923 with six units at work,[70] three new ones to supplement the existing Raymaker, Goulding, and Edwards units.[71] Neufeld would assume charge of the studio in the years that followed whenever both Julius and Abe were traveling.

Julius Stern (left) and Sig Neufeld, 1926.

And then there was Vance de Bar Colvig (1892-1967), better known by the more than seven million readers of newspapers supplied by the United Features Syndicate as "Pinto," the cartoonist and writer of clever captions. "Pinto" Colvig was added to the Sterns' gag writing team at the beginning of 1923 and assigned to Al Herman's unit.[72] In addition to his gag writing, Pinto would, on occasion, be pressed into service to act in small roles as well, in films such as *Quit Kiddin'*, *After a Reputation* (August 5, 1925), and *Buster Be Good* (October 28, 1925). "The funniest bit in this Century," wrote *Film Daily's* reviewer of *After a Reputation*, "occurs when Edna [Marian] takes a ride in a taxi driven by a cross-eyed driver. The fellow's name is not mentioned on the screen but he does the best bit of work in the comedy, really getting some laughs."[73] Unnamed, but my gut tells me this was Pinto in the role.

Within a year Pinto was made head of the newly-created Script Building department. "His work as head of the Script Building department will bring all original and purchased material under his jurisdiction, and before a script is turned over to the director for production it will undergo rigid alterations and building-up," wrote *Exhibitors Trade Review*. "This will make every Century story holeproof and as near-perfect as possible."[74] Or at least that was the goal, to streamline actual production time and eliminate a lot of decision-making downtime.

Buddy Messinger's in trouble, possibly from Al Herman's *Bringing Up Buddy*.
Tommy Hicks is perched on the bed at right, and Fred Spencer's the adult in the group.
Courtesy of Richard M. Roberts.

Diana Serra Cary described the typically haphazard process that existed prior to the introduction of the Script Building department. Storylines existed in only the most rudimentary form, to be fleshed out during actual production. Cast members would, more often than not, be provided with:

> some inkling of what you were going to wear as a costume, and what the movie is going to be about, but "about" is a big term. We didn't know, and we had a gag man, and he got $25 a week, for thinking of things just one step ahead of the camera. And we'd go out in the street in front of the studio, and there'd be a pause, and the cameraman would say "Well, which one do you want to shoot first?" He'd say, "Well, there's a manhole over here, why don't we take the cover off and have her fall in there? And then there's this, and then we can go to Westlake Park and the canoe chase." And pretty soon it all came together...sort of.[75]

Clearly not the most efficient method of production.

Another of Julius's innovations, and one that was inspired by his most recent trip to Europe, was the decision to have the prepared script for any new production read to the entire unit before a single shot was taken. This was the director's task, with the hope that each of the actors and actresses "can better visualize their respective parts."[76]

Doris Eaton. Courtesy of Kay Shackleton.

One of Julius's more highly touted acquisitions of 1923 was the signing of the Gorham Follies to star in six Century Comedies, to be directed by Archie Mayo and with Jack Cooper as the male lead. The package deal included lead Doris Eaton (1904-2010), formerly one of the principal dancers with the Ziegfeld Follies. Her husband Joseph K. Gorham was part of the deal, which included their company of twenty-five actresses and actors, and their properties and wardrobes—eighteen trunks worth—estimated at either $35,000 or $50,000, depending on the source. J.K. Gorham had originally directed the Ziegfeld productions for several years, but went into business for himself with the creation of the Gorham Follies.[77] Their first for Century was *High Kickers* (August 22, 1923), about which *Motion Picture News* commented:

> That exponent of feminine pulchritude, the bathing girl beauty, is with us again. The brand of entertainment which was made famous by Mack Sennett and the Sunshine producers has returned to the screen, this time under the banner of Century Comedies and with the diverting title of the Gorham Follies Girls. There are two featured players—Doris Eaton, former Ziegfeld star, and Jack Cooper.... While Doris and the girls are supplying the looks, Jack Cooper is furnishing the comedy gags.... Good entertainment of its kind.[78]

High Kickers was followed by *Round Figures* (September 12, 1923), and *Fashion Follies* (October 24, 1923), after which they were rebranded as the Century Follies Girls. As such they lost their previous director and male lead, and it would appear that Eaton and the Gorham Follies girls were shown the door as well. A new package of twelve films was announced, and "the bevy of pulchritude known as the Century Follies Girls" placed pretty much wherever some attractive girls were thought useful, as eye-candy or to pad out a weak script.

A second unit was created in mid-1924 to be confined to bathing girl comedies, and would be supervised by Abe. Julius would oversee the first unit, to appear in comedies set against backgrounds of cabaret sets, theatres, and revues.[79] At least sixteen titles have been confirmed released into early 1926, but there may have been several more; *Down to the Ship to See* (November 14, 1923; the title a word play on the previous year's feature *Down to the Sea in Ships*), *Pretty Plungers* (April 23, 1924), *Starving Beauties* (July 9, 1924), *Dancing Daisies* (November 26, 1924), *A Flivver Vacation* (March 31, 1926), and *Harem Follies* (December 10, 1924) were some of these titles.[80] This latter film had the distinction of having former Century star Alice Howell's daughter Yvonne as part of its cast. One film warrants mentioning, if only because of its amusing working title: *Yes, We Have No Pajamas*. An obvious play on Frank Silver and Irving Cohn's novelty song of 1923, *Yes! We Have No Bananas*, it is unknown what its final release title was or, for that matter, if it was ever even filmed.

Doris Eaton (seated) surrounded by the Gorham Follies Girls.

Bert Roach is spooked by Betty Welsh and Al Alt in Edward I. Luddy's *Harem Follies*.
Courtesy of Mark Johnson.

Julius, in one of his endless stream of publicity releases, announced his intention to insure the entire group of girls, to cover the company in the event of "illness, death, and other unlooked-for occurrences."[81] A month later Julius was also touting that Century was considering insuring Buddy Messinger for $100,000.[82] While I have little doubt regarding his intentions, a piece in one of those absurd "Joe Martin Soliloquizes" articles that ran in *Moving Picture Weekly* a few years earlier comes to mind. Martin's (or I should say the writer's) jaundiced and frequently caustic comments about the film industry never failed to amuse, and one wonders why studio head Carl Laemmle let them get by unedited. Anyway, Martin, complaining about the measly $25,000 insurance policy Universal had supposedly taken out on him, said:

> Why I ought to be insured for a thousand times twenty five hundred and the boss ought to be glad to pay the premium, even if he cancels the policy after he's got the newspapers to fall for the publicity stunt.[83]

Not that a studio would *ever* stoop that low for some publicity.

Another late arrival to Century was Pal, "The Intellectual Bulldog." Owned by the ex-service trainer Harry Lucenay, Pal was hired to replace the departing Brownie. Pal's first appearance was in Gillstrom's *Tips* opposite Baby Peggy, and would appear in nearly a dozen comedies over the course of the next season. Pal's efforts included *My Pal*, *The Rich Pup* (January 9, 1924), and *Mind the Baby*, the bulk of these turned over to Century's in-house animal whisperer Al Herman to direct, working in close collaboration with Lucenay.[84] As testament to Pal's abilities, the first annual Motion Picture Stars' Dog Show was held in June 1924, where Pal would compete against nearly thirty other mutts, among them Tom Mix's dog, Astor Von Thumshoche; Mary Philbin's $3,000 cocker spaniel, Billy Obo, Jr.; Rod La Roque's police dog, Dant; and Norma Shearer's daschund, Chewee. Rookies, all of them, Pal marching off with first place honors.[85] Lucenay decided to further cash in on Pal's popularity by placing a small ad in the *Los Angeles Times* offering that "a photograph of Pal, the dog actor, can be obtained by communicating with his owner, Harry C. Lucenay, 856 Hyperion Street."[86] At some point Pal took some time off to father a pup named Pete, who would go on to star in a large number of Century comedies as Buster Brown's dog Tige, and greater glory after that in Hal Roach's "Our Gang" comedies.

Trainer Harry S. Lucenay and his dog (and, evidently, chauffeur) Pal.

In late May 1923, Julius once again set sail for Europe for three months' vacation. While there he said he intended to search for a new comedian, "preferably one who can do 'stunts'," after a week spent in New York interviewing applicants had failed to turn up any likely candidates.[87] Before he left, Stern (or his ghostwriter) opined on the merits of comedy shorts in a piece titled "Comedy Necessary to Successful Program":

> It is an undisputed fact that comedy acts as the dessert of a good program, just as ice cream or a demitasse acts as the dessert of a fine dinner. Theater- goers usually feel something is missing if the comedy is not forthcoming, just as the banquet-goer feels something is lacking when the dessert is not forthcoming. I place these comparisons in the same category only because they are attended to last, although many a comedy has saved a show. For this reason, although a two reel comedy may or may not be called the dessert of a good show, I do contend that comedy can be used the most effectively as a drawing card—if properly advertised and exploited. A good instance is Baby Peggy, our little four year old comedienne. Many theatres are advertising her above the feature, which shows the dessert can sometimes be the whole dinner.
>
> Since my first picture, I have always contended…that comedy is absolutely a necessity. It is necessary not only to relieve the tension of two hours of

drama or comedy-drama, but to give to the movie goer something light and digestible. By that I mean the theme and action of a two reel comedy are not problematic or liable to be misunderstood. It is a light theme—told with comedic situations, so that adult and child may see and understand.[88]

Stern went on to claim that a recent count of theatre patrons showed that twenty-five percent of them came solely to see the short comedy being shown.

Pal poses as RCA's "Nipper" to fool a gullible cop, from an unidentified film.
Courtesy of Robert James Kiss.

Several things took place during Julius's absence in Europe, both at his direction and with the support of Abe. Plans for a series of buildings were drawn up to be known as Directors' Row. These would be a series of bungalows for use by the studio's directors "so that he may read and write undisturbed." Each bungalow was to be outfitted with a shower, small library, and a writing and reading table.[89] Not particularly luxurious sounding, but no doubt a step up from their current housing. Diana Serra Cary described the lot and its spartan lodgings at that time in graphic detail:

Century Studio occupied a full city block on the southwest corner of Gower Street and Sunset; it had been built in no style at all except what might be described as Early Hollywood. The buildings were mostly made-over barns dating from when it had been a humble farm. Remodeled frame California bungalows served as offices, relics of a slightly later period when L-KO (Lehrman's Knock-Out Comedies) had operated on this site.... Although the lot was not yet ten years old, including the brief reign of L-KO, it was in an advanced state of decay. Once-gaily-striped awnings hung in sun-bleached shreds over windows fogged with grime. The owners-producers toiled in cubicles euphemistically referred to as offices, but their raw lumber walls, door jambs, and windowsills had yet to be framed, painted, or sealed. A dressing room at Century was nearly as bare as a jail cell. My own—despite the star on the door—was windowless, uncarpeted, and all of ten feet square. It was equipped with a rough-hewn make-up bench and mirror framed in wire-caged light bulbs, an unyielding army cot... two straight chairs, a curtained pole to serve as a closet, and an antique kerosene stove for chilly dawns and nights when we worked overtime. These spartan quarters bespoke the studio's philosophy of total commitment to the product. Everything and everyone had been stripped for action, every needless creature comfort jettisoned to ensure expediency, speed, and profit. At Century time was money, and one always had the uneasy feeling that both were running out.[90]

One of the more complimentary things Cary had to say about Julius, who she once referred to as a "fiscal tyrant," was that "Julius Stern allowed himself no more creature comforts or perquisites as president than his lowliest employee.... His penuriousness was thoroughgoing and evenhanded, and while it scorned preferential treatment, it also made grousing about one's own stark accommodations an exercise in futility."[91] Cary's descriptions suggest that the directors' existing quarters were more of the same, and in need of improvement if the Sterns wanted to keep them on the lot.

Another change was the vote at a stockholders' meeting on July 10 to increase the company's capital stock from the current seven hundred fifty shares of the par value of $100 ($75,000) to five thousand shares of the par value of $100 ($500,000). Julius was absent from this meeting, but was represented by Sigmund Neufeld, now Century's vice president (or at least according to his signature on the official certificate), and Abe, Century's secretary.[92]

By September Julius had returned to the U.S. and the Century studios, overseeing affairs while Abe now spent some time over in France. Julius did not return from Europe empty handed, having purchased nine short stories and one play, to be reworked into scenarios for upcoming two-reelers. The short stories included "Come With Me," "The Old Butcher," "The Chimney Climber," "Herr Pup," "One Cold Night," "Three Sneers," "Welcome Ladies," "We Want Women," and "Don't Say No," and the play "The Shins of Society" by a fellow named Hans Henry Sneider.[93] Best of luck trying to associate any of those titles with the Century releases to follow, however.

"Once-gaily-striped awnings hung in sun-bleached shreds…" Julius Stern poses with Baby Peggy at the Century studios. Courtesy of Marc Wanamaker and Bison Archives.

With Abe's return the brothers hooked up in New York for a series of meetings with Universal officials, while Sig Neufeld remained in charge of the studio.[94] With the meetings behind them, the two brothers headed back to the West Coast, with stops in several principal key cities where they called on their exchanges and exhibitor friends.[95]

Left-to-right: Jack Earle, Hilliard Karr, and Harry McCoy in ad
for director Robert Kerr's *Hit 'Em Hard*.

Chapter 11: Too Many Cooks in the Kitchen (The 1923-1924 Season)

The upcoming 1923-1924 season's stars had been promoted as Baby Peggy, Buddy Messinger, Jack Cooper, the Billy Engle-Jack Earle team ("the long and short of comedy"), the new house canine Pal, and, of course, the Century Follies Girls ("Your patrons will want to see them again and again! Advertise them—and then try to keep the crowds away!"). It didn't work out quite that way. Jack Cooper, announced by Century as having re-signed and scheduled for a series of twelve comedies with those Follies Girls, only appeared in *Round Figures* before heading back to Sennett. Billy Engle only appeared in a handful of the Jack Earle comedies before jumping ship to hook up with the Roach studios.

As far as exhibitors were concerned, Century was by now producing a reliably dependable schedule of two-reel comedies, serviceable and sufficient to meet their needs, but for the most part undistinguished. "Just ordinary comedies," wrote an exhibitor in South Dakota. "Haven't been ashamed of any of them yet, but haven't had any one ask me when I was going to run another."[1] The rental costs were comparatively affordable, however, and the films filled a definite need.

Jack Earle pressed on, with more than a dozen comedies to his credit. Earle's occasional teaming with Harry McCoy resulted in *Sons-In-Law* (March 5, 1924), *Hit 'Em Hard* (April 2, 1924), *A Lofty Marriage* (April 30, 1924), and *Lost Control* (July 2, 1924), as well as those mentioned earlier.

A review for *Hit 'Em Hard* suggests something out of the norm, a precursor of sorts to *The Flintstones*:

> Jack Earle and Harry McCoy furnish the fun in this one. The action
> is in the prize ring and is fast. Part of the picture reverts to the stone-age

where clubs are used to great advantage. Stone-age taxis and baby carriages are shown along the "Main Street" and the prehistoric method of bootlegging is interestingly told. It is a good comedy.[2]

We'll have to take his word for it, since the film does not appear to have survived. Exhibitors didn't mince with words when a film failed to please them and their customers, with a Louisiana-based exhibitor offering up this scathing critique of the same film:

> Notice to all exhibitors who are using Universal's comedies: Look out for this one. Whoever directed this comedy [Robert Kerr] should be arrested and sent to Atlanta or some other Federal penitentiary for ten years for having nerve to get something like this on the screen. It's an insult to the general public. Rotten, nothing to the comedy and I can't see how some of these so-called picture men buy such stuff. About the worst I ever saw, and I certainly have seen some rotten ones.[3]

They don't come any more blistering than this one!

An article appeared in June that itemized the actors and actresses then at work on the films for the upcoming season. This affords a snapshot of a number of the lesser known talents at work for Century at that moment who never made it into the advertised credits: "Among the better known," as the article put it, "are Joe Bonner, Frank Earl, Jack Cooper, Jack Earle, Billy Engle, Ford West, Jack Henderson, Joe Moore, Fred Spencer, Tad Ross, Maurice Canon, Hyman Bernard, Sadie Campbell, Marjorie Marcel, Edith Lee Grant, Jewel and Neva Lynn, Lucille DuBois, and Marjorie Welch."[4] Within a few months Lillian Hackett, the aforementioned Harry McCoy, William Irving, and the child star Dawn O'Day (latter billed as Anne Shirley) were added to Century's stock company.[5]

The Sterns ran a tight, businesslike ship, and nothing went to waste. In conjunction with their purchasing and office managers, Julius and Abe would review all of the company's vouchers and requisitions. Julius described the process in detail in the article "Should 'System' Dominate Screen Art?"

> In the Century studios, to keep our people steadily and efficiently moving, we have created a rather elaborate requisition system.
>
> Nothing is bought or rented—in fact nothing enters our studio—without a written order passed by the requisition department and obeyed by my brother or myself.

Each requisition is investigated, and when it comes from our purchasing head we know by whom the article is needed, the picture it is for and the director in charge. We give each picture a working number and every requisition must bear it.[6]

A lot of those requests never went very far: "It goes without saying that most of these requests are turned down as unnecessary," added Julius.[7] Diana Serra Cary told a story that is suggestive of this. One of the serial directors making a Western needed a mountain lion for one of his scenes, and balked when Julius told him to use one of the studio's two African lions. "They have big ruffs around their necks," explained the director. "What I need is a mountain lion—you know, the kind with a short, sleek coat." He went on to state just how absurd an African lion would look in a film set in the plains of Montana, and said that they'd need to hire a mountain lion from Gay's Lion Farm. Julius cut him off, screaming "Shave 'em! Disguise 'em! But Goddammit, use 'em!"[8]

Abe discounted the various stories—such as this one—about their insistence on using the animals at hand rather than ones more appropriate, as pure bunk: "We should worry," he said. "We don't use lions when we should use wolves. We get them."[9] As *Picture-Play Magazine* put it, "If all the stories, which are always told in dialect, ridiculing the Sterns, were laid end to end, they would extend from the city hall in Whittier, California, to the right elbow of the Statue of Liberty."[10]

As a further step to ensure the success—or perhaps the acceptability—of their upcoming comedies, the Sterns instituted a policy where every new comedy would be given an unannounced preview at a local neighborhood theatre in Los Angeles, to gauge audience reaction. Tweaks would be made to each film where deemed necessary before shipping it off to the East Coast for printing and distribution.[11] "Title changes, action deletions and additions, as well as a new set of subtitles" were among the tweaks made at the direction of Julius, "who studies all effects of advance showings."[12] "I have always maintained that to discover the true entertaining value of such a picture it must be shown to a regular audience in a regular movie house in order to find the real reaction it will have," stated Julius in his response to *Film Daily*'s series "How to Show Them: Opinions of the Important Producers and Distributors Relative to Projecting Shorts."[13]

Two of Century's more promotable customers were the U.S. Army and Navy, who now included the company's releases in their weekly programs, shown for the amusement of the service men. "This is done in the line of worth-while entertainment," touted *Universal Weekly*, "and it is said that committees of discriminating judges pass on or condemn all subjects shown…. Thus Century Comedies have passed muster.…"[14]

In spite of their success, or perhaps because of it, both Julius and Abe continued to be the subjects of good-natured (mean spirited?), if frequently unflattering, stories and quotes. One such tale, likely apocryphal, was recounted by James Quirk and printed in *Photoplay*:

A scenario writer applied for a job.

"You an educated man?" demanded Julius.

"Yes, sir."

"You don't look it—prove it," said the doubting Julius.

"How can I prove I'm educated?" asked the unfortunate college graduate.

"Show your diploma," said Julius.

The victim tried to explain that people didn't carry their diplomas around with them.

"Well, then," said Julius scornfully, "say me a big woid."[15]

"Woid"? "Verd" would have been more like it, but I'm not buying it, and I suspect that Julius wasn't amused when he read this, good-natured or not. Another story about Julius and his seeming obliviousness to the obvious was relayed by Diana Serra Cary. According to her, Julius initially tinkered with the idea of naming the company Miracle Pictures. His motto for the company? You guessed it: "If it's a good picture, it's a Miracle!" This one's just a little too pat to be believed, and it's a bit of comical patter that would appear time and again over the years in films like Universal's 1941 *Hellzapoppin* and Joe Dante's 1976 *Hollywood Boulevard* for Roger Corman.

The 1923-1924 season was represented by a similar, if slightly reduced, roster of directors than that of the previous season. Al Herman once again headed the pack with a whopping twenty-four of the season's fifty-seven releases to his credit. Noel Smith and Alf Goulding handled another five each, while Arvid Gillstrom directed another four. The remaining films were handled by Archie Mayo, Harry Edwards, Herman Raymaker, and newcomers Robert Kerr, Edward Luddy, and Charles Lamont.

Robert Kerr (1892-1960) had been hired by the Sterns in 1917 to direct for L-Ko, lured away from Sennett where he had his directorial start a year earlier; among his trio of films for L-Ko were the Gale Henry-Hughie Mack co-starrers *A Flyer in Folly* and *Her Movie Madness* (both 1918). Leaving L-Ko that same year, Kerr bounced around for a few years directing comedies for Roach, Mermaid, and Quality before rejoining the Sterns at Century, if only for a mere four comedies before moving on.

Russian-born Edward I. Luddy (1899-1982; born Isidor Irving Litwack) was hired by Century in 1923. Initially he was to assist Al Herman in coming up with plotlines and gags for Herman's films, the Buddy Messinger vehicles *Bringing Up Buddy* and *The Young*

Tenderfoot among them. The Sterns liked what they saw, and promoted Luddy to writer-director of his own films shortly thereafter. *Tired Business Men* (May 21, 1924) with Al Alt was the first of these, which *Moving Picture World* deemed "one of the very best of the recent Century comedies." Luddy's six releases towards the end of the season would be followed by another twenty-six shorts over the following two seasons. Leslie Goodwin (1899-1969), a Brit who had relocated to Hollywood, was assigned to assist Luddy with his upcoming films.[16]

Director Robert Kerr.   Director Edward I. Luddy.

Luddy had emigrated from Russia in his youth, and had received schooling in both Canada and the U.S. After a stint managing Brooklyn's Flatbush Theatre, Luddy landed at Vitagraph where he was assigned a variety of tasks, acting and stunt work among them. He ended up with director Gil Pratt where he functioned as gag man and assistant director on the Montgomery and Rock Comedies. Luddy had the opportunity to co-direct a feature in 1921, the independently produced Ward Lascelle Production *Rip Van Winkle*, which he followed in 1922 with the Western *The Man Who Waited* for Playgoers Pictures. A brief stint writing for Popular Pictures preceded his signing with Century as a gag man.

Luddy would toil away at Century for three years before going freelance, directing comedy shorts for a dizzying number of different studios. Among these were one or more films for the "Winnie Winkle" and "Hairbreadth Harry" comedies for the West Brothers and Weiss Brothers-Artclass, Sunkist Comedies for J.R. Bray, Jack White's Cameo, F.B.O. and Robertson-Cole, and RKO, as well as the Larry Semon feature *Spuds* (1927) before eventually returning to Universal to direct Arthur Lake in his "Horace of Hollywood" series; the delightful *Whose Baby?* (1928) is one of the surviving entries in this latter series. By the mid-1930s Luddy had made the switch to feature film direction, accompanied by a name switch to Edward Ludwig, perhaps to distance himself professionally from fifteen years of short comedy direction. These later films ran the gamut from lower budget fare to more prominent offerings, the latter including the John Wayne vehicles *The Fighting Seabees* (1944), *Wake of the Red Witch* (1948), and the Commie-busting *Big Jim McLain* (1952). Other notable offerings included RKO's musical *Old Man Rhythm* (1935), the Edward G. Robinson gangster flick *The Last Gangster* (1937), and RKO's *Swiss Family Robinson* (1940). Ludwig even dipped his toes into the 3D craze with 1954's *Jivaro* for Paramount. He would continue in the industry into the mid-1960s, his last decade spent helming episodes for a variety of television series.

Edward Luddy's Century unit. Luddy (sitting at left), assistant director Leslie Goodwin (extreme right), cameraman Irving Ries, and seated, Al Alt (left) and Joe Bonner.

Gertrude Messinger and Arthur Lake in the "Horace of Hollywood" series entry *Whose Baby?* (1928). Courtesy of Richard M. Roberts.

Charles Lamont (1895-1993) was similarly hired in late 1923, as assistant director to Noel Smith on *That Oriental Game* (March 12, 1924) and *Checking Out* (April 9, 1924), both of which co-starred Harry Sweet and Pal. Lamont's previous experience was with Grand Asher where he directed a series of Sid Smith comedies in 1923—*The Big Game, The Lucky Rube,* and *Hollywood Bound* among them—as well as acting as gag man along with fellow directors Dick Smith, Archie Mayo, Arvid Gillstrom, Reggie Morris, and Harry Edwards.[17] The Sterns promoted him to full director and gave him his own unit in April 1924,[18] his first released short, *Her City Sport* (July 23, 1924), appearing near the season's end. "There is considerable rough and tumble and slapstick work," wrote *Moving Picture World's* reviewer, "with several situations that will amuse patrons who like comedies of this type, as it is well up to the Century standard."[19]

Director Charles Lamont, before he grew his little mustache.

Hailing from San Francisco, Lamont had a brief stint with the legitimate stage before making a career change at the conclusion of the First World War, when he went to work for Universal.[20] Somewhere along the line he married—and divorced—the actress Dixie Lamont (1906-1983; born Hazel Richardson). Dixie worked at Century in 1920 and 1921 after a few films for Vitagraph and Jimmy Aubrey, and evidently so did Charles, presumably in an assistant director capacity. According to the *Los Angeles Daily Times* in August 1920:

> Mr. Lamont was working at the Century studio, about a fortnight ago, as director of comedies, when suddenly on the set walked Dixie Lamont. Mr. Lamont looked up, blushed, stammered, and didn't say anything; but Dixie was calmer. "I'm your new star," she explained, "assigned by the president of the company." Mr. Lamont just swallowed hard as he looked at his former wife.
>
> Gradually, since then, he's been taking notice of what an awfully nice girl she is, even if they did used to quarrel; and all of a sudden yesterday, when the two were left alone together on the set, he exclaimed: "Dixie, we made a mistake, didn't we?"
>
> "Yes," she blushed, "we did." And then and there they eagerly decided to try it over again.[21]

Robert Anderson (left) and Dixie Lamont in Century's *Loose Lions*,
directed by William Watson.

The hitch, as it turned out, was that they hadn't yet been divorced for an entire year, and would have to wait until a year had passed to remarry. Luckily for Charles, it didn't pan out, Dixie instead married a fellow named Charles E. Phillipi, who later filed a suit for divorce in 1926, charging her with "improper conduct" (with B movie Western actor Buddy Roosevelt) and entertaining "boisterously."[22]

Lamont would have a lengthy and prolific career following his work for the Sterns, continuing to direct shorts well into the 1930s, eventually transitioning into feature direction which lasted into the late 1950s. Numerous entries in Universal's Abbott and Costello and Ma and Pa Kettle series predominated during that final decade.

There was another behind-the-scenes newcomer to the studio, a fifteen year old named Max Alexander who had just emigrated from Germany, his birthplace, to the U.S. Alexander was made Century's property manager, replacing Harry Gross, who left for Paramount's Eastern studios.[23] Promotions to casting director and technical supervisor followed, and within four years Alexander's status would be elevated to assistant to President Julius Stern, and Eastern Representative.[24] And why should such a young man be given such plum opportunities? Max was Julius and Abe's nephew, the son of their sister Frieda and her husband, Sigmund Alexander. Like I said earlier, Laemmle didn't have a corner on nepotism.

Julius Stern and his nephew, a youthful Max Alexander. Courtesy of Gilbert Sherman.

Over the course of the season new talent would be added to the Century stock company, some with prior stage and film experience, and others new to film. Among these were Hilliard Karr, Harry Murdock, Al Alt, Spec O'Donnell, Martha Sleeper, Wanda Wiley, Joe Bonner, and James "Bubbles" Berry.

Hailing from Houston, Texas, Hilliard Sinclair "Fatty" Karr (1899-1945), a plus-size comedian and a poor man's Roscoe Arbuckle, got his first taste of show biz with a two year stint in Gus Edwards's all-kid show, or at least according to a promotional piece in *Universal Weekly*.[25] A move into film followed, with leads in Master Pictures' Lion Comedies in Houston in 1917 for Josh Binney in films that included *Nathan Busts Into the Movies* and *An Account of a No-Account Count* (both 1917), where he was billed as Nathan Dewing. The locals still referred to him as Hilliard, as an article in a mid-July issue of the *Houston Post* indicates. This covered a presentation of the play *The Womanless Wedding* which was performed locally as a fundraiser for a local church's building fund. Its cast was made up of locals, each of whom parodied a famous personage or character. It concluded with:

> Hilliard Karr, Master Motion Picture actor, who played the role of Snookums, afforded constant merriment. He weighs 300 pounds, but he was dressed in a white frock and employed a pacifier and rattler and a large bottle of milk.
>
> Manager Binney of the Master Motion Picture company has taken a view of the "Womanless Wedding."[26]

In 1918 Karr followed Binney to Jacksonville, Florida, and his Florida Film Corporation comedies, where he played the character of Funny Fatty Filbert in *Fatty's Fast Flivver* and *Fatty's Frivolous Fiancee* (both 1918) among others. "His reputation as a laugh getter," wrote *Motion Picture News* of Dewing, "has placed him in the very foremost ranks of the funny fat men of the screen."[27] There was additional work for Mark Dintenfass's Cuckoo Comedies and a part in the Harold Lockwood feature *The Landloper* (1918); "Hilliard Karr A Houston Boy in the Supporting Cast" ran one of the *Houston Post*'s ads for this latter film.

Karr eventually packed up and headed off to Hollywood. There he would abandon the "Nathan Dewing" alias and appear in all future films as Hilliard Karr, the nickname "Fatty" soon added as a self-explanatory descriptive. A small part in the Western feature *Shadows of Conscience* in 1921 was followed by work for Fox supporting Al St. John in *Ain't Love Grand?* and *Out of Place* (both 1922). That same year Karr mused about his career to date, which displayed his reverence for the work of Roscoe Arbuckle, and his refusal to be cast as an imitator of same:

CENTURY COMEDY
BUDDY MESSINGER
in
"HIS FIRST DEGREE"

Buddy Messinger snoops on Hilliard Karr and Betty Welsh in *His First Degree*,
Edward Luddy director. Courtesy of Mark Johnson.

I had always wanted to go on the screen, but I realized that it would have to be in comic roles since nature had cast me in so generous a mould. I went to see almost every picture Arbuckle made. I analyzed them.

[In California a] producer wanted me to make comedies in imitation of Arbuckle films, but I refused because I didn't want to find myself at the climax of my film career as an imitator, even though I would have been paid well.

In making these comedies I do not feel that I am an imitator. I want to develop my own individual style of comedy. Then I may be able to achieve the popularity that once was Arbuckle's. He would not have gained that popularity had his comedy not been distinctive and individual.[28]

A little more than a year later Karr hooked up with Century under a short term contract. Karr's first for Century was the previously mentioned *Hit 'Em Hard* opposite Jack Earle and Harry McCoy. Numerous others, where he was frequently co-starred with Harry McCoy and Al Alt, included *Taxi! Taxi!* (May 7, 1924), *Fearless Fools* (June 4, 1924), and

Eat and Run (August 27, 1924). As the following season neared, Wanda Wiley became Karr's frequent co-star in *Her City Sport*, *Her Fortunate Face* (August 6, 1924), *Snappy Eyes* (October 1, 1924), and others. Subsequent teamings with Buddy Messinger and Edna Marian placed Karr in films like *Broadway Beauties* and *His First Degree* (December 31, 1924), but like everyone else at Century Karr was placed wherever he was needed.

Karr would star in nearly three dozen comedies for the Sterns well into the 1925-1926 season before departing to co-star with Frank Alexander and William "Kewpie" Ross as one of the Three Fatties in Joe Rock's "Ton of Fun" series for F.B.O., 1926-1928. His career pretty much petered out with the conclusion of that series. A series of jobs outside the industry followed, Karr passing on in 1945 in Dallas, Texas. He was buried back in his hometown of Houston.

Newlyweds Hilliard Karr and Lucille Hutton are shown an apartment by landlady Louise Carver, while Buddy Messinger struggles to get out of a headlock. From Edward Luddy's *The Aggravatin' Kid*. Courtesy of Mark Johnson.

Alexander "Al" Alt (1897-1992) was another Gus Edwards child protégé.[29] Alt had served as Fred Fishback's assistant director at Century in 1919, after which he got the acting bug and teamed with Helen Howell in two-reel comedies. The first of these, *Marked Women* (1921), was released on a state rights basis through Reelcraft, but that arrangement fell apart shortly thereafter. They quickly worked out a deal with Allied Distributing Corporation, with *Pure and Simple* and *Liquorish Lips* (both 1921) making it onto screens before the Alt-Howell Comedies venture folded.

Reelcraft stars Alexander Alt and Helen Howell.

Another Alt teaming followed with Zip Monberg, the duo portraying "Percy" and "Ferdie" in at least one of CBC's Hallroom Boys Comedies, after which Alt returned to Century to star. What set Alt apart from most of his fellow comedians at Century were his comparative good looks, debonair in fact, sporting a little mustache akin to the sort then being popularized by Douglas Fairbanks. Alt's first for the Sterns was Noel Smith's *Checking Out*, sharing acting honors with Pal and the recently returned Harry Sweet, who stayed long enough to make several other shorts before departing yet again. Numerous other films would follow for Alt, with Harry McCoy, Hilliard Karr, and Wanda Wiley his frequent co-stars, *Fearless Fools* (June 4, 1924), *The Trouble Fixer* (September 24, 1924), and *Some Tomboy* among them. Unfortunately for Alt, it would be his co-stars that were usually singled out for mention in reviews for many of the films in which he appeared, but he eventually advanced to leads—and recognition—in films such as *Dancing Daisies*,

A Dangerous Peach (February 18, 1925), *Helpful Al* (January 27, 1926), and *Al's Troubles* (March 10, 1926). While a pleasant and capable onscreen presence, Alt never really seemed to click with reviewers: "Alt is his usual self" was about the best that one reviewer could come up with for *Helpful Al*. Alt would remain with Century for a full three years and more than thirty films, followed by stints for Rayart and Jack White.

Anita Garvin checks out Al Alt while Larry Richardson observes with disapproval, in Jess Robbins's *A Dangerous Peach*. Courtesy of Mark Johnson.

Henry Murdock (1891-1928), a slight, bespectacled man with a tiny mustache and frequently sour expression, was brought over after three years on the Christie lot. His earliest years were spent with various stock companies and on vaudeville, followed by roles for Kalem in the mid-teens. Murdock was hired to support Fred Spencer,[30] and would appear in smaller roles in at least a dozen comedies during the season, with the occasional lead in films such as director Al Herman's *You're Next* (February 13, 1924), and *Scared Stiff* (August 13, 1924) opposite Al Alt. Director Edward Luddy's *Paging Money* (July 30, 1924) provided another starring role for Murdock, as a persistent book salesman who has grown numb to endless rejections. They've become the norm, so assistant Harry Mann accompanies him with a fireman's life net, set up to provide a soft landing each time Murdock is bodily tossed out of another prospective buyer's home. Burly Bill Blaisdell is on board as the owner of an exporting company—impatient with Murdock's hard-sell—along with Spec O'Donnell, seemingly in the cast to help pad out the film. (A heavily-watermarked fragment of this film survives, and is viewable on YouTube.[31]) When Murdock's contract with Century expired, he bounced around the industry taking roles in comedies for whoever needed him, with the occasional return appearance at Century. His career came to an abrupt end with his death in 1928 when he strangled on an awkwardly consumed piece of beefsteak that became lodged in his throat.[32]

Baby Peggy prays for a better part in Al Herman's *Little Miss Hollywood*.
Courtesy of Heritage Auctions, Ha.com.

British-born Joe (Joseph Adam) Bonner (1882-1959) had a lengthy run with Century spanning the years 1922 into 1927, with more than thirty films to his credit. Bonner got his start on the English stage before coming to the U.S. where he was a vaudeville headliner. Bonner made the switch to film with some work for Vitagraph before hooking up in 1919 with (Milburn) Moranti Comedies for Bulls-Eye. Some more work for Billy West and others preceded his hiring by the Sterns, his first for them backing up Queenie the horse in *True Blue*. In this one the forty year old played, of all things, a boy. While he appeared with most of Century's comedians over the years, Bonner frequently supported Baby Peggy in films that included *Peg o' the Movies, Carmen, Jr., Little Miss Hollywood* (October 31, 1923), and *Such Is Life* (January 30, 1924).

And then there were the kids. The Century Kids, a move on the Sterns part to jump on the youth comedy wagon then so popular as the result of Roach's "Our Gang" series of comedies, came into their own during the season. Buddy Messinger and Sadie Campbell were the constants in these shorts, or at least up to a point. The Kids were beefed up with the addition of freckle-faced "Spec" O'Donnell, cute-as-a-button Martha Sleeper, and a tiny little black kid with an infectious smile and oversized cheeks named James Berry.

Spec" O'Donnell. Courtesy of Drina Mohacsi.

Walter "Spec" O'Donnell (1911-1986) was signed to an eighteen month contract at the beginning of 1924. Several small roles in features for Warners and CBC preceded his hiring, but it was his lead in William Beaudine's *The Country Kid* that grabbed the Sterns' attention. They needed a talented kid, so they signed him. He was to be paid a graduated salary: $200 a week for the first six months, $300 a week for the next six months, and $400 a week for the final six months.[33] While he would be used in others' productions such as the Pal comedy *Delivering the Goods* (May 28, 1924), it was with the other Kids that he'd find the most rewarding work, in films like *The Racing Kid* (April 16, 1924), *Trailing Trouble* (May 14, 1924), and *Please, Teacher!* (June 18, 1924).

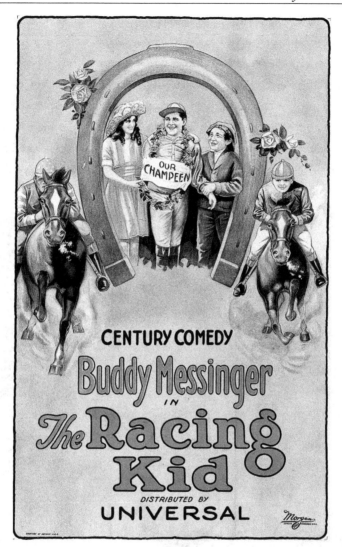

Poster for Al Herman's *The Racing Kid*, Buddy Messinger (center) flanked by Martha
Sleeper and "Spec" O'Donnell. Courtesy of Heritage Auctions, Ha.com.

Martha Sleeper (1910-1983), the enthusiastic and very funny young lady most
remembered today from her many appearances in Hal Roach's comedies, was another
addition. Sadie Campbell had departed Century after fourteen films with Buddy
Messinger, so the Sterns found thirteen year old Martha Sleeper, a newcomer with little
prior experience, as her replacement. Sleeper filled Campbell's place for the next six films,
in titles such as *Budding Youth* and *Low Bridge* (September 17, 1924). Sleeper's stint with
Century was brief, set loose when Campbell returned to the studio in May after a six

month absence. If anyone worried about Sleeper's future after her dismissal, they shouldn't have, since she was snapped up by Roach and blossomed into a charming and full-fledged comedian in a series of films opposite Charley Chase. "She has plenty of pep but is inclined to do things a bit too quickly," wrote one reviewer of her first role in Century's *The Racing Kid*,[34] her later work for Roach evidence that she was a fast learner. As for Campbell, press releases reported that she would make her reappearance with Messinger in stories then under development,[35] but since no further titles have been associated with her after *The Young Tenderfoot*—her last for Century before that six month absence—it's difficult to say whether her return actually amounted to anything.

Martha Sleeper in her pre-Roach days.

James "Bubbles" Berry (1915?-1969) was another addition, and a successful one at that. Hired by the Sterns in early 1924, press releases touted that he was five years old, although other sources place him a few years older. Purported to have previously "appeared in comedies for many of the producers on the coast," Century's casting department needed "a little colored boy" for a part in one of Messinger's films, and Berry was hired. Work in a second Messinger film convinced the Sterns to sign him for ten more films,[36] with an option for twelve more to follow. The Sterns quickly nicknamed Berry as "Bubbles," after the cheek-swelling, mouth-popping affectation that peppered his appearances.[37] The first after the signing, *The Blow Out* (August 20, 1924), was rapturously received by critics and really proved Berry's worth: "a little negro boy called Bubbles has been given greater opportunities to get the laughs and really 'walks away with the picture,'" wrote one reviewer.[38] Another reviewer concurred, stating that "in this reviewer's opinion [Bubbles] steals the acting honors clean away from Buddy."[39] Buddy must have been thrilled.

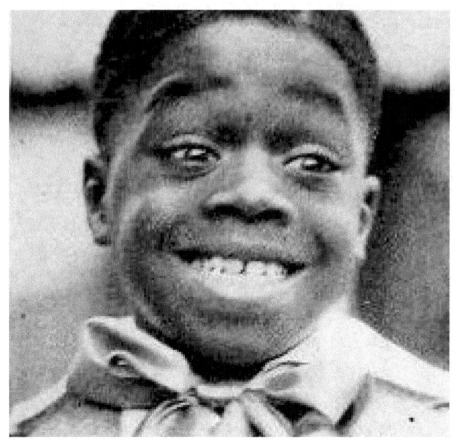

James "Bubbles" Berry.

Sailing Along (February 25, 1925) was another of Berry's appearances, this one sans O'Donnell. Al Herman's *Speed Boys* (November 12, 1924), which survives, teamed Berry—whitened lips here of the minstrel sort—with O'Donnell, as well as Arthur Trimble (who spends the later part of the film dressed as a cute little girl, and uncomfortably convincingly so) and roly-poly eight year old Tommy Hicks. Shot primarily on the Venice Miniature Railroad, Berry has a lot to do in this one, and even gets to flirt with and pick up a cute little black girl. One gag has him carrying a length of stove pipe when one small dog enters the back but gets stuck trying to emerge from its front, only his head and front legs exposed. A second dog gets stuck entering the back, with only his hind legs and tail exposed. Berry sees this and is astonished at just how long this "dog" is. Later aboard the train, some nearby kids throw rocks at conductor Berry and engineer O'Donnell, and they respond by throwing coal back at them. It's Berry who is the first to catch on that it's all just a ruse to get some free coal for heating. When an oversized woman boards the train—and at the very back, forcing Bubbles to walk its length to collect her fare—Bubbles observes her girth and decides to charge her two nickels rather than the standard one: "One nickel per hip" he announces, and she pays.

Sadie Campbell, Buddy Messinger, and nerd Donald Hughes in Al Herman's
Buckin' the Line. Courtesy of Richard M. Roberts.

With his eventual departure from Century, Berry made the occasional appearance as "Bubbles" in shorts for Jack White's Juvenile Comedies, the Bray studios, and the Weiss Brothers before disappearing from film for the next fifteen years. He resurfaced in the early 1940s as a dancer in easily trimmed segments in several musicals for M-G-M, a depressing necessity in those days for deep South release.

The Sterns' biggest catch of the season was unquestionably the newcomer Wanda Wiley (1901-1987), an attractive and athletic young lady with very limited prior film experience. Born Roberta Prestine Wiley on April 21 in New Boston, Bowie County, Texas to James Alexander Wiley and Ida Ione Barnett, family members all knew her as "Robbie" or "Bob." Wanda was one of twelve children, four of whom died young. Relocating to Dallas, Wanda was fourteen when she was enrolled in St. Mary's Hall in San Antonio, an all-girls boarding school attended by all of the Wiley girls at one time or another. Wanda's life during the several years that followed is somewhat hazy, but it is known that in 1920 she married a fellow named Robert Knopp in Fredericksburg, Texas. The marriage was short-lived, and likely was over by the time Wanda headed out to Hollywood. But more on that in a moment.

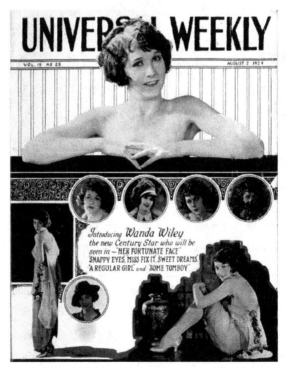

Century's new star Wanda Wiley, gracing the cover of the August 2, 1924 issue of *Universal Weekly*.

In March 1923, a dance contest was held in San Antonio, which Wanda and her dance partner, Lesandro Forseck, took part, dancing the Argentine Tango; the two of them, it was reported, were "from the best families in town." Actor Rudolph Valentino and his wife sponsored the contest as part of a managed and heavily-promoted nation-wide tour with an "advertising adjunct," charging a $2 admission. Wanda and her partner won the contest, and for their efforts were awarded "a doll's miniature of [Valentino] and wife."[40] According to family lore, Valentino was impressed with Wanda, suggested that she go to Hollywood, and wrote her a letter of introduction. She packed her bags.

Wanda Wiley (right) showing off some of her dance steps, in Edward Luddy's
Sweet Dreams. Courtesy of Robert James Kiss.

According to one of Universal's later promotional pieces on Wiley, she was discovered by an unnamed movie producer scouting locations in San Antonio near the dental college she was supposed to have attended. He gave her a bit part and, based on the results, suggested she head to Los Angeles.[41] Again, according to Universal, but none of this has been verified, and is in part at odds with Wanda's later recollections, so it remains suspect.

Once in Hollywood, Wanda set out to be a star. She entered the Motion-Picture Exposition—Goldwyn Beauty Contest held in July 1923, the promise of a screen test and potential Paramount studio contract dangled before the star-struck participants.[42] Wanda was promoted in the press as being "one of the leaders in the film contract contest," and when Douglas Fairbanks, Jr. visited to eye potential faces for inclusion in his upcoming first credited film for Paramount, *Stephen Steps Out*, Wanda was there lobbying hard along with a young lady named Esther Garcia. Both Wanda and Esther were sufficiently photogenic to make the papers gazing at the boyish Fairbanks.[43] Unfortunately, Wanda came in second.

Undaunted, Wanda eventually landed up on the Universal City lot where a director spotted her and asked her if she'd like to be in movies. Silly question. He immediately had his assistant take her to the wardrobe department and she was on the stage within the hour, cast in a film already in progress. She was later reported to have had small parts in several episodes of *The Leather Pushers* series, so these may have been her first roles.[44] Impressed with her screen presence, the Sterns hired her and placed her in six initial films, soon giving her starring roles with the Century Follies Girls in *Sailor Maids* (June 11, 1924), *Starving Beauties*, and *Her City Sport*.

Wanda Wiley showing off her legs (and a rather unusual costume) in this signed photo.

Wiley's comparative lack of experience as an actress was noted by several reviewers, especially for her acting in *Snappy Eyes*. "Miss Wiley looks very well but moves somewhat too quickly, making the movements look jerky at times," observed *Film Daily*.[45] *Exhibitors Trade Review* was more forgiving, and took note of her potential:

> Wanda Wiley cute and vivacious lends the role of country lass in straw bonnet and overalls quite a deal of personal charm. She has pretty teeth and takes pains all the time she is acting to give you the impression that this is not a comedy but a dental ad sign. Further she has eyes—they are sharp and snappy as the title. But, why does she blink, so continuously?
>
> Aside from these correctable limitations we think that Wanda will soon improve her business, and then we expect to see big possibilities in Wanda and her comedy films.[46]

Wiley's physicality was another matter, and reviewers were quick to note: "Wanda Wilie [sic] is fast becoming one of the foremost fun makers in the short subject field," wrote one of *Starving Beauties*. "Her appearance is always a signal for action and she takes her bumps like a man that comes up smiling."[47] The public reaction to Wiley didn't escape the Sterns, who now peeled her off of the Century Follies Girls and made her the featured performer in her own series. *Her Fortunate Face*, *Snappy Eyes*, *Some Tomboy* (October 22, 1924), and *Sweet Dreams* (November 5, 1924) were the first of these to be filmed.

Wanda Wiley collared while Harry McCoy makes time with a "society vamp"
in Edward Luddy's *Sweet Dreams*.

So enthusiastic was the response to *Her Fortunate Face* that the Sterns quickly bumped the Al Alt-Jack Earle comedy *Sahara Blues* (October 15, 1924) from its originally announced September 24 slot and replaced it with Wiley's *The Trouble Fixer*, another film already in the can.[48] Competitor producers took note and started barraging Wiley with attractive offers to play in their upcoming productions, but Julius beat them to the punch. He signed her to a long term contract, and then sent the exhausted actress back to Texas for a three-to-four week vacation and much needed rest.[49] Carl Laemmle's hopes for a "female Charlie Chaplin" years earlier appeared to have finally come to pass, albeit six years after the fact.

Baby Peggy remained the studio's biggest draw, appearing in nearly a dozen more comedies during the season, along with loan-outs to star in the occasional feature. Among her Century shorts not previously mentioned were *Nobody's Darling* (September 26, 1923), *Miles of Smiles* (November 28, 1923), and then, on a ramped up, every-two-week basis, *Our Pet* (May 11, 1924), *The Flower Girl* (May 25, 1924), *Stepping Some* (June 8, 1924), and *Poor Kid* (June 22, 1924). Aside from the much-delayed *Red Riding Hood*, which wouldn't be patched together and released at the end of 1925, *Poor Kid* would be the final Baby Peggy comedy released by Century.

"Rough Rider" Baby Peggy in Arvid Gillstrom's *Stepping Some.*

Miles of Smiles survives, the story of twins accidentally separated during infancy, one raised by their wealthy parents, and the other, "Peggy," raised by the owner of a miniature railway who had rescued her from the tracks. Years later Peggy's adoptive father spots her well-dressed twin, and wondering where his ward got the fancy clothes, follows her back to her parents' lavish home. Ejected from that home as an intruder, he rounds up eight cohorts to help him retrieve the twin, the girl he thinks to be his ward. In the meantime, Peggy has made her way to the house and discovered her twin, and a series of mistaken identity incidents follow involving Peggy, her twin, the maid and butler, and the confused parents. It's all eventually sorted out, Peggy reunited with her twin and parents, and her adoptive father leaving with a tidy reward for all his past efforts.

This cute little comedy is efficiently handled by Peggy's frequent director, Alf Goulding, although the goofy cavorting of the eight cohorts is rather thin and wearisome, somewhat reminiscent of the gaggle of reporters racing about in Goulding's Baby Peggy vehicle *The Kid Reporter* of a few months earlier. There's some really nice footage of the Venice Miniature Railroad, its car barn and turntable, and its various stops throughout Venice. The twin stuff is handled well enough, but there are only a few shots with both Baby Peggys in them at the same time, understandable given the time and budgetary constraints of the two-reel comedy format. A good copy of *Miles of Smiles* can be found on Undercrank Productions' *The Family Secret* DVD, which also includes the Baby Peggy short *Circus Clowns*.

Baby Peggy holds her "adopted" dad's cohorts at gunpoint, Joe Bonner at far right, in Alf Goulding's *Miles of Smiles*. Courtesy of Robert James Kiss.

Abe had spent six months in New York working in close collaboration with Universal officials on the campaigns for two of Baby Peggy's upcoming features, *The Darling of New York* (1923) and *The Law Forbids* (1924), for which the Sterns had loaned out the young actress's services.[50] These were Universal-Jewel productions made jointly by Universal and Century, and would be followed by a third, *The Family Secret* (1924).

Abe and his wife returned to California in early April, but his stay there was short-lived, since European vacations had by now become an annual event for the Sterns. Abe and his brother could count on a comparatively worry-free vacation this year since so much of the upcoming season's films were already in the can or midway through production, with films scheduled "way into the winter months" completed.[51] Abe sailed on July 5 on the *Leviathan*, expecting to be in Europe for six weeks, joined on this voyage by brother-in-law Carl Laemmle.[52]

Julius had sailed the previous week on the *Berengaria* for his combined business and pleasure trip, accompanied by his nephew Max Alexander, now described as Stern's production aide. Julius's stated goal was to secure the services of one of the Follies Bergère beauties in Paris to star in a new edition of the Century Follies Girls. Another goal: negotiate for story material suitable for Wanda Wiley's future films, referring to Wiley as "the greatest box-office find he has made in his entire career."[53] The brothers hooked up in Carlsbad, Czechoslovakia, where they probably joined Laemmle, whose annual trips back to Germany always included the curative waters of Carlsbad Spa and his hometown of Laupheim as destinations.[54] The Sterns would then head to Germany, and from there Julius would continue on to Paris and London.[55]

If the Sterns now thought they had found the future path for the output of their studio—specifically a return to the "Star Series" approach they had adopted late in L-Ko's life—that notion would soon prove to be true, or at least as far as exhibitor acceptance and an increase in bookings was concerned. What they wouldn't have expected, however, was that this whole approach would be upended shortly, and that the future would be totally redefined in a manner wholly at odds with their current beliefs.

The marriage of Herman Stern and his bride Hannah took place on September 1, 1924.
Top row, left-to-right: Arthur Alexander, unidentified, Rosabelle Laemmle,
Carl Laemmle Jr. The boy in front of Arthur is Alfred Stern. Middle row, left-to-right:
Frieda Strauss Stern, Max Alexander, unidentified woman, Abe Stern, Hannah Stern,
Herman Stern, Carl Laemmle. Bottom row, left-to-right: Unidentified woman, Malchen
Herzberger Stern, Loeb Stern, Irma Stern, Julius Stern. Courtesy of Gilbert Sherman.

Chapter 12: The Star Series Plan Redux (The 1924-1925 Season)

The marriage of Herman Stern—Julius and Abe's older brother—to his bride Hannah took place on the first day of the new 1924-1925 season. The newlyweds were there, of course, along with Julius and Abe, with other family members in attendance as well. The other attendees included: parents Loeb and Malchen Herzberger Stern; Frieda Strauss Stern, widow of deceased older brother Joseph, and her two children, Alfred and Irma Stern; nephews Max and Arthur Alexander, the children of sister Frieda and her husband Sigmund Alexander, who lived in Germany; and brother-in-law Carl Laemmle, along with his children, Carl Jr. and Rosabelle. There are two other women featured in the group photo taken after the wedding—one young, the other older—but they remain unidentified.

The upcoming 1924-1925 season's output had been ballyhooed back in mid-May by Julius before his departure for Europe. "It is the most ambitious program that Century has ever had the honor to announce," he claimed, "and every picture has been made with an eye to the eventual recognition of short product as the back-bone of every theatre's program."[1] Lofty claims, indeed.

Century, however, wasn't Universal's sole supplier of comedies. In 1924 alone, Universal would produce its own series of Universal Single-Reel Comedies to supplement (or potentially compete with?) Century's output. One such short-lived series to be released bi-weekly was Bryan Foy's "Hysterical History Comedies," which lampooned the stories of various historical figures with titles that included *William Tell*, *Benjamin Franklin*, *Rip Van Winkle*, and *Pochahontas and John Smith*. "Virtually every phase of American history will be satirized, so that every section of the country will see its development treated in a humorous and inoffensive vein."[2]

Neely Edwards, Bert Roach, and Alice Howell all shared the screen in another entry in the Universal Comedies series, as did Slim Summerville and Bobby Dunn in a third. Then there was the "Sweet Sixteen" series co-starring Arthur Lake and Olive Hasbrouck, some re-issues of Lyons and Moran's best shorts, and those two final Joe Martin comedies.

They'll Bring the House Down!

DON'T be alarmed if you hear a roar from your operator when you run these single reels. Everybody will laugh at the foolish antics of these side-splitting tramp comedians. They'll bring your house down — and the whole town to your house with their hilarious humor. At your Universal Exchange—NOW!

NEELY EDWARDS

BERT ROACH

CHUCK REISNER

UNIVERSAL
ONE REEL COMEDIES

Universal One Reel Comedies ad appearing in the February 2, 1924 issue
of *Universal Weekly.*

The longest-lived series, however, was "The Gumps," which premiered a year earlier and lasted into 1928. Based on Sidney Smith's popular comic strip series which had debuted back in 1917, the films co-starred Joe Murphy as Andy Gump—Murphy a physical ringer for the character—and Fay Tincher as his wife Min. These two-reelers were Samuel Von Ronkel Productions, produced for Universal release. The Sterns had first approached Richard F. Outcault about securing the rights to his "Buster Brown" series a year before the initial Gump comedy was released, so the success of the Gump films likely made the Sterns feel more confident in acquiring the rights for the series that would go into release in late 1925.

By the end of August, Century was promoting the new season's roster of stars to be featured through the end of the year. The list included Baby Peggy, Wanda Wiley, Buddy Messinger, Hilliard Karr, Al Alt, Pal, the Century Kids, and the Century Follies Girls. All of the four months' films, it was noted, were "in all Universal Exchanges now—*ready for your inspection!*"[3]

While in Europe, Julius had purchased a number of short stories from the French humorist Georges Fouret, to be translated and adapted for use in a new Wanda Wiley series, with Al Alt her co-star.[4] "So convinced am I that I have made one of the greatest, if not the greatest discovery, of my career in Wanda Wiley," said Julius, "that I decided to sign her up for a long term contract…" And long term it was, reported as a five-year contract.[5]

In November 1924, Abe announced that a new sales manager position had been created, and that H.M. Herbel, formerly a sales executive for Universal, had been hired to fill the spot. His first assignment was to get out there and push those three Baby Peggy Universal-Jewel features, with secondary orders to push the Century shorts along with the studio's other offerings.[6]

By year's end, and with Baby Peggy off filming features, Century was promoting that it now had four big stars on their roster for 1925: Wanda Wiley, Al Alt, and the newcomers Edna Marian and Eddie Gordon. Hilliard Karr's and the Century Follies Girls' names were added as well, seemingly so that no feathers were ruffled by this press release.[7] Announced by Julius as the studio's new "Star Series Plan," the studio would soon report a positive response to the announcement from exhibitors in both the U.S. and Canada. Sales manager Herbel confirmed that the announcement had "a decided effect on sales."[8] While this "Star System" decision might seem to be a poke in the eye of Laemmle, who was once firmly against the so-called star system—he had deemed it "a ruinous practice"[9]—the Sterns' lower salaries, and the shorter duration of each "star's" contract, were in a different league than those of the bigger studios.

Production had been put into high gear during the spring of 1925 so that product would be ready well in advance of release. This afforded exhibitors the opportunity to review the films before committing themselves to contracts, a change that seemed eminently fair and displayed a high degree of confidence in the quality of Century's current output. "Heretofore it has been the custom of exhibitors to buy comedies blindly," said Julius. "They would contract for a series of pictures not knowing just what they were going to receive from a quality viewpoint."[10] Now they would know.

Century managed to keep its roster of directors to a more manageable size for the new season. Edward I. Luddy had by now become the studio's top director, with nineteen of the season's fifty-two films to his credit. Charles Lamont helmed another ten, Al Herman eight, and Noel Smith five. William Watson returned from elsewhere in the Universal family for six films, and Arvid Gillstrom made a brief return for another two. Jess Robbins was rehired as well, ostensibly to direct that new Wanda Wiley series based on the Fouret stories,[11] but it appears that he only directed one, *Looking Down* (January 7, 1925), before being reassigned to other actors' projects. By year's end there were five units at work, headed by Herman, Watson, Luddy, Lamont, and Robbins.[12] By January Herman was gone, replaced by Noel Smith.[13]

Wanda Wiley holds on for dear life in Jess Robbins's *Looking Down*, the first of her films based on the Georges Fouret stories. Courtesy of Mark Johnson.

Production continued at the usual frenetic pace, and as a result the occasional accident was unavoidable. Wanda Wiley was injured while filming *Present Arms* (December 17, 1924) when the horse she was riding was spooked by the noise from a wind machine and bolted, throwing her to the ground. She ended up in the hospital with a severely sprained ankle and a fractured right arm. For the several weeks that she was incapacitated, director Edward Luddy was shunted over to another new production.[14] Accidents weren't confined solely to the comedians starring in the Centuries, however. Production manager Sig Neufeld joined their damaged ranks during the filming of another of Wiley's comedies. "He mounted the lofty camera stand so that he could view the filming of the scene and accidentally backed off," wrote the *Los Angeles Times*. A broken left arm was the result, after which he swore that he'd view all subsequent filming from solid ground.[15]

With Wiley's return, the first of her Georges Fouret-based stories went into production, the aforementioned *Looking Down*. Others based on Fouret's stories included

Nobody's Sweetheart (February 4, 1925) and the extant *The Queen of Aces* (May 13, 1925). In this latter film Wiley is both charming and amusing in a role that required her to dress (unconvincingly) as a man in an effort to crash a party to be closer to boyfriend Al Alt. This lands her in a poker game along with Alt's father, and when the game is raided by the cops the two of them make a hair-raising escape. Later on, and armed with the knowledge of the raided poker game, Wiley now has sufficient "dirt" on dad to quietly coerce him to permit her marriage to his son.

Wanda Wiley, ready to take on all opponents, in director William Watson's *The Queen of Aces*. That's Zip Monberg at far left in a brief appearance shortly before his death. Courtesy of Mark Johnson.

This is a nice little comedy, ably directed by William Watson and featuring an amusing comedy of errors and mistaken identities. Back at the mansion, Wiley is thought to be a man in Alt's sister's bedroom, but Alt is taken into custody since he's the only man around. The dual plunges of both Wiley and her future father-in-law as they elude the police are slickly executed, the two falling the many stories from the top of a skyscraper, landing in two conveniently placed barrels of water, safe and sound, as could only happen in the world of slapstick comedy.

Wiley took up fencing as part of her training for this film, and as a way to keep fit. "Miss Wiley says that for keeping slender and for acquiring graceful lines as well as graceful movements, there is nothing to be compared with the exercise derived from fencing."[16] And publicists never lie.

Always eager to capitalize on the rare popularity of one of their stars, the Sterns entered into an agreement with the makers of Orange Kist orange drink. It wasn't long before newspapers were peppered with the following ad:

> You are offered a remarkable opportunity to get into the movies through Orange Kist—the greatest orange drink in the world. Imagine a contract with Universal Century Pictures to act in Wanda Wiley's Company with a fine salary and expenses paid, all for bottle caps from a drink you'll love to drink, and coupons clipped from this paper. Clip the coupon in this ad and enter the contest now.[17]

The winner, a Connie Loranger, was unanimously selected from the hundreds of entrants, with the possibility of a three-year contract dangled before her. And talk about coincidences: Miss Loranger just happened to be the San Diego Soda works' Orange Kist Girl![18]

"Your Chance to Be a Movie Star!" An OrangeKist ad promising the winner a role in an upcoming Wanda Wiley comedy. Courtesy of Michael Hayde.

Another Wiley film that survives—or at least its second reel—is the Edward Luddy-directed *Flying Wheels* (March 3, 1926). The absence of reel one pretty much precludes any sort of extended character development, but reel two makes up for it in a typical, Wileyesque action sequence. The race car driver scheduled to pilot her father's car in the Annual Dealer's Cross Country Auto Race fails to show. Wiley takes matters in her own hands, commandeering the race car without permission and heading off to the race. Having a late start, Wiley intends to catch up, but encounters numerous obstacles along the way: She drags a traffic cop a block or two; she plows through a row of tents, leaving their long-johned tenants hopping mad; she clips a lineman's ladder, depositing him into a water trough; she gets a flat tire, but encourages a fellow using snuff to repeatedly sneeze into a funnel which re-inflates the tire; she plows into a huge haystack which covers the car until knocked loose by a tree, leaving Wiley to toss out "passenger" chickens left and right; and finally drives between two quarreling lovers, whisking the woman's skirt and the fellow's pants away with her. And then she wins the race.

An interruption in Wanda Wiley's attempt to win the cross country auto race in Edward Luddy's *Flying Wheels*. Courtesy of Robert James Kiss.

Public acceptance aside, the *Los Angeles Times* gave a qualified assessment of Wiley's abilities as a comedian, and on Century comedies in general as well. "Century comedies as a rule are nothing to get excited over," wrote reviewer Kenneth Taylor.

Once in a while you will strike one that is funny. The one on the Cameo bill this week tags along with the rest in this respect. It has a few laughs, well scattered. It also has Wanda Wiley, who possesses one of the most expressive sets of features in comedy today. A series of situations that ramble around aimlessly forms the plot. And while Miss Wiley is not exceptional as a comedienne, she has personality enough to bind all the many parts into one compact whole.[19]

The film referred to was most likely *Looking Down*, released five days earlier. As part of this film's action, and rather typical of many of Wiley's stunt-filled films, Wiley chases a fire engine on her bike, picks up a cop on her handlebars along the way, lands at a construction site where the cop falls into a vat of plaster while she is whisked high above on a raised beam, then returns to ground where she slips on a hot bolt—that sort of action.

Wanda Wiley during a break from driving in *Flying Wheels*. Courtesy of Mark Johnson.

Wiley's willingness to take risks while filming led to another accident that held up production, this one during the filming of *Her Lucky Leap* (January 20, 1926). A spill resulted in her being dragged behind a motorcycle, once again landing her in the hospital with cuts, bruises, and a sprained back.[20] "Her recent hospital experience, a three weeks lay-up, seems to have made her impatient rather than cautious," wrote *Universal Weekly* upon her release.[21] "She is never scared," added Walter Haviland, having interviewed Wiley for *Movie Monthly*, "and doesn't know how she gets away with things that would destroy the nerve of a husky man. She balances her body correctly by instinct and that's all there is to it, she says."[22]

Wanda Wiley flirts with a cop while Max Asher looks on, in Edward Luddy's *Her Lucky Leap*. Courtesy of Robert James Kiss.

Director Edward Luddy's *A Speedy Marriage* (November 18, 1925), which survives, provides ample evidence of Wiley's daredevil motorcycle driving, as she speeds up and down steep hills on narrow dirt paths while pursued by a small army of cops. Her physicality is otherwise on display in the hoary plotline where she needs to be married by five o'clock or lose her inheritance, with only seventeen minutes remain, of course. The result is nearly two reels of her mad dash, first to her lawyer's office, and then to collect husband-to-be Charles King for a trip to the preacher. At one point Wiley is buffeted about by a violent wind storm, wire work slamming her against one wall after another. She's dangled headfirst out her apartment building's window, blown off a radiator and onto her lawyer's desktop, slides under automobiles, and survives a gasp-inducing header off a bicycle she has attempted to ride down a storeroom's stacked mountain of crates, among other leaps, dashes, and spills too numerous to enumerate. If she didn't emerge from the filming of this film with a number of bruises, I'd be surprised. In one stunning shot Wiley slams on the brakes of her speeding roadster, fishtailing to a stop a mere few feet in front of the camera. Gags abound, and there's one cute sequence where King, seated at the opposite end of a sofa from Wiley, thinks the pig licking his neck is Wiley's kisses: "Your skin is like velvet…your breath like perfume," he sighs in a fit of ecstasy. Which raises the question: What's a pig doing in her living room?

Full-page promotional ad for the new Eddie Gordon series.
From the February 21, 1925 issue of *Exhibitors Herald*.

Small and wiry Eddie Gordon (1889-1943; born Pietro Armandi[23]), another of those four big stars trumpeted by Century, was born in Naples, Italy. Armandi had become an acrobat at age nine, and stayed with the same troupe for ten years. A name change to Pete Gordon accompanied the forming of his own troupe, The Bounding Gordons, which toured the vaudeville circuits for several years. Gordon made the leap to film, hooking up with Larry Semon at Vitagraph as part of the "Big V Riot Squad" in 1918, such as *Huns and Hyphens* and *Bears and Bad Men* (both 1918). Gordon continued with Semon in supporting roles in films such as *The Grocery Clerk* (1919) and *The Bakery* (1921) until early 1924. He then headed to Santa Rosa to make a comedy short for the independent Eldorado Film Company, where he was to co-star with heavyweight Frank Alexander in the Earl Olin-directed film titled *Bumpers*.[24] Viewing the completed film, a copy of which survives at USC School of Cinematic Arts' Hugh M. Hefner Moving Image Archive, it would appear that Gordon was replaced by another actor.

Hilliard Karr and Beth Darlington wait for Eddie Gordon to complete yet-another crossword puzzle, in Charles Lamont's *Puzzled By Crosswords*.

Gordon was hired by the Sterns in November 1924, when he—or the Sterns—decided to change his first name to Eddie, and for reasons that elude me.[25] His former considerable acrobatic skills, Century was quick to note, would allow him to "do many laugh-provoking stunts that other comedians would find impossible."[26]

Eddie Gordon and Larry Richardson in Noel Smith's *Itching for Revenge*.
Courtesy of Jim Kerkhoff.

Larry Richardson kneels before Eddie Gordon in Jess Robbins's *Crowning the Count*.
Courtesy of Robert James Kiss.

Gordon had some baggage in his background that the Sterns were probably unaware of. Back in 1905 when he was going by the name Peter Armando, Gordon had been arrested and charged with sodomy. Given his youthful age of sixteen, the jury took pity on him and returned a verdict of assault with intent to commit sodomy. This carried a potential maximum sentence of five years, half that of the original charge. Gordon lucked out when the judge reduced his sentence to one year, and the youth was shipped off to Anamosa penitentiary.[27] Gordon returned to his former profession, presumably with some culinary skills acquired during his year working in the prison's kitchen.

Gordon maintained a low profile from that time on—or at least as far as the press was concerned—resurfacing in 1917 as a shill for New York City-based Surpass Drug Corp.'s "miracle" product Cyaline. The ad touted Gordon as unemployed for the past four years, deemed an "incurable cripple" suffering from a malignant blood disorder.[28] That is until he tried Cyaline, after which he bounced back to full health and resumed his acrobatic career and work for Larry Semon. I hope he got paid well for this endorsement.

After appearing in several films in support of Edna Marian, Gordon was promoted to star of his own series. The first of these was the topical *Puzzled By Crosswords* (April 1, 1925), wherein crossword fanatic Gordon's sweetheart (Beth Darlington) loses patience with his addiction and drags him off to be married; Charles Lamont directed. *Itching for Revenge* (May 6, 1925) followed, with others such as *Kicked About* (June 10, 1925), *The Polo Kid* (July 22, 1925), and *Crowning the Count* (February 10, 1926) among the dozen released by Century into early 1926, with Noel Smith and Jess Robbins usually taking turns directing. In *Crying for Love*, diminutive Gordon was teamed with towering Blanche Payson as his overbearing spouse, a teaming that elicited this comment from *Moving Picture World*'s reviewer: "Although Eddie Gordon is the star…Blanche Payson walks away with the picture and really makes Eddie only a foil for her comedy."[29]

Given his film experience prior to joining Century, it comes as little surprise that one writer reported that "Gordon is said to resemble [Larry] Semon in the style of his work."[30] Probably assuming that his position with Century was secure, Gordon went out and splurged on a 1925 Hudson coach, photos of him proudly standing beside his new acquisition appearing in papers nationwide. Security is fleeting, however, and Gordon's reception as a lead comic was tepid at best, so he was let go in late 1925 after a mere twelve films for the Sterns. Gordon would go on to make a series of two-reel comedies for Sava Film over the next three years before moving on to the Hal Roach studios. With the coming of sound Gordon would plod on in numerous supporting roles, often uncredited, up until his death in 1943.

Gordon's supporting actor in a number of these was a stocky three hundred and sixty pound fellow named Larry Richardson. Born Laurence Richardson Jossenberger (1894-1935) in Fort Worth, Texas, Richardson was the son of a former stage carpenter, film editor, and (it was claimed) a Hollywood film player who went by the name Victor Rich.[31] Early work in stock was followed by appearances in film from 1914 as Lawrence Jossenberger, in films such as Pike Peak Photoplay's *The White Trail* (1915), eventually landing at Century as Larry Richardson in support of Gordon, Wanda Wiley, Edna Marion, and Al Alt. He later claimed to have appeared in at least fifty-two comedies for Century—I've only been able to track down credits for eleven of them—as well as having supported Harold Lloyd, Snub Pollard, and others at various times in the past. By 1928, however, Richardson had given up on his film career and made the permanent move to vaudeville, although he did appear in several early sound Vitaphone shorts. One iteration of this was as Larry Rich and His Friends, featuring his wife Cheri.[32] Richardson was stricken with stomach cancer in 1935 (according to his obituary; other sources cite a combination of diabetes and heart problems), and by August was dead at age forty-one.[33]

Larry Richardson plays poker with a heavily-disguised Wanda Wiley
in *The Queen of Aces*. Courtesy of Library of Congress.

Edna Marian (1906-1957; born Edna Hanam) was a dainty little blonde of seventeen and the last of the four big stars announced at the end of 1924.[34] Another graduate of Gus Edwards Revue on the Orpheum circuit, Edna's first roles were in the independent Puppy Love Series of college life, where she co-starred with another newcomer, eighteen year old

Gordon White. Major Leland S. Ramsdell, the head of producing company Hollywood Photoplay Productions, explained his choice of leads:

> I wanted a crowd of young folk who looked and acted like college students—a crowd hitherto greatly distorted on the screen. I wanted 'em clean and unaffected, spirited but well-behaved on the set.[35]

Edna Marian, distracted while milking a cow, in William Watson's *Uncle Tom's Gal.*
Courtesy of Library of Congress.

At least three of these were filmed, but it is not known if any of them actually made it to the screen. At any rate, Century snapped her up, gave her a new name, and issued a promotional piece that provided additional details about her background. It claimed that Marian had played in "a number of comedy series and has played many featured roles in feature length productions."[36] We'll take their word for it, but evidence as such has yet to surface.

After Marian's initial appearances opposite Eddie Gordon and as one of the Century Follies Girls in *Broadway Beauties* (December 24, 1924) and *Her Daily Dozen* (January 21, 1925), Marian got her first big starring role in *My Baby Doll* (February 11, 1925). In this one Marian accidentally breaks the large mechanical doll she was to deliver, forcing her to pose as the doll to avoid having her pay docked. Arthur Lake, then star of Universal's "Sweet Sixteen" series, was borrowed to act as the film's male lead. *My Baby Doll* survives in a print held by the Museum of Modern Art, or at least a good portion of it; both opening and closing footage are missing. Tiny but spunky Marian is a delight in the lead, a natural born comedian now provided the opportunity to showcase her talents. Still thought to be a doll and seated at a dinner table next to Lake, she sneaks one mouthful of food after another from Lake's fork when he isn't watching, the final bite so huge that she can barely close her mouth around it. Marian saves the day when she spots Lake about to "borrow" cash from his parents' wall safe, Marian pocketing the money before he can do so. When the "theft" is discovered, Lake is accused, but gets off the hook after Marian sneaks the money back into the safe.

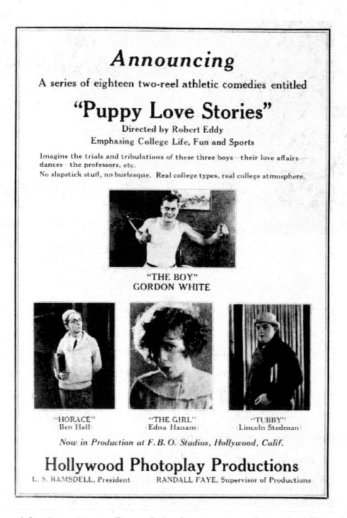

Full-page ad for the upcoming Puppy Love Stories series of comedies, Edna Marian bottom center as Edna Hanam. From the May 3, 1924 issue of *Exhibitors Herald*.

Marian's herky-jerky movements when pretending to be the automaton aren't terribly convincing, but a healthy dollop of suspension of disbelief overcomes that hurdle. As for Lake, he's such a cowering wimp in this film that it is almost impossible to sympathize with him or, for that matter, even like him at all. This role aside, the Sterns would borrow Lake again to star in *Putting on Airs* (April 8, 1925) and *Love Sick* (May 20, 1925).

Other of Marian's films include *Powdered Chickens* (March 11, 1925), *Putting On Airs*, and *Plenty of Nerve* (July 1, 1925), as well as the extant and delightful spoof *Uncle Tom's Gal* (October 7, 1925), in which farm girl Marian is pressed into service when the movie company shooting "Uncle Tom's Cabin" on her farm loses their lead actress. This one's a hilarious satire on filmmaking and the melodramatic "Uncle Tom's Cabin," with Marian as the wide-eyed innocent who can't act a lick. Marian's comedic talents are in full display here, seamlessly transitioning from glam to goofball without batting an eyelash. A prime example is in the opening fantasy scene where Marian's character imagines herself as a rich and pampered socialite surrounded by a bevy of hopeful suitors, and a few moments later the reality, farm girl Marian energetically milking a cow, and appearing about as dimwitted as imaginable.

Edna Marian, Jane "Cuddles" Shirley, and Arthur Lake in Edward Luddy's *My Baby Doll*.

Poster for *Uncle Tom's Gal.* Courtesy of Heritage Auctions, Ha.com.

Some of the film's other sequences notable for the laughs they generate include "Eva"s death scene and her ascension to heaven suspended in front of a ludicrous "cloud" backdrop, the prop fellow accidentally moving the clouds in the wrong direction ("Reverse it," yells the director, "She's a *good* girl!"). Another has Edna, now as "Topsy," looking absurd in black cloth sleeves and pullover headpiece rather than blackface. The funniest bit is her trek over the "ice floes," here clearly-labeled Fels Naptha product boxes topped with melting paraffin, two of them sticking to her feet and clumsily carried onto land. If only all Century comedies had been this good!

So pleased were the Sterns with the results that they immediately made plans for Marian and a "Romeo and Juliet" follow-up spoof, but needed a lead for her they described as a "lovely young man" who must "not be less than five feet ten inches in height, must be of good physique and passably good-looking, and must have a slender waistline."[37] Evidently none of their current stock company filled the bill, and it would appear that perhaps a search didn't result in a likely candidate either, for the film was never made. Marian's films for Century would last through the end of 1926.

Uncle Tom's Gal's approach to blackface. Courtesy of Library of Congress.

Edna Marian can't find any images on the exposed film taken at her farm, and is proving it to the film's director, Harry Martell, from *Uncle Tom's Gal*. Courtesy of Library of Congress.

By early 1925, the response to the Star Series was sufficiently encouraging that "the 1925-1926 production policy of the company is expected to be changed materially from past methods," it was reported. "We are determined to take our comedies out of the filler class," said Abe, putting his best spin on the situation currently at hand.

> We are putting more time, money, and care into production. As an indication of this, we now have five directors working at the Century studio, an almost unprecedented situation for a two-reel comedy company.... We are taking every possible means to build up our four stars. The best means is by putting them in good comedies. This we are doing.... Exhibitors are reacting to our progressiveness by signing up under our star series plan to a far greater degree than ever before.[38]

Beth Darlington, here posed with Charley Chase at the Roach studios.
Courtesy of Rob Arkus.

Another, albeit brief, addition to Century's roster of female leads was Beth Darlington (1904-1951), who signed at the end of 1924. Darlington's first film role had been with Shirley Mason in Fox's *The Lamplighter* (1921), and more recently roles with Eddie Lyons, Roach's Our Gang, Charley Chase, and Will Rogers, with a few Pete Morrison Western features thrown into the mix. Darlington's first three for Century were *Raisin' Cain* (March 18, 1925), *Clear the Way* (March 25, 1925), and *Puzzled By Crosswords*, all released contiguously, perhaps to give her some immediate audience exposure. Darlington appeared in only a handful of comedies for Century before retiring from the industry in 1925, her last film for the Sterns appearing to have been *Captain Suds* (December 16, 1925) in support of Eddie Gordon. This isn't definite, however, since there was so much confusion in the trades between Darlington and her supposed successor, the similarly named (and similar in appearance) Constance Darling. One example of this was *Too Much Mother-In-Law* (September 16, 1925) with Charles King playing the husband and Blanche Payson the mother-in-law. Darlington's and Darling's names were interchangeable depending on which trade magazine a review appeared in, and the same confusion applied to some articles and cast lists associated with the film. I've opted for Darling, in that she was the one credited in both a photo and review that appeared in *Universal Weekly*, Universal having released the film. This wasn't the only film in which the two actresses were confused, not only in reviews but in photo captions and ads as well; *Married Neighbors* (June 24, 1925) is another example of this confusion.

Beth Darlington, mid-hazing at her fashionable boarding school,
in Charles Lamont's *Raisin' Cain.*

Another hire in early 1925 was Texan Charles Lafayette King Jr. (1895-1957), whose resume included prior roles for a dizzying number of different studios. These dated back to at least 1918, and if unconfirmed reports are to be believed, as early as 1915. Julius lumped Charles King into a group he called "a better class of actors" in his article "Better Class of Actors Turning to Film Colony." Julius hinted at a shift in the type of comedy to be expected from Century in the near future, writing that:

> During the past few months we have added to our stock company of players three or four actors of national reputation, including Charles King, formerly a featured player with Universal; Jack Singleton, for many years a popular leading man of the speaking stage; and Tony Hayes, erstwhile musical comedy star.... These artists received their training on the legitimate stage and in screen dramatic work, and they bring to the motion picture comedy and artistry heretofore unknown. The day of the ordinary clowns and buffoons in screen comedies is gone and in their stead have come a new class of stellar comedians.[39]

Sounded good, but Hayes and Singleton failed to make much of an impression. King, on the other hand, proved to be an inspired choice.

Hailing from Hillsboro, Texas, King's father had wanted Charles to follow in his professional footsteps as a physician. King opted to be an actor instead, so he headed to Hollywood. In film since an unconfirmed bit part in D.W. Griffith's *The Birth of a Nation*, King had appeared in roles both large and small in a number of features and short comedies in films that included *Singing River* (1921; Fox), *Motion to Adjourn* (1921; Arrow), *The Price of Youth* (1922; Berwilla), and von Stroheim's *Merry-Go-Round* (1923; Universal) before signing with the Sterns.

King proved to be a comfortable fit at Century, starring in approximately three dozen shorts over the next three years. A number of these were as lead in several of the series that would become the studio's mainstay come the 1926-1927 season. King's first for Century came at the end of the 1924-1925 season, director Charles Lamont's *Paging a Wife* (August 12, 1925) with Al Alt and Lillian Worth. Most of King's earliest parts were in support of leads Alt and Wiley, but he was finally given a starring role opposite screen spouse Constance Darling in *Too Much Mother-In-Law*. Blanche Payson, described by one reviewer as "a woman of unusually large proportions," portrayed the overbearing in-law. This threesome reappeared in the follow-up *Too Many Babies* (April 28, 1926), King and Darling playing a childless couple visited by his mother-in-law Payson. The couple scrambles to acquire some stand-in tykes, having led Payson to believe that they already have two children. "The idea has been overworked by other comedy directors," sniffed *Film Daily*'s reviewer,[40] an observation that probably didn't escape a large segment of filmgoers. King would reappear with Darling in the follow-up *Honeymooning with Ma* (May 26, 1926), and opposite others in films such as Wanda Wiley's *Twin Sisters* (June 16, 1926) and *Motor Trouble* (June 23, 1926). King proved a likeable presence, handling the comedic aspects in a wholly acceptable fashion, and not beneath playing the fool when required. As for his appearance, while not what you would call debonair, King still had comparative youth going for him and was far better looking than he would appear in his later, more familiar weather-beaten "heavy" (in both senses of the word) roles in endless B Westerns throughout the thirties and forties.

Century comedian Charles King, sans mustache.

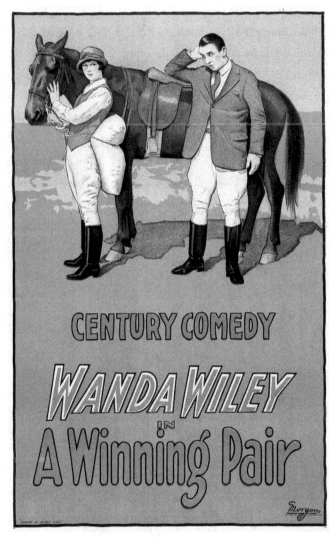

Poster art for Wanda Wiley and Charles King's *A Winning Pair*, Charles Lamont director. Courtesy of Heritage Auctions, Ha.com.

Looking forward to the 1925-1926 season, the Sterns were confident enough in their four Star Series releases and the "unprecedented success being had this spring" to up the budget to $500,000 for productions commencing "early next fall through the following winter," wrote *Exhibitors Trade Review*.[41] "A lavish schedule of production has been prepared…and it will be carried out under the personal direction of Sig Neufeld, production manager of the fun film plant."[42] Julius's stated goal: "I will not rest until our product is so far ahead of all others that they will be the humorous touchstones of the screen world."[43]

Wiley's popularity had taken off to the point where she was now a big draw in Germany as well as stateside. So popular was she there that a delegation from UFA began negotiations with the Sterns for a loan-out so that she could star in a few of their productions. Director F.W. Murnau, fresh off *The Last Laugh*, led the delegation and deemed Wiley "a Norma Talmadge type." Julius took their request under consideration, with an eye toward her upcoming production schedule and whether or not it could be arranged to accommodate UFA's offer.[44] It would appear that it couldn't—or perhaps Julius held out in hopes of a better offer—since nothing more came of this. Wiley watched any dreams she may have had for a European trip, work in feature films, and a shot at greater international stardom go up in flames. Julius re-signed her to a new long-term contract in May (so much for that "five year contract" reported a year earlier), sent her back to Texas for another vacation, and slapped a check in her hand "to cover all of your vacation expenses as a token of our sincere appreciation of your work for this company during the past two years."[45] Or so it was reported.

Wanda Wiley swoons between Harry McCoy (left) and bald Bynunsky Hyman, in Edward Luddy's *Sweet Dreams*. That's Louise Carver in the background left. Courtesy of Jim Kerkhoff.

In July, Century celebrated its six hundred comedies produced since 1914, L-Ko's output included in the mix. During this all-day reunion, anyone employed by the Sterns over the eleven year period was invited to attend.[46] It's unknown, but highly doubtful, that Henry Lehrman was one of the attendees. Preceding this event in June was the open house held by Century for those attending the Shrine convention in Los Angeles. Julius, a Shriner himself, organized the event that would allow attendees to witness the filming of comedies.[47] And while Julius was not a bad looking guy—broken nose aside—he wisely chose Wanda Wiley to serve as hostess.[48]

The previous year's decision, which afforded exhibitors the opportunity to preview completed comedies before their release, had been a success, so production was ramped up in the spring to create a stockpile of the 1925-1926 season's releases. As a result, by June all films scheduled for September through the following January release were at the exchanges, available for exhibitor preview. "We are finding out that the exhibitor is just as willing to preview a comedy as a feature, and that in contracting for a season's output, he wants to know what he is getting," said sales manager H.M. Herbel. "He does not want to buy a cat in a bag on his comedies any more than he wants to buy a block of features unsold."[49]

As a result of Century's adoption of the Star Series, and the ability of exhibitors to preview a representative sample of their efforts, bookings for the studio's output was now at an all-time high. The Sterns had high hopes for the upcoming 1925-1926 season, and their hopes would soon be answered with one of the biggest series successes of their careers. What they didn't—*couldn't*—anticipate was the unexpected "Act of God" (or of man?) that was soon to befall their studio.

Chapter 13: The Planting of a Seed (The 1925-1926 Season)

Under Century's new four-star plan, the studio's productions would be divided into two classes: situation comedies and slapstick comedies. The former would feature Wanda Wiley and Edna Marian—Marian returning to the studio after a loan-out to film Universal's *The Still Alarm* (1926)—and the latter Eddie Gordon and Al Alt, described by sales manager H.M. Herbel as "old-timers at rough-and-tumble slapstick." Herbel elaborated: "We have found that the South, with the exception of a few larger centres prefers slapstick comedies, while Chicago and everything East, prefers straight situation type. The West, with the exception of the four large Coast towns, prefer slapstick," added Herbel.[1]

There was to be a significant shift in the scheduled output this season. While both Wanda Wiley and Edna Marian were to appear in twelve films each, Eddie Gordon and Al Alt would be reduced to six each, and Charles King another four. Alt's releases included *Piping Hot* (October 14, 1925), *Helpful Al*, and *Her Ambition* (August 25, 1926) opposite Bartine Burkett, with a remaining two films spilling into the following season, by which time Alt was long gone from the studio. Eddie Gordon's stay with the studio was short-lived as well, his remaining six releases including *Officer Number Thirteen* (September 9, 1925), *A Taxi War* (November 11, 1925), and *Captain Suds* (December 16, 1925).

The remainder of the season's fifty-two comedies would be filled with twelve of Century's newest series—the series that would have a profound impact on all of the subsequent seasons' output—the "Buster Brown" Comedies.[2]

Film companies had been pursuing purchase of the rights to cartoonist Richard F. Outcault's syndicated comic strip since the mid-teens, but he had been protective of his popular creation and felt the various film companies would not do it justice. The character of Buster Brown had made sporadic appearances on film since his introduction in 1902, first announced in the March 26, 1904 issue of *New York Clipper* as "Buster Brown and His Dog Tige in a Series of Very Funny Pranks;" picture rights had been secured by Edison and sold as a group. Several entries from this early series—*Buster's Dog to the Rescue* and *Buster and the Dude*, both from March 1904—are available for view on YouTube.

Blanche Payson attempts to keep Eddie Gordon from spanking Tommy Hicks in Noel Smith's *A Flivver Vacation.* Courtesy of Robert James Kiss.

Al Alt (center left) and Hilliard Karr check out the girls in Charles Lamont's *Piping Hot.* Courtesy of Richard M. Roberts.

Another oddity appeared in May 1913, Essanay's *Buster Brown, Tige and Their Creator, R.F. Outcault*, this time with the two comic characters interacting onscreen with their creator; Theodore Wharton directed. Edison regained the rights to the series again in mid-1914, with twelve split-reel entries to follow.[3] These included *Buster Brown and the Treatment of Goats, Buster Brown's Education, Buster Brown and the German Band*, and *Buster Brown Causes a Commotion*; Charles H. France directed. By 1915 the series had grown to twenty-five entries.[4]

The Sterns managed to convince Outcault that they could do filmic justice to his character, and in late October or early November 1924 had secured the exclusive rights. "Century announces that they will make of this comic page a series of two-reel comedies unequalled in the history of two-reel production," wrote *Universal Weekly* in its typically overblown and boastful fashion.[5]

Arthur Trimble and Doreen Turner pose for camera-dog Pete in this publicity still for the Stern Brothers' "Buster Brown" series. Courtesy of Robert James Kiss.

Oddly enough, it had been reported two years earlier that the Sterns had then acquired the rights to Buster Brown, and at that time the part of Buster's dog Tige was to be played by Brownie.[6] It is unclear if and how that deal fell through, or if it took a long two years to work out the details, but either way nothing more was heard about the series until late in 1924. "It's a great 'scoop' for Century," commented Julius. "Clean and wholesome comedy subjects are at a premium these days...."[7] And to clear up any potential misconceptions in the minds of exhibitors, Julius was quick to note that the films would be straight comedies, and not animated cartoons.

Born in Lancaster, Ohio, Richard Felton Outcault (1863-1928) was the creator of the *Yellow Kid*, the cartoon series widely credited as influencing the development of the comic strip. An early contributor to humor magazines, by 1885 Outcault was drawing comic cartoons for Joseph Pulitzer's *New York World*. It was there in 1895 that he created the character that would come to be known as the "Yellow Kid," a bald street urchin clad in a bright yellow nightshirt. Outcault was lured away by William Randolph Hearst's *New York Journal* that same year and was forced to leave his creation behind. A year later Outcault moved over to the *New York Herald* where in 1902 he created his most popular and enduring character and comic strip, *Buster Brown*. As presented, Buster Brown was a mischievous kid from a well-to-do family, outfitted in the somewhat prissy "Little Lord Fauntleroy" style. Along with him in his antics was his bull terrier Tige, as drawn a rather bizarre looking canine with a wide head and far too many teeth. Outcault took his characters with him when he moved over to Hearst's *New York American* in 1906, but by 1918 had turned the series over to others and retired from the newspaper business. He spent the last ten years of his life painting.

Cartoonist Richard F. Outcault.

The choice to play Buster was, in retrospect, an easy one. Eight year old Arthur Trimble (1917-?) had appeared in Century comedies for the better part of two years, his first opposite Baby Peggy in the yet-to-be-released *Red Riding Hood*. The public first eyeballed Trimble in a small part in Harry Sweet's *Hee! Haw!* in early 1923, and the lead in *That's Rich* (March 26, 1924). As one of the Century Kids, Trimble appeared in *Trailing Trouble, Please, Teacher!*, *Here He Comes!*, and *Speed Boys*. In this latter film Trimble dresses up as a little girl to lure "Spec" O'Donnell away from their mutual girl Josephine Adair, and given Trimble's decided effeminacy he was utterly convincing in drag. Supposedly chosen for the role of Buster out of ten finalists, Trimble was signed to a long term contract.

Trimble, it should be noted, was somewhat of a trouper given his unsettling experience as a six year old. While filming *The Adventures of Prince Courageous* (1923) for director Frederick G. Becker, Trimble was required to take part in a scene where both his hands and feet were tied and he was tossed into an Orange County Park lake. When Trimble, who was expected to come back up to the surface, didn't, Becker dove in and dragged the submerged boy back to land where he was revived. The boy's mother offered the explanation that he must have become "excited under the strain of actual filming as he had rehearsed the scene on several occasions."[8] Whatever the case, the scare would have been enough to convince many six year olds that filmmaking was not for them. Evidently Trimble's mother didn't feel that way.

Arthur Trimble, Doreen Turner, and Pete in another publicity pose for the Stern Brothers' "Buster Brown" series. Courtesy of Rob Arkus.

Along with Arthur Trimble, six year old Doreen Turner was signed to star as Mary Jane, along with Pete the dog assuming the role of Tige. Katherine Young was to play Buster's mother, Charles King his father, Emily Gerdes the maid, and Dorothy Vernon the cook. Charles Lamont was to direct from stories and continuities by George McWilliams,[9] and the series would be filmed by cameraman William Hyer.[10] As with all of Century's announcements, these specifics would undergo many changes over the next four years of the successful series' run.

Doreen Turner (1918-1994) brought an impressive resume to the series given her young age. Her first big role was in the Mary Pickford feature *Through the Back Door* in 1921, followed by a series of comedy shorts for director William Campbell at Educational. Here she starred opposite Coy Watson, Jr. and a shifting cast of animals in films that included *The Stork's Mistake* (1921) and *Monkey Shines* (1922). Roles in features followed for studios that included F.B.O.—*Speed Wild* (1925)—and Universal—*Lorraine of the Lions* (1925)—before she was hired by the Sterns for what must have appeared to be a dream role.

Pete the Pup makes the big time, featured on the December 4, 1926 cover
of *Universal Weekly*.

PETE

Pete the pup in a photo signed by trainer Harry Lucenay. Note that the image
was flipped, the ring around Pete's right eye here appearing around his left.

Predating all this was Turner's first appearance in the press, when she was among
seven thousand entrants in the *Los Angeles Express*'s Best Babies contest of November
1920. Turner competed as well, and managed to be one of seventeen best babies awarded a
silver medal, selected by the judges as those "who would make ideal screen babies." Small
potatoes compared to her future co-star, four year old Trimble, who won the second prize
of a gold medal and $300 in merchandise credit.[11] First steps in future screen "immortality."

Pete the dog, who looked as much as any live canine could look like Outcault's odd
looking Tige (which wasn't much), was alternately referred to as "Peter" and "Petey" in the
early days of his career. Pete was born into show biz, his father Century's earlier dog star, Pal.

Educating Buster, the first of the series' twelve for the season, was released on September
23, 1925. There wasn't much of a plot as such, rather a series of humorous incidents that
take place when Buster first wakes up, during his later walk to school accompanied by Mary
Jane and Tige, and the problems arising once they arrive. Some of the gags commented

upon after its release included a fly that landed on sleeping Buster's face that Tige, unable to chase it away, actually smashes with his paw. Buster, denied breakfast, gets on some stilts, masquerades as a cop, and acquires a pie in the process (the pie ends up thrown in Tige's face). And later, after Tige has had a run-in with a skunk, he walks by a fence with three birds sitting atop it, each one falling dead as he passes. Those sort of gags.

Evidently a lot of care was lavished on this first, series-selling entry, and by all accounts director Lamont rose to the occasion, creating a crowd- and reviewer-pleasing film. The reviewer for *Exhibitors Trade Review* was sold:

> If the remainder of the series are up to the high standard set by this one, screen patrons are in for some highly enjoyable entertainment, for the comedies will be something new and different. They have a special appeal for children, but are not too childish to bring smiles to the lips of the grown-ups.... The direction is excellent, and the kids deserve much credit for their interpretations. Tige is a great asset and supplies more than his share of the humor with which the film is loaded.[12]

Motion Picture News concurred, stating that if this entry "is to be taken as a criterion of what is to follow this should be a very popular set of pictures,"[13] and *Moving Picture World* one-upped the others, calling it "one of the most genuinely amusing comedies the writer has ever seen."[14]

Buster Be Good was the second in the series, again directed by Lamont. The first entry proved to be a tough act to follow, as evidenced by reviewer comments. "This one is not so funny as the first of the series, but nevertheless is superior to many short comedies and holds special appeal for the juvenile trade," wrote *Exhibitors Trade Review*, adding that "Tige the dog, deserves much credit for making these comedies a success. He is a wonderful animal, and his little bag of tricks are good for many a laugh."[15] *Moving Picture World* agreed, stating "While not as clever or spontaneous in its humor as 'Educating Buster Brown,' this subject...is a good comedy."[16]

Gus Meins, a newcomer to the Century lot, took over direction for the series' third—*Oh! Buster!* (November 25, 1925)—and the remainder of the season's entries. The season's other ten films included *Buster's Bust-Up* (January 13, 1926), *Buster's Nose Dive* (February 24, 1926), *Buster's Skyrocket* (April 14, 1926), and *Buster's Mix-Up* (May 12, 1926), all of which survive.

Buster's Bust-Up is one of those high-and-dizzy films. Buster, his mind elsewhere over a breakup with Mary Jane, sits on a construction site's girder which is then hauled up into the heavens. It's the usual skyscraper stuff here, no better, no worse, but marred by several absurdly spinning girders. Poor Pete, who appears in a number of shots high up on the mockup skyscraper, looks borderline traumatized having to navigate those narrow girders, and even more so when Trimble yanks him by the collar, pulling him down from a higher girder to a lower one. The film ends in the same fashion as the strips, with another of Buster's resolves: "Resolved: That all women are alike, except that some are different from others. Buster."

Is it smallpox, or merely splattered paint? A spotted Arthur Trimble sits with Pete, post-crash, while Doreen Turner looks on. From Gus Meins's *Buster's Bust-Up*. Courtesy of Robert James Kiss.

Buster's Nose-Dive has Buster and Tige accidentally taking off in his father's newly-invented air plane, and experiencing all sorts of aerial thrills before it turns out that it was all a dream. This one is a comparatively ambitious little film, loaded with lots of special effects, some of them better than others. One of the better of these is the plane's exit crash through the wall of his father's building, which is nicely executed. The various shots of the flight over the city's streets are uneven, some through an oddly positioned double exposure, others from a plane mockup seemingly hung beside the camera car, and others offering

Buster's point-of-view of the flight, the mockup mounted on the front of the camera car. And there's the trick shot, animated, of the plane crashing through the tall building's tower. A change of pace, for sure, that benefits from the more lavish budgets allotted these early series entries.

Buster's Skyrocket, like so many of the other entries in the series, is filled with a number of incidental little sequences that, while amusing, do little to further the plot. These include Tige's run-in with a storefront mechanical bulldog; Buster and Mary Jane's golf game which starts on the street but ends up inside, demolishing Buster's house; and their dealings with their unfortunate tutor. All this before they end up in the back of some robbers' car along with Tige, the fireworks therein exploding and causing the car to crash. There are (as always) lots of cute close-ups of Tige in this one, and it's his antics that once again steal the show and were, perhaps, the primary drawing power of this series. There's one very cleverly executed trick shot early on, when Buster's golf swing connects with Tige, sending him sailing through the air for a block or two, landing far down the sidewalk.[17] All in all, it's the usual kid antics, the two of them repeatedly getting in trouble, the results softened somewhat by Tige's presence and anthropomorphized contributions. And, as always, Trimble mugs a lot.

Century Comedy
BUSTER'S BUST UP

Doreen Turner and Arthur Trimble realize they are being hauled sky-high atop a girder in *Buster's Bust-Up*. Courtesy of Richard M. Roberts.

It's Tige's show once again in the enjoyable *Buster's Mix-Up*, Tige spending the bulk of the film attempting to mend a rift between Mary Jane and Buster. The film opens with a bang, Mary Jane unleashing a hailstorm of thrown dishes at a cowering Buster for some slight which is never revealed. Turner rises to the occasion in this one, truly convincing as she unleashes her fury on wimpy little Buster, and later demonstrating her dancing chops by performing the Charleston at her party. She turns to nerdy freckled kid Leon Holmes for companionship, but when a ride on his bike turns scary when he's accidentally ejected, it's Tige and Buster who rescue her. Tige, not surprisingly, garners the most laughs, early on with his bewilderment over the dish-throwing, and later in his attempts to find a new home, first by ejecting a poodle from a chauffeur-driven limo and taking its place, and later by faking a runaway baby carriage rescue. Consumption of a brick of chewing tobacco, mistaken for chocolate, leaves the poor dog heaving behind Mary Jane's piano. It's a great little film.

A portion of *Buster's Orphan Party* (July 21, 1926) survives as well. After a cute bit where Tige serves Buster and Mary Jane some tea, Mrs. Brown points out to the kids that it's Orphans' Day. The kids decide to take matters in hand and head out to gather up a carload of orphans. Meanwhile, Tige chips in and finds another lone kid, and proceeds to haul him back to the Brown residence in a cart. Heading up a steep hill proves to be too much of a struggle for Tige, however, the cart, kid, and Tige now rolling backwards down the hill towards a cliff. Buster and friends intercede and rescue Tige and the kid at the last moment. All head back to the Brown's home and seat themselves around the dining table for a promised feast. As they await their meal, a fat kid sneaks some fruit, only to end up with a mouthful of wax. And there this fragment ends, but according to a contemporary review:

> A riot is in progress when Buster appoints Tige to keep order. The clever dog is used in a stunt whereby a hole is sawed in the table and Tige steals the chicken. He does some great work in dodging the kids till he has time to finish the chicken. The colored boy does a fine Charleston on the table, but the arrival of Buster's mother into the wrecked house means that Buster is ready for a licking. He plays safe by placing a plate in the seat of his pants. As usual, all the principal honors go to Tige. The dog is a wonder.[18]

As usual!

Meanwhile, Edna Marian, who was named a Wampas Star of 1926,[19] didn't last long with the studio after her recent return. During her break she'd had roles in a pair of features—Fox's *The Desert's Price* (1925) with Buck Jones, and Universal's *The Still Alarm* (1926)—and faced with offers for more starring roles decided that features provided a more challenging, fulfilling, and lucrative future than with shorts. To that end she bought out her five-year contract[20] from the studio, which still had several years to run, freeing her up to free-lance in roles with feature productions.[21] Marian's remaining films for the Sterns included *A Haunted Heiress* (May 5, 1926), *Dare Devil Daisy* (July 7, 1926), *His Girl Friday* (July 28, 1926), and her final, *A Second Hand Excuse* (December 8, 1926).

Marian's shoes would be filled by Constance Darling, who had come to the studio the previous year and would remain there for two years. Little is known about Darling's life before or after her two-year stint with Century or, for that matter, during that short period of time as well. Let it suffice to say that her most frequent co-star in the dozen or so films that she appeared in was Charles King, with whom she seemed to have a nice on-screen rapport. More than half of the following season's thirteen "The Excuse Maker" films would feature Darling, but by the time of the release of the final of these—*Keeping His Word* (May 11, 1927)—she was no longer with the studio. Her only other known credit during this period was for a loan-out to Universal to star in one of their Mustang brand Westerns, *The Show Cowpuncher* (November 13, 1926).

Bald Bynunsky Hyman wants a kiss from Constance Darling, Al Alt directly behind him, and Hilliard Karr far right. Lobby card for Charles Lamont's *A Rough Party*. Courtesy of Richard M. Roberts.

GUS MEINS

Formerly with Mack Sennett

HAS JUST
COMPLETED
DIRECTING
A SERIES
OF

BUSTER
BROWN
COMEDIES

FOR
CENTURY
FILMS

Director Gus Meins.

Renowned film historian Steve Massa has proffered an interesting theory regarding actresses Beth Darlington and Constance Darling, the possibility that the two were actually the same person. Darlington's final film was presumably the aforementioned Century's *Captain Suds*, ending her five year run starring in comedy shorts, her marriage at the beginning of 1926 the accepted explanation for retirement. Constance Darling first appeared on the scene in 1925 as well in Century's *A Rough Party* (July 8, 1925), the first in her brief two-year career as outlined above. What brought him to this theory is the similarity of their looks, and comparisons of images of the two actresses seem to bear this out. There are admittedly some slight differences between the two, Massa observing that Darling appears "just a little thinner and made over as more of a flapper as Constance Darling." The fact that writers and reviewers tended to confuse the two adds some heft to this theory, and since Massa's facial recognition abilities are, in a word, uncanny, I though it worthwhile to mention this for future consideration and study. The obvious question that arises, though, is *why*? Why would a seemingly successful actress change her credited identity at this point in her career? There are several conceivable answers to this, such as a contractual conflict that would otherwise have disallowed her from making any more films for Century. But for now we should forget about the "why" until it has actually been determined that they were indeed one and the same, and I'll leave that potential discovery for others with a deeper knowledge of the two actresses' work, and more archival resources at their disposal.

The "Buster Brown" comedies were an immediate hit, and boosted Century's bookings. The series' new director, Gus Meins (1893-1940), was born Gustave Peter Ludwig Luley in Frankfurt, Germany, and came to the U.S. at age nine. Educated in St. Louis and Los Angeles, Meins had taken courses at a Minneapolis art school, which led to a job as cartoonist and illustrator with the Life Publishing Co. in New York; his work appeared in *Life* and *Judge* magazines. A brief stint with Vitagraph followed, and by 1919 he was writing scenarios and gags for Fox Sunshine Comedies.[22] Assistant direction and, it was claimed, some full direction followed at Famous Player-Lasky, Fox Sunshine, and Chester Productions before moving to the Sennett lot.[23] There he served as an assistant director before a promotion to full director in 1922, with only a handful of credits to his name, such as *Step Forward* and *Home Made Movies* (both 1922). Perhaps it was that cartoonist experience that tipped the decision-making scale to assign Meins to the "Buster Brown" series, but in any case Meins handled the series, and the kids and dog within it, in a creditable fashion. Exhibitors were pleased with the results, as one Chicago-based theatre owner gushed in a letter to Universal:

> They are in my estimation a real comedy chuck full of funny situations and are real money-makers according to my receipts on the days I run them. At least twenty adults wanted to know when we were going to run another Buster Brown, showing that they appeal not only to the children but have 100 per cent appeal.[24]

Towards year's end, Carl Laemmle declared the weeks of December 13-26 to be the 3rd Annual Universal Joy Week, stating that "the vast resources of Universal City have been placed at the exhibitors' disposal to enable them to offer their patrons the best short subjects available." The "Buster Brown Comedies" were touted as part of this, and exhibitors were encouraged to take advantage of the "more than ten" Buster Brown product tie-ins already in place. These included Kellogg's Corn Flakes, Carnation Milk, and the various commodities marketed under the Buster Brown trademark, such as Buster Brown shoes, socks, scooters, bicycles, tricycles, cartoon books, overalls, clothing, toys, food, and so forth.[25] The series, needless to say, was helping to put more money into Outcault's already bulging pockets.

"Universal Joy Week" promoted on the cover of *Universal Weekly*, December 12, 1925.

And as if Joy Week wasn't enough, Universal also took part in National Laugh Month, joining other producing and distributing companies in providing one- and two-reel comedies for release in January. Of Universal's total thirty-six reels, Century contributed four two-reel shorts, along with two Gumps Comedies, four Bluebird Comedies, five Mustang Westerns (any laughs there?), and an adventure serial.[26] Within a month of the original announcement, however, Century shifted gears and offered the eight Buster Brown comedies then completed to any exhibitor who wished to book them during the month. Additionally, Century offered any and all of their comedies currently at the exchanges for preview, included all of those not officially scheduled for release through the end of April.[27] National Laugh Month might as well have been called National Flood the Market with Century Comedies Month.

With the stunning and almost immediate success of the "Buster Brown" series, the Sterns' hopes—and perhaps prayers—were realized. Said Julius:

When we launched the Buster Brown comedies last Fall, we knew we had something that should be a hit. We had never made comedies of this type before. It was a gamble for us. However, from the start, the Buster Brown comedies took hold. They became very popular and were so much in demand that we realized we had a gold mine in this series. The Buster Brown comedies cost much more than any comedies we had made up to that time, and when we realized what a greater success they were proving than any of our past product, we decided then and there to change our entire production policy and make only high-class series of comedies.[28]

And with that realization and decision to make only "high-class" comedies, that meant capitalizing on the success of the series: if one series, and a comic strip series at that, was such a success, why not make the switch from star-based series to comic-based series with stars? And, as it would turn out in subsequent years, it was the series that really mattered, the stars within them in many cases expendable. So at the beginning of 1926 the Sterns now had big plans for the upcoming 1926-1927 season.

The first big change was a corporate reinvention of sorts. If there was still any whiff of Henry Lehrman and his L-Ko studio left lingering with its offspring Century, it would soon evaporate with the coming season, as the Century name would be jettisoned in favor of the new name: Stern Brothers Comedies. This change, it was reported, "is a great forward step on the part of the two Sterns and marks their complete advent into the top ranks of comedy producers."[29] The new production company was incorporated as the Stern Film Corporation.[30] All new comedies produced from the time of the announcement in January would be made under the new brand name, and by the end of February the new brand name would begin to appear, intermingled with the Century name in the weekly releases. Reviewers were slower to acknowledge the change, stubbornly clinging to the Century name for the better part of the remaining season.

The second change included plans for "at least five…first-class" comedy series. Their collective budgets, earlier estimated at $500,000, would in time be jacked up by fifty percent to $750,000. The first new series to be announced was "The Adventures of Jane" series of thirteen releases, with Wanda Wiley to star in stories written by Roy Evans.[31] The series name would be changed to "What Happened to Jane?" shortly thereafter.

The next announced was the "The Newlyweds and Their Baby" series, based on the cartoon series by George McManus, with whom a contract was signed early in the year. Thirteen of these were planned as well.[32] "In order to obtain the screen rights for the

McManus comic characters," wrote *Exhibitors Herald*, "they had to pay an exceptionally high price but they say that this is well justified by the excellent quality of the series they plan to turn out." Recently signed comedian Sid Saylor was announced to assume the role of "Mr. Newlywed," while Ethlyne Clair, a discovery of Abe's, would play the part of "Mrs. Newlywed."[33] A week later plans were shuffled a bit, with the announcement that Saylor would be placed elsewhere, and that the role of "Mr. Newlywed" would now go to Jed Dooley, brother of popular comedian Billy Dooley of Christie Comedies. Gus Meins would juggle directorial chores for this series as well as the Buster Browns, but the start of the series was delayed while a search was on for a kid to play the part of "Baby Snookums," and intended star Dooley recovered from an attack of influenza. The first three films were completed and in New York by the start of June.

Full-page ad for the Stern Brothers' "Let George Do It" series, from the June 4, 1927 issue of *Universal Weekly*.

Another new series in the planning stages was the "Let George Do It" series, based on another of McManus's cartoon strips. Saylor, previously slated to appear in the role of "Mr. Newlywed," was quickly deemed more suitable for McManus's sad sack character George. "George is an amiable easy-going somewhat boastful easy mark," wrote *Moving Picture World*, "who finds himself in places where he gets various irksome jobs wished upon him and somehow manages to muddle through."[34] The first of Saylor's comedies were to be filmed by Scott Pembroke, and would be available later in the spring for exhibitor preview.[35]

Cartoonist George McManus (1884-1954), the creator of these previous two series, was born in San Diego, Missouri, where he would eventually ditch high school to go to work for the local paper, the *St. Louis Republic*. At first nothing more than an errand boy, his talents as a cartoonist were soon noted and led to a comic strip titled *Alma and Oliver*. By the turn of the century McManus had relocated to New York City where he landed a job with Joseph Pulitzer's *New York World*. There he would create *The Newlyweds and Their Baby* strip in 1904, followed by other comic strips of varying success. Among these were *Let George Do It, Nibsy the Newsboy, Panhandle Pete, Spare Ribs and Gravy, Cheerful Charlie*, and a number of others. McManus took the "Newlyweds" characters with him when he was lured over to William Randolph Hearst's *New York American* in 1913. His most popular and enduring strip, however—*Bringing Up Father*— was created there, which followed the home life of embattled Irish-American couple Maggie and Jiggs. The strip would continue on up to McManus's death in 1954, after which it lived on under the pens of other cartoonists.

George McManus

Cartoonist George McManus.

The final of the upcoming season's new series was touted as "The Excuse Maker" series, based on the stories by William Anthony, "one of the best comedy writers in Hollywood." These were described as "stories dealing with the predicaments and escapades of a young lady-killer before and after marriage."[36] Charles King was to play the "lady-killer."

By April 1926 five units were busy at work creating the following season's product. Gus Meins was directing the "The Newlyweds and Their Baby" series, Charles Lamont the "Let George Do It" series, newcomers Sam Newfield and Francis Corby separate entries in the "What Happened to Jane?" series, and Scott Pembroke "The Excuse Maker" series. By May, nearly two-thirds of the following season's films had been completed, and shipped east for exhibitor preview. "Reports from Universal exchanges indicate that exhibitors are welcoming the opportunity to see these comedies with their own eyes before they book," said Beno Rubel, Century's new secretary.[37]

Wanda Wiley in Charles Lamont's *Cupid's Victory*. Courtesy of Heritage Auctions, Ha.com.

A shocker of sorts was announced in April 1926, one that flew in the face of so many of the studio's previous claims: Wanda Wiley's contract with Century had been terminated.[38] No definitive reason for this decision was provided to the press, aside from Louella Parsons's claim that Wiley was leaving "short reel comedies to play in features."[39] Along with the current season's twelve releases, which included *Cupid's Victory* (September 30, 1925), *Yearning for Love* (March 24, 1926), *Painless Pain* (April 21, 1926), *Playing the Swell* (May 19, 1926), and *A Thrilling Romance* (July 14, 1926), Wiley had already completed six of the upcoming season's "What Happened to Jane?" films by the time she was canned. With Wiley's departure, Thelma Daniels, Ethlyne Clair, and Marjorie Marcel would each take turns in the lead as "Jane" in the last of the series' twelve entries before it was shelved.

Larry Richardson is aunt Julia Griffith's choice for a suitor, professing his love for Wanda Wiley in Edward Luddy's *Yearning for Love*. Courtesy of Mark Johnson.

A Thrilling Romance, a print of which survives in the archives of the Library of Congress, was one of the current season's last Wiley vehicles to be released, and it's a pip. Directed by Jess Robbins and written by T. Page Wright, Wiley stars as a writer who just can't seem to get published. Her latest rejection arrives: "I'm returning your manuscripts as they have no thrills, romance or intelligence. Outside of that they are all right." Attempts to toss the pile of manuscripts out her window result in her landlady ejecting her from the rooming house. She meets and falls for a cabbie (Earl McCarthy), and they unwittingly get involved with a jewel thief and his girl, and a wild chase is on. The jeweler, discovering the theft, flags down a motorcycle cop, and they too join the chase. Wiley ends up alone in the cab as it disintegrates around her, its chassis all that remains. The chase terminates at the edge of a huge seaside cliff—the same location that was used numerous times before and after in other thrill comedies—where both Wanda and the cabbie are knocked over the edge. As they plummet to certain death, we cut back to Wanda at her typewriter, finishing up her latest effort; evidently all that preceded was the story she was typing. "Suddenly everything seemed to give way beneath them," she types, "and the two amazingly found themselves falling through the air, down, down, down the side of the cliff. On, on, they fell and fell and fell..." Wiley pauses, searching for a proper ending. The landlady, who has been reading over Wanda's shoulder, offers her two cents worth of opinion. Wanda concludes the sentence: "...until at last, they fell...**in love.**" It's a charming little conclusion, and the ending to a film that once again demonstrates just how good some of the Century comedies could be, and just how good a comedian Wiley had become.

Clean-shaven rival suitor Charles King attempts to spirit Wanda Wiley away from her dozing aunt Julia Griffith in *Yearning for Love*. Courtesy of Robert James Kiss.

Wanda Wiley has writer's block in Jess Robbins's *A Thrilling Romance*.
Courtesy of Library of Congress.

Wanda Wiley and Earl McCarthy, the object of her affections, in *A Thrilling Romance*.
Courtesy of Library of Congress.

Wiley's tenure with Century had come to a seemingly abrupt end, however, and Louella Parsons's claim that Wiley had departed for feature work was either erroneous or wishful thinking on Wiley's part. Instead, Wiley hooked up with the J.R. Bray studios where she made another handful of shorts in their Fistical Culture Comedies series. Those lasted for about a year into 1927, after which she had a near-brush with death when a fire engulfed her home later that same year.

In 1929 Wanda remarried, this time to a fellow named Thomas Saffarons. It would appear that Wanda was a popular girl, as several more marriages were in her future, one to a David Gillespie in New Mexico, and a final one to a Dr. Donald T. Atkinson back in Texas. Her marriage to Atkinson was the one that clicked, ending with his death in 1959; Wanda never had any children by any of these marriages. After a period in the 1930s where she studied under Eva La Gallienne at New York's Fourteenth Street Theatre and had some parts on Broadway, Wanda finally had enough of it; what had once been exciting was by now just a job, and Wiley decided to retire from the business. Wanda spent the better part of her remaining years travelling internationally, but by 1987 Wanda was suffering from Alzheimer's. She passed on a year later on January 2, 1988 in Las Vegas, Nevada. She was buried in Grove Hill Cemetery in Dallas, Texas.

Wanda Wiley hands out business cards for her boss's dental practice in Edward Luddy's *Painless Pain*. Hilliard Karr at far right, and Villie Latimer second from left.
Courtesy of Heritage Auctions, Ha.com.

With production well in hand for the 1926-1927 season, Century temporarily shut down production while the Stern brothers once again embarked on their annual European vacation, Julius at the beginning of July, and Abe a week later.[40] Carl Laemmle headed for Europe around this time as well, but had been taken ill two days out of New York. An operation was put off until arriving at Southampton, where he was rushed by train to London for the emergency appendectomy. Abe and Julius were summoned to London from Prague, where they remained until Laemmle's recovery was well under way.[41] If they thought that this would be the sole interruption of their respective vacations, however, they were dead wrong.

Group photo taken in Carlsbad, 1926. Abe Stern, front row center, and Julius Stern, right.
Courtesy of Rachael Rose-Stern.

The Century studio, which by now extended along Sunset Boulevard from Gower Street to El Centro Avenue, had a frontage of approximately two hundred fifty feet by one hundred fifty feet down the two side streets, and was of frame construction. It sat on property leased to the Sterns by its owner, Marie Blondeau, who still lived in a cottage to the rear of the studio. On August 15, the Snub Pollard Company had been shooting at the otherwise empty studio, but had departed by around 1:00 P.M., leaving only watchman David Frankel on duty. Two hours later around 3:00 P.M. Frankel discovered a fire in the southwest corner of the building, of such intensity that the entire studio, with the exception of a small office, was leveled within an hour. The studio's contents didn't help matters, with heavy explosions caused by the chemicals, films, flares, smoke bombs, canned gunpowder, and blank cartridges stored in the studio arsenal, "For a time the entire central part of Hollywood was endangered," wrote the *Los Angeles Times*, "as the fire was extremely hot and great curling rolls of tar-roofing and burning film were swept on to the roofs of residences by a high wind," One residential cottage was destroyed, and the roofs of the Christie and Chadwick studios caught fire but were extinguished. The loss was estimated at between $400,000 and $500,000 by studio manager Sig Neufeld, who added that it was fully insured.

The Century studios on fire, August 15, 1926.
Courtesy of Marc Wanamaker and Bison Archives.

True to form, six other motion picture studios rushed cameramen to the scene to shoot footage for use in future productions. Actor Cullen Landis, midway through filming Rayart's *The Smoke Eaters*, arrived decked out in his fireman's costume for some action shots.[42]

Arson was initially suspected, since several months earlier three other fires had been started there, the handiwork of an unhinged woman who was, as *Variety* described her, "mentally deranged and suffering from the delusion that her daughter had been ruined in the movies."[43] Or as another paper put it, "her daughter had been wronged in the movie plant," readers left to their own imaginations as to what exactly "wronged" meant.[44] Arson was soon ruled out, but the actual cause was never ascertained. "The fact that we are so far ahead of schedule saved the day for us as regarding negatives," said secretary Rubel.

"When work stopped for the summer, all comedies then in the making were completed and shipped to New York. The fire, therefore, did not set us back even by one day in our current release schedule…. The far-sightedness of the Stern Brothers in keeping their production so far ahead is well evidenced in the present situation."

The Century sound stages engulfed in fire, August 15, 1926.
Courtesy of Marc Wanamaker and Bison Archives.

Julius and Abe were expected to return from Europe to supervise the next steps towards rebuilding or locating a new studio. Rubel added that they had "plenty of time to look over the ground and re-establish things before we have to start work on the last half of our 1926-1927 product.[45]

Given that the studio was unoccupied when the fire broke out; that negatives for all films produced to date were already on the East Coast for processing; that the current release schedule would not be impacted in the least; and that the rambling old studio was fully insured, it wouldn't have been totally surprising if skeptics suspected a more home-grown effort—an insurance job, if you will. If those suspicions ever existed, however, there wasn't a peep of it in the press.

The day after the fire, Sig Neufeld sent a telegram to the Sterns, then currently staying at the Claridge Hotel in Paris:

Prop carpenter shop wardrobe all stages completely destroyed by fire.

Fortunately cameras front offices vault & all records saved not even touched. Nobody knows how fire started watchman made rounds half hours before and everything was okay. I left studio half hour before fire started. Generator okay. Wired Rubel Come here immediately. Behrendt man here will keep you posted please don't worry will do best I possibly can. Fire happened three o-clock Sunday afternoon = SIG =[46]

And if it is to be believed, Abe supposedly sent a terse telegram back to Neufeld. It read:

"Fire the watchman."[47]

The home of the new Stern Brothers Studios, 6040-6048 Sunset Boulevard.
Abe Stern in center of doorway, and Max Alexander with bow tie at left of doorway.
Courtesy of Marc Wanamaker and Bison Archives.

Chapter 14: Like a Phoenix Rising….
(The 1926-1927 Season)

If the Sterns were expected to return from Europe to oversee the rehabilitation of their studio, those expectations were not met. The brothers assigned the task to Beno Rubel, who had rushed out to the coast to supervise, assisted by Sig Neufeld. Technical manager Max Alexander was instructed to help as well, if only to give the eighteen-year old youth something to do. They didn't fool around, and in less than a month, according to *Universal Weekly*, had "acquired a new studio property, constructed sets, purchased new equipment, costumes and other properties, engaged new production forces and…launched into what is termed the greatest picture-making drive of its career." The new studio was located at 6040-6048 Sunset Boulevard between the corners of Beachwood Drive—number 6048—and Gordon Street—number 6040—two blocks from the wreckage of their old studio.[1] The studio had three large stages, a large water tank, and was said to have been equipped with "every modern appurtenance for the making of pictures." Rubel had up-to-date offices and dressing rooms built as well.

The burnt remains of the Sterns' old studio were cleared, and became the future location of the Sunset-Gower Field baseball stadium.

The new Stern Brothers Studio building, according to historian Marc Wanamaker, was actually two identical two-story buildings, constructed side by side, with common studio space in the rear for use by both office buildings. Built by producer Louis Burston and his star and co-producer Francis Ford, the new studio had been officially inaugurated at a grand opening ceremony back on May 31, 1919; Julius and Abe were among the attendees.[2] The Hank Mann Company had leased space at 6040 Sunset in 1920, followed by Webster

Cullison's Clever Comedies in 1921. By 1922 another portion of the studio was being leased to Sanford Productions at 6046-6048 Sunset where their five-reel Pete Morrison Westerns were being filmed by director Marcel Perez,[3] as well as Perez's own starring series of Tweedy comedies.[4] Choice Productions had space there as well at 6044 Sunset in 1922. The studio was sold by Ford shortly thereafter in August 1923 to film distributor Morris R. Schlank, but current tenants were able to remain. By 1924, 6040 Sunset was the home of a Gavaert Film raw stock distributor.

Max Alexander flanked by Doreen Turner and Arthur Trimble in the new studio's doorway. This doorway would be redressed and serve as the entrance to the dental parlor in the final entry in the "Buster Brown" series, 1929's *Stop Barking*.
Courtesy of Marc Wanamaker and Bison Archives.

After three months abroad, the Sterns returned to America in mid-October,[5] and with their new ownership of the building would continue to lease space to other production companies in the years that followed.

The Sterns' decision to switch to clearly defined series was for the most part a success. There were thirteen new Gus Meins-directed Buster Brown comedies released during the course of the season, Universal acknowledging their newfound popularity by now tagging them as Universal-Jewel Comedies. These were released on the first Monday of each month, independent of the Stern Brothers Comedies which continued to occupy the weekly Wednesday slot. These Universal-Jewels would up the Sterns' output to sixty-five films for the current season, and the Sterns were so excited about the upcoming season's output that they had the National Screen Service create five trailers for promotional purposes, one for each of the new series.[6]

Ingenue Ruby McCoy adds some cheesecake to the new studio's front walk.
Courtesy of Mark Johnson.

Exhibitors were enthusiastic about the direction the Stern Brothers Comedies were taking, so much so that within a month contract business had doubled since September 1. The jump, according to secretary Beno Rubel, was "unprecedented in the history of the Stern organization and [showed] the present high status of short product," reported *Exhibitors Herald*. Rubel was quoted as saying:

> We felt the reaction immediately after release date. In many localities, the big first run houses or big circuits spot booked one or more of these comedies, for showing in early September. The extent to which these houses and circuits have come back after playing the spot-booked

comedies, in order to sign up the entire series, or the entire Stern Brothers product, has been remarkable. The exceptional and sudden popularity of the Buster Brown Comedies last year has been surpassed by The Newlyweds and Their Baby series.[7]

The "Let George Do It" series with Sid Saylor had thirteen entries, Francis Corby directing the bulk of these. "The Excuse Maker" series had thirteen releases as well, directing honors shared between Corby and newcomers Scott Pembroke and Sam Newfield, while the Gus Meins-directed "The Newlyweds and Their Baby" led the pack with fourteen releases. "What Happened to Jane" had the aforementioned twelve releases, various entries helmed one time or another by every one of the studio's directors who had been pressed into service, after which it was scrapped from the following season's schedule.

The season's Buster Brown comedies included *Buster, Watch Tige* (October 4, 1926), *Buster's Narrow Escape* (November 1, 1926), *Buster's Sleigh Ride* (February 7, 1927), *Look Out—Buster!* (April 4, 1927), and *Buster's Initiation* (July 4, 1927), among others. *Look Out—Buster!* begins with a cute little dream sequence, Buster and Tige sitting at a butler-attended dining table, Tige decked out in suit and tie. After feasting on turkey, Tige assists as a weary Buster attempts to open a bottle of champagne, resulting in a face full of sprayed bubbly. He awakens to find Tige squirting a water hose in his face. This is followed by the kids learning that all dogs are to be quarantined due to the hot weather. They hastily dress Tige as a baby just before the animal control officer visits. Detected, the trio escapes and hides in some barrels, which leads to a second reel wherein they find themselves hauled to a crooks' cave-based hideout, and their efforts to escape. It is Tige who effects their escape, having dispatched the bad guys, one by one, by dropping boulders onto their heads. Tige, not unexpectedly, provides most of the film's cute bits: the lengthy sequence of Tige growing drowsy, yawning, and finally falling asleep after the dream's big meal; Tige's reactions, in close-up, to the animal control officer's arrival and search; Tige's cautious approaches and retreats from the cave's entrance where the trio of club-wielding crooks await him; and Tige's eyes rolling about after being conked on the head by a boulder. Tige also performs some impressive climbs and leaps as well in and around the cave, a rather impressive set either constructed for this production, or more likely borrowed from an earlier one.

Buster's Initiation survives as well, and as typical with the series has a number of cute little set pieces. Buster is late awakening for school, and matters aren't helped when the wheel falls off his Tige-powered car. Passenger Mary Jane shows just how fickle she is, leaving Buster in the lurch when she accepts a ride in a chubby rival's car. Finally arriving late to school, Buster sneaks to his desk with Tige's assistance, the latter making a return trip to retrieve Buster's books. Discovered, Buster is exiled to the room's corner, and Tige to the coat closet. Tige proceeds to eat all of the other kids' boxed lunches. Come lunch time Tige's antics become evident, so the chubby rival organizes the other boys outside, and armed with boards they wait for Buster to emerge so that they can give him a sound thrashing. Buster and Mary Jane escape out a side window, and along with Tige take off in Buster's little car. The others pursue them, or at least until Tige jumps out and approaches them menacingly, scaring the kids away. *Film Daily*'s reviewer loved the film:

Arthur Trimble, Pete, Doreen Turner, and a pair of bums in Gus Meins's *Buster's Frame-Up*. Courtesy of Mark Johnson.

Undoubtedly, the youngsters will eat this one up alive, concerned as it is with the never-failing entertainment device of putting a school out of commission. The grown-ups, too, will appreciate the genius of the dog, Tige, who is a trooper par excellence.[8]

One of the film's comedic highlights takes place when the teacher, having already smashed his own pocket watch in a failed attempt to rap Buster's knuckles with a ruler, decides to lead the class in some physical exercises. They all dutifully mimic his actions, but when Tige's fleas get into his clothes and get the best of him, the students follow, mimicking his wild gyrations. Everyone finally collapses into their respective seats, exhausted.[9]

Tige, Buster, and Mary Jane annoy another theater patron in *Buster's Frame-Up*.

"The Newlyweds and Their Baby" was unquestionably the season's biggest success among the newbies. The initial search for a kid to play Snookums was proving fruitless after hundreds of babies of all ages failed to click, so the Sterns made a radio appeal. Scores responded to this appeal, but it was Sunny McKeen, "with no screen experience but with a well defined personality and a cuteness that won the Sterns at once"[10] who caught their eye and was chosen to play the strip's mischievous infant. The identity of McKeen was initially held from the press, Julius only willing to say that his name was Sunny and that "I have found a baby who seems to have been born for a role of this kind. He is 15 months old and his tests and work in the first comedy made me certain that he is a greater find than even Baby Peggy was."[11] That's arguable, for sure, but to each, his own.

George McManus, whose popular comic strip the "Newlyweds" series was based on, was pleased with the on-screen results:

> I certainly have to congratulate the Stern Brothers for the great comedies
> they have turned out from my cartoons. I have seen several of "The Newlyweds
> and Their Baby" pictures and they are everything I hoped for and more. Where
> did they ever find that remarkable baby? I could watch that kid for hours. He
> seems too good to be true. I wonder if he knows that he is acting? He actually

seems to bubble over with the joy of making these comedies. If there ever was a "'find" he is it.[12]

George McManus has Lawrence "Snookums" McKeen under tight control, if only briefly. Courtesy of Robert James Kiss.

Reviewers were just as happy with the series as was McManus, and equally taken with the child playing Snookums. "If the first numbers are indications of what is to follow, it looks like a clean-up for Universal," wrote *Motion Picture News*. "These two-reelers are surely the finest juvenile blue devil chasers that have been put on the market in many moons; the comedies are teeming with action, are capably directed and can boast of an ideal cast."[13] As for Snookums, the reviewer praised the little tyke by stating that "his spontaneous propensity for mischievous pranks is nothing short of amazing.... The kid is irresistibly funny."[14] And that pretty much sums up the typical plotline of a Newlyweds film: Mischievous Snookums causes trouble, but escapes punishment because he is so darn cute.

The Newlyweds' Neighbors (September 1, 1926), the first in the series, sounds typical of the series as a whole: Snookums throws a lot of tin cans over the fence into the neighbor's yard, and the neighbor, thinking Snookums' father to be the culprit, retaliates. Soon the entire neighborhood is in an uproar, the ringleaders promptly arrested and taken to the patrol wagon for a trip to the station. There they find little Snookums sound asleep, and as *Universal Weekly*'s synopsis put it, "He is so cute that the cops haven't the heart to disturb him. They all sit on the curb and wait for him to finish his nap."[15]

Jed Dooley, Lawrence "Snookums" McKeen, and Ethlyne Clair set out to do some gardening in Gus Meins's *The Newlyweds' Neighbors*. Courtesy of Mark Johnson.

"Cute" is in the mind and eye of the beholder, and not everyone finds this monstrous little kid to be cute, but you have to give him his due and admit that he had personality. The character of Snookums was played (or should I say, walked through) by Lawrence "Sunny" McKeen, Jr. (1924-1933), a mere toddler whose on-screen persona is best summed up by that curious stalagmite of hair sticking straight up from the crown of his head. Born in California, McKeen's career in silent comedy consisted solely of these "Newlyweds" comedies for Century, although he did manage to bridge the divide into sound, if only for a very short while. McKeen, or at least his character of Snookums, is an acquired taste, a taste I have yet to acquire. My taste—or lack thereof—is beside the point, however, since the public at large in the late 1920s seemed to have been totally enamored with this child. But enough of McKeen.

Group photo taken during the production of *Snookums' Tooth*. Left-to-right: unknown, Ethlyne Clair, Lawrence McKeen, Jed Dooley, and director Gus Meins.
Courtesy of Mark Johnson.

Appearing approximately once a month, other titles in the Newlyweds series included *Snookums' Tooth* (September 22, 1926), in which Snookums goes missing during a party to celebrate his first tooth; *The Newlyweds Quarantined* (October 6, 1926), where Snookums places glue on his parents' guests' chairs, then saws off the legs and backs (cute, huh?); *The Newlyweds Build* (February 2, 1927), with Snookums' parents, Lovey and Dovey, assembling a pre-fab house, followed by their brat kid who disassembles it almost as quickly; and *Snookums Buggy Ride* (November 3, 1926), which has Snookums hiding from his mother at his father's workplace, creating havoc there, and later lifted skyward in his baby carriage by balloons, taking a nap atop a telegraph pole. That sort of thing.

"No doubt the series will build a large following among the movie fans," wrote reviewer M.T. Andrews:

> ...chiefly because of the presence of that precocious, diapered infant, Snookums. Where have the Stern Brothers found this screen prodigy is a mystery but a mystery worth any price. "Sunny," as he is officially cast, plays

the elfish youngster with Kewpie hair, a pair of prominent teeth and a roguish grin, and known as Snookums, a calamity personified.[16]

Jed Dooley consults with inept construction worker Sid Saylor while Ethlyne Clair teeters on a ladder. From Gus Meins's *The Newlyweds Build*. Courtesy of Mark Johnson.

Ethlyne Clair has lost her clothes somewhere along the line in *The Newlyweds Build*; Snookums and Jed Dooley assist. Courtesy of Robert James Kiss.

The actor chosen to play Snookums' father was a fellow named Jed Dooley (1884-1973). Dooley was no newcomer to show business, having been a staple in vaudeville on the Keith Circuit for the past twenty-two years. In his teens he was a trick bicycle rider for a carnival, a talent he parlayed into a solo bicycle act in vaudeville. By the mid-teens Dooley was partnered with his wife Ethel. A split and divorce led to a teaming with his brother Billy, eight years Jed's junior. "The Dooleys, Bill and Jed, rode out on unicycles, sang a little ditty and scored from the start," wrote *New York Clipper*. "The turn includes almost everything—some singing, talking, rope-spinning, and slap-stick comedy."[17] Within a year the team split and both created solo acts, Jed's described as a "juvenile Will Rogers act.... His opening displays a bit of versatility, and his asides to the house were a welcome relief from the majority of the 'wise cracks' which have been inflicted upon long suffering audiences from across the footlights of late."[18] Said Dooley, modestly, of his act, "After you have seen the other acts, you'll wish that I was still on."[19] Reviewers were quick to comment on the speechless young lady who accompanied Dooley and handed him his props—new wife and former Follies beauty Audree Evans—one describing her as "a mighty good-looking girl looking mighty good in tights."[20]

Snookums and Jed Dooley in an unidentified "Newlyweds" comedy.
Courtesy of the Eileen Bowser FOOF Collection.

Snookums, Ethlyne Clair, and Jed Dooley in another unidentified "Newlyweds" comedy.
Courtesy of Mark Johnson.

Sid Saylor has taken over as Mr. Newlywed, here with Ethlyne Clair, Santa Claus, and
Snookums. From Gus Meins's *Snookums' Merry Christmas*. Courtesy of Mark Johnson.

It's unknown what Jed's reaction was when his younger sibling was hired by Christie in 1925 to star in short comedies, but one article suggests that there might have been some envy, stating that Jed "has never appeared on the screen. If he ever gets an offer, he predicts he will be a second Charlie Chaplin."[21] Dooley now had his chance. Bearing a strong physical resemblance to his younger brother and, for that matter, a passing resemblance to Harry Langdon, Dooley's screen career proved to be very short lived, returning to the stage after appearing in only seven of these films. Sid Saylor, originally announced for the role, now found himself back in it and slated for the remaining six, in *Snookums' Merry Christmas* (December 22, 1926), *Snookums Disappears* (March 2, 1927), and others.

Snookums' mother was played by a titian-haired southern beauty named Ethlyne Clair (1904-1996; born Ethlyne Clair Williamson). Clair was born in Talladega, Alabama, and had gone on to win an Atlanta-based beauty contest. After attending the National Academy of Fine and Applied Arts in Washington, D.C., Clair had gone to New York where she was "discovered," landing small supporting roles in the features *Sandra* (1924), *The Golden Bed*, *Chickie*, and *The Necessary Evil* (all 1925). The latter film's director, George Archainbaud, described her as the "perfect movie type. She has every photographic quality, in abundance."[22] Clair made no bones about her dogged intention to become a movie star:

> I don't cook and I don't sew. That's not my business. I'm going in for the movies, and I'm trying to study the art of the thing to the exclusion of all else. That doesn't mean that I pore over books and that sort of thing. I take exercise just as regularly and religiously as the business man keeps in touch with affairs at his office or factory. I swim and play tennis and ride horseback in order to keep myself fit, my mind alert and my ambition and enthusiasm keen.[23]

Sid Saylor, of course, was busy filming McManus's "Let George Do It" series, so having the Newlyweds films added to his chores kept him rather busy. During the 1926-1927 season he had twenty films in release at different times. Born in Chicago, Syd Saylor (1895-1962; born Leo Sailor, and for some reason credited as "Sid" in the Stern Brothers Comedies) joined an acting troupe when he was fourteen, and at various times was on the stage, in vaudeville and the circus as an acrobat, trick bicycle rider and wire artist.[24] With experience Saylor found that he had a knack for comedy and making people laugh. He eventually headed to Hollywood, landing his first job in film with the Sterns. The first in the series, *George the Winner* (September 8, 1926), has George boasting to Thelma Daniels— here billed as Ouida Hill—his prowess as a race car driver, only to find himself pressed into service when the scheduled driver quits. "[The] acting and personality of Sid Saylor who is a newcomer and an ideal type for the title role, makes the subject thoroughly amusing," wrote *Moving Picture World's* reviewer.[25] Other entries in the series' first season included *George's In Love* (November 24, 1926), *And George Did!* (December 29, 1926), *By George* (January 26, 1927), and *George Leaves Home* (April 27, 1927). "Sid Saylor has a gay, sprightly sense of comedy entirely individualistic," wrote *Film Daily's* reviewer of this latter film, wherein George heads to the big city in search of his girl, and encounters vamps, crooks, and others along the way. "How he finally finds her makes for any number of twittering sequences which are the salt of this young fellow's pictures."[26]

Ethlyne Clair, outdoors girl. Courtesy of Michael G. Ankerich.

Production shot from the set of *Snookums' Merry Christmas*. Left-to-right: Sid Saylor, Charles King, Snookums, director Gus Meins, and Ethlyne Clair. Courtesy of Sam Gill.

Race car driver Sid Saylor is congratulated on his win by Ouida Hill—soon to change her name to Thelma Daniels—in Francis Corby's *George the Winner*. Courtesy of Mark Johnson.

According to Kalton Lahue, it was Julius rather than Abe who had met her in New York at a theatrical event in the Astor Hotel—not that it really makes a difference—and signed her to a $100 a week contract to star. Anyway, true to the strip's characters, Mrs. Newlywed was a beauty, while her husband was rather goofy looking.

And George Did!, which was directed by newcomer Scott Pembroke and survives, is representative of the series. In this one, George has two roles, first as an apartment building's handyman—"furnace man to chamber maid" reads one intertitle—who thinks a tenant is giving him the come-on, only to run afoul of her irate husband. The second job is the elevator operator at a construction site, reassigned to help high up with the red hot rivets. Not only does this lead to the usual height-induced thrills, but a return to ground results in a second encounter with the irate husband, and both end up back atop that half-finished skyscraper. Exhibitors by and large were extremely happy with the results, as evidenced by the comments of E.A. Rhoades of the Grand Theatre in Story City, Iowa: "They laughed themselves sick at this one."[27] There was, of course, the occasional dissenter, as shown in this caustic review from hyper-Puritanical exhibitor Philip Rand of Salmon, Idaho's Rex Theatre:

> The director of this filthy comedy ought to be roped and tied to the bottom of the city garbage truck and be covered with the day's refuse. Only some such drastic action will ever cure these foul-minded directors of what ails them. I had to cancel Mack Sennett comedies because they were so raw, and I'll have to cancel the Snookum and Georges unless they get a heap cleaner.[28]

Which, if one really thought about it, would soon leave the Rex Theatre without *any* comedy shorts.

Regardless of Philip Rand's opinion of the film, *And George Did!* is one of the better "high-and-dizzy" shorts, boasting a fair amount of edge-of-the-seat thrills. After all of the tricked-up stuff set atop the skyscraper under construction, there are several shots that are obviously *not* faked, those of Saylor riding a rope down many stories between the girders of an actual construction site, shot from above and quite clearly filmed on location. And there's no doubt about it: that's Saylor riding the rope. Thrills aside, Saylor manages plenty of laughs in this one, at one point losing his suspenders and forced to navigate the girders while his overalls keep falling down around his ankles. His lunch sandwich filled with chewing tobacco rather than meat is a highlight, his slow reactions and increasing nausea, which is mirrored by the "woozy" camerawork as well, an extended hoot.

Chauffeur Sid Saylor has had better days, in Francis Corby's *By George.*
Courtesy of Mark Johnson.

There's one obvious visual false note in this film, however, likely a result of the studio's incessant cost-cutting: The construction site's elevator is incongruously set beside a clabbered-sided building, evidently a mock-up built next to one of the Sterns' old wooden buildings and not very convincing as a result. As for the skyscraper set, it appears to be the same one that was used in *Buster's Bust-Up* released earlier that same year, not that anyone would have noticed. Compare the two films, however, and you'll see that the Meins-directed *Buster's Bust-Up* benefits from more creative camera work, usually shot from above and showing more of the buildings and roads far below, enhancing the sense of height and danger; Pembroke's *And George Did!* is mostly shot straight on, lessening the visual impact of the height. The "Let George Do It" series, it should be noted, was very popular and would continue to be a draw for three seasons, up until the studio's doors were shuttered. As *Universal Weekly* so indelicately put it, "Even fat and forty housewives fall for Sid Saylor's engaging smile."[29]

Director Scott Pembroke (1889-1951; born Percy Stanley Pembroke) had a rather interesting background that preceded his move into film. Born in Oakland, California to Samuel J. Pembroke and his wife, Marian Scott Pembroke, Percy soon fell in with a gang of his peers which came to be known as the "Jim Crow" gang. This didn't end up well, when

Pembroke and two of his friends were charged with the robbery and grizzly murder of an employee of a grocery store that took place in 1905, one of a series of crimes the youths were involved in. Pembroke turned on his two friends and gave evidence that resulted in their life sentences in prison.[30] After two hung juries, sixteen year old Pembroke was acquitted during a third trial. The law didn't give up on him, however, charging him in connection with a robbery that took place two years earlier. Found guilty and awaiting sentencing, the seemingly unfazed Pembroke made an unusually brazen and self-confident announcement, as reported in the *San Francisco Call*:

> Percy Pembroke today announced his intention to go on the stage as soon as he has obtained his freedom. He said that there was no necessity of a youth working hard who had had the advertising he had secured during the course of his five trials, and that he intended to utilize his notoriety to the best advantage.
>
> "There are plenty of courts this thing can go through," said Percy in speaking of his chances of appealing his case. "There is even the Supreme Court at Washington. If the bond is not too high—that is, in the neighborhood of $40,000 or $50,000—I can easily have my freedom while I can go on the road with a stock company which I have been planning to organize."[31]

Pembroke's plans would be delayed for awhile, however, when the now seventeen year old was sentenced in March 1907 to ten years in San Quentin.

As it turned out, Pembroke did have some previous stage experience, having acted in actress Olga Nethersole's production of *Sapho* back in 1906. Four years later in 1910, Nethersole came to his aide and successfully applied to Governor Gillett for a pardon for Pembroke,[32] and by 1914 he had received a full pardon. With his release, Pembroke resolved to stay on the straight and narrow, and by 1913 was working as a traveling sales rep for an Oakland-based outlet of the Regal Motor Car Company. There was some theatre work as well with roles at San Francisco's Alcazar Theatre.

Pembroke's first film work was for Essanay at their Niles studio late that same year, remaining with that company up until its close in 1916, with some side jobs for the Liberty Film Company in San Mateo in early 1915. Described as a "strong, manly type," Pembroke found his way over to Kalem in 1916 where he starred in their *The Hazards of Helen* serial. By 1917 he was with Universal, where he described his duties as "racing driver and actor," and avoided being drafted by claiming exemptions of "dependents and crippled hand."[33]

Pembroke would continue to appear in films into the mid-1920s for Universal, Metro, Balboa, and Bison, as well as directing and appearing in shorts for Roach. Pembroke landed with the Sterns when he was cast in their *Adventures of Tarzan* serial in 1921, resulting in lead roles in various Century comedies such as director James Davis's *Tee Time* (January 12, 1921), *Seeing is Believing* (March 30, 1921), and *On with the Show* (April 20, 1921), as well as *A Small Town Derby* for director Al Herman.

Scott Pembroke and his (third) bride, actress Gertrude Short, 1926.

Hal Roach provided Pembroke with additional opportunities to direct, with future assignments as such for F.B.O. and Joe Rock. Stan Laurel was his frequent star for Rock, with titles such as *Monsieur Don't Care* (1924), *Pie-Eyed*, and *Dr. Pyckle and Mr. Pryde* (both 1925) among them. During these years Pembroke would alternately be billed as "Perc," "Percy," and in the earliest years as "Stanley" and "P.S. Pembroke." Pembroke married actress Gertrude Short in 1926, his two previous marriages of 1916 and 1920 merely trial runs. By 1927, Pembroke had adopted his mother's pre-marriage surname, now going by Scott Pembroke.

Lured over to Century, Pembroke's first as director there was the Charles King-

Constance Darling vehicles *Too Many Babies* and *Honeymooning with Ma*, as well as King's *Motor Trouble*. With *And George Did!*, Pembroke was teamed with Saylor, if only briefly, to also direct *George Runs Wild* (February 23, 1927) and *George's Many Loves* (June 15, 1927). He was then reassigned to "The Excuse Maker" series where he directed *Some More Excuses* (March 9, 1927), which one reviewer noted that Pembroke, "consciously or otherwise," plagiarized Harry Langdon's *His Marriage Wow*. Other Pembroke efforts in this series included *Keeping His Word*, *That's No Excuse* (June 8, 1927), and *Please Don't* (August 24, 1927), as well as several entries in the "What Happened to Jane?" series. And with that, Pembroke left Century for Columbia Pictures, where he co-directed the feature *For Ladies Only* (1927) with Henry Lehrman. Pembroke would stick with feature direction into the later 1930s with a mix of dramas, comedies, and Westerns.

Charles King has called in the cops when he and his bride think their house is haunted. From Scott Pembroke's *That's No Excuse*. Harry Martell at left. Courtesy of Mark Johnson.

Pembroke's *Some More Excuses* wasn't the only derivative comedy to come out of the Sterns' studio, by far. Francis Corby's *The Newlyweds' Court Trouble* (October 31, 1928) features an extended, and escalating, street-based crème puff battle that is uncomfortably similar to (and seemingly a blatant rip-off of) Roach's *The Battle of the Century*'s climatic pie fight from ten months earlier; evidently the gag writers weren't feeling overly creative that day. The film does boast one satisfying closing shot, however. Their neighbor, disgruntled over having his not-unreasonable suit against the Newlyweds dismissed, heads out to the street, picks up a couple of rocks, and tosses them one after the other, first striking Mr. Newlywed Jack Egan, and then his wife Derelys Perdue, a distant block away. It's too bad he didn't aim for Snookums, the sole cause of everyone's troubles, which would have been far more satisfying.

Soda fountain clerk Charles King, falling for an heiress portrayed by Phyllis Kaufman, "daughter of A.J. Kaufman, one of the executives of the Lubliner and Trinz-Balaban and Katz Circuits." Or at least according to a publicity blurb. From Francis Corby's *What'll You Have?* Courtesy of Jim Kerkhoff.

"The Excuse Maker" series did not meet with the same success as the "Newlyweds" and "George" series, lasting only the one season before cancellation. The first of these to be released, *Love's Hurdle* (September 29, 1926), co-starred Charles King and Constance Darling in a story about a shoe clerk whose social climbing boasts land him as a jockey in an important horse race. His chances with the girl of his dreams hinge on his winning the race, as if you couldn't have guessed.

Film Daily's reviewer was sufficiently impressed by director Corby's and his unit's handling of this film. "This is the first of 'The Excuse Maker' series and is a wow," he wrote.

They cranked their brains as well as the camera on this one. And it shows. From every angle—direction, situations, gags, tempo, and the snappy comedy work of Charley King. The whole atmosphere is as crisp and breezy as the cross-country hurdle race it features.[34]

Other titles in the series included *Keeping His Word*, *Please Excuse Me* (November 10, 1926), *What'll You Have?* (January 12, 1927), *What's Your Hurry?* (February 9, 1927), and *She's My Cousin* (April 13, 1927), all with Darling opposite King, as well as *Some More Excuses* and *Be My Wife* (March 23, 1927) with Ethlyne Clair assuming the female lead. *That's No Excuse* and *What an Excuse* (July 13, 1927) both substituted Thelma Daniels in the lead.

One would presume that *Please Excuse Me*, which survives, is representative of the series. In this one King plays a broker who is habitually late to the office. Here he attempts to worm his way out of being docked by concocting a fanciful yarn about rescuing the boss's daughter (Darling)—who is also King's girl—from marauding Indians on his way to work. His yarn is shown in flashback, and is the film's highlight. Darling's arrival reveals the phoniness of his excuse, but the boss gives him a second chance: repossess a diamond ring from the feared Mr. Sandow, here played by Bud Jamison. With an assist from the wily Darling, the couple manages to lure Sandow back to the office where King's co-workers take control and retrieve the ring. The boss, impressed with King's resourcefulness, quietly hands King the ring, an apparent wedding engagement offering.

Charles King rescues Constance Darling from a bunch of marauding Indians, in Sam Newfield's *Please Excuse Me*.

Directed by newbie Sam Newfield, this is enjoyable viewing. The Indian confrontation sequence is full of laughs, culminating with King's suspenders doubling as a makeshift slingshot, downing one Indian after another while attempting to hold up his pants. His rickety Ford provides a number of gags that are interspersed throughout the film as well, an intertitle advising "Bring her flowers and she'll not smell your Ford," a line that must have thrilled Henry Ford back in Detroit. One of these has King coming up with a clever method of extricating his Model T from a tight spot by opening the fire hydrant next to it, the gushing water sliding the car out into the street. Jamison, as usual, makes for a satisfyingly imposing heavy, merrily tossing King about his apartment like an oversized rag doll before succumbing to Darling's charms.

Fiancé Tony Hayes takes Wanda Wiley for a ride in Sam Newfield's *Jane's Engagement Party*. Courtesy of Heritage Auctions, Ha.com.

STERN BROTHERS COMEDY
JANE'S HUBBY

"Jane," now portrayed by Thelma Daniels, attempts to shield her eloped hubby
Charles King from her angry father, in Scott Pembroke's *Jane's Hubby*.
Courtesy of Richard M. Roberts.

Wanda Wiley's distracting Eddie Baker in Francis Corby's *Jane's Flirtation*.
Courtesy of Jim Kerkhoff.

The "What Happened to Jane" series, discussed briefly in the previous chapter, was the other series to last only the current season and its twelve entries. The Sterns' increasing lack of interest in this series likely was due to Wanda Wiley's departure from the studio. This resulted in a lack of consistency in the subsequent entries, in no small part a result of the ongoing replacement of the actresses portraying the lead, as well the directors helming the entries. Francis Corby, Jess Robbins, and Charles Lamont each directed two of the series' shorts, while newcomers Scott Pembroke and Sam Newfield each directed three. *Jane's Inheritance* (September 15, 1926) was the first of Wiley's starring vehicles, followed by *Jane's Troubles* (October 20, 1926), "a rough and tumble slap-stick with plenty of knock-abouts and hilarious business" declared *Film Daily*'s reviewer.[35] *Exhibitors Herald*'s reviewer's reaction was not quite as enthusiastic: "It's a pretty rough and tumble thing with the laughs well separated and, in the case of the thinning audience observed, not volcanic."[36]

Other of the Wiley entries included *Jane's Engagement Party* (November 17, 1926), *Jane's Predicament* (December 15, 1926), *Jane's Flirtation* (January 19, 1927), and *Thanks for the Boat Ride* (February 16, 1927), after which the remaining six were divvied up between Ethlyne Clair, Thelma Daniels, and Marjorie Marcel. All of the initial entries were well received by reviewers and public alike, but by the end of the series' run it had run out of steam. A review for the final entry, Scott Pembroke's *Plain Jane* (August 17, 1927) starring Marjorie Marcel, was tepid at best: "The story, the action, incident and acting take pretty much the line of least resistance, without anything unusual in the line of comedy, plot or humor taking place."[37]

Bronx-born Sam Newfield (1899-1964; born Samuel Neufeld) was Sigmund Neufeld's younger brother. Enchanted by the stories that Sigmund sent back to New York, and the money that accompanied them, Sam eventually made the move out to California as well, and joined Sigmund in Los Angeles. Sam changed his last name first to "Newfeld" and later to "Newfield," and in 1919 took whatever job he could find with the Sterns, as a runner, set assistant and occasional actor, the latter in one of the Sterns' Rainbow Comedies, *Off His Trolley*. By 1923 Sam was writing gags and plotlines with Al Herman for films like *Oh Nursie!* (May 2, 1923), *Fare Enough* (June 6, 1923), and *Hold On*. Unlike his older brother, who was drawn to the business side, Sam soon found that he preferred the production side, and had a talent for dealing with actors. This led to his promotion to director and his handling of ten films for the 1926-1927 season, spread across the "Excuse Maker," the "Jane," and the "George" series. Newfield directed another fifteen films the next season, and seventeen films the final season. Regarding Newfield's direction of *Jane's Engagement Party*, reviewer Paul Thompson said that "Sam Newfield saw to it that enough amusing situations were staged to hold the numerous followers of Jane's adventures."[38] Not a glowing review, but one suggesting an acceptably workmanlike job.

Director Sam Newfield, later in life.

Three winning series out of five was enough to convince the Sterns to go for broke, which resulted in their decision to increase the budgets for the following season's sixty-four films. Announced seemingly everywhere—*Universal Weekly, Exhibitors Herald, Motion Picture News,* and *Moving Picture World* among others—the Sterns were now touting a new budget for the 1927-1928 season of $1,500,000, double the previous year's budget which had ended up in the reported neighborhood of $750,000. "The increase will go into better stories, better directors, scenarists, stars, players, technicians, and studio equipment, including settings," claimed Julius. Additionally, another $100,000 was reported spent during their European vacation to purchase costumes, props, novelties, and other material for their upcoming films. Julius proceeded to brag about their purchases, and in exhaustive detail:

In the Persian shops, we purchased an amazing array of gowns for Mrs. Newlywed and our other female leads, as well as the latest in lingerie, silken pajamas and the newest tricky styles and modes. In London we purchased an array of outfits for Mr. Newlywed and our other male leads, running the gamut of sartorial furnishings. In Belgium we purchased many fine lace curtains and other lace, velvet and other hangings. We also bought many carpets in Belgium and a number of Persian rugs in Paris.

Then we went to Nuremburg, the toy centre of Germany, where we bought the latest in novelties and trick toys for use in the Newlyweds and Buster Brown comedies. Among them were many mechanical and electrical toys of unusual make, including mechanical animals, which are amazingly life-like.

In Czecho-Slovakia we bought many pieces of fine statuary, art stuff and antiques, for use in dressing up our sets. We also made many purchases of objets d'art, antiques, and period furniture in Paris. One of the most unusual things we bought was a special suit of medieval armor, which we had made by a famous German armorer, especially for Snookums, the baby in the Newlyweds comedies.

All this material, in addition to that purchased for us in New York and in Los Angeles, will give our productions a class quite unique in the two-reel field.[39]

Next time you view a Stern Brothers Comedy released in 1928 or 1929, see if you can spot any of this described opulence on screen. Bets are you can't.

"We are making five series for the coming year," wrote Julius. "Several of them are repeats on earlier experiments with this type of screen comedy. They proved so popular we dropped from our schedule two well-received series not made from cartoon strips and replaced them with two comic strips."[40] Stern went on to explain the benefits of such a policy for exhibitors:

All of our product for the coming year is based on long-popularized newspaper comic strips. Thus, with one stroke, we have solved the entire comedy pulling power for the exhibitor. We have guaranteed maximum patron interest, and have placed ourselves in the position of offering a product that is as widely known as Ivory Soap, as widely read as any five of the most popular magazine authors and universally popular.[41]

With the jettisoning of "The Excuse Maker" and "What Happened to Jane" series, the Sterns had made the rounds trying to drum up two suitable replacements. The first success in this quest was Abe's acquisition of the screen rights for Pop Momand's popular "Keeping Up with the Joneses" comic strip then appearing in the *New York Telegram* and hundreds of other newspapers throughout the country.[42] Appearing first in 1913, the daily strip featured the social climbing McGinis family—husband and wife Aloysius and Clarice, their daughter Julie, and housekeeper Bella Donna—and their ongoing struggle to keep up with their neighbors, the unseen Joneses. Gus Meins, by now the Sterns' most dependable director with the twin successes of the "Buster Brown" and "Newlyweds" series under his belt, was assigned to direct, and comedy writer Page Wright was to assist Meins with the scripts.[43]

Ads for the Stern Brothers' upcoming "Keeping Up with the Joneses" and "Mike and Ike" series. From the June 4, 1927 issue of *Universal Weekly*.

The second replacement series was announced shortly thereafter in late December, this one based on Rube Goldberg's Popular "Mike and Ike (They Look Alike)" comic strip, introduced in the *San Francisco Bulletin* back in 1907, and now syndicated by the McClure Syndicate. Arrangements had been made several months earlier, but not finalized until recently. The premise of the strip was that Mike and Ike, identical twins of questionable intellect, get into all sorts of predicaments, as *Universal Weekly* put it, "brought about by their resemblance and the laughable errors of mistaken identity." Charles King was assigned a new starring role, this one as Mike, while Charles Dorety was brought back to the studio to play Ike. Francis Corby was slated to direct, and well known comedy story writer and gag man Roland Asher was engaged to adapt the strips to the screen. If promotional pieces are to be believed, Goldberg had this to say about the upcoming series: "After I saw what bully comedies they were putting out from the George McManus strips, 'The Newlyweds and Their Baby' and 'Let George Do It,' I felt that this firm was the one to do justice to my strips. I am looking forward with great anticipation to the outcome. I predict an excellent series."[44] From his lips to God's ears.

Rube Goldberg (1883-1970) is best remembered today for his cartoons of the outrageous inventions of "Professor Lucifer Gorgonzola Butts," which solved the simplest of tasks in the most outrageously inefficient ways. Born in San Francisco, Reuben Garret Lucius Goldberg's earliest cartoons appeared in the *San Francisco Chronicle* and *San Francisco Bulletin*, one of which was the one that the Sterns acquired the rights to—*Mike and Ike (They Look Alike)*. It was with his move to New York to hook up with the *New York Evening Mail* that he created several other comic strips of varying duration. Along with the aforementioned *The Inventions of Professor Lucifer Gorganzola Butts* (which likely inspired Charley Bowers' invention-laden comedies of 1926-27), these included *Boob McNutt, I Never Thought of That*, and *Foolish Questions*, all of which were syndicated throughout the country. By the late 1930s Goldberg had added editorial cartoons to his repertoire as well.

Cartoonist Rube Goldberg.

As initially planned, each of the five series would consist of thirteen shorts, for a total of sixty-five films for the season. It didn't work out that way, however, only the "Mike and Ike" series meeting the projected total. "Let George Do It" led with fifteen entries, while the other three fell one short each, ending with only sixty-four films for the season.

An upcoming Special Christmas Holiday Comedy was announced in November for the following month, one to star little Sunny McKeen. Titled *Snookums' Merry Christmas*, the film had a plot that evoked the Christmas spirit, albeit in an odd fashion. In this one a burglar breaks into the Newlyweds' home and is discovered, fleeing the joint dressed as Santa. Mr. Newlywed, here played by Sid Saylor, dresses as Santa to surprise Snookums, but a cop spots him and mistakes him for the burglar, "with the result that he is badly beaten up by the cop who is chasing the burglar," wrote *Universal Weekly*.[45] How's that for a cheerful Christmas offering? The Sterns later claimed that the film broke all records for simultaneous showings.

Sometime during 1926, Julius—a frequent smoker of fine cigars—was presented with an expensive humidor by the executives at Universal. On its lid was engraved "To Julius, From the Universal Boys, '26." It is unknown what prompted this thoughtful presentation, but my guess would be the stunning success of the "Buster Brown" comedies, and the studio's rebranding and shift in production policy that accompanied it.

For the upcoming Laugh Month of January 1927, the Sterns collaborated with Universal to make all of their two-reelers scheduled for release in January through May of that year—twenty-one of them—available for January booking. The decision, they said altruistically, "means a sacrifice on the part of the producers and distributors, because the same comedies would amass greater rentals by spot bookings over a period of four or five months than they can possibly bring in during January. However, the Sterns and Universal are 100 per cent behind Laugh Month, and are willing to go to great extremes to help the exhibitor in making Laugh Month programs of maximum box-office value."[46] How's that for a magnanimous gesture?

Construction on the Sterns' new digs continued apace, the new year ushering in studio enhancements intended to be able to accommodate simultaneous production by several additional comedy units. These included a large new stage, one hundred thirty five feet long, eighty three feet wide, and thirty nine feet high; ten new dressing rooms; and an eight foot deep, eighteen by sixteen foot swimming pool; a new projection room had already been completed.[47] Tangible evidence, it would seem, of where some of that $1,500,000 budget was being used. By March of 1927 any delay that had been caused by the previous year's fire had been erased, and nearly twenty-five percent of the following 1927-1928 season's product was already completed.[48] Unfortunately, the haste under which the studio expansion was undergoing led to one fatal accident, when a wooden girder broke and a carpenter fell forty feet to his death on the studio floor below.[49]

Carl Laemmle had grown extremely proud and protective of his son, Carl Laemmle, Jr., or at least that was the name his son was now going by. Born on April 28, 1908, his son was originally named Julius Laemmle, the name "Julius" an affectionate nod to Carl's beloved brother-in-law and trusted right-hand-man (and wife Recha's brother), Julius Stern.[50] Young Julius was brought up living and breathing all things Universal, and as he grew into his teens Carl made it a point to include him in articles and, more prominently, photos within the pages of *Universal Weekly*. By mid-1924 he was still referred to as "Julius Laemmle" in the trades, and then, all of a sudden, he was rechristened "Carl Laemmle, Jr." Two years later, shortly after Junior had turned eighteen, it was announced that he was to make his official debut as a producer on his own series of screenplays, "The Collegians." "The young producer will not only take charge of the units making the pictures but will select the casts and the directors," reported *Motion Picture News*.[51] Starring George Lewis, this series of two-reel Universal Junior Jewels—the highest rating which could be given to a Universal short subject—lasted into 1929.

Carl Laemmle and his fourteen year old son, Julius Laemmle, in 1922, before the latter's name was changed to Carl Laemmle, Jr.

According to historian Neal Gabler, "Laemmle himself occasionally complained that he wasn't sure what would happen to Junior," who was described as easygoing and carefree; "Some thought him irresponsible."[52] As a result of Laemmle's emergency appendectomy and near death experience during that summer trip to Europe, coupled with his advancing age, Laemmle bit the bullet and made the decision that would ultimately impact the fate of his company and bring an end to the Laemmle regime. Towards the end of 1926, Carl Laemmle announced that he was going to train his eighteen year old son in all aspects of the motion picture business. "He will work in every department of the studio, learning not only the intricacies of successful film production from the standpoint of the executive, but from the standpoint of the director, the actor, and the technician as well," reported *Universal Weekly*. "According to his father's present plans, he will be attached to one of the units at Universal City as an assistant to the director for the present time, to learn the actual making of pictures on the sets."[53] The message was clear: Laemmle was grooming his son to take over the business, allowing the aging Laemmle to become an elder statesman of sorts and to enjoy the fruits of his many labors.

Carl Laemmle, Jr., age nineteen, flanked by the cast and crew of his "The Collegians" series. Series stars Dorothy Gulliver and George Lewis to either side of him.

According to Stern family lore—and the accuracy of this is up for debate and will never be known for certain—it was Julius Stern whom Carl Laemmle had originally foreseen as the eventual inheritor of the reigns of Universal.[54] Their history together would seem to bear this out, since Stern had been with Laemmle from the very beginning, overseeing production at the Imp studios and eventually all of the East Coast studios up until he "left" Universal to head to the West Coast and L-Ko.

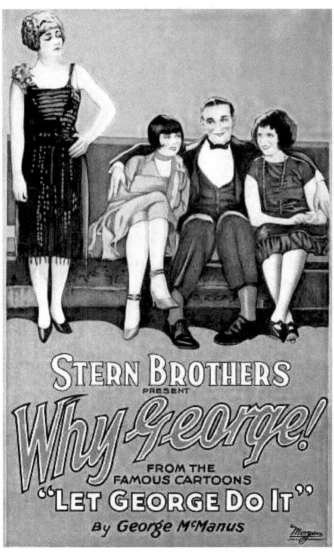

Sid Saylor in Charles Lamont's *Why George!* Bartine Burkett is in the film as well,
but if one of the women pictured on this poster is supposed to be her,
your guess is as good as mine.

Stern, of course, never really left Universal. His ongoing ties through the production of shorts, serials, and the occasional feature helped keep the Universal release schedule full, and with comparatively respectable product. And as we've seen, Laemmle continued to rely on Stern to carry out his wishes for Universal while Laemmle was a continent away on the East Coast. Stern yielded considerable power and, for better or worse, leeway in the decision-making process out at Universal City, with instructions to cut costs, eliminate waste, and make for a leaner, and more profitable Universal. Stern was eventually made one of the company's vice presidents, but it was his zealousness in carrying out what he thought were Laemmle's dictates that eventually ran him afoul of his brother-in-law, a compromising of trust and, perhaps, a humiliation that led to his resignation. The two would continue to collaborate on a strictly-business basis after that, although family ties remained reasonably strong with the two vacationing in Europe annually at the same time, and frequently travelling on the same ship. All that said, though, the deep-seated conviction remained with the Sterns that any long-term plans Laemmle may have had for Stern evaporated with Stern's resignation. In a fit of pique, Laemmle made the decision to anoint his son as heir to the studio at some near-future date, changed his son's name to "Carl Laemmle, Jr." to more closely carry on the family tie in the minds of others, and began intensive grooming of his son for that future position. And, when Carl Jr. turned twenty-one, his birthday present (if you want to call it that) was the turning over of a lot of the keys to the studio for his leadership.

With the ongoing grooming of Carl Jr., Laemmle decided to move into accommodations more suitable to a film mogul of his status. To that end he purchased Casa Grande del Monte, the forty room mansion the late Thomas Ince had built on Benedict Canyon Drive. In February 1927, Laemmle hosted a gala housewarming at his new estate, with daughter Rosabelle and her aunt, Anna Fleckles (Julius and Abe's sister) serving as hostesses. Julius attended, of course, as did Abe and his wife, accompanied by the now seemingly ever-present Max Alexander. The rest of the guest list was a regular Who's Who of Hollywood's notables, but I'll resist naming them here.[55]

With the following season's output well under way and on the eve of the Sterns' annual European vacation, Julius took time out to expound on his approach to the "Buster Brown" comedies, and the Stern Brothers Comedies in general:

> In none of these comedies, or the Buster Browns, will we permit any
> malicious or destructive pranks by the children, even for the sake of a laugh. It
> must all be clean, harmless fun—and this applies to all our comedies. Also, there

must be no offensive or unpleasant characters, and in bringing these cartoon characters to the screen we have avoided repulsive and grotesque make-ups or characters that might resemble the cartoonist's caricatured figures but would be unpleasant to look at.[56]

One could argue that there were plenty of "destructive pranks" in the "Buster Brown" comedies, although usually presented as the unintentional consequences of an otherwise preoccupied kid. One only need look at *Buster's Skyrocket* where Buster and Mary Jane first trash the downstairs of his home in a spirited, if somewhat clumsy, game of indoor golf, after which they proceed to make their tutor's life a living hell. In *Buster's Bust-Up* Buster inadvisably rides his self-pedaled fire engine along the sidewalks of his hometown, bowling over one pedestrian after another, a mailman his first casualty, followed by a fruit vendor, and then an old man with a cane, ending up with a trio of irate pursuers. "Harmless fun," as Julius put it, unless you were on the receiving end.

Jed Dooley struggles with a donkey, with a back-end assist by Ethlyne Clair,
in Gus Meins's *Snookums' Playmates*; Earl McCarthy and Constance Darling try to help.
Courtesy of Mark Johnson.

And then there was Tige. Tige—or should I say Pete—was the big draw in these comedies, since nominal star Trimble had the personality of someone with a noticeable *lack* of personality. Tige had it in spades, however; his impressive and frequently surprising antics always crowd pleasers. Alas, Tige could not always escape the soft-pedaled violence that would occasionally take place in these films, such as the aforementioned incident in *Buster's Skyrocket* when Buster's golf swing connected with the poor dog, sending him sailing through the air for a block or two in a cleverly executed shot. *Buster's Initiation* features another trick shot along these same lines. In this one Buster's toy car is powered by Tige's four feet, the dog lured by a dangling string of sausages. The car breaks loose and rolls down a steep hill, Tige's feet now smoking from the friction. It comes to an abrupt stop when it hits a curb, ejecting Tige high through the air, but all is well: Tige lands on his feet a distance away. In *Look Out—Buster!* a falling boulder lands on the dog's head, followed by a close-up of Tige's dazed face, his eyes rolling in circles within their sockets. This is, of course, typical silent comedy slapstick stuff which no one took seriously or ever felt that any real physical harm came to the characters within, but it did leave Julius's pledge sounding rather silly and self-serving.

The Sterns' trip to Europe may have been put on the fast track when they learned that their older sister, Frieda Alexander, was ill. Two months earlier in April 1927, Max Alexander—Frieda's son—had headed to her home in Fulda, Germany when he first learned that she was terminally ill. Julius set sail in mid-June and was at Frieda's bedside when she died. Abe followed several weeks later, sailing on the S.S. *Aquitania*, arriving in time to attend her funeral. Julius and Abe's older brother Herman, who had by now become sales manager for Stern Brothers Comedies, accompanied Abe.[57] The studio remained on vacation hiatus during this period, production resuming in mid-August.

As the upcoming season approached, exhibitors were at odds regarding the quality of Universal's various comedy offerings, and didn't mince with words. Among the positive comments were those from an exhibitor in West Virginia who cited perceived improvement, stating that "Universal comedies are running better this year than last." An exhibitor in Idaho agreed, and in a more detailed fashion: "Good. Universal is making them better and cleaner, too. Had to cancel Pathe comedies as they were too tough. Universal's Pee Wee Holmes Western comedies, the Gumps, Edna Warran and most of the Stern Brothers are good. Also Buster Browns. Try a few and see." Others disagreed, however. An Alabama-based exhibitor put it bluntly: "These Universal comedies are pitiful. That's putting it mildly." Another West Virginian had similar feelings, warning "Brother exhibitors, before you contract for next year's comedies with Universal, make sure they're better than last year's or you're licked. They were naturally terrible."[58] As they say, you can't please everyone. The Stern Brothers Comedies continued to sell, however, so evidently they were doing something right and getting it up there on the screen.

By the end of 1927, the studio's personnel included the following: Julius and Abe were President and Vice President, respectively; Max Alexander was now Studio Manager; Sigmund Neufeld was Production Manager and Scenario Editor; Bert Sternbach was Casting Director, Location Chief, and Purchasing Agent; Henry Bate, Publicity Director; Al Martin, Title Writer; Dave Rothchild, Film Editor; Charles Gould, Technical Director and Chief Electrician; Eve Harman, Paymaster; and Dave Frankel was Chief of Props. The studio's Scenarists were listed as William Weber, Page Wright, and Roland Asher; and the Cameramen as Henry Forbes, Edgar Lyons, and Victor Scheurich.[59]

Snookums, Jack Bartlett, and Addie McPhail hit the beach in Gus Meins's
The Newlyweds' Servant. Courtesy of Richard M. Roberts.

Chapter 15: The Ascendancy of Snookums (The 1927-1928 Season)

The newly shuffled Universal release schedule for the 1927-1928 season made it clear that "The Newlyweds and Their Baby" series was now the "big dog" in the Sterns' kennel, having supplanted the Buster Brown Comedies as the Universal Junior Jewel offering released on the first Monday of each new month. Additional resources had been funneled into the production of the series, and with that promotion, Trimble and company were now back on the Sterns' weekly Wednesday schedule. Gus Meins would direct the first eight Newlyweds episodes, Francis Corby taking over once Meins was reassigned to the "Keeping Up with the Joneses" series. Along with Sam Newfield, this trio represented the Sterns' new, leaner directorial staff, responsible for sixty-one of the season's sixty-four films. Gag writer Roland Asher was given the opportunity to direct the remaining three, but it would appear that he was either inadequate for, or unhappy with, the job since they would prove to be the sole directing credits of his career.

"There seems to be a definite let-up in the extent to which the better class houses have been going in for prologues and presentation acts," said the studio's sales manager Herman Stern. "This has resulted in a corresponding opening of the market for short subjects, with good two-reel comedies getting the break."[1] A void that the Stern Brothers were hoping to fill, with "The Newlyweds and Their Baby" leading the charge.

Saylor continued in the lead as Mr. Newlywed, described with perhaps a bit of exaggeration by one writer as "almost an exact likeness of Mr. Newlywed of the celebrated George McManus cartoons." Saylor's entries included *The Newlyweds' Troubles* (September 5, 1927) and *The Newlyweds' Surprise* (October 3, 1927). Saylor, still heading the "Let

George Do It" series as well, was spread too thin and scheduling was proving a challenge, so the search went out for a new lead.

And, for that matter, a new Mrs. Newlywed as well, since Ethlyne Clair had defected from the Sterns to star in features for Universal, F.B.O., and the Warners. That defection ultimately didn't amount to much, since her voice was deemed unsatisfactory for sound films and she retired from the business. Years later when asked to name her favorite film, Clair responded "I didn't like any of them…. I hated them. You see, I wanted to do big things and become a big star….I thought I was above all that. I just wanted to be a beautiful vamp."[2]

Little McKeen as Snookums was the real, breakout star of the series, the actor and actress playing his parents deemed of less importance and replaceable, so it wasn't long before new faces appeared in those roles. First hired were Jack Bartlett and Addie McPhail, who appeared in a half dozen of the season's shorts, including *The Newlyweds' Christmas Party* (December 5, 1927), *The Newlyweds' Servant* (February 6, 1928), and *The Newlyweds' Happy Day* (June 4, 1928).

The Newlyweds' Christmas Party survives, and while there's little of real note about this film (aside from the Christmas season tie-in), it does warrant comment. After an extended opening where Snookums manages to lose his diapers, climb into a fish bowl, and torture the fish therein, we learn that it is Christmas Eve. At bedtime, Bartlett and McPhail admonish Snookums for being selfish after he bores them both to tears with an endless recital of all the things he wants Santa to bring him. Taking their comments to infant-sized heart, Snookums sneaks out and heads to the toy store where he invites all sorts of street kids back to the house for Christmas. They all follow him home and enter the house, much to his parents' surprise. A Santa impersonator clumsily arrives down the chimney, and proceeds to hand out a bunch of un-PC gifts for Snookums to pass on to the kids. Things like a small ironing board for the Chinese kid, a chicken for the black kid, that sort of thing. And then the unfunny topper, when Snookums presents his parents with Snookums-sized gifts: a tiny pipe for dad, and a tiny china set for mom. His parents (and the viewing audience, I'm sure it was hoped) are charmed. Julius Stern, of course, gave the film his usual promotional hype: "Our Christmas comedy last year was said to be the best thing on the Christmas market. We set out to make sure of a similar reputation for this year, because we know that our exhibitor patrons appreciate getting special pictures at the right time. The new picture is without a doubt the finest thing we ever turned out at our studio."[3] The "finest thing" overstates the case just a wee bit, but in the spirit of Christmas I'll let him slide here.

Little is known about Bartlett aside from the fact that after appearing as Mr. Newlywed in six films, he disappeared as quickly as he had appeared. Addie McPhail (1905-2003; born Addie Oakley Dukes) was hired by the Sterns to appear in the new "Keeping Up with the Joneses" series, but was tagged to add her good looks to this series as well. "Addie, who is rather tall for pictures, features the shortest bathing suit in Hollywood in this picture," commented one writer about her appearance in *The Newlyweds' Servant*. McPhail's only known pre-Sterns experience was in 1925, as one of the lovelies gracing Chicago's Capitol Theatre stage in the pre-film overture "American Fantasy," described as "Depicting Woman's crowning glory from the Garden of Eden to the 1925 flapper." Not much glory for McPhail here, though, stuck in the second part's "Forum of the Pageant of Beauty" along with forty-two other young ladies.[4] McPhail would star in both Stern series through the 1928 season, after which she moved on to star in shorts for the Weiss Brothers, Sennett, and Jack White and Educational well into the 1930s, marrying comedian Roscoe Arbuckle along the way.

Snookums and Addie McPhail in an unidentified "Newlyweds" comedy.
Courtesy of Robert James Kiss.

Jack Egan and Derelys Perdue would assume the roles of Mr. and Mrs. Newlywed for the 1928-1929 season, but two of their earliest filmed episodes—*The Newlyweds' Advice* (January 2, 1928) and *The Newlyweds' False Alarm* (July 2, 1928)—found their way intermingled into the current season's schedule. Neither of these later pairings ever warranted mention in the numerous reviews of these films, with only McKeen as Snookums the writers' continual focus. At least Saylor, in his short stint as Mr. Newlywed, managed to garner any sort of attention, as in *Film Daily*'s review of *Stop Snookums* (June 1, 1927): "Sid Saylor, as Mr. Newlywed left at home to do the domestic act, is an excellent foil for the little child actor, who is developing real talent, apart from his cuteness."[5] A shame, it would seem, that Saylor was tied up with the other series and unable to lend his talents to this one for a few more entries.

Jack Egan and Derelys Perdue are now saddled with this little monster, in another unidentified "Newlyweds" comedy. Courtesy of Robert James Kiss.

It was originally announced that Joe Young would be Perdue's partner in the next teaming. "He is regarded by the Sterns as an ideal choice for Mr. Newlywed. He not only looks the part, being the exact type of the character as made famous in the George McManus newspaper comic strip from which the comedies are adapted, but also is up to the whimsical style of acting the part demands." Or so claimed *Universal Weekly*, which is rather similar to what they wrote about Saylor and the same role. No matter, as Young was instead moved to the "Mike and Ike" series and would continue there for the upcoming 1928-1929 season.[6]

Panic set in at the studio in early January 1928, when little McKeen was rushed by his parents back from a vacation in the California mountains, stricken by what turned out to be pneumonia. "[F]or a week or more his condition was precarious," it was reported. "About the middle of the month, however, the crisis had passed and since that time he has been mending rapidly."[7] After what the Sterns had gone through to locate a kid with his talents, the two of them must have been beside themselves until the fate of their little cash cow was determined.

The "Let George Do It" series returned with its fifteen entries, and remained as popular as ever. Sam Newfield directed the bulk of these, although Gus Meins would step in and take over as needed. The season's episodes included *George Steps Out* (September 28, 1927), *Picking On George* (October 26, 1927), and *Model George* (December 28, 1927)—all directed by Meins—as well as *On Deck* (November 30, 1927), *High Flyin' George* (January 25, 1928), *George's False Alarm* (February 29, 1928), *Sailor George* (May 9, 1928), and *Big Game George* (July 18, 1928)—these latter films all directed by Newfield. "Quite on a par with previous pictures of this unit, which means fair entertainment," wrote *Motion Picture News*[8] of this latter film.

Sid Saylor has gotten hitched to Jane Manners in a rather unconventional location, in Sam Newfield's *High Flyin' George*. Courtesy of Robert James Kiss.

Studio manager Sig Neufeld spoke in early 1928 of the perceived change in the public's attitude toward comedies, a change that demanded "comedies packed with thrills, and danger sequences." No longer was the public "satisfied with straight comedy and ordinary humorous situations," he claimed.

> The stunts which used to cause gasps of horror and breath-taking suspense in the old-time thrillers now are considered excruciatingly funny, when performed by a comedian. The situation may be just as nerve-racking or as dangerous as it ever was, but it now produces paroxysms of laughter where it used to curdle the blood.... There is no question as to the danger our players now are subjected in order to inject the thrill element into comedies.[9]

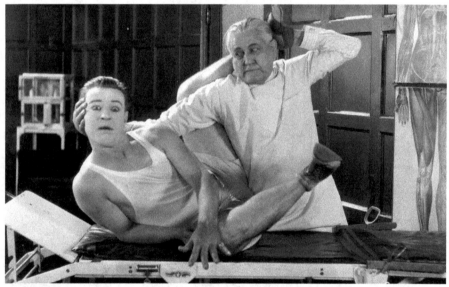

Sid Saylor getting adjusted by Silas Wilcox in an unidentified "Let George Do It" comedy. Courtesy of Mark Johnson.

One could easily argue that this was really nothing new, and only need to point to any number of comedies that preceded it. Regardless, Neufeld went on to describe a near calamity while filming the "Let George Do It" comedy *Big Game George*:

> Sid Saylor, the star, was suspended high over the deck of a departing ocean liner by a derrick. The boat was supposed to go out from under him as he dangled in the air. It so happened that the after flag staff of the ship fouled some of the lines and began to drag Saylor's cable out of position. There was no

stopping the huge boat, and it was only a question of a few seconds before the cable might snap, letting Saylor fall to the deck. He would have been killed or maimed for life in such an event. Luckily, the lines were cleared in the nick of time, just a second or two before the movement of the boat would have thrown its full power against the cable. It was a narrow escape and Saylor thought he was a goner. So did all of us.[10]

Film Daily's reviewer was taken with Saylor's performances: "This lad, Sid Saylor, who stars in the 'Let George Do It' comedies, has a knack of repeating his grimaces and droll expressions in a way that never palls. He takes falls like a circus rider, is ten gags ahead of the top-notch comedy constructionists, and all told is the kind of trouper that short subjects need."[11] *Motion Picture News* concurred, stating that "Sid Saylor is rapidly coming to the front as a purveyor of slapstick and rough and tumble comedy."[12] The series would be renewed for the following season.

Sid Saylor as salesman-turned-cop, ignoring bum Joe Bonner in Sam Newfield's *Rushing Business*. Courtesy of Robert James Kiss.

The "Buster Brown" series remained as popular as ever, even though "demoted" from a Universal Junior Jewel to a Stern Brothers Comedy. The sameness of the series' entries, while probably a plus in the minds of the wee ones in the audience, was beginning to lose some of its charm for at least some of the exhibitors, such as H.S. Boyd and his Community Theatre in Woodbury, Connecticut: "This series gets rather monotonous. Buster is too much of a girl to suit most folks."[13]

Doreen Turner, Arthur Trimble, and Pete in an unidentified "Buster Brown" comedy.
Courtesy of Mark Johnson.

Ten year old Albert Schaefer, a one hundred thirty-eight pound ball of pork, was added to the Buster Brown cast as Buster's rival. Hoping that lightning would strike twice, the Sterns hired Sunny McKeen's little fourteen month-old sister Merry Mae McKeen to appear in the *Buster Minds the Baby* (June 27, 1928). "She is roly-poly and full of capers" wrote one promo piece, but given that she only appeared in one more known entry, *Teacher's Pest* (November 14, 1928), it would appear that Merry's film career was a brief one. Aside from those two minor additions, the series was just more of the same, with Francis Corby directing seven of the twelve entries. His efforts included *Buster, Come On!* (September 14, 1927), *Buster's Home Life* (October 12, 1927), *Run Buster!* (December 14, 1927), and *Buster Steps Out* (February 8, 1928).

"Mike and Ike (They Look Alike)". Well, not really, since the two Charles—King and Dorety—bore only a vague resemblance aside from their slicked-back hair and tiny mustaches, but that's beside the point since audiences probably didn't care. Francis Corby, one of the studio's two most overworked directors, handled ten of the new series' twelve entries, while Roland Asher, the series' story and gag writer, was trusted to film the other two films, and little more after that.

Lawrence "Snookums" McKeen's little sister, Merry Mae McKeen, with Jerry,
Pete's second-rate replacement as Tige. From Sam Newfield's *Teacher's Pest*.
Courtesy of Robert James Kiss.

The Dancing Fools (September 21, 1927) was the first of the "Mike and Ike" shorts to be released, wherein Mike (King) and Ike (Dorety) take their girls—one fat and one lean—to a tough cabaret and take part in a "roughest dance" contest; Mike and his chubby partner are the winners. "This is one of the initial starts in the 'Mike and Ike' series, and if the rest continue of a grade with this, exhibitors may well book the whole series now," wrote *Film Daily*. "Charles King and Charles Dorety are pretty much as two peas in a pod in playing the title roles, and besides, manage to squeeze a lot of deft comics into every situation."[14]

Given that Mike and Ike were on the make in most of the series' entries, the Sterns made sure to cast them with a number of attractive actresses. Among these were Ethlyne Clair, Thelma Daniels, Marjorie Marcel, Dolores May, Charlotte Dawn, Marie Woods, Marny Elwyn, Doris Eaton, and Jean Doree. Doree was signed to a contract based on the strength of her performances in three of the "Let George Do It" army and navy comedies, *The Disordered Orderly* (November 9, 1927), *On Deck*, and *On Furlough* (July 27, 1927);[15] her first "Mike and Ike" was *No Blondes Allowed* (March 21, 1928).

The series' primary director, Francis Corby (1893-1960), was an experienced and respected cameraman long before he turned to direction. A member of the American Society of Cinematographers, early work behind the camera included films for Universal and the Sterns at Century, as well as director Robert Hill's feature *The Brand of Courage*, entries in the Star Comedy series, and others. By later 1922 he had gone to work in Fred Fishback's unit for Jack White's Mermaid Comedies, where he received a real education in short comedy construction. Corby lensed films starring Cliff Bowes, such as *Plus and Minus* and *The Limit* (both 1923), and others starring Lige Conley, which included *Air Pockets* and *Neck and Neck* (both 1924).

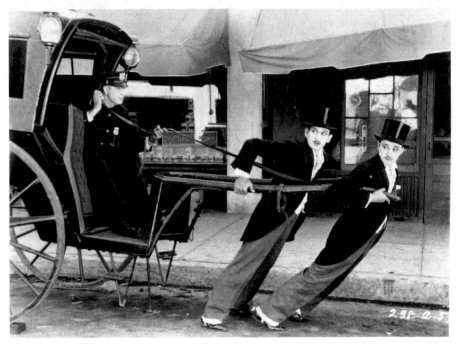

Charles King and Charles Dorety as Mike and Ike, forced into servitude by an unsmiling cop, in an unidentified "Mike and Ike" comedy. Courtesy of Sam Gill.

Hired by Universal in 1925, Corby was given the opportunity to direct several episodes in "The Gumps" series, and was loaned out to Sierra Pictures to shoot the Earle Douglas comedy *Here He Comes*. He then went to work for the Sterns at Century, specifically to direct. He was assigned to the Edna Marian unit, where he was responsible for *The Big City* (February 3, 1926), *Say It With Love* (March 7, 1926), *Movie Madness* (June 2, 1926), and *Wait a Bit* (August 11, 1926), among others. Having adequately demonstrated his capabilities with the Marian unit, Corby was then bounced around to whichever series needed assistance. Some diverse examples include *Jane's Inheritance*, *George the Winner*, *A Second-Hand Excuse* (December 8, 1926), and *Buster, Come On!*. Corby's next ongoing assignment was directing the new "Mike and Ike" series, his contributions including the aforementioned *The Dancing Fools*, *All for Uncle* (October 9, 1927), *There's a Will* (December 21, 1927), and *No Blondes Allowed*.

Cameraman Francis Corby (right) poses with director Fred Fishback in 1924.

An element of raciness was added in some of the entries, such as *Oh! Mabel!* (November 23, 1927), wherein Mike is married rather than single. In these films Mike's extra-marital affairs, either genuine or imagined by his jealous spouse, provide an additional complication to his philandering. The frenetically paced *No Blondes Allowed* is an example of the former, and is a delightful showcase for the teaming of Charles King and Charles Dorety as the cartoon twins. In this one King, as Mike, attempts to get his wife onto a train and off on a vacation so that he and Dorety, as Ike, can make time with the two blondes hidden in Dorety's closed rumble seat. Speeding back to King's house, a motorcycle cop stops them and listens to their flimsy excuse of rushing back to the aid of King's ailing wife and infant. Not quite buying their story, the cop insists on accompanying them. Dorety hastily convinces one of the blondes to pose as the wife, and provides her with a tiny monkey dressed in infant clothes. Independent of this, King convinces the other blonde to pose as well while he manipulates a hand puppet as the supposed infant. The cop is fooled at first, imagining a resemblance of King to the monkey—a subtle and very funny double-exposure—but is soon on to them. And when King's wife returns home unexpectedly—she missed her train—all hell breaks loose, culminating in an extended chase and free-for-all as the twins repeatedly attempt to hide the blondes from both the cop and King's wife.

King and Dorety make for a very amusing and likable team in this funny, very fast-paced outing, which drives home the point that they were both seasoned comedians by this time and thoroughly comfortable in their roles. Mike and Ike, They Really Don't Look Alike, but that's all the better since the viewer can readily tell them apart and recognize, and admire, them for their respective talents. The comedy itself is a good one, with lots of laughs and a climactic free-for-all that doesn't wear out its welcome. One of the funnier parts occurs when each of the blondes is escorted from the rumble seat, in which they've been trapped, to the mansion, moving slowly on wobbly legs and held up solely by one of the twins. The two actresses, one of whom is Jean Doree, more than hold their own while being squashed into closed Murphy Beds, drenched in a shower, and pushed out a window to the lawn below. This delightful film survives in a print held by the Museum of Modern Art.

Charles Dorety (left) and Charles King (in drag) in Francis Corby's *All for Uncle*.
Courtesy of Jim Kerkhoff.

All for Uncle, which also survives, provides another nicely representative example of the series. Ike's fiancé dumps him when she thinks he's a philanderer and a cheapskate, which causes a big problem when Uncle Dudley sends a telegram offering $10,000 if he approves of the fiancé. In a panic over Dudley's imminent arrival, Mike is forced to dress in drag as "Mildred." Dudley falls for "Mildred" and flirts shamelessly with her, much to Mike's discomfort.

Cartoonist Arthur "Pop" Momand.

While filled with a lot of familiar situations and gags, *All for Uncle* is competently handled by Corby as well, and provides plenty of laughs. There's some nice camera work likely added at Corby's insistence, one a backward tracking shot as the duo walks down the sidewalk, reversing course as Mike stops and follows a pretty girl headed the other way. A later scene where Ike holds a little girl upside down and violently shakes her to retrieve the engagement ring she has swallowed, is at once both funny and rather startling, the little girl clearly sobbing at this humiliating treatment. All in all, a pleasant, laugh-filled little comedy. A contemporary review speaks volumes about Corby's film: "Francis Corby, who directed this third one of the 'Mike and Ike' series, [knows] how to get the best of the material and principals he has to work with, and they—the principals, at least—in turn make his job none too distressing, for Charles King and [Charles] Dorety in the roles of the twins, are troupers down to their toes."[16] Well said.

The "Keeping Up with the Joneses" series, based on Pop Momand's popular comic strip, was the other of the season's two new introductions. Harry Long was hired to play the part of the family patriarch, Aloysius P. McGinis, and Stella Adams his wife Clarice. Addie McPhail lent her good looks to the part of their daughter Julie, while heavyweight Gene Layman assumed the role of their black female cook Bella Donna. Given his impressive track record over the past two seasons, director Gus Meins was given carte blanche as far as casts and crew were concerned, and would helm all of the season's twelve entries. Al Martin was assigned to write the comedies' titles.

On the set of *Passing the Joneses*. Director Gus Meins, sitting, with white cap and whitened lips. Stella Adams to the left of him, and Harry Long standing to the right in tophat, Gene Layman in blackface over Long's shoulder. Courtesy of Robert Birchard.

San Diego-born Arthur Ragland "Pop" Momand (1886-1987) spent his childhood and was educated in New York City. Soon after the turn of the century, Momand was hired as a sketch artist for the *New York World* and later the *Evening Telegram*, creating comic strips for both papers. It was in 1913 that he created his most famous comic strip, *Keeping Up with the Joneses*, the title quickly adopted as a commonplace phrase describing an attempt to keep up with the standards and lifestyles of one's neighbors and acquaintances. Momand, who lived in Cedarhurst, a village on New York's Long Island at the time, later claimed that the strip was inspired by his experiences there before he and his wife fled the stifling, upper-class community for Manhattan. *Keeping Up with the Joneses* was soon syndicated, each strip signed solely as "Pop Momand," and would run until 1945 in the *New York World* and several hundred other papers both here and abroad. Momand would eventually retire from cartooning and become a portrait painter, for which he had trained at Paris's Académie Julian. Momand lived to the ripe old age of one hundred and one.

Stella Adams seems concerned by the attention hubby Harry Long is getting in Gus Meins's *Her Only Husband*. Courtesy of Richard M. Roberts.

Keeping in Trim (September 7, 1927) was the first in the series to be released. In this one Mr. and Mrs. McGinis, who exercise daily to a radio fitness show, decide to join an athletic club to keep pace with their neighbors, the Joneses. Reviewer Chester J. Smith had mixed feelings about the results:

> Director Gus Meins surely tried to crowd everything he could think of along slapstick and knockabout comedy lines into this one of the "Keeping Up with the Joneses" series. In fact if he had eliminated a little bit of the rougher knockabout stuff he would probably have had a much better comedy. There is such a thing as overplaying your shots.[17]

Evidently not a fan of slapstick, Smith tended to be dismissive of the various series entries he reviewed, although he was observant enough to admit that the series "more or less accurately portrays the comic strip from which it is moulded and that probably is its main objective." Other reviewers were more charitable. *Film Daily* deemed the series "sufficiently diverting and enlivened by the pranks of Harry Long in the principal role to be worth a booking." For *Passing the Joneses* (October 2, 1927), where the two couples compete in a mountain climbing contest, that same publication declared that "The gag man is up to snuff in this one, the situations and backgrounds are varied, and the principals are 'out front' working every minute of the way, and so a good measure of entertainment results."[18] Other entries in the "Joneses" series included *Society Breaks* (October 5, 1927), *Showing Off* (December 7, 1927), *Indoor Golf* (March 7, 1928), *A Full House* (June 13, 1928), and *McGinis vs. Jones* (August 8, 1928).

Gene Laymon, in the Two Star Comedy *Are Golfers Cuckoo?* (1926).

Harry Long's pre- and post-Stern history is a mystery, but let it suffice to say that he was highly regarded in his handling of the role of Aloysius. Texas-born Stella Adams (1883-1961) came to the Sterns with a wealth of experience under her belt, both on stage and in film. As part of the Oakland Stock Company as early as 1899, Adams would also play in the Cummings and Lee Comedy Co. and the People's Stock Co. during the first decade of the 1900s. Adams's first film role was for Selig in 1909, after which she appeared in several shorts for Éclair before settling in at Universal's Nestor brand in 1912, appearing in numerous films for Al Christie, *His Nobs the Duke* (1915) and *Cupid Trims His Lordship* (1916) representative titles. Following Christie after his departure from Nestor in 1916 to set up his own studio, she'd remain with him into the following year in films such as *Cupid's Uppercut* (1916) and *Those Wedding Bells* (1917) before taking a nine year break from the industry. She made a return in 1926, and was hired a year later by the Sterns for the "Joneses" series.

Former vaudevillian Gene Laymon's (1889-1946) first film appearance was in 1920 as "Sentimental Joe" in J. Stuart Blackton's *Forbidden Valley*. He eventually headed to Germany where he worked for Aden Film, returning to what turned out to be an aborted deal to make twelve two-reel comedies for producer George E. Kann and his Verity Films in 1924.[19] Laymon rebounded by signing in 1925 to co-star with Charles Dorety in another series of twelve two-reel comedies for the Tennek Film Corporation, to be named Two Star Comedies. When Tennek went under, Sava Films, Inc. was formed with Laymon its president to take over Tennek's production contracts.[20] The term "comedies" really isn't appropriate here, since the paltry budgets and sparse, very humorless, scripts sank the series after only two entries actually co-starring the duo, *The Inventors* and *Are Golfers Cuckoo?* (both 1926). Laymon was rescued from this disaster by the Sterns, who for whatever reason promoted and billed him with the last name spelling of "Layman." Laymon's role in the "Joneses" series was fairly prominent, made up in blackface and dressed in drag as the McGinis's hefty maid Bella Donna.

Twelve of the "Keeping Up with the Joneses" series were produced during the season before it too was shelved by the Sterns. For what it's worth, its director and cast remained consistent for the duration, with the exception of McPhail, who was moved over to the "Newlyweds" unit. Harriett Mathews was hired and announced as her replacement,[21] but ended up in the "Mike and Ike" series; Derelys Perdue assumed the role—briefly.

The Stern Brothers Comedies had in the past two years moved into the big leagues. A comparison of the output—sixty-five two-reelers for the 1926-1927 season, and sixty-four two-reelers for the 1927-1928 season—to that of some of their major competitors puts things in perspective. Hal Roach had a total of fifty-five shorts in 1927 and another forty-four in 1928, for release through Pathé and later, M-G-M, while Sennett had thirty-four in 1927 and another thirty in 1928, all released through Pathé. Apples to oranges? Perhaps, but the Sterns' output during this later period was staggering, and the acceptability of the releases therein was, for the most part, of a reasonably high level.

The future should have looked promising.

Group photo taken at a Stern Brothers function. Max Alexander seated left with hand in lap. To the right of him seated: Lawrence McKeen, Jack Egan, Abe Stern, Ned LaSalle with arm resting on chairback, Sig Neufeld, and Sid Saylor. Joe Young at right in front of cop Harry Martell, Julia Griffith on right side of table at left, next to last woman at far back. The fellow at far left seems more interested in the brunette than the photographer. Courtesy of Marc Wanamaker and Bison Archives.

Chapter 16: Decided Make Our Own Comedies (The 1928-1929 Season)

The lead-in to the 1928-1929 season was marked by some conflicting announcements regarding the Sterns' plan for their studio. First of all, the current 1927-1928 season's earlier-announced budget of approximately $1,500,000 was now reduced by roughly a third to $1,000,000 for the upcoming 1928-1929 season, although it was presented to the press that the "Sterns are to increase their production budget materially."[1] Which leaves one wondering: Was that $1,500,000 budget pure puffery, or were they attempting to put a "happy face" on the upcoming reduced budget, with the hope that no one would remember those budget announcements of a year and a half earlier?

Back in early 1928, Julius had issued a vague but reassuring statement to the press: "Although I may have some surprising news concerning our plans for 1928-29 to be announced within a few weeks, I am not prepared to go into details at this time, except to state that the present popular line-up of Stern Brothers comedies probably will be continued."[2] Probably.

By mid-year another article appeared, putting a positive spin on a major policy change. Titled "New Faces Mark Line-Up of Stern Brothers Comedies," the subtitle promised "Larger Casts Including New Comedians Presage Faster and Funnier 1928-29 Product." What this amounted to, however, was the company-wide dumping of all but the most important of their stars, replacing them with new faces. Of the so-called stars, only Arthur Trimble, Sid Saylor, and Sunny McKeen would be spared, the rest of the usual casts for the most part now gone. "With great care, the Sterns have picked an array of principals and supporting players of established comedy experience and with distinct screen personalities," the article went on to say. "This change in casts, coupled with the engagement of new gag-men and other studio experts, combines to assure comedies for the new season on a much higher plane than ever before turned out, Stern asserts."[3] And what would you expect him to say?

Doreen Turner and Arthur Trimble (far right) look on in horror as the sheriff administers a spanking to Albert Schaefer, possibly from Francis Corby's *Buster Steps Out*.

For the "Buster Brown" series, Stern promised "two-reelers…on a scale far greater than ever before, with a large cast of kids, black, white and yellow, in support of the juvenile principals."[4] Trimble would remain as Buster Brown, but Doreen Turner was gone, replaced by Lois Hardwick. Pete was to return as "Tige" as well, but would be replaced in short order with a mutt named Jerry, his substandard and truly bizarre looking fill-in. That "large cast" would include chubby Albert Schaefer, Hannah Washington, Bobby Newman—chubby, but not in Schaefer's league—and a few other nameless kids. For the "Newlyweds" series, McKeen's "Snookums" would have a new pair of parents, Jack Egan and Derelys Perdue having replaced the short-termers Jack Bartlett and Addie McPhail. Sid Saylor's popularity ensured that he would remain as "George," but the series was beefed up with the addition of Harry Martell and Dorothy Coburn. "Mike and Ike" continued with the previous season's replacements, Joe Young and Ned La Salle—they appeared in that season's final six installments—now filling the shoes of Charles King and Charles Dorety, respectively; Harriett Mathews and Betty Welsh were now added to the cast in support.[5] Whether or not this was the "surprising news" alluded to five months earlier is questionable, but no other news of significance was forthcoming. What this shift clearly demonstrated, however, was that with only a few exceptions it was the comic strip that was the star here, and the participants merely afterthoughts.

Significantly, there were now only the four series on the release schedule, the "Keeping Up with the Joneses" series having been discontinued. There were thirteen episodes of each, for a total of fifty-two shorts. The "Newlyweds" series would continue as Universal Junior Jewel releases, but was now included in the weekly Wednesday Stern Brothers slot, appearing every fourth Wednesday.

Francis Corby, Gus Meins, and Sam Newfield were now the studio's sole—and presumed overworked—directors, each responsible for seventeen films, along with a fifty-second film co-directed by Corby and Meins. Never before had so few been responsible for so many films. And I'm guessing that, compensation aside, they weren't happy about it.

Francis Corby was the primary director of "The Newlyweds and Their Baby," handling ten of the episodes. *The Newlyweds' Hard Luck* (September 5, 1928) kicked off the new season, a typically absurd story with the family attending a dinner where father is to demonstrate his invention for making rain. Disastrous results follow when Snookums gains control, soaking everyone. "A merry mix-up of fun is supplied in this newest Stern Brothers Snookums comedy, presenting the talented 'kid' actor Sunny McKeen," wrote reviewer George J. Reddy. "The young comedian aided by his usual good surrounding cast, makes of this release one of the best comedies in this series."⁶ A promising start to the new season, it would seem.

As the new Mr. Newlywed, actor Jack Egan (1904-1982) had early experience on stage as both a singer and actor before turning to film. One notable performance was as the juvenile lead in *The White Peacock* opposite Olga Petrova.⁷ "Jack Egan, looking juvenilish, did straight and warbled a ballad acceptably" wrote *Variety* of a 1924 appearance at the Palace Theatre.⁸ Egan had been recruited from the stage for a prominent role in Frank Tuttle's romantic comedy *Love 'Em and Leave 'Em* (1926), followed by more comedic roles in features such as *The Potters* (1927), *The Big Noise, Mad Hour*, and most recently *Harold Teen* (both 1928).

As the new Mrs. Newlywed, Derelys Perdue (1902-1989) had several prior years experience on stage as dancer, in stock, and in road shows. Arriving in California as one of the Marion Morgan dancers, the tall, pretty brunette had a credit-less start acting and dancing in a trio of Olive Thomas features for Triangle. Another early uncredited role followed in *Man-Woman-Marriage* (1921), after which Perdue received credit for roles in the Warner Bros. serial *A Dangerous Adventure* (1922), and features that included *The*

Bishop of the Ozarks (1923), F.B.O.'s *Daytime Wives* (1923), Chadwick's *Paint and Powder* (1925), and Universal's *Quick Triggers* (1928). Egan and Perdue were paired in series entries that included *The Newlyweds Unwelcome* (October 3, 1928), *The Newlyweds Lose Snookums* (November 28, 1928), *The Newlyweds' Headache* (January 23, 1929), *The Newlyweds in Society* (April 17, 1929), and *The Newlyweds' Angel Child* (July 10, 1929).

Derelys Perdue. Courtesy of Kay Shackleton.

The Newlyweds' Headache, which survives in a print held by the Museum of Modern Art (and currently misidentified as *The Newlyweds' Advice*), is typical of the series. Snookums accompanies his father to the Household Exhibition, and then proceeds to turn one display after another into a shambles. The exhibition ends up a total wreckage while Snookums sits off to one side, chowing down on pilfered cakes, his belly now huge and swollen from all the consumed sweets. An earlier sequence takes place in the hotel in which the Newlywed family resides. Snookums pours ink down a communication tube, spraying the man at the front desk downstairs. He retaliates, but hits Egan instead. This goes back and forth, involving the hotel manager, the Newlyweds' maid, another guest, and so forth, the free-for-all dragging on just a little too long. Egan, Perdue, and Snookums beat a hasty retreat from the apartment building. Uninspired comedy, but it does manage to generate a few mild laughs.

Jack Egan is the surprise here, a round-faced, pint-sized comedian who more than holds his own in the on-screen antics. He's a good replacement in the lead, and refreshing in that he barely tolerates his obnoxious son, teetering on the verge of throttling him in several instances...which many viewers probably would like to have seen! Derelys Perdue, an extremely attractive brunette, repeatedly stands up to and dominates her perpetually frustrated hubby. Sadly she has far too little to contribute, or at least in this episode.

Snookums, Jack Egan, and Derelys Perdue meet Jimmy Durante-look-alike Hugh Saxon in this unidentified "Newlyweds" comedy; Martin Kinney at far left.
Courtesy of Robert James Kiss.

In general, the thirteen "Newlyweds" entries received passable reviews, with the occasional standout balanced by the occasional pan. *Motion Picture News* reviewer Raymond Ganly didn't mince words in his review of the Corby/Meins co-directed *The Newlyweds in Society*:

They've put about everything into this one in an attempt to cull the laughs, but the gags are stale and unbelievably old. They are poor imitations of material from other and better comedies. Lots of repetition, punk humor from everyone in the cast except the kid, "Snookums," and a lot of flips and falls, pie-throwing and other twaddle that gets the comedy nowhere. This Newlywed is an unappealing mixture of ancient celluloid puns. There is little in it to recommend.[9]

Ganly was perceptive enough to point out one of the series' arguable failings, and that was its use of Sunny McKeen. McKeen comes across as a little monster in most of these films, and no matter how "cute" they try to make him at a given film's conclusion, he still comes across as a rather unpleasant and unmanageable brat. "The producers have made of little Sunny just a rough, bouncing boy," wrote Ganly. "His performance would be greatly enhanced if ever so often they would have him come across with a touch of wistfulness or baby tenderness. As it is his talent is not being realized to its proper extent."[10] And not the best of role models for the little tykes out there in the audience.

Derelys Perdue, Snookums, and Jack Egan go for a ride in Francis Corby's *The Newlyweds Need Help*. Courtesy of Richard M. Roberts.

Egan and Perdue would continue on as Mr. and Mrs. Newlywed through the 1928-1929 season, their final teaming in *The Newlyweds' Angel Child*. There was one last entry in the series, this one teaming Joe Young with Molly Malone as Mrs. Newlywed in *The Newlyweds' Pests* (August 7, 1929); Harry Martell and Art Rowlands appeared as salesmen.

Molly Malone, Snookums, and Joe Young upset a typist in Gus Meins's *The Newlyweds' Pests*, the final entry in the series. Courtesy of Robert James Kiss.

The final year of the "Let George Do It" comedies were a mixed bunch, relying heavily on the antics and charm of Sid Saylor to get them over. Harry Martell appeared throughout as his buddy, usually named "Steve," and based on reviews the two made an appealing team. The series' other addition, Dorothy Coburn, usually appeared as one of their girls or as the object of their lust. The biggest complaint about the series seemed to be the lack of material and gags provided to Saylor. "Saylor is a hard worker," wrote reviewer George J. Reddy, "and when given material to work with usually turns out commendable results."[11] Raymond Ganly concurred, commenting about Gus Meins's *The Cross Country Bunion Race* (November 7, 1928) that "Saylor has a lot of ability, but he is not given so very many gags with which to work."[12]

Harry Martell is another one of those actors about whom little is known. Formerly a "heavy" in comedies and more recently as a straight comedian, some of his pre-Stern credits include *A Peaceful Riot* (1925) and *What! No Spinach?* (1926) for Joe Rock; Christie's *Dizzy*

Sights (1927), *Say Uncle,* and *Hold 'Er Cowboy;* and the Weiss Brothers' *Holding His Own* with Ben Turpin, and *Fare Enough* (all 1928) with Poodles Hannaford.

Harry Martell gives runner Sid Saylor some pithy advice, in Gus Meins's *The Cross-Country Bunion Race.*

Dorothy Coburn (1905-1978) had a slightly higher profile due to her multiple appearances in the comedies of Hal Roach from 1926 to 1928, frequently appearing with Stan Laurel and Oliver Hardy. Some of her better known appearances with the popular team included *The Second Hundred Years, Putting Pants on Philip, The Battle of the Century* (all 1927), and *The Finishing Touch* (1928), although usually in minor parts. When she was let go by Roach, the Sterns snatched up the spunky, blue-eyed, black-haired cutie for the "George" series. Coburn showed up in *Rubber Necks* (September 12, 1928), *All for Geraldine* (December 5, 1928), and *Sailor Suits* (January 2, 1929), among others. Reviewers never commented upon either her or Martell, or at least by name, focusing instead primarily on series lead Saylor.

The plots tended to fall along similar lines, but would occasionally delve off into something more interesting. In *The Cross Country Bunion Race,* George and his pal take part in the titular race hoping to raise some funds to pay off damage to some neighbors' homes. *Television George* (February 27, 1929) had a plot built around the then-experimental and crude device, which was presented as an everyday home appliance; a visit to a broadcasting station figured into the story as well. Raymond Ganly again, reviewing this latter film: "This…comedy contains some good fun patterned after the usual 'dumb' comedy style of its star, Sid Saylor, who does effective work.… The number releases a high proportion of merriment. It will go over in neighborhood theatres."[13]

"ALL FOR GERALDINE"
A Stern Brothers Comedy

Dorothy Coburn, Sid Saylor, and Harry Martell in Gus Meins's *All for Geraldine*.
Courtesy of Mark Johnson.

The "Mike and Ike" series had acquired Joe Young and Ned La Salle as leads midway through the previous season, and they would continue with the series up until its conclusion. Chicago-born Joe Young (1900-1980) was the older brother of more famous actor Robert Young. He was recruited by the Sterns from the Sennett lot where he had appeared in numerous comedies, primarily in supporting roles—often uncredited—and frequently hidden by layers of makeup, from the early 1920s. "Joe Young…is not a newcomer to Sennett films," wrote *Moving Picture World* in 1926. "But his face is new to comedy fans, for Joe seldom has been seen as his real self. He is a clever makeup artist, and appears in nearly every Sennett comedy released by Pathé, in the guise of an old sheriff, country postman or other eccentric character."[14] During these years he would also occasionally appear in films for the Weiss Brothers, Robertson-Cole, Rayart, and others as well. Young would appear sans makeup in the Sterns comedies, and would change his name to Roger Moore much later on in his career, likely to distance himself from his earlier career as a comedy actor, and for the Sterns no less.

Sid Saylor in an unidentified "Let George Do It" comedy. Courtesy of Mark Johnson.

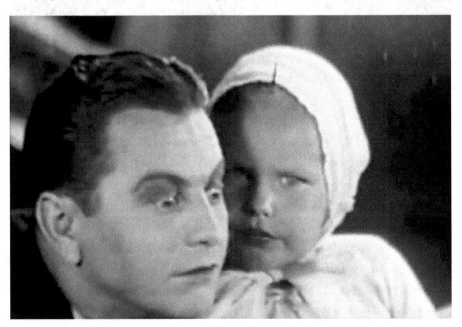

Joe Young, here listening to Lawrence "Sunny Jim" McKeen's attempts to be intelligible, from the early 1929 talkie *Baby Talks*. Courtesy of Ralph Celantano.

As for his co-star Ned La Salle, nothing is known about his past or future aside from a single appearance he made while on break from the "Mike and Ike" series. Titled *Scrapped, a Life Story in Tabloid*, the single-reel film was shot on the streets of Los Angeles for a reported miserly $297. Written and directed by H.A. Woodmansee, and filmed by Joe Darrell, the cast of three included Mignon Rittenhouse and Baby Jimmie Kellar, along with La Salle.[15] It is not known whether it was ever actually released, but if it was it certainly wouldn't have added any luster to La Salle's dead-end career.

Betty Welsh, Harriet Matthews, Ned La Salle, and Joe Young in Gus Meins's *Fish Stories*. Courtesy of Robert James Kiss.

The first of the "Mike and Ike" series to feature the new team was *Women Chasers* (May 16, 1928), with the twins hired by a rich client to retrieve incriminating letters from a vamp blackmailer. "The twins, Mike and Ike, do their stuff in dress clothes as usual, and are considerably funnier than the material they are allowed to work with," wrote one reviewer.[16] Another in their series was *Whose Wife* (June 6, 1928), another of the few to actually have the unnamed stars receive a modicum of praise: "Lively fun, with the twin comedians doing good work."[17] Francis Corby's *Husbands Won't Tell* (August 29, 1928) received some qualified praise as well: "The credit for the humor supplied, rests on the players and the director, whose hard work brighten a thin script."[18] *Fish Stories* (November 21, 1928), *She's a Pippin* (March 13, 1929), *Chaperones* (June 5, 1929), and the series' final release, *Good Skates* (August 28, 1929), were among the other series entries. Curiously, while all of the listings in the trades credited Young and La Salle as the co-stars of *Good Skates*, *Motion Picture News*'s reviewer observed that "one of the twins is a newcomer, by the way."[19] Which begs the question: Did the Sterns substitute yet another unnamed actor in one of the leads? Meins and Newfield split the directorial duties for the most part, with Corby stepping in for a final two.

Corby's run at direction effectively ended with the Sterns, returning to cinematography for both shorts and features throughout the 1930s into the early 1940s. He stepped back behind the megaphone for two final shorts in the early 1940s as well, after which he put active production aside to become a partner in the newly-incorporated Cinema-Craft Productions, to manufacture photographic supplies and motion picture film.

One of the later entries in the "Mike and Ike" series was Sam Newfield's *Hold Your Horses* (January 16, 1929), and demonstrates just how far the series had fallen. Here the twins run into a pair of young ladies at an equestrian shop, and proceed to boast about their respective abilities as horsemen. When push comes to shove, however, their lack of riding ability becomes painfully evident, as demonstrated in one sequence after another where they are kicked through barn walls, repeatedly tossed from their mounts, and end up in a wild ride through picnickers and a camp site's tents. The opening rooming house sequence seems rather incongruous in that it appears to be set in an opulent mansion, an unlikely setting for such a motley group of ill-mannered and slovenly tenants. This so-called comedy is a total yawn, with only one or two tiny laughs buried in it, and most of them cheap and stale laughs at that. As the twins, Young and La Salle have vaguely similar appearances with their tiny, pencil-thin mustaches, slicked back hair, and matching tuxedos, so much so that it's frequently impossible to tell which is which. Since both actors are lacking any sort of charisma—or at least in this viewer's opinion—and deliver barely adequate, humorless performances, it really doesn't matter much. Viewing this teaming makes one realize just how accomplished and likable King and Dorety were in these same roles. For what it's worth, a print survives in the archives of the Museum of Modern Art.

There were some criticisms lobbed at the four series that, it would appear, likely pertained to a lot of the final season's entries. "This line-up of comic films have pretty nearly all given off an appearance of being 'machine made,' and the same old stereotyped gags are used to vamp the giggles in this new one," wrote *Motion Picture News* of *She's a Pippin*.[20] A later review noted that "The use of a new set wouldn't hurt these Stern comedies in the least."[21] An exhibitor out in Oregon was just a bit less diplomatic in his assessment of the current crop of Stern Brothers Comedies: "Stern Brothers said a nose-bag full when they said, 'Our comedies are not to be laughed at!' We second the motion. Most of them are just a waste of time, carbons, electricity, and several dollars!"[22] Not a fan, needless to say.

It was, perhaps, the "Buster Brown" series' final season that fell the furthest in terms of quality. As the new Mary Jane, however, Lois Hardwick (1917-1968) proved to be an adequate replacement. Selected from a reported field of five hundred applicants to fill Doreen Turner's little shoes, Hardwick came to the series with a comparatively impressive resume for a girl of her age. As the fourth actress to portray "Alice" in Walt Disney's half-animated/half-live action "Alice in Cartoonland" series, Hardwick starred in the final ten entries released in 1927. These included *Alice's Circus Daze, Alice's Picnic, Alice's Medicine Show*, and *Alice in the Big League*. Hardwick also had minor—and frequently uncredited—appearances in the features *Seventh Heaven, The Enemy* (both 1927), *The Crowd*, and *Lilac Time* (both 1928). Hardwick's first appearance was late in the 1927-1928 season's *Buster Minds the Baby*.

The "Buster Brown" comedies' new cast of Lois Hardwick, Arthur Trimble, and Jerry the dog in Sam Newfield's *Watch the Birdie*. Courtesy of Drina Mohacsi.

It was the character of Tige who suffered dearly during the final season. Pete was now gone, having jumped ship for better prospects over at the Roach studio, and in his stead appeared another dog named Jerry. Jerry's questionable talents aside, it was the absurd makeup applied to his face that stood out like a sore thumb. Gone was the distinctive dark ring around Pete's right eye, not that it was there in the original comic strip, but that trademark ring had over the past three seasons become the accepted norm. Instead, some moron at the Sterns' studio must have thought it would be cute to instead draw in really dark arched eyebrows with grease paint, leaving the poor mutt with a perpetual look of surprise. The result is laughable (and not in a good way), and very distracting. Perhaps the choice was director Sam Newfield's, who helmed eleven of the final thirteen episodes, but one would hope he had better taste and instincts than that.

Jerry as "Tige," sporting those absurd looking eyebrows. From Sam Newfield's
Buster's Spooks.

Another, more important addition to the series was little Hannah "Oatmeal" Washington (1923-1933). A Stern promotional release described her as "small and dark, a little colored boy discovered by Julius Stern while playing a diminutive role in the plantation scenes in 'Uncle Tom's Cabin'," and then went on to describe "him" as "This little dash of chocolate...."[23] Washington had previous roles in a number of the Bray studios' "McDougall Kids" series 1927-1928 (where she was also misleadingly identified as a "he") in films that included *The Big Pie Raid* (1927) and *Fowl Play* (1928), and with Billy Dooley in *A Gallant Gob* (1928) where she was actually promoted as a girl. Washington appeared as "Hambone Johnson" in several of the "Mickey McGuire" series, and in an uncredited part in Universal's feature *Uncle Tom's Cabin*. The Sterns would credit Washington simply as "Oatmeal."

Hannah "Oatmeal" Washington. Courtesy of Drina Mohacsi.

Knockout Buster (March 6, 1929) survives, and demonstrates the depths to which the series had fallen. The first reel of the Corby-directed "comedy" involves a prize fight between Buster and a chubby kid, played by Albert Schaefer. Mary Jane, as now portrayed by Lois Hardwick, serves as the timekeeper, and little Oatmeal the referee. Buster wins only because Tige, here played by Jerry, sticks him in the rear with a pin, sending him into the air and landing on his opponent, who is knocked silly. Reel two involves a camping trip that Buster's dad plans for Buster, Mary Jane, and Tige, but tells Oatmeal that she cannot join them. "Ah'll be quiet as a rat," pleads Oatmeal, but to no avail. So she hides under a tarp in the trailer and ends up at the camp grounds with the others. Discovered, dad sends her out for firewood, a trek that soon involves her in a pursuit of a chicken, stealing (and losing) an egg, and an eventual feast in a water melon patch. The remainder of the film involves an extended chase by the farm's irate, shotgun-wielding farmer.

What is significant about this particular entry, and one would argue its saving grace, is that the entire second reel consists primarily of the humorous antics of Oatmeal, an adorable and scene-stealing natural. Trimble has been shunted to the sidelines, with only a short and painfully unfunny bit where he's confronted with a folding chair, and later on when both he and Hardwick join Oatmeal in the flight from the farmer, the three of them jockeying for position within their respective hiding places in a trio of haystacks. There's little to recommend this film aside from the antics of Oatmeal. A highlight involves her outrageously distended belly, presumably a result of pigging out on watermelon, instead turning out to just be another watermelon hidden under her shirt. The film survives in part in the archives of the Museum of Modern Art, and in fairness I should mention that most of reel one is missing, and may have shown Trimble and Hardwick in a better light. "Just average fun" and "Will score a few laughs" was about the most enthusiasm that reviewers could muster up for this middling entry.

Hannah "Oatmeal" Washington in *Buster's Spooks*.

As Tige, newcomer Jerry would look cute enough if he didn't have those ridiculous eyebrows. Regardless, he seemingly has little of Pete's talents or training, and what meager abilities he has are on display when he drinks some hard cider. He stumbles about in slow motion—some shots filmed in reverse—in a painfully lame display of canine inebriation. (If you want to see just how an inebriated animal should be handled on film, see Hal Roach's *High Society* (1924) which closes with some very amusing shots of an inebriated parrot!) The two other remaining gags both involve fake legs and paws, operated by an off-screen individual, first holding the safety pin and later eating a chunk of watermelon. Pete's considerable talents are sorely missed! Jerry could, however, rise to the occasion when needed, as in *Tige's Girl Friend* (April 3, 1929), where he was coupled with another dog: "There's not so much of Buster Brown and Mary Jane in this new Stern opus—Tige, a clever dog, and another little canine performer carry the brunt of it. As a result of the dogs' work it is considerably above the usual cut-and-dried funfilms in which Arthur Trimble is so often ineffective."[24] Jerry 1, Trimble 0.

Jerry sporting those fake legs, in Sam Newfield's *Watch the Birdie*.
Courtesy of Library of Congress.

Long gone were the glowing reviews of some of the earlier seasons. While this final crop of Buster Browns would occasionally garner a positive review, as often as not they were lukewarm. These frequently boiled down to comments stating that undiscriminating kids might laugh at some of the juveniles' antics, but adults will be bored to tears. "Adult audiences will probably yawn through the screening of this," wrote George J. Reddy of *Half-Back Buster* (September 19, 1928), "but the antics of Buster, Mary Jane and the little darkey 'Oatmeal' will no doubt take the juveniles over."[25] An Ohio-based exhibitor took it a step further in his opinion of this film: "A rather poor imitation of Roach's Gang comedies. Sterns don't seem to realize that you can't take a bunch of kids and make another Our Gang just like that. Drew some laughs, of course, but lacks the true snap."[26] And Raymond Ganly did not mince words in his review of the Meins-directed *Getting Buster's Goat* (July 24, 1929):

> It's hard to determine whether even a trifle of brain work or acumen for laughs went into the making of this comedy. In comparison with other juvenile comedies it takes a back seat. Certainly the kids are not demanding comedies of poor construction. Even their youthful minds deserve a break and should not be fed with a punk assortment of gags. Lament the fate of this one. It goes pottering around and doesn't make much headway.[27]

Ganly was more charitable in his review of the late "Buster Brown" comedy, *Buster's Spooks* (June 26, 1929), stating that "a good idea is successfully played with in this new Buster Brown comedy." This one, directed by Sam Newfield, fared somewhat better than the previously mentioned *Buster's Knockout*, following the antics of Trimble, Hardwick, Hannah "Oatmeal" Washington, and Jerry, who think they have accidentally drowned a fat kid, played by Albert Schaefer. He's actually okay, and follows them as they take refuge in an empty home, which Schaefer proceeds to "haunt." What follows is a lot of typical "spook house" gags, many of them recycled from earlier films of this type and rather stale by this late period. Still, the kids' and dog's antics provide some amusement, most of the laughs supplied by Tige and Oatmeal. There's a lot of knee-knocking, which leads to Oatmeal's pants continually falling but little else. The biggest laughs, however, are once again courtesy of Tige, proving that, eyebrows aside, he was a marginally acceptable replacement for Pete: peering out through the raised visor of the helmet of the suit of armor in which he is hiding; a mask perched on his rear end, his wagging tail sticking out of its mouth hole as if a long, furry tongue; and chased throughout the house by an animated bolt of lightning.

That bolt also burns a zig-zag "scar" on the top of Oatmeal's head, and she elicits the film's final laugh when, ejected through a window in an attempt to escape, lands head first in a watering can. All mild laughs, admittedly, but better than so many of the tepid titters resulting from a viewing of *Knockout Buster*.

Arthur Trimble, pushing thirteen years of age and outgrowing those sissified duds, as "Buster Brown" in Sam Newfield's *Buster's Spooks*.

I don't wish to give the impression that all of the reviews for the Sterns' final season of comedies were negative, because they weren't. There were many that garnered glowing reviews—as Ganly's comments on *Buster's Spooks* demonstrate—others that were deemed routine, and still others that were dismissed outright, just as had been the case with previous years' output. The difference was the marked increase in the lackluster, bordering on negative, reviews this final season. And even if the reviewers tempered some of their comments in an effort to not bite the hand that, in a roundabout way, fed them, exhibitors felt no such restraint. Exhibitors, after all, had their respective livelihoods to think of, and if a given film failed to perform, and in an especially dismal fashion, they let other exhibitors know about it in *Exhibitors Herald-World*'s "What the Picture Did for Me" column. Here's a sampling of some of their comments, broken down by the four series.

For "The Newlyweds and Their Baby" series, some exhibitor comments included:

The Newlyweds' Holiday: "Snookums is waning fast. These subjects becoming very weak;" and "Average Newlywed comedy, which nobody stayed to see twice."

The Newlyweds Unwelcome: "The public seems to be getting tired of this line of comedies"

The Newlyweds Need Help: "Stern Brothers, you will have to step on it to keep up with the rest."

The Newlyweds' Visit: "Can't give these comedies much. Not many laughs and not big outbursts of enthusiasm."

The Newlyweds in Society: "The day you are to play this, play something else. It is terrible. No laughs."

The "Buster Brown" series garnered some similar exhibitor comments:

Teacher's Pest: "Nothing but cheap hokum."

Out At Home: "Just as bad as they were last season;" and "Rotten. All of Universal comedies invariably are."

Good Scout Buster: "These things are not to be laughed at. Their slogan should be 'Not a Laugh in a Carload'."

Watch the Birdie: "Not any comedy that you would remember."

Busting Buster: "Not much. Some dog was substituted for the regular Tighe [sic], one indecent scene but luckily very short;" and "Disgusting. A few of the kids liked it."

The "Mike and Ike (They Look Alike)" series wasn't spared:

Shooting the Bull: "And still we contend that anyone who can laugh at these is weak-minded."

No Blondes Allowed: "Just two thousand feet of film wasted."

Finishing School: "Another Mike and Ike comedy that might just as well have been left in the can. A few morons tittered and that was all."

She's a Pippin: "An alleged comedy with Mike and Ike which comes as near zero as we ever hope to have. Get the hook!"

Hold Your Horses: "Just a poor comedy offering."

Nor was the "Let George Do It" series spared:

Man of Letters: "This was terrible;" and "Another lemon."

George's False Alarm: "Not to be laughed at."[28]

Big Game George: "As poor as the others."

Look Pleasant: "Not so good. You can see better comedy on the street any day than these two boys play. Terrible. Better pay for same and not play it."

The Cross Country Bunion Race: "Merely two reels of what is ordinarily accepted as comedy. Not many real laughs."

Close Shaves: "Same old gags and they're losing their kick."

There could be any number of explanations for the decline in quality of the final season's entries. One could be budgetary, a tightening of the Sterns' belt due to previous over-extension of their monetary resources. They had, it would appear, dropped the season's projected budget by a third, if those earlier claims are to be believed.

Another possible explanation could be the demands put on their three remaining directors and their gag men. Each unit had to come up with a staggering amount of product within the seemingly unreasonable time constraints placed upon them. This could have impacted the results, the former creativity now taking a back seat to expediency and the recycling of older plots and gags. Potentially sloppy or inadequate visuals may have been a byproduct of these harried schedules as well. The studio's directors had always attempted to adhere to the Sterns' dictate that as little footage be used as possible, a policy that resulted in making do with the contents of a first take, regardless of its quality.

Or perhaps there was a growing rift between the Sterns and Laemmle that was hidden from the trades, planting the seed of retirement in their minds, and a festering disinterest in the studio and its output the unfortunate result. It wouldn't have been surprising, after all, if Abe had burnt out after fifteen years on the firing line. Burdened with a decade of direct responsibility for keeping the product flowing out to the East Coast lab, Abe had finally passed the studio's management and the day-to-day headaches and pressure that went with it, on to others. Still, the buck ultimately stopped with him, and he was—they both were—wealthy men by now, and could afford to leave this all behind them, willingly or begrudgingly.

The industry-wide conversion to sound may have had something to do with it as well, perhaps a daunting prospect that the brothers were unsure they wished to undertake. Unlike some of the bigger film studios, Universal did not have an affiliated theatre chain in which they could exhibit their product. With only limited access to first-run houses in the major cities, Universal was forced to rely on independent theatres. The majority of these theatres were rural based and were among the last theatres to be wired for sound. As a result, the Sterns had had a reliable outlet for their silent comedy shorts, but the writing was now on the wall: sound films were here to stay, and silents soon to be a thing of the past.

Faced with the tide of change sweeping over the industry with the stunning acceptance and demand for sound film, the Sterns wrestled with the next step in their careers as producers. One argument in the favor of making the leap to sound was the increase in movie attendance over the past seven years: theatres that had been drawing forty million patrons per week back in 1922 were now in 1929 drawing more than double that amount, with a hefty ninety million patrons per week. Entertainment dollar spending had peaked at $4.3 billion dollars per year, with money spent for movie attendance more than ten times that spent on sports.

The argument against transitioning into sound was the growing acceptance of commercial radio. Introduced back in November 1920 by Pittsburgh station KDKA, national network broadcasting followed in 1926 with the National Broadcasting Company, and a year later with the Columbia Broadcasting System. And now, by 1929, more than a third of all households owned a radio,[29] a surprising statistic given that nearly three quarters—72%—of all households had annual incomes less than $2,500, the family income deemed necessary for a decent standard of living.[30] But it was free entertainment, and it didn't cost a dime; its growth in popularity sent shivers up the spines of the Hollywood bigwigs.

Julius gathered his employees and gave them a quick speech about the future, starting by telling them that he currently "knew nothing about talking pictures.... We must drift with the tide," said Stern. "If it must be talkers it must be talkers. We will have to make them even though the expense will be more."[31] He sounded more resigned to the fact than excited about it. And that increase in expense....

Regardless, Stern made the first baby step towards acquiescing to a shift to sound. In October 1928 Stern closed a deal with noted humorist and writer Ring Lardner, for the full rights to the "You Know Me Al" series of baseball stories, along with three other series.[32] Abe had acquired the silent rights to "You Know Me Al" for eight thousand dollars back in December 1925, with plans for Eddie Gribbon to star: "Everyone here sold on Eddie Gribbon—think he best type for this material" wrote Abe to Julius.[33] Needless to say, nothing ever came of those earlier plans. According to an October 1928 press release, the Sterns had additionally held the silent screen rights to three other Lardner series for over a year, the new deal now including the talking picture rights to those series as well. The arrangement, it was claimed, was the "largest picture rights deal ever consummated by this organization."[34]

Julius (left) and Abe Stern bookend Rosabelle Laemmle Bergerman after her January 2, 1929 wedding. Courtesy of Gilbert Sherman.

On a social level, or at least according to the occasional report in the trades, the Sterns and Laemmle were still on seemingly friendly terms. When Julius was suddenly taken ill on the East Coast in late October, Carl Laemmle delayed a trip to the West Coast, ostensibly out of concern for his brother-in-law "who is very close to the U. president."[35] By January 2, 1929, all were back in California to attend the wedding of Laemmle's daughter Rosabelle to Stanley Bergerman. Abe's wife served as one of Rosabelle's attendants, and Abe, Julius, and Max Alexander were all guests at the wedding.[36] Alfred Stern, son of Julius and Abe's oldest brother Joseph, attended as well.

Whatever the state of the Sterns' current relationship with their brother-in-law, it wasn't long before the bombshell was dropped that caught the industry—and the Sterns—by surprise. On February 16, 1929, Carl Laemmle sent a terse telegram to the Sterns. Its brief content simply stated:

> Decided make our own comedies.[37]

Carl Laemmle had severed Universal's business ties with the Sterns. Severed it, and in a stunningly abrupt and cold-hearted fashion.

Within a week the news made the pages of the February 26 issue of *Film Daily*:

> Universal City—Contract of Stern Film Co., with Universal will not be renewed, THE FILM DAILY learns. The Sterns for years have supplied comedies for the Universal program. New releases now is being negotiated. A new company is being formed, it is understood, headed by Julius Stern with Abe Stern reported planning to retire from the picture business.[38]

An article in *Variety* offered a bit more information, some of it rather startling:

> Universal will discontinue releasing Century Comedies made by Stern Brothers, in-laws to Carl Laemmle. Decision was made prior to his departure for Hot Springs.
>
> Meanwhile the brothers, one of whom does not speak to Laemmle, have had a quarrel among themselves as to whether they shall persist as producers with their release channel shut off.[39]

Film Daily summed it up in one short, straight-faced sentence: "Now who would have thought such a thing could have happened!"[40]

So what happened, and why? Julius had a relationship with Laemmle that dated back to 1903, and had been an integral part of Laemmle's expanding film business from 1906, a twenty-three year association. Brother Abe's relationship with Laemmle was almost as long, dating back to 1910. The trust between the three of them was complete and unwavering, or at least up until 1922 when Julius resigned his position as vice president of Universal. The business relationship continued, however, the Sterns providing a reliably steady stream of two-reel product to round out the Universal schedule. It's unknown whether the switch from Century to Stern Brothers Comedies played any sort of part in a further straining of relations, since it is not unlikely that the Sterns renegotiated the terms under which Universal would buy their product when they upgraded that same product. So what happened?

In 1929, Universal was having some cash flow issues. Laemmle, having a pretty good sense of Julius's worth by this time, asked Julius for a loan, and Julius, not unreasonably, said that he required a payback date. Laemmle took this as a personal affront, and he refused to provide one. So Julius refused to extend a loan, and one can infer that it was Julius who was referred to in the above article as "one of whom does not speak to Laemmle."

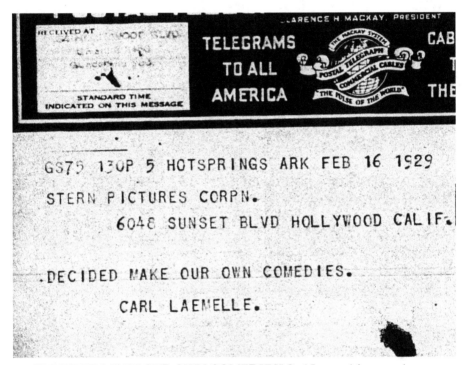

"DECIDED MAKE OUR OWN COMEDIES" Carl Laemmle's terse telegram of February 16, 1929. Courtesy of Andrew Stern.

With Universal no longer an outlet for releasing the Sterns' films, Julius probably muttered "Scheiß drauf," severed all ties, and sold his considerable Universal stock. Which worked out rather well since the sale preceded the stock market crash of October by months. Rather well and, as the story goes, far better than the approximately $5,500,000 Carl Laemmle received when he was forced to sell to J. Cheever Cowdin and Standard Capital.[41] With the sale of his stock in Universal, Julius had cut all ties with the company.[42]

And from that time on there would be no further promotional items about the Stern

Brothers Comedies appearing in the trades, even though there was another half year's worth of releases remaining.

No one really worried about the Sterns' future, however. As *Variety* put it, the "Sterns have extensive realty holdings in Hollywood and are rated in the millionaire division. Picture making is a side line with them."[43]

Chapter 17: From Here to Eternity

Laemmle made good his threat, snapping up a number of former Stern employees, now all available since the season's output had all been in the can and shipped East by the time of Laemmle's telegram. Among these were the actors Sid Saylor and Sunny McKeen, as well as Sig Neufeld, Sam Newfield, and Gus Meins.

Saylor was signed to star in a new series of two-reel comedies for Universal, with both Newfield and Meins slated to direct, and Sig Neufeld supervising. These would all be released as silents,[1] *Universal Weekly* touting that "Saylor's droll mannerisms and pantomime need no accompanying sound to make them excellent entertainment."[2] Included among this group were *Burning Youth, Too Many Women* (all 1929), *Outdoor Sports, Make It Snappy, Traffic Troubles, French Leave, Fellow Students, Foul Ball, Step Right Up, Sid's Long Count, All Wet,* and *Plane Crazy* (all 1930). *Burning Youth,* the first of these to be released and which survives, landed with a thud, or at least as far as reviewers were concerned. "This is a terrible tragic affair," wrote Raymond Ganly, "and the spectator is liable to moan in bereavement with its melancholy attempts at comedy."[3] *Film Daily*'s reviewer was even more dismissal of the film:

> Nearly all the old hooey ever known to comedy business is included in this two reel comedy about the youth who goes fireman. You know the flock of moss-grown gags worked around the fire station and then the inevitable Firemen's Drill Day, with the bum hose connection, men jumping off into nets, and the general excitement over nothing at all.[4]

An inauspicious start for the new series, it would appear.

With his series for Universal completed, Saylor would move on to an impressively lengthy career in film lasting into the early 1960s, usually billed as "Syd" Saylor. From that time on, Saylor appeared in more than three hundred fifty features, shorts, and television programs, both in credited and (frequently) uncredited bit parts. Perhaps best remembered today as the humorous sidekick in an endless stream of Westerns, Saylor's character roles spanned the spectrum of genres before his death in 1962 from a heart attack at age sixty-seven.

Syd Saylor in later years as the dependable but grizzled sidekick in dozens of westerns.

Lawrence McKeen was to star in his own series of two-reel "Sunny Jim" comedies, with direction by Gus Meins and released in both sound and silent versions. "His antics are to be heightened by his childish voice and his exuberant laughter," wrote *Universal Weekly*,[5] and Sig Neufeld was to supervise the production of this series as well.[6] Meins was sidelined and replaced by Harold Beaudine, and McKeen's films included *Baby Talks, No*

Boy Wanted, Christmas Cheer (all 1929), *Sister's Pest, Neighbors, Mush Again, His Bachelor Daddy, She's a He, Brother for Sale,* and *Stop That Noise* (all 1930). Reel two of *Baby Talks* survives, McKeen stiff and awkward in his delivery, and just as annoying as before as he proceeds to disrupt "magician" Charles King's performance at a house party. Reviewer Raymond Ganly dismissed this film as "haphazard and sour," but was generous enough to deem its follow-up, *No Boy Wanted,* as "good movie fare for kids and adults alike." As for McKeen's delivery, Ganly added that "the only fault apparent is that Sunny Jim speaks with too much restraint; his diction is clear but it shows that he received some stiff coaching. A more naturally childish delivery would suit him better."[7] That's expecting a lot from a kid not quite five years of age, but an accurate assessment nonetheless.

With the completion of those films, McKeen was now officially a has-been. McKeen's life wasn't nearly as lengthy as Saylor's, succumbing from an attack of measles and blood poisoning on April 2, 1933 at the tender young age of eight.[8]

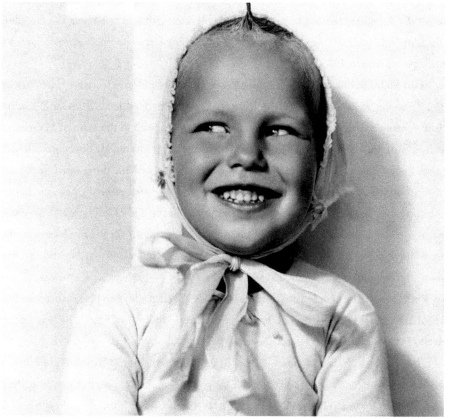

Lawrence McKeen, rechristened as "Sunny Jim" for the new Universal talkie series.
Courtesy of Robert James Kiss.

Arthur Trimble, who was not picked up by Universal, saw his career in film evaporate with the end of the "Buster Brown" series. An article appeared in the August 4, 1948 issue of the *Los Angeles Times* that recounted how an auto mechanic named Arthur Trimble had shot and killed his wife, and then turned the gun on himself. There were a number of details in this and a subsequent article in *The San Bernardino County Sun*, along with some other sources that suggest that this was the same Arthur Trimble who starred in those "Buster Brown" comedies, but conflicting evidence proves otherwise; this was a different Arthur Trimble.

Sig Neufeld and his younger brother Sam Newfield fared far better. After producing dozens of films through the 1930s for Tiffany, Tower, Ambassador, and Puritan Pictures, Neufeld would end up producing hundreds of additional low-budget programmers through his own Producers Releasing Corporation beginning in 1939. Brother Sam would direct the lion's share of these latter films for PRC, so many in fact that he resorted to using the aliases of Peter Stewart and Sherman Scott to hide from the filmgoing public the reality that one person was responsible for so much output. Newfield would continue directing into 1964, his career coming to an abrupt end with his death that same year. His last film, *The Long Rifle and the Tomahawk*, would be brother Sig's last as producer as well. Sig died fifteen years later in 1979.

Gus Meins would eventually leave the Universal family and go to work for Hal Roach in 1932, directing dozens of comedies starring the likes of Charley Chase, Our Gang, Thelma Todd—teamed with both ZaSu Pitts and Patsy Kelly—as well as the team of Laurel and Hardy. Breaking with Roach in 1937, Meins moved in feature comedy direction, helming lower budget programmers primarily for Republic Pictures. With the positive reception of his most recent film, Meins was reported to have anticipated receiving new and better contracts to follow. This all came to a screeching halt at the end of July in 1940, however, when Meins was arrested on a morals charge stemming from his alleged involvement with six youths aged ten to fifteen. Meins called the charges "ridiculous and outlandish," but soon after being released on $5,000 bail told his son "You probably won't see me again," and took off.[9] Meins drove off to La Crescenta where he attached a hose to his exhaust pipe and killed himself, his body discovered three days later. Beside him was a note: "I had no chance to combat this thing because I am a German."[10]

This brings us back to Julius and Abe. In April 1929 the Sterns had Phil Goldstone's National Film Recording Company install Biophone sound recording equipment at their studio on its largest stage, and rebranded it as the National Film Recording Studios; nephews Max and Arthur Alexander were put in charge of the new sound installation.[11] By June, producer Trem Carr was leasing space at the studio and filmed his first all-talking film, *Handcuffed*, at the facility.[12] Ownership of the studio was transferred to the Alexanders, which had by 1933 been renamed the Alexander Brothers Studio.

In addition to continuing to rent out a portion of the studio to Trem Carr and Monogram Pictures, the brothers decided to go into production that same year.[13] The premier release of M & A Alexander Productions—the name given to their first production company—was the low budget crime drama *I Can't Escape*, followed by the Westerns *Thunder Over Texas*, *Cowboy Holiday* (all 1934), and a string of other cut-rate offerings, primarily Westerns, into 1938. The Alexanders would produce more than one hundred features through the 1940s— both as a team or independent of the other—releasing through Producers Releasing Corp.,[14] Grand National, and other smaller companies. Former Century directors would occasionally resurface directing features for the Alexanders, among these Charles Lamont for *International Crime* (Grand National; 1938), Sam Newfield for *Queen of Burlesque* (PRC; 1946), and Al Herman for *Dawn Express, The Rangers Take Over* (PRC; both 1942), and *Badmen of Thunder Gap* (PRC; 1943).

Also in late 1929 came the renaming of several of the Sterns' New York corporations. Stern Enterprises, Inc. was changed to Stern Film Productions, Inc., and Stern Pictures and Finance Corporation was switched to Stern Pictures and Industrial Corporation.[15] There seemed to be no end to the numerous businesses the Sterns would incorporate—and rebrand—over the years.

The brothers maintained a low profile for the next several years, and speculation as to their future plans would, on occasion, surface in the trades. In a July 1930 article titled "Where's J. and A.?", *Variety* reported that it was "understood" that they were in the banking business, "Loaning dough on interest."[16] Additional reports surfaced in 1932 stating that the brothers were considering plans to return to production with a new company, and within a month Julius's Ring Lardner properties "You Know Me Al," "The Real Dope," and "Treat 'Em Rough" were named as the first subjects, with possible release through Universal.[17] It didn't happen.

What did happen, however, led Julius further into the real estate ownership arena. Henry Bergman, a supporting comedian who gained public recognition over a twenty year period through his participation in the films of Charles Chaplin, had opened a popular eatery named "Henry's." Located at 6315 Hollywood Boulevard a half block off Vine Street, Chaplin had set up Bergman in this new side business sometime in the mid-1920s, and according to Julius, Bergman "did about a half a million dollars a year business."[18] In spite of the restaurant's popularity, Bergman became ill with neuritis, and went broke in 1932.[19] When Bergman went belly up, the bank approached the Sterns to see if they were interested in buying the property, which they did for $35,000. "I had a chattel mortgage on the equipment," stated Julius in a much later interview, and likely an example of *Variety's* "Loaning dough on interest" comment. "I made up my mind. I will not open up a restaurant," continued Julius. "What happened was I decided to build a motion picture house, in the height of the depression, in 1933."[20] The result was the $60,000, seven hundred-seat Vine Theatre, built in 1940 for the Stern Brothers Realty Co. There were two stores on either side of the theatre as well, a jewelry store to the left and an Orange Julius (no connection) franchise to the right. Julius retained ownership of the theatre and property up until his death, twenty-six years after his brother Abe had passed on.[21]

More speculation about the Sterns' plans surfaced in mid-1935. The brothers were to set sail on the *Ile de France* for a trip to France and London, where they were "seriously contemplating entering feature production."[22] Feature production never happened, either, and for all intents and purpose the Sterns were by now effectively retired from the film business.

There was another reason for Julius's frequent trips to Europe during this period beyond mere rest and relaxation. His daughter Susan reflected on this:

> During those years, Hitler was making his infamous march across Europe, and hints of dire deeds were leaking across the Atlantic. Dad decided to do something about it and began his pilgrimages. He traveled between the United States and Germany many times, for several years. He continued until it became quite dangerous to do so. At first he was mainly concerned with getting his relatives out, and later he brought friends, their relatives, and generally anybody he knew who could be convinced to leave. In all, he brought some seventy-five Jews to safety. A cousin's cousin [named Larry] told me the following story.
>
> "I remember, when I was a little boy, Uncle Julius came to our house in Germany. He had me sitting on his lap, and he was begging my mother and father to go with him to America. They refused, and then Uncle Julius pleaded with them to let him take me—'the boy', he called me. But they insisted that a child belongs with his parents, and eventually he gave up." Larry survived the camps; his parents did not.[23]

It would appear that by 1942 Julius had moved out of his long-term lodging at the Ambassador Hotel, and into shared lodging with his brother Herman and Herman's wife and two sons at 331 ½ N. Genesee Street in Hollywood.[24] This didn't last long, as during that very same year Julius had fallen in love. Edith Betty Steiner, "a graduate of Skidmore College and…well known in New York social circles,"[25] was the object of his affection. Daughter Susan told the story of their meeting:

Julius Stern and adopted daughter Susan, circa 1942. Courtesy of Gilbert Sherman.

[My mother, who was in Reno at the time with a friend,] ran into a friend who subsequently introduced her to two men, one of whom was Julius Stern. In a magnanimous gesture, Julius reached in his pocket, handed each of the women two silver dollars, said, "Have a good time at the tables," and walked away. Later in the day, Mother chanced to see Julius again. "Listen, Mister," said she, tapping him on the shoulder, "I don't want your money!"

With which she handed him back his two bucks, and then SHE walked away. From all accounts, that did it. He was so enthralled with the idea that there was a woman in the world who wouldn't take his money that he couldn't wait to shower her with it (moderately). He brought her nylon stockings. Even though nylons were like gold during the war, Mother stuck to her guns and refused to take them. But they say that every man has his price (and every woman hers). Mother's undoing was the carton of cigarettes Dad bought as a going-away gift (she was on her way back to New York). A month later Julius followed her there…[26]

The two were married on November 30, 1942.[27] With that New York state-based decree of 1921 forbidding remarriage without consent of the court in mind, Julius and Edith packed up and headed to East Orange, New Jersey, where a rabbi performed the ceremony at the home of a friend.[28] Julius, age fifty-six, and his new bride, twenty-five years his junior, moved into apartment 11D located at 33 E. 70th Street in Manhattan.[29] Edith already had a five year old daughter, Susan Frances Bokor, from a previous marriage to Edwin Bokor. Julius and Edith had a single child, Marie Grace Stern, born a year after their marriage. Years later, Susan's first marriage to Paul Engel bore two children, Gilbert and Judy, but ended in divorce. She would remarry in 1967 to a fellow named Lewis Sherman, who adopted Gilbert and Judy a year later.[30]

While active production was now fifteen years behind him, Julius managed to keep one toe in the business, if only on the periphery. Unaffiliated Independent Exhibitors, Inc., a group of Brooklyn, Queens, and Manhattan independent "subsequent run" operators formed in 1943, was self-described as the "little man's" or "forgotten exhibitors" organization.[31] Lobbying for the "fifth, sixth and subsequent-run exhibitors," their primary gripe was the high film rentals being charged by the major film companies. When they received what they felt was an unsatisfactory response by the film companies contacted, a delegation of fifteen exhibitors headed to Washington to plead their cases before the Office of Price Administration and Department of Justice officials.[32] Deeming the sales policies "illogical and ruinous," their argument was that the present policies would drive the small exhibitor out of business.[33]

Julius, well aware that the independent exhibitor had been the primary outlet for so much of Universal's output, and in no small part a major reason for his old comedy companies' success, joined the group and took part on a committee along with Jesse L. Stern (no relation), Max Wallach, and Jacob Leff that met with representatives from Universal,

RKO, and Paramount. Neil Agnew, Paramount's general sales manager, was swayed by their concerns and agreed that operators who could demonstrate that their operating expenses were out of line with their gross income could expect an adjustment from his company. He further agreed to "liberalize the policy on reissues and promised to eliminate any discrimination in favor of circuits as to the availability of reissues or revivals."[34]

Julius and wife Edith take a stroll through Manhattan, circa 1945.
Courtesy of Gilbert Sherman.

Aside from the Vine Theatre, Julius and Abe had several other real estate holdings that provided a steady flow of income. As time went on, Abe sold all of his shares in these properties to Julius save one, located on Lankershim. This property eventually ended up in Julius's hands as well, either through an outright sale or upon Abe's death in 1951. Regardless, in 1953 Julius sold the Lankershim property to four of his nephews, Max and Arthur Alexander along with his brother Herman's sons, Larry and Arnold Stern. Arnold was the sole surviving owner upon his death in 2019, after which it was sold.

Abe Stern in later years. Courtesy of Gilbert Sherman.

Somewhere along the line Julius incorporated the Sternbros Realty Corporation to handle these real estate holdings. By the 1970s this had been reorganized and reincorporated as Sternbros Motion Picture Enterprises, Inc., and it's likely that some of the other corporations had been reorganized as well and folded into this all-encompassing corporation. It held only five leases by 1978: Columbia Pictures Corp. for a hundred year lease on premises at 6040 Sunset Blvd, next to the old L-Ko lot ($3,630 per month); Rubeck Realty Corp. for a lease on the Vine Theatre premises ($2,500 per month); Joung Hoon Lee and Soon Myoung Lee for a lease on Lee's Hot Dog Store premises ($375 per month—the former Orange Julius store); Harvey and Frances Cohn, lease on C & H Jeweler premises ($375 per month—the other store aside the Vine Theatre); and Gaylord Wagner, owner of Hollywood Knickerbocker Hotel, for a lease on an alleyway adjacent to the hotel.[35]

By the 1950s, the Alexander brothers had made the pragmatic switch from motion picture to television production. Their first syndicated show in 1952 was the thirteen episode half-hour *Renfrew of the Mounted* Telepix series based on the *Renfrew of the Royal*

Mounted radio series. Their follow-up production was to be another thirteen half-hour shows based on Ring Lardner's "You Know Me Al" series, the rights of which were acquired from their uncle Julius, who had sat on the rights since 1928. Production was planned for the following January, but it is doubtful that the show ever got beyond the planning stages. Still working out of their 6040 Sunset Boulevard location, the Alexanders were also supplementing their income by selling older feature films to television stations, owning the rights to one hundred twenty-five films which included many of their own indie features as well as forty other British productions.[36]

Julius and Edith sometime in the early 1950s. Courtesy of Gilbert Sherman.

The Alexanders did produce one final film, this one made in England under the working title *That Woman Opposite*. Co-starring Phyllis Kirk and Dan O'Herlihy, Julius traveled over to England to confer with the Alexanders regarding the distribution of the film. Released in 1957 as *City After Midnight*, distribution was handled in the U.S. by RKO.[37] In later years, Max would promote that before coming to the U.S. in 1923 he had been associated with both UFA studios and Universal and gained "a reputation in several European capitals,"[38] but given that he was only fifteen when he arrived here, those claims seem a bit overblown. Max's life came to an end in 1964 when he was only fifty-six years old, his production company still positioning itself as a "National distributor of feature films, Westerns and half-hour filmed TV shows, cartoons and comedies."[39] His younger brother Arthur would follow in 1989.

Julius and Edith, vacationing in Rome, 1957. Courtesy of Gilbert Sherman.

Julius's later years were very comfortable, continuing to reside with Edith in their New York apartment. "He generally lived a pretty quiet life, at least in the last twenty years of his life," recalled grandson Gilbert Sherman. "They were extraordinarily comfortable and lived well...lived large, as we would say. But not ostentatious."[40] Not a religious man during those early years in Hollywood, with marriage Julius embraced Judaism. He would attend synagogue on Friday night, Saturday morning, and again on Saturday night. Fifth Avenue Synagogue became his default synagogue, a mere eight block walk from the apartment. Congregation Shearith Israel, often called The Spanish and Portuguese Synagogue, was his frequent choice for the high holy days, however. Given that it was located on the far side of Central Park and more of a chore to reach on foot, he would stay with friends rather than make the lengthy trek back home.

Julius, probably flirting with the ticket taker in the Vine Theatre's box-office, 1967.
Courtesy of Gilbert Sherman.

Julius belonged to several clubs, the Harmonie Club on East 60th Street, and the City Athletic Club overlooking Central Park among them. He loved to play gin rummy, and his cigar smoking had now grown to a two-or-three-Churchill-a-day habit. He preferred a Macanudo or a Montecristo, which he'd pick up every day or so at the Harmonie, and would frequently smoke one each in the morning, afternoon, and evening. "He could be very articulate, but his English wasn't so hot when he was old," recalled Gilbert. "It wasn't uncommon for him to revert to German or Yiddish, absolutely for swearing!"[41]

Physically fit well into his old age, Julius would walk most everywhere, with regular stops at the stock exchange. He said that during one period of his life he was investing $5,000 a year in the market, and was eventually receiving $100 a week in dividends as a result. He owned a Chevrolet Impala but rarely used it, aside from his trips out to Long Island to the Inwood Country Club they belonged to. Still very sociable, Julius and Edith would vacation most summers at the Beverly Hills Hotel. Bungalow number eight was their bungalow, and they had an assigned cabana by the pool. In 1968 when Julius's grandchildren accompanied them on a six-week vacation, Jack Benny had the cabana on one side, and Jackie Gleason the other, with Johnny Carson nearby. The kids, needless to say, must have been star struck! Daughter Susan recalled meeting Eddie Cantor and George Jessel as well during vacations several decades earlier, either at the Beverly Hills Hotel or in Palm Springs, where Stern frequently vacationed during the earlier years.

Julius and Edith on vacation at the Beverly Hills Hotel, circa 1968.
Courtesy of Gilbert Sherman.

Nearly a half century after his active involvement in the film industry, however, it was a topic that Julius preferred not to talk about. Gilbert's take on it? "Maybe it was humility, maybe it was just age. Been there, done that; been done with that for fifty years; leave me alone." Daughter Susan reflected on this, and her father's lack of any sort of self-promotion, both in his later years as well as during the decades that followed the dissolving of his and his brother's studio. He would say, as Susan paraphrased it, "I never wanted screen credit. It was just a business to me. I didn't want to get mixed up with it. I never wanted the screen credit." Susan elaborated:

> The feeling he conveyed was that indeed he avoided screen credit whenever possible, considering it to be an encumbrance. The attitude was borne out, perhaps, in his retiring from the business in the late 1920's. He had made all the money he felt he could make from pictures (without making huge investments in sound equipment), and the glamour didn't interest him.[42]

A final thought on the origins of the earlier L-Ko studio: While history and surviving evidence strongly suggest that the studio was the result of an agreement between Laemmle and Henry Lehrman, there's another possibility. Julius Stern would go on to claim in various promotional pieces that it was he who formed the company, including one in the December 3, 1921 issue of *Exhibitors Herald*: "[Julius] started his career as general manager of the old Imp studio on Tenth Avenue, New York. When the studios moved to California he went there as general manager and while there he formed his own company called the LKO. After two years he formed Century of which he is the head."

Stern had originally hired Lehrman back in 1911 as Imp's first scenario editor, and eventually let him direct at least one known short comedy, the split-reel *Beat At His Own Game* (March 2, 1912). "Pathe Lehrman…was in the scenario department when I encouraged him to do a picture," wrote Stern in 1915. "It was a slap-stick comedy and I must admit that it wasn't well thought of at the time of its premiere about four years ago. That was because Lehrman was ahead of his time: slap-stick of that order is today the demanded film of the business."[43]

Jack Cohn, later one of the founders of what would become Columbia Pictures, had worked in Imp's darkroom during that same period. Cohn later stated that "Henry Lehrman made a couple of half-reel comedies. He was years ahead of the crowd on slapstick comedies, but there was no one in the organization who appreciated these pictures, and he was laid off before he ever screened his work."[44]

Given Cohn's assertion that Lehrman was laid off from Imp before any of his films had been screened, it's possible that Stern came to recognize Lehrman's talents as both a writer and director of comedies after his release from Imp. Later, perhaps at Laemmle's direction, Stern may have decided to create a comedy company as a competitor to Sennett's Keystone, one to back up Universal's Joker brand and eventually serve as a replacement to the floundering Sterling brand. Stern may have negotiated with Lehrman and come to a mutually acceptable agreement, rounded up some investors, and put his brother Abe in charge to oversee the operations. This Stern would have done as he did most everything else for Laemmle back then: dutifully, quietly, and behind the scenes. All conjecture, of course, with nothing tangible aside from Stern's few later comments to back it up, but a possibility nonetheless.

So while there may have been some (or a lot of) truth to Julius Stern's claims that he had started L-Ko, I've found no independent evidence of this aside from his later claims, and have—for better or worse—chalked it up to Stern's attempts to erase Lehrman's earlier connection to the studio. I remain unconvinced otherwise, but in fairness to Stern I've offered this "alternative" history.

Whatever the case, by the 1950s the L-Ko was a distant memory to both Julius and Abe. Little is known about Abe Stern's later years aside from the fact that he and his wife Hortense had only the one child, daughter Barbara. Barbara announced her engagement to a Louis Albert Stern in August, 1946, and the nineteen year old was married in December; at least she didn't need to change her surname. Abe died when only sixty-three on July 12, 1951 in Los Angeles, and Hortense passed on three years later in 1954.

Julius died in New York on April 26, 1977, age ninety-one. Services were held at the Riverside Memorial Chapel at 76th Street and Amsterdam Avenue, and he was buried at Beth Olam, the Shearith Israel Cemetery in Ridgewood, Queens County, New York.

None of the industry trades noted his passing.

Julius in 1973, four years before his death. Courtesy of Gilbert Sherman.

Chapter 18: C'est La Vie

"But Mr. Stern, fast nickels are better than slow quarters."

So said the proprietor of the Orange Julius franchise, one of two small stores inside the Vine Theatre building, during a discussion about just how hard it was to make a living.

Julius suggested that he raise his prices.

And that was the fellow's response.

This wasn't news to Julius, since these were words that both Julius and Abe had lived by all through their stewardship of the L-Ko, Century, Rainbow, and Stern Brothers brands. They were, after all, businessmen first and creative entities a distant second; their goal was to turn out a decent product as efficiently and cost-effectively as possible, and to get these films into the hands of exhibitors at affordable prices. This was due more to necessity rather than any sort of altruistic stance on their part, since their distributor, Universal, did not own a chain of theatres. Unlike some of the bigger players, such as Paramount, Metro-Goldwyn-Mayer, Fox, and Warners, Universal did not have a direct outlet for its considerable product. Universal's films were for the most part shown in unaffiliated theatres in rural areas or urban neighborhoods, and had to be sold on merit and price, price frequently predominating.

What is surprising is just how good so many of their surviving films are, given the budgetary and time constraints under which their casts and crews had to operate. Add to that the Sterns' unstated "policy" of short-term contracts, which resulted in an ongoing turnover of the studio's stars. While this helped to keep costs under control, it had an obvious impact on the continuity—or lack thereof—of the faces gracing the screen in Century's comedies. The few actors and actresses (and dogs) who really clicked with the audiences, however, had, by comparison, staying power, and the Sterns were savvy enough to retain them and reward them as such.

Wanda Wiley's *The Queen of Aces* and *A Thrilling Romance* are both crowd pleasers, and arguably as good as the best of what Roach and Sennett were producing. The films of Baby Peggy Montgomery were huge hits and in a category all their own due to the youngster's undeniable talents and charm, from her earliest Brownie co-starring roles such as *Playmates* to her more "mature" spoofs like *Peg O' the Mounted*. So good was Peggy that the Sterns found it more profitable to hire her out for starring roles in features, both ones in which they were involved as well as others on loan-out. Brownie, of course, was the Sterns' pint-sized, scrappier answer to Sennett's heroic Teddy, and able to carry entire films on his own; no need for the support of a Gloria Swanson or Bobby Vernon!

With their comparatively beefed-up budgets, the later cartoon-inspired "Buster Brown" and "Newlyweds" series were quite good, or at least the earliest entries before they became tired rehashes of by-then familiar plots. *Buster's Bust-Up* and *Buster's Nose Dive* are both thoroughly enjoyable examples of the former series, and *The Newlyweds' Headache* a humorous example of the latter. All that said, perhaps the reason that so many of the surviving films are so good is for that very reason: they survived *because* they were so good, and were originally chosen over much of the less successful output to be offered by catalog for non-theatrical and home-use rental or sale. But that could be said of Sennett's output as well.

What is not arguable is the fact that the films of Century, Rainbow, and the Stern Brothers Comedies filled a necessary void, providing lower-cost fare for those thousands of rural theatres and their less demanding audiences. The Sterns' output of reliably entertaining two-reelers accompanied the endless stream of Westerns and dramas churned out by Universal and its affiliates. It was what Laemmle wanted—what Laemmle *needed*—and they didn't disappoint, or at least in terms of providing him with two-reel comedies and multi-part serials. Where they did disappoint, it would seem, was in acceding to Laemmle's incessant demands on their time, being his go-to guys when he was otherwise spread too thin work-wise. It was a delicate balancing act that worked for a while, but eventually the demands on the Sterns—on Julius specifically—proved to be too much. The stress and strain of keeping their own businesses functioning smoothly while being at Laemmle's beck and call led to the eventual falling out, which cast a pall over the final few years of their relationship with their brother-in-law, until it reached the eventual breaking point.

The Sterns' successful fifteen year run as producers of comedies speaks for itself, however; their output rivaling that of Roach and Sennett in quantity, if not always quality, their studios demonstrating a staying power that outlasted numerous other shorter-lived comedy brands and studios. That they decided to pack it in at the end of the twenties and not undertake the expensive transition to "talkies" was, in retrospect, a sound one; both Sennett and Roach had opted to make the transition, but only Roach managed to hang on into the forties. The Sterns, it would appear, seemed to realize that they had had their day, and quietly exited the filmic scene.

"The one thing I'll say, and I'm not bragging," mused Stern much later in life, "we had the reputation: the Stern Brothers' word is as good as their signature; we never broke a contract."

Shortly after Julius's death in 1977, his daughter Susan summed up her father's life in three brief sentences:

> Dad was a German Jew who came to this country around the turn of the century. In true Horatio Alger style he made his bundle. Unlike many, he retired and spent the rest of his life reaping the rewards.[1]

And when you stop to think about it, a quarter century spent in the business followed by a half century of comfortable, stress-free retirement, that's not a bad life, is it?

Afterword

When I was born in 1960, Julius Stern, "Grampy" (to me and my sister), was 74 and had been retired from the day-to-day of the motion picture business (his phrase for the movie industry) for 25 years. During the 17 remaining years of his life, I can only remember a few occasions when he made even a passing mention of his time in the business. Every once in a while, he proudly beamed about Baby Peggy, Buster Brown, and Tarzan, but I never got the sense that he was the motion picture pioneer that he clearly was. I am pretty sure that I did not really know that he had been in the movie business at all. He mostly talked about his 99-year lease to Columbia Studios and his other California properties. We were also consistently regaled with stories about his first U.S. job that paid $5 per week in the clothing store. This, of course, is merely derivative of the maxim that "time is money".

It was after he died that I began to put two and two together and realized that he had been more than simply "involved" in the movies. Long before I had the pleasure to meet Tom Reeder, I spent many years gathering historical and anecdotal information about Julius Stern, and by extension, Abe, if for no other reason than to satiate a growing hunger to understand this part of where "I came from". Neither my cousins (Abe's grandchildren), nor my mother and aunt (Julius's children), knew much of anything until about 15 years ago. At that time, my aunt commissioned Marc Wanamaker to research and produce a thorough history of Stern Bros. (in all its iterations), Universal and Julius and Abe's involvement in the business. Were it not for that superb effort, much of this history might have been lost to time, because despite Julius's tendency to seek the accolades of the press while in the business, once he was done…he was done.

Over the years, I learned that Julius, in particular, was instrumental in the founding and early success of the nickelodeons, the film distribution business, the IMP and of course,

Universal Studios and all the various brands of two-reel comedies he and Abe produced. Julius was a tireless, extraordinarily gifted and entrepreneurial business leader, who despite having only an 8th grade education, achieved a great deal. His efforts and successes were certainly evident in his businesses, but moreover, in the lives of his family members and the many people he encountered throughout his long life. I am sure that much of the same can be said of Abe. This having been said, both men were true products of 19th century Germany and their manifest rigidity was felt by some, even those they loved. To me, Julius was simply "Grampy".

My family and I would especially like to thank Tom Reeder for his exhaustive work in publishing this history of Julius and Abe Stern, their lives and their substantial and significant contributions to the motion picture industry. There is no doubt in my mind that Universal Studios would not have become what it became without these two men.

Gilbert Sherman
Cleveland, Ohio
October 29, 2020

Century, Rainbow, and Stern Brothers Comedies: Their Films

What follows is a complete chronological listing of the known films of the Century, Rainbow, and Stern Brothers Comedies. Brief summaries are included for each film where a plot synopsis could be found. The Rainbow Comedies are noted with the words **Rainbow Comedy** in bold as an aid to locating them among the Century Comedies.

These films were released every week on Wednesday from September 1919 through August 1929. The "Buster Brown" series was elevated to Universal Junior Jewel status and released on the first Monday of each month during the 1926-1927 season, after which it reverted back to Wednesdays as a Stern Brothers Comedy. "The Newlyweds" series was then promoted as a Universal Junior Jewel release, replacing the Buster Browns on that first Monday slot for the 1927-1928 season. For the final 1928-1929 season "The Newlyweds" was "demoted" to once again being a Stern Brothers Comedy, now appearing every fourth Wednesday. Release dates have been adjusted to accurately reflect the actual day of release rather than the "week of" dates frequently given in other sources.

The Rainbow Comedy *The Jail Breaker* is the only film for which I could not confirm an accurate release date, so I've used the one found at the Internet Movie Database (IMDb) and labeled it as "unconfirmed." This film and its actual release date is an anomaly in that there were no "open" release dates remaining after the other films were assigned to their proper dates on the schedule. It remains to be determined what its actual release date was, if not the one provided at the IMDb.

The names given for actors and crew members can be a source of confusion, both in a film's credits and as they appeared in the trades. Alternate spellings would appear, and former names were occasionally discarded for new. Some examples: director Edward I.

Luddy changed his name to Edward Ludwig in later years after his stint with the Sterns; the same applies to actor Joe Young, who "reinvented" himself as Roger Moore. Ouida Hill changed her name to Thelma Daniels early on while at Century, and the same goes for Louise Fortune who switched to Louise Lorraine. Fred Bretherton switched to Fred Spencer, Harry Swett underwent a tweak to Harry Sweet, and Consuela Henley anglicized her first name to Connie; in each of these instances you'll find one or the other name appearing throughout these credits. Bessie Welsh changed her name to Betty Welsh midstream, so you'll find both in the credits below (her name was occasionally misspelled as Bessie Welch, but that's been corrected to the Welsh spelling). George Monberg's screen name alternated between Zip Monberg and Zip Monty, and in at least one instance as George Monte. Lillian Biron appears in the Century credits as Lillian Byron, and Edna Marion as Edna Marian. Syd Saylor appears in the credits as Sid Saylor. Pete Gordon became Eddie Gordon when he became part of Century's roster of comedians, but would revert back to Pete later in his career. And then there were the spellings and misspellings of names: Buddy Messinger vs. Buddy Messenger, Tad Ross vs. Ted Ross, and Wanda Wiley vs. Waunda Wiley; in these instances I have used the former spelling.

The comedy shorts of Joe Martin are appended to the bottom of this filmography. While the Sterns were not actually involved with these productions, I've included them anyway since there's previously been some confusion as whether or not they were. Diana Serra Cary places Joe at the studio, and he may have been borrowed from Universal for the random appearance, but it's possible that she was confusing Joe with the missus. This is a topic for further research.

Lastly there are two additional films appended to the bottom, the all-canine production *The Eternal Triangle*, and the kid fantasy *Sinbad the Sailor*, both from 1919 and directed by Norman Dawn. I've found the random reference connecting these films to the Sterns, but nothing conclusive; another issue warranting further research.

The Two-Reel Comedies of the Stern Brothers:

Balloonatics: Released 09/01/1917. © Century Comedies 08/16/1917. Century Comedy. Cast: Alice Howell, Fatty Voss, Dick Smith, Joe Moore. Director, Story, Editor: John G. Blystone (State Rights Production/Longacre Distributing Co.) (working title **The Balloon Bandits**)

Maid Howell elopes with the son of the house. Cook Voss, in love with Howell, takes off in a hot air balloon, its dangling anchor causing much havoc before picking up the bungalow with Howell and the groom inside, taking it for a long ride before it crashes to the trees below.

Automaniacs: Released 10/01/1917. © Century Comedies 09/11/1917. Century Comedy. Cast: Alice Howell, Fatty Voss, Robert McKenzie. Director, Story, Editor: John G. Blystone (State Rights Production/Longacre Distributing Co.)

Howell and Voss are auto mechanics in a small town garage.

Neptune's Naughty Daughter: Released 11/01/1917. © Century Comedies 10/16/1917. Century Comedy. Cast: Alice Howell, Robert McKenzie, Eva McKenzie, Joe Moore, Fatty Voss, Ida Mae McKenzie, Coo-Coo the Dog. Director, Story, Editor: John G. Blystone (State Rights Production/Longacre Distributing Co.) (working title **The Worshippers of the Cuckoo Clock**)

Fisherman's daughter Howell is shanghaied. The boat is involved in a smash-up and collision, and takes on water. Howell is rescued by her lover, who takes her to safety in his rowboat. Their pursuers make one last attempt to capture them from atop a lighthouse, but instead fall to earth when the lighthouse is pulled over.

Her Bareback Career: Released 12/01/1917. © Century Comedies 11/27/1917. Century Comedy. Cast: Alice Howell, Eva McKenzie. Director, Editor: John G. Blystone (State Rights Production/Longacre Distributing Co.) (working title **Alice of the Sawdust**)

"Miss Howell had never tackled any out and out 'circus stunts' in real circus surroundings, and it is believed that never before upon the screen has any woman so callously disregarded the laws of gravity and the heels of an ill-tempered horse. She has soared to the circus-peak on invisible wire, swung through space on swaying handle-bars and performed aerial 'stunts' that woman has never before attempted." (*Motography*, 07/21/1917)

She Did Her Bit: Released 12/30/1917. © Century Comedies 01/16/1918. Century Comedy. Cast: Alice Howell. Director: John G. Blystone (State Rights Production/Longacre Distributing Co.) (working title **The Village Blacksmith**)

Blacksmith's daughter Howell falls in love with a "city feller," marries him, and bursts into high society.

Oh, Baby!: Released 02/14/1918. © Century Comedies 02/11/1918. Century Comedy. Cast: Alice Howell, Bert Roach, James Finlayson, William Irving, Russell Powell, Eddie Barry, Neal Burns, Eva Novak. Director: John G. Blystone (State Rights Production/Longacre Distributing Co.) (working title **School Days**)

Just released from prison, Minnie Grabit (Howell) poses as a Salvation Army girl to collect some money, and later becomes a nurse and finally a servant girl.

What's the Matter with Father?: Released 04/01/1918. © Century Comedies 03/22/1918. Century Comedy. Cast: Alice Howell, Eva Novak, Eddie Barry, Neal Burns, Harry Griffith. Director: John G. Blystone (State Rights Production/Longacre Distributing Co.) (Last film distributed through Longacre, although **Her Unmarried Life** had previously been listed as a Longacre product)

Her Unmarried Life: Released 05/29/1918. © Century Comedies 05/09/1918. Century Comedy. Cast: Alice Howell, Dick Smith, Bert Roach, Eva McKenzie, Arthur Thalasso. Director: John G. Blystone (First film distributed through Universal as a result of Universal combining all exchanges.)

Peter Pickles learns that the school teacher has an inheritance coming, so he plans to marry off his daughter Pansy (Howell) to him. She has other plans, though, and switches places with another girl. The inheritance turns out to be a pig, so Peter is overjoyed to find that Pansy did not marry the teacher. He finds her a new bridegroom to her liking, and they are married.

In Dutch: Released 06/26/1918. © Century Comedies 05/24/1918. Century Comedy. Cast: Alice Howell, Eddie Barry, Hughie Mack, Billy Armstrong, Neal Burns, James Finlayson, Russell Powell. Director: John G. Blystone.

Stowaway Dutch girl Hulda (Howell) is discovered and forced to work in the kitchen with its lecherous cook. She is saved from his advances by Tommy Little, and they are married. In America, Tommy takes a job as a waiter, and Hulda as a dancer. She turns out to be popular, and earns an enormous salary. Another fellow attempts to abduct her, but Tommy comes to the rescue once again.

Choo Choo Love: Released 07/17/1918. © Century Comedies 06/27/1918. Century Comedy. Cast: Alice Howell, Hughie Mack, Russell Powell, Billy Armstrong, Edith Kelly, Neal Burns, L-Ko Beauty Girls. Director: John G. Blystone.

Howell, her father Powell, and sister Kelly head to the beach. Howell falls for traveling salesman Armstrong, much to father's annoyance. On the train ride home, Howell and Armstrong foil father by uncoupling his part of the train from theirs.

Hey, Doctor!: Released 07/31/1918. © Century Comedies 07/24/1918. Century Comedy. Cast: Alice Howell, Russell Powell, Eddie Barry, Neal Burns, Billy Armstrong, Edith Kelly, James Finlayson, Marvin Loback. Director: John G. Blystone.

Howell, assistant to doctor Powell, and janitor Barry are on the hunt for patients when she meets and falls for Armstrong. Now a patient, the doctor thinks Armstrong's good for an easy $2,000. There's a masquerade ball, and a wild chase ensues when the doctor goes to collect his $2,000.

Bawled Out: Released 08/14/1918. © Century Comedies 08/17/1918. Century Comedy. Cast: Alice Howell, Hughie Mack, Vin Moore, Helen Gibson. Director: James Davis.

Howell arranges an escape for imprisoned sweetheart Mack, but fellow prisoner Moore and his gang break out as well. Mack is recaptured but released providing he bring back the escaped prisoners. Mack falls for Gibson, Queen of the Crooks, but Howell cleverly manages to lock them in a house, then uses her flivver to push the house back to the prison grounds.

Hoot Toot: Released 08/28/1918. © Century Comedies 08/06/1918. Century Comedy. Cast: Alice Howell. Director: James Davis.

Unsuccessful in her attempts to join the Red Cross and the army, Howell decides she needs some training using her overweight husband "as the goat." He gets an invite to a poker game and needs her money to take part. Howell is furious, a chase follows, hubby ends up in jail, and Howell tries once again to join the army.

Cupid vs. Art: Released 09/11/1918. © Century Comedies 09/14/1918. Century Comedy. Cast: Alice Howell, Hughie Mack. Director: Vin Moore.

Howell's father turns her over to Scraggs, owner of a sanitarium, in return for forgiveness of his mortgage debt. Alice falls in love with Mack, so Scraggs has him imprisoned and forces Howell to plan for marriage. She gets word to Mack, who escapes and rescues Howell. A big chase and a happy ending follow.

Untamed Ladies: Released 10/09/1918. © Century Comedies 09/30/1918. Century Comedy. Cast: Alice Howell, Hughie Mack.

Escaped gypsy Howell falls for an artist, who plans to make her a society belle. At the debutante party that follows, Howell is accused of stealing a wealthy woman's necklace. Her gypsy lover tracks her down and poses as the minister at her wedding to the artist. She recognizes him, and a lively chase follows before she is reunited with the artist.

The Cabbage Queen: Released 12/18/1918. © L-Ko 12/09/1918. Century Comedy. Cast: Alice Howell, Hughie Mack, Phil Dunham, William Irving. Director: Vin Moore (working title **A Liberty Cabbage Queen**)

German spies Dunham and Irving determine to steal Howell's secret formula for sauerkraut. Assisted by her sweetheart Mack, Howell manages to foil all of the spies' attempts, thereby starving the German Army of its supply of sauerkraut.

The Geezer of Berlin: Released 08/15/1918. © Jewel Productions, Inc. 07/19/1918. Jewel Comedy. 3 reels. Cast: Ray Hanford, Jack Stewart, Marvin Loback, Walter Bytell,

Earl Lynn, Hughie Mack, Bartine Burkett, Monty Banks, Bert Roach. Director: Arthur Hotaling. Story: Frank Howard Clark.

A travesty on Universal's popular feature **The Kaiser, the Beast of Berlin**, the hero ropes the Kaiser, flies away with him in an airplane, and drops him through the roof of Mack's bakery where he is pelted by pies before being shoved into a lit oven. "To Hell with the Kaiser" reads the intertitle.

Behind the Front: Released 02/12/1919. © Century Comedies 01/29/1919. Century Comedy. Cast: Alice Howell, Hughie Mack, Brownie the Dog. Director: Vin Moore and/or Noel Smith.

The war board decides to draft fat men, Mack included, for use in place of sand bags during bomb and hand grenade tests. Back home, his wife Howell falls for the milkman, but gives him the brush-off when she learns of hubby's new role in the armed forces.

Society Stuff: Released 03/12/1919. © Century Comedies 03/03/1919. Century Comedy. Cast: Alice Howell. Director: Vin Moore.

Mr. and Mrs. Kash head to the seashore, taking their maid Maisie and hired man Harold with them. They grow bored, however, and head back home, their help to follow the next day. Maisie and Harold impersonate the Kashes at a grand ball held that evening, Maisie donning her mistress' jewels. The jewels are the target of a couple of crooks.

A Jungle Gentleman: Released 04/09/1919 © Century Comedies 03/18/1919. Century Comedy. Cast: Jimmie Adams, Esther Wood, Forrest Robinson, Charles Dudley, Mrs. Joe Martin the Monkey. Director, Story: Fred Fishback.

Dr. Cutup (Adams) hires Mrs. Joe Martin, dresses her as an office boy, and has her scatter banana peels outside his office in a successful attempt to drum up new patients.

Looney Lions and Monkey Business: Released 04/23/1919. © Century Comedies 04/08/1919. Century Comedy. Cast: Dot Farley, Charles Dorety, The Century Lions. Director: Fred C. Fishback (Vin Moore in copyright). Animal Trainer: Charles Gay.

Light-Fingered Luke finds himself back in prison after his escape leads him to Fifi, who turns out to be the warden's daughter. A second escape results in a job at the zoo tending the lions, who manage to escape.

Frisky Lions and Wicked Husbands: Released 05/28/1919. © Century Comedies 05/10/1919. Century Comedy. Cast: Dot Farley, Charles Dorety, The Century Lions. Director: Fred Fishback (Vin Moore in copyright). Animal Trainer: Charles Gay.

Susie, sheriff of Parched City, shoots her revolver through each package that arrives at the express office to determine whether or not it contains explosives. Shooting off the lock on Al Cohol's shipment has unintended consequences, however, when it unleashes the ferocious lion inside.

Howling Lions and Circus Queens: Released 06/25/1919. © Century Comedies 06/13/1919. Century Comedy. Cast: Dot Farley, Billy Bevan, The Century Lions. Director: Fred C. Fishback (Vin Moore in copyright). Animal Trainer: Charles Gay.

Rube lovers Salindy Simp (Farley) and Billy Bifkins (Bevan) find their relationship challenged when the circus comes to town and she falls for lion tamer Buffalo Bull. She follows the circus when it leaves, and Bifkins follows her. A visit to the lion's cage results in a hair-raising pursuit.

A Lion Special: Released 07/30/1919. © Century Comedies 07/16/1919. Century Comedy. Cast: Chai Hong, The Century Lions. Director: Fred Fishback (Jim Davis in copyright). Animal Trainer: Charles Gay.

Two crooks' plan to steal Pop Hebenezer's new invention fall short when they are greeted by the lion that Pop's daughters have substituted in the invention's place.

Lonesome Hearts and Loose Lions: Released 08/27/1919. © Century Comedies 08/10/1919. Century Comedy. Cast: Dan Russell, Marjorie Ray, Harry Sweet, The Century Lions. Director: Fred C. Fishback (William Watson in copyright). Animal Trainer: Charles Gay.

A blacksmith's assistant (Sweet) wants to prove his bravery to his new girl Trixie by entering a cage full of lions, intending to inject them with an "anti-pep" drug. Rival Harry switches the drug to the "pep" version with the expected results, and the lions run loose throughout the town.

Beginning of 1919-1920 Season

The Jail Breaker: Released 09/02/1919 (unconfirmed). © Century Comedies 12/09/1919. **Rainbow Comedy.** Cast: Frank Coleman, Billy Engle, Edna Gregory, Evelyn Nelson. Director: Charles Parrott.

When the mayor receives a threatening letter from Goofee Gus, he calls in the Chief of Police for protection. Gus is arrested, but breaks out of prison, dresses as a woman, vamps a pursuing policeman, and sets the mayor's house on fire. The chief's son Sweety, lover of the mayor's daughter, rescues her by swinging on a rope to an adjacent building.

A Village Venus: Released 09/03/1919. © Century Comedies 07/30/1919. Century Comedy. Cast: Edith Roberts, Jimmie Adams. Director: Fred Fishback.

Roberts is lured away from her husband, child, and mortgage by a wily artist, but soon finds she's the object of the affections of both the artist and his valet. Her husband follows, accompanied by his little daughter and her sweetheart, and locates the studio. He beats up the artist and rescues his wife.

A Roof Garden Rough House: Released 09/10/1919. © Universal Film Mfg Co. 09/02/1919. **Rainbow Comedy.** Cast: Zip Monberg, Lois Neilsen. Director: James Davis.

"The plot has to do with the downfall of a motor cop whose persistence in winning the affections of another man's wife leads to all kinds of complications, which carry through the dance on a roof garden, to the skating rink and also the top of the building." (*Motion Picture News*, 07/19/1919)

A Lion in the House: Released 09/17/1919. © Century Comedies 09/03/1919. Century Comedy. Cast: Zip Monberg, Cliff Bowes, Merta Sterling The Century Lions. Director: Fred Fishback. Animal Trainer: Charles Gay.

Zip, his cute nagging wife, and mischievous son go to the beach. He sells illegal liquor to fisherman from his hidden stock on the ocean floor. A detective is on to him, and brings his lion to help with the lawbreakers. A chase ensues in the amusement center.

An Oriental Romeo: Released 09/24/1919. © Universal Film Mfg Co. 09/12/1919. **Rainbow Comedy.** Cast: Chai Hong. Director, Story: Jess Robbins.

Mr. and Mrs. Hookworm take their infant to the beach. Dad's dalliance with Lovely Lily ends when she makes off with his watch and chain. He meets waiter Charlie (Hong), but they are soon at odds. Charlie "hides" by dressing up as a pretty little lady, but is soon surrounded by admirers.

Chasing Her Future: Released 10/01/1919. © Century Comedies 09/26/1919. Century Comedy. Cast: Jimmie Adams, Edith Roberts. Director: Fred Fishback.

Detective Edith (Roberts) is on the trail of a "bull-shivik" crooks, as are detectives Peek and Boo. She gets hold of their plans to bottle up a canal. Everyone attends an evening affair where the crooks start tossing bombs, Peek and Boo eventually capturing them.

Dainty Damsels and Bogus Counts: Released 10/08/1919. © Universal Film Mfg Co. 09/27/1919. **Rainbow Comedy.** Cast: Lois Neilson, Zip Monberg. Director, Story: Walter Stevens.

A pair of hoboes crash a party and assume the clothes and identities of two counts. They rise to the occasion when a baby girl is kidnapped, giving pursuit in a baby aeroplane. They effect a rescue and return the baby to its mother.

Daring Lions and Dizzy Lovers: Released 10/15/1919. © Century Comedies 10/02/1919. Century Comedy. Cast: Jimmie Adams, Esther Wood, Bud Jamison, The Century Lions. Director: Fred Fishback (Director, Story William Watson in copyright) (working titles **Lions and Tin Horn Sports** and **Lions and Lingerie**)

Millionaire's daughter is sent off to a private girls' school, much to the chagrin of her tiddley-winks champ beau. He follows her train by car. Once she is settled in the girls' dormitory, a doctor arrives to look things over. Several African lions escape from a nearby wharf and invade the dormitory, the girls cowering behind a "wall" of bedsprings. All ends well, and the girl marries her beau.

Romeos and Jolly Juliets: Released 10/22/1919. © Universal Film Mfg Co. 10/17/1919. Century Comedy. Cast: Merta Sterling, Cliff Bowes, Century Bathing Girls. Director, Story: William Watson.

Farmer Thimothy Clover takes leave to observe a bunch of Campfire Girls at a nearby swimming hole. Later, the farmer sleeps in the barn's loft, and a storm forces the girls to take refuge there as well. His wife discovers them, and accidentally(?) sets fire to the barn with a dropped lamp.

A Popular Villain: Released 10/29/1919. © Universal Film Mfg Co. 10/17/1919. **Rainbow Comedy.** Cast: Chai Hong. Director: J.A. Howe.

Pursued by his employer for flirting with his wife, cook Charlie (Hong) stumbles across a film company shoot and is hired to act. Hubby arrives and takes the place of another actor who is supposed to throttle Charlie's character. He does so, and convincingly.

Brownie's Doggone Tricks: Released 11/05/1919. © Century Comedies 11/11/1919. Century Comedy. Cast: Dot Farley, Phil Dunham, Lois Neilson, Brownie the Dog, Baby Ruth. Director: Vin Moore.

Behind wife Minnie's (Farley) back, hubby (Dunham) attempts to flirt with the new arrival (Neilson) at their boarding house. "Bob" Brownie, their dog, has Minnie's best interests at heart, and repeatedly thwarts hubby's attempts at love-making.

A Tight Fix: Released 11/12/1919. © Universal Film Mfg Co. 11/03/1919. **Rainbow Comedy.** Cast: Chai Hong, Claire Alexander, Harry Sweet. Director, Story: Alf Goulding. Assistant Director: David Smith.

Newlywed (and penniless) Harry has a brick thrown at him by a rival, and upon returning it the brick breaks a plate glass window. Pursued by a cop, Harry takes refuge in a Chinese laundry run by Hong, who accidentally burns the cop and ends up pursued as well. Hong hides in a trunk which is delivered to Harry's home, his wife shocked upon opening it. Harry arrives and, seeing Hong with his wife, comments "My wife with an armful of Chop-suey!"

African Lions and American Beauties: Released 11/19/1919 © Century Comedies 10/25/1919. Century Comedy. Cast: Jimmie Adams, Esther Wood, The Century Lions. Director, Story: Fred Fishback. Animal Trainer: Charles Gay.

"Jimmy Austin [sic] and Esther Woods are announced as the featured performers in this two-reel Century comedy which has some novelty in that three lions prowl about and act in a tame manner. Austin has very little to do in the production and the leading woman is also out of the foreground for a considerable amount of time. Fred C. Fishback is credited with writing this, but it is difficult to see just what he wrote, for there is hardly any story at all—in fact, what little plot was begun, was left unfinished. This is nothing but a number of bits of business joined together into a sort of patchquilt." (*Film Daily*, 01/11/1920)

Oh! You East Lynn: Released 11/26/1919. © Century Comedies 11/15/1919. **Rainbow Comedy.** Cast: Phil Dunham, Dot Farley, Lois Nelson, Billy Engle. Director, Story: J.A. Howe.

Prop boy Lynn's wife is forced to take the lead in a traveling troupe's show when the star performer fails to appear. A chorus girl reminds Lynn that he promised to make her a star if she'd run off and marry him, but his wife's arrival quickly puts an end to that notion.

A Barnyard Romance: Released 12/03/1919. © Century Comedies 11/26/1919. **Rainbow Comedy.** Cast: Chai Hong, Billy Engle, Louise Lorraine. Director: Jess Robbins.

Tramp Owata Hobo (Hong) captures the bandits who had robbed Louise, winning the farm girl's love. Later, her tyrant father tracks her down at the artist's studio in which she is posing, drags her home and starts to beat her. Hong rescues her and they escape on a buckboard, but when it overturns she is rescued by, and leaves with, the artist.

A Lucky Dog's Day: Released 12/10/1919. © Century Comedies 12/03/1919. Century Comedy. Cast: Brownie the Dog. Director, Story: William Watson.

The newlyweds are at odds with their landlord neighbor, matters not helped when the former's dog Brownie chases the landlord's cat. After a particularly violent row, the newlyweds awaken to find that the landlord has dragged their home from its foundation and set it adrift in the sea. An overturned lamp sets the structure ablaze, but they are rescued from its roof at the last moment.

The Good Ship Rock 'n' Rye: Released 12/17/1919. © Century Comedies 12/06/1919. Universal Jewel. Cast: Jimmie Adams, Mrs. Joe Martin the Monkey, Edith Roberts. Director, Story: Fred Fishback.

Mrs. Joe Martin impersonates a sailor lad on a pirate ship. The captain imprisons the sweetheart of the girl (Roberts) he's in love with and forces her to work in the ship's galley. She puts gun powder in the cake dough and blows up Martin, then helps her sweetheart escape. Rescued by a cruiser, guns are aimed at the pirate's ship and sink it. Martin manages to escape in a rowboat, and sheds her sailor clothes.

Weak Hearts and Wild Lions: Released 12/24/1919. © Century Comedies 12/13/1919.

Century Comedy. Cast: Jimmie Adams, Lois Nelson, Billy Engle, The Century Lions. Director, Story: Fred Fishback. Animal Trainer: Charles Gay (alternately referred to as both **Weak Minds and Wild Husbands** and **Wild Lions and Weak Minds** in the trades)

Adams is hired as all-around help by a circus. Adams, the lion tamer, and the manager all fall for the Queen of the Circus, so to get even Adams frees the lions, and all hell breaks loose in the circus.

Charlie Gets a Job: Released 12/31/1919. © Century Comedies 12/20/1919. **Rainbow Comedy.** Cast: Chai Hong, Louise Fortune (Lorraine). Director, Story: Jess Robbins (working title **Charley in Society**).

Kale and his daughter hire Charlie (Hong) as butler. Johnny, enraged that Kale won't let him near his daughter, enlists the aid of a bunch of rough-necks to assume the clothes and identities of a group of noblemen invited to dinner. Jonny and the girl elope, and Charlie's attempt to stop their speeding car ejects him into a mud puddle.

Adam and Eve a la Mode: Released 01/07/1920. © Century Comedies 12/27/1919. **Rainbow Comedy.** Cast: William Franey, William Irving, Rainbow Beauties. Director: Jess Robbins.

Mr. Sweettooth and his neighbor Philip de Glass stumble across a bevy of lovely young animal skin-clad ladies waiting for the arrival of dance instructor Prof. Jim-Jam. The girls, assuming the two fellows to be the professor and his friend, begin dancing for them. The arrival of the professor and the two fellows' wives quickly puts an end to that.

A Baby Doll Bandit: Released 01/12/1920. © Century Comedies 12/31/1919. Universal Jewel. Cast: Edith Roberts, Jimmie Adams, Mrs. Joe Martin the Monkey. Director, Story: Fred Fishback.

Betsy Beautiful arrives in the Western town of Weazel Tail Bend and is quickly given a job as the school's teacher. She is followed by her sweetheart, Hiram Biff. Pineapple Pete robs the local bank, and the sheriff arrives and demands half the cash. Hiram shows up, rounds up the crooks, grabs the money and his girl Betsy, and the two head out of town. Mrs. Joe Martin is headwaiter at a saloon, and later attends school.

Naughty Lions and Wild Men: Released 01/14/1920. © Century Comedies 01/05/1920. Century Comedy. Cast: Jimmie Adams, The Century Lions. Director, Story: Fred Fishback. Animal Trainer: Charles Gay.

Attempting to win his love Lois Killsome's hand by taking place in a lion hunt, Adams runs afoul of King Fadeum and finds himself being stewed for dinner. Queen Bangle takes a shining to Adams, who is ultimately rescued when Lois and competing lion hunters arrive on the scene.

All for the Dough Bag: Released 01/21/1920. © Century Comedies 01/09/1920. **Rainbow Comedy.** Cast: Phil Dunham, Bartine Burkett, Zip Monberg, Brownie the Dog, Eddie Baker. Director, Story: J.A. Howe.

Dancing professor Dunham attempts to elope with neighbor Burkett, but his grip with Brownie's dog collar gets mixed up with a crook's jewel-filled grip. After a wild chase the crook is caught, and Burkett's mother forgives Dunham.

Brownie's Busy Day: Released 01/28/1920. © Century Comedies 12/31/1919. Century Comedy. Cast: Brownie the Dog, George Jaeschke. Director: Jay A. Howe (working title **Brownie's Taking Ways**)

Crooked salesman Jaeschke woos grocery clerk June Love, much to the annoyance of head clerk Louie Prune. He steals from the store's cash register, but when suspected hides the stolen loot in Louie's pockets. He is caught in the act by Brownie, the store's pet.

Over the Ocean Wave: Released 02/04/1920. © Century Comedies 01/30/1920. **Rainbow Comedy.** Cast: Chai Hong, Charles Inslee, Harry Luderman, Bartine Burkett, Harry Sweet. Director, Story: Jess Robbins.

A ship's owner (Luderman) and his captain (Inslee) conspire to kidnap an heiress (Burkett), but conflicts arise when the captain falls for her. Charlie (Hong), the boat's chef, intervenes, rescuing the girl and blowing up the ship with a keg of dynamite.

Over the Transom: Released 02/09/1920. © Century Comedies 01/30/1920. Universal Jewel. Cast: Jimmie Adams, Esther Wood, Patrick Herman, Mrs. Joe Martin the Monkey. Director, Story: Fred Fishback.

Hotel clerk Jimmie (Adams) is in love with hotel milkmaid Esther (Wood). Esther falls for a count (Herman) and elopes with him, unaware that he's stolen the hotel's cash. They are followed by Jimmie and the bell hop (Mrs. Joe Martin), assisted by the female fire department.

Good Little Brownie: Released 02/11/1920. © Century Comedies 02/05/1920. Century Comedy. Cast: Brownie the Dog, Merta Sterling, Cliff Bowes, Virginia Warwick. Director: William Watson.

When Billy lures Henry's (Bowes) girl Virginia (Warwick) away at the beach, Henry gets even by setting up a competing near beer business next to Billy's, even surreptitiously tapping Billy's keg. Lota Fat (Sterling) arrives and asks for a sandwich, but Henry's attempts to steal one from Billy are thwarted by Brownie. Henry has his pals kidnap Virginia and drag the sack she's in to a Justice of the Peace to be married, but after the ceremony realizes it's Lota in the sack, not Virginia.

The Bull Thrower: Released 02/18/1920. © Century Comedies 02/09/1920. **Rainbow Comedy.** Cast: Phil Dunham, Edna Gregory, Billy Engle. Director, Story: J.A. Howe.

After inadvertently bring a Mexican bandit to justice, Dunham is made Chief of Police. Both Dunham and the former chief love the mayor's daughter, who decides that the winner of a bullfight may have her hand. Dunham emerges victorious.

Loose Lions and Fast Lovers: Released 02/25/1920. © Universal Film Mfg Co. 02/19/1920. Century Comedy. Cast: Bud Jamison, Lois Neilson, Harry Swett, Dan Russell, Marjorie Ray, The Century Lions. Director, Story: Fred Fishback (working title **Tiger Rose and Dandy Lions**)

Cirus (Sweet) is in love with one of his mother's boarders (Neilson). Some crooks arrive by boat and sweet-talk him into a tour of town, during which some stowaway lions emerge from the boat and terrify the town. Everyone ends up atop Cirus' kitchen stove, surrounded by the six lions.

A Red Hot Finish: Released 03/03/1920. © Universal Film Mfg Co. 02/24/1920. **Rainbow Comedy.** Cast: Virginia Warwick, Pat Harmon, Cliff Bowes. Director: William H. Watson.

Dirty Mike kidnaps a naive heiress and makes her his servant. When she learns from Moon, Mike's confederate, that a bathing pavilion belongs to her, she disposes of the villains and takes ownership of the pavilion. The villains return, but with an assist by her lover, Joe, manage to thwart their plans, sending them over a cliff.

My Dog Pal: Released 03/10/1920. © Universal Film Mfg Co. 02/25/1920. Century Comedy. Cast: Lois Neilson, Merta Sterling, Bud Jamison, Billy Engle, Brownie the Dog. Director, Story: Fred Fishback.

Farmer "Pop" Walker inherits the Lily White Café, so he takes his grandchildren Bud and Merta and their dog Brownie along to help run it. The manager and head waiter plan to rob Pop, but Brownie spoils their plans by returning the bomb they've planted, blowing them both to smithereens.

A Roaring Love Affair: Released 03/17/1920. © Universal Film Mfg Co. 03/04/1920. **Rainbow Comedy**. Cast: Zip Monberg, Harry Swett, Consuela Henley. Director, Story: Jess Robbins.

Farmhand Sapolio (Swett) follows when the farmer's daughter he's in love with, Paulino, takes off with a smooth-talking actor. Sapolio takes action when he thinks Paulino is being attacked, only to find that they are making a film. He doesn't give up, but awakens to find it's all a dream.

A Lion's Alliance: Released 03/24/1920. © Universal Film Mfg Co. 03/15/1920. Century Comedy. Cast: Merta Sterling, Bud Jamison, The Century Lions. Director, Story: Fred Fishback.

Mert and Bud go to the circus and chase each other about, accidentally letting loose some lions. The lions find their way to a beauty parlor/athletic club where Blue, the black masseuse and his young son both work. The son is chased about until Blue returns, the lions falling into parlor's water tank.

Light Hearts and Leaking Pipes: Released 03/31/1920. © Universal Film Mfg Co. 03/16/1920. **Rainbow Comedy**. Cast: Zip Monberg, Virginia Warwick. Director: William H. Watson.

Plumber O'Reilly finds himself in the middle of it when a woman customer is visited by one lover after another, hiding each one from the next. Then her husband arrives and the battle ensues. Cops are called, and two taking refuge in a eucalyptus tree are felled by the other two.

A Champion Loser: Released 04/07/1920. © Universal Film Mfg Co. 03/25/1920. **Rainbow Comedy**. Cast: Harry Sweet, June Love, Billy Engle. Director: Chuck Reisner.

A pugilist visiting a rural town puts on an exhibition.

"This has several funny bits that will get the desired results, but much of it is old stuff. The material linked about the exhibition and the pugilist who visits the rural town and some of the animal bits help it along considerably." (*Film Daily*, 03/21/1920)

Dog-Gone Clever: Released 04/14/1920. © Universal Film Mfg Co. 04/01/1920. Century Comedy. Cast: Brownie the Dog, Charles Dorety, Chris Rube, Lillian Byron, Robert Gray. Director: Chuck Reisner.

Napoleon (Brownie) escapes from jail and responds to a "Dog Wanted" sign at a livery stable. Its proprietress Byron finds some valuable plans inside Napoleon's collar, but is soon kidnapped and held prisoner at a blacksmith's shop. Napoleon effects a rescue.

A Jazzy Janitor: Released 04/21/1920. © Universal Film Mfg Co. 04/07/1920. **Rainbow Comedy**. Cast: Zip Monberg, Virginia Warwick, William Irving. Director: William H. Watson.

Hotel chauffeur Monberg is caught by his wife peeping into an attractive tenant's room, and gives chase. Monberg takes part in some illegal gambling and cleans up, but the Chief of Police raids the place. Monberg's wife arrives and knocks them all out with a sledge hammer, but revives her husband when she finds his pockets stuffed with money.

Lion Paws and Lady Fingers: Released 04/28/1920. © Universal Film Mfg Co. 04/16/1920. Century Comedy. Cast: The Century Lions. Director, Story: Fred Fishback.

Customer Heinie falls for Lady Finger, the sales girl at Luke McGluke's bakery. The kitchen help threatens to strike. When the circus pulls out of town and forgets to take the lions along, they escape and head into the bakery.

A Restaurant Riot: Released 05/05/1920. © Universal Film Mfg Co. 04/23/1920. **Rainbow Comedy.** Cast: Billy Engle, Merta Sterling, Lyn Cole, Celeste Zimlick. Director: J.A. Howe.

Restaurant owner Mutt N. Head threatens to fire kitchen help Engle unless he drums up some business. Engle heads outside and pretends to be drunk, is spotted by the crowd outside, who then rush the place thinking it's a speakeasy. Inspector Sterling pretends to be a customer, is actually given some "hard" tea, and wobbles out of the restaurant a bit tipsy.

My Salomy Lions: Released 05/12/1920. © Universal Film Mfg Co. 04/28/1920. Century Comedy. Cast: Billy Engle, Merta Sterling, Charles Dorety, Louise Lorraine, Bud Jamison, Hans Joby, The Century Lions. Director, Story: Fred Fishback.

In Turkey, a tourist (Dorety) and two honeymooners (Jamison and Lorraine) stumble across the palace of a sultan (Engle). He fancies the bride and takes the others prisoner, but her husband saves the day by unleashing some lions. Merta is in the harem as Fattemma.

He Loved Like He Lied: Released 05/19/1920. © Universal Film Mfg Co. 05/06/1920. **Rainbow Comedy.** Cast: William Irving, Consuela Henley, Joe Jacobs, Billy Engle. Director: Mal St. Clair.

Count Vampa Little (Irving) and Dirty Mike (Engle) impersonate soldiers for the purpose of separating war widows from their insurance money. Their new target: Mrs. Weeping Willow (Henley). The two imposters become competitors when Mike feels that he's being rooked on his share, but their respective attempts come to an abrupt end when Willow's husband Nicky (Jacobs) shows up, still very much alive.

The Tale of a Dog: Released 05/26/1920. © Universal Film Mfg Co. 05/13/1920. Century Comedy. Cast: Brownie the Dog. Director, Story: Tom Buckingham.

An Artist's Muddle: Released 06/02/1920. © Universal Film Mfg Co. 05/21/1920. **Rainbow Comedy.** Cast: Harry Mann, Dick Dickerson, Lillian Byron. Director: Noel Smith (working title **A Temperamental Artist**)

Two artists are in love with the same girl, unaware that she is married to a sailor. The sailor returns and the one artist attempts to get the other out of the way by setting him up for a fall at the sailor's hands. Several attempts lead to an extended chase.

Moonshines and Jailbirds: Released 06/09/1920. © Universal Film Mfg Co. 05/24/1920. **Rainbow Comedy.** Cast: Billy Engle, George Dickerson, Esther Jackson, Hans Joby. Director: Jay A. Howe.

During Prohibition, turtles are used to smuggle bootleg liquor across the Mexican border into the U.S. A revenue officer is framed by the bootleggers, so the revenuer's daughter's husband (Engle) accepts the blame and heads to prison. All ends well.

Lions' Jaws and Kittens' Paws: Released 06/16/1920. © Universal Film Mfg Co. 06/04/1920. Century Comedy. Cast: Harry Sweet, Edna Gregory, Zip Monberg, The Century Lions, Merta Sterling. Director, Story: William Watson.

A tailor (Monberg) flirts with his upstairs neighbor Ethel (Gregory) while fitting her for a gown, so his jealous wife (Sterling) calls Ethel's lion tamer husband (Sweet) who comes down and breaks it up. The two meet again at the zoo, so this time the husband unleashes his lions, which are recaptured after some scary moments. Ethel and her husband dream that lions are all over their bed, but awaken to find only kittens on the bed.

A He-Male Vamp: Released 06/23/1920. © Universal Film Mfg Co. 06/09/1920. **Rainbow Comedy.** Cast: Zip Monty, Harry Sweet, Connie Henley. Director: William H. Watson.

The stranger frames the girl's sweetheart for the extortion of her father's money, hoping to win her hand in marriage. The sweetheart dresses in women's clothing to get close to the stranger, forces a switch of clothing, who is then arrested for the extortion. He confesses all.

A Villain's Broken Heart: Released 06/30/1920. © Universal Film Mfg Co. 06/09/1920. **Rainbow Comedy.** Cast: Billy Engle, Celeste Zimlick. Director: J.A. Howe.

Guests at what first appears to be a hotel turn out to be the inmates of an asylum. Zimlick is there as well, detained by force by the superintendant who wants her to deed over her property. Enter a private detective (Engle) employed by relatives, who is the facial double of the asylum's janitor, leading to confusion.

Should Waiters Marry?: Released 07/07/1920. © Universal Film Mfg Co. 06/29/1920. **Rainbow Comedy.** Cast: George Ovey, Bud Jamison, Chai Hong, Eddie Lambert, June Love, Century Bathing Beauties. Director, Story: Thomas Buckingham.

Beachside restaurant waiter Ovey is in love with the owner's daughter Love. Dishonest lifeguard Jamison serves as a rival, his goal to dispose of her father and gain possession of the restaurant. Ovey foils Jamison, earning her father's gratitude and Love's hand and fortune.

Bear Skinned Beauties: Released 07/14/1920. © Universal Film Mfg Co. 07/01/1920. Century Comedy. Cast: Zip Monberg, Edna Gregory, Century Beauty Chorus. Director, Story: F.C. Windemere (working title **An Awful Skate**).

Roller skating messenger boy Monberg gets mixed up with a fashionable modiste shop's owner, Bull Slinger, when the latter tries to vamp Monberg's girl. Monberg is chased to a dental office and mistakenly gassed for an extraction, his gas-induced dreams ending when he awakens and sees Bull.

Off His Trolley: Released 07/21/1920. © Universal Film Mfg Co. 07/09/1920. Rainbow Comedy. Cast: Billy Engle, Dick Dickerson, Sam Newfield, Jessie Fox, Jack Wright. Director, Story: J.A. Howe.

Competition between a rural jitney bus and a trolley car results in increasingly creative fights for customers.

A Birthday Tangle: Released 07/28/1920. © Universal Film Mfg Co. 07/15/1920. Century Comedy. Cast: Connie Henley, Bud Jamison, Marvin Loback, Charles Dorety, Century Beauty Chorus. Director, Story: James Davis (working title **Home Brew**)

Old Crow, owner of the town hotel, has a weakness for drink that his daughter attempts to end by scaring him with a bevy of bedsheet-covered "ghosts." The same trick is pulled on Billy Monday, who has attended the daughter's birthday party. Billy is hired by her father to serve as the hotel's barber, but gets into trouble when he clips a gypsy's dog's hair and is accused of cruelty to animals.

Won By a Nose: Released 08/04/1920. © Universal Film Mfg Co. 07/21/1920. Rainbow Comedy. Cast: Charles Dorety, Connie Henley, Harry Keaton, Zip Monberg. Director: Fred Windemere.

Blacksmith's helper Dorety falls for a girl but loses her to a city chap, so he heads to the city to win fame, fortune, and the girl. A fortune teller advises him to bet on horses, but at the track he encounters his rival who attempts to disable the horse Dorety has bet on. Dorety accidentally ends up on the horse's back, and the frightened animal takes off and wins the race with flying colors. But Dorety doesn't win the girl!

An Oil Can Romeo: Released 08/11/1920. © Universal Film Mfg Co. 08/03/1920. Rainbow Comedy. Cast: Bud Jameson, Charles Dorety, Lillian Byron, Brownie the Dog. Director: James Davis.

Inn owner Joe is assisted by Aunt Emily, who has sent in a photo of her daughter Byron to a matrimonial agency in hopes of landing a man. Dorety, having seen the photo, comes to the inn, and he and Byron soon plan to elope. Aunt Emily gets wind of this, takes Byron's place wearing a heavy veil, and is about to be married to Dorety when Byron and her dad arrive and squelch Aunt Emily's plans.

A One Cylinder Love Riot: Released 08/18/1920. © Universal Film Mfg Co. 08/06/1920. Century Comedy. Cast: Bud Jamison, Billy Engle, Connie Henley, Lillian Byron. Director, Story: Tom Buckingham.

Engle and Byron are lovers, but her dad wants her to marry a villainous millionaire.

When the couple takes off, dad and the millionaire follow, but after a hayloft-set fight dad realizes that Byron will only have Engle, and settles for that.

Brownie, the Peacemaker: Released 08/25/1920. © Universal Film Mfg Co. 08/14/1920. Century Comedy. Cast: Brownie the Dog, Phil Dunham, Merta Sterling, Jessie Fox, Chai Hong. Director: Dan Taylor.

Sterling believes Brownie to be her reincarnated husband. Brownie drives a miniature car, handling brakes and wheel cleverly. The film ends with an auto chase and the villain's downfall.

Beginning of 1920-1921 Season

A Movie Hero: Released 09/01/1920. © Universal Film Mfg Co. 08/21/1920. Century Comedy. Cast: Jimmie Adams, Louise Fortune. Director, Story: Fred Fishback.

In a movie theater, the projected western stars Adams as the new sheriff, the former sheriff his rival for Fortune's hand. Her brother Hans steals their dad's money and splits it with the ex-sheriff, who abducts Fortune when she refuses his advances. A chase follows and Adams overcomes the ex-sheriff and gang, and rescues the girl. The film now over, Adams appears in front of the audience and applauds himself, boasting how clever he is.

You Tell 'Em, Lions, I'll Roar: Released 09/08/1920. © Universal Film Mfg Co. 09/03/1920. Century Comedy. Cast: Harry Sweet, Merta Sterling, Zip Monberg, George Ovey, The Century Lions. Director, Story: William Watson (working title **Wild Lions and Ferocious Cheese**)

Grocery store owners drive a villain away using limburger cheese. Crooks later rob the store's safe, so the owners follow them to the local vaudeville house where a lion tamer performs. They unleash the lions but are chased back to their store, but fend them off with the limburger.

The Profiteering Blues: Released 09/15/1920. © Universal Film Mfg Co. 09/08/1920. Century Comedy. Cast: Merta Sterling, Eddie Lambert, Bud Jamison. Director: Fred Fishback (working title **Cracked Wedding Bells**)

Two newlywed couples struggle to find overnight lodgings in a town short of available rooms. After a horrible night and multiple attempts to sleep both indoors and out, daybreak arrives. Sterling and her hubby build a house, and five years later are surrounded by "five little Mertas."

Love and Gasoline: Released 09/22/1920. © Universal Film Mfg Co. 09/09/1920. Century Comedy. Cast: Connie Henley, Bud Jamison, Harry Keaton, Harry Mann. Director: Noel M. Smith.

A villain kidnaps the girl when he finds that he's losing out to two rivals. A chase follows in multiple conveyances and smashups, but the hero finally overtakes them and rescues the girl.

His Master's Breath: Released 09/29/1920. © Universal Film Mfg Co. 09/17/1920. Century Comedy. Cast: Brownie the Dog. Director, Story: Fred Fishback.

Neighbors Rye and Rock are both heavy drinkers, the former successfully smuggled into his home each night by his dog Brownie, the latter less successfully so. They take refuge in a house for a surreptitious drink, but there's an illegal still inside and the place is raided by the cops, followed by the wives. Brownie, tied out front, protects the place but pulls the front of the house off. A chase follows, and the two couples make up.

A Shot-Gun Wedding: Released 10/06/1920. © Universal Film Mfg Co. 09/25/1920. Century Comedy. Cast: Harry Sweet, Merta Sterling. Director, Story: Fred Fishback.

Hired help Sweet is promised a half interest in the ranch if he will marry Sterling, the owner's daughter. Sweet loves othe daughter Inez, so his rival Jack orchestrates it so that the owner forces a shotgun wedding on Sweet and Sterling, Jack officiating. Finding the nuptials to be illegal, Sweet is reunited with Inez.

Loose Lions: Released 10/13/1920. © Universal Film Mfg Co. 10/07/1920. Century Comedy. Cast: Robert Anderson, Dixie Lamont, The Century Lions. Director, Story: William Watson.

Gambler Anderson is awarded a job as lion tamer at a movie star when he rescues an actress (Lamont) on a runaway horse. Later thinking the director has caused the actress' death by lion, he unleashes the beasts only to find her alive and well.

Should Tailors Trifle?: Released 10/20/1920. © Universal Film Mfg Co. 10/14/1920. Century Comedy. Cast: Charles Dorety, Peggy Prevost, Bud Jamison, Brownie the Dog. Director, Story: Tom Buckingham.

Tailor Dorety marries tailor Prevost. When his dog Brownie brings a baby into the shop, rival Jamison states that the baby is Dorety's by another woman. Enraged by his supposed infidelity, Prevost runs off with Jamison. The child's father gives Dorety a reward for rescuing the infant, so Dorety turns the tables and tells Prevost that Jamison's wife retrieved their baby and gave him the reward. Now furious with Jamison, Prevost returns to Dorety.

Uncle Tom's Caboose: Released 10/27/1920. © Universal Film Mfg Co. 10/25/1920. Century Comedy. Cast: Charles Dorety, Peggy Prevost, Zip Monberg, Lois Gibson, Dolly Stoddard. Director, Story: James Davis.

A travelling troupe puts on their version of Uncle Tom's Cabin, but with up-to-date methods rather than an old-time wagon show. During a performance, handy man Dorety and cook Chow Mein rob the show and the villagers' homes, but are arrested by the sheriff.

A Blue Ribbon Mutt: Released 11/03/1920. © Universal Film Mfg Co. 10/25/1920. Century Comedy. Cast: Charles Dorety, Lillian Byron, Bud Jamison, Brownie the Dog. Director, Story: Chuck Reisner.

Dorety finds Brownie and a pup and decides to enter the latter in a dog show. Former boss Byron has a poodle entered and it wins, so Brownie substitutes the pup for the poodle. Crooks steal the pup, but Byron thinks that it was her poodle that was taken; she's overjoyed when Brownie produces the missing dog. Dorety and Byron are reunited, and Brownie awarded a special prize.

A Lyin' Tamer: Released 11/10/1920. © Universal Film Mfg Co. 10/29/1920. Century Comedy. Cast: Cliff Bowes, Dixie Lamont, Charles Inslee, The Century Lions. Director, Story: Chuck Reisner.

A big game hunter, asleep en route to present his lions, loses his clothes to an escaped convict. Arriving at the destination, the convict assumes the hunter's role but accidentally unleashes the lions. The warden and his daughter are in attendance, the convict is recognized, and rearrested.

Twin Crooks: Released 11/17/1920. © Universal Film Mfg Co. 11/08/1920. Century Comedy. Cast: Charles Dorety, Lillian Byron, Bud Jamison. Director, Story: Tom Buckingham.

His animal act a bust, Dorety takes a job as janitor, his boss a brute with a pretty wife. Twin crooks abduct the couple's baby, so Dorety attempts to get it back, his motives and intentions frequently misunderstood. After a scene high atop a skyscraper, Dorety retrieves the baby.

A Fishy Story: Released 11/24/1920. © Universal Film Mfg Co. 11/15/1920. Century Comedy. Cast: Zip Monberg, Esther Jackson. Director: Fred Fishback.

A retired fisherman puts the three men who love his daughter Jackson to a difficult fishing test, resulting in many aquatic difficulties. The chief of police, one of the suitors, wins favor when he arrests the other two for robbing the father's safe. A young detective arrests Jackson and some other girls for their skimpy bathing attire, and ends up marrying her.

Hot Dog: Released 12/01/1920. © Universal Film Mfg Co. 11/20/1920. Century Comedy. Cast: Brownie the Dog, Zip Monberg, Lillian Byron, Harry Sweet, Brownie the Dog. Director, Story: Fred Fishback.

Heiress Byron's appointed guardian Duffy wants his son Monberg to marry her, so he locks up Monberg's wife and hides their child. Sweet, her lover, is kept at bay, but finally gets through and marries her. Brownie, meanwhile, has looked after and safeguarded the child.

Laughing Gas: Released 12/08/1920. © Universal Film Mfg Co. 11/27/1920. Century Comedy. Cast: Charles Dorety, Bud Jamison. Director, Story: Tom Buckingham (working title **A Doctor's Dilemma**)

Dorety takes a job as a doctor's assistant to get at the doctor's medicinal booze. When a crook swallows the doctor's money, laughing gas is administered, and he's operated on; his spirit floats away leaving the money behind. X-Rays reveal dice inside a black fellow's stomach. Dorety puts the cops onto the doctor's still, but he's arrested along with the doctor. The nurse saves him from prison to nurse him for his wounded heart.

Tails Win: Released: 12/15/1920. © Universal Film Mfg Co. 12/11/1920. Century Comedy. Cast: Harry Sweet, Dixie Lamont, Zip Monberg. Director, Story: William Watson.

A married theatrical agent falls for his stenographer, not realizing that she's married and that his new bookkeeper is her husband. Getting wind of this, the agent's wife hires a detective. Stenographer learns that she's inherited a circus, but only boxes full of lions arrive; they escape and the chase is on.

Trouble Bubbles: Released 12/22/1920. © Universal Film Mfg Co. 12/08/1920. Century Comedy. Cast: Billy Armstrong, Esther Jackson. Director: Billy Armstrong.

Cop Armstrong arrests a home brewer and his cohorts, taking all to jail, their home brew included. Armstrong is promoted, a party follows, the chief's wife gets drunk, and a band of home brewers kidnap the chief's daughter as reprisal. Armstrong rescues her and her kidnappers are arrested.

Their First Tintype: Released 12/29/1920. © Universal Film Mfg Co. 12/16/1920. Century Comedy. Cast: Bud Jamison, Merta Sterling, Inez McDonald, Billy Engle, Century Beauty Chorus. Director, Story: Bud Jamison.

A studio photographer goes to great lengths to get his subjects to smile. Gym scenes follow with girls and boys doing various acrobatic stunts. Village firemen attempt to douse a fire, but a dog grabs the hose and drags the firemen about.

Happy Daze: Released 01/05/1921. © Universal Film Mfg Co. 12/28/1920. Century Comedy. Cast: Cliff Bowes, The Century Lions. Director: Charles Reisner (working title **In Sultan Land**)

A boy takes a job as sailor to follow his girl to Turkey, creating mischief en route, and making the rest of the trip in a tub when the boat blows up. The girl is kidnapped by the sultan for his harem, so the boy follows and gets into the harem with two other sailors. The sultan unleashes his lions, creating mass havoc. The boy rescues the girl but is devastated when she embraces another sailor; it turns out to be her brother.

Tee Time: Released 01/12/1921. © Universal Film Mfg Co. 01/05/1921. Century Comedy. Cast: Percy Pembroke, Billy Armstrong, George Williams, Fay Holderness, Florence Lee, Century Lions. Director: James Davis (working title **Golf and Jail-Birds** and possibly **The Spirit of Twenty-One**)

Pembroke and Armstrong hold a golf contest, the winner getting Lee. Armstrong loads his golf ball with nitro-glycerin. A plot to kidnap a baby and place blame on the other results in both being jailed. After some encounters with lions, Pembroke wins the girl.

Fire Bugs: Released 01/19/1921. © Universal Film Mfg Co. 01/08/1921. Century Comedy. Cast: Jack Duffy, Harry Sweet, Brownie the Dog. Director, Story: Fred Fishback.

When the heroine's house catches fire, a hick fire department readies itself with an able assist from Brownie.

His Fearful Finish: Released 01/26/1921. © Universal Film Mfg Co. 01/15/1921. Century Comedy. Cast: Charles Dorety, Bartine Burkett, Bud Jamison, Loyal Underwood. Director, Story: Tom Buckingham.

Loan shark Jamison threatens to throw Underwood out of his home unless daughter Burkett will have him, but she loves Dorety. Fights follow between the two suitors, but when Dorety finds a roll of bills in a chimney he has smashed, the problem is settled. Jamison's revenge involves placing her youngster sibling on a runaway horse wagon, but the child is saved.

Puppy Love: Released 02/02/1921. © Universal Film Mfg Co. 01/22/1921. Century Comedy. Cast: Brownie the Dog, Cliff Bowes, Merta Sterling. Director, Story: Chuck Reisner (copyrighted as **His Puppy Love**)

A crook robs widow Haash's safe, but son Dinky and his dog Brownie observe and alert the police who erroneously arrest the bootblack next door. Dinky and Brownie are kidnapped by the crook, but Brownie stops the auto, the bootblack is released, and the crook arrested.

Fresh from the Farm: Released 02/09/1921. © Universal Film Mfg Co. 01/31/1921. Century Comedy. Cast: Harry Sweet, Bud Jamison. Director, Story: Tom Buckingham.

Relieved of all his valuables shortly after arriving in the city, rube Sweet gets a job in a boarding house. He falls for a female tenant, incurring the wrath of chef Jamison. After a number of altercations, Sweet and the girl make their escape to be married.

Leaping Lions and Jailbirds: Released 02/16/1921. © Universal Film Mfg Co. 02/01/1921. Century Comedy. Cast: The Century Lions, Harry Sweet, Billy Engle. Director, Story: William Watson.

When the condemned is found to have escaped, and not wanting to disappoint the guests invited to witness a hanging, the warden fools Birdie (Sweet) into taking the condemned's place. Birdie's wife lets loose some lions and in the ensuing panic Birdie is set free.

Vamps and Scamps: Released 02/23/1921. © Universal Film Mfg Co. 02/07/1921. Century Comedy. Cast: Zip Monberg, Century Bathing Beauties. Director, Story: James Davis.

Bunny Huge bets woman-hater Jack O'Ladden a thousand dollars that one of the girls in his hotel will make him fall. The girls attempt, one after another, in disguises, but fail. Frustrated, Bunny and Jack fight, cops are called, and Jack attempts an escape. He's arrested by a bunch of cops that turn out to be the girls in uniforms, and he loses the bet.

Her Circus Man: Released 03/02/1921. © Universal Film Mfg Co. 02/28/1921. Century Comedy. Cast: Baby Peggy, Harry Sweet, Harry Gribbon, The Century Lions. Director, Story: James Davis.

City swell Gribbon and rube Sweet vie for the same girl. Entering a circus, we see Turkish harem dancing scenes and a lion-taming act. Sweet wins $50 for riding the back of a mule, and ends up with the girl.

The Dog Doctor: Released 03/09/1921. © Universal Film Mfg Co. 02/25/1921. Century Comedy. Cast: Harry Sweet, Louise Lorraine, Brownie the Dog, Bud Jamison, Zip Monberg. Director, Story: Fred Fishback.

Sweet encounters trolley service issues rushing home to his wife and sick baby. The doctor is called he's but busy, so his assistant Brownie is sent instead. The baby turns out to be a pup, so Brownie takes the pup back to the hospital which is filled with other pup patients. A villain attempts to steal Brownie.

Stuffed Lions: Released 03/16/1921. © Universal Film Mfg Co. 03/07/1921. Century Comedy. Cast: Harry Sweet, Cliff Bowes, Dixie Lamont, The Century Lions. Director, Story: Chuck Reisner.

The animals in the taxidermist's shop are all filled with liquor. On the lam Sweet takes refuge there and is given a job. Sent to get a crate of lions, they escape and follow him back to the shop. Roller-skating police arrive and round them up.

A Bunch of Kisses: Released 03/23/1921. © Universal Film Mfg Co. 03/12/1921. Century Comedy. Cast: Charles Dorety, Louise Lorraine. Director, Story: Fred Fishback.

Auto repair shop owner Dorety takes off in pursuit when a rival makes off with Lorraine, his cashier girlfriend. After a wild pursuit in autos, Dorety gets the girl and off to the minister's they go to get married.

Seeing is Believing: Released 03/30/1921. © Universal Film Mfg Co. 03/19/1921. Century Comedy. Cast: Florence Lee, Percy Pembroke. Director, Story: James Davis.

Con artist Pembroke is exposed to the family he's trying to bilk by a photographer's filmed evidence. He abducts the daughter and takes her to the minister's, but the detectives arrest him in time. The daughter's sweetheart, the photographer, is there, so they decide to get married.

Tough Luck: Released 04/06/1921. © Universal Film Mfg Co. 03/29/1921. Century Comedy. Cast: Harry Sweet, Brownie the Dog. Director, Story: Tom Buckingham (working title **Superstition**)

Absurdly superstitious Sweet is given a note to deliver to a doctor, who promptly locks him up behind bars. A girl he met earlier turns out to be the doctor's daughter, Brownie helps Sweet to escape, and he and the girl are married.

Harem Scarem: Released 04/13/1921. © Universal Film Mfg Co. 04/01/1921. Century Comedy. Cast: The Century Lions, Harry Sweet. Director, Story: William Watson.

Passerby Sweet attempts to rescue the Rajah's favorite dancer, who is guarded by lions. Guards unleash some lions to stop Sweet, but he and the girl evade them and release other lions, which go after the Rajah. Imprisoning the guards, Sweet and the dancer make their escape.

On with the Show: Released 04/20/1921. © Universal Film Mfg Co. 04/07/1921. Century Comedy. Cast: Baby Peggy, Harry Gribbon, Percy Pembroke, Florence Lee, The Century Lions. Director, Story: James Davis.

City slicker Percy (Gribbon) acts in a rube's amateur film along with the rube's girl. Later spotting a safe's combination on screen, Percy robs it. A later showing of the film reveals Percy's identity to a Pinkerton detective in the audience, and he is arrested.

The Kid's Pal: Released 04/27/1921. © Universal Film Mfg Co. 04/13/1921. Century Comedy. Cast: Florence Lee, Bud Jamison, Billy Engle, Brownie the Dog. Director, Story: Tom Buckingham.

Brownie dotes on the little girl star (*not* played by Baby Peggy). The Weasel kidnaps the girl and hides her in a hay mow, and her pursuing older sister in a barn. Brownie rushes to the rescue, saving both the girl and her sister, and chasing The Weasel from the premises.

The Country Heir: Released 05/04/1921. © Universal Film Mfg Co. 04/22/1921. Century Comedy. Cast: Harry Sweet, Florence Lee. Director, Story: William Watson.

Willie Dye (Sweet) accidentally learns of the inheritance he is to receive from his uncle if he is located, and discovers that the uncle's lawyer and an adventuress plan to steal it. Willie heads to his uncle's home only to find that he is too late, the lawyer having made off with the safe's contents, $2 in Russian rubles!

Dandy Lions: Released 05/11/1921. © Universal Film Mfg Co. 04/27/1921. Century Comedy. Cast: The Century Lions. Director, Story: William Watson.

A fired reporter takes a job at a restaurant. He is fired from that job as well when the owner takes a liking to the guy's wife and hires her. Seeking revenge, the reporter frees a crate of lions which end up putting the restaurant out of business.

Playmates: Released 05/18/1921. © Universal Film Mfg Co. 05/06/1921. Century Comedy. Cast: Baby Peggy, Brownie the Dog, Florence Lee, Zip Monberg. Director, Story: Fred Fishback.

Betty (Lee) does the laundry for a bachelor, while Brownie dotes on Betty's child Baby Peggy and gives her a bath. Peggy roams off and is found by a cop, but Brownie intercedes before she is placed in the Children's Society Home. Betty and the bachelor decide to marry and make one big happy family.

A Dollar's Worth: Released 05/25/1921. © Universal Film Mfg Co. 05/14/1921. Century Comedy. Cast: Harry Sweet. Director, Story: Tom Buckingham.

Sweet enters a tough town and takes a dollar bill from one of the local lugs. Others attempt to get the dollar back, but Sweet is energized by a spray of pulverized goat glands and cleans up the joint. He rescues a young lady but loses both her (she's married) and the dollar to a passing cop.

For Sale: Released 06/01/1921. © Universal Film Mfg Co. 05/21/1921. Century Comedy. Cast: Harry Sweet. Director, Story: Tom Buckingham.

Sweet attempts to sell an ancient flivver that seems to have a mind of its own. To demonstrate what the aging vehicle can do, he agrees to take a girl and her family for a drive and picnic. When the girl is abducted by a former sweetheart, Sweet rescues her.

On Account: Released 06/08/1921. © Universal Film Mfg Co. 05/28/1921. Century Comedy. Cast: Baby Peggy, Charles Dorety, Olive Dale, Bert Roach. Director, Story: William Watson.

Dorety, his wife Dale, and infant Peggy live above their beer-brewing landlord Roach. The rent due, Dale instead gives Roach a bottle of beer, lifted from his own shelf by Peggy. Roach plans to catch the thief, but instead is instrumental in catching three crooks.

Pals: Released 06/15/1921. © Universal Film Mfg Co. 06/04/1921. Century Comedy. Cast: Baby Peggy, Brownie the Dog. Director, Story: Tom Buckingham.

"Brownie, the wonder dog, is the star of this two reel Century Comedy. He is, as has been said many times before, a consummate little actor. His wide variety of tricks that are worked reasonably into the plot are not short of marvelous. To say that he has appeal for any audience is superfluous. The little three year old tot who shares practically all of the scenes with Brownie increases the appeal of the picture. 'Pals' will fit onto any type of program and it will be especially well received in a theatre that caters to parents who bring their children." (*Moving Picture World*, 05/14/1921)

Custard's Last Stand: Released 06/22/1921. © Universal Film Mfg Co. 06/10/1921. Century Comedy. Cast: Zip Monberg, Florence Lee. Director, Story: William Watson.

Repeatedly ignored by the female guest he longs for, the Bilkmore Hotel's room-clerk is despondent. A nighttime fundraising benefit has an act wherein that same girl is "attacked" by a villain. Thinking it reality, the room-clerk begins throwing things at the stage, and the audience joins in.

Wood Simps: Released 06/29/1921. © Universal Film Mfg Co. 06/17/1921. Century Comedy. Cast: The Century Lions, Charley Dorety. Director, Story: William Watson.

Charley, his partner, and valets go rabbit hunting, track one to a hole, which turns out to be the rear entrance to a lion's den. The lions chase them back to and through their home.

Society Dogs: Released 07/06/1921. © Universal Film Mfg Co. 06/27/1921. Century Comedy. Cast: Brownie the Dog, Florence Lee. Director, Story: Fred Fishback.

Brownie, in Tuxedo, dines on an elegant meal, but it's a dream. Brownie's master is a glazier, and has trained the dog to break windows with a stone tied to his tail. A clothes cleaner has Brownie smear mud on potential customers. Brownie escapes a pursuing cop by posing as Nipper, the RCA dog.

The Smart Alec: Released 07/13/1921. © Universal Film Mfg Co. 07/02/1921. Century Comedy. Cast: Harry Sweet. Director, Story: Tom Buckingham.

Beaten senseless while attempting to rescue a nurse from a masher, Harry ends up in a hospital. Administered ether, he dreams he and the nurse are in a canoe heading for a 1,000 foot waterfall. He ends up saving the day, only to awaken with the nurse pouring water on his head. He tells her of the dream, and she promises to make his dream come true. They leave the hospital together.

Third Class Male: Released 07/20/1921. © Universal Film Mfg Co. 07/08/1921. Century Comedy. Cast: Baby Peggy, Charles Dorety, Florence Lee, Fred Spencer, Cupie Dolan. Director, Story: William Watson.

Baby Peggy escapes from a burning building. Dorety and Lee attempt to put out the fire, but Baby Peggy succeeds by attaching a cable to a locomotive which pulls down a water tower, extinguishing the flames.

The Whizz-Bang (aka **The Wizzbang** and **The Whiz-Bang**): Released 07/27/1921. © Universal Film Mfg Co. 07/16/1921. Century Comedy. Cast: Lige Conley, Florence Lee, Edna Gregory, Bud Jamison. Director, Story: Fred Fishback (working title **The Thinker**)

Conley's an inventive genius, but his inventions are more creative than efficient. Villain Jamison attempts to steal Conley's girl Gregory, but is repeatedly foiled by Conley's inventions. The Whizz-Bang is a machine that effectively cracks nuts!

Alfalfa Love: Released 08/03/1921. © Universal Film Mfg Co. 07/21/1921. Century Comedy. Cast: Brownie the Dog. Director, Story: Fred Fishback (working title **Three Wise Boobs**)

Brownie takes care of many of the farm's chores, both inside and out. Learning that the farm's new owner is a woman, three "boob" farmhands conspire to win her affections, only to learn that she is married. They head to the train tracks to end it all, but Brownie arrives and convinces them not to follow through. They leave the farm behind, Brownie wishing them a farewell, after which he returns to his chores.

In Again: Released 08/10/1921. © Universal Film Mfg Co. 07/29/1921. Century Comedy. Cast: Harry Sweet, Dixie Lamont. Director, Story: Tom Buckingham.

Harry and Dixie head to the city to elope. An escaped convict switches clothes with Harry, his striped convict outfit now attracting police. Harry manages to switch into an all-white painter's uniform.. He catches the convict, but later learns that Dixie and her dad are prisoners in the Blue Cat Café. Harry effects a rescue with the aid of the cops who had earlier pursued him.

The Clean Up: Released 08/17/1921. © Universal Film Mfg Co. 08/03/1921. Century Comedy. Cast: Baby Peggy, Charles Dorety. Director, Story: William Watson.

Dorety is the owner of a small bank. A bank robber enters and steals the money while Dorety is otherwise occupied, but young daughter Baby Peggy spots the crook. She later sees him again at the sea shore and overhears that he's going to make a return to the bank. She alerts the police, and the crook is soon apprehended.

Golfing: Released 08/24/1921. © Universal Film Mfg Co. 08/12/1921. Century Comedy. Cast: Baby Peggy, Brownie the Dog. Director, Story: Fred Fishback.

Dad and Baby Peggy take golf lessons in their house, with disastrous results. Out on the links with Brownie as caddy, a gypsy kidnaps Peggy and ties Brownie. Dad and wife are misdirected to the river, but Brownie escapes and rescues Peggy from the gypsy's tent, making a horseback escape.

Hold Your Breath: Released 08/31/1921. © Universal Film Mfg Co. 08/19/1921. Century Comedy. Cast: Charles Dorety, Bert Roach, Century Lions. Director, Story: William Watson.

Dorety and Roach, both drunk, clamber atop the roof of a 22 story building. Roach demands that Dorety pay up on a debt, leading to chase along a ledge overlooking a lion's den. Dorety slips and falls in, and Roach is surprised to find Dorety reclining comfortably on one of the biggest lions.

Beginning of 1921-1922 Season

Stealin' Home: Released 09/07/1921. © Universal Film Mfg Co. 08/24/1921. Century Comedy. Cast: Harry Sweet, Bartine Burkett, James T. Kelley. Director, Story: Alfred J. Goulding. Assistant Director: David Smith.

Office boy Sweet is fired by gruff boss Kelley. Promising to head home, he instead heads to the ball game, is mistaken for the new pitcher, is put in a uniform, and gets a home run for the team when it is badly needed.

Brownie's Little Venus: Released 09/14/1921. © Universal Film Mfg Co. 09/02/1921. Century Comedy. Cast: Baby Peggy, Brownie the Dog, Bud Jamison, Lillian Byron. Director, Story: Fred Fishback.

Husband and wife (Jamison and Byron), accompanied by young daughter Baby Peggy and Brownie, return from a closed theater. Later, Peggy stumbles across a burglar attempting to rob their safe, and after some confusion where Peggy is mistaken for the burglar, Jamison catches the thief.

High Life: Released 09/21/1921. © Universal Film Mfg Co. 09/12/1921. Century Comedy. Cast: Harry Sweet, Charles Dorety, Bartine Burkett. Director, Story: Alfred J. Goulding. Assistant Director: David Smith.

Sweet takes his girl Burkett for a ride. His hat blows off and lands on a girder, and when Sweet tries to retrieve it he is hauled high atop a building under construction. Burkett is soon similarly whisked into the air, followed by a clergyman who performs a ceremony atop the structure.

A Week Off: Released 09/28/1921. © Universal Film Mfg Co. 09/20/1921. Century Comedy. Cast: Baby Peggy, Charles Dorety. Director, Story: Fred Fishback.

Henpecked hubby Dorety, his freeloading boarder who is the wife's favorite, and a trio of children go on a week's vacation. All of the work falling on Dorety. After struggling with the tent and so forth, a bee stings Dorety's nose, and an ambulance is called and takes him to a hospital. The doctor's advice: You need a vacation.

Brownie's Baby Doll: Released 10/05/1921. © Universal Film Mfg Co. 09/23/1921. Century Comedy. Cast: Baby Peggy, Brownie the Dog, Bartine Burkett. Director, Story: Alfred J. Goulding. Assistant Director: David Smith.

Waif Baby Peggy is befriended by Brownie. Together they appropriate a wallet full of money, and proceed to acquire a new riding-habit, a pony she gets thrown from, and finally an auto that she gets to drive. After a series of hair-raising escapades, Peggy awakens to find it was all a dream.

Mama's Cowpuncher: Released 10/12/1921. © Universal Film Co. 09/28/1921. Century Comedy. Cast: Harry Sweet, Bartine Burkett, Joe Murphy, James T. Kelley, Bob O'Connor. Director, Story: Alfred J. Goulding. Assistant Director: David Smith.

Musical prodigy Sweet heads West but success eludes him, so he takes a job in a dance hall where he meets the Western Queen. His dumbness gets him into hot water, so he decides to toughen up, achieving success with the lariat, the gun, bronco busting, and finally wins the girl's hand. They marry, and years later they ride into his parents' drawing room on horseback, child in tow.

Seashore Shapes (aka **Sea Shore Shapes**): Released 10/19/1921. © Universal Film Mfg Co. 10/07/1921. Century Comedy. Cast: Baby Peggy, Teddy the Dog, Louise Lorraine, Bud Jamison. Director: Fred Hibbard/Alfred J. Goulding. Assistant Director: David Smith.

Lorraine is courted by two imposters posing as Counts, one of them a life-saver, the other an organ grinder-pickpocket. Teddy the Great Dane foils one of the latter's attempts, so he steals Baby Peggy and makes off on a motor boat. Teddy rescues Peggy.

Tin Cans: Released 10/26/1921. © Century Comedies 10/14/1921. Century Comedy. Cast: Brownie the Dog, Bud Jamison. Director: Fred Hibbard.

Two boys love the same girl, but one owns a flivver and takes her for a drive. The other boy ties tin cans to his dog Brownie's tail and has Brownie follow them. The first thinks his car is falling apart so he sells it and buys a horse and buggy – same problem. The rival acquires the discarded flivver, and the fickle girl drives off with him.

The Nervy Dentist: Released 11/02/1921. © Century Comedies 10/22/1921. Century Comedy. Cast: Charles Dorety, Bartine Burkett. Director, Story: Alfred J. Goulding. Assistant Director: David Smith.

Dorety is in love with Burkett, the assistant to a doctor whose business is faltering, so Dorety promises to drum up some patients. Using banana peels, he soon has a bunch of victims piled into the back of his auto, and takes them back to the doctor's office.

Around Corners: Released 11/09/1921. © Century Comedies 10/28/1921. Century Comedy. Cast: Brownie the Dog, Bud Jamison. Director: Fred Hibbard. (Misidentified as **Tin Cans** in the October 1994 issue #51/52 of *Griffithiana*)

Brownie's on the run from the dog catcher. He foils a burglary, carrying off the bomb intended to blow up a safe, and buries it. It blows, taking the dog catcher with it.

A Muddy Bride: Released 11/16/1921. © Century Comedies 11/05/1921. Century Comedy. Cast: Baby Peggy, Brownie the Dog, Jackie Morgan, Bud Jamison. Director: Fred Hibbard.

Baby Peggy plays dress-up when imitating her sister's wedding ceremony. While her frantic parents search for her, a good natured minister pretends to marry her to a "groom." The "newlyweds" get in a "smashup" in their toy auto, and are chased by their irate parents. Mud puddles enter into the picture.

Playing Possum: Released 11/23/1921. © Century Comedies 11/13/1921. Century Comedy. Cast: Harry Sweet, Charles Dorety, Bartine Burkett. Director, Story: Alfred J. Goulding. Assistant Director: David Smith.

Sweet and wife Burkett argue, so he decides to end it all. Repeated attempts at suicide fail, so when he's about to give up an auto hits him. He plays dead, and two undertakers fight over the body. The "corpse" comes to life when a lion enters the room. Sweet breaks up a spiritualistic séance and finally gets back with Burkett.

Teddy's Goat: Released 11/30/1921. © Universal Film Mfg Co. 11/22/1921. Century Comedy. Cast: Baby Peggy, Charles Dorety, Bud Jamison, Viola Dolan, Jackie Morgan, Dorothy Morgan, Teddy the Dog. Director: Fred Hibbard.

Teddy assists his milkman owner any way he can, tending the goat that gives 40 gallons of milk daily, and hauling the delivery cart. A rival milkman tries to sour the milk with a lemon, but Teddy switches bottles. His master weds his girl, and they head off for a honeymoon, Teddy assisting.

Get-Rich-Quick Peggy: Released 12/07/1921. © Century Comedies 11/29/1921. Century Comedy. Cast: Baby Peggy, Louise Lorraine, The Aubert Twins, Teddy the Dog. Director, Story: Alfred J. Goulding. Assistant Director: David Smith.

Farm girl Baby Peggy is kidnapped by gypsies, but Teddy rescues her. She's given a fine home by millionaires who mistake her for their niece, but send her away when they learn of their error. Gypsy queen Lorraine adopts her, and along with Teddy the three make a home.

A Family Affair: Released 12/14/1921. © Century Comedies 12/01/1921. Century Comedy. Cast: Charles Dorety, Louise Lorraine, Zip Monberg, Teddy the Dog. Director, Story: Alfred J. Goulding. Assistant Director: David Smith.

Dorety invites Lorraine for a drive, but they soon find dad, mom, granddad, grandma, kids, and Teddy along for the ride. They try to take refuge on a yacht, but the rest of the group is already there. Dorety overpowers a dangerous wrestler and wins the girl.

The Dumb Bell: Released 12/21/1921. © Century Comedies 12/09/1921. Century Comedy. Cast: Harry Sweet, Bartine Burkett. Director, Story: Tom Buckingham.

Sweet employs a doll to get a seat on the trolley. His later attempts to discard it are misunderstood by a cop who thinks he's abandoning a child, and by his sweetheart who thinks he's already married with child.

Chums: Released 12/28/1921. © Century Comedies 12/14/1921. Century Comedy. Cast: Baby Peggy, Brownie the Dog. Director, Story: Fred Hibbard.

When her mother is hounded by a rent collector, Baby Peggy and Brownie head out to earn some money. After a series of incidents which involve jumping freights and working in a film studio, Peggy becomes wealthy and returns home to find her mother selling papers. Peggy saves the old home.

Shipwrecked Among Animals: Released 01/04/1922. © Century Comedies 12/21/1921. Century Comedy. Cast: Harry Sweet, Alberta Vaughn, Zip Monty. Director, Story: Alfred J. Goulding. Assistant Director: David Smith (Parody of Universal's **Shipwrecked Among Cannibals**)

Shipwrecked on a South Sea Island, Sweet tries to win the heart of fur-clothed native Vaughan, but is repeatedly interrupted by wild animals, lions included. He wins the girl and dresses himself in lion skins. Monberg plays an Englishman.

The Straphanger: Released 01/11/1922. © Century Comedies 12/22/1921. Century Comedy. Cast: Lee Moran, Blanche Payson, Bartine Burkett, Baby Peggy. Director, Story: Fred Hibbard (working title **The Commuter**)

Moran is the henpecked husband of Payson. A hurried breakfast and the ordeal of catching a subway are followed by Moran's return home on the same conveyance, loaded with bundles. Friends arrive for dinner, and Payson is not happy about it. They employ a funny mechanical device for heating the baby's bottle.

An Idle Roomer: Released 01/18/1922. © Universal Film Mfg Co. 01/05/1922. Century Comedy. Cast: Harry Sweet, Thelma Dillerman, Bud Jamison, James Finlayson. Director, Story: Arvid E. Gillstrom.

Roomer Sweet awakens from a dream set in a Sultan's harem. He has a trick gas oven in his Victrola. He loves his landlady's daughter Dillerman. Her father wants her to marry Jamison, who puts dynamite in Sweet's pancake flour. Exploding bubbles float about. Sweet ends up marrying Dillerman.

Circus Clowns: Released 01/25/1922. © Universal Film Mfg Co. 01/11/1922. Century Comedy. Cast: Baby Peggy, Brownie the Dog, William Irving, Earl Montgomery, Dick Smith, Lillian Byron. Director, Story: Fred Hibbard.

Baby Peggy and Brownie are the stars of a tiny circus, having been kidnapped earlier. Her frantic parents hire detective Montgomery who finally tracks her down and returns Peggy and Brownie. Circus owner Irving follows hoping to get back his star act, but he is arrested.

The Touchdown: Released 02/01/1922. © Universal Film Mfg Co. 01/23/1922. Century Comedy. Cast: Lee Moran, Joe Murphy. Director, Story: Alfred J. Goulding. Assistant Director: David Smith.

Farm boy Moran heads to college where he and a dude are rivals for the professor's daughter. Initiation into a dormitory follows, the rival causing all sorts of problems for Moran. Moran accidentally finds himself in a big football game, scores the winning touchdown, and wins the daughter's hand.

Horse Sense: Released 02/08/1922. © Universal Film Mfg Co. 01/30/1922. Century Comedy. Cast: Harry Sweet, Queenie the Horse, Margaret Cloud, Bud Jamison, Harry Cornell. Director, Story: Fred Hibbard (possible working title **A Fast Life**)

Doug (Sweet) is in love with his girl Mary (Cloud). Doug has a horse trained to awaken him no matter what it takes. Mary's father wants her away from Doug, and puts her on a ship bound for a foreign port. Doug manages to get on board and avoid the Captain (Jamison), first mate, and the father. Arriving at the foreign port, Doug and Mary debark and escape their pursuers.

Little Miss Mischief: Released 02/15/1922. © Universal Film Mfg Co. 01/31/1922. Century Comedy. Cast: Baby Peggy. Director, Story: Arvid E. Gillstrom.

When a new baby brother arrives, Baby Peggy runs away from home. She is captured by a junk dealer and put to work, imitating a howling cat at night so that he can amass all of the junk thrown at her. She escapes and returns home, happy to be there, as are her worried parents.

Table Steaks: Released 02/22/1922. © Universal Film Mfg Co. 02/08/1922. Century Comedy. Cast: Brownie the Dog, Dick Smith, Bartine Burkett, Charles Dorety. Director, Story: Fred Hibbard.

Smith arrives at a hotel and falls for the owner's daughter, Burkett, who is also pursued by Dorety. Smith puts his final obstacle, a little brother, out of the way with a quarter. Smith and Burkett end up marrying. Brownie oversees all of this as the hotel's guardian, porter, playmate, etc.

Upper and Lower: Released 03/01/1922. © Universal Film Mfg Co. 02/15/1922. Century Comedy. Cast: Lee Moran, Alberta Vaughn, Zip Monberg, Betty May. Director, Story: Alfred J. Goulding. Assistant Director: David Smith.

On the lam from the law, Moran applies blackface and takes a strike-breaking job as a Pullman Porter. A black girl pursues him while he has his eyes on a white female passenger. Other Pullman-based gags. Closing shot: the train enters a tunnel, and when it emerges everyone's face is black.

A One Horse Town: Released 03/08/1922. © Universal Film Mfg Co. 02/24/1922. Century Comedy. Cast: Harry Sweet, Bud Jamison, James Finlayson. Director, Story: Tom Buckingham.

Penniless crooks Jamison and Finlayson pose as actors ready to put on a two-man show. They hire boob Sweet to post flyers, and later act as prop man and scene shifter. He manages to ruin the show, but emerges a hero when he thwarts the crooks' attempt to steal the hotel's savings. Sweet wins the girl, and her grateful father's permission to marry.

Peggy, Behave!: Released 03/15/1922. © Century Comedies 03/03/1922. Century Comedy. Cast: Baby Peggy, Blanche Payson, Fred Bretherton (Spencer), Dick Smith, Cameo the Dog. Director, Story: Arvid E. Gillstrom (working title **Peggy Be Good**)

Peggy is the mischievous ward of a cruel farm-based aunt, who sends Peggy back to her mother. En route by train, bandits attempt a holdup but are foiled by Peggy and some Roman Candles. Peggy later stops the train from careening off a draw bridge. She arrives home with a check from the railroad's grateful President.

Mutts: Released 03/22/1922. © Century Comedies 03/14/1922. Century Comedy. Cast: Brownie the Dog. Director: Fred Hibbard (working title **Putting On the Dog**)

All-dog cast with Brownie the manager, chief bartender, musician, and bouncer of Poodle Cafe. After bouncing a drunken mutt, the mutt returns later that night and sets fire to Brownie's house. The fire department arrives and saves women and children dogs first.

Two of a Kind: Released 03/29/1922. © Century Comedies 03/21/1922. Century Comedy. Cast: Harry Sweet, Bud Jamison, Jack Henderson. Director, Story: Tom Buckingham (working title **One of the Four Hundred**)

Plumber's helper Sweet and a millionaire's son (also) Sweet are spitting images of each other, and through multiple situations of mistaken identity the helper ends up marrying the girl that the millionaire wanted his son to marry.

The Rubberneck: Released 04/05/1922. © Century Comedies 03/29/1922. Century Comedy. Cast: Lee Moran, Jack Duffy. Director, Story: Alfred J. Goulding. Assistant Director: David Smith.

Rube Moran visits town and his uncle takes him to see the sights. Entering a rough café, Moran gets tangled in a fight with a bunch of toughs, stands to the side, lets them beat each other into insensibility, and emerges the "victor." He proposes to the café queen, and she accepts, lifting his bankroll while they embrace.

A Dark Horse: Released 04/12/1922. © Century Comedies 04/05/1922. Century Comedy. Cast: Charles Dorety, Ena Gregory, Sally the Horse. Director, Story: Jess Robbins.

Sally the horse is Dorety's valet. When he's coaxed into a crooked card game, Sally spots the cheating and aids Dorety into winning. Sally cleans up the place, chasing the gambler and his aids up a tree, finding a bomb, and blowing up the tree.

No Brains: Released 04/19/1922. © Century Comedies 04/07/1922. Century Comedy. Cast: Harry Sweet, Alberta Vaughn. Director, Story: Tom Buckingham (working titles **Nobody Home** and **The Sleepyhead)**

Sweet loves the owner's daughter Vaughn and gets a job. He finds a rival in the foreman, and a mighty conflict follows, much of it involving a freight elevator and its shaft. Sweet wins the daughter.

Cheerful Credit: Released 04/26/1922. © Century Comedies 04/12/1922. Century Comedy. Cast: Brownie the Dog, Bartine Burkett, Eddie Barry. Director, Story: Fred Hibbard.

Burkett grows tired of her cheap flat, so using credit moves into a Fifth Ave. mansion. Brownie takes care of the baby while the young couple live in luxury. The stay is cut short by the creditors and their moving van, hauling stuff out while Brownie hauls it back in.

Red Hot Rivals: Released 05/03/1922. © Century Comedies 04/24/1922. Century Comedy. Cast: Lee Moran, Bartine Burkett, Jimmie Adams, Bud Jamison, Sally the Horse. Director, Story: Fred Hibbard.

Village fire chief Moran and sheriff Adams are rivals for the hand of Burkett. Moran is more interested in playing checkers than putting out fires, so the lunch wagon owner rolls his flaming wagon to the station. A fire cuts short Moran's station house-based dinner with Burkett, but an explosion brings the burning house down, burying Moran and Adams in the debris.

Sic 'Em Brownie: Released 05/10/1922. © Century Comedies 04/27/1922. Century Comedy. Cast: Brownie the Dog, Jackie Morgan, Alberta Vaughn, Tom Murray, Bynunsky Hyman, Fred Peters. Director, Story: Alfred J. Goulding. Assistant Director: David Smith (working title **Three of a Kind**)

Heiress Vaughn and her little brother Morgan are saved from a life on the streets by her rich uncle. Burglars invade the millionaire's house and attempt to rob it, but Brownie comes to the rescue by shooting a revolver rigged with a piece of cord, and delivers them to the hands of the police.

Off His Beat: Released 05/17/1922. © Century Comedies 04/28/1922. Century Comedy. Cast: Harry Sweet, Lois Scott, Bert Roach, Ena Gregory, Tom Buckingham. Director, Story: Tom Buckingham.

Unintentionally ending up on the police force, Sweet joins in to help capture some burglars at the home of his girl, but is forced by one of them to turn over his uniform and change clothes. Sweet ends up falling off a building and flattening the crook, thereby saving the day. Sweet kisses his sweetheart, but then her husband enters with five kids, says he had a rough day, and they'll have to finish the film without her. Sweet appeals to the audience!

The Little Rascal: Released 05/24/1922. © Century Comedies 05/09/1922. Century Comedy. Cast: Baby Peggy, Nip the Dog, Blanche Payson, Fred Spencer, Dick Smith. Director, Story: Arvid E. Gillstrom (working title **The Little Angel**)

Baby Peggy is a little monster in this one, endlessly tormenting the help. They threaten to quit unless her father straightens her out, so he heads to her room for a spanking, but when he sees the sleeping girl tucked in bed, cannot fathom that she is the little rascal they say she is.

Three Weeks Off: Released 05/31/1922. © Century Comedies 05/09/1922. Century Comedy. Cast: Lee Moran, Alberta Vaughn, Johnny Fox. Director, Story: Alfred J. Goulding. Assistant Director: David Smith.

Moran pretends he is ill to get his boss to give him a vacation. He and his wife have a great time there until the boss shows up, requiring Moran to again feign illness. Prescribed medicines make him really ill. A trip to the chiropractor leaves him feeling great, so he applies the same chiropractic treatment to his boss when he suffers a headache. Successful, the boss gives Moran even more vacation time as a reward.

Some Class: Released 06/07/1922. © Universal Film Mfg Co. 05/25/1922. Century Comedy. Cast: Johnny Fox, Jack Henderson, Jackie Morgan, Brownie the Dog. Director, Story: Alfred J. Goulding. Assistant Director: David Smith.

Brownie drives his playmate kids to school each day, but his cleverness and mischievous pranks cause the teacher to quit. Brownie takes the teacher's place, but when a fire breaks out in the school Brownie rescues the kids and is rewarded for his bravery.

Speed 'Em Up: Released 06/14/1922. © Universal Film Mfg Co. 05/31/1922. Century Comedy. Cast: Harry Sweet, Alberta Vaughn, Jack Henderson, Fred Spencer, Johnny Fox. Director, Story: Arvid E. Gillstrom.

Farm hands Sweet and Fox have a bottle of "Pepo" that speeds things up, demonstrated here on motorcycle engines, chickens, well water, and eventually in a barn dance's punch resulting in overly-amorous old men and ladies. Sweet and farm girl Vaughn elope. Spencer is Roscoe the fat foreman, and Henderson the girl's father.

Ten Seconds: Released 06/21/1922. © Century Comedies 05/31/1922. Century Comedy. Cast: Lee Moran, Bartine Burkett, Bud Jamison, Betty May. Director, Story: Fred Hibbard.

Chauffeur Moran is in love with his boss' daughter Burkett, who inadvertently gets Moran involved in a prize fight with the champ. Moran, about to lose, is saved when someone plays the champ's favorite sob song on a violin, reducing him to tears. Moran lands some good punches, and wins.

Horse Tears: Released 06/28/1922. © Century Comedies 06/14/1922. Century Comedy. Cast: Queenie the Horse, Jackie Morgan, Pete Morrison. Director, Story: Fred Hibbard.

Queenie, the pal of schoolboy Morgan, is owned by a cop who is in love with a vamp from the city. The vamp heads to the city, so the cop sells Queenie to buy a ticket to follow her. Queenie hitches to the tail end of the train, and arrives in the city when her master does. The cop gets a job as a mounted police with Queenie. Queenie exposes the vamp, and reunites her master with his sweetheart.

Live Wires: Released 07/05/1922. © Universal Film Mfg Co. 06/21/1922. Century Comedy. Cast: Brownie the Dog, Johnny Fox, Jackie Morgan, Ena Gregory, Junior Delameter, Zip Monberg, Pal the Dog. Director, Story: Alfred J. Goulding. Assistant Director: David Smith.

Messenger boys Fox and Morgan are assisted by Brownie. One of them is sent for a birthday cake, but arrives at the little girl's party to find the cake crushed. Many party-based gags, both human and canine, but little plot.

Apartment Wanted: Released 07/12/1922. © Universal Film Mfg Co. 06/20/1922. Century Comedy. Cast: Lee Moran, Ena Gregory, Zip Monberg, Alberta Vaughn, Jackie Morgan. Director, Story: Alfred J. Goulding. Assistant Director: David Smith.

Family man Moran can't find an apartment that will take his children, so he takes a job as a janitor in return for the basement apartment. His wife doesn't like it, so he sets to work trying to drive some tenants out. After several failed attempts, he dresses as a ghost but scares his wife, who shoots him. This lands him in jail, but it's nicely appointed and just as he has grown accustomed to the place he is released.

You and Me: Released 07/19/1922. © Universal Film Mfg Co. 07/11/1922. Century Comedy. Cast: The Century Kids, Josephine Adair. Director: Jack Dawn (Director, Story: Arthur Hackett in copyright)

Four and five year olds populate the cast. A former sweetheart tests the heroism of some young men, and throws her doll in the water, which is rescued by a dog. Failing to make her former sweetheart jealous, she goes back to him and all ends well.

Hello, Mars: Released 07/26/1922. © Universal Film Mfg Co. 07/17/1922. Century Comedy. Cast: Harry Sweet, Johnny Fox, Alberta Vaughn, Ena Gregory, Fred Spencer. Director, Story: Alfred J. Goulding. Assistant Director: David Smith (working title **High Fliers**)

Sweet and Fox's home-made airplane goes out of control and lands them on Mars. There they encounter beautiful women, Gregory and Vaughn among them, and herculean men. After a series of attempts to pay off Mars' income tax, they awaken from their plane's crash to learn it was all a dream.

Short Weight: Released 08/02/1922. © Universal Film Mfg Co. 07/22/1922. Century Comedy. Cast: Johnny Fox, Brownie the Dog. Director, Story: Alfred J. Goulding. Assistant Director: David Smith.

Fox and Brownie are very hungry, so Fox gets a job. After a messy day Fox is fired, but hides in the store to sleep overnight after the boss leaves. Burglars break in to rob the place, but Brownie detains them while Fox calls the police. As a reward, Fox is rehired.

Henpecked: Released 08/09/1922. © Universal Film Mfg Co. 07/28/1922. Century Comedy. Cast: Lee Moran, Blanche Payson, Queenie the Horse, Bud Jamison, Maude the Mule. Director: Fred Hibbard.

Moran's domineering, oversized wife forces him to get a job with a blacksmith. He puts horseshoes on Queenie, but a disastrous encounter with a mule results in Moran's firing. He takes some Nervo, goes home, and commands his wife to get some firewood. When she returns the Nervo has worn off, she reasserts herself, and Moran jumps out the window onto Queenie, and rides away.

Bath Day: Released 08/16/1922. © Universal Film Mfg Co. 08/02/1922. Century Comedy. Cast: Harry Sweet, Queenie the Horse. Director, Story: Fred Hibbard.

Sweet struggles to give his kid brother a bath. A suitor for Sweet's sister kidnaps their horse Queenie, tries to camouflage it to look like another horse, then presents it to the girl as a gift "replacement." Queenie foils his plot. The house is flooded by the bathroom's overflow, but all ends happily.

Kid Love: Released 08/23/1922. © Universal Film Mfg Co. 08/10/1922. Century Comedy. Cast: The Century Kids. Director, Story: Jack Dawn.

Little Betty likes Tommy, Tommy loves Betty, and Betty's mom dislikes Tommy; she wants her daughter to play with Newton Mortimer. The Mortimers come to visit, but Betty's dad, a restaurant delivery man, manages to dump food all over the guests, and they leave.

Hickville's Romeo: Released 08/30/1922. © Universal Film Mfg Co. 08/18/1922. Century Comedy. Cast: Lee Moran, Rosie the Monkey. Director, Story: Albert Herman.

Hotel clerk Moran is in love with the owner's daughter, who in turn loves him. Another townie loves Moran, but when she is rebuffed turns to her blacksmith brother who says he'll force Moran to marry her. Almost successful, he's foiled when some boards fall on his head. Moran and the daughter embrace.

Beginning of 1922-1923 Season

Cured: Released 09/06/1922. © Universal Film Mfg Co. 08/25/1922. Century Comedy. Cast: Queenie the Horse, Rosie the Monkey, Maude the Mule, Cameo the Dog, Stripes the Zebra. Director, Story: Albert Herman.

Animal hospital doctor Queenie is assisted by Rosie, who is the nurse, cook, bookkeeper, and cashier. A man thinks he's purchasing a zebra, but actually it's a pony painted with stripes. Discovering the ruse, he first demands his money back then later plans to blow up the hospital with dynamite. Queenie saves the day.

Foolish Lives: Released 09/13/1922. © Universal Film Mfg Co. 09/01/1922. Century Comedy. Cast: Lee Moran, Ena Gregory, Blanche Payson, Fred Spencer. Director, Story: Arvid E. Gillstrom (working titles **Married Folks** and possibly **Too Much Family**)

Moran, Spencer, and their wives Gregory and Payson, all share an apartment, everything 50-50. When the wives argue, however, everything is split up, including the Ford. After a particularly combative day the husbands go home to find that their wives have made up, so the husbands head for Reno.

The Radio Hound: Released 09/20/1922. © Universal Film Mfg Co. 09/08/1922. Century Comedy. Cast: Brownie the Dog, Johnny Fox, Jackie Morgan. Director, Story: Arvid E. Gillstrom.

Morgan, Fox, and Brownie vacation at their uncle's farm, and he's not happy about it. They get into all sorts of mischief, but when uncle tries to punish them Brownie intervenes. Back in the city, Fox works in a tailor shop, assisted by Brownie. Enter uncle, who spanks the boys, but is chased off by Brownie.

The Kickin' Fool: Released 09/27/1922. © Universal Film Mfg Co. 09/14/1922. Century Comedy. Cast: Harry Sweet, Lillian Byron, Fred Spencer, Maude the Mule. Director, Story: Tom Buckingham.

Sweet is blamed for the antics of Maude, a trouble-making mule, but the mule actually belongs to Spencer, Sweet's rival for the hand of Byron. Sweet attempts to get rid of Maude, but with no success. He chases Maude, ends up on her back, wins a race, receives the prize, proves that Spencer is the real owner, and wins Byron.

Some Family: Released 10/04/1922. © Universal Film Mfg Co. 09/21/1922. Century Comedy. Cast: Lee Moran, Ena Gregory, Fred Spencer, Blanche Payson, Jackie Morgan. Director, Story: Arvid E. Gillstrom.

Moran has problems with his sweetheart Gregory's oddball family, which begin when he proposes to her. He buys a Ford and takes Gregory for a ride, but the whole family piles in. He can't get rid of them, so he cuts the car in half, separate from the family's side, and disappears with Gregory.

The Fresh Kid: Released 10/11/1922. © Century Comedies 09/29/1922. Century Comedy. Cast: Johnny Fox, Ena Gregory, Glen Cavender, James T. Kelley. Director: Norman Taurog (working title **Freshie**)

Troublemaker Fox interferes with the city fellow's lovemaking with Fox's sister Gregory. When the city fellow steals dad's grocery store money and elopes with Gregory, Fox overhears and brings them back.

Wedding Pumps: Released 10/18/1922. © Universal Film Mfg Co. 10/07/1922. Century Comedy. Cast: Brownie the Dog, Jackie Morgan, William Irving, Alberta Vaughn. Director, Story: Fred Hibbard.

Shoe salesman Morgan is assisted by Brownie in delivering shoes to Irving, who is to marry Vaughn. At the wedding supper Brownie intercepts a note from the groom to a former sweetheart, saying he married solely for her money, and will meet her in Cuba. The bride sees this and faints. Brownie and Morgan eat everything in sight, resulting in a dose of castor oil the next morning.

The Cabby: Released 10/25/1922. © Universal Film Mfg Co. 10/12/1922. Century Comedy. Cast: Maude the Mule, Louise Lorraine, Jackie Morgan, Jerry Mandy, William Irving, Hap Ward. Director, Story: Albert Herman (working title **Too Many Babies**)

Maude breaks up a poker game when she sees her cabby master being cheated. Later a tailor rides in the cab but skips out without paying. Maude places a bomb in the tailor's shop, blowing up a customer's suit. The customer wants it replaced, the tailor refuses, so the customer returns later to rob the till. The tailor recovers the money, but Maude picks his pocket and gives it to her master.

Ginger Face: Released 11/01/1922. © Universal Film Mfg Co. 10/21/1922. Century Comedy. Cast: Johnny Fox, Herbert Jenkins, William Irving, Vera White. Director, Story: Jimmie Adams (working title **Vanilla and Chocolate**)

Accidentally left behind when his parents go on vacation, Fox is "adopted" by Sammy (Jenkins), a young black kid, as "promising pugilistic material." Adventures follow, including an attempt to "fish" using dynamite, a plan that backfires when Sammy's dog retrieves the explosive, and it explodes.

Just Dogs: Released 11/08/1922. © Universal Film Mfg Co. 10/18/1922. Century Comedy. Cast: Century Dogs (Pal, Camisole [aka Cameo], Peaches, Mary), Little Joe the Monkey. Director, Story: Albert Herman. Cinematography: Blake Wagner (working title **The Flapper**)

Joe has trouble waking his buddy Pal. They cook breakfast, Joe milks a goat, Pal catches a fish. Joe rides into Barktown on Pal's back where Pal meets a beautiful white dog. Pal and the white dog end up getting married, a black dog minister officiating.

Hello, Judge!: Released 11/15/1922. © Universal Film Mfg Co. 10/28/1922. Century Comedy. Cast: Lee Moran, Ena Gregory, Jack Henderson, Blanche Payson, William Irving, Jack Morgan. Director, Story: Arvid E. Gillstron (working title **Guilty**)

Moran is on trial for choking his mother-in-law Payson and supposedly killing her pet parrot. Judge Henderson sentences him to life, but when Moran makes his plea and details Payson's abuse and mistreatment, the judge lets him off and banishes Payson (and her parrot) from Moran's home. Gregory is Moran's wife.

True Blue: Released 11/22/1922. © Universal Film Mfg Co. 11/02/1922. Century Comedy. Cast: Queenie the Horse, Edward Carlie, Betty May, Joe Bonner. Director, Story: Albert Herman (working title **My Horse Pal**)

First half reel shows hands only, playing cards, knocking at doors, etc. Queenie takes care of her bachelor master Bonner. Gets him to his sweetheart May's home in a less than sober condition, and gets them to the minister's to be married before her father Carlie catches them.

Rookies: Released 11/29/1922. © Universal Film Mfg Co. 11/02/1922. Century Comedy. Cast: Brownie the Dog, Jackie Morgan, The Century Kids. Director, Story: Alfred J. Goulding. Assistant Director: David Smith.

Two little boys, members of a scout troop that has Brownie as its mascot, are in love with the same girl. A bear attacks and Brownie fights him off, but one of the boys claims he killed it, using his mother's bearskin rug as "evidence." He wins the girl's love, and the other lover goes away with Brownie, brokenhearted.

Women First: Released 12/06/1922. © Universal Film Mfg Co. 11/04/1922. Century Comedy. Cast: Lee Moran, Alberta Vaughn. Director: Fred Hackett.

Hotel clerk Moran, in love with the owner's daughter, is jealous when a customer flirts with her. Moran goes through all sorts of mishaps and adventures attempting to rescue her when fire breaks out and the girl is caught in her room.

A Small Town Derby: Released 12/13/1922. © Universal Film Mfg Co. 11/04/1922. Century Comedy. Cast: Johnny Fox, Jackie Morgan, Ena Gregory, Scott Pembroke, Joe Bonner, Edward Carlie, Lillian Byron, Tom Dempsey, Maude the Mule. Director, Story: Albert Herman.(working titles **At the Fair** and **Slam! Bang!**)

Fox and his mule Maude attend a small town fair. Maude drinks a lot of soda and Fox enters and wins a pie-eating contest. Fox later slaps a caged lion without looking, thinking it's Maude. Maude is entered in a horse race, and wins when her main competitor drinks too much hard cider beforehand.

Me and My Mule: Released 12/20/1922. © Universal Pictures Corp. 12/05/1922. Century Comedy. Cast: Queenie the Horse, Maude the Mule, Spencer Bell, Joe Bonner, Betty May. Director, Story: Albert Herman (working title **Some Hero**)

A rebuffed villain arrives at the girl's farm, mortgage in hand, demanding either payment, the girl's hand, or pals Queenie and Maude instead. He gets the two animals, who later create havoc at his farm, and foil his plans to rob the bank by posing as ghosts and overpowering him and his cohorts.

The Tattle Tail: Released 12/27/1922. © Universal Pictures Corp. 12/09/1922. Century Comedy. Cast: Brownie the Dog, Jackie Morgan, Blanche Payson, Ena Gregory, Jack Henderson, Buddy Ross, George Monte (Monberg?). Director, Story: Arvid E. Gillstrom (working title **A Barking Sleuth**)

Brownie assists some detectives trying to get the goods on moonshiners. Brownie tracks them down and collects evidence by rolling in the moonshine, so the bootleggers toss him in a lake to rinse him off. Brownie keeps his tail above water, thereby saving some evidence.

American Plan: Released 01/03/1923. © Universal Pictures Corp. 12/14/1922. Century Comedy. Cast: Lee Moran, Betty May, Blanche Payson, Rosie the Monkey. Director, Story: Albert Herman (working title **The Boarder**).

Boarding house landlady Payson is in love with boarder Moran, who in turn loves fellow boarder May. Moran can't stand Payson's cooking, so he cooks his own meals in his room, against the rules, assisted by his monkey Rosie. He inherits an unassembled Ford, puts it together, then takes off with May for a drive, a cop and Payson in pursuit. He picks up a minister who marries the couple just before the Ford explodes.

Sting 'Em Sweet: Released 01/10/1923. © Universal Pictures Corp. 12/27/1922. Century Comedy. Cast: Brownie the Dog, Jackie Morgan, Ena Gregory, Jack Earle, Jack Cooper. Director: Herman C. Raymaker.

Sister has two beaus and Morgan delights in playing tricks on both of them. He sifts pepper on one's bouquet of flowers, then delivers a box of bees to the group. The remainder of the action revolves around a mad scramble to avoid being stung.

Hee! Haw!: Released 01/17/1923. © Universal Pictures Corp. 12/28/1922. Century Comedy. Cast: Harry Sweet, Zip Monberg, Arthur Trimble, Maude the Mule. Director, Story: Albert Herman.

Struggling book agent Sweet takes pity on Maude and her homeless, little girl friend. He determines to smuggle them into his hotel room, tying four pillows to Maude's hoofs to get her up the stairs. Once in the room, Maude delights in kicking the feathers out of the pillows. Maude sets off the hotel's fire alarm, and when the guests flee eats the food and drinks the home brew. Proprietor Monberg interferes, but is chased away by Maude.

Farm Follies: Released 01/24/1923. © Universal Pictures Corp. 01/10/1923. Century Comedy. Cast: Blanche Payson, Jack Cooper, Jack Earle, Ena Gregory, Betty May, Jean Hope, Lois Boyd, Century Beauties. Director, Story: Albert Herman (working title **Farmer-ettes**)

A lazy farmer and his hard-working wife accept a group of stranded chorus girls as boarders. The farmer now works hard to keep the girls entertained.

The Home Plate: Released 01/31/1923. © Universal Pictures Corp. 01/24/1923. Century Comedy. Cast: Lee Moran, Betty May, Blanche Payson. Director, Story: Albert Herman (working titles **Out of Home** and **Atta Boy**)

Reluctant Moran is forced to marry his long-term girl by her brother. He escapes while they are shopping, but finds himself at a ball park where he is mistaken for the pitcher. When he gets thrown out, his wife and her brother chase and catch him. She tells her brother to give Moran a chance, and that she is the only one privileged to beat him up!

Boyhood Days: Released 02/07/1923. © Universal Pictures Corp. 01/25/1923. Century Comedy. Cast: Buddy Messinger, Marjorie Marcel. Director, Story: Harry Edwards (working titles **School Room Romance**, **When Boyhood Was in Flower** and **Me for You**)

Eleven year old Buddy loves Alice, and Buddy's father, who owns the town store, loves

Alice's mother. Buddy is put to work in the store, creating all sorts of havoc with spilled tar, shoes full of tacks, and setting off a bunch of fireworks. The fireworks lead to the capture of a couple of crooks.

Pleasure Before Business: Released 02/14/1923. © Universal Pictures Corp. 01/27/1923. Century Comedy. Cast: Jack Cooper, Century Beauties. Director, Story: Alfred J. Goulding.

Collegian Cooper is in love with the college principal's daughter, but complications follow when she mistakes a look-alike tramp (also played by Cooper) for her sweetheart.

The Game Hunter: Released 02/21/1923. © Universal Pictures Corp. 02/07/1923. Century Comedy. Cast: Lee Moran, Queenie the Horse. Director, Story: Albert Herman.

A pair of newlyweds embark on a hunting trip, their journey completed with assistance by Queenie. A chopped tree wrecks the camp, and a merry chase involving a bear ends up interrupting the initiating ceremonies of the Order of the "Bears."

A Howling Success: Released 02/28/1923. © Universal Pictures Corp. 02/14/1923. Century Comedy. Cast: Jack Cooper, Brownie the Dog, Buddy Messinger, Jack Earle, Betty May, Vera White. Director, Story: Harry Edwards. Assistant Director Zion Myers. Camera: George Crocker (working title **Detective K. Nine**)

Professor Cooper has a solution that will kill dogs instantly, so Brownie and bell hop Messinger steal the formula, evading detective Earle. Brownie returns to a meeting of dogs with the formula and is presented with a medal for bravery.

A Spooky Romance: Released 03/07/1923. © Universal Pictures Corp. 02/20/1923. Century Comedy. Cast: Jack Cooper, Inez McDonald, Jack Earle, Billy Engle. Director: Albert Herman. Asst Director: Mark Sandrich. Story: Al Herman and Sig Neufeld. Camera: Billy Williams (possible working title **Flivver Follies**).

"The story of 'A Spooky Romance,' centers around a flapper and her favored beau who try to get rid of another suitor through a series of spooky sequences calculated to chill the ardor of the bold rival." (*Motion Picture News*, 02/10/1923)

Sweet and Pretty: Released 03/14/1923. © Universal Pictures Corp. 03/03/1923. Century Comedy. Cast: Brownie the Dog, Joe Moore, Eddie Barry, Lois Boyd, Billy Engle, Century Beauties. Director: James Davis. Story: James Davis, Sig Neufeld.

A superstitious suitor loses his bride-to-be to a rival, all due to the tricks played upon him by his rival, aided and abetted by Brownie.

Smarty: Released 03/21/1923. © Universal Pictures Corp. 03/06/1923. Century Comedy. Cast: Buddy Messinger, Sadie Campbell, Fred Spencer, Charles Hatton, Blanche Payson, Merta Sterling, Tiny Ward. Director: Harry Edwards (working title **Teacher's Pest**)

Messinger's pranks keep everyone on edge, particularly the schoolmaster. Ruffled feathers are smoothed when the teacher falls in love with Messinger's pretty sister.

Peg o' the Movies: Released 03/28/1923. © Universal Pictures Corp. 01/27/1923. Century Comedy. Cast: Baby Peggy, Alf Goulding Jr., Max Asher, Joe Bonner, Lillian Hackett. Director: Alfred J. Goulding.

Baby Peggy, traveling in a hammock under a freight car, arrives at Universal City. There she causes disruption among films being shot, but finally gets a chance to act when she plays the role of a vamp.

Vamped: Released 04/04/1923. © Universal Pictures Corp. 03/16/1923. Century Comedy. Cast: Jack Cooper, Marjorie Meadows, Billy Engle, Jack Earle, Jimmie Adams, Lois Boyd. Director: Albert Herman. Story: Sig Neufeld, Albert Herman.

Cooper is a country store clerk, and Marcel is a milliner-vamp. Some diner action involving oysters on the half shell that are very athletic. Later, chloroform is placed in a bottle of smelling salts.

Sunny Gym: Released 04/11/1923. © Universal Pictures Corp. 03/24/1923. Century Comedy. Cast: Brownie the Dog, Joe Bonner, Billy Engle, Tiny Sanford, Century Beauties. Director, Story: Herman C. Raymaker (working title **Straighten 'Em Out**)

Sanford is the trainer in a gymnasium, ably assisted by Brownie, who guards unwilling recruits Engle and Bonner. The gym is divided in two, the men on one side and the Century Beauties on the other.

Dad's Boy: Released 04/18/1923. © Universal Pictures Corp. 03/29/1923. Century Comedy. Cast: Buddy Messinger, Eddie Barry, Merta Sterling, Ross "Tiny" Ward, Dick Smith, Bynunsky Hyman. Director, Story: Harry Edwards.

Messinger is the son of a widow who is beset by two suitors, neither of whom meet Messinger's approval.

Sweetie: Released 04/25/1923. © Universal Pictures Corp. 03/29/1923. Century Comedy. Cast: Baby Peggy, Jerry Mandy, Louise Lorraine, Max Asher, James T. Kelley, Jennie the Monkey. Director, Story: Alfred J. Goulding (working title **Peggy Immigrates**)

Poor newsgirl Baby Peggy becomes a street musician with monkey and barrel organ. She is adopted by a wealthy woman over her husband's protests. During a society fete Peggy dresses as Salome and performs along with her monkey.

Oh Nursie!: Released 05/02/1923. © Universal Pictures Corp.03/16/1923. Century Comedy. Cast: Jack Cooper, Jack Earle, Marjorie Marcel, Joe Bonner, Century Beauties, Charles Dudley. Director: Albert Herman. Assistant Director: Mark Sandrich. Camera: Billy Williams. Story: Albert Herman, Sam Neufeld.

Nervy insurance salesman Cooper ends up in a hospital where he is surrounded by beautiful nurses (The Century Beauties). He has several altercations with a doctor he previously attempted to sell insurance to. Finally a strong fan blows his hospital bed out of the hospital, into the street, and into a lake, picking up a pretty nurse along the way.

Why Dogs Leave Home: Released 05/09/1923. © Universal Pictures Corp. 03/16/1923. Century Comedy. Cast: Brownie the Dog, Billy Engle. Director: Archie Mayo (working title **Try to Get It**)

Brownie is thrown out of a house and manages to substitute himself for a millionaire's dog.

Ain't Love Awful?: Released 05/16/1923. © Universal Pictures Corp. 03/24/1923. Century Comedy. Cast: Bobby Dunn, Ernie Adams, Frank Earl, Lillian Worth. Director: Eugene De Rue, Zion Myers. Story: Bobby Dunn, Eugene De Rue (working title **The Poor Boob**)

The father of Dunn's intended is against their marriage, and hires One Round Ed to trounce Dunn when he shows up. After beating up a number of potential financiers, Ed recognizes Dunn as his old sparring partner and lets him go. Dunn's rich pa says he'll finance the girl's father's promotion if Dunn can marry the girl, and all of a sudden all of the father's objections to Dunn fall by the wayside.

All Over Twist: Released 05/23/1923. © Universal Pictures Corp. 04/03/1923. Century Comedy. Cast: Buddy Messinger, Jack Cooper, Fred Spencer, Jack Henderson, Sadie Campbell. Director: Archie Mayo (working title **The Bus Boy**)

Messinger is put to work in the kitchen of his father's restaurant, but quickly gets in trouble with the chef. The film ends with Messinger sailing off in a fantastic toy balloon, his girl beside him.

The Kid Reporter: Released 05/30/1923. © Universal Pictures Corp. 03/31/1923. Century Comedy. Cast: Baby Peggy, Buddy Williams, James T. Kelley, William Irving, Zip Monberg, Blanche Payson, Albert Willis. Director, Story: Alfred J. Goulding (working titles **The Scoop** and **The Cub Reporter**)

Newspaper stenographer Baby Peggy, learning that any reporter who can discover the culprit whole stole some jewels will be made editor, dons a checkered suit, cane and monocle. It turns out the butler did it, and Peggy recovers the jewels.

Fare Enough: Released 06/06/1923. © Universal Pictures Corp. 04/18/1923. Century Comedy. Cast: Jack Cooper, Joe Bonner, Jeanne Hope, Jack Earle, Marjorie Marcel, Ford West, Emily Gerdes. Director: Albert Herman. Assistant Director: Mark Sandrich. Story: Albert Herman, Sam Neufeld. Camera: Billy Williams.

Promoter Cooper and trolley conductor Earle compete against rival bus runner Marcel. The film ends when one of the runaway conveyances breaks into a powder warehouse with all principals on board…with disastrous results.

The Imperfect Lover: Released 06/13/1923. © Universal Pictures Corp. 05/03/1923. Century Comedy. Cast: Brownie the Dog, Ena Gregory, Bobby Dunn, Vernon Dent. Director, Story: Archie Mayo (working title **The Leather Slingers**)

"The story…has its theme based on the prize ring. Brownie proves himself a friend and ally of Bobby Dunn, several pounds lighter than his heavy opponent, Vernon Dent, who tips the scales at 275 and who challenges him to a fight in the ring for the hand of blonde Ena Gregory, as well as for her homestead. Brownie proves how a brindled pup may be a most unfair referee as he continuously steps in to ring the bell and save his friend from being knocked out." (*Motion Picture News*, 04/28/1923)

Don't Get Fresh: Released 06/20/1923. © Universal Pictures Corp. 05/21/1923. Century Comedy. Cast: Buddy Messinger, Sadie Campbell. Director: Archie Mayo.

The installment man repossesses Messinger's mother's furniture, but all ends up happily when Messinger saves the life of that same man's daughter. There's a kids' party where a blindfolded Messinger ends up walking high above the street on a ledge. He makes it safely back to the party.

Taking Orders: Released 06/27/1923. © Universal Pictures Corp. 03/27/1923. Century Comedy. Cast: Baby Peggy, Dick Smith, Fred Spencer, Juanita Vaughn, Max Asher. Director: Alf Goulding (working title **Peggy's Busy Day**)

Baby Peggy works for her father in his cafeteria and next-door dental parlor. She administers laughing gas with a heavy hand, the patients floating up to the ceiling. A dog inhales the gas and floats out the window, so Peggy follows, lifted by a bunch of toy balloons. Father's enemies put dynamite in some apples to be baked, and when Peggy puts them in the oven they explode. Peggy quickly performs a hula dance to keep the cafeteria customers from leaving.

Hold On: Released 07/04/1923. © Universal Pictures Corp. 05/25/1923. Century Comedy. Cast: Billy Engle, Jack Earle, Marjorie Marcel. Director: Albert Herman. Assistant Director: Mark Sandrich. Story: Albert Herman, Sam Neufeld. Camera: William Hyer.

A wife and her brother try to make a man out of her husband. Swinging on a horizontal bar, hubby sends him into the neighbor's wife's bedroom. The brother-in-law and neighbor are lodge brothers, so they decide to initiate hubby into the lodge, a process that involves a lot of wild animals.

Speed Bugs: Released 07/11/1923. © Universal Pictures Corp. 06/04/1923. Century Comedy. Cast: Fred Spencer, Ernie Adams, Fay Wray, Glen Cavender, Billy Engle. Director: Archie Mayo. Camera: George Larson (working titles **Step On It** and **Gasoline Love**)

Spencer is the portly sweetheart of a garage owner's daughter, and proves his worth by winning an auto race. The race is plagued by the usual stunts the various racers pull on the others in hopes of getting the upper hand.

Buddy at the Bat: Released 07/18/1923. © Universal Pictures Corp. 06/27/1923. Century Comedy. Cast: Buddy Messinger, Sadie Campbell, Fred Spencer, Jean Laverty, Frank Earl, Lillian Worth, Donald Hughes, Frank Weatherwax. Director: Albert Herman. Story: William A. Friedle (working title **Present Arms**)

Baseball team captain Buddy and his team's opponents draft Buddy's automobile dealer dad as the game's umpire. A poor decision causes dad to be mobbed, dragging his son back to the dealership. Buddy demos a car to a woman and her young daughter, the latter taking a shining to Buddy.

Tips: Released 07/25/1923. © Universal Pictures Corp. 03/24/1923. Century Comedy. Cast: Baby Peggy, Fred Spencer, Jack Henderson, Inez McDonnell, Pal the Dog. Director: Arvid E. Gillstrom.

Baby Peggy's father puts her to work in a big hotel as a bellboy, carrying suitcases, taking guests' pets outside, and vacuuming with disastrous results to the hotel cat and the guests' shoes left outside their doors.

Spring Fever: Released 08/01/1923. © Universal Pictures Corp. 06/09/1923. Century Comedy. Cast: Fred Spencer, Lois Boyd, Henry Murdock. Director: Harry Edwards. Assistant Director: William Quinlan. Camera: Billy Williams (working title **Hay! Hay!**)

Farm-based comedy with Spencer competing with a rival to gain favor with the village belles. At the end, the rival loosens the nut holding the wheel of the wagon in which Spencer is hauling some guests and his girl, dumping the guests into a stream but leaving Spencer and his girl safe on the drivers' seat.

Lots of Nerve: Released 08/08/1923. © Universal Pictures Corp. 06/16/1923. Century Comedy. Cast: Pal the Dog, Henry Murdock, Otto Fries, Violet Shelton. Director: Noel M. Smith (working title **His Master's Curse**)

Pal outwits the landlady looking to collect rent from his master Murdock. Pal later aids Murdock in winning the girl he loves by keeping his rival away.

So Long, Buddy: Released 08/15/1923. © Universal Pictures Corp. 07/07/1923. Century Comedy. Cast: Buddy Messinger, Ella McKenzie, Ida McKenzie, Frank

Weatherwax, Frank Earles, Jean Laverty. Director: Noel M. Smith (working title **Slide Kelly Slide**)

Messinger, son of a country hotel's owner, is uncomfortable when the rival for his girl puts itching powder in his clothes. A troupe of actors comes to the hotel, and during a nighttime rehearsal Messinger dons a huge false head and frightens the hotel's black servants.

High Kickers: Released 08/22/1923. © Universal Pictures Corp. 06/19/1923. Century Comedy. Cast: Doris Eaton, Jack Cooper, Gorham/Century Follies Girls. Director: Archie Mayo (working title **The Folly Girl**)

Hired girl Eaton longs to join the chorus girls staying at the boarding house, following and imitating their various dance moves. Their coach is taken with her good looks, so he tries to kidnap her. She is rescued by photographer Cooper, another lodger.

Carmen, Jr.: Released 08/29/1923. © Universal Pictures Corp. 06/02/1923. Century Comedy. Cast: Baby Peggy, Lillian Hackett, Inez McDonnell, Tommy Wonder, Joe Bonner, Buddy Williams, Ernest McDonald, Bynunsky Hyman, Gus Leonard, Max Asher, Jack Cooper, Ena Gregory, Alf Goulding Jr., Joe Moore, Tad Ross, John Ralesco. Director: Alfred J. Goulding. Titles: Joe W. Farnham (working titles **The Senorita** and **Sunny Smiles**)

In Mexico, senorita Peggy wanders into a café and clumsily joins a young boy doing the Tango. She later vamps some senors, and ends up in a bull ring as replacement for the matador; she triumphs.

Beginning of 1923-1924 Season

Back to Earth: Released 09/05/1923. © Universal Pictures Corp. 08/01/1923. Century Comedy. Cast: Jack Earle, Billy Engle. Director, Story: Albert Herman (possible working title **Hold On**)

Two real estate con men have a "flying bungalow" that they fly to a vacant lot, sell to a sucker, then fly off to find another lot and sucker. The bungalow is equipped with all sorts of ingenious devices. The swindlers finally get swindled by "a giant of a fellow," Earle.

Round Figures: Released 09/12/1923. © Universal Pictures Corp. 08/04/1923. Century Comedy. Cast: Jack Cooper, Marjorie Marcel, Gorham/Century Follies Girls. Director: Archie Mayo.

A young lady pretends she's a dog in order to get a free meal. She's sold to a cabaret manager who, upon discovering that she's not a dog, gives her a job as cigarette girl. She's helped by a stranger, they fall in love, and after some adventures are blown into a minister's home and are married.

Bringing Up Buddy: Released 09/19/1923. © Universal Pictures Corp. 08/09/1923. Century Comedy. Cast: Buddy Messinger, Sadie Campbell, Marjorie Marcel, Dorothy Vernon, James Kelley, Rudoplh Friml, Jr.. Director: Albert Herman. Story: Al Herman, Edward Luddy.

Messinger's the mischievous son of a newly-rich couple who are vainly attempting to break into society. Messinger makes a mess of things, though, so they send him off to military school. There he finds that he needs to prove himself through fisticuffs, knocking down one student after another before accidentally knocking down his tutor. He gets into so much trouble there that he's chased back home, the exasperated superintendant in hot pursuit.

Nobody's Darling: Released 09/26/1923. © Universal Pictures Corp. 07/13/1923. Century Comedy. Cast: Baby Peggy, Harry Clifford, Lillian Worth, Charlotte Rich, John Ralesco. Director: Alfred J. Goulding. Assistant Director: Leslie Goodwin. Story: Harry Edwards. Camera: Jerry Ash (working title **The Orphan**)

Baby Peggy plays some practical jokes, gets into a negro orphan asylum, holds up traffic with a dummy policeman, and is chased into a toy store where she pretends to be a doll. She is bought by a rich little girl, but frightens the household and flees, asking a policeman to take her home.

One Exciting Day: Released 10/03/1923. © Universal Pictures Corp. 08/28/1923. Century Comedy. Cast: Billy Engle, Jack Earle, Joe Moore. Director: Albert Herman.

The hero is forced by some Bolsheviks to deliver a bomb, and almost gets caught by the law doing so. He is captured and put to work in a powder factory and proceeds to mess things up.

A Regular Boy: Released 10/10/1923. © Universal Pictures Corp. 08/28/1923. Century Comedy. Cast: Buddy Messinger. Director: Albert Herman.

Inventor Messinger has scattered his electrical and other devices around the house, much to the discomfort of his mother's guests. Exploding peanuts, squirting cakes, revolving chairs, trick sofas, and so forth are among them, followed by a scheme for removing the goldfish lodged in the back of his mother's dress.

Don't Scream: Released 10/17/1923. © Universal Pictures Corp. 09/22/1923. Century Comedy. Cast: Pal the Dog, Ernie Adams, Marjorie Marcel, Fred Spencer. Director: Albert Herman. Story: Al Herman and Harry Lucenay (working title **Pal Puts It Over**)

Pal is valet to his master Adams, who attempts to win Marcel's affections. Obstacles get in his way, including poverty, husky rival Spencer, and a bunch of crooks. With Pal's assistance, however, Adams wins out.

Fashion Follies: Released 10/24/1923. © Universal Pictures Corp. 09/10/1923. Century Comedy. Cast: Zip Monberg, Henry Murdock, Doris Eaton, Gorham/Century Follies Girls, Fred Spencer, Sunshine Hart. Director, Story: Albert Herman.

An ambitious male modiste decides to stage a fashion show, but one thing after another goes wrong, and all at his expense. Enter Murdock and his pal in their specially equipped flivver. The modiste gives them the boot, so they disguise themselves as display models to regain entry.

Little Miss Hollywood: Released 10/31/1923. © Universal Pictures Corp. 08/28/1923. Century Comedy. Cast: Baby Peggy, Fred Spencer, Dick Smith, Joe Bonner, Florence Lee. Director, Story: Al Herman. Titles: Joe W. Farnham.

Movie struck orphan Baby Peggy reaches Hollywood, gets her first glimpse of the big studios and many big name artists, including Mary Pickford, Douglas Fairbanks, and Charles Ray.

Golfmania: Released 11/07/1923. © Universal Pictures Corp. 09/10/1923. Century Comedy. Cast: Billy Engle, Jack Earle, Jean Laverty, Henry Murdock, Fred Spencer, Spec O'Donnell. Director: Albert Herman.

Golf enthusiasts Engle and Earle are amateurs at the sport, and it shows in their inept performances. Their game comes to an end when a black bear arrives on the scene and creates havoc at the country club.

Down to the Ship to See: Released 11/14/1923. © Universal Pictures Corp. 10/13/1923. Century Comedy. Cast: Pal the Dog, Roscoe Karns, Century Follies Girls. Director, Story: Albert Herman (working titles **Any Old Port** and **Ship Ahoy**)

At a girls' camp, Karns' sweetheart Mary is sent away by the camp's chaperone so that she can vamp Karns. Pal sets things straight. Later, Karns is chased aboard a ship by an irate sailor, and Pal rescues Karns from a number of scrapes. Mary comes aboard and she and Karns are married.

She's a He: Released 11/21/1923. © Universal Pictures Corp. 09/01/1923. Century Comedy. Cast: Buddy Messinger. Director: Albert Herman.

Plumber's assistant Messinger is working for a young couple who have told their relatives they have a young daughter. They don't, so when their aunt arrives Messinger masquerades as the daughter. He's not very good at it.

Miles of Smiles: Released 11/28/1923. © Universal Pictures Corp. 09/10/1923. Century Comedy. Cast: Baby Peggy, Joe Bonner. Director: Alfred J. Goulding.

Baby Peggy as twins, one who wanders off and is raised by a train engineer, the other raised by her wealthy parents. Circumstances place the former twin at her sister's house, resulting in identity confusion. The wealthy couple finally realizes that this is their long lost daughter, and the engineer willingly gives her up, happy to have her reunited with her birth parents.

A Corn-Fed Sleuth (aka The Corn-Fed Sleuth): Released 12/05/1923. © Universal Pictures Corp. 10/26/1923. Century Comedy. Cast: Jack Earle. Director, Story: Albert Herman (working title **The Detective**)

Farm boy Earle takes a correspondence course to become a detective, and heads to the city. He falls prey to a gang of crooks who use him to obtain his own brother-in-law's furniture. Eventually catching on, he succeeds in getting the furniture back.

My Pal: Released 12/12/1923. © Universal Pictures Corp. 10/24/1923. Century Comedy. Cast: Pal the Dog, Ernie Adams, Alice Day, Fred Spencer, Harry Pringle, Roscoe Karns. Director: Albert Herman. Story: Al Herman, Harvey Jackson. Camera: William Hyer (tentative release title **The Water Dog**)

Dick flirts with Molly in a rather brazen fashion using a tricked-up rumble seat. Later, assisted by Pal, he rescues her from drowning. He and Pal go to a movie studio where they cause all sorts of disruption, but eventually land jobs with the production company.

Buckin' the Line: Released 12/19/1923. © Universal Pictures Corp. 10/29/1923. Century Comedy. Cast: Buddy Messinger, Sadie Campbell, Donald Hughes. Director, Story: Albert Herman.

Buddy's team practices in his parlor, wrecking the place. Pal substitutes for Buddy, who is practicing the violin. Working in his dad's store, mischievous Buddy is made delivery boy and sets out on his bike. He spots a football game and joins in, winning the game. His jubilant teammates carry him back to his dad's store on their shoulders. A demonstration is staged, the store wrecked, and Buddy is made to clean up the mess…much to his friends' amusement.

Hansel and Gretel: Released 12/26/1923. © Universal Pictures Corp. 08/28/1923. Century Comedy. Cast: Baby Peggy, Jack Earle, Fritzi Fern, Buddy Williams, Blanche Payson, James T. Kelley, Johnny Fox. Director: Alfred J. Goulding.

Hansel and Gretel are abandoned in the woods by their father. After birds eat their trail of bread crumbs, the kids head to a witch's house. She wants to make gingerbread out of them, but they outwit her and push her into the oven. Their mother, now having second thoughts about abandoning them, leads the neighbors in a rescue.

Obey the Law: Released 01/02/1924. © Universal Pictures Corp. 11/22/1923. Century Comedy. Cast: Jack Earle, Harry McCoy, Marjorie Marcel, Tiny Sanford, Yorke Sherwood. Director, Story: Robert Kerr. Assistant Director: A. Linkoff. Camera: William Hyers (working title **The Process Server**)

The judge gives a court order to attach the property of J. Smith to movers Earle and McCoy. They are told by none other than Smith himself that Smith lives next door, so they clean out that house, only to find that it's the judge's house!

The Rich Pup: Released 01/09/1924. © Universal Pictures Corp. 11/28/1923. Century Comedy. Cast: Pal the Dog, Henry Murdock, William Irving, Mary O'Brien, Baby Dawn O'Day, Bynunsky Hyman. Director, Story: Albert Herman. Camera: Billy Williams.

Baby Dawn O'Day is left in the care of Pal, who rescues her from drowning and an auto accident. She has two suitors; Pal likes one of them and the other turns out to be a jewel thief. Pal helps out the one he likes and frustrates his unworthy rival.

The Caddy: Released 01/16/1924. © Universal Pictures Corp. 12/24/1923. Century Comedy. Cast: Buddy Messinger. Director, Story: Arvid E. Gillstrom. Assistant Director: Leslie Goodwin. Camera: Victor Sherrick (working title **Boys Will Be Boys**)

Messinger escapes the orphan asylum and the two keepers who have mistreated him. He takes a job as a caddy for a golfer in a championship game.

Own a Lot: Released 01/23/1924. © Universal Pictures Corp. 12/21/1923. Century Comedy. Cast: Harry Sweet, Thelma Hill, Vernon Dent, Century Follies Girls. Director, Story: Noel M. Smith. Camera: Harry Forbes (working titles **Own a Home** and **The Tourists**)

Besieged by land and home salesmen, a newlywed couple breaks down and purchases a tiny bungalow. So tiny is it that when they have a celebratory party, the wildly dancing guests burst the walls and the bungalow is destroyed, leaving the couple with a lot but nothing else.

Such Is Life: Released 01/30/1924. © Universal Pictures Corp. 09/10/1923. Century Comedy. Cast: Baby Peggy, Joe Bonner, Tommy Wonder, Jack Henderson, Arnold MacDonald, Paul Stanhope. Director: Alfred J. Goulding.

London waif Baby Peggy is snubbed by the woman whose car almost hit her, but later is adopted by that same woman when Peggy saves her small daughter from a fire.

Keep Going: Released 02/06/1924. © Universal Pictures Corp. 12/21/1923. Century Comedy. Cast: Jack Earle, Harry McCoy, Marjorie Marcel, Billy Franey. Director, Story: Robert Kerr (working title **Keep Moving**)

Traffic cop Earle and McCoy are rivals for the hand of Marcel. Marcel falls into a pond, and McCoy beats Earle to the rescue by using a passing iceman as a bridge. Rescued, she sees only Earle and falls into his arms crying "My hero!" McCoy gives up and keeps going.

You're Next: Released 02/13/1924. © Universal Pictures Corp. 12/21/1923. Century Comedy. Cast: Henry Murdock, Walter Irving, Helen Stocking, Bynunsky Hyman, Joe Bonner, Frank Alexander. Director: Albert Herman. Story: Dave Bader (working title **Next, Please**)

Spurned by his girl until he makes good, Murdock builds a motorcycle-based barbershop that is successful. The film ends with the girl, Murdock, and his rival Oscar aboard the shop which crashes into a telephone pole, depositing the girl in Murdock's arms, and Oscar atop the pole.

Quit Kiddin' (aka **Kidding**): Released 02/20/1924. © Universal Pictures Corp. 01/08/1923. Century Comedy. Cast: Buddy Messinger, Sadie Campbell, Joe Bonner, Fred Spencer, Ella McKenzie, Pinto Colvig, Anita Garvin. Director, Story: Albert Herman. Assistant Director: John Ralesco. Camera: William C. Hyer (working title **Captain Applesauce**)

Messenger boy Messinger is to deliver a message to a famous pirate's grandson. Without Messinger's knowledge, thieves substitute the message with a death threat. Messinger arrives at the house and encounters what appears to be a haunting. He eventually recovers the original message, the whereabouts of a vast fortune hidden in the house, and captures the would-be thieves.

Peg O' the Mounted: Released 02/27/1924. © Universal Pictures Corp. 09/22/1923. Century Comedy. Cast: Baby Peggy, Jack Earle, Bert Sterling, Tiny Tim the Pony. Director: Alfred J. Goulding. Assistant Director: David Smith. Camera: Jerry Ash. Story: Bert Sterling.

Mounted Policeman's daughter Baby Peggy jumps into action during her father's absence, trailing some moonshiners. She's captured but escapes, then returns, captures the entire gang, and marches them back to headquarters.

Sons-In-Law: Released 03/05/1924. © Universal Pictures Corp. 01/09/1924. Century Comedy. Cast: Jack Earle, Harry McCoy. Director, Story: Robert Kerr (copyrighted as **His Sons-In-Law**)

Earle and McCoy are in love with sisters, but the girls' father disapproves. They try various schemes to gain entrance to the house, and their chance comes when father hits McCoy with his car, McCoy feigning near death and taken to the house. Father discovers the deception, so McCoy masquerades as a baby in a carriage, and Earle as his maid. Father tries to seduce the "maid," but gets wise when he finds the "baby" smoking a cigar.

That Oriental Game: Released 03/12/1924. © Universal Pictures Corp. 01/17/1924. Century Comedy. Cast: Pal the Dog, Harry Sweet, Zip Monberg. Director, Story: Noel M. Smith. Assistant Director: Charles Lamont. Camera: Harry Forbes (working title **Putting It Over**)

Sweet and Pal play Mah-Jongg. Sweet and his rival both head to the girl's house, and she demands candy. Sweet contacts Pal, who brings a box of candy, but the rival steals it. Pal switches the candy for a brick, and the girl is enraged upon receipt. The rival calls in some roughnecks to kill Sweet, so they try to use dynamite, but Pal returns it to the rival and the roughnecks, leaving Sweet and the girl to their love-making.

The Young Tenderfoot: Released 03/19/1924. © Universal Pictures Corp. 01/21/1924. Century Comedy. Cast: Buddy Messinger, Sadie Campbell, Tad Ross, Herbert Sherwood, Fred DeSilva. Director, Story: Albert Herman. Story: Edward I. Luddy, Albert Herman (working title **Wilder and Woolier**)

Misbehaving Messinger is sent west by his father. Enroute he and his bodyguard meet bandit Terrible Pete, capture him, and turn him over to the sheriff. Pete escapes and vows revenge on Messinger, but failing at that kidnaps Messinger's sweetheart Campbell. Messinger follows and after a fight knocks out Pete, rescues Campbell, and recaptures the bandit.

That's Rich: Released 03/26/1924. © Universal Pictures Corp. 02/27/1924. Century Comedy. Cast: Arthur Trimble, Ella McKenzie. Director: Noel M. Smith.

Mistreated foster child Trimble is suddenly showered with affection when his foster parents learn from a stranger he's to inherit a million dollars. The stranger turns out to be an escaped inmate, so the mistreatment resumes. Trimble runs away, and is pursued by his foster father until the latter is blown up in a blast.

Hit 'Em Hard: Released 04/02/1924. © Universal Pictures Corp. 01/22/1924. Century Comedy. Cast: Jack Earle, Harry McCoy, Hilliard Karr, Marjorie Marcel, Frank Alexander. Director: Robert Kerr. Story: Pinto Colvig (working title **Past and Present**; copyrighted as **Hit Him Hard**)

Part of the film is set in stone-age times, with stone-age taxis and baby carriages and a prehistoric method of bootlegging. Another part of the film is set in the prize fight ring.

Checking Out: Released 04/09/1924. © Universal Pictures Corp. 01/22/1924. Century Comedy. Cast: Pal the Dog, Harry Sweet, Al Alt, Leslie Goodwins, Betty Young,

Vernon Dent. Director, Story: Noel M. Smith. Assistant Director: Charles Lamont. Camera: Harry Forbes (working title **Checking In**)

Rival hot dog stand owner Dent drives Sweet out of business. Sweet and Pal take jobs as bell hops in a hotel. Dent arrives and throws Sweet out a window. Sweet and Pal later foil Dent's attempt to burglarize the hotel safe. Sweet marries the telephone operator, his sweetheart.

The Racing Kid: Released 04/16/1924. © Universal Pictures Corp. 03/04/1924. Century Comedy. Cast: Buddy Messinger, Martha Sleeper, Spec O'Donnell, Joe Bonner, Max Mogi, Mary Land, Bynunsky Hyman. Director: Albert Herman. Camera: William C. Hyer (working title **The Jockey**)

Messinger, son of a horse owner, learns that the jockey to ride his dad's horse in a big race is in cahoots with a gambler. Aided by pals Sleeper and O'Donnell, they waylay the jockey and Messinger takes his place. Loading the horse into a taxi midway for part of the ride, Messinger wins.

Pretty Plungers: Released 04/23/1924. © Universal Pictures Corp. 03/14/1924. Century Comedy. Cast: Al Alt, Bartine Burkett, Hilliard Karr, Century Follies Girls, Joe Bonner, Bill Blaisdell, Leslie Goodwin. Director: Noel M. Smith (working titles **Pools First** and **The Movie Queen**)

Bitter rivals Alt and Karr are both in love with Burkett. She leads them to a swimming pool where they encounter swim instructor Blaisdell, also in love with her. He pursues the two suitors with violence in mind, but through their swimming and running ability manage to outwit him.

A Lofty Marriage: Released 04/30/1924. © Universal Pictures Corp. 03/21/1924. Century Comedy. Cast: Jack Earle, Harry McCoy, Bartine Burkett, Henry Murdock. Director: Harry Edwards (possible working titles **Sky High** and **Down to Earth**).

Earle and McCoy are rivals for the hand of Burkett, continuously attempting to outwit and outmaneuver each other. Earle finally gets the upper hand and is about to wed Burkett when the two rivals find themselves suspended over a cliff. They both fall, leaving only two holes in the ground.

Taxi! Taxi!: Released 05/07/1924. © Universal Pictures Corp. 03/14/1924. Century Comedy. Cast: Harry McCoy, Al Alt, Hilliard Karr, Betty Young, Bessie Welsh, Bernard Hyman, George Gyton, Director: Noel M. Smith (working title **Stranded**)

McCoy and Alt are pals, and while they hate work they break down and take jobs as cabbies. Problems arise when a hated stout bully, also a cabbie, vies for customers. McCoy and Alt win the customers through a series of clever ruses, and harass the bully mercilessly. They win in the end.

Our Pet: Released 05/11/1924. © Universal Pictures Corp. 12/27/1923. Century Comedy. Cast: Baby Peggy, Newton Hall, Winston Radom, Verne Winter, Donald Condon. Director, Story: Herman C. Raymaker (working titles **Too Many Lovers** and **Five After One**)

Baby Peggy's suitors arrive one at a time, and she hides each one from the next. When another arrives in a Packard, Peggy goes off with him, the left-behind suitors now discovering each other. She is saved from a spanking when she returns due to an officer's arrival with reward money for her capturing a burglar.

Trailing Trouble: Released 05/14/1924. © Universal Pictures Corp. 03/14/1924. Century Comedy. Cast: Buddy Messinger, Martha Sleeper, Spec O'Donnell, Arthur Trimble, Harry Pringle, Countess Mariana Moya. Director, Story: Albert Herman. Camera: William C. Hyer (working title **The Jazz Boy**)

Amateur detective Messinger, aided by pal O'Donnell and sweetheart Sleeper, go to the aid of her detective father in tracking down some crooks. The crooks enter Sleeper's house where the trio of youths manage to frighten and capture them, Messinger earning her father's admiration.

Tired Business Men: Released 05/21/1924. © Universal Pictures Corp. 04/14/1924. Century Comedy. Cast: Al Alt, Joe Bonner, Marjorie Marcel, Bartine Burkett, Betty Young, William Blaisdell, Century Follies Girls. Director, Story: Edward I. Luddy, Leslie Goodwin (working title **Hikers**)

Escaping from a pursuing cop, flirt Alt stumbles into a business and is given a job. He manages to demoralize the employees, and convinces them to run away for a picnic. The boss follows and is persuaded to join in. Alt and his pal go hunting, are chased by a bear, and are mistakenly shot by the Century Girls, dressed as Boy Scouts. A terrific windstorm buries them all in a collapsed tent.

The Flower Girl: Released 05/25/1924. © Universal Pictures Corp. 01/18/1924. Century Comedy. Cast: Baby Peggy, Billy Franey, Jack Earle, Joe Moore. Director, Story: Herman C. Raymaker. Asst Director: Dave Smith. Titles: Bob Hopkins. Camera; Jerry Ash (working title **Kissable Tess**)

Homeless Parisian girl Baby Peggy and her dog Buddy make the acquaintance of a famous artist while on one of their strolls. He invites them back to his studio where he paints her portrait. This becomes a critical success, winning both Peggy and the artist fame.

Delivering the Goods: Released 05/28/1924. © Universal Pictures Corp. 04/22/1924.

Century Comedy. Cast: Pal the Dog, Spec O'Donnell, Marjorie Marcel, Henry Murdock, Gerry O'Dell, James T. Kelley. Director, Story: Edward I. Luddy; Assistant: Leslie Goodwins.

Grocery store delivery boy O'Donnell is assisted by Pal. They shoot packages from a cannon to customers. Pal stops a runaway, handles canned goods in the store, and foils a villain who tries to double-cross the hero.

Fearless Fools: Released 06/04/1924. © Universal Pictures Corp. 04/29/1924. Century Comedy. Cast: Harry McCoy, Al Alt, Hilliard Karr. Director: Noel M. Smith.

McCoy and Alt accidentally annoy Karr's wife, but Karr is too fat to chase them along the outside window ledge. Later they inherit a fortune, only to find that Karr is their chauffeur. He takes them on a wild ride that ends up depositing them in a heap at the base of a huge cliff.

Stepping Some: Released 06/08/1924. © Universal Pictures Corp. 01/05/1924. Century Comedy. Cast: Baby Peggy. Director: Arvid E. Gillstrom (copyrighted as **Steppin' Some**)

Baby Peggy, her father believed lost at sea, ekes out a meager existence for her mother. Delivering a message to a hilltop home, she finds her grandparents. Peggy and her ma move there, where a bogus count attempts to seduce ma. Father, still alive, returns and tracks down his family where he finds Peggy being spanked and the bogus count trying to kiss his wife. He settles things and the family is now reunited.

Sailor Maids: Released 06/11/1924. © Universal Pictures Corp. 05/07/1924. Century Comedy. Cast: Wanda Wiley, Century Follies Girls, Joe Bonner, William Irving, William Blaisdell, Betty Young. Director, Story: Albert Herman. Camera: William C. Hyer (working title **Water Waves**)

The manager of a stranded troupe tries to get his chorus back home without paying fares. Smuggled as mail in sacks, they are put on a ship. They foil a burglar but are accused of the robbery, leading to a wild chase on the ship. They disguise themselves as sailors, but are discovered by the captain. They vamp him and he agrees to let them ride for free.

Please, Teacher!: Released 06/18/1924. © Universal Pictures Corp. 04/29/1924. Century Comedy. Cast: Buddy Messinger, Martha Sleeper, Spec O'Donnell, Arthur Trimble, Ernie Adams, James "Bubbles" Berry. Director, Story: Albert Herman (working titles **Playing Hookey** and **Happy Days**; copyrighted as **Happy Days**)

Messinger heads to school each day on his combination aeroplane-bicycle, but this day he crashes into a telegraph pole. Once in school, he and his classmates, along with sweetheart Sleeper, create such havoc that their teacher dismisses them. They have a wonderful time.

Poor Kid: Released 06/22/1924. © Universal Pictures Corp. 01/05/1924. Century Comedy. Cast: Baby Peggy, Pal the Dog, Max Asher. Director, Story: Arvid E. Gillstrom.

Thrown out by their landlord, Baby Peggy, her father, and her dog Pal head to the park. There she picks up a bag of jewels tossed by some robbers who were evading the cops. The cop follows the crooks, who follow Peggy, and before they know it all have walked into the police station. Peggy receives a reward.

A Royal Pair: Released 06/25/1924. © Universal Pictures Corp. 05/20/1924. Century Comedy. Cast: Al Alt, Jack Earle, Hilliard Karr, Joe Bonner, Tad Ross, Henry Murdock, Marjorie Marcel, Betty Young, Elizabeth Kavane, Century Follies Girls. Director: Noel M. Smith. Story: Noel Smith, Dean Hawkins (working title **Araby Bound**)

Detectives Earle and Alt are hired to track down the kidnapped daughter of King Boola. They finally track her down in the cave hideout of a brigand chief and his cohorts. He manages to outwit them numerous times, but eventually they overcome the whole tribe of brigands and rescue the princess.

Lost Control: Released 07/02/1924. © Universal Pictures Corp. 05/23/1924. Century Comedy. Cast: Jack Earle, Harry McCoy, Hilliard Karr, Bessie Welsh, Marjorie Marcel, Betty Young, Bartine Burkett, James T. Kelley. Director: Noel Smith (working title **The Runaway Car**)

"The action of the story is built around a one-horse town and its gangling, dilapidated street car. How it runs away, how it brings three couples back to amicable terms once again is the fundamental basis of the story." (*Universal Weekly*, 04/12/1924)

Jack and the Beanstalk: Released 07/06/1924 (possibly Christmas week 1924). © Universal Pictures Corp. 01/16/1924. Century Comedy. Cast: Baby Peggy, Jack Earle, Blanche Payson, Buddy Williams. Director, Story: Alfred J. Goulding.

Jack (Baby Peggy) is sent to the market to sell the old cow but returns instead with some beans. Ma tosses them away but the next morning Jack finds they have sprouted and grown to a giant beanstalk. He climbs it a finds the kingdom of terrible giant Earle. After a series of dangerous adventures, Jack kills the giant.

Starving Beauties: Released 07/09/1924. © Universal Pictures Corp. 05/23/1924. Century Comedy. Cast: Wanda Wiley, Joe Bonner, Century Follies Girls. Director: Edward I. Luddy (Director, Story: Al Herman in copyright) Camera: William C. Hyer.

Wiley and the rest of a troupe of stranded show girls create a fire scare to escape, and are pursued by the hotel's proprietor and the police. After a wild chase that utilizes various modes of transportation, they are caught and put in jail where they now have free room and board.

Budding Youth: Released 07/16/1924. © Universal Pictures Corp. 06/04/1924. Century Comedy. Cast: Buddy Messinger, Tommy Hicks, L.J. O'Connor, Martha Sleeper, Pete the Dog, James "Bubbles" Berry, Century Kids. Director: Arvid E. Gillstrom.

Messinger and his gang tangle with a short-tempered attorney (O'Connor) who has chased them off his property. Messinger gets even with him with a pail of water balanced over the front door, is chased and eventually caught, and forced to apologize. Pete arrives with a lit stick of dynamite which blows a hole in the seat of the attorney's pants.

Her City Sport: Released 07/23/1924. © Universal Pictures Corp. 06/17/1924. Century Comedy. Cast: Wanda Wiley, Harry McCoy, Hilliard Karr, Century Follies Girls. Director: Charles Lamont (working title **The Farmyard Flapper**)

Dissatisfied with her fat lover Karr, country girl Wiley falls for city boy McCoy. Karr doesn't take this sitting down, and after a wild pursuit McCoy gives up and leaves Wiley to Karr.

Paging Money: Released 07/30/1924. © Universal Pictures Corp. 06/25/1924. Century Comedy. Cast: Henry Murdock, Harry Mann, Bill Blaisdell, Spec O'Donnell. Director, Story: Edward I. Luddy (working title **Good Morning**)

A frustrated book agent resorts to all sorts of devious methods to gain entrance to prospective customers' houses, including dressing as a woman which gets him thrown from a window. He overinflates the balloon tires on his flivver, resulting in its rise into the air and eventual explosion.

Her Fortunate Face: Released 08/06/1924. © Universal Pictures Corp. 06/04/1924. Century Comedy. Cast: Wanda Wiley, Harry McCoy, Hilliard Karr. Director, Story: Edward I. Luddy (working title **Her Face Value**; copyrighted as **Her Face Value**)

Arrested for a theft she did not commit, Wiley is chosen by McCoy who has made a bet that a crook can be reformed if placed in the proper environment. He makes her his maid, she makes love to him, is exonerated when a necklace is stolen, and finally wins his heart.

Scared Stiff: Released 08/13/1924. © Universal Pictures Corp. 06/25/1924. Century Comedy. Cast: Al Alt, Henry Murdock, Bessie Welsh. Director, Story: Albert Herman (working title **Hip! Hip! Hurrah!**).

College boys Alt and Murdock are expelled after creating havoc with a giant pushball. In a restaurant they have problems with some clams. They later help a girl in a haunted house, and discover the "haunting" to be the work of a jealous heir hoping to scare her away.

The Blow Out: Released 08/20/1924. © Universal Pictures Corp. 07/07/1924. Century Comedy. Cast: Buddy Messinger, Spec O'Donnell, Willie McDonald, James "Bubbles" Berry, Century Comedy Kids. Director, Story: Edward I. Luddy.

Messinger and Bubbles rescue the former's sweetheart from a runaway auto. They attend a party at her house, and Bubbles humiliates Messinger. The two, along with rival O'Donnell, hide in a piano which rolls down a hill, the girl's father in pursuit since some bonds are hidden in the piano.

Eat and Run: Released 08/27/1924. © Universal Pictures Corp. 07/07/1924. Century Comedy. Cast: Al Alt, Harry McCoy, Max Davidson, Max Asher, Bessie Welsh, Hilliard Karr. Director, Story: Albert Herman (working title **Full of Pep**)

"The story tells of the difficulties encountered by two young men in love with the same girl, the daughter of a restaurant owner. Max Davidson, as the girl's father, tells the two young men that they must each prove their worth to his satisfaction before they can have his daughter. The one who finally wins does so through a traveling lunch wagon he has opened. The father sees a good business man in him and makes him his partner." (*Universal Weekly*, 08/02/1924)

Beginning of 1924-1925 Season

Traffic Jams: Released 09/03/1924. © Universal Pictures Corp. 07/28/1924. Century Comedy. Cast: Harry McCoy, Hilliard Karr, Bessie Welsh, Joe Bonner, Ernie Adams. Director: Noel M. Smith. Assistant Director: Charles Lamont. Story: Noel Smith, Pinto Colvig.

Frustrated in his attempts to cross a busy street, McCoy climbs inside a huge steel cage ball and succeeds, but creates havoc doing so. Later, a rival's runaway car crashes into McCoy's girl's house and chases everyone about. McCoy escapes in a race car, accidentally enters a big race, and not only wins the race but the girl as well; the rival is covered with soot from the race car's exhaust.

Mind the Baby: Released 09/10/1924. © Universal Pictures Corp. 08/11/1924. Century Comedy. Cast: Pal the Dog, Ernie Shields, Fred Spencer, Louise Lorraine, Earl Marsh, Tad Ross. Director, Story: Albert Herman. Story: Pinto Colvig (working titles **Some Pal** and **Some Tail**)

A villain, learning of an inheritance, plots to abduct a foundling baby from its foster mother. The baby wanders off, and it's Pal to the rescue, saving the infant from an alligator, the villain, and from a clothes basket afloat in a lake and heading for the falls.

Low Bridge: Released 09/17/1924. © Universal Pictures Corp. 08/15/1924. Century

Comedy. Cast: Buddy Messinger, Martha Sleeper, James "Bubbles" Berry, Eddie Hughes, Spec O'Donnell. Director: Arvid E. Gillstrom (working title **Rocking the Boat**).

Bubbles boasts to Sleeper of Messinger's yacht, and invites her for a cruise. Since there is no yacht, Bubbles and Messinger build one in their bathroom. The room floods, the house is drenched, and the two builders along with Sleeper sail out of the house, Messinger's irate parents in pursuit.

The Trouble Fixer: Released 09/24/1924. © Universal Pictures Corp. 07/19/1924. Century Comedy. Cast: Wanda Wiley, Al Alt, Harry McCoy. Director, Story: Albert Herman.

Newlywed Wiley poses as her husband's unmarried groom's wife when his father, thinking him married, comes to town. When her husband's uncle visits, Wiley is forced to act as twins, and "borrows" a baby to satisfy the uncle's expectations. The baby turns out to be black, and its mother rather annoyed. After much running about and back and forth between the two households, the ruse is exposed.

Snappy Eyes: Released 10/01/1924. © Universal Pictures Corp. 07/14/1924. Century Comedy. Cast: Wanda Wiley, Harry McCoy, Al Alt, Hilliard Karr, Century Follies Girls. Director, Story: Albert Herman (working title **Oh You Girls**)

Father sends country girl Wiley off to finishing school to get her away from the city chap who's wooing her. The city chap follows her and they leave the school to be married, but before the minister can do so her former country sweetheart arrives with the chap's wife! All ends well.

What an Eye!: Released 10/08/1924. © Universal Pictures Corp. 08/15/1924. Century Comedy. Cast: Buddy Messinger, Hilliard Karr. Director, Story: Edward I. Luddy.

Newspaper office boy Messinger, his reporter brother, and the brother's stenographer fiancé take action on the editor's assignment: get the dope on a so-called haunted house and its head-sized "mysterious eye" terrorizing the neighborhood. Messinger finds out that the "eye" is a doctor who treats nervous patients, "creating" patients by first making them nervous via the "mysterious eye." He gives credit of the discovery to his brother and the fiancé.

Sahara Blues: Released 10/15/1924. © Universal Pictures Corp. 08/20/1924. Century Comedy. Cast: Al Alt, Hilliard Karr, Jack Earle, Bartine Burkett, Elisabeth Kavane, Century Follies Girls. Director: Noel M. Smith and Al Herman.

Egyptologists Alt and Earle, lost in the desert, stumble upon the court of an Arab sheik and his harem. They nearly lose their lives but emerge victorious, and are given the pick of the harem for their wives.

Some Tomboy: Released 10/22/1924. © Universal Pictures Corp. 08/20/1924. Century Comedy. Cast: Wanda Wiley, Al Alt, Harry McCoy, Hilliard Karr, Mary Land, James T. Kelley, The Century Kids. Director: Edward I. Luddy (working title **The Tomboy**; copyrighted as **The Tom-Boy)**

Pursued by wealthy Alt, tomboy Wiley is invited to his mother's party to serve as the mother's hairdresser. She makes a disaster of this and flees, but discovers two burglars and courageously captures them. For this she is forgiven the disastrous hairdressing.

Here He Comes!: Released 10/29/1924. © Universal Pictures Corp. 08/25/1924. Century Comedy. Cast: Buddy Messinger, Spec O'Donnell, James "Bubbles" Berry, Arthur Trimble. Director, Story: Edward I. Luddy (working title **A Hospital Riot**)

Buddy rescues Dolores from the runaway horse he was thrown from, via a motorcycle. Buddy takes his friends Arthur, Bubbles, Spec, and Donald all for a ride on his motorcycle, ending up in a hospital's quarantine ward. All climb in bed and are pulled out of the hospital by Buddy's motorcycle.

Sweet Dreams: Released 11/05/1924. © Universal Pictures Corp. 07/19/1924. Century Comedy. Cast: Wanda Wiley, Harry McCoy, Spec O'Donnell, Mary Land, Louise Carver. Director, Story: Edward I. Luddy (working title **Her Bridegroom**)

Poor girl Wiley is in love with lawyer McCoy whose mother is forcing him to marry a society vamp. Wiley discovers that she, and not the vamp, is the rightful heir due to an ID mixup at birth. She rushes to the wedding, kidnaps the minister and groom, and marries the latter herself.

Speed Boys: Released 11/12/1924. © Universal Pictures Corp. 08/25/1924. Century Comedy. Cast: Spec O'Donnell, James "Bubbles" Berry, Arthur Trimble, Josephine Adair, Tommy Hicks The Century Kids. Director: Albert Herman (copyrighted as **Speed, Boys!**)

O'Donnell, Trimble, and Bubbles step in to help run a miniature railroad. After a number of mishaps and adventures, Bubbles is sidetracked by a cute young passenger. O'Donnell woos Trimble's girl Adair, so Trimble dresses up as a girl and successfully attracts O'Donnell. Having succeeded at that, the two go on an amusement ride, O'Donnell emerging with a black eye, and further annoyed when Trimble's disguise is revealed.

Don't Fall: Released 11/19/1924. © Universal Pictures Corp. 09/05/1924. Century Comedy. Cast: Buddy Messinger, James "Bubbles" Berry, Spec O'Donnell. Director: Arvid E. Gillstrom.

Messinger and Bubbles set out to make a fortune. After adventures on a boxcar, a van, and a passing auto, they end up in a movie studio. Bubbles is pressed into service as an actor when another proves unsuitable, and is a success. Messinger becomes his manager, and their fortune is made.

Dancing Daisies: Released 11/26/1924. © Universal Pictures Corp. 08/25/1924. Century Comedy. Cast: Al Alt, Century Follies Girls. Director, Story: Albert Herman (working title **Pretty Flappers**)

Penniless dance instructor Alt and his showgirls are thrown off a train and land at a beachside hotel where the pretty girls are put to work to draw crowds. Now flush, the hotel owner takes off and is pursued to a train by Alt and the girls. There they encounter the same conductor who earlier threw them off the train. They jump on him and take some tickets.

The Family Row: Released 12/03/1924. © Universal Pictures Corp. 09/15/1924. Century Comedy. Cast: Buddy Messinger, Hilliard Karr, Bartine Burkett, Dolores Brinkman, Grace Woods, Dorothy Vernon. Director, Story: Edward I. Luddy (working title **The Kid Brother**)

Messinger and his older brother court two sisters, the brother eventually marrying. Messinger and his girl proceed to play tricks to arouse his brother's jealousy. They dress up several girls as young men and have them enter the wife's house, the brother thinking them to be lovers.

Harem Follies: Released 12/10/1924. © Universal Pictures Corp. 10/20/1924. Century Comedy. Cast: Bert Roach, Bessie Welsh, Al Alt, Lucille Hutton, Yvonne Howell, Century Follies Girls. Director, Story: Edward I. Luddy (working title **Be Yourself**)

Roach and a dashing sheik smoke hookahs and watch a bunch of dancing girls. They become woozy and dream all sorts of exciting adventures set in contemporary times involving street cars, autos, cops, and a spooky inventor.

Present Arms: Released 12/17/1924. © Universal Pictures Corp. 10/31/1924. Century Comedy. Cast: Wanda Wiley, Al Alt, Hilliard Karr. Director, Story: Edward I. Luddy. Camera: William Hyer (working title **On Duty**)

Housemaid Wiley is in love with her mistress' son, but he's not moved by her. She saves him before his auto crashes off a cliff. When his mother gets sick, Wiley goes to the son, who is on guard duty at the fort, switches clothes with him, and assumes his duty. A spy steals some radio plans, so she pursues him in uniform and recovers the plans. The son is believed to be the hero, and realizing she's responsible begs her forgiveness, which she accepts.

Broadway Beauties: Released 12/24/1924. © Universal Pictures Corp. 11/07/1924. Century Comedy. Cast: Edna Marian, Eddie Gordon, Hilliard Karr, Century Follies Girls, Joe Moore, Cameo the Dog. Director, Story: Edward I. Luddy.

Country lass Marian heads to the city to seek her fortune, eventually followed by her sweetie Karr. She gets a job as dancer in a cabaret. Karr arrives and spots her dancing, infuriating the proprietor. Karr won't give up until he learns that Marian is now married to the proprietor.

His First Degree: Released 12/31/1924. © Universal Pictures Corp. 01/03/1925. Century Comedy. Cast: Buddy Messinger, Max Asher, Hilliard Karr, Bessie Welsh, Dolores Brinkman, Edward J. Lambert. Director: Edward I. Luddy.

Looking Down: Released 01/07/1925. © Universal Pictures Corp. 12/02/1924. Century Comedy. Cast: Al Alt, Wanda Wiley, Joe Moore, Dorothy Vernon. Director: Jess Robbins. Story: Jess Robbins, George Fouret (working titles **Up In The Air** and **Coming Down**)

Wiley chases a fire engine on her bike, picking up a cop on her handlebars along the way. Landing on a construction site, he falls into a vat of plaster while she is whisked high above on a raised beam. She returns to ground but slips on a hot bolt, splashing a vamp with the plaster. The cop arrests the vamp. A young engineer asks her to go riding with him, and they end up in a roadhouse with the vamp and her villain boyfriend. The villain appropriates the engineer's flivver, but ends up driving into a swimming pool. The engineer drives it out, Wiley on board.

The Aggravatin' Kid: Released 01/14/1925. © Universal Pictures Corp. 10/20/1924. Century Comedy. Cast: Buddy Messinger, Hilliard Karr, Lucille Hutton, Louise Carver, Arthur Thalasso. Director, Story: Edward I. Luddy (working title **Uncle's Reward**)

Messinger unsuccessfully attempts to prevent Karr's marriage to his sister. They head to Florida for their honeymoon. Uncle writes that he'll give them $30,000 if Karr is prosperous, so they move into an expensive home to fool him. He discovers their ruse but also reconnects with an old sweetheart, and gives them the money anyway.

Her Daily Dozen: Released 01/21/1925. © Universal Pictures Corp. 12/10/1924. Century Comedy. Cast: Edna Marian, Eddie Gordon, Hilliard Karr, Century Follies Girls. Director, Story: Edward I. Luddy (working title **Keep Fit**).

Marian is a slavey in a boarding house. Boarder Gordon is in love with her, and owes rent. He gets a job in a gym when its owner Karr is talked into it by Marian, who he has taken a shine to. Gordon and Karr are at continuous odds with each other, leading to an extended battle from which Gordon emerges victorious.

Taming the East: Released 01/28/1925. © Universal Pictures Corp. 12/04/1924. Century Comedy. Cast: Buddy Messinger, Hilliard Karr, Lois Boyd, Dolores Brinkman, Joe Bonner. Director, Story: Edward I. Luddy (working title **The Wooly West**)

Rookie cowboys Messinger and Karr foil a robbery, and are invited to the bank owner's home back East. The robber follows them and causes so much trouble that they decide that the East is wilder than the West, so they head back West with the banker's two daughters.

Nobody's Sweetheart: Released 02/04/1925. © Universal Pictures Corp. 12/10/1924. Century Comedy. Cast: Wanda Wiley, Harry McCoy. Director, Story: William Watson, Georges Fouret (working titles **What's the Use?** and **Nobody's Girl**)

Hungry and homeless Wiley schemes with a cop to get a free meal, but the plan backfires. She seeks refuge in a detective agency, and is put to work, assigned to recover stolen jewels from a notorious café. She is successful, and ends up marrying the boss.

My Baby Doll: Released 02/11/1925. © Universal Pictures Corp. 12/17/1924. Century Comedy. Cast: Arthur Lake, Edna Marian, Larry Richardson, Jane (Anne) "Cuddles" Shirley. Director, Story: Edward I. Luddy (working title **The Doll Baby**).

Arriving late to work, Marian is told to deliver a large mechanical doll. She breaks it, so she takes its place to avoid having her pay docked. Spotting the boy robbing the family safe, Marian manages to get hold of the money and replace it, thereby saving the boy from disgrace. She reveals herself.

A Dangerous Peach: Released 02/18/1925. © Universal Pictures Corp. 12/10/1924. Century Comedy. Cast: Al Alt, Hilliard Karr, Larry Richardson, Anita Garvin. Director, Story: Jess Robbins.

Shipping clerk Alt finds himself locked in a crate to be delivered to Mrs. Wilson (Garvin). His boss is in love with the woman, so his boss delivers the crate and makes love to her. Hearing a noise, she shouts that her husband is coming, so the boss hides. Hubby opens the crate, finds Alt, and fires a volley of shots. A dozen admirers emerge from various rooms, all making a dash for the door. Alt joins them.

Sailing Along: Released 02/25/1925. © Universal Pictures Corp. 12/02/1924. Century Comedy. Cast: Buddy Messinger, Martha Sleeper, Stella Doyle, Harry McCoy, Donald Hughes, James "Bubbles" Berry. Director, Story: Charles Lamont. Assistant Director: Robert Tansey (working title **Sailing**)

Sailor Messinger tries to woo pretty passenger Doyle, but finds that one of the ship's officers (McCoy) is a rival.

Don't Worry: Released 03/04/1925. © Universal Pictures Corp. 12/26/1924. Century Comedy. Cast: Wanda Wiley, Max Asher, Hilliard Karr, Al Alt. Director, Story: William Watson.

Country girl Wiley comes to live with her rich uncle, a cough drop manufacturer, and later succeeds in capturing several rival manufacturers attempting to steal his formula.

Powdered Chickens: Released 03/11/1925. © Universal Pictures Corp. 12/10/1924. Century Comedy. Cast: Edna Marian, Hilliard Karr, Max Asher, Dorothy Vernon. Director, Story: Edward I. Luddy.

Country girl Marian's father invents a formula to make hens lay. A city chap puts TNT into it, so after the hens lay the eggs they explode whenever anyone picks them up.

Raisin' Cain: Released 03/18/1925. © Universal Pictures Corp. 12/19/1924. Century Comedy. Cast: Beth Darlington, Whitney Raymond. Century Follies Girls. Director, Story: Charles Lamont.

Darlington's wealthy father finally grows tired of bailing her out of her numerous traffic messes, so he sends her to a boarding school. She is hazed by the other girls, so her sweetheart rescues her, they elope, and she wins her father's forgiveness.

Clear the Way: Released 03/25/1925. © Universal Pictures Corp. 12/04/1924. Century Comedy. Cast: Buddy Messinger, Beth Darlington. Director, Story: Charles Lamont (working title **Ain't Love Grand?**)

Buddy and his girl's shopping trip is cut short when her packages fall in a river. Later, Buddy and his rival fight in the latter's flivver, which comes to an end when the flivver crashes and the two are swept into a sewer. After that, Buddy gives his girl's wheelchair-bound father a ride pulled behind his motorcycle, which doesn't go well until the old man finds that he can now walk, so everyone is happy.

Puzzled by Crosswords: Released 04/01/1925. © Universal Pictures Corp. 03/03/1925. Century Comedy. Cast: Eddie Gordon, Beth Darlington, Hilliard Karr, Edna Marian. Director, Story: Charles Lamont.

Crossword fanatic Gordon's sweetheart loses patience with him and drags him off to be married. After a number of exciting experiences they end up in a police station where Gordon makes converts of the cops. His girl drags him off to the minister's house after relieving him of his pencils and puzzles.

Putting on Airs: Released 04/08/1925. © Universal Pictures Corp. 12/26/1924. Century Comedy. Cast: Edna Marian, Arthur Lake, Dorothy Vernon, Frank Whitson. Director, Story: Edward I. Luddy (working title **Rich Ideas**)

Trying to impress her sweetheart Lake, Marian points out a mansion and claims she lives there. Lake insists they go inside, forcing her to carry on the bluff. He organizes a big party and invites all of their friends. The mansion's owners turn up, and it turns out they are Lake's parents.

Getting Trimmed: Released 04/15/1925. © Universal Pictures Corp. 01/07/1925. Century Comedy. Cast: Wanda Wiley, Al Alt, Alice Belcher, Jack Singleton. Director,

Story: Edward I. Luddy.

Barber shop owner Wiley makes a mess of everything she tries to do, so she takes a job at a lunch counter. A runaway truck runs amuck and carries the counter through crowded streets and alleys. She ends up dropped into a fire engine, crawling out blackened.

Tourists De Luxe: Released 04/22/1925. © Universal Pictures Corp. 12/27/1924. Century Comedy. Cast: Tony Hayes, Hilliard Karr, Bessie Welsh, Billy Engle, Edgar Kennedy. Director, Story: Charles Lamont (working title **Winning Ways**)

When gypsies abduct the daughter of the proprietor of an auto camp, travelling salesmen Hayes and Karr give chase in their flivver and overtake it. The gypsies' wagon comes loose from the horses pulling it, and it careens down a hill, rescuers and rescued on board. It lands on a blast site and explodes, leaving everyone hanging from a rock high up.

Almost a Husband: Released 04/29/1925. © Universal Pictures Corp. 12/26/1924. Century Comedy. Cast: Buddy Messinger, Beth Darlington. Director, Story: Charles Lamont (working title **Too Young to Marry**)

Messinger and Darling's youthful attempts to marry are daunted by their respective fathers. Donning disguises to look older, they manage to acquire a marriage license, but arriving at the minister's house they find he's been alerted by their fathers. The fathers rush in and give their respective children a sound spanking.

Itching for Revenge: Released 05/06/1925. © Universal Pictures Corp. 01/22/1925. Century Comedy. Cast: Eddie Gordon, Fay Holderness, Larry Richardson, Bartine Burkett. Director, Story: Noel M. Smith.

Gordon purchases a radio control set for his car, but when he goes to summon the car a number of other cars show up as well, their owners having purchased the same radio set. Gordon goes to visit his girl but encounters a rival, so he dons a gorilla suit and scares him away.

The Queen of Aces: Released 05/13/1925. © Universal Pictures Corp. 01/13/1925. Century Comedy. Cast: Wanda Wiley, Al Alt, George A. Williams, Robert Paige, Larry Richardson, Century Follies Girls, Zip Monberg. Director: William Watson. Story: William Watson, Georges Fouret (working titles **You Cute Little Devil** and **Queen of Hearts**; rereleased as **His Taking Ways**)

Wiley is banned from her prospective father-in-law's social party because she is far too athletic. She gets in anyway by dressing as a man, and ends up attending a poker game with him. It's raided and they escape, and she later overcomes his objections to marriage with the subtle threat of revealing his weakness for poker.

Love Sick: Released 05/20/1925. © Universal Pictures Corp. 01/14/1925. Century Comedy. Cast: Arthur Lake, Beth Darlington, Ben Hall, Anita Garvin. Director, Story: Charles Lamont (working title **Who's to Blame**)

Lake uses his dog to drive away rivals from Darlington, but she still spurns his advances. Giving up, he writes her a note that he's going to kill himself, but his attempts to do so all fail until he is accidentally hit by an ambulance. Feigning injury, he's rushed to the hospital where Darlington puts her arms around him. When he comes to she tells him she loves him, and everything is all right.

Slick Articles: Released 05/27/1925. © Universal Pictures Corp. 01/16/1925. Century Comedy. Cast: Billy Engle, Hilliard Karr, Trilby Clark, Joe Bonner. Director, Story: Albert Herman (working title **It's All Wrong**)

Sailor Engle and Karr, his captain, pose as artists. A girl they have rescued poses for them. In order to pay their rent they steal a painting and sell it to the girl's father. The painting's rightful owner claims the painting and the two artists end up in jail.

Speak Freely: Released 06/03/1925. © Universal Pictures Corp. 01/16/1925. Century Comedy. Cast: Edna Marian, Al Alt, Hilliard Karr. Director, Story: William Watson.

When his wife storms out after a quarrel, hubby has to have his maid Marian pose as his wife to prove he's married to his visiting parents. The maid's iceman sweetheart shows up as does his wife, who now poses as the maid and makes life hell for her husband.

Kicked About: Released 06/10/1925. © Universal Pictures Corp. 01/22/1925. Century Comedy. Cast: Eddie Gordon, Larry Richardson. Director, Story: Noel M. Smith.

Arrested for depriving a fruit dealer of his livelihood, Gordon has a choice: 30 years in jail or become a cop and arrest the town's chief criminal. Choosing the latter, Gordon gets the worst of it before effecting an arrest. As a reward Gordon is assigned to the bomb squad.

Gridiron Gertie: Released 06/17/1925. © Universal Pictures Corp. 03/11/1925. Century Comedy. Cast: Wanda Wiley, Joe Bonner, Les Bates, Fred Peters. Director, Story: Edward I. Luddy.

Taken ill, a young fellow is forbidden by his stepmother from playing in the big football game. Sweetheart Wiley steps in, dons his uniform and doubles for the lad to protect his reputation. She scores the winning points.

Married Neighbors: Released 06/24/1925. © Universal Pictures Corp. 01/17/1925. Century Comedy. Cast: Billy Engle, Beth Darlington (Constance Darling according to some sources), Hilliard Karr, Max Asher. Director, Story: Charles Lamont.

It is bachelor Engle's last night of freedom, and he's out on a tear with a bunch of married friends. They commandeer a hansom but end up driving it off a bridge. Seeing the chilly reception each of his friends receives from their wives, Engle almost has second thoughts about marriage. He is late to his wedding, so bride Darlington starts out after him. An accident while crossing a bridge lands him in Darlington's car, and soon they are off on their honeymoon.

Plenty of Nerve: Released 07/01/1925. © Universal Pictures Corp. 01/25/1925. Century Comedy. Cast: Edna Marian, Billy Engle, Dorothy Vernon. Director, Story: William Watson (possible working title **Plain Luck**).

Marian's mother Vernon disapproves of sweetheart Engle's cowardice. Vernon inherits a sanitarium, so the manager, wanting to keep the place under his control, locks Marian and Vernon in a padded cell. Engle arrives, overcomes his cowardice, thwarts the villain's plans, and wins Marian.

A Rough Party: Released 07/08/1925. © Universal Pictures Corp. 01/24/1925. Century Comedy. Cast: Al Alt, Hilliard Karr, Constance Darling, Hyman Bynunsky. Director, Story: Charles Lamont.

Karr and Alt have a dilapidated flivver that they make over. They meet Darling and she invites them to a party where all the adults dress like kids.

Just in Time: Released 07/15/1925. © Universal Pictures Corp. 01/29/1925. Century Comedy. Cast: Wanda Wiley, Joe Bonner, Bynunsky Hyman. Director, Story: Edward I. Luddy.

Reporter Wiley sets out to rescue the editor's son who was kidnapped and held for ransom. Assuming the disguise of one of the gang's female members, Wiley rescues the son. She's chased by the gang, and leads them back to the newspaper office where the police capture them.

The Polo Kid: Released 07/22/1925. © Universal Pictures Corp. 12/27/1924. Century Comedy. Cast: Eddie Gordon, Larry Richardson, Beth Darlington. Director, Story: Jess Robbins (working title **Cleaning Up**)

Street cleaner Gordon incurs the wrath of a politician. Later Gordon rescues Darlington from a runaway horse and delivers her to her mansion, finding that her father is that same politician. Gordon foils a household robbery by the butler and a cohort, thereby earning the politician's gratitude.

Dry Up: Released 07/29/1925. © Universal Pictures Corp. 02/16/1925. Century Comedy. Cast: Jack Singleton, Bartine Burkett. Director, Story: Albert Herman.

Aspiring lawyer Singleton can't pass the boards and finds himself broke. Posing as a lawyer, he agrees to serve divorce summons to Burkett's husband. After serving the wrong man, Singleton finally gets it right but is now turned down by a repentant Burkett.

After a Reputation: Released 08/05/1925. © Universal Pictures Corp. 03/29/1925. Century Comedy. Cast: Edna Marian, Matty Roubert, Pinto Colvig. Director: William Watson. Story: William Watson, Pinto Colvig.

Unsophisticated youth Roubert wants to become a man of the world, the kind of fellow his sweetheart Marian likes. He manages to get a few chorus girls to act lovingly to him in front of Marian, who finally forgives him.

Paging a Wife: Released 08/12/1925. © Universal Pictures Corp. 03/25/1925. Century Comedy. Cast: Al Alt, Lillian Worth, Hilliard Karr, Charles King. Director, Story: Charles Lamont.

Alt's wife is away on a trip, so Karr picks him up and the two speed off. Stopped by a cop, Alt claims to be a doctor rushing to aid a sick mother and child. The suspicious cop decides to follow them, requiring Alt to persuade a flapper to pose as the mother. This works, until Alt's wife returns and senses another woman hiding in the house. It turns out to be a friend of hers, so all is well until the cop overhears this and arrests Alt and Karr.

Won by Law: Released 08/19/1925. © Universal Pictures Corp. 03/13/1925. Century Comedy. Cast: Wanda Wiley, Bob Reeves, Lillian Worth, Frank Whitson, John Brown the Bear. Director, Story: Edward I. Luddy.

Lazy girl Wiley falls for a handsome young Northwest Mounted Policeman. They go on a trip and encounter difficulties, leading to his abduction by moonshiners. She rescues him, marries him, and promptly subdues him.

Crying for Love: Released 08/26/1925. © Universal Pictures Corp. 04/23/1925. Century Comedy. Cast: Eddie Gordon, Blanche Payson, Tad Ross, Joe Bonner. Director, Story: Noel M. Smith.

Gordon suffers ongoing humiliation and abuse at the hands of wife Payson. Learning of some strength-giving pills, these transform him with the result that he is now the real master of the house. The tables turned, Payson now becomes totally submissive.

Beginning of 1925-1926 Season

Stranded: Released 09/02/1925. © Universal Pictures Corp. 04/11/1925. Century Comedy. Cast: Edna Marian, Hilliard Karr, Pete the Dog, Century Follies Girls. Director, Story: William Watson.

Gertie (Marian) and Karr are rival cabbies. She drives a homemade bus, and he drives a Ford. They scramble when a train arrives, but she emerges victorious with a bus filled with a theatrical troupe. She takes them to the local hotel, but after their stay they attempt to skip without paying their board. Gertie and Karr pursue them and appropriate their baggage, leaving the troupe dejected. Gertie and Karr make up.

Officer Number Thirteen: Released 09/09/1925. © Universal Pictures Corp. 04/23/1925. Century Comedy. Cast: Eddie Gordon, Frank Whitson, Betty Browne, Nan Conner. Director, Story: Edward I. Luddy (working title **Guilty Conscience**; copyrighted as **Officer No. 13**)

Erroneously thinking the police are after him, Gordon risks life and limb to evade them. Stumbling across a safecracker puts the police on his trail, and a melee results in his wearing a cop's outfit sizes too large. He leads a riot squad towards a gang fight and licks them all, but ends up in the can along with the gang for impersonating an officer. The sergeant's daughter pleads for his release, which is granted when another cop announces that he's a hero.

Too Much Mother-in-Law: Released 09/16/1925. © Universal Pictures Corp. 04/11/1925. Century Comedy. Cast: Constance Darling (Beth Darlington according to some sources), Blanche Payson, Charles King. Director, Story: Noel M. Smith.

Newlyweds Darlington and King pick up mother-in-law Payson, who takes an immediate dislike to him. She now rules the house and him. Old ladies come to visit, so he spikes their tea with scotch. He finally loads Payson into his motorcycle, runs her ragged, then dumps her at the train station.

Educating Buster: Released 09/23/1925. © Universal Pictures Corp. 06/12/1925. Century Comedy. Cast: Arthur Trimble, Doreen Turner, Pete the Dog, Hilliard Karr, Charles King, Emily Gerdes, Leon Holmes, Albert Schaefer. Director, Story: Charles Lamont. Camera: William Hyer. Based on Richard F. Outcault's comic strip "Buster Brown."

Buster (Trimble), on stilts, impersonates a policeman to get some free pie from a cook. Arriving late to school along with Mary Jane (Turner), Tige (Pete) follows and is thrown out along with another kid's smelly Limburger cheese. Cheese in mouth, Tige returns to the schoolroom, throwing the place into chaos.

Cupid's Victory: Released 09/30/1925. © Universal Pictures Corp. 05/07/1925. Century Comedy. Cast: Wanda Wiley, Earl McCarthy, Tony Hayes, Century Beauties. Director, Story: Charles Lamont.

Wiley tries to make a fellow jealous by surrounding herself with a lot of fellows. He dresses as a vamp, lures them one-by-one into the next room, then disposes of them. He then surrounds himself with chorus girls to make Wiley jealous. Despondent, she attempts suicide, but without any success. She tries driving blindfolded, but ends up crashing into the fellow's car, the two of them landing in a balcony, her in his lap.

Uncle Tom's Gal: Released 10/07/1925. © Universal Pictures Corp. 04/21/1925. Century Comedy. Cast: Edna Marian, Larry Richardson, Les Bates, Joe Bonner, Harry Martel. Director, Story: William Watson.

Movie company comes to Marian's father's farm to film "Uncle Tom's Cabin." When the lead actress quits, the director hires Marian to play Little Eva, Topsy, and Eliza. The filming is a disaster, the icing on the cake when Marian naively opens the cans of exposed negatives.

Piping Hot: Released 10/14/1925. © Universal Pictures Corp. 04/10/1925. Century Comedy. Cast: Al Alt, Hilliard Karr. Director, Story: Charles Lamont (working title **A Leadpipe Cinch**)

Sleepwalker Alt walks a rope across the street to an adjacent building, and descends to safety atop a safe. Plumbers Alt and Karr go to a house to fix the pipes, but make a horrible mess of things and are thrown out.

A Winning Pair: Released 10/21/1925. © Universal Pictures Corp. 04/23/1925. Century Comedy. Cast: Wanda Wiley, Charles King, Henry Murdock. Director, Story: Charles Lamont.

Wiley wakens from a high-diving dream. Infatuated by a fellow, she joins him in a horseback ride, faking a runaway and fall to arouse his sympathy. Unconscious, she is revived by kisses from the fellow, now her lover.

Buster Be Good: Released 10/28/1925. © Universal Pictures Corp. 06/12/1925. Century Comedy. Cast: Arthur Trimble, Doreen Turner, Pete the Dog, Pinto Colvig. Director, Story: Charles Lamont. Assistant Director: Gus Meins. Based on Richard F. Outcault's comic strip "Buster Brown."

Buster (Trimble) goes to Mary Jane's (Turner) house where her father is holding a meeting of spiritualists. Buster rounds up his gang and they all dress up, first as spooks to frighten the spiritualists, and later as Buster himself to confuse the lead spiritualist. Buster ends up getting spanked.

Nursery Troubles: Released 11/04/1925. © Universal Pictures Corp. 05/14/1925. Century Comedy. Cast: Edna Marian. Director, Story: William Watson.

Tramp Marian, dressed as a boy, emerges from a train's brakebeam and is chased by a cop. She gets a job in a department store's nursery. She gives the babies to the wrong mothers but sets matters right, is promoted to head of the department, and wins the love of the boss.

A Taxi War: Released 11/11/1925. © Universal Pictures Corp. 05/14/1925. Century Comedy. Cast: Eddie Gordon, Anita Garvin, Larry Richardson. Director, Story: Noel M. Smith (working title **For Hire**).

Gordon and his pal escape from their rent-demanding landlady. Gordon takes a job with a taxi company, and his pal for a rival taxi company. As a result, the two play tricks on each other to lure customers away from the other.

A Speedy Marriage: Released 11/18/1925. © Universal Pictures Corp. 06/16/1925. Century Comedy. Cast: Wanda Wiley, Charles King. Director, Story: Edward I. Luddy.

Wiley is informed by her lawyer that she must be married by 5:00 to inherit her late uncle's estate. She arranges to meet her fiancé but encounters all sorts of obstacles on her way. She and her fiancé finally arrive at the minister's house, and they are married at the stroke of 5:00.

Red Riding Hood: Released 11/21/1925. © Universal Pictures Corp. 06/05/1925. Century Special. Cast: Baby Peggy, Arthur Trimble, Louise Lorraine, Johnny Fox, Alf Goulding, Jr., Peter the Great the Dog. (Originally titled **Little Red Riding Hood** and scheduled for release on 11/06/1922 and shot as a feature). Director, Story: Alfred J. Goulding.

Trimble is the favored contender for Baby Peggy's hand, and after the first few scenes which show her social life, the film closely follows the fairy tale.

Oh! Buster!: Released 11/25/1925. © Universal Pictures Corp. 10/28/1925. Century Comedy. Cast: Arthur Trimble, Doreen Turner, Pete the Dog, Pinto Colvig. Director: Gus Meins. Assistant Director: William Mull. Camera: William Hyer. Based on Richard F. Outcault's comic strip "Buster Brown."

Buster (Trimble) and Mary Jane (Turner) are invited to spend the weekend at his grandfather's, but Tige is not invited. Tige shows up anyway and wins over the grandfather by chasing a book agent away. But not for long. When grandfather's committee of bankers show up carrying the same type of briefcases as the book agent, Tige goes after them as well.

Scandal Hunters: Released 12/02/1925. © Universal Pictures Corp. 04/21/1925. Century Comedy. Cast: Al Alt, Larry Richardson, Marie Torpie. Director, Story: Jess Robbins.

When all the other reporters refuse the assignment to interview the mayor, Alt accepts it. He keeps being thrown out of the mayor's house, but when he finally lands the story the other reporters jump on him, leaving him a wreck.

Eighteen Carat: Released 12/09/1925. © Universal Pictures Corp. 05/14/1925. Century Comedy. Cast: Edna Marian. Director, Story: William Watson.

When she loses a diamond to a hen, Marian heads to the city to earn money to pay her father back. She's to deliver packages containing clothes, but loses them to a slick crook. Recovering them, she delivers them and spots the diamond near the gizzard of a roast chicken and departs happily.

Captain Suds: Released 12/16/1925. © Universal Pictures Corp. 05/18/1925. Century Comedy. Cast: Eddie Gordon, Beth Darlington, Larry Richardson, Lillian Worth. Director, Story: Noel M. Smith.

Gordon is abused by his stepmother, and later abused by his big rival when he calls on his girl. When the rival strangles Gordon, he is dispatched by a spectator who bounces a brick off his head. Gordon gets covered with mud and then embraces his girl.

Buster's Nightmare: Released 12/23/1925. © Universal Pictures Corp. 11/12/1925. Century Comedy. Cast: Arthur Trimble, Doreen Turner, Pinto Colvig, Pete the Dog. Director: Gus Meins. Based on Richard F. Outcault's comic strip "Buster Brown."

Buster (Trimble), Mary Jane (Turner), her baby brother, and Tige are left alone in the house to play. After much mischief, including Tige frozen solid and needing thawing in the oven, darkness comes and the kids are terrified of ghosts.

Going Good: Released 12/30/1925. © Universal Pictures Corp. 05/29/1925. Century Comedy. Cast: Wanda Wiley, Jack Singleton. Director, Story: Edward I. Luddy.

Wiley's friend invents a formula to convert water to gas, and some foreigners want to steal it. The villains pursue them and they are chased into a haunted house. They finally make their escape by way of the roof.

The Honeymoon Squabble: Released 01/06/1926. © Universal Pictures Corp. 08/01/1925. Century Comedy. Cast: Edna Marian, Jack Singleton, Victor Rottman, Valerie Lavella, Hilliard Karr. Director, Story: William Watson.

Newlywed Marian and hubby, now at odds, take separate rooms at a hotel, as does another squabbling couple. The house detective suspects hanky panky, unaware of the couples' true status. After a lot of mixups, marriage licenses are produced and everyone is now cleared of suspicion.

Buster's Bust-Up: Released 01/13/1926. © Universal Pictures Corp. 11/02/1925. Century Comedy. Cast: Arthur Trimble, Doreen Turner, Pete the Dog. Director: Gus Meins. Based on Richard F. Outcault's comic strip "Buster Brown."

Buster (Trimble) and Mary Jane (Turner) have a falling out. Paint splattered on his face leads mom to think he has smallpox and puts him to bed. He and Tige sneak out and accidentally end up high atop a building under construction. Buster and Tige parachute to comparative safety, falling through a skylight and into his bed. Mom looks in on Buster and thinks he's resting peacefully.

Her Lucky Leap: Released 01/20/1926. © Universal Pictures Corp. 04/21/1925. Century Comedy. Cast: Wanda Wiley, Whitney Raymond, Joe Bonner, Max Asher, Eddie Clayton, Les Bates. Director, Story: Edward I. Luddy (working title **Met By Accident**)

Aboard a ship, jewelry thieves hise a necklace down Wiley's back. A detective keeps his eyes on the thieves while they keep an eye on Wiley, eventually following her to land. They pursue her to her aunt's house, so she leads a chase that ends at the police station, the thieves arrested.

Helpful Al: Released 01/27/1926. © Universal Pictures Corp. 05/14/1925. Century Comedy. Cast: Al Alt, Charles King, Lillian Worth, Tony Hayes, Ouida Hill (Thelma Daniels). Director, Story: Charles Lamont.

Alt and his pal find a kidnapped baby in their car. Attempting to care for it becomes a challenge when it first walks a cliff-side plank, and later is carried aloft by some balloons. The baby descends into its parents' car. Alt receives the $5,000 reward, but the wind blows it away.

The Big City: Released 02/03/1926. © Universal Pictures Corp. 11/20/1925. Century Comedy. Cast: Edna Marian. Director: Francis Corby. Story: Tad Ross.

Country girl Marian heads to the big city and runs into all sorts of problems before landing in the home of her aunt. The aunt makes Marian her maid with instructions not to touch the canary. The canary escapes and Marian wrecks the house attempting to capture it.

Crowning the Count: Released 02/10/1926. © Universal Pictures Corp. 01/07/1925. Century Comedy. Cast: Eddie Gordon, Larry Richardson. Director, Story: Jess Robbins.

In dutch for owing back rent at the hotel, Gordon adds whiskers as a disguise and is mistaken for the expected count by a mysterious stranger. Gordon is honored until asylum attendants arrive and grab the stranger. Gordon feigns craziness and is hauled away as well.

Accidents Can Happen: Released 02/17/1926. © Universal Pictures Corp. 06/11/1925. Century Comedy. Cast: Al Alt, Hilliard Karr. Director, Story: Charles Lamont.

Aviators Alt and Karr crash and suffer some delusions as a result. Hearing the call for help from the girl they both love, they enter an abandoned house where all sorts of weird things happen. It is finally explained that they've been part of a lodge initiation conducted by the girl's father.

Buster's Nose Dive: Released 02/24/1926. © Universal Pictures Corp. 11/20/1925. Century Comedy. Cast: Arthur Trimble, Doreen Turner, Pete the Dog. Director: Gus Meins. Based on Richard F. Outcault's comic strip "Buster Brown."

Buster (Trimble) sneaks a ride to his father's airfield along with Mary Jane (Turner) and Tige. Playing with a model of his dad's airplane, it takes off with them in it, crashing through the wall and sailing over town, his dad below in pursuit. The plane finally falls into the back seat of dad's car.

Flying Wheels: Released 03/03/1926. © Universal Pictures Corp. 12/02/1925. Century Comedy. Cast: Wanda Wiley, Alfred Hewston, Joe Bonner, Consuelo Dawn. Director, Story: Edward I. Luddy.

Wiley tries to play golf while two tormentors try to gum up her game. Later she enters an auto race driving the tiny car of her auto dealer father, and after a number of incidents emerges the winner.

Al's Troubles: Released 03/10/1926. © Universal Pictures Corp. 12/14/1925. Century Comedy. Cast: Al Alt, Jack Singleton, George Barton. Director, Story: Charles Lamont.

Alt and his pal escape from a raided poker game, having lost everything but their underwear. They join a cross country foot race and Alt wins a silver cup. They take it to a pawn shop in exchange for clothes. They drop down a chimney to escape the cops still pursuing them. Emerging covered with soot, they are mistaken by the two black brides as their respective grooms, and barely manage to escape marriage. They are arrested.

Buster's Hunting Party: Released 03/17/1926. © Universal Pictures Corp. 12/18/1925. Century Comedy. Cast: Arthur Trimble, Doreen Turner, Pete the Dog. Director: Gus Meins. Based on Richard F. Outcault's comic strip "Buster Brown."

Buster (Trimble), Mary Jane (Turner), and Tige accompany Buster's uncle to the country for a hunting and fishing trip. Tige has bad encounters with a speckled carp and a skunk, the latter leaving the dog stinking. A bear enters their cabin and climbs in uncle's bed, uncle fleeing when he too tries to climb in the bed. Buster is left behind, hiding in a corner with Tige and his skunky smell.

Yearning for Love: Released 03/24/1926. © Universal Pictures Corp. 05/14/1925. Century Comedy. Cast: Wanda Wiley, Charles King, Larry Richardson, Julia Griffith. Director: Edward I. Luddy. Story: George Fouret.

Wiley's prim aunt wants her to marry an undesirable suitor, but Wiley prefers another of her own choosing. Forced to the alter by her aunt, the rival dresses as the minister and blackjacks the intended groom, and the two run off to be married. The aunt, meanwhile, marries the poor rejected sap.

A Flivver Vacation: Released 03/31/1926. © Universal Pictures Corp. 12/04/1925. Century Comedy. Cast: Eddie Gordon, Blanche Payson, Tommy Hicks, Century Follies Girls. Director, Story: Noel M. Smith.

Henpecked Gordon, his domineering wife Payson, a lazy brother-in-law, and mischievous son Hicks go on their annual flivver vacation. Hicks causes the most problems, and Gordon bears the brunt of most everything. Gordon and Payson end up tumbling down a high embankment.

Say It with Love: Released 04/07/1926. © Universal Pictures Corp. 12/18/1925. Century Comedy. Cast: Edna Marian, Earl McCarthy, Mary Land. Director: Francis Corby. Story: Tad Ross.

Poor girl Marian spots an ideal job at an employment agency, but lacking paper writes the address on the collar of the fellow in front of her. Her memory faulty, she follows him all over town only to find the address she seeks is his house. A romance follows and she loses her job, but when a fire breaks out they stage an elopement.

Buster's Skyrocket: Released 04/14/1926. © Universal Pictures Corp. 12/18/1925. Century Comedy. Cast: Arthur Trimble, Doreen Turner, Pete the Dog. Director, Story: Gus Meins. Based on Richard F. Outcault's comic strip "Buster Brown."

Buster (Trimble), Mary Jane (Turner), and Tige play indoor golf, making a mess. Their tutor arrives, but after some pranks they manage to escape and hide in a stolen munitions car. It's pursued by the police, and their gunfire sets off the fireworks. The car explodes and Buster rolls down the hill in a tire, close on Tige's heels.

Painless Pain: Released 04/21/1926. © Universal Pictures Corp. 02/08/1926. Century Comedy. Cast: Wanda Wiley, Hilliard Karr, Villie Latimer, Jack Singleton. Director, Story: Edward I. Luddy (working title **Toothaches**).

Seeking to drum up business for her customer-less dentist sweetheart, Wiley hires a tough to punch out passersby. She then hands out business cards for the dental practice. This works, but her sweetheart isn't at the now-crowded office, so Wiley takes over and collects a handsome fortune.

Too Many Babies: Released 04/28/1926. © Universal Pictures Corp. 12/28/1925. Century Comedy. Cast: Charles King, Constance Darling, Blanche Payson. Director: Scott Pembroke.

Childless couple King and Darling are visited by his stern mother-in-law Payson, who believes they have two children. Both rush out to round up a couple of kids. Returning with four, Payson is on to them and proceeds to maul King until a cop intervenes, and she fools the cop into thinking King the aggressor.

A Haunted Heiress: Released 05/05/1926. © Universal Pictures Corp. 12/28/1925. Century Comedy. Cast: Edna Marian. Director, Story: Francis Corby.

When a crooked lawyer advices her to sell the dilapidated property she's inherited from her grandfather, Marian decides to live in it instead. He hires a gang to "haunt" the place and scare her away, but with the help of the lawyer's clerk she outwits the gang and keeps the house.

Buster's Mix-Up: Released 05/12/1926. © Universal Pictures Corp. 01/22/1926. Century Comedy. Cast: Arthur Trimble, Doreen Turner, Pete the Dog, Leon Holmes. Director: Gus Meins. Based on Richard F. Outcault's comic strip "Buster Brown."

Buster (Trimble) and Mary Jane (Turner) are at odds, so she turns to Freckles for companionship. Tige does his canine best to mend the rift, but unsuccessfully. When Freckles takes her on a bicycle ride and it gets out of control, Buster and Tige rescue her and he wins her favor.

Playing the Swell: Released 05/19/1926. © Universal Pictures Corp. 12/18/1925. Century Comedy. Cast: Wanda Wiley, Earl McCarthy, Virginia Bushman. Director: Francis Corby. Story: Tad Ross.

Wiley tries to impress a fellow by claiming that the roadster and the mansion she drives to are hers, but it turns out they are his. He invites her to a party, so she creates an outfit using the lace curtains. When it starts to fall apart, she becomes the laughing stock. In spite of this, she and the fellow end up engaged.

Honeymooning with Ma: Released 05/26/1926. © Universal Pictures Corp. 02/26/1926. Century Comedy. Cast: Charles King, Constance Darling. Director: Scott Pembroke.

King's mother-in-law arrives for a stay, and takes an immediate dislike to him. She pummels him, but when others pass through she pretends to be dancing with him. Along with wife Darling, they all go on a picnic, and here all sorts of things happen to his abuser to even the score. She ends up in a lake.

Movie Madness: Released 06/02/1926. © Universal Pictures Corp. 01/22/1926. Century Comedy. Cast: Edna Marian, Henry Murdock, Earl McCarthy. Director: Francis Corby. Story: Tad Ross.

Farm girl Marian's house is chosen for a movie location, and she's chosen as the lead when the former quits. The movie people make all sorts of "alterations" to the house, including holes in the roof. They leave, a terrific rainstorm comes and floods the place, and her father returns to the disaster.

Buster's Heart Beats: Released 06/09/1926. © Universal Pictures Corp. 04/05/1926. Century Comedy. Cast: Arthur Trimble, Doreen Turner, Pete the Dog. Director: Gus Meins. Based on Richard F. Outcault's comic strip "Buster Brown."

Tige assists Buster (Trimble) in the recital of a poem. Tige pours tar down the chimney to rout the guests. Another child recites "The Boy Stood on the Burning Deck," and Tige adds realism by pulling an oil stove under the boy's chair.

Twin Sisters: Released 06/16/1926. © Universal Pictures Corp. 01/11/1926. Century Comedy. Cast: Wanda Wiley, Charles King. Director: Jess Robbins. Story: T. Page Wright.

Wiley as twin sisters, one homeless and the other a stage star. The two are repeatedly confused by their pursuers, one a stage door Johnny, and the other a count. All is eventually set straight, and the twins plan for a double wedding.

Motor Trouble: Released 06/23/1926. © Universal Pictures Corp. 03/25/1926. Stern Bros Comedy. Cast: Charles King. Director: Scott Pembroke.

Newlywed and penniless King takes a job as a chauffeur even though he can't drive. His employer is his mother-in-law, whom he has never met. Their first drive is a disaster, and she chases him back to his house. He hides in a shower curtain, but his wife soon recognizes him.

There She Goes: Released 06/30/1926. © Universal Pictures Corp. 01/30/1926. Stern Bros Comedy. Cast: Wanda Wiley, Joe Bonner. Director: Jess Robbins. Story: T. Page Wright.

Dancer Wiley's photo is accidentally published as that of notorious gunman Chicago Sal. She applies for a job, the manager thinks her to be Sal, and alerts the cops. She's chased all over the city until she uncovers the real Sal, the wig-wearing leading lady of a show Wiley'd applied to.

Dare Devil Daisy: Released 07/07/1926. © Universal Pictures Corp. 01/22/1926. Century Comedy. Cast: Edna Marian, Matty Kemp. Director: Francis Corby. Story: Tad Ross.

Marian is to inherit her grandfather's fortune, but only if she marries the man of his choice. She balks at this and elopes with her lover, whose parents have chosen another for him to marry. All ends well when it is discovered that the groom is the same fellow that grandfather had chosen.

A Thrilling Romance: Released 07/14/1926. © Universal Pictures Corp. 01/30/1926. Century Comedy. Cast: Wanda Wiley, Earl McCarthy, Joe Bonner, Al Hallett. Director: Jess Robbins. Story: T. Page Wright.

Authoress Wiley is despondent over her faltering career, but pounds away at the typewriter nonetheless. Fade to all sorts of exciting and romantic adventures involving jewel thieves, taxi driver McCarty, and found money. Fade back to Wiley finishing the story we've just viewed.

Buster's Orphan Party: Released 07/21/1926. © Universal Pictures Corp. 04/10/1926. Stern Bros Comedy. Cast: Arthur Trimble, Doreen Turner, Pete the Dog. Director: Gus Meins. Based on Richard F. Outcault's comic strip "Buster Brown."

It's Orphans' Day, so Buster (Trimble) and Mary Jane (Turner) invite a bunch of poor orphans to a party. Things get out of hand and the place is a shambles, so Buster puts a plate in the seat of his pants anticipating his mother's return and a spanking.

His Girl Friend: Released 07/28/1926. © Universal Pictures Corp. 03/25/1926. Century/Stern Bros Comedy. Cast: Edna Marian, Earl McCarthy. Director, Story: Francis Corby. Story: Tad Ross.

Father has kicked all of Marian's suitors out of his house, so McCarthy returns dressed as a girl. Father starts to get romantic with him, but discovering the ruse chases him out of the house. The cops arrest father for assaulting a "girl," leaving Marian and McCarthy free to elope.

Mixed Brides: Released 08/04/1926. © Universal Pictures Corp. 03/25/1926. Century/Stern Bros Comedy. Cast: Wanda Wiley, Hal Ford. Director: Jess Robbins. Story: T. Page Wright.

Wiley heads to the city to marry her sweetheart. Another family has sent for the stout girl who is to marry their son, sight unseen. Wiley is mistaken for the stout girl, and the stout girl thinks Wiley's sweetheart is her intended. Confusion reigns until things are finally straightened out, and Wiley and her sweetheart are married in a motorcycle's sidecar by a minister.

Wait a Bit: Released 08/11/1926. © Universal Pictures Corp. 03/25/1926. Stern Bros Comedy. Cast: Edna Marian, Earl McCarthy. Director: Francis Corby. Story: Tad Ross.

Marian loves McCarty, but father wants her to marry a Duke. McCarthy dons whiskers and poses as father's brother, but things get dicey when the real brother arrives. The Duke finally gives up, and McCarty demonstrates that he is of sufficient financial means to comfortably support Marian.

Buster Helps Dad: Released 08/18/1926. © Universal Pictures Corp. 04/13/1926. Stern Bros Comedy. Cast: Arthur Trimble, Doreen Turner, Pete the Dog. Director: Gus Meins. Based on Richard F. Outcault's comic strip "Buster Brown."

To help out his financially strapped father, Buster (Trimble) takes Tige to a movie studio. There Tige outperforms the film's canine star, Ring Tin Can, and is hired as the dog's replacement. Later Tige condescendingly throws a bone to Ring Tin Can from his fancy car.

Her Ambition: Released 08/25/1926. © Universal Pictures Corp. 04/30/1926. Stern Bros Comedy. Cast: Bartine Burkett, Al Alt, Art Rowlands, Dorothy Vernon, Frank Earl, Silas Wilcox. Director, Story: Charles Lamont. Story: Roy Evans.

A theatrical manager takes country girl Burkett to the big city. Alt, her country lover, follows, fearing the worst. Alt repeatedly breaks into rehearsals to try to rescue her. Finally, covered with soot, the producer hires him to play Uncle Tom opposite Burkette's Eva.

Beginning of 1926-1927 Season: The Stern Brothers Comedies Replaces the Century Comedies

The Newlyweds' Neighbors: Released 09/01/1926. © Universal Pictures Corp. 06/18/1926. Stern Bros Comedy. Cast: Jed Dooley, Ethlyne Clair, Lawrence McKeen. Director: Gus Meins. Based on George McManus' comic strip "The Newlyweds and Their Baby."

Snookums (McKeen) tosses tin cans over the fence into the neighbor's yard. The neighbor thinks that father Dooley is the culprit and confronts him, and soon the whole neighborhood is up in arms. The patrol wagon arrives and arrests the two presumed perpetrators, but find Snookums asleep in the wagon. They sit on the curb and wait for him to finish his nap.

Buster's Girl Friend: Released 09/06/1926. © Universal Pictures Corp. 06/12/1926. Stern Bros Comedy; released as a Junior Jewel Comedy. Cast: Arthur Trimble, Doreen Turner, Pete the Dog. Director: Gus Meins. Based on Richard F. Outcault's comic strip "Buster Brown."

A fat boy ruins the show put on by Buster (Trimble), then takes Mary Jane (Turner) to a fun palace. Buster follows with Tige, the dog stealing the money to buy tickets. Riding on the chute-the-chutes, the attendant attempts to toss Tige out, but is foiled.

George the Winner: Released 09/08/1926. © Universal Pictures Corp. 05/29/1926. Stern Bros Comedy. Cast: Sid Saylor, Ouida Hill (Thelma Daniels), Art Rowlands. Director: Francis Corby. Based on George McManus' comic strip "Let George Do It."

George (Saylor) boasts to Daniels of being a race car driver. When the real driver quits and leaves Daniels' father driverless, George is pressed into service. After a wild ride, he wins.

Jane's Inheritance: Released 09/15/1926. © Universal Pictures Corp. 05/06/1926. Stern Bros Comedy. Cast: Wanda Wiley, Al Alt. Director: Francis Corby. Story: Roy Evans. "What Happened to Jane" series.

Wiley learns of an inheritance and the plan of the villain to marry her. Her sweetheart Alt masquerades as Wiley, and rescues her when the villain attempts to take her away in a taxi.

Snookums' Tooth: Released 09/22/1926. © Universal Pictures Corp. 05/15/1926. Stern Bros Comedy. Cast: Jed Dooley, Ethlyne Clair, Lawrence McKeen, Leon Holmes. Director: Gus Meins. Based on George McManus' comic strip "The Newlyweds and Their Baby" (working title **Snookums' First Tooth**)

To celebrate Snookums' (McKeen) new tooth, the Newlyweds (Dooley and Clair) throw a party. Finding Snookums missing, the party breaks up and sets out in search of the missing infant. His parents discover him asleep in the car in which they are searching for him.

Love's Hurdle: Released 09/29/1926. © Universal Pictures Corp. 04/26/1926. Stern Bros Comedy. Cast: Charles King, Adrienne Dore, Constance Darling. Director: Francis Corby. Story: William Anthony. Based on "The Excuse Maker" stories by William Anthony.

Aspiring social climber and shoe clerk King is visited by the daughter of an owner of thoroughbreds, so he pretends to be the store's owner. Invited to the track, her father, having been fooled into thinking King an excellent rider, presses him into service when a jockey backs out due to the horse's violent nature. The horse kicks King through the roof and all over the track, but he somehow manages to win the race. He marries the girl.

Buster, Watch Tige: Released 10/04/1926. © Universal Pictures Corp. 06/12/1926. Stern Bros Comedy; released as a Junior Jewel Comedy. Cast: Arthur Trimble, Doreen Turner, Pete the Dog. Director: Gus Meins. Based on Richard F. Outcault's comic strip "Buster Brown."

Buster (Trimble) and Mary Jane (Turner) try to plant seed, but Tige gets in their way. Tied to a chicken coop, Tige drags it into the house and the chickens escape. Tige makes a mess of the place trying to round up the chickens.

The Newlyweds Quarantined: Released 10/06/1926. © Universal Pictures Corp. 06/01/1926. Stern Bros Comedy. Cast: Jed Dooley, Ethlyne Clair, Lawrence McKeen. Director: Gus Meins. Based on George McManus' comic strip "The Newlyweds and Their Baby."

Mischievous Snookums (McKeen) wants to make his parents' (Dooley and Clair) guests comfortable by putting glue on their chairs and sawing off the legs and backs. He finds a "Quarantine" sign and places it on the door, forcing the guests to remain at the Newlyweds' home.

Which Is Which?: Released 10/13/1926. © Universal Pictures Corp. 04/26/1926. Stern Bros Comedy. Cast: Charles King. Director: Sam Newfield. Story: William Anthony. Based on "The Excuse Maker" stories by William Anthony.

After mistaking his girl's father for a wanted bank robber and turning him into the police, King gets in deeper when the real robber, a look-alike of the father, tries to rob the father's house. A mixup follows, and King tries to capture the robber but beats up the father instead. The crook is finally captured and King is forgiven.

Jane's Troubles: Released 10/20/1926. © Universal Pictures Corp. 06/22/1926. Stern Bros Comedy. Cast: Wanda Wiley. Director: Jess Robbins. Story: Roy Evans. "What Happened to Jane" series.

Father favors Percy for his daughter Jane (Wiley) while mother favors Algernon. Neither favor George, who is Jane's pick. She does everything to avoid the other two, but a fight follows to decide who will win Jane. George extricates himself and elopes with Jane, leaving the other two.

Why George!: Released 10/27/1926. © Universal Pictures Corp. 05/08/1926. Stern Bros Comedy. Cast: Sid Saylor, Bartine Burkett. Director: Charles Lamont. Based on George McManus' comic strip "Let George Do It."

Saylor plays timid professor George as well as his prize fighter twin brother (and also their father!) who are continuously confused for each other. George finds himself in the prize ring, so to protect himself he fills his shirt with sponges. They soak up water, and when he is hit they squirt water into the face of his opponent, allowing George to make a knockout punch.

Buster's Narrow Escape: Released 11/01/1926. © Universal Pictures Corp. 06/18/1926. Stern Bros Comedy; released as a Junior Jewel Comedy. Cast: Arthur Trimble, Doreen Turner, Pete the Dog. Director: Gus Meins. Based on Richard F. Outcault's comic strip "Buster Brown."

After wrecking a photo studio, Buster (Trimble), Mary Jane (Turner), and Tige find themselves on a farm due to a flat tire. Tige tries to milk a bull, gets drunk on hard cider, and shoots the farmer in the seat of the pants.

Snookums' Buggy Ride: Released 11/03/1926. © Universal Pictures Corp. 05/29/1926. Stern Bros Comedy. Cast: Jed Dooley, Ethlyne Clair, Lawrence McKeen. Director: Gus Meins. Based on George McManus' comic strip "The Newlyweds and Their Baby."

Snookums (McKeen) hides from his mother (Clair), and later creates havoc at his father's (Dooley) office, the two of them ejected by the irate boss. Later Snookums, in his perambulator, is lifted skyward by balloons, enjoying a nap atop a telegraph pole.

Please Excuse Me: Released 11/10/1926. © Universal Pictures Corp. 06/26/1926. Stern Bros Comedy. Cast: Charles King, Constance Darling, Bud Jamison. Director: Sam Newfield. Story: William Anthony. Based on "The Excuse Maker" stories by William Anthony.

Late to work at the collection agency, King spins a wild tale about rescuing the boss' daughter Darling from Indians as the cause of his delay. Proven a liar, he's assigned to collect payment on a diamond ring from strong man Jamison, and along with Darling the two use their wits to accomplish the task.

Jane's Engagement Party: Released 11/17/1926. © Universal Pictures Corp. 05/18/1926. Stern Bros Comedy. Cast: Wanda Wiley, Tony Hayes. Director: Sam Newfield. Story: Roy Evans. "What Happened to Jane" series.

Hayes rescues his love Jane (Wiley) from her engagement to a man who is actually a wanted bigamist. He pays a bunch of kids to show up and claim the fellow is their father, and dresses as a woman to claim to be one of the wives.

George's in Love: Released 11/24/1926. © Universal Pictures Corp. 07/06/1926. Stern Bros Comedy. Cast: Sid Saylor, Thelma Daniels. Director: Francis Corby. Based on George McManus' comic strip "Let George Do It."

Fireworks salesman George (Saylor) is followed by his dog with a time bomb in its mouth. When his girl's father is kidnapped, they set out in pursuit, the dog close behind. The kidnappers get stuck on the edge of a cliff, George drives below and catches the father when he's thrown from the car in a tussle. The dog gives George the bomb, he tosses it into the kidnappers' car, and they are blown sky high.

Snookums' Outing: Released 12/01/1926. © Universal Pictures Corp. 06/22/1926. Stern Bros Comedy. Cast: Jed Dooley, Ethlyne Clair, Lawrence McKeen. Director: Gus Meins. Based on George McManus' comic strip "The Newlyweds and Their Baby."

The Newlyweds go camping. Dooley tries to milk a bull and gets the worst of it. Snookums (McKeen) hooks Dooley's bathing suit, leaving him naked. Snookums steals some clothes from a line and gives them to Dooley, but the irate owner shows up, retrieves his clothes, and drives them away at gunpoint.

Buster's Prize Winner: Released 12/06/1926. © Universal Pictures Corp. 07/15/1926. Stern Bros Comedy; released as a Junior Jewel Comedy. Cast: Arthur Trimble, Doreen Turner, Pete the Dog. Director: Gus Meins. Based on Richard F. Outcault's comic strip "Buster Brown."

Tige enters a dog show and wins. A crook dognaps him, so Buster (Trimble) and Mary Jane (Turner) follow him on their scooters. Tige attacks his dognapper, and the fellow flees from his car. Tige is reunited with his pals.

A Second Hand Excuse: Released 12/08/1926. © Universal Pictures Corp. 05/08/1926. Stern Bros Comedy. Cast: Charles King, Edna Marian, Leon Holmes, Frank Earle. Director: Francis Corby. Story: William Anthony. Based on "The Excuse Maker" stories by William Anthony.

King's pants get splattered with mud on his drive to his girl's house, so he sends a kid into the cleaners with them. When a cop tells him to move his car, pantless King emerges to crank it to a start. King lures a pedestrian into his car and steals his pants, then it's off to his girl's he goes. Her family is there, and they force him to take them for a drive. Fat Effie wrecks the flivver with her weight.

Jane's Predicament: Released 12/15/1926. © Universal Pictures Corp. 06/22/1926. Stern Bros Comedy. Cast: Wanda Wiley, Earl McCarthy. Director: Sam Neufield. Story: Roy Evans. "What Happened to Jane" series.

Cosmetic demonstrator Jane (Wiley) is fired. Her boyfriend McCarthy's uncle is coming and thinks him to be married, so Jane marries him. McCarthy's furniture is in the process of being repossed. Uncle plans to disinherit him until he meets, and is taken with, Jane.

Snookums' Merry Christmas: Released 12/22/1926. © Universal Pictures Corp. 11/08/1926. Stern Bros Comedy. Cast: Sid Saylor, Ethlyne Clair, Lawrence McKeen, Charles King. Director: Gus Meins. Based on George McManus' comic strip "The Newlyweds and Their Baby."

After some Christmas shopping, the Newlyweds struggle to get a tree home on the bus. A burglar breaks into the house and is discovered, so he flees dressed as Santa. Saylor dresses as Santa for Snookums, but a cop spots him, thinks he's the burglar, and beats him up.

And George Did!: Released 12/29/1926. © Universal Pictures Corp. 05/12/1926. Stern Bros Comedy. Cast: Sid Saylor, Dorothy Gulliver, Colin Chase, Madalynne Field. Director: Scott Pembroke. Based on George McManus' comic strip "Let George Do It."

Fleeing the room of a married woman, George (Saylor) takes a job on a building being constructed. An accident propels him back into the room of the woman, so her irate husband chases George high up onto the building's girders. George pushes the husband off, then accidentally falls as well.

Buster's Picnic: Released 01/03/1927. © Universal Pictures Corp. 07/22/1926. Stern

Bros Comedy; released as a Junior Jewel Comedy. Cast: Arthur Trimble, Doreen Turner, Pete the Dog. Director: Gus Meins. Based on Richard F. Outcault's comic strip "Buster Brown."

Heading to a picnic, Buster's (Trimble) little brother feeds the contents of the basket to Tige, leaving nothing to eat. Tige makes amends by stealing another family's lunch, but the cream cake's frosting on Tige's mouth leads picnickers to believe him to be rabid. A dislodged hornets' nest ends the day.

Snookums' Playmates: Released 01/05/1927. © Universal Pictures Corp. 08/25/1926. Stern Bros Comedy. Cast: Lawrence McKeen, Jed Dooley, Ethlyne Clair, Earl McCarthy, Constance Darling. Director: Gus Meins. Based on George McManus' comic strip "The Newlyweds and Their Baby."

Snookums' (McKeen) parents (Dooley and Clair) get into a debate with the parents of a neighboring girl over whose child is superior. Their discussion is cut short when they are confronted with the destruction created by Snookums and the girl in an adjacent room.

What'll You Have?: Released 01/12/1927. © Universal Pictures Corp. 04/30/1926. Stern Bros Comedy. Cast: Charles King, Constance Darling. Director: Francis Corby. Story: William Anthony. Based on "The Excuse Maker" stories by William Anthony.

Soda fountain clerk King falls for an heiress, but scrambles to avoid discovery when she enters the store. He later beats up a couple of burglars at her house, receiving a check from her father for his heroism, and the girl's hand as well.

Jane's Flirtation: Released 01/19/1927. © Universal Pictures Corp. 07/06/1926. Stern Bros Comedy. Cast: Wanda Wiley, Earl McCarthy, Eddie Baker, Madalynne Field. Director: Francis Corby. Story: Roy Evans. "What Happened to Jane" series.

A hefty, muscle bound chap takes Jane (Wiley) for a drive, picking up one end of the auto to see what is troubling the motor. As the film progresses they encounter numerous issues with the vehicle.

By George: Released 01/26/1927. © Universal Pictures Corp. 07/15/1926. Stern Bros Comedy. Cast: Sid Saylor, Art Rowlands. Director: Francis Corby. Based on George McManus' comic strip "Let George Do It."

To be near his girl and frustrate her crafty pursuer, George (Saylor) goes to work in her household as butler, chauffeur, maid, and cook.

The Newlyweds Build: Released 02/02/1927. © Universal Pictures Corp. 08/12/1926. Stern Bros Comedy. Cast: Lawrence McKeen, Jed Dooley, Ethlyne Clair, Sid Saylor. Director: Gus Meins. Based on George McManus' comic strip "The Newlyweds and Their Baby."

Evicted from their home, the Newlyweds (Dooley and Clair) attempt to erect a build-it-yourself house. Snookums (McKeen) disassembles almost as fast as they assemble the place. The result is less than perfect, and that night's rain causes the place to shrink.

Buster's Sleigh Ride: Released 02/07/1927. © Universal Pictures Corp. 07/24/1926. Stern Bros Comedy; released as a Junior Jewel Comedy. Cast: Arthur Trimble, Doreen Turner, Pete the Dog. Director: Gus Meins. Based on Richard F. Outcault's comic strip "Buster Brown."

Buster (Trimble), Mary Jane (Turner), and Tige go on a sleigh ride and find themselves under the snow almost as much as on top, and dodge huge snowballs that seem unusually attracted to them.

What's Your Hurry?: Released 02/09/1927. © Universal Pictures Corp. 04/30/1926. Stern Bros Comedy. Cast: Charles King, Constance Darling. Director: Sam Newfield. Story: William Anthony. Based on "The Excuse Maker" stories by William Anthony.

King goes into the gasoline business to impress his girl Darling's father, but the place explodes before it even opens. Later her father is kidnapped, so the couple gives pursuit, and after losing the kidnappers in a sea of Fords, finally rescue father through a series of implausible coincidences.

Thanks for the Boat Ride: Released 02/16/1927. © Universal Pictures Corp. 07/08/1926. Stern Bros Comedy. Cast: Wanda Wiley, Al Alt, Art Rowlands, Betty Baker. Director: Charles Lamont. Story: Roy Evans. "What Happened to Jane" series.

Having eloped on a boat, Alt loses his ticket and has to evade the captain. Alt poses as a girl, vamps the captain, gets a compromising photo, and "persuades" the captain to officiate his marriage to Jane (Wiley), promising to keep mum.

George Runs Wild: Released 02/23/1927. © Universal Pictures Corp. 07/08/1926. Stern Bros Comedy. Cast: Sid Saylor, Ethlyne Clair. Director: Scott Pembroke. Based on George McManus' comic strip "Let George Do It."

Flirtatious husband George (Saylor) falls for another woman, not realizing it is his wife Clair in disguise. She follows him home where she alternately poses as both wife and the other woman, with his wife "shooting" the other woman. His flirting habit is broken when a cop arrives and Clair explains all.

Snookums Disappears: Released 03/02/1927. © Universal Pictures Corp. 11/01/1926. Stern Bros Comedy. Cast: Lawrence McKeen, Sid Saylor, Ethlyne Clair. Director: Gus Meins. Based on George McManus' comic strip "The Newlyweds and Their Baby."

After creating havoc in a painter's studio, Snookums (McKeen) escapes to a nearby apartment. Father Saylor follows and encounters a blonde, and is "discovered" by her jealous husband. Saylor encounters the husband on numerous occasions, while Snookums runs wild in an elevator.

Buster's Dark Mystery (aka **Buster's Dark Secret**): Released 03/07/1927. © Universal Pictures Corp. 08/17/1926. Stern Bros Comedy; released as a Junior Jewel Comedy. Cast: Arthur Trimble, Doreen Turner, Pete the Dog. Director: Gus Meins. Based on Richard F. Outcault's comic strip "Buster Brown."

Buster (Trimble), Mary Jane (Turner), and Tige set out to recover a stolen painting of Tige. They track down the thieves' hiding place and after a number of harrowing experiences manage to recover the painting and trap the thieves.

Some More Excuses: Released 03/09/1927. © Universal Pictures Corp. 07/15/1926. Stern Bros Comedy. Cast: Charles King, Ethlyne Clair, Bud Fine. Director: Scott Pembroke. Story: William Anthony. Based on "The Excuse Maker" stories by William Anthony.

Lawyer King and wife Clair are summoned by a mysterious fellow to his house to draw up a will. Once there they realize that they are in danger, confronted with exploding drinks, a wild ape, a mummy, and the fellow himself ready to operate on King. It turns out the fellow is a lunatic earlier sent to an asylum by King. His keepers arrive in the nick of time, rescue King, and haul the lunatic away.

Jane's Honeymoon: Released 03/16/1927. © Universal Pictures Corp. 06/24/1926. Stern Bros Comedy. Cast: Thelma Daniels, Earl McCarthy, Lillian Worth. Director: Charles Lamont. Story: Roy Evans. "What Happened to Jane" series.

Newlywed McCarthy is inundated at work by calls from his wife Daniels, annoying his boss. McCarthy claims the calls were to invite his boss and wife to dinner, something Daniels has never prepared before. Dinner is so bad that the boss accuses the couple of trying to poison him, and stomps out of the house. Hot words follow between the couple, leading to a divorce, but sentimentality results in a rush to the church to remarry.

Be My Wife: Released 03/23/1927. © Universal Pictures Corp. 08/23/1926. Stern Bros Comedy. Cast: Charles King, Ethlyne Clair, Ena Gregory, Fred Spencer. Director: Francis Corby. Story: William Anthony. Based on "The Excuse Maker" stories by William Anthony.

King's boss is resistant to giving him a raise, but he softens when King's maid appears at his office and is thought to be his wife. Raise granted, King can't say no when the boss invites himself to dinner. He convinces the maid to pose as his wife, incurring the wrath of both his actual wife and the maid's big sweetheart Spencer. All ends in a hail of crockery.

Backward George: Released 03/30/1927. © Universal Pictures Corp. 12/23/1926. Stern Bros Comedy. Cast: Sid Saylor, Viola Bird, Harry Martin, George Merrill, Helen Lynch. Director: Gus Meins. Based on George McManus' comic strip "Let George Do It."

Farm hand George's (Saylor) love of the farmer's daughter is threatened by a city slicker out to gain possession of the farm by wooing her. The slicker hires a vamp to sidetrack George, but she falls for the farmer, reveals the slicker's plot to George, and the slicker is exposed.

Look Out—Buster!: Released 04/04/1927. © Universal Pictures Corp. 08/25/1926. Stern Bros Comedy; released as a Junior Jewel Comedy. Cast: Arthur Trimble, Doreen Turner, Pete the Dog. Director: Gus Meins. Based on Richard F. Outcault's comic strip "Buster Brown."

Running away from home, Buster (Trimble) and Mary Jane (Turner) hide Tige in a box that ends up in a robbers' cave. The robbers attempt to kill him but Tige dispatches them by rolling boulders down on them. Detectives pick up the trail, arrest the robbers, and reward Tige.

Fishing Snookums: Released 04/06/1927. © Universal Pictures Corp. 12/11/1926. Stern Bros Comedy. Cast: Lawrence McKeen, Sid Saylor, Ethlyne Clair. Director: Gus Meins. Based on George McManus' comic strip "The Newlyweds and Their Baby."

Left with the maid when his parents (Saylor and Clair) go fishing, Snookums (McKeen) hides in their car. When they hear of a child falling from a window, they rush back home only to find him safe and sound. Snookums later commandeers a motor boat with his parents aboard.

She's My Cousin: Released 04/13/1927. © Universal Pictures Corp. 04/30/1926. Stern Bros Comedy. Cast: Charles King, Constance Darling, Hal Ford, Roli Roxi. Director: Francis Corby. Story: William Anthony. Based on "The Excuse Maker" stories by William Anthony.

Newlywed King takes bride Darling back to his bachelor pad and finds himself making excuses for the old flames that show up and the letters he has received from them. One persistent former admirer causes Darling to dress as her husband and confront the woman.

Jane's Hubby: Released 04/20/1927. © Universal Pictures Corp. 03/21/1927. Stern Bros Comedy. Cast: Thelma Daniels, Charles King, Max Asher. Director: Scott Pembroke. Story: Roy Evans. "What Happened to Jane" series.

Having eloped, King is thrown out of the house by Jane's (Daniels) father. He disguises himself as a black maid to get back into the house, but after numerous incidents the couple gets arrested for speeding and finds peace in jail. That is, until her parents end up in the adjacent cell.

George Leaves Home: Released 04/27/1927. © Universal Pictures Corp. 03/01/1927. Stern Bros Comedy. Cast: Sid Saylor. Director: Francis Corby. Based on George McManus' comic strip "Let George Do It."

Country rube George (Saylor) heads to the city looking for his girl Nell, and runs into vamps, crooks, and others before meeting with success.

Buster Don't Forget: Released 05/02/1927. © Universal Pictures Corp. 08/25/1926. Stern Bros Comedy; released as a Junior Jewel Comedy. Cast: Arthur Trimble, Doreen Turner, Pete the Dog. Director: Gus Meins. Based on Richard F. Outcault's comic strip "Buster Brown."

Buster (Trimble) and Mary Jane's romance is threatened by an attractive little blonde vamp, but Tige foils her plans after evading a dog catcher.

The Newlyweds' Shopping Tour: Released 05/04/1927. © Universal Pictures Corp. 02/28/1927. Stern Bros Comedy. Cast: Lawrence McKeen, Sid Saylor, Ethlyne Clair. Director: Gus Meins. Based on George McManus' comic strip "The Newlyweds and Their Baby."

Leaving Snookums (McKeen) with father Saylor at his office while his mother (Clair) goes shopping, the child makes a wreck of the place. Father takes the kid to find his mother at the store, and the child once again puts the place out of commission.

Keeping His Word: Released 05/11/1927. © Universal Pictures Corp. 04/30/1926. Stern Bros Comedy. Cast: Charles King, Constance Darling. Director: Scott Pembroke. Story: William Anthony. Based on "The Excuse Maker" stories by William Anthony.

King and his sweetheart ignore her mother's dislike for him and elope. His mother-in-law now separates them, but King manages to win her over by orchestrating a fake burglary and emerging as a "hero."

Jane Missed Out: Released 05/18/1927. © Universal Pictures Corp. 03/24/1927. Stern Bros Comedy. Cast: Violet Bird, Thelma Daniels, Earl McCarthy. Director: Jess Robbins. Story: Roy Evans. "What Happened to Jane" series.

Jane (Bird) sets her sights on bashful McCarthy, and eventually wins him over.

Kid George: Released 05/25/1927. © Universal Pictures Corp. 03/08/1927. Stern Bros Comedy. Cast: Sid Saylor, Ethlyne Clair. Director: Francis Corby. Based on George McManus' comic strip "Let George Do It."

Dressed as a kid for a masquerade party, George (Saylor) has a lot of town to cross to get there, encountering mishaps with a horse, a rival suitor, and a cop.

Stop Snookums: Released 06/01/1927. © Universal Pictures Corp. 03/28/1927. Stern Bros Comedy. Cast: Lawrence McKeen, Sid Saylor, Ethlyne Clair. Director: Gus Meins. Based on George McManus' comic strip "The Newlyweds and Their Baby."

With wife Clair away, hubby Saylor attempts to have a poker game. It's a disaster, of course, due to the presence of mischievous Snookums (McKeen). Clair returns prematurely, so the other poker players hide in a closet, stuck there for hours when Snookums falls asleep outside the door.

Buster's Frame Up: Released 06/06/1927. © Universal Pictures Corp. 03/08/1927. Stern Bros Comedy; released as a Junior Jewel Comedy. Cast: Arthur Trimble, Doreen Turner, Pete the Dog. Director: Gus Meins. Based on Richard F. Outcault's comic strip "Buster Brown."

Buster (Trimble) and Mary Jane (Turner) smuggle Tige into a movie theater dressed as a baby. When they are thrown out, they stumble across a film shoot full of "Indians," and when they are at the point of being scalped, awake to find it was all a dream.

That's No Excuse: Released 06/08/1927. © Universal Pictures Corp. 03/21/1927. Stern Bros Comedy. Cast: Charles King, Thelma Daniels, Harry Martel. Director: Scott Pembroke. Story: William Anthony. Based on "The Excuse Maker" stories by William Anthony.

Newlyweds King and Daniels can't escape the number thirteen, honeymooning in a house that appears to be haunted. In addition to their superstitions, there's a crazed caretaker in charge, black cats, and all sorts of things to upset them. The police are called to solve the situation.

George's Many Loves: Released 06/15/1927. © Universal Pictures Corp. 03/29/1927. Stern Bros Comedy. Cast: Sid Saylor, Thelma Daniels, Harry Martin, Madalynne Fields, Eleanor Fredericks, Ena Gregory, Stern Brothers Beauties. Director: Scott Pembroke. Based on George McManus' comic strip "Let George Do It."

Thrown from his house for spoiling his father's game of checkers, George (Saylor) arrives at a summer hotel and is mistaken for a champion prizefighter due to arrive. The champ arrives and George leaves, and walking home falls for a girl who turns out to be his father's choice of a mate.

Jane's Sleuth: Released 06/22/1927. © Universal Pictures Corp. 03/31/1927. Stern Bros Comedy. Cast: Ethlyne Clair, Charles Dorety, Dorothy Wolbert. Director: Sam Newfield. Story: Roy Evans. "What Happened to Jane" series.

Aspiring detective Oscar (Dorety) has run-ins with a real detective shadowing two crooks intent on stealing a diamond necklace. Dorety emerges victorious in capturing the crooks. Jane is portrayed by Clair.

My Mistake: Released 06/29/1927. © Universal Pictures Corp. 05/05/1927. Stern Bros Comedy. Cast: Charles King, Florence Allen, Lillian Worth, Baby Wally. Director: Sam Newfield. Story: William Anthony. Based on "The Excuse Maker" stories by William Anthony.

His wife away, King scrambles after a drunken party at his house when he hears that she's returning. Rushing to the station, he's handed a baby to hold by a kidnapper who takes off. His wife arrives, sees the bay, and accuses him of leading a double life. The baby's mother arrives and sets things straight.

Buster's Initiation: Released 07/04/1927. © Universal Pictures Corp. 04/04/1927. Stern Bros Comedy; released as a Junior Jewel Comedy. Cast: Arthur Trimble, Doreen Turner, Pete the Dog. Director: Gus Meins. Based on Richard F. Outcault's comic strip "Buster Brown."

Buster (Trimble) and Mary Jane (Turner) head to school in the little Tige-powered auto. Tige causes trouble at school, and angry at Buster for incurring the teacher's wrath, the rest of the boys decide to get him. The trio manages to escape, but just barely.

Snookums Asleep: Released 07/06/1927. © Universal Pictures Corp. 03/28/1927. Stern Bros Comedy. Cast: Lawrence McKeen, Sid Saylor, Ethlyne Clair. Director: Gus Meins. Based on George McManus' comic strip "The Newlyweds and Their Baby."

Dad Saylor struggles mightily to put Snookums (McKeen) to sleep, and keep him there. First a loud horn is demanded by the child, annoying the neighbors. Next a lengthy quest for two cats. Finally succeeding and heading off to bed himself, Saylor is reawakened by the singing of wife Clair's glee club.

What an Excuse: Released 07/13/1927. © Universal Pictures Corp. 03/29/1927. Stern Bros Comedy. Cast: Charles King, Thelma Daniels, Max Asher, Bud Fine. Director: Sam Newfield. Story: William Anthony. Based on "The Excuse Maker" stories by William Anthony.

Daniels' father hires a detective to keep sweetheart King away, the latter trying all sorts of ploys to outwit the sleuth. The couple finally tricks both dad and the detective, by ditching one and sending the other on a wild goose chase after another couple.

Jane's Relations: Released 07/20/1927. © Universal Pictures Corp. 05/21/1927. Stern Bros Comedy. Cast: Marjorie Marcel, Earl McCarthy, Joe Bonner. Director: Scott Pembroke. Story: Roy Evans. "What Happened to Jane" series.

McCarthy and Marcel's two sets of in-laws arrive for a stay at the same time, leaving the couple no place to sleep. Both clans make plans to outstay the other.

On Furlough: Released 07/27/1927. © Universal Pictures Corp. 06/09/1927. Stern

Bros Comedy. Cast: Sid Saylor, Jean Doree, Ethan Laidlaw. Director: Sam Newfield. Based on George McManus' comic strip "Let George Do It."

Out on furlough, buck private George (Saylor) and his girl Doree are pursued by his future father-in-law, angered over having been bumped into the mud, and the hard boiled sergeant who also desires Doree. They finally outwit their pursuers.

Buster's Handicap: Released 08/01/1927. © Universal Pictures Corp. 03/28/1927. Stern Bros Comedy; released as a Junior Jewel Comedy. Cast: Arthur Trimble, Doreen Turner, Pete the Dog. Director: Gus Meins. Based on Richard F. Outcault's comic strip "Buster Brown."

After Buster (Trimble) and Mary Jane (Turner) avoid the amorous advances of others, Buster enters an auto race. All sorts of vehicles are put into the race, but Buster manages to win.

Snookums Cleans Up: Released 08/03/1927. © Universal Pictures Corp. 12/23/1926. Stern Bros Comedy. Cast: Lawrence McKeen, Sid Saylor, Ethlyne Clair. Director: Gus Meins. Based on George McManus' comic strip "The Newlyweds and Their Baby."

Finally earning a day off for working so hard, Saylor soon finds that his day of supposed relaxation includes a lot of "home work" assigned by spouse Clair, along with providing amusement for Snookums (McKeen). As usual, Snookums gets into all sorts of mischief.

Oh, Taxi!: Released 08/10/1927. © Universal Pictures Corp. 05/27/1927. Stern Bros Comedy. Cast: Sid Saylor, Dolores May, Harry Martel. Director: Francis Corby. Based on George McManus' comic strip "Let George Do It."

George (Saylor) inherits an ancient taxi from his uncle, with hopes of making good for his sweetheart. It ends with a wild ride for all concerned, his girl's father bearing the brunt of the mishaps. Regardless, George wins the girl.

Plain Jane: Released 08/17/1927. © Universal Pictures Corp. 05/21/1927. Stern Bros Comedy. Cast: Marjorie Marcel, Earl McCarthy, Helen Gilmore. Director: Scott Pembroke. Story: Roy Evans. "What Happened to Jane" series.

A variation of the old story of the "ugly duckling" turning into a "beautiful swan." One would assume that it was Marcel portraying the girl in question.

Please Don't: Released 08/24/1927. © Universal Pictures Corp. 05/21/1927. Stern Bros Comedy. Cast: Charles King, Marjorie Marcel, Helen Gilmore. Director: Scott Pembroke. Story: William Anthony. Based on "The Excuse Maker" stories by William Anthony.

When King overhears his wife (Marcel) and mother-in-law talking about life insurance, he gets the idea they are planning to do away with him. Several accidents help to confirm his suspicions, so he decides to accommodate them and hire a professional assassin to do the job.

Rushing Business: Released 08/31/1927. © Universal Pictures Corp. 06/09/1927. Stern Bros Comedy. Cast: Sid Saylor, Joe Bonner. Director: Sam Newfield. Based on George McManus' comic strip "Let George Do It."

Dressed as a cop for a masquerade party, George (Saylor) is pressed into service by real cops after a crook. George poses along with some police dummies outside a clothing store, but the crook carts him away, planning to use his outfit as a disguise. George captures the crook and wins the girl.

Beginning of 1927-1928 Season

The Newlyweds' Troubles: Released 09/05/1927. © Universal Pictures Corp. 06/04/1927. Stern Bros Comedy; released as a Junior Jewel Comedy. Cast: Lawrence McKeen, Sid Saylor, Ethlyne Clair, Harry Martell. Director: Gus Meins. Story: George McManus. Based on George McManus' comic strip "The Newlyweds and Their Baby."

Parents Saylor and Clair are required to buy a sleeper ticket when they pursue Snookums (McKeen) onto a train. Snookums plays with a shotgun, Saylor is almost arrested when he takes the gun from his child and is mistaken for a bandit. No one sleeps when Snookums marches the aisle beating on his drum, and commotion reigns until the train finally makes its stop.

Keeping in Trim: Released 09/07/1927. © Universal Pictures Corp. 05/02/1927. Stern Bros Comedy. Cast: Harry Long, Stella Adams, Addie McPhail, Gene Layman. Director: Gus Meins. Based on Arthur "Pop" Momand's comic strip "Keeping Up with the Joneses."

The McGinis family (Long and Adams) is dedicated to physical fitness, following the radio routines each morning. They enroll in a swank athletic club to keep up with the Joneses.

Buster, Come On!: Released 09/14/1927. © Universal Pictures Corp. 05/17/1927. Stern Bros Comedy. Cast: Arthur Trimble, Doreen Turner, Pete the Dog. Director: Francis Corby. Based on Richard F. Outcault's comic strip "Buster Brown."

The Brown family goes on summer vacation, leaving Tige behind. Tige follows and outwits them, arriving at the camp along with the rest. Adventures with bulls, bees, wild pussy cats, and other nice pets befall Buster (Trimble), Mary Jane (Turner), and Tige during their stay.

The Dancing Fools: Released 09/21/1927. © Universal Pictures Corp. 05/02/1927. Stern Bros Comedy. Cast: Charles King, Charles Dorety, Ethlyne Clair, Madalynne Field.

Director: Francis Corby. Story: Roland Asher. Based on Rube Goldberg's comic strip "Mike and Ike."

Evading their landlady, twins Mike and Ike (King and Dorety) take their girls, one fat and one lean, to a rough dance hall. A prize is offered for the roughest dance, and Mike and his fat flapper are the winners.

George Steps Out: Released 09/28/1927. © Universal Pictures Corp. 05/21/1927. Stern Bros Comedy. Cast: Sid Saylor. Director: Gus Meins. Based on George McManus' comic strip "Let George Do It."

George (Saylor) woos the girl, bumps into numerous setbacks, and is chased by a cop before he wins her.

The Newlyweds' Surprise: Released 10/03/1927. © Universal Pictures Corp. 06/04/1927. Stern Bros Comedy; released as a Junior Jewel Comedy. Cast: Sid Saylor, Ethlyne Clair, Lawrence McKeen. Director: Gus Meins. Based on George McManus' comic strip "The Newlyweds and Their Baby."

Applying at an apartment that discourages young children, Saylor and Clair hide Snookums (McKeen) in a parrot cage. This cage gets confused with an old maid's real parrot cage, and the mistakes are discovered. A free-for-all breaks out in the apartment's hallway among its residents.

Society Breaks: Released 10/05/1927. © Universal Pictures Corp. 05/17/1927. Stern Bros Comedy. Cast: Harry Long, Stella Adams, Addie McPhail, Gene Layman. Director: Gus Meins. Based on Arthur "Pop" Momand's comic strip "Keeping Up with the Joneses."

Aloysius McGinis (Long) is forced to go to a dance with his socially ambitious wife Adams. His feet hurt so he takes off his tight shoes, sneaks into the kitchen to dance with a good looking serving maid, then feigns illness when his wife catches him at it. Not falling for it, his wife subjects him to the usual beating.

Buster's Home Life: Released 10/12/1927. © Universal Pictures Corp. 05/11/1927. Stern Bros Comedy. Cast: Arthur Trimble, Doreen Turner, Pete the Dog. Director: Francis Corby. Based on Richard F. Outcault's comic strip "Buster Brown."

Buster (Trimble), Mary Jane (Turner), Tige, and a pet monkey make life miserable for Hannah the maid when she refuses to let the dog in the house. A block and tackle is employed to gain entrance, after which they mess up the place. Buster's mom returns and blames Hannah for the mess.

All for Uncle: Released 10/19/1927. © Universal Pictures Corp. 05/03/1927. Stern Bros Comedy. Cast: Charles King, Charles Dorety, Thelma Daniels, Dorothea Wolbert,

Harry Martel, Lorraine Rivero, Joe Bonner. Director: Francis Corby. Based on Rube Goldberg's comic strip "Mike and Ike."

Twins King and Dorety face a potential wedding gift of $10,000 from Uncle Dudley if he approves of Dorety's intended. She has married another, however, thinking him a bigamist. With no bride in sight, King masquerades as Dorety's wifein an attempt to fool uncle. Their plan misfires when uncle takes a shine to the new "bride.".

Picking on George: Released 10/26/1927. © Universal Pictures Corp. 05/17/1927. Stern Bros Comedy. Cast: Sid Saylor. Director: Gus Meins. Based on George McManus' comic strip "Let George Do It."

George (Saylor) is pursued by a jealous husband after his actress wife has made love to him. The chase leads to a beach and numerous complications, George needing to disguise himself to escape.

Passing the Joneses: Released 11/02/1927. © Universal Pictures Corp. 06/09/1927. Stern Bros Comedy. Cast: Harry Long, Stella Adams, Addie McPhail, Gene Layman. Director: Gus Meins. Based on Arthur "Pop" Momand's comic strip "Keeping Up with the Joneses."

The McGinises (Long and Adams) attempt to outdo the Joneses in a mountain climbing contest. In spite of a series of mishaps they manage by sheer blundering to win the prize.

The Newlyweds' Mistake: Released 11/07/1927. © Universal Pictures Corp. 06/09/1927. Stern Bros Comedy; released as a Junior Jewel Comedy. Cast: Addie McPhail, Joe Young, Lawrence McKeen. Director: Gus Meins. Based on George McManus' comic strip "The Newlyweds and Their Baby."

Mr. Newlywed (Young) is arrested for failing to make payments on his piano. Snookums goes to the jail with him, and after charming the chief and the other cops, manages to lock them all in jail and release his father.

The Disordered Orderly: Released 11/09/1927. © Universal Pictures Corp. 06/09/1927. Stern Bros Comedy. Cast: Sid Saylor, Jean Doree. Director: Sam Newfield. Based on George McManus' comic strip "Let George Do It." (copyrighted as **A Disordered Orderly**)

Buster, What's Next?: Released 11/16/1927. © Universal Pictures Corp. 07/27/1927. Stern Bros Comedy. Cast: Arthur Trimble, Doreen Turner, Pete the Dog. Director: Gus Meins. Based on Richard F. Outcault's comic strip "Buster Brown."

Buster (Trimble), Mary Jane (Turner), and Tige (Pete) attempt to get rid of an obnoxious girl by various means, including locking her in a closet and shoving her down a coal shute. She always returns. Buster proposes a boxing match, but a stiff left punch leaves him reeling. He's thankful when her relatives arrive and take her away.

Oh! Mabel!: Released 11/23/1927. © Universal Pictures Corp. 08/03/1927. Stern Bros Comedy. Cast: Charles King, Charles Dorety, Thelma Daniels. Director: Francis Corby. Based on Rube Goldberg's comic strip "Mike and Ike."

Mike's wife is jealous when he receives a call from Mabel, actually intended for Ike. Mabel tries to blackmail Ike with a breach of promise threat. Mike agrees to help, but his car crashes into Mabel's on the way and he takes her to his office. His wife arrives, so he hastily settles with Mabel to avoid further confrontation. He later poses as Ike and heads to Mabel's where he makes love to her, but his wife arrives and he has difficulty explaining that his actions were on behalf of Ike.

On Deck: Released 11/30/1927. © Universal Pictures Corp. 06/09/1927. Stern Bros Comedy. Cast: Sid Saylor, Jean Doree. Director: Sam Newfield. Based on George McManus' comic strip "Let George Do It."

George (Saylor) masquerades as a sailor to impress his girl. Encountering a marching squad of sailors, George is compelled to join. He's confronted by Ensign Harry, his rival for the girl, so Harry proceeds to make George's life on board miserable. After many unfortunate experiences, George's luck changes and he wins the heart of his girl.

The Newlyweds' Christmas Party: Released 12/05/1927. © Universal Pictures Corp. 10/17/1927. Stern Bros Comedy; released as a Junior Jewel Comedy. Cast: Jack Bartlett, Addie McPhail, Lawrence McKeen. Director: Gus Meins. Based on George McManus' comic strip "The Newlyweds and Their Baby."

After a day of Christmas shopping, there is a wild ride home on a runaway trolley. While the tree is trimmed, Snookums (McKeen) sneaks out and brings back a bunch of ragged urchins to share the presents.

Showing Off: Released 12/07/1927. © Universal Pictures Corp. 07/07/1927. Stern Bros Comedy. Cast: Harry Long, Stella Adams, Addie McPhail, Gene Layman. Director: Gus Meins. Based on Arthur "Pop" Momand's comic strip "Keeping Up with the Joneses."

The McGinises (Long and Adams) prepare for a society theatrical presentation, taking the leads. Adams' role of a beauty is a washout, but she blames Long for the first act's failure. Long messes up as John the Baptist, Adams comes on as a dancing flapper, and Long makes another mistake when they chop off his head. The show comes to a halt when the McGinises break into a fight.

Run Buster!: Released 12/14/1927. © Universal Pictures Corp. 08/05/1927. Stern Bros Comedy. Cast: Arthur Trimble, Doreen Turner, Pete the Dog. Director: Francis Corby. Based on Richard F. Outcault's comic strip "Buster Brown."

Buster (Trimble) masquerades as an adult admirer and manages to get a pie from Bertha, the cook. Mary Jane (Turner) flirts with a lot of boys to make Buster jealous, one of whom is Gus. Buster comes to her house, gets rid of his rivals, and makes up to Mary Jane.

There's a Will: Released 12/21/1927. © Universal Pictures Corp. 06/09/1927. Stern Bros Comedy. Cast: Charles King, Charles Dorety, Thelma Daniels. Director: Francis Corby. Based on Rube Goldberg's comic strip "Mike and Ike."

Twins Mike and Ike (King and Dorety) are involved in a case of mistaken identity.

Model George: Released 12/28/1927. © Universal Pictures Corp. 07/29/1927. Stern Bros Comedy. Cast: Sid Saylor. Director: Gus Meins. Based on George McManus' comic strip "Let George Do It."

The Newlyweds' Advice: Released 01/02/1928. © Universal Pictures Corp. 12/06/1927. Stern Bros Comedy; released as a Junior Jewel Comedy. Cast: Lawrence McKeen, Derelys Perdue, Jack Egan. Director: Francis Corby. Based on George McManus' comic strip "The Newlyweds and Their Baby."

Horse Play: Released 01/04/1928. © Universal Pictures Corp. 11/23/1927. Stern Bros Comedy. Cast: Harry Long, Stella Adams, Addie McPhail, Gene Lyman. Director: Gus Meins. Based on Arthur "Pop" Momand's comic strip "Keeping Up with the Joneses"

Finding horseback riding to be fashionable, Ma McGinnis (Adams) forces the family to take it up. Pa (Long), on board an old fire department horse, gets the ride of his life when the horse responds to an alarm.

Buster's Big Chance: Released 01/11/1928. © Universal Pictures Corp. 07/27/1927. Stern Bros Comedy. Cast: Arthur Trimble, Doreen Turner, Pete the Dog. Director: Francis Corby. Based on Richard F. Outcault's comic strip "Buster Brown."

Dates for Two: Released 01/18/1928. © Universal Pictures Corp. 06/09/1927. Stern Bros Comedy. Cast: Charles King, Charles Dorety. Director: Francis Corby. Based on Rube Goldberg's comic strip "Mike and Ike."

Twins Mike and Ike (King and Dorety) make dates but get into all sorts of trouble as each tries to keep his appointment with the wrong girl. It ends in a double marriage.

High Flyin' George: Released 01/25/1928. © Universal Pictures Corp. 09/10/1927. Stern Bros Comedy. Cast: Sid Saylor, Jane Manners. Director: Sam Newfield. Assistant Director: Robert Laszlo. Based on George McManus' comic strip "Let George Do It." (working title **Up in the Air**)

"Sam Newfield directed the George Comedy, which is an aeroplane picture filled with stunts and comedy flying. It has as many thrills as the bigger aeroplane features and is a decided innovation in two-reel entertainment." (*Universal Weekly*, September 10, 1927)

Start Something: Released 02/01/1928. © Universal Pictures Corp. 12/03/1927. Stern Bros Comedy. Cast: Harry Long, Stella Adams, Addie McPhail, Gene Layman. Director: Gus Meins. Story: William Weber, T. Page Wright. Based on Arthur "Pop" Momand's comic strip "Keeping Up with the Joneses."

The McGinises (Long and Adams) visit a fortune teller and are told that they will have a mysterious visitor in their home that night. This leads to a nerve-wracking night full of weird noises and strange sights. An agent arrives to have some papers signed, becomes implicated in the rough and tumble stuff, but eventually manages to calm things down with an explanation.

The Newlyweds' Servant: Released 02/06/1928. © Universal Pictures Corp. 10/05/1927. Stern Bros Comedy; released as a Junior Jewel Comedy. Cast: Lawrence McKeen, Jack Bartlett, Addie McPhail. Director: Gus Meins. Based on George McManus' comic strip "The Newlyweds and Their Baby."

The Newlyweds (Bartlett and McPhail) go to the beach, accompanied by a nurse for Snookums (McKeen). Snookums makes life hell for her, first strolling into the ocean and later leading her in a merry chase through the seaside amusement park.

Buster Steps Out: Released 02/08/1928. © Universal Pictures Corp. 06/20/1927. Stern Bros Comedy. Cast: Arthur Trimble, Doreen Turner, Pete the Dog, Albert Schaefer. Director: Francis Corby. Based on Richard F. Outcault's comic strip "Buster Brown."

Buster (Trimble) and Mary Jane (Turner) chase an escaped canary throughout the house, leaving the place a shambles. Next the children take the neighborhood kids for a wild, traffic-disrupting ride through the city and out into the country where they go fishing.

A Man of Letters: Released 02/15/1928. © Universal Pictures Corp. 09/20/1927. Stern Bros Comedy. Cast: Sid Saylor, Marie Wood, Dorothy Vernon, James T. Kelley. Director: Sam Newfield. Based on George McManus' comic strip "Let George Do It."

Mail clerk George's (Saylor) girlfriend awaits an important letter, unaware that a pair of crooks are nearby hoping to grab it. Somehow it gets stuck to George's shoe, who starts his rounds pursued by the crooks. The crooks pounce and make off with the letter in spite of both George's and his girl's best efforts, but George then reveals that they only got the envelope, while he has its contents.

What a Party!: Released 02/22/1928. © Universal Pictures Corp. 09/20/1927. Stern Bros Comedy. Cast: Charles King, Charles Dorety. Director: Francis Corby. Based on Rube Goldberg's comic strip "Mike and Ike."

Twins Mike and Ike (King and Dorety) think they are responsible for the death of an Italian fruit vendor the night before. They finally decide to give themselves up, only to find that the death they read about was in a six year old newspaper, and the culprit of the previous night's murder already caught.

George's False Alarm: Released 02/29/1928. © Universal Pictures Corp. 01/18/1928. Stern Bros Comedy. Cast: Sid Saylor, Marny Elwyn, Max Asher. Director: Sam Newfield. Based on George McManus' comic strip "Let George Do It."

A failed suicide attempt lands George (Saylor) a job in the fire department. He takes his girl Mary for a ride on the hook and ladder. Fire breaks out in her apartment, and Mary rushes in when they arrive. George makes several attempts to rescue her before meeting with success, Mary carrying her badly burnt biscuits with her.

The Newlyweds' Success: Released 03/05/1928. © Universal Pictures Corp. 06/04/1927. Stern Bros Comedy; released as a Junior Jewel Comedy. Cast: Lawrence McKeen, Addie McPhail, Jack Bartlett. Director: Gus Meins. Based on George McManus' comic strip "The Newlyweds and Their Baby."

Having impressively impersonated a cowboy and Charlie Chaplin at a baby show, Snookums (McKeen) is rushed out to Hollywood. His first day on set is chaos, culminating with the escape of a leopard and Snookums donning a leopard skin rug.

Indoor Golf: Released 03/07/1928. © Universal Pictures Corp. 12/10/1927. Stern Bros Comedy. Cast: Harry Long, Stella Adams, Derelys Perdue, Gene Layman. Director: Gus Meins. Based on Arthur "Pop" Momand's comic strip "Keeping Up with the Joneses."

McGinis (Long) is blackmailed by a gold digger who has a staged "incriminating" photo of him. His wife (Adams) shows up, so McGinis says the woman is giving golf lessons. The house is reduced to shambles as efforts to learn golf inside demolishes things, any that survive falling under McGinis' attempts to rescue the photo from the woman.

Buster Shows Off: Released 03/14/1928. © Universal Pictures Corp. 06/14/1927. Stern Bros Comedy. Cast: Arthur Trimble, Doreen Turner, Pete the Dog. Director: Roland Asher. Based on Richard F. Outcault's comic strip "Buster Brown."

No Blondes Allowed: Released 03/21/1928. © Universal Pictures Corp. 10/05/1927. Stern Bros Comedy. Cast: Charles King, Charles Dorety, Jean Doree. Director: Francis Corby. Based on Rube Goldberg's comic strip "Mike and Ike" (working title **Blonde Babies**)

Twins Mike and Ike (King and Dorety) are followed by a cop who doesn't buy their explanation of rushing to treat a patient. With two blondes in tow, both are independently convinced to pose as the patient, a problem further complicated when Mike's wife returns prematurely from her aborted vacation.

Watch, George!: Released 03/28/1928. © Universal Pictures Corp. 10/06/1927. Stern Bros Comedy. Cast: Sid Saylor, Charlotte Dawn. Director: Sam Newfield. Based on George McManus' comic strip "Let George Do It."

New cop George (Saylor) is assigned to guard his girl Mary's father's valuable mummy during his absence. Thieves arrive and disguise themselves as mummies in order to scare George. After the general mixup, George subdues the crooks right before father returns with a purchaser for the mummy.

The Newlyweds' Friends: Released 04/02/1928. © Universal Pictures Corp. 10/05/1927. Stern Bros Comedy; released as a Junior Jewel Comedy. Cast: Lawrence McKeen, Jack Bartlett, Addie McPhail. Director: Gus Meins. Based on George McManus' comic strip "The Newlyweds and Their Baby."

Snookums creates havoc at a wedding in which he is page to the bride. He redeems himself when he discovers the hiding place of the crook who has stolen the bride's diamond necklace, and locks him in.

Her Only Husband: Released 04/04/1928. © Universal Pictures Corp. 12/28/1927. Stern Bros Comedy. Cast: Harry Long, Stella Adams, Addie McPhail, Gene Layman, Harry Martell. Director: Gus Meins. Based on Arthur "Pop" Momand's comic strip "Keeping Up with the Joneses."

McGinis (Long) heads to a business appointment at a cabaret, forgetting that his wife had earlier hidden his pants. His wife (Adams) enters with the Joneses, and McGinis is mistakenly assigned as a waiter to their table. Wife chases hubby from then on, making a shambles of the cabaret.

That's That: Released 04/11/1928. © Universal Pictures Corp. 01/11/1928. Stern Bros Comedy. Cast: Arthur Trimble, Doreen Turner, Pete the Dog. Director: Francis Corby. Based on Richard F. Outcault's comic strip "Buster Brown."

Mr. Brown heads to demonstrate his new bombing plane, unaware that Buster (Trimble), Mary Jane (Turner), and Tige are hiding in the car. The demo is almost a disaster due to Buster's placing TNT in the plane, but failure turns to success when the plane saves the committee's chairman from toppling off a cliff. He signs a contract on the spot for all the planes Brown's company can deliver.

Taking the Count: Released 04/18/1928. © Universal Pictures Corp. 10/05/1927. Stern Bros Comedy. Cast: Charles King, Charles Dorety, Doris Eaton, Jean Doree. Director: Francis Corby. Based on Rube Goldberg's comic strip "Mike and Ike."

Having so little luck at love, interior decorators Mike and Ike (King and Dorety) each agree to pay the other $1,000 if he fails again. Their first job is in a house with two beautiful daughters, and the boys try to hide from the other the fact that each is falling hard for one of them. Enter a Count who was lined up to marry one of them, and sensing the competition he instead decides to make off with their mother's diamonds.

When George Hops: Released 04/25/1928. © Universal Pictures Corp. 10/19/1927. Stern Bros Comedy. Cast: Sid Saylor, Ruby McCoy, Charlie Meakin, George Morrell, Allan Sears. Director: Sam Newfield. Based on George McManus' comic strip "Let George Do It."

George (Saylor) gets a job as a bellhop only to find that his girl's father owns the place. Circumstances keep placing George in the girl's room where he's discovered by her father, requiring some fast thinking to get out of a jam. George is ordered to walk a guest's dogs, who all break loose.

A Big Bluff: Released 05/02/1928. © Universal Pictures Corp. 01/03/1928. Stern Bros Comedy. Cast: Harry Long, Stella Adams, Addie McPhail, Gene Layman. Director: Gus Meins. Based on Arthur "Pop" Momand's comic strip "Keeping Up with the Joneses" (copyrighted as **Meet the Count**)

Pa McGinis (Long) tries to bust into society by holding a reception for a count. A detective arrives and claims the count an imposter, so McGinis tries to palm off the detective as the count. This doesn't go over very well, and becomes a complete flop when the detective's jealous sweetheart arrives and turn the party into a free-for-all.

The Newlyweds' Imagination: Released 05/07/1928. © Universal Pictures Corp. 10/19/1927. Stern Bros Comedy; released as a Junior Jewel Comedy. Cast: Lawrence McKeen, Jack Bartlett, Addie McPhail Director: Gus Meins. Based on George McManus' comic strip "The Newlyweds and Their Baby."

The Newlyweds (Bartlett and McPhail) are on board a ship where Snookums (McKeen) creates the usual amount of havoc. Snookums finally ends up in the pilot house fast asleep, his parents now happy once again.

Sailor George: Released 05/09/1928. © Universal Pictures Corp. 02/03/1928. Stern Bros Comedy. Cast: Sid Saylor. Director: Sam Newfield. Based on George McManus' comic strip "Let George Do It."

Discharged from the navy, George (Saylor) takes a job as soda clerk where his girl works. The ship's ensign is his rival, and insists on George returning to the ship when the latter cannot prove that he was discharged.

Women Chasers: Released 05/16/1928. © Universal Pictures Corp. 10/15/1927. Stern Bros Comedy. Cast: Joe Young, Ned La Salle. Director: Francis Corby. Based on Rube Goldberg's comic strip "Mike and Ike."

Mike and Ike (Young and La Salle) are hired by a rich client to retrieve letters from a vamp blackmailer. They finally track her down in a cabaret and after a lot of turmoil manage to secue the letters for their client.

Buster's Whippet Race: Released 05/23/1928. © Universal Pictures Corp. 01/11/1928. Stern Bros Comedy. Cast: Arthur Trimble, Doreen Turner, Jerry the Dog. Director: Francis Corby. Based on Richard F. Outcault's comic strip "Buster Brown."

Buster (Trimble) and Mary Jane (Turner) prep Tige for entry in a whippet race. The race itself is very exciting, but it ends up in the living room of Buster's parents. Buster receives his usual licking for the trouble he has caused.

George's School Daze: Released 05/30/1928. © Universal Pictures Corp. 11/23/1927. Stern Bros Comedy. Cast: Sid Saylor. Director: Sam Newfield. Based on George McManus' comic strip "Let George Do It."

George (Saylor) accidentally ends up as a rookie cop assigned to a tough neighborhood. A gang steals his girl's purse and the regular cops arrive, but through dumb luck George manages to come out on top as the hero.

The Newlyweds' Happy Day: Released 06/04/1928. © Universal Pictures Corp. 11/14/1927. Stern Bros Comedy; released as Junior Jewel Comedy. Cast: Lawrence McKeen, Jack Bartlett, Addie McPhail. Director: Francis Corby. Based on George McManus' comic strip "The Newlyweds and Their Baby."

Their camping trip cut short when they are chased by a bear, the Newlyweds (Bartlett and McPhail) learn that Snookums' (McKeen) wealthy grandfather is coming to visit. Elaborate plans to entertain the old fellow are compromised by Snookums' antics, but the grandfather is so tickled by the child's mischievousness that he declares the youngster his sole heir.

Whose Wife?: Released 06/06/1928. © Universal Pictures Corp. 11/02/1927. Stern Bros Comedy. Cast: Joe Young, Ned La Salle. Director: Francis Corby. Based on Rube Goldberg's comic strip "Mike and Ike"

Mike (Young) marries, only to find that the rich uncle coming to visit will make him his sole heir if he remains single. So Mike pretends that Ike (La Salle) is the happy groom, but awkwardness and confusion soon follow aboard the train's sleeper car as Mike tries to get to his wife.

A Full House: Released 06/13/1928. © Universal Pictures Corp. 12/13/1927. Stern Bros Comedy. Cast: Harry Long, Stella Adams, Addie McPhail, Gene Layman. Director: Gus Meins. Based on Arthur "Pop" Momand's comic strip "Keeping Up with the Joneses."

Pa McGinis' (Long) poker game is cut short by Ma (Adams), who drags him to the costumer's to select a costume for the masked ball. Pa tries to escape in a sailor suit but a cop mistakes him for an escaped nut. Pa manages to return to the ball and is joined by his poker buddies who have crashed it. They resume their poker game until discovered once again by Ma, who physically breaks up the game.

When George Meets George: Released 06/20/1928. © Universal Pictures Corp. 12/20/1927. Stern Bros Comedy. Cast: Sid Saylor, Thelma Daniels. Director: Sam Newfield. Based on George McManus' comic strip "Let George Do It" (copyrighted as **George Meets George**)

"With the clever comedy work of Sid Saylor, this succeeds in being very entertaining. In addition, the plot is quite substantial and works up to a lot of suspense with natural laughs. Moves fast, with some nice comedy bits." (*Film Daily*, 05/20/1928)

Buster Minds the Baby: Released 06/27/1928. © Universal Pictures Corp. 05/15/1928. Stern Bros Comedy. Cast: Arthur Trimble, Lois Hardwick, Jerry the Dog, Merry Mae McKeen, Hannah "Oatmeal" Washington. Director: Sam Newfield. Based on Richard F. Outcault's comic strip "Buster Brown."

Buster (Trimble) and Mary Jane (Hardwick) head to the neighborhood bazaar, leaving Tige behind to mind the baby. At the bazaar "Oatmeal" gets in trouble with the knife thrower, requiring Buster and Mary Jane to rescue him.

The Newlyweds' False Alarm: Released 07/02/1928. © Universal Pictures Corp. 12/13/1927. Stern Bros Comedy; released as a Junior Jewel Comedy. Cast: Lawrence McKeen, Derelys Perdue, Jack Egan. Director: Francis Corby. Based on George McManus' comic strip "The Newlyweds and Their Baby."

The Newlyweds (Egan and Perdue) and the neighbors inspect the new hotel while Snookums gets into all sorts of trouble. When the proprietor takes the visitors to see the best bedrooms, he finds that Snookums has already been there, and the room afloat.

Reel Life: Released 07/04/1928. © Universal Pictures Corp. 01/17/1928. Stern Bros Comedy. Cast: Harry Long, Stella Adams, Addie McPhail, Gene Layman. Director: Gus Meins. Based on Arthur "Pop" Momand's comic strip "Keeping Up with the Joneses."

Cash Customers: Released 07/11/1928. © Universal Pictures Corp. 12/13/1927. Stern Bros Comedy. Cast: Joe Young, Ned La Salle. Director: Roland Asher. Based on Rube Goldberg's comic strip "Mike and Ike."

Dress salesmen Mike and Ike (Young and La Salle) are told by their boss to take two elderly customers to lunch. A prohibition officer appears causing a guest at the next table to dump his booze into the water carafe. The two elderly women get drunk, and then their husbands appear.

Big Game George: Released 07/18/1928. © Universal Pictures Corp. 12/16/1927. Stern Bros Comedy. Cast: Sid Saylor. Director: Sam Newfield. Based on George McManus' comic strip "Let George Do It."

Wealthy big game hunter George (Saylor) is on the way to Africa, but through an accident misses the boat. Wandering the streets in his white hunting suit, circumstances force him to act as a street cleaner. He's spotted by his girl who now thinks he's an imposter, and the copy trailing him continues to make his life miserable.

Good Scout Buster: Released 07/25/1928. © Universal Pictures Corp. 05/15/1928. Stern Bros Comedy. Cast: Arthur Trimble, Lois Hardwick. Director: Sam Newfield. Based on Richard F. Outcault's comic strip "Buster Brown."

Buster (Trimble) is sent to camp where his father hopes he'll learn some discipline. Tige follows and they find Mary Jane (Hardwick) already there as a fellow camper. Discipline quickly turns to mayhem, a movie company's wind machine not helping matters.

Broke Out: Released 08/01/1928. © Universal Pictures Corp. 12/06/1927. Stern Bros Comedy. Cast: Joe Young, Ned La Salle. Director: Roland Asher. Based on Rube Goldberg's comic strip "Mike and Ike."

McGinis vs. Jones: Released 08/08/1928. © Universal Pictures Corp. 12/28/1927. Stern Bros Comedy. Cast: Harry Long, Stella Adams, Addie McPhail, Gene Layman. Director: Gus Meins. Based on Arthur "Pop" Momand's comic strip "Keeping Up with the Joneses."

A golf game is scheduled at the club between Pa McGinis (Long) and Mr. Jones. Pa doesn't know much about golf, but he's aided by Ma (Adams) and caddy Bella Donna (Layman). Pa is so weary by the 18th hole that he's wheeled from shot to shot in a wheel barrow, but a miraculous hole-in-one at the final hole establishes him as the winner.

Busting Buster: Released 08/15/1928. © Universal Pictures Corp. 05/15/1928. Stern Bros Comedy. Cast: Arthur Trimble, Lois Hardwick, Jerry the Dog, Hannah "Oatmeal" Washington,. Director: Sam Newfield. Based on Richard F. Outcault's comic strip "Buster Brown."

The Newlyweds' Anniversary: Released 08/06/1928. © Universal Pictures Corp. 01/05/1928. Stern Bros Comedy; released as a Junior Jewel Comedy. Cast: Jack Egan,

Derelys Perdue, Lawrence McKeen. Director: Francis Corby. Story: William Weber, T. Page Wright. Based on George McManus' comic strip "The Newlyweds and Their Baby."

She's My Girl: Released 08/22/1928. © Universal Pictures Corp. 01/05/1928. Stern Bros Comedy. Cast: Sid Saylor. Director: Sam Newfield. Based on George McManus' comic strip "Let George Do It."

Cub reporter George (Saylor) is assigned to cover an exclusive society wedding from which reporters have been banned. Finally managing to sneak into the place, he finds that the bride is his childhood sweetheart, and is being forced into the marriage. George decides to break up the affair.

Husbands Won't Tell: Released 08/29/1928. © Universal Pictures Corp. 05/22/1928. Stern Bros Comedy. Cast: Joe Young, Ned La Salle. Director: Francis Corby. Based on Rube Goldberg's comic strip "Mike and Ike."

As part of his initiation into the Married Men's Protective Club, Mike is instructed to "flirt" with a fellow candidate who is dressed as a woman. Mike's wife, unaware of this initiation, gets wind of this flirtation and heads to the club where she proceeds to wreck the place.

Beginning of 1928-1929 Season

The Newlyweds' Hard Luck: Released 09/05/1928. © Universal Pictures Corp. 05/28/1928. Stern Bros Comedy; released as a Junior Jewel Comedy. Cast: Jack Egan, Derelys Perdue, Lawrence McKeen. Director: Francis Corby. Based on George McManus' comic strip "The Newlyweds and Their Baby."

After Snookums (McKeen) wrecks the house playing golf, and is suspected of swallowing his mother's (Perdue) diamond ring, the family heads to a dinner where father (Egan) is to demonstrate his invention for making rain. Snookums gains control, soaking everyone in a downpour.

Rubber Necks: Released 09/12/1928. © Universal Pictures Corp. 01/20/1928. Stern Bros Comedy. Cast: Sid Saylor, Jean Doree, Dorothy Coburn, Harry Martell. Director: Gus Meins. Based on George McManus' comic strip "Let George Do It."

George (Saylor) and his pal lose their flapjack-making jobs, but land new ones as detectives in a flirtatious woman's father's hotel. On night duty, they are first spooked by a monkey's shadow, and later when the father returns in costume from a masquerade ball. They flee the hotel.

Half-Back Buster: Released 09/19/1928. © Universal Pictures Corp. 05/28/1928. Stern Bros Comedy. Cast: Arthur Trimble, Lois Hardwick, Jerry the Dog, Hannah

"Oatmeal" Washington,. Director: Sam Newfield. Based on Richard F. Outcault's comic strip "Buster Brown."

"A rather poor imitation of Roach's Gang comedies. Sterns don't seem to realize that you can't take a bunch of kids and make another Our Gang just like that. Drew some laughs of course, but lacks true snap. Cut out the mob stuff and let Buster and Tige do their stuff. Good print and photography." (*Exhibitors Herald World*, 01/19/1929, Wolfe & Williams, Screenland theatre, Nevada)

Just Wait: Released 09/26/1928. © Universal Pictures Corp. 05/28/1928. Stern Bros Comedy. Cast: Joe Young, Ned La Salle, Betty Welsh, Harriett Mathews. Director: Gus Meins. Based on Rube Goldberg's comic strip "Mike and Ike."

Hired as waiters to cover the Van Camp party, Mike and Ike are sidelined by a pair of pretty girls they meet along the way. Pretending to be millionaires and "borrowing" a car they find at a dealer's lot, they show the girls a good time, but when they take them home they find that they are the Van Camp's daughters.

The Newlyweds Unwelcome: Released 10/03/1928. © Universal Pictures Corp. 06/06/1928. Stern Bros Comedy; released as a Junior Jewel Comedy. Cast: Jack Egan, Derelys Perdue, Lawrence McKeen. Director: Francis Corby. Based on George McManus' comic strip "The Newlyweds and Their Baby."

The Newlyweds (Egan and Perdue) inherit a ranch. Arriving in the latest cowboy attire, they are the butt of the jokes of the locals. Snookums (McKeen) takes off on the back of a fast pony with everyone in hot pursuit. They finally find him and the pony in the dining room, eating dinner.

Look Pleasant: Released 10/10/1928. © Universal Pictures Corp. 05/28/1928. Stern Bros Comedy. Cast: Sid Saylor, Dorothy Coburn, Harry Martell. Director: Gus Meins. Based on George McManus' comic strip "Let George Do It."

Tossed from their boarding house, George and his pal take jobs as insurance agents. Frustrated by each new attempt to gain a customer, George drops a flower pot on his newest prospect's head only to find that the fellow himself is an insurance agent; he gives chase. The pair climb through a window, and when confronted by the room's charming occupant, present themselves as window cleaners. And then her husband, their latest victim, arrives.

Buster Trims Up: Released 10/17/1928. © Universal Pictures Corp. 06/06/1928. Stern Bros Comedy. Cast: Arthur Trimble, Lois Hardwick, Hannah "Oatmeal" Washington. Director: Sam Newfield. Based on Richard F. Outcault's comic strip "Buster Brown."

Buster and his friends' flirtatious nurse is distracted by her sweetheart, a cop. The baby carriage rolls into the lake and bystanders rush to the rescue, only to find the infant unharmed, under a tree playing with Tige.

Shooting the Bull: Released 10/24/1928. © Universal Pictures Corp. 05/28/1928. Stern Bros Comedy. Cast: Joe Young, Ned La Salle. Director: Gus Meins. Based on Rube Goldberg's comic strip "Mike and Ike."

Sporting goods department salesmen Mike and Ike impress two female customers, who invite them on a hunting expedition. Their father decides that the boys are a couple of pikers, so he dresses in a gorilla outfit and throws a scare into them. The boys attempt to explain their lack of courage.

The Newlyweds' Court Trouble: Released 10/31/1928. © Universal Pictures Corp. 06/08/1928. Stern Bros Comedy; released as a Junior Jewel Comedy. Cast: Lawrence McKeen, Jack Egan, Derelys Perdue. Director: Francis Corby. Based on George McManus' comic strip "The Newlyweds and Their Baby."

Snookums (McKeen) and his monkey cause so much trouble for the neighbors that the Newlyweds (Egan and Perdue) are hauled into court. But in court Snookums touches the judge's heart and his parents are let off scot-free.

The Cross Country Bunion Race: Released 11/07/1928. © Universal Pictures Corp. 05/29/1928. Stern Bros Comedy. Cast: Sid Saylor, Dorothy Coburn, Harry Martell, Harriett Mathews. Director: Gus Meins. Based on George McManus' comic strip "Let George Do It."

To pay off damages done to neighbors' houses, George's (Saylor) fellow acrobat friend enters him in a cross country race. George would rather get some sleep than run, but when chased by a bear he manages to win the race and the prize money.

Teacher's Pest: Released 11/14/1928. © Universal Pictures Corp. 06/15/1928. Stern Bros Comedy. Cast: Arthur Trimble, Lois Hardwick, Merry Mae McKeen, Jerry the Dog. Director: Sam Newfield. Based on Richard F. Outcault's comic strip "Buster Brown."

When a mischievous pupil drops a box of sneezing powder during a visit by the school board of trustees, Buster (Trimble) is blamed for this prank. Tige and the neighborhood dogs come to his assistance.

Fish Stories: Released 11/21/1928. © Universal Pictures Corp. 06/13/1928. Stern Bros Comedy. Cast: Joe Young, Ned La Salle, Betty Welsh, Harriet Mathews. Director: Gus Meins. Based on Rube Goldberg's comic strip "Mike and Ike."

Mike and Ike (Young and La Salle) try to impress two girls (Welsh and Mathews) by posing as wealthy sportsmen, but when their father invites them to join in a fishing party, their ineptitude becomes readily apparent.

The Newlyweds Lose Snookums: Released 11/28/1928. © Universal Pictures Corp. 06/15/1928. Stern Bros Comedy; released as a Junior Jewel Comedy. Cast: Jack Egan, Derelys Perdue, Lawrence McKeen. Director: Francis Corby. Based on George McManus' comic strip "The Newlyweds and Their Baby."

The Newlyweds (Egan and Perdue), fearing that Snookums (McKeen) has been kidnapped, finally find him taking a continuous ride in the elevator. They rush him to the baby parade where he was overdue, and he jockeys his decorated auto into first place while wrecking the parade.

All for Geraldine: Released 12/05/1928. © Universal Pictures Corp. 06/13/1928. Stern Bros Comedy. Cast: Sid Saylor, Dorothy Coburn, Harry Martell. Director: Gus Meins. Based on George McManus' comic strip "Let George Do It."

George (Saylor) and his friend Steve call on the latter's girl friend. George makes a hit with her, and Steve is jealous. George takes her motoring with Steve in pursuit, but that comes to an abrupt halt when Steve is pinched by a cop for tying up traffic.

Watch the Birdie: Released 12/12/1928. © Universal Pictures Corp. 06/20/1928. Stern Bros Comedy. Cast: Arthur Trimble, Lois Hardwick, Jerry the Dog. Director: Sam Newfield. Story: William Weber, T. Page Wright. Based on Richard F. Outcault's comic strip "Buster Brown."

When the Browns rent an apartment that doesn't accept dogs, Buster (Trimble) sneaks Tige in hidden in a suitcase. It ends up in the wrong apartment, so Tige seeks out Buster and Mary Jane (Hardwick), causing much disruption in the building. The landlord gives chase, but Tige ends up imprisoning him in a chest.

And Morning Came: Released 12/19/1928. © Universal Pictures Corp. 07/05/1928. Stern Bros Comedy. Cast: Joe Young, Ned La Salle. Director: Francis Corby. Based on Rube Goldberg's comic strip "Mike and Ike."

Mike and Ike (Young and La Salle) face the wrath of their girls' mother when they get them home late. They get mixed up in a kidnapping and find themselves stuck with an unwanted baby, and then face their girls who aren't convinced by their explanations.

The Newlyweds Need Help: Released 12/26/1928. © Universal Pictures Corp. 06/20/1928. Stern Bros Comedy; released as a Junior Jewel Comedy. Cast: Jack Egan, Derelys Perdue, Lawrence McKeen. Director: Francis Corby. Based on George McManus' comic strip "The Newlyweds and Their Baby."

When Snookums (McKeen) disrupts their bridge party, the Newlyweds (Egan and Perdue) send him out with the maid. While she flirts with a cop, Snookums' carriage is hoisted atop a moving van. The kid gets the ride of his life before being rescued by his frantic parents.

Sailor Suits: Released 01/02/1929. © Universal Pictures Corp. 05/28/1928. Stern Bros Comedy. Cast: Sid Saylor, Dorothy Coburn, Harry Martell. Director: Gus Meins. Based on George McManus' comic strip "Let George Do It."

George (Saylor) and his buddy (Martell) pose as sailors to get a date. They both fall for and fight over the same girl (Coburn), but this is interrupted when a Navy MP, thinking them to be real sailors, orders them back to the ship. They get out of this mess only to find that the girl is marrying a real sailor.

Out at Home: Released 01/09/1929. © Universal Pictures Corp. 06/20/1928. Stern Bros Comedy. Cast: Arthur Trimble, Lois Hardwick, Hannah "Oatmeal" Washington. Director: Sam Newfield. Story: William Weber, T. Page Wright. Based on Richard F. Outcault's comic strip "Buster Brown" (working title **Kitchen Mechanic**)

Buster (Trimble), Mary Jane (Hardwick), and Oatmeal wander into dad's lab and start the mechanical maid he was perfecting. Buster rescues Oatmeal from nearly being crushed by the thing, and removesg its innards. The kids hear father telling his guests that the mechanical maid will be serving dinner, so Buster and Oatmeal climb inside the thing and attempt to do so. The kids are discovered when the thing catches fire, and Buster catches another spanking.

Hold Your Horses: Released 01/16/1929. © Universal Pictures Corp. 07/10/1928. Stern Bros Comedy. Cast: Joe Young, Ned La Salle, Dick Smith. Director: Sam Newfield. Based on Rube Goldberg's comic strip "Mike and Ike."

Evicted from their boarding house, Mike and Ike (Young and La Salle) meet two girls who suggest they all go horseback riding. Their ineptitude soon becomes apparent, and after the girls help them remount several times they finally grow tired of these two rookies and give them the brush-off.

The Newlyweds' Headache: Released 01/23/1929. © Universal Pictures Corp. 06/20/1928. Stern Bros Comedy; released as a Junior Jewel Comedy. Cast: Lawrence McKeen, Jack Egan, Derelys Perdue. Director: Francis Corby. Based on George McManus' comic strip "The Newlyweds and Their Baby."

Egan has the Electrical Household Goods display at the Household Exhibition, but is saddled with Snookums. Snookums makes a disaster out of his father's display, and then moves on to wreck a vacuum cleaner display. He wrecks a pillows display as well, placing a Free Sample sign which results in a mad rush. Feathers are everywhere, then blown about when Snookums turns on the fans at another exhibit. The exhibition ends in total disaster.

Crushed Hats: Released 01/30/1929. © Universal Pictures Corp. 06/20/1928. Stern Bros Comedy. Cast: Sid Saylor. Director: Gus Meins. Based on George McManus' comic strip "Let George Do It."

George (Saylor) and his pal work in a hat shop, and to drum up customers George shoots the hats off passersby, after which his pal drives a steam roller over the hats. George hands out his business card, and business is booming until the customers discover the trick. George and his pal make a hasty retreat.

Have Patience: Released 02/06/1929. © Universal Pictures Corp. 07/05/1928. Stern Bros Comedy. Cast: Arthur Trimble, Lois Hardwick. Director: Sam Newfield. Based on Richard F. Outcault's comic strip "Buster Brown."

Buster (Trimble), Mary Jane (Hardwick), and Tige create havoc in a doctor's office. Mr. Brown decides to take a trip alone, but Tige and the others follow him onto the train. Tige creates more havoc in the baggage, dining, and sleeper cars. The porters and conductor unceremoniously escort Tige and the Browns off the train.

Take Your Pick: Released 02/13/1929. © Universal Pictures Corp. 07/23/1928. Stern Bros Comedy. Cast: Joe Young, Ned La Salle. Director: Sam Newfield. Based on Rube Goldberg's comic strip "Mike and Ike."

Mike and Ike (Young and La Salle) arrive to pick up their chorus girl dates, sneaking in the stage entrance. They put on costumes and mingle with the chorus girls to evade the manager, but he's finally on to them and tosses them out on their ears.

The Newlyweds' Visit: Released 02/20/1929. © Universal Pictures Corp. 11/01/1928. Stern Bros Comedy; released as a Junior Jewel Comedy. Cast: Jack Egan, Derelys Perdue, Lawrence McKeen. Director: Sam Newfield. Based on George McManus' comic strip "The Newlyweds and Their Baby."

Tossed from their home when Snookums (McKeen) hits the landlord with a rotten tomato, the Newlyweds (Egan and Perdue) are invited to occupy a relative's house. They think it's haunted, but soon discover they are in the wrong house, surrounded by men in masquerade costumes thinking these "intruders" were burglars.

Television George: Released 02/27/1929. © Universal Pictures Corp. 01/15/1928. Stern Bros Comedy. Cast: Sid Saylor, Derelys Perdue. Director: Francis Corby. Based on George McManus' comic strip "Let George Do It."

George (Saylor) leaves his television-addicted wife at home to join a pal and a couple of girls at a television broadcasting room. As it turns out, his wife watches his "performance" on the TV, so she rushes to the station to pummel her guilty spouse.

Knockout Buster: Released 03/06/1929. © Universal Pictures Corp. 07/10/1928. Stern Bros Comedy. Cast: Arthur Trimble, Lois Hardwicke, Jerry the Dog, Bobby Newman, Hannah "Oatmeal" Washington, Albert Schaefer. Director: Francis Corby. Based on Richard F. Outcault's comic strip "Buster Brown."

With Mary Jane (Hardwick) the timekeeper and Oatmeal the referee, Buster (Trimble) is pitted against a fat boy in a front yard prize fight, and somehow manages to win. Later they all head off on a camping trip, Oatmeal hiding out among the luggage. The kids explore a nearby farm, and are chased by a farmer who believes they have stolen his watermelons.

She's a Pippin: Released 03/13/1929. © Universal Pictures Corp. 12/21/1928. Stern Bros Comedy. Cast: Joe Young, Ned La Salle, Emily Gerdes. Director: Sam Newfield. Based on Rube Goldberg's comic strip "Mike and Ike."

On shore leave, sailors Mike and Ike (Young and La Salle) finally connect with two young ladies. Arriving at the girls' house, they see a stranger sneaking in the window. The boys try to make heroes of themselves, but it backfires when it turns out the "stranger" is the girls' father, having lost his keys.

The Newlyweds' Holiday: Released 03/20/1929. © Universal Pictures Corp. 12/26/1928. Stern Bros Comedy; released as a Junior Jewel Comedy. Cast: Jack Egan, Derelys Perdue, Lawrence McKeen, Hannah "Oatmeal" Washington. Director: Francis Corby. Based on George McManus' comic strip "The Newlyweds and Their Baby."

Mrs. Newlywed's (Perdue) sewing circle is disrupted when Snookums (McKeen) and the child of one of her friends get into a pillow fight, leaving feathers everywhere. Later the family goes on a picnic, and Oatmeal is smuggled in in the family's lunch basket.

Seeing Sights: Released 03/27/1929. © Universal Pictures Corp. 07/13/1928. Stern Bros Comedy. Cast: Sid Saylor. Director: Gus Meins. Based on George McManus' comic strip "Let George Do It."

George (Saylor) and his buddy Steve are assisted by their girls running a sight-seeing bus. George stages a fight with a dummy and the girls drum up additional trade with bus-filling results. An opened snuff box causes a lot of sneezing, and a fight breaks out; chaos rules.

Tige's Girl Friend: Released 04/03/1929. © Universal Pictures Corp. 01/18/1929. Stern Bros Comedy. Cast: Arthur Trimble, Lois Hardwick. Director: Sam Newfield. Based on Richard F. Outcault's comic strip "Buster Brown."

Tige beats up the English bull dog that took a bone away from Mary Jane's (Hardwick) dog Fluffy. Buster (Trimble), Mary Jane, and Tige visit the hospital where grandpa is sick, and turn the ward upside down.

This Way Please: Released 04/10/1929. © Universal Pictures Corp. 01/08/1929. Stern Bros Comedy. Cast: Joe Young, Ned La Salle. Director: Sam Newfield. Based on Rube Goldberg's comic strip "Mike and Ike."

Chased by a cop, Mike and Ike (Young and La Salle) take refuge in a dentist's office, don white coats, and administer laughing gas to that same cop. They escape to a hotel and become bell hops, get mixed up in a girl's room, and end up with both of them wearing a single pair of pants.

The Newlyweds in Society: Released 04/17/1929. © Universal Pictures Corp. 12/26/1928. Stern Bros Comedy; released as a Junior Jewel Comedy. Cast: Jack Egan, Derelys Perdue, Lawrence McKeen. Director: Francis Corby and Gus Meins. Based on George McManus' comic strip "The Newlyweds and Their Baby."

The Newlyweds (Egan and Perdue) and Snookums (McKeen) attend a fashionable party with predictable results. A couple of thieves sneak in and attempt to steal some jewels, but Snookums stumbles across them and by accident traps them. Snookums is now the hero of the party.

Private Business: Released 04/24/1929. © Universal Pictures Corp. 01/07/1929. Stern Bros Comedy. Cast: Sid Saylor. Director: Gus Meins. Based on George McManus' comic strip "Let George Do It."

George (Saylor) and his buddy finally meet up with two French mademoiselles after some mistaken identity-filled meetings. They go for a dip in a nearby pool but get into an altercation with an attendant. It isn't long before the place is in an uproar, people in the wrong bath houses, sharing the wrong clothes, and so forth. George and his pal quietly slip away from the place.

Magic: Released 05/01/1929. © Universal Pictures Corp. 01/31/1929. Stern Bros Comedy. Cast: Arthur Trimble, Lois Hardwick. Director: Sam Newfield. Based on Richard F. Outcault's comic strip "Buster Brown."

Buster (Trimble), Mary Jane (Hardwick), and Tige interrupt and expose the tricks a magician is performing at a house party. His birds get loose, create a hurricane of feathers, and drive the guests from the room.

Finishing School: Released 05/08/1929. © Universal Pictures Corp. 01/07/1929. Stern Bros Comedy. Cast: Joe Young, Ned La Salle. Director: Gus Meins. Based on Rube Goldberg's comic strip "Mike and Ike."

Two girls are sent out to find some waiters for a school luncheon, and run across Mike and Ike (Young and La Salle). They have such a good time that they are delayed in their errand, so the boys agree to pose as waiters. Arriving back at the school, however, they encounter real waiters who were brought in when the girls failed to return in a timely fashion. The luncheon turns into a disaster, so the girls pack their bags and leave the boys to face the music.

The Newlyweds' Excuse: Released 05/15/1929. © Universal Pictures Corp. 01/07/1929. Stern Bros Comedy; released as a Junior Jewel Comedy. Cast: Jack Egan, Derelys Perdue, Lawrence McKeen. Director: Francis Corby. Based on George McManus' comic strip "The Newlyweds and Their Baby."

Snookums (McKeen) gets into trouble with a paint brush, then wrecks the bathroom giving his dog a bath. The Newlyweds (Egan and Perdue) head to an auction house where Snookums proceeds to wreck numerous pieces, and his dad is forced to buy them.

Close Shaves: Released 05/22/1929. © Universal Pictures Corp. 01/10/1929. Stern Bros Comedy. Cast: Sid Saylor. Director: Francis Corby. Based on George McManus' comic strip "Let George Do It."

Fired from their jobs as bricklayers, George (Saylor) and his pal take over a barber shop whose owner has been arrested. Jealous that his pal is showing too much attention to a female arrival, George takes it out on her father seated in his barber chair. The two pals end up in jail over an argument about the girl's handbag.

Delivering the Goods: Released 05/29/1929. © Universal Pictures Corp. 01/31/1929. Stern Bros Comedy. Cast: Arthur Trimble, Lois Hardwick. Director: Sam Newfield. Based on Richard F. Outcault's comic strip "Buster Brown."

Buster (Trimble), Mary Jane (Hardwick), and Tige help out at Buster's father's grocery store. In father's absence they cause the usual havoc, smashing eggs in pants pockets, releasing red pepper into the air, culminating with Tige involved in a "mad dog" false alarm.

Chaperones: Released 06/05/1929. © Universal Pictures Corp. 01/15/1929. Stern Bros Comedy. Cast: Joe Young, Ned La Salle. Director: Sam Newfield. Based on Rube Goldberg's comic strip "Mike and Ike."

Fooled once before when Mike and Ike (Young and La Salle) returned their girls to their home, the chaperone now follows the girls to a party. Mike tries several schemes to get rid of the chaperone, an Apache dance included. Unsuccessful, the boys abandon the girls and take up with two others, only to find that they too have a humorless chaperone.

The Newlyweds Camp Out: Released 06/12/1929. © Universal Pictures Corp. 02/07/1929. Stern Bros Comedy; released as a Junior Jewel Comedy. Cast: Jack Egan, Derelys Perdue, Lawrence McKeen. Director: Francis Corby. Based on George McManus' comic strip "The Newlyweds and Their Baby."

When Mrs. Newlywed's (Perdue) relatives arrive and take over the house, Snookums

(McKeen) and his dad (Egan) are forced to sleep in a back yard tent. Snookums' antics finally drive the relatives out of the house.

Hot Puppies: Released 06/19/1929. © Universal Pictures Corp. 07/10/1929. Stern Bros Comedy. Cast: Sid Saylor, Derelys Perdue. Director: Gus Meins. Based on George McManus' comic strip "Let George Do It."

George (Saylor) and his pal, at odds over a pretty stenographer, run afoul of their boss. He sends them out to peddle fireworks, which ends in disaster when a hot dog salesman mistakes some fire crackers for hot dogs, and places them on his grill.

Buster's Spooks: Released 06/26/1929. © Universal Pictures Corp. 02/07/1929. Stern Bros Comedy. Cast: Arthur Trimble, Lois Hardwick, Hannah "Oatmeal" Washington, Jerry the Dog, Albert Schaefer. Director: Sam Newfield. Based on Richard F. Outcault's comic strip "Buster Brown." (working title **Buster's Choice**)

When they think they have accidentally drowned the fat boy who has been bothering them, Buster (Trimble), Mary Jane (Hardwick), Oatmeal, and Tige avoid a cop and take refuge in an unoccupied house. They think it's haunted, but it turns out that it is only the doing of the fat boy who is trying to get even with them.

Early to Wed: Released 07/03/1929. © Universal Pictures Corp. 01/21/1929. Stern Bros Comedy. Cast: Joe Young, Ned La Salle. Director: Gus Meins. Based on Rube Goldberg's comic strip "Mike and Ike."

Jewelry clerks Mike and Ike (Young and La Salle) deliver a necklace to one of their girls, who is about to wed a duke. The duke pummels them both out of jealousy, so they lock him in a closet. One of the twins dons his clothes, and ends up married to his girl.

The Newlyweds' Angel Child: Released 07/10/1929. © Universal Pictures Corp. 12/06/1927. Stern Bros Comedy; released as a Junior Jewel Comedy. Cast: Jack Egan, Derelys Perdue, Lawrence McKeen. Director: Francis Corby. Based on George McManus' comic strip "The Newlyweds and Their Baby."

Snookums (McKeen) creates havoc in a photographer's studio. He then commandeers an auto, landing him and his parents (Egan and Perdue) in jail. Snookums gets out of the cell and turns the place into a shambles. Releasing his parents from their cell, the three beat a hasty retreat.

Fly Cops: Released 07/17/1929. © Universal Pictures Corp. 01/15/1929. Stern Bros Comedy. Cast: Sid Saylor. Director: Francis Corby. Based on George McManus' comic strip "Let George Do It."

Rookie cops George (Saylor) and his pal are dismissed as hopeless after accompanying the others on a raid on a crooks' hideout. The two get wind of a $10,000 reward, and after a skirmish and a dose of dumb luck find that they've captured the gang, and the reward as well.

Getting Buster's Goat: Released 07/24/1929. © Universal Pictures Corp. 02/07/1929. Stern Bros Comedy. Cast: Arthur Trimble, Lois Hardwick. Director: Gus Meins. Based on Richard F. Outcault's comic strip "Buster Brown."

Buster (Trimble), accompanied by Mary Jane (Hardwick) and Tige, brings home a goat he has won as a prize. The goat proceeds to wreck his home and break up a dinner party.

Just the Type: Released 07/31/1929. © Universal Pictures Corp. 01/31/1929. Stern Bros Comedy. Cast: Joe Young, Ned La Salle. Director: Gus Meins. Based on Rube Goldberg's comic strip "Mike and Ike."

Movie lovers Mike and Ike (Young and La Salle) elude the watchman and sneak into a movie studio. Bluffing their way as a pair of extras, they break up scene after scene, causing no end of exasperation to the studio's directors.

The Newlyweds' Pests: Released 08/07/1929. © Universal Pictures Corp. 02/13/1929. Stern Bros Comedy; released as a Junior Jewel Comedy. Cast: Joe Young, Molly Malone, Lawrence McKeen, Harry Martell, Art Rowlands. Director: Gus Meins. Based on George McManus' comic strip "The Newlyweds and Their Baby."

Snookums (McKeen) causes disruption at his father's (Egan) office, so the board of directors leave in a huff. Returning home, they find a food utensil salesman giving a demonstration in the parlor to invited neighbors. Snookums wrecks the demo.

The Cut-Ups: Released 08/14/1929. © Universal Pictures Corp. 01/18/1929. Stern Bros Comedy. Cast: Sid Saylor. Director: Francis Corby. Based on George McManus' comic strip "Let George Do It."

George (Saylor) and his pal learn of an inheritance, so they invite the pal's girl to dinner; George serves as butler, waiter, and chef. Her whole family arrives to eat, so George scrambles in the kitchen. Then he learns that his inheritance is one dollar. The film ends with creditors having stripped the house bare.

Stop Barking: Released 08/21/1929. © Universal Pictures Corp. 02/07/1929. Stern Bros Comedy. Cast: Arthur Trimble, Lois Hardwick. Director: Sam Newfield. Based on Richard F. Outcault's comic strip "Buster Brown."

Finding the dentist out to lunch, Buster (Trimble) and Mary Jane (Hardwick) decide to remove Tige's bad tooth themselves. Later on the kids and Tige head to Buster's dad's hotel and make nuisances of themselves.

Good Skates: Released 08/28/1929. © Universal Pictures Corp. 02/13/1929. Stern

Bros Comedy. Cast: Joe Young, Ned La Salle. Director: Francis Corby. Based on Rube Goldberg's comic strip "Mike and Ike."

A jealous husband chases Mike and Ike (Young and La Salle) to a roller skating rink where they are mistaken for skating masters. Since they can't skate, one of the twins maneuvers the other around the rink suspended from an overhead wire, with mixed results. The jealous husband arrives and a skating melee follows.

Working Titles Not Yet Associated with Final Release Titles, or for Films That Were Never Released:

Camping Out: Cast: Buddy Messinger, Martha Sleeper, James "Bubbles" Berry, Donald Hughes, Tommy Hicks. Director: Arvid Gillstrom (*Universal Weekly*, May 17, 1924)

Step Lively: Cast: Buddy Messinger, Joe Bonner. Director: Arvid Gillstrom (*Universal Weekly*, June 14, 1924)

The Freshman, retitled as **The College Flapper**: Cast: Joe Bonner, Zack Williams, Century Beauties. Director: Alfred J. Goulding. Announced in production in *Exhibitors Trade Review* (October 21, 1922) and having been retitled in *Motion Picture News* (November 23, 1922). Possibly released as **Pleasure Before Business** (February 14, 1923).

Stern Brothers Production Not Released as L-Ko, Century, Rainbow, or Stern Brothers Comedy.:

A Kaiser There Was: Released 12/16/1918. © Universal Film Mfg Co. 12/31/1918. Master Comedies. Cast: Billy Armstrong, Chai Hong, Eva Novak, Bill White, Charles Inslee, James Donnelly. Director: Charles Avery.

Armstrong and his valet Hong go to war, and in Europe he falls for Novak, the colonel's daughter. He's told that he can have her hand, but only if he can capture or kill the Kaiser. Inslee is a rival in love, and through his machinations Armstrong and Hong end up in the Kaiser's palace. They avoid a firing squad, and later disguised as trees enter the palace, kill the guards, and pursue the Kaiser. After a chase on horseback, the Kaiser falls off a cliff and ends up tarred and feathered. Armstrong and Hong are heroes, and Armstrong wins the hand of Novak.

Joe Martin Comedies

Monkey Stuff: Released 07/07/1919. © Universal Film Mfg Co. 06/16/1919. Universal Jewel. Cast: Joe Martin, Harry Lorraine, Phyllis Allen, Beatrice Lovejoy, Harry

Burns, Lucille Smith, Charlie the Elephant. Director, Story: William Campbell. Assistant Director: Harry Burns.

Harry Ostermoore (Lorraine) has a wandering eye, first pursuing his maid Phyllis (Smith) and later Rosie Bloom (Lovejoy), and all to the consternation of his wife (Allen). Meanwhile, Joe Martin foils purse-snatching crook Swat Dugan (Burns) and a lion's attempt to kidnap a baby, and finally rescues Harry, his wife, and the crooks from the lion.

The Jazz Monkey: Released 07/21/1919. © Universal Film Mfg Co. 06/16/1919. Universal Jewel. Cast: Joe Martin, Neal Burns, Dora Rogers, Rube Miller, Bob McKenzie, Ross Letterman, George Allen, Charlie the Elephant. Director, Story: William Campbell. Assistant Director: Harry Burns.

Vaudevillians Heavy Ham (McKenzie) and Dotty Dainty (Rogers) plan to rob the local bank while the populace attends the show, but are thwarted by Joe Martin (working title **And the Elephant Still Pursued Her**)

A Prohibition Monkey: Released 09/13/1920. © Universal Film Mfg Co. 04/06/1920. Universal Jewel. 2 reels. Cast: Joe Martin, Dora Rodgers, Robert McKenzie, Larry McGrath, Frank Hayes, Alfred McKennon, Arthur Nowell, Ida McKenzie, Charlie the Elephant. Director: William S. Campbell. Assistant Director: Harry Burns (working title **Wild Lions and Loose Bandits**).

A spoof of westerns wherein saloon owner Riley (McKenzie) seeks to keep the boarded-up church closed for business reasons. Joe Martin aids a travelling evangelist to reform the town, assisted by Charlie the elephant and Buster the horse. Riley sends a dance hall girl (Rodgers) to vamp the preacher, but the latter overcomes her charms and the assembled thugs, with an able assist from his animal friends.

A Wild Night: Released 10/11/1920. © Universal Film Mfg Co. 10/07/1920. Universal Jewel. 2 reels. Cast: Joe Martin. Director: Al Santell (working title **Lower Four and Upper Three**)

In Paris, Joe Martin and his pal McGinis assume disguises to rob a posh party, but find another pair of impersonating crooks as competitors. Some lions are set loose and the police are called. An attempted escape is foiled, and all of the crooks end up in jail.

No Monkey Business: Released 02/28/1921. © Universal Film Mfg Co. 03/03/1921. Universal Jewel. 2 reels. Cast: Joe Martin.

After a long night of heavy drinking, Joe Martin returns home to be confronted by visions of the devil, a crocodile, ostrich, snake, and other wild animals. After this experience he swears off drinking and no more "monkey business"

A Monkey Hero: Released 04/19/1921. © Universal Film Mfg Co. 04/06/1921. Universal Jewel. 2 reels. Cast: Joe Martin, Hap Ward, Arthur Nowell, George Gudell, Rex De Roselli, Dorothy Vernon, Curley Stecker, Roy Stecker, Carl Stecker, Ethel Stecker, Ethel the Lion, Chance the Great Dane, Charlie the Elephant, Roger the Hound. Director, Story: Harry Burns and Curley Stecker. Camera: Lee Garmes (working title **The Monkey Fireman**)

Joe Martin thwarts Cheatem's Circus manager's attempts to first steal cash and later kidnap the owner's baby for ransom. Joe and his animal friends later rescue the baby when a fire breaks out in the circus tent.

A Monkey Movie Star: Released 07/04/1921. © Universal Film Mfg Co. 06/25/1921. Universal Jewel. 2 reels. Cast: Joe Martin. Director: Harry Burns.

Joe Martin, abused by his keeper, escapes and wanders into the office of the Hi-Tone Film Company. He's hired to star in a film, but arrives "fashionably" late the first day. An elephant hoses down the cast and crew. Joe wakes up: it was only a pleasant dream.

A Monkey Bell Hop: Released 11/28/1921. © Universal Film Mfg Co. 11/22/1921. Universal Jewel. 2 reels. Cast: Joe Martin. Director: Harry Burns.

"Just about as poor a comedy as it is possible to make. Not funny and at times disgusting. Martin is poorest of the monkey actors." (*Exhibitors Herald*, 10/07/1922, Ben L. Morris, Temple theatre, Bellaire, O.)

A Monkey Schoolmaster: Released 01/02/1922. © Universal Film Mfg Co. 12/31/1921. Universal Jewel. 2 reels. Cast: Joe Martin. Director, Story: Harry Burns.

School teacher Joe Martin tells his students of a cannibal island where he was king, but blown up by travelers who they earlier attempted to stew. After the story is recess, and Joe plays a drum during orchestra rehearsal. A wind storm blows a lion from the zoo into the school. After a terrific fight where Joe overpowers the lion, he wakes up to find it was a dream.

A White Wing Monkey: Released 01/07/1924. © Universal Pictures Corp. 01/04/1924. Universal Jewel. 1-reel. Cast: Joe Martin. Director: Harry Burns.

Jungletown street cleaner Joe Martin foils a pickpocket organ-grinder's theft. Later, a runaway baby carriage is headed towards some escaped lions, but Joe snatches the child away in the nick of time and returns it to its mother.

Down in Jungle Town: Released 01/28/1924. © Universal Pictures Corp. 01/16/1924. Universal Jewel. 1-reel. Cast: Joe Martin. Director: Harry Burns.

Enraged by the visit of his mother-in-law, a man shoots up the town, so Joe Martin and an elephant arrest him. An anarchist tries to blow up Joe, but ends up blown apart instead. A hungry bear chases a child, so Joe mounts the elephant, lassos the bear, and rescues the baby.

Possible Stern Brothers Productions

Sinbad the Sailor: Released 09/08/1919. © Universal Film Mfg Co. 08/26/1919. L-Ko Special; released as Universal Jewel. 1 reel. Cast: George Hupp, Raymond Lee, Zoe Rae. Director: Norman Dawn.

A boy (Lee) falls asleep while reading about Sinbad the sailor (Hupp), and dreams of himself in those adventures.

The Eternal Triangle: Released 11/10/1919. © Universal Film Mfg Co. 10/27/1919. Universal Jewel. Director: Norman Dawn. Story: James H. Finn

All-dog comedy: Bill Shepherd's wife Lisette attracts the attention of cad Reggie Van Airdale. She ends up running off with him when her husband's jealousy annoys her. Accompanied by the gossipy neighbors who had alerted him to his rival, Bill tracks down Reggie, who backs down when confronted. Reggie swears off women for life.

Endnotes

Introduction

[1] For whatever reason, the Sterns would change the spelling of some of their actors' and actresses' names, and rename others. For example, Edna Marion had her last name spelled as "Marian," Pete Gordon has his first name changed to "Eddie," Lillian Biron's last name was spelled "Byron," and Syd Saylor had his first name spelled "Sid."

Chapter 1: The Origins of L-Ko

[1] "All Century Comedies Must Be Absolutely Clean, Says Stern," *Moving Picture World*, November 26, 1921, p.400

[2] "Lehrman Starts Production Work," *Moving Picture World*, August 15, 1914, p.946

[3] One of Behrendt's less laudible moves while affiliated with L-Ko was to take pity of a fellow named George Kelly, a self-described "second-story man" who wished to go straight. Behrendt hired Kelly to work at L-Ko, but Kelly took advantage of his new position, made off with one of the company's automobiles, and used it to try to help some of his former pals break out of jail. He was caught and, instead of breaking others out of jail, landed back inside instead. ("He Went Straight—to Jail," *New York Morning Telegraph*, June 10, 1917, page unknown)

[4] Victor Heerman interviews by Kalton C. Lahue on February 21, 1969, and Sam Gill on July 22, 1967 and December 3, 1971.

[5] Heerman interviews by Kalton C. Lahue and Sam Gill

[6] "Fashion Note," *Los Angeles Times*, August 31, 1915, page unknown

[7] "Coast Picture News," *Variety*, August 17, 1917, p.22

[8] J.C Jessen, "In and Out of West Coast Studios," *Motion Picture News*, April 1, 1916, p.1894

[9] "Author Van Loan Gets One Hundred Dollars a Word," *Motion Picture News*, June 17, 1916, p.3762. Van Loan, in his autobiography *How I Did It* (Los Angeles: The Whittingham Press, 1922, p.112), claimed that he sold the title to Julius Stern for $250.

[10] "Henry Lehrman Sells Interest in L-Ko," *Motion Picture News*, July 22, 1916, p.410

[11] "Lehrman Returns to Coast," *Moving Picture World*, December 4, 1915, p.1811

Chapter 2: The Brothers Stern

[1] John Drinkwater, *The Life and Adventures of Carl Laemmle* (London: William Heinemann Ltd, 1931), pp.8, 20, 26

[2] Drinkwater, *The Life and Adventures of Carl Laemmle*, pp.41-49

[3] "List or Manifest of Alien Passengers for the U.S. Immigration Officer at Port of Arrival," S.S. *Kaiser Wilhelm II*, sailing from Bremen, Germany to New York, dated September 8, 1903.

[4] Susan Stern Sherman, *Remembering*, an unpublished memoir about life with her father Julius Stern, 1977, p.2

[5] Undated audio interview with Julius Stern, circa 1975

[6] Ibid.

[7] Sherman, *Remembering*, p.2. "The funny thing is," continued her memoir, "to my knowledge that particular uncle had no name other than the familiar S.O.B. title to which we were accustomed. There were other S.O.B.'s in Dad's life, but they all had names. For instance, 'For the first two terms, Roosevelt was all right. I voted for him, But after that, that anti-Semitic sonofabitch…' Or, 'Joseph Kennedy, that sonofabitch, tried to sell us out to Hitler.' And of course, 'That sonofabitch Harry Cohn is giving me trouble with the Columbia lease.' But whenever that sonofabitch was not identified by an accompanying name, we knew it was uncle." As for "spifs and pm.'s", "spif" stood for "sales performance incentive fund;" "p.m." remains a mystery.

[8] Undated audio interview with Julius Stern

[9] Drinkwater, *The Life and Adventures of Carl Laemmle*, pp.53-59. Terry Ramsaye, in his *A Million and One Nights* (New York: Simon and Schuster, Inc., 1925, pp.448-449), offers a slightly different account, saying that their initial thoughts were to open a small clothing store, given their collective experience in that line of business

[10] Drinkwater, *The Life and Adventures of Carl Laemmle*, p.59

[11] Undated audio interview with Julius Stern

[12] "Julius Stern, General Manager of the Imp Films Company," *The Implet*, January 27, 1912, p.2

[13] Undated audio interview with Julius Stern

[14] Ibid.

[15] Neal Gabler, *An Empire of Their Own* (New York: Anchor Books/Doubleday, 1988), p.54

[16] Drinkwater, *The Life and Adventures of Carl Laemmle*, pp.60-61

[17] "Julius Stern, General Manager of the Imp Films Company," p.2

[18] "Julius Stern," *Billboard*, December 26, 1908, p.11

[19] Julius Stern, "Reminiscences of a Studio Manager, Part 1," *Moving Picture World*, June 5, 1915, p.1591

[20] Drinkwater, *The Life and Adventures of Carl Laemmle*, p.62

[21] Undated audio interview with Julius Stern

[22] Sherman, *Remembering*, p.4

[23] Drinkwater, *The Life and Adventures of Carl Laemmle*, pp.72-77

[24] Gabler, *An Empire of Their Own*, p.61

[25] "Bright-Light Pictures Make a Hit at Poli's," *Moving Picture News*, February 11, 1911, p.10

[26] "Julius Inspects His 'Circuit'," *New York Clipper*, July 25, 1914, p.7

[27] "Petition for Naturalization" November 12, 1913

[28] Julius Stern, "Reminiscences of a Studio Manager, Part 2," *Moving Picture World*, June 12, 1915, p.1763

[29] "Wanted: Attractive Ingenue and Leading Lady," *Variety*, May 1, 1914, p.28

[30] "Imp Employees Check Big Blaze," *Moving Picture News*, September 9, 1911, p.23

[31] "Julius Stern Engaged," *Moving Picture News*, November 18, 1911, p.22

[32] Gabler, *An Empire of Their Own*, p.59

[33] Drinkwater, *The Life and Adventures of Carl Laemmle*, p.95

[34] Telegram from Carl Laemmle to Universal Vice President William H. Swanson, dated December 12, 1912

[35] "Stern Back from California," *Moving Picture World*, April 13, 1912, p.141

[36] "Accuse Universal Directors of Fraud," *Motography*, February 15, 1913, p.126

[37] "Universal European Company Home," *Moving Picture World*, November 15, 1913, p.720

[38] Ibid.

[39] "No Film Directors to Order," *Variety*, December 19, 1913, p.17

[40] Letter from Carl Laemmle to Julius Stern, dated March 30, 1915

[41] "$300,000 Film Fire in Colonial Hall," *New York Times*, May 14, 1914, p.4

[42] "List or Manifest of Alien Passengers for the United States Immigration Officer at Port of Arrival," S.S. *Kaiser Wilhelm*, September 20, 1910.

[43] "Chicago Letter," *Moving Picture News*, October 28, 1911, p.26

[44] "Chicago Letter," *Moving Picture News*, February 10, 1912, p.22

[45] List or Manifest of Alien Passengers for the United States Immigration Officer at Port of Arrival," September 10, 1912.

[46] Drinkwater, *The Life and Adventures of Carl Laemmle*, p.261

[47] "Lubin Trio Comes Over to Universal," *The Atlanta Constitution*, August 16, 1914, p.B8

[48] "Stern Supervising Victor Work," *Moving Picture World*, September 12, 1914, p.1488

[49] "Moving Scenario Department," *Moving Picture World*, September 12, 1914, p.1492

[50] Norbert Lusk, "I Love Actresses, Chapter III," *National Board of Review Magazine*, May 1946, p.13

51 Lusk, "I Love Actresses," p.44
52 "Universal Head Visits Riverside," *Riverside Daily Press*, July 12, 1915, p.4
53 "Universal Studio in East Vies with City in West," *Motion Picture News*, June 26, 1915, p.57
54 "Just to Make Talk," *Motion Picture News*, November 6, 1915, pp.73-74
55 "Hush! It Was Rush in Slush at 'U' from Snow Mush," *Motion Picture News*, January 8, 1916, p.52
56 Letter from Carl Laemmle to Julius Stern, March 30, 1915
57 Stern, "Reminiscences of a Studio Manager, Part 2," p.1764
58 "Film Flashes," *Variety*, August 13, 1915, p.16
59 Although not for long; Goldwyn Pictures Corporation, having outgrown its studio at the Solax plant, leased Universal's larger Fort Lee studios in early 1917. "Goldwyn Leases Studio," *Moving Picture World*, April 14, 1917, p.252
60 "Universal Concentrates in West," *Moving Picture World*, June 10, 1916, p.1862; "Removal of 'U' Studios to West Definitely Decided," *Motion Picture News*, June 10, 1916, p.3585
61 "Greater Number of Eastern 'U' Players Now in the West," *Motion Picture News*, June 24, 1916, p.3921
62 "Los Angeles Film Brevities," *Moving Picture World*, May 27, 1916, p.1517
63 "L-Ko Comedy Companies Greet Stern," *Motion Picture News*, July 15, 1916, p.241
64 Telegram from Julius Stern to Carl Laemmle, dated July 28, 1916.

Chapter 3: The Birth of Century Comedies

1 "Los Angeles Film Brevities," *Moving Picture World*, October 7, 1916, p.60
2 Telegram from Julius Stern to Abe Stern, 1916 (day and month unknown)
3 "Julius Stern," *Moving Picture World*, November 4, 1916, p.633
4 "Just to Make Talk," *Motion Picture News*, October 7, 1916, p.2212
5 "Close-Ups," *Photoplay*, September 1918, p.67
6 King Vidor, *A Tree is a Tree* (New York: Harcourt, Brace and Company, 1952), p.11. There are several variations to the wording of this quote, but this is the version that has gained the most traction over the years.
7 "Some L-Ko Announcements," *Moving Picture World*, May 19, 1917, p.1152
8 "Laemmle to Start New Film Company, Is Report," *New York Clipper*, October 14, 1916, p.32
9 "L-Ko Adopts Star System for Comedy Companies," *Motion Picture News*, December 15, 1917, p.4184
10 "J.G. Blystone and Alice Howell," *Moving Picture Weekly*, November 25, 1916, pp.4-5
11 According to Anthony Slide in his book *She Could Be Chaplin!* (Jackson: University Press of Mississippi, 2016). Other sources give May 5, 1888 as her birth date, and her grave stone in Forest Lawn Memorial Park states July 1, 1885.
12 Marjorie Howard, "Her Face is Your Fortune," *Moving Picture Weekly*, August 25, 1917, p.8
13 "Romance That Began in the City of Eau Claire," *The Eau Claire Ledger*, July 9, 1915, p.5
14 "Has a Quiet Job," *Motography*, June 16, 1917, p.1269
15 "L-Ko Announces Comedy Releases," *Motion Picture News*, January 13, 1917, p.277; "Activities of L-Ko," *Moving Picture World*, January 13, 1917, p.250
16 "Los Angeles Film Brevities," *Moving Picture World*, March 3, 1917, p.1366
17 "He's Not so Very Ill," *New York Morning Telegraph*, August 19, 1917, page unknown
18 "Fail to Pass Examinations," *New York Morning Telegraph*, August 19, 1917, page unknown
19 "New Brand of Comedies Ready," *Motography*, May 12, 1917, p.1004
20 "Brand New Comedy Series," *Motography*, May 19, 1917, p.1050
21 "Alice Howell Howls," *New York Morning Telegraph*, May 13, 1917, page unknown
22 "Alice Howell Pictures to Be Known as Century Comedies," *Motion Picture News*, May 26, 1917, p.3282
23 "Century Comedies Attract Buyers," *Moving Picture World*, May 19, 1917, p.1465
24 "Exhibitors Demand Comedies," *New York Morning Telegraph*, June 17, 1917, page unknown
25 "Showing of Century Comedies July 27," *Moving Picture World*, August 4, 1917, p.817
26 "Alice Howell Comedies for Showing on 27ᵗʰ," *Motion Picture News*, August 4, 1917, p.837
27 "Without Fear or Favor By An Old Exhibitor," *New York Dramatic Mirror*, August 11, 1917, page unknown
28 "Long Acre Will Market Centuries," *Moving Picture Weekly*, July 28, 1917, p.33
29 "Longacre Distributing Century Comedies," *Moving Picture Weekly*, August 18, 1917, p.38
30 By 1920 it was reported that approximately 75% of pre-release titles reported in the trades were working titles, and would be changed by the time of a film's release. "Quite frequently the unsuspecting story is given to understand from the beginning that it will not retain its cognomen forever, but just as frequently what is supposed to be a permanent appellation doesn't satisfy everybody who must be

satisfied on the question, and much argument follows." ("Recording Title Changes," *New York Morning Telegraph*, June 6, 1920, page unknown)

[31] "Alice Howell in Runaway Balloon," *Motion Picture News*, December 2, 1916, p.3461

[32] "Reviews of Current Productions," *Moving Picture World*, July 7, 1917, p.76

[33] "Comments on the Films," *Moving Picture World*, June 30, 1917, p.2120

[34] "Reviews of Current Productions," *Moving Picture World*, July 14, 1917, p.253

[35] "What the Picture Did for Me," *Motography*, January 5, 1918, p.4

[36] Joe Moore's tenure with Century came to an abrupt end when he was drafted and sent to training camp in September. ("Moore Drafted," *New York Morning Telegraph*, September 23, 1917, page unknown)

[37] "Los Angeles Film Brevities," *Moving Picture World*, April 7, 1917, p.80

[38] "Century Gossip," *Universal Weekly*, October 20, 1917, p.20

[39] "L-Ko Notes," *Moving Picture Weekly*, September 8, 1917, p.26

[40] "Brandt Gains Merited Promotion," *Motography*, January 19, 1918, p.1

[41] "Universal Combines All Its Exchanges," *Moving Picture Weekly*, May 25, 1918, p.10

[42] "Alice Howell Release To Be Issued Monthly," *Moving Picture World*, May 25, 1918, p.1165

[43] "Tribute to Fatty Voss," *New York Morning Telegraph*, May 6, 1917, page unknown

[44] "All Releases Postponed Four Weeks," *Moving Picture Weekly*, October 26, 1918, p.3

[45] "Jack Blystone Joins Henry Lehrman," *Motion Picture News*, December 21, 1918, p.3707

Chapter 4: Regrouping

[1] "Wanted: A Female Chaplin," *Motion Picture News*, May 18, 1918, p.2978

[2] "'The Geezer of Berlin' Will Be Released Soon," *Moving Picture World*, July 20, 1918, p.456

[3] "Reviews," *Exhibitors Herald and Motography*, August 24, 1918, p.26

[4] "Death of Mrs. Carl Laemmle Following Pneumonia Attack," *Moving Picture World*, January 25, 1919, p.453

[5] "He's In the Army Now," *New York Morning Telegraph*, November 18, 1917, page unknown

[6] Undated audio interview with Julius Stern

[7] "Century Comedies That Are in the Making," *Motion Picture News*, October 25, 1919, p.3169

[8] "Sifted from the Studios," *Motography*, June 3, 1916, p.1287

[9] "Century Lion Injures Trainer on Coast," *Motion Picture News*, April 17, 1920, p.3494

[10] "Pickups By the Staff," *Camera!*, May 14, 1921, p.7

[11] "Reviews and Advertising Aids," *Moving Picture World*, May 17, 1919, p.1077

[12] "Century and L-Ko Companies Expand," *Moving Picture World*, August 10, 1918, p.815

[13] "Vin Moore's Lion Comedies," *Camera! 1919 Yearbook*, p.71

[14] "Fred Fishback," *Camera! 1919 Yearbook*, p.66

[15] "Universal Monkey Hailed from Singapore; Was Venice Attraction at One Time," *Camera!*, January 26, 1924, p.9

[16] "They're Married Now," *Moving Picture Weekly*, December 27, 1919, p.5

[17] "Wild Lions and Loose Bandits," *Camera!*, August 16, 1919, p.3

[18] Burns was also a writer, responsible for the "Chit, Chat and Chatter" and "Assistant Directors' Association Notes" columns that appeared in *Camera!* magazine, and would later publish and edit *Hollywood filmograph*. He was an on again-off again actor as well, beginning in the mid-teens and, after a break during the 1920s, would resume his acting career in the 1930s, lasting up until his death in 1948. His wife was Dorothy Vernon, comedian Bobby Vernon's mother.

[19] "Burns Signs with Universal," *Camera!*, January 8, 1921, p.6

[20] "Harry Burns Completes First Joe Martin Comedy," *Camera!*, January 22, 1921, p.7

[21] "What the Picture Did for Me," *Exhibitors Herald*, October 7, 1922, p.78

[22] "Straight from the Shoulder Reports," *Moving Picture World*, March 4, 1922, p.78

[23] "Joe Martin's Popularity," *Moving Picture Weekly*, September 1, 1917, p.17

[24] "Movie Monk on Rampage," *Moving Picture Weekly*, September 13, 1919, p.1

[25] Diana Serra Cary, *What Ever Happened to Baby Peggy?* (New York: St. Martins Press. 1996), p.35

[26] "Veteran Screen Actor Injured By Ape," *Motion Picture News*, May 13, 1922, p.2692

[27] "Universal Moviegrams," *Universal Weekly*, January 26, 1924, p.11

[28] "Joe Martin, Noted Monkey, Deserts Screen for Circus," *Universal Weekly*, January 26, 1924, p.32

[29] "Los Angeles Film Brevities," *Moving Picture World*, October 23, 1915, p.605

[30] Lindsay Squier, "How Do They Do It," *Photoplay*, December 1919, p.30

[31] "Trainer Injured When Mad Elephant Charges," *Motion Picture News*, May 5, 1923, p.2152

[32] "Taps for Charlie," *Picture-Play Magazine*, January 1924, p.86

[33] Jimmy Starr, *Barefoot On Barbed Wire* (Lanham, MD: The Scarecrow Press, Inc., 2001), p.59

[34] Harry Hammond, "West Coast Theatres Acquires Number of New Houses," *Exhibitors Herald*, January 12, 1924, p.26

[35] Harry Hammond Beall, "Curly Stecker Dead," *Exhibitors Herald*, July 5, 1924, p.30

[36] "New Century Policy in the Fall Announced," *Motion Picture News*, July 5, 1919, p.353

[37] "First Paramount Comedy October 2," *Motography*, September 23, 1916, p.723

[38] "Rainbow Comedies," *Motion Picture News*, November 23, 1918, p.3014

[39] "L-Ko Changed to Century," *Moving Picture World*, July 19, 1919, p.363

[40] The number of shares would be further increased three years later to five thousand shares. (*Certificate of Increase of Capital Stock of L-Ko Motion Picture Kompany*, August 25, 1920; *Certificate of Increase of Capital Stock of Century Film Corporation*, April 23, 1923)

[41] "Stern Succeeds Powers as Universal Treasurer," *Motion Picture News*, May 1, 1920, p.3823. While Abe had "never held an official position with Universal," stated the article, "he has been closely allied with the big film company ever since its organization."

[42] *In the Matter of the Petition of L-Ko Motion Picture Kompany, a Corporation, for a Change of Name*, October 26, 1920

Chapter 5: The Serials and Other Distractions

[1] "Universal Eastern Forces Thinning," *Moving Picture World*, June 24, 1916, p.2244

[2] "Universal Quits Producing in the East This Week," *New York Clipper*, June 3, 1916, p.34

[3] "Abe Stern Marries," *Moving Picture World*, May 27, 1916, p.1517

[4] "Mr. Stern's Honeymoon," *New York Morning Telegraph*, May 14, 1916, page unknown

[5] "Report a New Producing Company," *Moving Picture World*, May 20, 1916, p.1372

[6] Cal York, "Plays and Players," *Photoplay Magazine*, July 1916, p.102

[7] "Sifted from the Studios," *Motography*, June 10, 1916, p.1347

[8] "Sifted from the Studios," *Motography*, June 17, 1916, p.1404

[9] "L-Ko Announces Comedy Releases," *Motion Picture News*, January 13, 1917, p.277

[10] "Lincoln Signs with Great Western," *Moving Picture World*, June 14, 1919, p.1636

[11] "Henry McRae Starts New Serial," *Moving Picture World*, March 3, 1919, p.1185

[12] "Elmo Lincoln Starts on a New Serial, 'Fighting Through'," *Motion Picture News*, December 6, 1919, p.4114

[13] "Elmo the Fearless" two-page ad, *Moving Picture Weekly*, January 31, 1920, pp.6-7

[14] "Start Crusoe Serial," *Moving Picture Weekly*, January 14, 1922, p.31

[15] As it turned out, Harry Myers eventually landed the lead.

[16] Telegram from Julius Stern to Abe Stern at 1600 Broadway, April 18, 1922

[17] "New Tarzan Serial on Market," *Motion Picture News*, June 18, 1921, p.3697; "Numa Pictures to State Right New 'Tarzan' Serial Featuring Lincoln," *Exhibitors Herald*, June 25, 1921, p.77

[18] "'Tarzan' Serial Complete," *Motion Picture News*, August 13, 1921, p.860

[19] "Hill Says 'Adventures of Tarzan' Is His Greatest Directorial Achievement," *Exhibitors Herald*, August 27, 1921, p.48

[20] "Tarzan's $5,000 Shave," *Variety*, March 31, 1922, p.6

[21] "Pacific Producing Co. Making a Serial," *Motion Picture News*, August 30, 1919, p.1831

[22] "Cuts and Flashes," *Wid's Daily*, October 27, 1919, p.2

[23] "Wanted Stories," *Wid's Daily*, March 20, 1920, p.4

[24] "Julius Stern Insists on 'Censor Proof' Comedies, *Exhibitors Trade Review*, November 26, 1921, p.1798. The actual Pacific Film Company was located in Culver City and was producing short comedies featuring George Ovey.

[25] "Negro Films Soon on the Market," *Los Angeles Times*, October 12, 1919, p.43

[26] "Injustice," AFI Catalog of Feature Films: The First 100 Years 1893-1993. https://catalog.afi.com/Film/2024-INJUSTICE?sid=35bec916-e4b7-411e-91d1-d4d853029e76&sr=1.8468649&cp=1&pos=0

[27] "Brief Theater Notes," *Motography*, September 8, 1917, p.536

[28] "Orpheum Company Adds To Theatres In Beloit," *Exhibitors Herald*, March 12, 1921, p.63

Chapter 6: Competing With Oneself (The 1919-1920 Season)

[1] "Rainbow Comedies Latest Addition to Universal's Brands," *Exhibitors Herald*, June 14, 1919, p.69

[2] "Abe of the Stern Brothers Returns East," *New York Morning Telegraph*, September 14, 1919, page unknown

[3] "Soon: Rainbow Comedies" full-page ad, *Moving Picture Weekly*, July 26, 1919, p.37

[4] J.C. Jessen, "In and Out of West Coast Studios," *Motion Picture News*, July 19, 1919, p.759

[5] Mae Laurel preceded Neilson, but given that she was still legally married to someone in her native Australia, Stan and Mae's relationship was that of a common-law couple.

[6] "New Pictures on the Screen," *Los Angeles Times*, July 13, 1919, p.41

[7] Cal York, "East and West," *Photoplay*, July 1925, p.45

[8] "Short Reels," *Film Daily*, January 18, 1920, p.32

[9] Bartine Burkett interview by Mark Jungheim in her Burbank, California apartment, November 28, 1984

[10] Gilbert Sherman correspondence with author, March 21, 2020

[11] Sam Gill correspondence with author, June 9, 2020

[12] "Harry Sweet an Acrobat as Well as All Around Player," *Exhibitors Trade Review*, February 4, 1922, p.674

[13] "Merta Sterling Laughs at Fate," *Moving Picture Weekly*, March 10, 1917, p.15

[14] "Many Stunts in Century Comedy," *Moving Picture World*, July 30, 1921, p.524

[15] "Reviews of Current Short Subjects," *Exhibitors Trade Review*, September 10, 1921, p.1035

[16] "Sennett Makes a Discovery," *Moving Picture World*, September 14, 1918, p.1596

[17] "What the Picture Did for Me," *Exhibitors Herald*, June 10, 1922, p.72

[18] Laurence Reid, "The Complete Plan Book," *Motion Picture News*, October 16, 1920, p.3075

[19] "Tuchman, Little Feller, Measures Up to Big U Job," *Motion Picture News*, October 30, 1915, p.56

[20] Julius Stern's 1908 *Petition for Naturalization*

[21] "6 Comebackers," *Variety*, May 27, 1942, p.3

[22] Not to be confused with the other, older Florence Lee (1888-1962), whose film career began in 1911 and lasted through the silent era.

[23] Harry Burns, "Chit, Chat and Chatter," *Camera!*, June 8, 1919, p.7

[24] "Edith Roberts Joins Fisback [sic] Organization, *New York Morning Telegraph*, April 27, 1919, page unknown

[25] "Jimmy Adams Will Direct Johnny Fox," *Motion Picture News*, June 17, 1922, p.3254

[26] "Reviews of Current Short Subjects," *Exhibitors Trade Review*, November 11, 1922, p.1523

[27] Cary, *What Ever Happened to Baby Peggy?*, pp.4-5

[28] "Director For Music Hall Star," *Los Angeles Times*, October 10, 1920, p.42

[29] Actor Edgar Washington (1898-1970), whose film career began in the late 1920s and lasted up until 1961 where he had an uncredited part in *The Hustler*. Edgar was occasionally billed under variations of his name, such as Blue Washington, Edgar Blue Washington, and Edgar Blue

[30] "Short Reels," *Film Daily*, March 21, 1920, p.28

[31] "News of the Film World," *Variety*, March 5, 1920, p.64

[32] "Among the Sunshine-Drama Factories," *Motography*, October 14, 1916, p.890; and *Motography*, September 8, 1917, p.504

[33] "Film Men Take Vacation," *Moving Picture World*, April 21, 1917, p.441

[34] "Hollywood Hokum," *Motion Picture News*, June 29, 1918, p.3920

[35] "Film Chief Gets Rest But Hides," *San Diego Union and Daily Bee*, January 17, 1916, p.5

[36] "Laemmle on Vacation," *New York Morning Telegraph*, August 24, 1919, page unknown

[37] "Looping the Loop in the Windy City," *Motion Picture News*, December 13, 1919, p.4245

[38] "Bon Voyage Dinner and Dance to Carl Laemmle and Abe Stern," *Moving Picture Weekly*, July 24, 1920, pp.20-21

[39] "Universal Comedies to Carry Only One Brand," *Exhibitors Herald*, May 22, 1920, p.63

[40] "Centuries Only," *Moving Picture Weekly*, June 12, 1920, p.4

Chapter 7: A Girl and Her Dog (The 1920-1921 Season)

[1] "Editorials: Sterns Return from Europe," *Moving Picture Weekly*, November 6, 1920, p.10

[2] "Some Short Reels," *Film Daily*, November 9, 1919, p.28

[3] "Most Popular Animal Actor in Films," *Moving Picture Weekly*, April 23, 1921, p.36

[4] "Screen Pets," *Blue Book of the Screen 1923*, 1924, p.324

[5] "New 'Brownie' Films Funnier Than Ever," *Moving Picture Weekly*, April 9, 1921, p.32

[6] "The Very Best Actor in the Movies," *Moving Picture Weekly*, June 18, 1921, pp.20-21

[7] "Great Day Dawns for Upper Dogs," *Los Angeles Times*, February 12, 1922, p.53

[8] "The Very Best Actor in the Movies," p.21

[9] Cary, *What Ever Happened to Baby Peggy?*, pp.6-8. Julius Stern, true to form, took credit for discovering Baby Peggy. In a widely circulated article titled "The True Story of How Baby Peggy Became a Star at the Age of Three," Stern claimed that Fishback was at wits end trying to find a tyke suitable to star with Brownie, and it was Stern to the rescue. "'Wait a minute,' said Stern. 'I just saw a baby go down

the street with its mother. The kid looked good to me.' And he ran out of the gate and down the road after a trim-figured young woman and a very young child." You get the idea. ("The True Story of How Baby Peggy Became a Star at the Age of Three," *Salinas Daily Index*, January 31, 1924, p.4) Regardless, it appears that Peggy had roles in at least two other films released several months before *Playmates*, and both directed by James Davis, *Her Circus Man* (March 2, 1921) and *On with the Show* (April 20, 1921), but these may have been filmed after *Playmates*. Cary says that the Sterns paid her the standard $5 per day, but that Fishback threw in an additional $2.50 per day when her father balked at the lesser amount. (p19)

[10] "Short Reels," *Film Daily*, May 1, 1921, p.20

[11] Cary, *What Ever Happened to Baby Peggy?*, p.20

[12] "Most Popular Animal Actor in Films," *Moving Picture Weekly*, April 23, 1921, p.36

[13] "Dog-Star Injured Making Century Comedy," *Motion Picture News*, August 27, 1921, p.1111

[14] "What the Picture Did for Me," *Exhibitors Herald*, October 14, 1922, p.82

[15] "Brownie to Show 'em How He Earns His $300 Per," *Exhibitors Trade Review*, May 13, 1922, p.1723

[16] "Brownie Is Ill," *Universal Weekly*, January 6, 1923, p.25

[17] "Brownie, 'The Wonder Dog'" full-page ad, *Camera!*, March 31, 1923, p.2

[18] "'Pal' Heads New Noel Smith Comedy," *Motion Picture News*, May 12, 1923, p.2302

[19] "Do You Like Them?," *Moving Picture Weekly*, November 27, 1920, p.34

[20] "Beauty and the Beast," *Moving Picture Weekly*, January 22, 1921, p.37

[21] "Century Comedy Company Changes Plans," *Moving Picture Weekly*, October 8, 1921, p.23

[22] "Carey to Make Universal-Jewel Pictures After Finishing Three Five-Reel Films," *Moving Picture World*, March 26, 1921, p.394

[23] "What the Picture Did for Me," *Exhibitors Herald*, September 30, 1922, p.74

[24] "'Century' Popularity Grows, *Moving Picture Weekly*, February 19, 1921, p.37

[25] Julius Stern, "Plans for Century's Eighth Anniversary," *Motion Picture News*, July 22, 1922, p.402

[26] "What the Picture Did for Me," *Exhibitors Herald*, September 30, 1922

[27] "Director and Dog Star Renew Contract," *Motion Picture News*, April 9, 1921, p.2478

[28] Mary Mae, "Reel Chatter," *Fort Wayne News and Sentinel*, May 15, 1921, page unknown

[29] "Julius Stern of Century Leaves U.S. for Three Months Tour of Europe," *Exhibitors Herald*, June 25, 1921, p.65

[30] "Century Comedies Plant Is Being Enlarged," *Motion Picture News*, July 23, 1921, p.574

[31] "Europe in Need of Comedies, Writes Stern," *Motion Picture News*, August 27, 1921, p.1101

Chapter 8: The Return of Henry Lehrman, Albeit a Brief One (The 1921-1922 Season)

[1] "Century Comedies Plan Six Producing Companies in West," *Exhibitors Herald*, September 10, 1921, p.69

[2] "New Century Comedy Star," *Motion Picture News*, October 1, 1921, p.1751

[3] "Baby Peggy in Cast of Neilan Production," *Motion Picture News*, February 25, 1922, p.1256

[4] "Sweet Renews Contract with Century Film," *Motion Picture News*, October 15, 1921, p.2015

[5] "Looking for New Director for Harry Sweet," *Motion Picture News*, October 29, 1921, p.2353

[6] "Arvid Gillstrom Will Direct Harry Sweet," *Motion Picture News*, December 10, 1921, p.3063

[7] "Baby Peggy Holds Record as Youngest Star Yet 'Loaned'," *Exhibitors Trade Review*, February 25, 1922, p.897

[8] "Universal Moviegrams," *Moving Picture Weekly*, March 4, 1922, p.10

[9] Diana Serra Cary, *Hollywood's Children*. (Boston: Houghton Mifflin Company, 1979), pp.110-111

[10] Cary, *What Ever Happened to Baby Peggy?*, p.43

[11] Kalton C. Lahue, *Bound and Gagged*. (New York: Castle Books, 1968), p.297

[12] "Louise Lorraine Signs for Three Century Comedies," *Moving Picture Weekly*, October 1, 1921, p.18

[13] Cary, *What Ever Happened to Baby Peggy?*, p.47

[14] "Goulding and Smith Celebrate," *Exhibitors Trade Review*, August 26, 1922, p.856

[15] "Lee Moran with Century," *Motion Picture News*, October 29, 1921, p.2312

[16] "Some Short Reels," *Film Daily*, January 15, 1922, p.19

[17] "Short Subject and Late Feature Reviews," *Motion Picture News*, January 21, 1922, p.640

[18] "Reviews of Current Short Subjects," *Exhibitors Trade Review*, March 11, 1922, p.1040

[19] "Lee Moran's New Century Comedies," *Moving Picture Weekly*, January 21, 1922, p.11

[20] "Jail Girls in Death Mystery," *Los Angeles Times*, October 10, 1921, p.II1

[21] "Of Acute Alcoholism," *Los Angeles Times*, October 13, 1921, p.II10

[22] Fishback's grand nephew, Jason Engle, provided an interesting anecdote about the Fishbacks. He wrote: "Fred's brother Harry, is Harry Fischbach the founder of Fischbach and Moore, an international elec-

trical company which at one point was the largest electrical firm in the nation, both private and public. Fischbach and Moore is also the same company that was at the center of the insider trading scandal of the late 1980's which brought the company down and as a result sent Ivan Boskey and Michael Milken to prison. I guess scandals found a way of involving Fischbach's." (Correspondence with the author, August 10, 1911)

23 "Jessen's Studio Notes By Wire," *Motion Picture News*, September 16, 1922, p.1382

24 "Sales Drive for Century," *Motion Picture News*, December 17, 1921, p.3224

25 "Hold 'Century Week' During Holidays," *Exhibitors Herald*, December 24, 1921, p.72

26 "Christmas Week-Century Week," *Exhibitors Trade Review*, December 24, 1921, p.249

27 "Big Returns from Holiday Drive of Century Comedies," *Exhibitors Trade Review*, February 4, 1922, p.674

28 "To Produce Independently," *Camera!*, January 28, 1922, p.17

29 "Some Short Reels," *Film Daily*, January 8, 1922, p.19

30 "Century's Sally is Now Queenie," *Exhibitors Trade Review*, April 29, 1922, p.1553. Curiously, Century had claimed in February that their new horse was owned by director Jess Robbins, and had been temporarily named "Jessie" in his honor. ("Century Comedy's Equine Star Is Ready to Be Seen," *Exhibitors Trade Review*, February 25, 1922, p.897). Named, perhaps after Abe's wife, who had just dragged Abe through divorce court hell?

31 For clarity's sake it should be noted that *Universal Weekly* and *Moving Picture Weekly* were both the same publication. Released weekly, it was provided to industry trade publications and exhibitors to promote current and upcoming studio releases. It was published under the *Universal Weekly* title through June 1915, after which it was changed to *Moving Picture Weekly*, a title it would retain for the next seven years. By June 1922 it had reverted back to the former title.

32 "Making Animal Comedies No Joke," *Universal Weekly*, September 9, 1922, p.30

33 Stuart Gibson, "Reviews of Latest Short Subject Releases," *Motion Picture News*, November 4, 1922, p.2316

34 "Demand Prompts Making of New Century Comedy Featuring All Animals," *Exhibitors Herald*, November 18, 1922, p.66

35 David N. Bruskin, *The White Brothers: Jack, Jules, & Sam White* (Metuchen, NJ: The Scarecrow Press, Inc., 1990), p.61

36 "True Blue," *Universal Weekly*, November 11, 1922, p.40

37 "New Directors Signed for Century Comedies," *Universal Weekly*, June 10, 1922, p.10

38 "Stern Engages Lehrman as Century Comedy Producer," *Exhibitors Trade Review*, February 25, 1922, p.897

39 "Pulse of the Studios," *Camera!*, April 15, 1922, p.10

40 Harry Burns, "Chit, Chat and Chatter About Southland Film Folks," *Camera!*, June 17, 1922, p.8

41 Burns, "Chit, Chat and Chatter About Southland Film Folks

42 "Minimum Rental is Promised By Stern," *Exhibitors Herald*, March 18, 1922, p.62

43 "Century-Universal Contract Renewed," *Exhibitors Trade* Review, May 13, 1922, p.1721

44 "Julius Stern May Take Lee Moran to England," *Exhibitors Trade Review*, May 13, 1922, p.1722

45 "Lee Moran and His Century Lineup," *Motion Picture News*, July 22, 1922, p.402

46 "Film Funmaker Accused By Wife," New York *Evening Telegram*, July 11, 1922, page unknown

47 "Lee Moran Starts Across Continent in Auto to Make Personal Appearances at Many Houses," *Universal Weekly*, August 18, 1922, p.23

48 "Pickups By the Staff," *Camera!*, September 23, 1922, p.7

49 "Century Bookings Gain," *Exhibitors Trade Review*, February 18, 1922, p.827

50 "Rotarians Visit Comedy Studios," *Los Angeles Times*, June 11, 1922, p.60

51 "Abe Stern in New York on Way to Europe," *Motion Picture News*, April 29, 1922, p.2460; "Abe Stern Sails for Europe," *Exhibitors Trade Review*, May 20, 1922, p.1805

52 "People," *Camera!*, June 24, 1922, p.18

Chapter 9: Julius Stern, Carl Laemmle, and the Ties That Bind

1 Letter from Julius Stern to Carl Laemmle, dated November 12, 1919. Laemmle was at the time vacationing at the French Lick Hotel in Indiana.

2 "Eddie Polo's New Contract," *New York Morning Telegraph*, February 8, 1920, page unknown.

3 Letter from Julius Stern to Carl Laemmle, dated November 12, 1919. Laemmle and P.A. Powers had taken over the theatre in early 1917, to "run Bluebird pictures exclusively" ("Universal Heads Buy Theatre," *New York Morning Telegraph*, March 25, 1917, page unknown)

4 "Laemmle Names Stern to Succeed Powers as Universal's Treasurer," *Exhibitors Herald*, May 8, 1920, p.51

5 "Three Men Govern Universal," *Motion Picture News*, June 5, 1920, p.4632

6 Letter from Carl Laemmle to Julius Stern, dated November 18, 1921

7 Undated audio interview with Julius Stern

8 "Laemmle Denies He Will Shakeup Coast," *Exhibitors Herald*, November 12, 1921, p.32

9 Ibid.

10 "Stern Now Chief at 'U' City, Thalberg Production Manager," *Exhibitors Herald*, November 19, 1921, p.43

11 Renee Beeman, "Live News of The West Coast," *Exhibitors Trade Review*, November 21, 1921, p.1797

12 "Julius Stern 2nd Vice-President of 'U'," *Motion Picture News*, November 26, 1921, p.2835

13 "The Harlequin Players," *Los Angeles Herald*, November 23, 1921, p.8

14 "Shake-Up at 'U'," *Los Angeles Herald*, November 21, 1921, p.B-8

15 Letter from Carl Laemmle to Julius Stern, dated November 18, 1921

16 Ibid.

17 Telegram from Carl Laemmle to Julius Stern, dated December 10, 1921

18 Harry Hammond Beall, "Tempting Bait Fails to Lure Producers from West Coast," *Exhibitors Herald*, December 24, 1921, p.102

19 "New General Manager Upsets Universal City," *Variety*, December 23, 1921, p.38

20 Letter from Julius Stern to Irving Thalberg, dated December 17, 1921

21 Ibid.

22 "Stern Goes to New York," *New York Morning Telegraph*, January 1, 1922, page unknown

23 "Thalberg Joins Mayer," *Camera!*, February 3, 1923, p.16

24 According to Thalberg biographer Samuel Marx, Thalberg's decision to leave Universal was prompted by his refusal to marry Laemmle's daughter Rosabelle, incurring his boss' wrath. Thalberg was making $400 per week at Universal when he left in 1923, his new job for Louis B. Mayer paying $600 per week. Within three short years Thalberg would be making $4,000 per week at M-G-M, with a minimum annual guarantee of $400,000. (Samuel Marx, *Mayer and Thalberg: The Make-Believe Saints*. New York: Random House, 1975, p.92)

25 "'Foolish Wives' Cut to Ten Reels," *Moving Picture Weekly*, January 28, 1922, p.11

26 Telegram from Carl Laemmle to Julius Stern, dated December 10, 1921

27 It was reported that Ripley received a $40,000 bonus for his tireless work in reducing the film to its shortened length, although this particular article stated that it was now sixteen reels rather than fourteen. ("'Foolish Wives' Completed In Coast to Coast Trip," *Exhibitors Herald*, December 17, 1921, p.38)

28 "Von Stroheim's 'Foolish Wives' Not So Foolish," *New York Tribune*, January 22, 1922, p.48

29 "Julius Stern's Dynamic Energy and Efficiency Speeds Editing of Universal's 'Foolish Wives'," *Moving Picture World*, January 14, 1922, p.175

30 "'Foolish Wives' Cut to Ten Reels," *Moving Picture Weekly*

31 By 1928, however, Universal decided that even further cuts were necessary for a revival; Editorial department head Maurice Pivar assigned the task to Ted Kent, an editor since 1922. This version never went into general release, but remained for subsequent non-theatrical releases.

32 Telegram from Carl Laemmle to Julius Stern, dated October 3, 1919

33 "Wife Sues Film Company Chief," *Los Angeles Times*, September 17, 1921, p.23

34 "Divorce Given Wife of L.A. Official of Film Firm," *Los Angeles Herald*, November 28, 1921, p.1

35 "Newsy Notes on Short Subjects," *Moving Picture World*, March 24, 1923, p.466; "Abe Stern Plans Home for Bride," *Los Angeles Times*, April 11, 1923, p.24

36 "Rosabelle Laemmle Made a Godmother," *Universal City Bulletin*, November 12, 1927, page unknown

37 *Interlocutory Judgment, Sylvia B. Stern, Plaintiff, against Julius Stern, Defendant*, dated March 26, 1921

38 It would be another year before the "Enoch Arden" bill was passed in 1922, expanding the grounds for divorce to include five years of desertion.

39 Sherman, *Remembering*, pp.5, 18

40 "Divorce Judge Favors Strict National Law," *New York Times*, February 24, 1923, p.6

41 "Stern Introduces Army Methods at Universal City," *Exhibitors Trade Review*, January 21, 1922, p.523

42 "Pictures," *Variety*, March 10, 1922, p.43

43 "Stars Leave Universal," *New York Morning Telegraph*, December 25, 1921, page unknown

44 Ibid.

45 "Universal City 'Shake-up' Denied By Julius Stern, Film Executive," *Moving Picture Weekly*, January 14, 1922, p.33

Chapter 10: From Filler to Focus (The 1922-1923 Season)

1 "Century-Universal Contract Renewed," *Exhibitors Trade Review*, May 13, 1922, p.1721

[2] "Clever French Clowns," *Melbourne Table Talk*, January 18, 1923, p.42

[3] "Blue Ribbon Winner Enlist as Canine Actor," *Motion Picture News*, October 7, 1922, p.1777

[4] New Talent Secured for Baby Peggy Comedies," *Motion Picture News*, October 7, 1922, p.1777

[5] "Julius Stern Outlines Future Plans," *Exhibitors Trade Review*, November 4, 1922, p.1466

[6] Ibid.

[7] "Abe Stern Making College Story with Many Pretty Girls," *Exhibitors Trade Review*, October 21, 1922, p.1353. It's possible that this film, which had the earlier working title of *The College Flapper*, ended up being released as *Pleasure Before Business* (February 14, 1923), which was advertised as starring Jack Cooper and the Century Beauties. This film had two distinct parts, the first set on stage with a burlesque company, and the second set at a college campus. One review commented on its "lack of cohesiveness," so it's possible that the Bonner and Williams film footage was cobbled together with more footage starring Jack Cooper and released as such.

[8] "'Universal Joy Week' Great Slogan,'" *Universal Weekly*, November 11, 1922, p.10

[9] "Universal Moviegrams," *Universal Weekly*, November 18, 1922, p.11

[10] "Universal Signs New Contract with Century," *Moving Picture Weekly*, May 13, 1922, p.17

[11] "Century Announces Season's Program," *Exhibitors Trade Review*, September 16, 1922, p.1060

[12] "Talang Working for Century," *Exhibitors Trade Review*, June 24, 1922, p.213

[13] "New Stages for Century," *Exhibitors Trade Review*," July 1, 1922, p.271

[14] "Sandrich Saga," *Motion Picture Herald*, January 1, 1941, p.51

[15] "Reviews of Current Short Subjects," *Exhibitors Trade Review*, May 29, 1922, p.1813

[16] "Reviews," *Exhibitors Herald*, November 4, 1922, p.61

[17] "Reviews of Current Short Subjects," *Exhibitors Trade Review*, October 28, 1922, p.1411

[18] "Some Short Reels," *Film Daily*, July 23, 1922, p.13

[19] "Reviews of Current Short Subjects," *Exhibitors Trade Review*, June 10, 1922, p.87; June 24, 1922, p.214; August 5, 1922, p.699

[20] "Full Particulars of Universal's Product for Coming Year," *Universal Weekly*, July 15, 1922, p.34

[21] "Baby Peggy Films Placed on Regular Universal Program," *Moving Picture World*, January 20, 1923, p.265

[22] "Senorita Baby Peggy," *Universal Weekly*, November 18, 1922, p.36. The San Gabriel Mission is cited as the filming location in "Six Baby Peggy Comedies Now Ready for Release," *Universal Weekly*, January 27, 1923, p.9, so it is unclear whether one of these locations is incorrect, or if filming took place at both

[23] "Baby Peggy Recovering from Serious Illness," *Motion Picture News*, December 2, 1922, p.2811

[24] "What the Picture Did for Me," *Exhibitors Herald*, June 21, 1924, p.76 (Roy W. Adams, Pastime theatre, Mason, Michigan)

[25] "Reviews," *Exhibitors Herald*, June 30, 1923, p.65

[26] Renee Beeman, "Live News of the West Coast," *Exhibitors Trade Review*, August 19, 1922, p.816

[27] "Plans for Century's Eighth Anniversary," *Motion Picture News*, July 22, 1922, p.402

[28] "Casting for 'Little Bo Peep'," *Universal Weekly*, August 26, 1922, p.15

[29] "200 Extras Lend Color to 'Jack and the Beanstalk'," *Universal Weekly*, July 29, 1922, p.37

[30] "Makes Unusual Sets for New Century Fairy Story," *Exhibitors Herald*, September 2, 1922, p.72

[31] "Century Film Corporation," *Exhibitors Herald*, January 27, 1923, p.62

[32] "Baby Peggy Films Placed On Regular Universal Program," *Moving Picture World*, January 20, 1923, p.265; "Baby Peggy Ill With Pneumonia," *Universal Weekly*, November 25, 1922, p.35

[33] "Red Riding Hood' Released As Special Two-Reeler by Century," *Moving Picture World*, December 5, 1925, p.459

[34] "What the Picture Did for Me," *Exhibitors Herald*, January 16, 1926, p.94 (C.H. Moulton, Bijou theatre, Beach, North Dakota)

[35] Cary, *What Ever Happened to Baby Peggy?*, p.63

[36] According to Earle's birth certificate, a facsimile of which was reproduced in the April 5, 1924 issue of *Universal Weekly*, p.36. Other sources vary, including Earle's biographer, nephew Andrew Erlich. (Andrew Erlich, *The Long Shadows: The Story of Jake Erlich* [Multicultural Publications, 2012])

[37] "Century to Produce 'Jack and the Beanstalk'," *Universal Weekly*, July 8, 1922, p.39. Other sources have Earle topping out at a towering eight feet, six and one-half inches.

[38] Diana Serra Cary says that Earle was discovered by director Fred Fishback, but I'll stick with the more detailed Erlich family lore regarding this.

[39] "The Pep of the Program," *Moving Picture World*, January 20, 1923, p.267

[40] "Reviews of Current Short Subjects," *Exhibitors Trade Review*, May 10, 1923, p.755

[41] "Engle Joins Century and Will Play in Herman Unit," *Exhibitors Trade Review*, February 17, 1923, p.610

[42] Roger Ferri, "Additional Short Subject Reviews," *Motion Picture News*, November 17, 1923, p.2384

[43] "The Pep of the Program," *Moving Picture World*, November 10, 1923, p.255

[44] "Harry McCoy Signs Long Term Contract," *Universal Weekly*, February 9, 1924, p.30

[45] "Short Subjects," *Film Daily*, February 10, 1924, p.8

[46] "Baby Peggy Company is Off for Yosemite," *Motion Picture News*, July 29, 1922, p.535

[47] "ASC On Parade," *American Cinematographer*, December 1942, p.518

[48] Erlich, *The Long Shadows: The Story of Jake Erlich*, p.527

[49] "Betty May to Star in Al Herman Comedy," *Motion Picture News*, September 30, 1922, p.1239

[50] "'Al' Series," *Variety*, December 22, 1922, p.39

[51] "Ring Lardner Feature Reaches Screen at Last," *Camera!*, August 11, 1923, p.11

[52] "Ena Gregory Signs New Contract With Century," *Exhibitors Herald*, December 2, 1922, p.66

[53] Phil M. Daly, "And That's That," *Film Daily*, October 14, 1927 p.10

[54] "Aubrey and Avery Directing Comedy," *Moving Picture World*, July 9, 1921, p.228

[55] "Fred Spencer to Star," *Camera!*, April 7, 1923, p.14

[56] *Moving Picture World*, July 14, 1923, p.173

[57] Fay Wray, *On the Other Hand* (New York: St. Martin's Press, 1989), p.50

[58] "Buddy Started Career in His Perambulator," *Universal Weekly*, February 9, 1924, p.30

[59] "One Regular Boy," *Universal Weekly*, February 24, 1923, p.17

[60] "'Buddy' Now With Century," *Universal Weekly*, November 18, 1922, p.36

[61] "Buddy Messinger Rising," *Universal Weekly*, December 9, 1922, p.6

[62] "Harry Edwards to Direct Messinger at Century Studios," *Exhibitors Trade Review*, December 2, 1922, p.25

[63] "English Beauty in Century Comedies," *Universal Weekly*, December 9, 1922, p.18

[64] "Reviews of Current Short Subjects," *Exhibitors Trade Review*, February 10, 1923, p.557

[65] "First Messinger of 1923 Will Be shown at Rialto," *Exhibitors Trade Review*, February 24, 1923, p.657

[66] "Gus Edwards' Protégé Back with Century Comedies," *Motion Picture News*, June 9, 1923, p.2775

[67] "Sadie Campbell Returns to Lot," *Universal Weekly*, May 17, 1924, p.28

[68] Wheeler Winston Dixon, *Cinema at the Margins* (New York: Anthem Press, 2013), p.63. This sort of seat-of-the-pants film construction might explain why some of the shorts' first and second reels have absolutely nothing to do with each other, seeming two disparate films.

[69] "Stern Bros. Appoint Production Manager," *Motion Picture News*, December 2, 1922, p.2812

[70] "Sterns Improving Studios," *Camera!*, December 30, 1922, p.13

[71] "Three More Companies for Century," *Moving Picture World*, December 23, 1922, p.779

[72] "Cartoonist and Writer Gag Man for Century," *Motion Picture News*, February 3, 1923, p.590

[73] "Short Subjects," *Film Daily*, July 25, 1925, p.12

[74] "Made Head of Century Script Building Department," *Exhibitors Trade Review*, February 2, 1924, p.29

[75] Diana Serra Cary, interviewed in Sacile, Italy, 2006. https://www.youtube.com/watch?v=44AHfafOKFU

[76] Renee Beeman, "Live News of the West Coast," *Exhibitors Trade Review*, February 10, 1923, p.558

[77] "Gorham Follies in Six Comedies," *Motion Picture News*, April 14, 1923, p.1815

[78] "Opinions On Current Short Subjects," *Motion Picture News*, September 1, 1923, p.1070

[79] "Bathing Girl Unit for Century Comedies," *Motion Picture News*, April 19, 1924, p.1798

[80] A group photo of the girls was identified as coming from both *Starving Beauties* in some trade magazines, and *Dancing Daisies* in others; the latter was the correct credit

[81] "Century Girls to Be Insured," *Exhibitors Trade Review*, September 1, 1923, p.610

[82] "To Insure Boy Star," *San Francisco Chronicle*, October 28, 1923, p.3

[83] "Joe Martin Soliloquizes," *Moving Picture Weekly*, July 5, 1919, p.29

[84] "First of Century's New Dog Comedy Series Under Way," *Motion Picture News*, September 1, 1923, p.1071

[85] "Filmdom Pets Back Home Again," *Los Angeles Times*, June 26, 1924, p.21

[86] Marjorie Perry La Force, "Who's Who and What's What," *Los Angeles Times*, June 29, 1924, p.60

[87] "Julius Stern Sails For Europe on Vacation," *Motion Picture News*, May 26, 1923, p.2545

[88] "Comedy Necessary to Successful Program," *Film Daily*, June 3, 1923, p.23

[89] "Century Plans Bungalows for All Directors," *Motion Picture News*, June 23, 1923, p.2954

[90] Cary, *Hollywood's Children*, p.78

[91] Cary, *What Ever Happened to Baby Peggy?*, pp.5, 26. Cary made another telling comment about the condition of the Sterns' lot, this one to film historian Sam Gill. According to Gill, Cary once told him "that the Century lot was such a dirty and filthy place, her parents decided early on they did not want to park their beautiful new car on such a dirty space, and would park about a half-block up Gower, right outside the Christie Studio." Even though it was a public street, Gill thought that Al and

Charles Christie might have had objections to their parking where the Christie personnel night need to park. Cary said that the Christies were okay with it. "Since the Christies had such old ties with Carl Laemmle and Universal," surmised Gill, "that may be one reason the Christies were so nice about that." (Sam Gill correspondence with author, August 20, 2020)

[92] *Certificate of Increase of the Capital Stock of Century Film Corporation*, July 19, 1923, pp.1-6
[93] "Stern Buys Ten Vehicles for Century Comedies," *Motion Picture News*, October 23, 1923, p.1767
[94] "Stern Brothers to Meet," *Moving Picture World*, September 29, 1923, p.403
[95] "Stern Brothers Planning Continental Tour," *Motion Picture News*, October 20, 1923, p.1881

Chapter 11: Too Many Cooks in the Kitchen (The 1923-1924 Season)

[1] "Short Subjects," *Exhibitors Herald*, September 8, 1923, p.83 (Charles Lee Hyde, Grand theatre, Pierre, South Dakota)
[2] "The Big Little Feature," *Exhibitors Trade Review*, April 5, 1924, p.29
[3] "What the Picture Did for Me," *Exhibitors Herald*, July 26, 1924, p.70. (M.J. Babin, Fairyland theatre, White Castle, Louisiana)
[4] "Many Return to Century Studio," *Exhibitors Trade Review*, July 28, 1923, p.382
[5] "Century Signs Dawn O'Day New Child Star," *Motion Picture News*, November 17, 1923, p.2360
[6] "Should 'System' Dominate Screen Art?," *Exhibitors Trade Review*, October 6, 1924, pp.836-837
[7] Ibid.
[8] Cary, *What Ever Happened to Baby Peggy?*, p.36
[9] "Inside Stuff: Pictures," *Variety*, October 10, 1928, p.44
[10] "Hollywood Rides Its Goats," *Picture-Play Magazine*, September 1930, p.109
[11] "Previews for Century," *Moving Picture World*, February 23, 1924, p.673
[12] "Century Announces Two Title Changes," *Universal Weekly*, March 29, 1924, p.38
[13] "How to Show Them: Opinions of the Important Producers and Distributors Relative to Projecting Shorts," *Film Daily*, September 14, 1924, p.17
[14] "Army and Navy Laud Centuries," *Universal Weekly*, March 29, 1924, p.38
[15] James Quirk, "Speaking of Pictures," *Photoplay*, March 1924, p.94
[16] "Luddy Starts Directing Initial Century Comedy," *Universal Weekly*, April 12, 1924, p.37. Leslie Goodwin would later become an established and respected director of both film and television, in a career that lasted into the late 1960s.
[17] "Gags Are What Make Wheels Go," *Los Angeles Times*, July 13, 1923, p.27
[18] "Lamont Gets New Century Comedy Unit," *Motion Picture News*, April 26, 1924, p.1910
[19] "The Pep of the Program," *Moving Picture World*, August 2, 1924, p.400
[20] "Who's Who With Lupino Lane: Charles Lamont," *Moving Picture World*, February 26, 1927, p.635
[21] Grace Kingsley, "Flashes," *Los Angeles Daily Times*, August 10, 1920, p.30
[22] "Mountain Party Gets Blame in Complaint for Filmland Divorce," *San Bernardino County Sun*, May 11, 1926, p.19
[23] "The Film Mart," *Exhibitors Herald*, October 13, 1923, p.61
[24] "Max Alexander Named Eastern Executive of Stern Film Corporation," *Exhibitors Herald*, December 24, 1927, p.51
[25] "Gus Edwards' Trio of Proteges Make Good in 2-Reelers," *Universal Weekly*, May 10, 1924, p.39
[26] "Farcical Wedding a Laugh Producer," *Houston Post*, June 13, 1917, p.7
[27] "Binney to Produce Comedies," *Motion Picture News*, May 4, 1918, p.2696
[28] James W. Dean, "'Man vs. Beast' is a Thrilling Drama of the Jungle," *Wausau Daily*, October 11, 1922, p.8
[29] "Gus Edwards' Trio of Proteges Make Good in 2-Reelers," *Universal Weekly*
[30] "Henry Murdock Signed By Century," *Motion Picture News*, April 28, 1923, p.2074
[31] Under "Comedy Caper About a Salesman, 1910s – Film 44402"
[32] "Actor Strangles," *Baltimore Sun*, September 30, 1928, p.56
[33] "Spec O'Donnell Signs Movie Contract," *Madera Mercury*, March 26, 1924, p.3
[34] "Short Subjects," *Film Daily*, April 13, 1924, p.12
[35] "Sadie Campbell Returns to Lot," *Universal Weekly*
[36] "Colored Comedy Child Is Signed by Century," *Motion Picture News*, April 12, 1924, p.1660
[37] "Studio Executives Rename Century's Colored Comedian," *Universal Weekly*, June 14, 1924, p.37
[38] "The Pep of the Program," *Moving Picture World*, August 30, 1924, p.734
[39] "Short Subjects," *Film Daily*, August 17, 1924, p.8
[40] "Valentinos Touring Country With Advertising Adjunct," *Variety*, March 29, 1923, p.5
[41] "Wanda Wiley Comes to Screen from Dental College," *Universal Weekly*, September 27, 1924, pp.14-15

[42] "Exposition Has Beauty Test," *Los Angeles Times*, July 1, 1923, p.25; "Ballots May Be Cast for Contract Contestants," *Los Angeles Evening Express*, July 19, 1923, p.14

[43] "Young Fairbanks Sees 15 Entrants Photographed," *Los Angeles Evening Times*, July 23, 1923, p.7

[44] "Wanda Wiley, Rudy's Choice With Century," *Universal Weekly*, May 17, 1924, p.28. "Rudolph Valentino chose her as the finest dancer, as well as one of the most beautiful girls, in the State of Texas," or at least according to this article.

[45] "Short Subjects," *Film Daily*, September 28, 1924, p.11

[46] "The Big Little Feature," *Exhibitors Trade Review*, October 11, 1924, p.37

[47] "The Big Little Feature," *Exhibitors Trade Review*, July 26, 1924, p.33. Curiously, many of the press releases and ads for Wanda's films spelled her first name as "Waunda."

[48] "Advance Date of Wiley Film," *Universal Weekly*, August 23, 1924, p.36

[49] "Producers Angle for Wanda Wiley," *Universal Weekly*, August 9, 1924, p.23

[50] "Century Official Returns to Coast," *Universal Weekly*, April 5, 1924, p.36. In her autobiography *Whatever Happened to Baby Peggy?*, Cary says that Laemmle paid her a staggering $10,000 per week for these three features. (p56)

[51] "Century Announces Fall Program," *Exhibitors Trade Review*, August 9, 1924, p.57

[52] "Abe Stern Takes Vacation Abroad Announcing New Production Plan," *Universal Weekly*, July 19, 1924, p.37

[53] "Julius Stern Goes Abroad," *Universal Weekly*, July 19, 1924, p.37

[54] Gabler, *An Empire of Their Own*, p.72

[55] "Stern Brothers in Carlsbad," *Universal Weekly*, August 2, 1924, p.35

Chapter 12: The Star Series Plan Redux (The 1924-1925 Season)

[1] "Fall Program Is Century's Biggest, Says Julius Stern," *Moving Picture World*, May 17, 1924, p.273

[2] "Universal Announces Release of 'Hysterical History Comedies'," *Universal Weekly*, March 29, 1924, p.17

[3] "Century Comedies" full-page ad, *Universal Weekly*, August 23, 1924, p.37

[4] "Julius Stern On Way to California," *Universal Weekly*, October 18, 1924, p.19

[5] "Stern Signs Wanda Wiley," *Moving Picture World*, November 15, 1924, p.256

[6] "Sales Manager Appointed for Century Comedies," *Universal Weekly*, November 8, 1924, p.25

[7] "Century Comedies Now Have Four Stars," *Universal Weekly*, December 6, 1924, p.26

[8] "Exhibitors Pleased with Four Star Series Plan of Century," *Moving Picture World*, January 24, 1925, p.381

[9] "Bluebird Photoplays," *Motion Picture World*, March 10, 1917, p.1550

[10] "Large Program is Planned for Century Films," *Los Angeles Times*, January 18, 1925, p.73

[11] "Jess Robbins Engaged to Direct Wanda Wiley," *Universal Weekly*, November 1, 1924, p.13

[12] "Five Units At Work in Century Studios," *Universal Weekly*, December 20, 1924, p.29

[13] "Four Companies Now at Work on Century Lot," *Universal Weekly*, January 24, 1925, p.29

[14] "Wanda Wiley's Horse Put Her in Hospital," *Universal Weekly*, September 13, 1924, p.15

[15] "Century Film Official Breaks an Arm in Fall," *Los Angeles Times*, April 4, 1925, p.67

[16] "Takes Up Fencing to Keep in Trim," *Universal Weekly*, January 3, 1925, p.27

[17] "Your Chance to Be a Movie Star!," *Mount Carmel Item*, June 3, 1925, p.7

[18] "Former Havre Girl Selected for Film Play," *Great Falls Tribune*, October 1, 1925, p.4

[19] Kenneth Taylor, "Mystery Fails to Mystify," *Los Angeles Times*, January 12, 1925, p.25

[20] "Wanda Wiley Injured in Accident," *Exhibitors Trade Review*, March 14, 1926, p.55; "Actress Is At Work Again After Accident," *Los Angeles Times*, March 15, 1925, p.72

[21] "Century to Make 'The Iron Pony'," *Universal Weekly*, April 4, 1925, p.22

[22] "Movie Monthly Editor Interviews Wanda Wiley," *Universal Weekly*, December 12, 1925, p.23

[23] Armandi's last name has appeared with the alternate spellings of Armanda and Armando, so the actual spelling of his birth name is in question

[24] Agnes Kerr Crawford, "Flashes from Frisco," *Camera!*, January 26, 1924, p.14

[25] "Century Signs Famous Acrobat," *Universal Weekly*, November 15, 1924, p.31; "Century's Acrobat Changes His Name," *Universal Weekly*, November 29, 1924, p.29

[26] "Century Comedies Now Have Four Stars," *Universal Weekly*

[27] "Is Found Guilty of Lesser Crime," *Quad City Times*, October 20, 1905, p.9; "Peter Armando to Penitentiary," *Quad City Times*, October 23, 1905, p.9; "Prisoners Taken to Penitentiary," *Quad City Times*, October 29, 1905, p.14

[28] "Physicians Astonished," *Pittsburgh Press*, July 22, 1917, p.4

[29] "The Pep of the Program," *Moving Picture World*, August 15, 1925, p.732

[30] "Century Reports Find in Eddie Gordon," *Universal Weekly*, February 14, 1925, p.33

[31] "Larry Rich Dead," *Film Daily*, August 7, 1935, p.2

[32] "Larry Rich Next At Golden Gate," *San Francisco Examiner*, April 18, 1928, p.15

[33] "Obituaries: Larry Rich," *Variety*, August 7, 1935, p.62. In her autobiography *Whatever Happened to Baby Peggy?*, Cary has fond memories of her interactions with Rich during her post-Century and -Sol Lesser days in vaudeville during the later 1920s. Rich took interest in the youngster and taught her a number of song and dance routines that she would add to her existing act, one of which included a crowd-pleasing imitation of Sir Harry Lauder (pp.90, 95-96)

[34] Edna Marian would be later billed as Edna Marion in her post-Century films

[35] "Puppy Love Series Different," *Freeport Journal-Standard*, May 6, 1924, p.13

[36] Ibid.

[37] "'Romeo' Wanted for Edna Marian," *Universal Weekly*, March 21, 1925, page unknown

[38] "Century Comedies Are of First Run Quality," *Universal Weekly*, January 21, 1925, p.25

[39] "Better Class of Actors Turning to Film Colony," *Los Angeles Times*, March 10, 1925, p.29

[40] "Short Subjects," *Film Daily*, April 25, 1926, p.12

[41] "Century Has $500,000 Budget," *Exhibitors Trade Review*, April 4, 1925, p.58

[42] "Big Outlay for Century," *Exhibitors Trade Review*, March 21, 1925, p.50

[43] "Century Plans Excellent Comedy Releases," *Motion Picture News*, June 6, 1925, p.2793

[44] "German Screen Builders Seek Wanda Wiley," *Oakland Tribune*, March 29, 1925, p.43

[45] "Petite Comedy Star Leaves to Visit Olde Home," *Los Angeles Times*, May 4, 1925, p.35

[46] "Century to Fete 11th Birthday," *Exhibitors Herald*, April 18, 1925, p.66

[47] Julius was a member of other fraternal societies and athletic clubs as well around this time, including the Two-Thirty-Three Club, whose membership was made up of individuals affiliated with the film industry; the Commercial Club of Southern California, boasting a membership of "leaders in the business and professional circles of Southern California"; the Breakers Club of Los Angeles, described as "Southern California's Finest Beach, Social and Athletic Club"; and the Hollywood Olympic Club, another athletic organization ("Personalities: Julius Stern," *Exhibitors Daily Review*, May 10, 1927, p.2

[48] "Century Chief Will Entertain Shrine Friends," *Los Angeles Times*, April 20, 1925, p.25

[49] "Century Establishes New Preview System," *Motion Picture News*, July 4, 1925, p.88

Chapter 13: The Planting of a Seed (The 1925-1926 Season)

[1] "Slapstick or Situation Comedies, Century Will Have Both," *Universal Weekly*, April 11, 1925, p.35

[2] "Century Announces Ambitions of Comedies for Next Season," *Moving Picture World*, May 9, 1925, p.208

[3] "Edison Will Film 'Buster Brown'," *Motion Picture News*, May 9, 1914, p.51

[4] "Film Flashes," *Variety*, April 16, 1915, p.18

[5] "Century Succeeds In Purchasing Film Rights to Buster Brown," *Universal Weekly*, November 8, 1924, p.14

[6] "Stern Brothers Get Right to Buster Brown Cartoons," *Exhibitors Herald*, December 30, 1922, p.130

[7] "Buster Brown Coming in Screen Comedies," *Universal Weekly*, May 9, 1925, p.31

[8] "Baby Film Hero Nearly Drowns," newspaper unknown, September 15, 1922, page unknown

[9] "Century Has Lengthy Program," *Motion Picture News*, May 2, 1925, p.1957

[10] "Here's Buster, Mary of Screen," *Los Angeles Times*, May 4, 1925, p.13

[11] "Barbara Jean Bennett, Scientifically Fed Child, Wins Express Best Babies Contest," *Los Angeles Evening Express*, November 24, 1920, p.10

[12] "The Big Little Feature," *Exhibitors Trade Review*, August 29, 1925, p.28

[13] "Opinions on Current Short Subjects," *Motion Picture News*, August 29, 1925, p.1047

[14] "The Pep of the Program," *Moving Picture World*, August 29, 1925, p.920

[15] "The Big Little Feature," *Exhibitors Trade Review*, August 29, 1925, p.28

[16] "The Pep of the Program," *Moving Picture World*, August 29, 1925, p.920

[17] Not everyone ewas happy about these trick shots inserted in an otherwise "live" film. According to one exhibitor complaining about *Buster Minds the Baby*, "Just as the other 283 Stern Bros. comedies I have played. Why won't they learn that fake photography cheapens a picture and never gets a laugh?" (*Exhibitors Herald and Moving Picture World*, October 27, 1928, p.65. J.S. Walker, Texas theatree, Grand Prairie, Texas)

[18] "Wide Range of Entertainment Embraced in New Short Subjects," *Film Daily*, August 22, 1926, p.11

[19] Along with Mary Astor, Dolores Costello, Joan Crawford, Sally O'Neil, Dolores Del Rio, Fay Wray, Janet Gaynor, Sally Long, Joyce Compton, Marceline Day, Mary Brian, and Vera Reynolds

[20] "Wanda Wiley, Ed [sic] Marion in Century," *The Eugene Guard*, May 7, 1925, p.17

[21] "Wampas Star Joins Freelance Ranks," *Los Angeles Times*, February 28, 1926, p.69

[22] H.E.N., "Happenings on the Pacific Coast," *Exhibitors Herald and Motography*, August 30, 1919, p.84

23 "Sennett Signs Meins," *Camera!*, August 4, 1922, p.6

24 Sol Best, Chicago, Illinois, as reprinted in *Universal Weekly*, December 12, 1925, p.37

25 "Third Annual Joy Week to Stimulate Business," *Universal Weekly*, December 12, 1925, p.13. Universal secured a tie-in with Buster Brown Hosiery to place a seven by thirteen inch window or counter display featuring the series' three stars in the company's 10,000 merchants' stores. In return, Century provided Universal's Exchanges with displays promoting the hosiery company, to be distributed to any exhibitor who wanted them. ("Hosiery Company Puts Out Buster Brown Tie-Up Cards," *Universal Weekly*, December 12, 1925, p.32)

26 "Strong Short Product Ready for Laugh Month," *Universal Weekly*, December 12, 1925, p.13

27 "Eight 'Buster Browns' Ready for Laugh Month," *Universal Weekly*, January 2, 1926, p.38

28 "Million Dollar Program Laid Out By Stern Brothers for 1926-27," *Universal Weekly*, May 15, 1926, p.18

29 "Sterns Announce New Comedy Policy," *Universal Weekly*, January 30, 1926, p.29

30 The corporation would be referred to as the Stern Bros. Film Corporation at various times as well, and may have been the true legal name

31 "Stern Bros. Announce New Comedy Policy; 'Century' Dropped From 1926-27 Product," *Moving Picture World*, January 23, 1926, p.340

32 "Stern Brothers Buy 'Newlyweds and Baby' Press Comic for Series," *Exhibitors Herald*, February 7, 1926, p.50

33 "McManus' 'Newlyweds' to Be Screened By Sterns for Universal Release," *Exhibitors Herald*, March 20, 1926, p.66

34 "'Let George Do It'," *Moving Picture World*, June 19, 1926, p.630

35 "Stern Brothers Sign Sid Saylor," *Moving Picture World*, April 10, 1926, p.454

36 "New Stern Brothers Comedy Series Has Hearty Reception At Colony," *Universal Weekly*, May 29, 1926, p.415

37 "Stern Brothers Comedy Production Far Advanced for Coming Season," *Universal Weekly*, July 10, 1926, p.24

38 "Wanda Wiley's Contract Ends," *Film Daily*, April 16, 1926, p.1

39 Louella O. Parsons, "Lillian Gish Not Worried By Any Shortage of Plays," *Tampa Tribune*, July 18, 1926, p.49

40 "Stern Brothers Sail for Vacations Abroad," *Universal Weekly*, July 10, 1926, p.24

41 "Carl Laemmle Definitely on Road to Recovery, Universal is Advised," *Motion Picture News*, July 24, 1926, p.302

42 "Landmark of Film Industry Lies in Smoking Ruins," *Los Angeles Times*, August 18, 1926, pp.19-20

43 "No Arson in Century Studio Blaze Say Officials," *Variety*, August 25, 1926, p.13

44 "Angry Mother is Sought as Blaze Razes Studio," *San Pedro News Pilot*, August 16, 1926, p.1

45 "Fire Razes Stern Bros. Hollywood Studio But Will Not Effect Release Schedule," *Universal Weekly*, September 4, 1926, p.17

46 Telegram from Sigmund Neufeld to Julius and Abe Stern in Paris, France, dated August 16, 1926

47 Gene Fowler, *Father Goose: The Story of Mack Sennett* (New York: Covici-Friede Publishers, 1934), pp.368-369

Chapter 14: Like a Phoenix Rising…. (The 1926-1927 Season)

1 "Stern Brothers Start Work in New Studio," *Universal Weekly*, October 2, 1926, p.23

2 "Good Luck Symbol Hangs High at Francis Ford Studio Celebration," *Camera!*, June 8, 1919, p.5

3 "Sanford Productions Presents Pete Morrison," *Motion Picture News*, May 27, 1922, p.2918. Coincidentally, former Century assistant director Al Alt served as assistant director on some of these as well.

4 "Samford [sic] Completes Second," *Exhibitors Trade Review*, June 10, 1922, p.91

5 "Sterns Returning," *Moving Picture World*, October 9, 1926, p.4

6 "Screen Trailers Made for Sterns' Comedies," *Exhibitors Herald*, September 11, 1916, p.45

7 "Contracts Since Sept'ber: Rubel," *Exhibitors Herald*, October 16, 1926, p.46

8 "Short Subjects," *Film Daily*, June 26, 1927, p.10

9 The survival of a number of the Buster Brown comedies is due in part to their recycling as segments of the *Mischief Makers* television series syndicated by National Telepix in 1960-61. For these, Buster became "Sparky," and the titles changed from the originals. For example, *Buster's Initiation* became *Sparky at School*, *Buster's Skyrocket* became *Sparky and the Tutor*, and *Buster's Bust-Up* became *Sparky Rides High*. Several other entries in the Buster Brown series were recycled as well.

10 "Stern Brothers Sign 'Snookums' to New Long Term Contract," *Moving Picture World*, January 22, 1927, p.279

[11] "Million Dollar Program Laid Out By Sterns for 1926-27," *Universal Weekly*, May 15, 1926, p.18

[12] "'Newlyweds' and 'Let George Do It' Creator Goes to Coast to Assist With Production," *Universal Weekly*, August 14, 1926, p.30

[13] "Opinions on Current Productions," *Motion Picture News*, June 19, 1926, p.2876

[14] Ibid

[15] "A Page of Synopses," *Universal Weekly*, February 12, 1927, p.40

[16] M.T. Andrews, "Opinions on Current Productions," *Motion Picture News*, June 26, 1926, p.2972

[17] "Vaudeville," *New York Clipper*, April 16, 1919, p.10

[18] "Jed Dooley," *Variety*, March 24, 1920, p.26

[19] "Frills and Fashions," *Variety*, February 11, 1921, p.7

[20] "23RD Street," *Variety*, March 4, 1921, p.20

[21] "Jed Dooley," *Variety*, December 30, 1925, p.9

[22] "'Mr. and Mrs. Newlywed' Signed for New Stern Brothers Series," *Universal Weekly*, April 3, 1926, p.31

[23] "Wants Slow Rise to Fame Says Ethlyne Williamson," *Atlanta Constitution*, July 2, 1927, p.8

[24] "Thrill Comedies the Latest Public Demand Says Sig. Newfield, Stern Studio Manager," *Universal Weekly*, February 4, 1928, p.26

[25] "Reviews of Little Pictures with a Big Punch," *Moving Picture World*, June 19, 1926, p.630

[26] "Reviews of New Short Subjects," *Film Daily*, April 10, 1927, p.7

[27] "What the Picture Did for Me," *Exhibitors Herald*, December 3, 1927, p.65

[28] "What the Picture Did for Me," *Exhibitors Herald*, October 29, 1927, p.56. Rand didn't mince words in his comments on other Stern films, asking this of *Snookums Disappears*: "Why does Carl Laemmle allow it? Why does Will Hays? Must our comedies be made for the smutty?" (October 29, 1927, p.56)

[29] "Six Comedy Releases During February Announced By the Stern Brothers," *Universal Weekly*, February 11, 1928, p.33

[30] "Back to Life to Tell of Assailants," *Oakland Tribune*, July 28, 1905, p.1; "Confesses to Murder," *Oakland Tribune*, August 3, 1905, pp.1-2

[31] "Percy Pembroke, Felon, Plans to Go on Stage," *San Francisco Call*, April 7, 1907, p.49

[32] "Olga Nethersole Asks the Governor for Pardon of Percy Pembroke, the Famous 'Boy Thug' in San Quentin," *Oakland Tribune*, January 10, 1910, p.2

[33] Percy Pembroke Draft *Registration Card*, dated June 5, 1917

[34] "Short Subjects," *Film Daily*, May 9, 1926, p.9

[35] "Short Subjects," *Film Daily*, September 26, 1926, p.13

[36] "What Happened to Jane," *Exhibitors Herald*, October 23, 1926, p.65

[37] "Short Subjects," *Film Daily*, July 17, 1927, p.9

[38] Paul Thompson, "Opinions on Current Productions," *Motion Picture News*, October 30, 1926, p.1682

[39] "$1,500,000 Production Budget Planned For Stern Brothers Comedies Next Year," *Universal Weekly*, October 23, 1926, p.26

[40] Julius Stern, "The Producer Must Do His Share," *Motion Picture News*, May 27, 1927, p.2073

[41] Ibid.

[42] "Sterns Buys Another Famous Cartoon Strip, 'Keeping Up With Joneses,' for 1927-28 Series," *Universal Weekly*, December 4, 1926, p.33

[43] "Meins, Maker of Buster Brown and newlyweds, Is to Direct 'Keeping Up With the Joneses'," *Universal Weekly*, February 26, 1927, p.19

[44] "Rube Goldberg's 'Mike and Ike' Cartoons Purchased by Sterns for 1927 Comedy Series," *Universal Weekly*, December 25, 1926, p.23

[45] "A Page of Synopses," *Universal Weekly*, December 4, 1926, p.40

[46] "Stern Bros. Generous 'Laugh Month' Proposal," *Moving Picture World*, January 8, 1927, p.128

[47] "Big New Stage Being Built by Stern Bros.," *Universal Weekly*, January 15, 1927, p.31

[48] "Reorganized Stern Bros. Studio Clicking 100% in Production," *Universal Weekly*, March 19, 1927, p.22

[49] "Fall Kills Carpenter," *Exhibitors Herald*, January 29, 1927, p.9

[50] This is based on speculation on the part of Julius's grandson, Gilbert Sherman, although it's very convincing speculation. Carl Sr.'s father's name was Julius as well, so an argument could be made that Junior was named after his grandfather. That seems unlikely, however, given that Carl Sr. eventually had his son's name legally changed in the mid-1920s; would he have done so if his son was named after his father?

[51] "Laemmle, Jr., to Make Debut As Producer," *Motion Picture News*, May 22, 1926, p.2458. One example of just how far Laemmle would go to promote his son to the rest of the industry occurred during an interview conducted in early 1928. Laemmle was asked which of his organization's productions had

given him the greatest satisfaction, and he provided two titles: *The Hunchback of Notre Dame* and *The Collegians* series! It's rather unlikely that anyone else would consider the latter of those two as one of Universal's top achievements to that date. (Adelaide E. Beckman, "Carl Laemmle, Picture Pioneer," *Universal Weekly*, February 4, 1928, pp.15, 40, in a reprint of the article appearing in *The Jewish Tribune*, date unknown)

52 Neal Gabler, *An Empire of Their Own*, p.73
53 "Carl Laemmle to Train Son in All Branches of Film Business," *Universal Weekly*, December 11, 1926, p.12
54 Gilbert Sherman phone conversation with author, June 26, 2019
55 "Housewarming Given," *Los Angeles Times*, February 27, 1927, p.57
56 "Stern Sees Changing Taste," *Motion Picture News*, April 29, 1927, p.1576
57 "Abe Stern Sails for Germany," *Film Daily*, June 23, 12927, p.2; "Sister of Stern Bros. Dies in Germany," *Motion Picture News*, July 1, 1927, p.2547
58 "Short Subjects," *Exhibitors Herald*, October 22, 1927, p.71
59 "Personnel of Studios: U.S. and Canada," *Film Daily Yearbook 1928*, pp.412-413

Chapter 15: The Ascendancy of Snookums (The 1927-1928 Season)
1 "Comedy Sales Chief Reports Increased Demand for Shorts," *Universal Weekly*, September 10, 1927, p.27
2 "Ethlyne Clair, 91, Silent Screen Star," *South Florida Sun Sentinel*, March 2, 1996, p.32
3 "Special Christmas 'Newlyweds' Issued by the Stern Brothers," *Moving Picture World*, October 29, 1927, p.554
4 "Big First Run Presentations," *Moving Picture World*, July 11, 1925, pp.154, 156
5 "Short Subjects," *Film Daily*, May 1, 1927, p.16
6 "New Series of 'Newlyweds' Started by Stern Brothers," *Universal Weekly*, April 7, 1928, p.15
7 "Snookums Recovers from Pneumonia," *Universal Weekly*, February 11, 1928, p.29
8 "Opinions On Pictures," *Motion Picture News*, September 1, 1928, p.737
9 "Thrill Comedies the Latest Public Demand Says Sig. Newfield, Stern Studio Manager," *Universal Weekly*, February 4, 1928, p.26
10 Ibid.
11 "Reviews of New Short Subjects," *Film Daily*, September 4, 1927, p.22
12 "Opinions on Pictures," *Motion Picture News*, March 31, 1928, p.1043
13 "What the Picture Did for Me," *Exhibitors Herald*, November 12, 1927, p.56
14 "Reviews of New Short Subjects," *Film Daily*, September 4, 1927, p.22
15 "Jean Doree Signed By Stern Bros. For Leads," *Moving Picture World*, September 24, 1927, p.221
16 "Short Subjects," *Film Daily*, October 30, 1927, p.13
17 Chester J. Smith, "Opinions on Current Productions," *Motion Picture News*, August 19, 1927, p.526
18 "Short Subjects," *Film Daily*, October 9, 1927, p.7
19 "Vaudevillian, Gene Laymon, Star of New Comedies," *Exhibitors Trade Review*, March 29, 1924, p.28
20 "72 Shorts from 'Sava'," *Film Daily*, May 9, 1926, p.1
21 "Harriett Mathews [sic] To Play 'Julie' in 'Joneses' Series," *Universal Weekly*, December 10, 1927, p.28

Chapter 16: Decided Make Our Own Comedies (The 1928-1929 Season)
1 "Five Stern Brothers Units in Work Soon," *Film Daily*, January 23, 1928, p.7
2 "Julius Stern Goes to Coast to Launch Comedy Production for Coming Season," *Universal Weekly*, January 28, 1928, p.40
3 "New Faces Mark Line-Up of Stern Brothers Comedies," *Universal Weekly*, June 9, 1928, p.22
4 "Buster Brown' Comedies," *Exhibitors Herald and Moving Picture World*, April 28, 1928, p.73
5 "New Faces Mark Line-Up of Stern Brothers Comedies"
6 George J. Reddy, "Opinions on Pictures," *Motion Picture News*, August 18, 1928, p.549
7 Ralph Wilk, "A Little from the Lots," *Film Daily*, January 3, 1928, p.1
8 "Vaudeville Reviews," *Variety*, October 22, 1924, p.33
9 Raymond Ganly, "Opinions on Pictures," *Motion Picture News*, September 9, 1928, p.994
10 Raymond Ganly, "Opinions on Pictures," *Motion Picture News*, March 30, 1929, p.988
11 George J. Reddy, "Opinions on Pictures," *Motion Picture News*, December 28, 1928, p.1766
12 Raymond Ganly, "Opinions on Pictures," *Motion Picture News*, October 13, 1928, p.1164
13 Raymond Ganly, "Opinions on Pictures," *Motion Picture News*, May 11, 1929, p.1646
14 "Mack Sennett Gives Young a Chance," *Moving Picture World*, August 21, 1926, p.489
15 "1-Reel Life Story for $297," *Variety*, September 26, 1928, p.10

16 "News of the Latest in Short Subjects," *Film Daily*, April 22, 1928, p.9

17 "Short Subjects," *Film Daily*, May 6, 1928, p.10

18 George J. Reddy, "Opinions on Pictures," *Motion Picture News*, September 1, 1928, p.737

19 "Opinions on Pictures," *Motion Picture News*, August 10, 1929, p.605

20 George J. Reddy, "Opinions on Pictures," *Motion Picture News*, February 9, 1929, p.436

21 Raymond Ganly, "Opinions on Pictures," *Motion Picture News*, May 11, 1929, p.1646

22 "What the Picture Did for Me," *Exhibitors Herald-World*, January 19, 1929, p.65

23 "New Faces Mark Line-Up of Stern Brothers Comedies," *Universal Weekly*, June 9, 1928, p.23

24 George J. Reddy, "Opinions on Pictures," *Motion Picture News*, March 16, 1929, p.846

25 George J. Reddy, "Opinions on Pictures," *Motion Picture News*, February 9, 1929, p.436

26 "What the Picture Did for Me," *Exhibitors Herald-World*, January 19, 1929, p.65 (Wolfe & Williams, Screenland theatre, Nevada, Ohio)

27 Raymond Ganly, "Opinions on Pictures," *Motion Picture News*, July 24, 1929, p.125

28 Several of the aforementioned exhibitor comments would clearly indicate that the quip "Our comedies are not to be laughed at" had become known industry-wide by this time, and was frequently bandied about.

29 Jerome McDuffie, Gary Piggrem, Steven E. Woodworth, *United States History* (Piscataway, New Jersey: Research and Education Association, 2004), p.159

30 Jerome McDuffie, Gary Piggrem, Steven E. Woodworth, *United States History*, p.157

31 "Inside Stuff: Pictures," *Variety*, September 5, 1928, p.24

32 The "Treat 'Em Rough" series, "The Real Dope" series, and the Jack Keefe series. ("Sterns Get Rights to 4 Story Series," *Exhibitors Herald and Moving Picture World*, November 24, 1928, p.39)

33 Telegram from Abe Stern to Julius Stern, dated December 24, 1925.

34 "Stern Buys Sound Film Rights to Lardner Tales," *Exhibitors Herald and Moving Picture World*, October 20, 1928, p.29; "'Al' Series With Talk," *Variety*, October 24, 1928, p.9

35 "Laemmle's Return Indef.," *Variety*, November 7, 1928, p.4

36 "Society of Cinemaland," *Los Angeles Times*, December 30, 1928, p.51

37 Telegram from Carl Laemmle, Hot Springs Ark, to Stern Pictures Corporation., 6048 Sunset Blvd, Hollywood Calif., dated February 16, 1929

38 "Not Renewing," *Film Daily*, February 26, 1929, p.1

39 "Laemmle Shuts Off Sterns," *Variety*, February 27, 1929, p.89

40 "Bombshell," *Film Daily*, March 3, 1929, p.12

41 "Cowdin Group Pays $5,500,000 Cash in 'U' Deal," *Film Daily*, March 16, 1936, p.1

42 Gilbert Sherman phone conversation with author, June 26, 2019

43 "Laemmle Shuts Off Sterns," *Variety*

Chapter 17: From Here to Eternity

1 According to some reports, *Outdoor Sports*, *Traffic Troubles*, and *Fellow Students* were released with sound.

2 "Universal Two-Reel Comedies," *Universal Weekly*, July 13, 1929, p.29

3 Raymond Ganly, "Opinions on Pictures," *Motion Picture News*, August 10, 1929, p.605

4 "Short Subjects," *Film Daily*, August 25, 1929, p.9

5 "Universal Two-Reel Comedies," p.28

6 "Sid Saylor Starts New Comedy Series," *Universal Weekly*, April 13, 1929; "Universal Moviegrams," *Universal Weekly*, April 20, 1929, p.8

7 Raymond Ganly, "Opinions on Pictures," *Motion Picture News*, October 5, 1929, p.1264

8 "Obituary," *Variety*, April 11, 1933, p.54

9 "Movie Director Held on Morals Charge," *Huntsville Times*, August 1, 1940, p.4; "Film Director Found Suicide," *Los Angeles Times*, August 5, 1940, p.7

10 Meins Estate Valued at $2000," *Los Angeles Times*, September 10, 1940, p.30

11 "National Film Takes Over Century Studios for Sound," *Variety*, April 3, 1929, p.7

12 "Trem Carr Filming First All-Dialogue Feature Production," *The Film Mercury*, June 14, 1929, p.1

13 "Alexander Brothers Planning to Produce," *Film Daily*, May 26, 1933, pp.1, 7

14 While the Alexanders were producers for PRC, rights for the "Keeping Up with the Joneses" comic strip were reacquired for use as the basis of a new series of feature comedies. It would appear that none of these were ever produced. (Ralph Wilk, "Hollywood Speaking," *Film Daily*, October 21, 1945, p.8)

15 "Changes in Names," *Variety*, November 6, 1929, p.42

16 "Where's J. and A.?," *Variety*, July 23, 1930, p.5. One recipient of Stern's loans was the director William Wyler, yet another relative of Laemmle's. A cancelled check for the amount of $150 remained among Stern's mementos up until his death. (Susan Stern Sherman, *Remembering*, p.5)

¹⁷ "Julius and Abe Stern Returning to Production," *Film Daily*, January 24, 1932, p.1; "Hollywood: Stern Resuming," *Variety*, February 23, 1932, p.41

¹⁸ Undated audio interview with Julius Stern

¹⁹ "Hollywood," *Variety*, January 10, 1933, p.27

²⁰ Undated audio interview with Julius Stern

²¹ "Stern Bros. Plan New Hollywood Blvd. House," *Boxoffice*, January 6, 1920, p.73; "Field Reports 143 Houses in Quarter," *Boxoffice*, January 6, 1940, p.21. As part of Julius's estate after his death, daughters Susan and Marie sold the property in the early 1990s.

²² "Abe, Julius Stern Here on Way Abroad," *Motion Picture Daily*, June 26, 1935, p.2

²³ Sherman, *Remembering*. P.6

²⁴ Julius Stern draft registration card, 1942. It lists him as self-employed by Stern Film Prod. Inc., 6040 Sunset Blvd, Hollywood, Calif.

²⁵ "Wedding Bells," *Film Daily*, December 14, 1942, p.3. Julius's daughter Marie questions just how "well known in New York social circles" Edith actually was, as she had been selling stockings at Macy's shortly before meeting Julius, and hated it.

²⁶ Sherman, *Remembering*. P.7

²⁷ "Wedding Bells," *Film Daily*, December 14, 1942, p.3

²⁸ Heman M. Purdy, Rockland County Clerk, New York, had issued a certification a mere ten days earlier referring to the Interlocutory Judgment of March 26, 1921, stating "that no order or direction of the Court in any way affecting said judgment , or application for such order or direction, has since been filed in this office." This suggests that Julius may have checked to see if that earlier decree was still in effect, and finding that it was made the decision to remarry in New Jersey. (Heman. M. Purdy certification, dated November 20, 1942)

²⁹ Julius had the opportunity to buy a nice brownstone across the street on 70th, but passed when he learned that the owner had committed suicide by throwing himself out the window. "He was superstitious," recalled his grandson, Gilbert Sherman

³⁰ Susan Stern Sherman, although actually Julius's step daughter, always referred to him as Dad. Similarly, Gilbert Sherman always refers to Julius as his grandfather since that was the role he played in Gilbert's life

³¹ Sol Title, "Titles in the News," *The Exhibitor*, December 30, 1942, p.4b

³² "Unaffiliated Plans Plea to Government," *Motion Picture Daily*, June 18, 1943, p.7

³³ "Majors Sales Policies Hit By Unaffiliated Exhibitors," *Showmen's Trade Review*, May 22, 1943, p.6

³⁴ "Neil Agnew Assures Indie Rental Relief," *Film Daily*, January 7, 1944, pp.1, 3

³⁵ Letter to Arnold Stern from Ira S. Karlstein of Zalkin, Rodin & Goodman, Counselors at Law, New York, NY, dated March 8, 1978; re Sternbros Motion Picture Enterprises, Inc.

³⁶ "Alexanders Prep Lardner Vidpix," *Variety*, March 5, 1952, p.29

³⁷ "Kirk and O'Herlihy Film Soon to Show," *Los Angeles Times*, April 2, 1957, p.42

³⁸ "Television Film Producer and Distributor Personalities," *The Radio Annual and Television Yearbook*, 1956, p.1085

³⁹ "Radio and Television Program Producers and Distributors," *Yearbook of Radio & Television*, 1964, p.675

⁴⁰ Gilbert Sherman phone conversation with author, June 26, 2019

⁴¹ Ibid.

⁴² Sherman, *Remembering*. p5

⁴³ Julius Stern, "Reminiscences of a Studio Manager, Part II," *Moving Picture World*, June 12, 1915, p.1763

⁴⁴ Jack Cohn, "Fourteenth Street," *The Film Daily*, February 28, 1926, p.57

Chapter 18: C'est La Vie

¹ Sherman, *Remembering*, p.1

Bibliography

Books:

Bruskin, David N. *The White Brothers: Jack, Jules, & Sam White*. Metuchen, New Jersey: The Directors Guild of America & The Scarecrow Press, Inc, 1990.

Cary, Diana Serra. *Hollywood's Children*. Boston: Houghton Mifflin Company, 1978.

——————. *What Ever Happened to Baby Peggy?* New York: St. Martin's Press, 1996.

Dixon, Wheeler Winston. *Cinema at the Margins*. New York: Anthem Press, 2013.

Doyle, Billy H. *The Ultimate Directory of the Silent Screen Performers*. Metuchen, NJ: The Scarecrow Press, Inc., 1995.

Drinkwater, John. *The Life and Adventures of Carl Laemmle*. London: William Heinemann Ltd, 1931.

Edmonds, I.G. *Big U: Universal in the Silent Days*. South Brunswick and New York: A.S. Barnes and Company, 1977.

Erlich, Andrew. *The Long Shadows: The Story of Jake Erlich*. Scottsdale Arizona: Multicultural Publications, 2012.

Fowler, Gene. *Father Goose*. New York: Covici-Friede Publishers, 1934.

Gabler, Neal. *An Empire of Their Own*. New York: Anchor Books/Doubleday, 1988.

Hirschhorn, Clive. *The Universal Story*. New York: Crown Publishers, Inc., 1983.

Kiehn, David. *Broncho Billy and the Essanay Film Company*. Berkeley, CA: Farwell Books, 2003.

Lahue, Kalton C. *Bound and Gagged: The Story of the Silent Serials*. New York: Castle Books, 1968.

——————. *Continued Next Week*. Norman, Oklahoma: University of Oklahoma Press, 1964.

Marx, Samuel. *Mayer and Thalberg: The Make-Believe Saints*. New York: Random House, 1975.

Massa, Steve. *Lame Brains & Lunatics*. Albany, GA: BearManor Media, 2013.

——————. *Slapstick Divas*. Albany, GA: BearManor Media, 2017.

McDuffie, Jerome, and Piggrem, Gary, and Woodworth, Steven E. *United States History*. Piscataway, New Jersey: Research and Education Association, 2004.

Ramsaye, Terry, *A Million and One Nights*. New York: Simon and Schuster, Inc., 1925.

Reeder, Thomas. *Mr. Suicide: Henry "Pathé" Lehrman and the Birth of Silent Comedy*. Albany, Georgia: BearManor Media, 2017.

Starr, Jimmy. *Barefoot on Barbed Wire*. Lanham, Maryland: The Scarecrow Press, Inc., 2001.

Stephens, E.J. and Wanamaker, Marc. *Early Poverty Row Studios*. Charleston, South Carolina: Arcadia Publishing, 2014.

Sherman, Susan Stern. *Remembering*. Unpublished, 1977.

Vidor, King. *A Tree is a Tree*. New York: Harcourt, Brace and Company, 1952.

Walker, Brent E. *Mack Sennett's Fun Factory*. Jefferson, NC: McFarland & Company, Inc, 2010.

Wray, Fay. *On the Other Hand: A Life Story*. New York: St. Martin's Press, 1989.

Articles:

Massa, Steve. "Edward I. Luddy: Forgotten Foot Soldier of Silent Comedy," *SlapStick!*, Spring 2006.

Stern, Julius. "Reminiscences of a Studio Manager, Part 1," *Moving Picture World*, June 5, 1915.

──────. "Reminiscences of a Studio Manager, Part 2," *Moving Picture World*, June 12, 1915.

Newspapers, Trade Publications, Periodicals:
American Cinematographer, 1942
Atlanta Constitution, 1927
Baltimore Sun, 1928
Billboard, 1908
Blue Book of the Screen, 1923
Boxoffice, 1920, 1940
Camera!, 1919-1924
Eau Claire Leader, 1915
Exhibitors Herald, 1919-1927
Exhibitors Herald-World, 1928-1929
Exhibitors Trade Review, 1921-1926
Film Daily, 1919-1929, 1933-1936, 1942-1945
Film Daily Yearbook, 1928
Fort Wayne News and Sentinel, 1921
Great Falls Tribune, 1925
Freeport Journal-Standard, 1924
Houston Post, 1917
Los Angeles Evening Express, 1920
Los Angeles Herald, 1921
Los Angeles Times, 1919-1928, 1940, 1957

Madera Mercury, 1924

Melbourne Table Talk, 1923

Motion Picture Daily, 1935, 1943

Motion Picture Herald, 1941

Motion Picture News, 1915-1929

Motion Picture World, 1917

Motography, 1913, 1916-1918

Mount Carmel Item, 1925

Moving Picture News, 1911-1912

Moving Picture Weekly (see *Universal Weekly*)

Moving Picture World, 1912-1927

National Board of Review Magazine, 1946

New York Clipper, 1914, 1916, 1919

New York Dramatic Mirror, 1917

New York Evening Telegram, 1922

New York Morning Telegraph, 1916-1917, 1920-1922

New York Times, 1914, 1923

New York Tribune, 1922

Oakland Tribune, 1905, 1910, 1925

Photoplay, 1916-1919

Picture-Play Magazine, 1924, 1930

Pittsburgh Press, 1917

Quad City Times, 1905

Riverside Daily Press, 1915

San Bernardino County Sun, 1926

San Diego Union and Daily Bee, 1916

San Francisco Call, 1907

San Francisco Chronicle, 1923

San Francisco Examiner, 1928

San Pedro News Pilot, 1926

Showmen's Trade Review, 1943

SlapStick!, 2007-2008

South Florida Sun Sentinel, 1996

The Atlanta Constitution, 1914

The Exhibitor, 1942

The Film Mercury, 1929

The Implet, 1912

The Jewish Tribune, date unknown

The Radio Annual and Television Yearbook, 1956

Universal City Bulletin, 1927

Universal Weekly/Moving Picture Weekly, 1916-1929
Variety, 1920-1935, 1942, 1952
Wausau Daily, 1922
Yearbook of Radio and Television, 1964

Audio/Video Interviews:
Jungheim, Mark. Bartine Burkett video interview, Burbank, California, November 28, 1984.
Interviewer unknown. Diana Serra Cary video interview, Sacile, Italy, 2006
Interviewer unknown. Julius Stern audio interview, New York, circa 1975.

Miscellaneous Sources:
AFI Catalog of Feature Films (afi.com)
Internet Archive (archive.org)
Lantern: Search, Visualize and Explore the Media History Digital Library (lantern. mediahist.org)
Library of Congress (chroniclingamerica.loc.gov)
Media History Digital Library and the University of Wisconsin-Madison Department of Communication Arts (mediahistoryproject.org)
Newspaper Archive (newspaperarchive.com)
Newspapers by Ancestry (newspapers.com)
Niles Essanay Film Museum (nilesfilmmuseum.com)
NitrateVille (nitrateville.com)
Old Fulton NY Post Cards (fultonhistory.com)
Silent Comedy Mafia Forum (silentcomedymafia.com)
Silent Comedy Watch Party (YouTube channel)
The Statue of Liberty—Ellis Island Foundation, Inc. (heritage.statueofliberty.org)

Index

101 Bison Film Company 315
Abbott and Costello 223
Absinthe 24
Académie Julian 349
Adair, Josephine 273
Adam and Eve a la Mode 93, 413
Adams, Ernie 200
Adams, Jimmie xiii-xix, 66-67, **69**, 104, 109, **110**, 156, 178
Adams, Stella 348, **349**, 350
Aden Film 351
Adventures of Jane series 284
Adventures of Prince Courageous, The 273
Adventures of Robinson Crusoe, The 79, **82**, 173
Adventures of Tarzan Serial Sales Corporation, The 81
Adventures of Tarzan, The 81, **83-84**, 50, 139, 315
African Lions and American Beauties 111, 411
After a Reputation 205, 472
After Her Millions 4
Agnew, Neil 387
Ain't Love Grand? 224, 468
Air Pockets 344
Al. G. Barnes Circus 73
Al's Troubles 228, 478
Alexander Brothers Studio 383
Alexander, Arthur **242**, 243, 382, 387
Alexander, Frank 226, 253
Alexander, Frieda 332
Alexander, Max **223**, 241, **242**, 243, **296**, 297, **298**, 330, 332-333, 352, 375, 382, 387, 390
Alexander, Sigmund 223, 243
Alice in Blunderland 188
Alice in Cartoonland series 365
Alice in Society 7, 40
Alice in the Big League 365
Alice in Wonderland 177, 188
Alice of the Sawdust 50, 405
Alice's Circus Daze 365

Alice's Medicine Show 365
Alice's Picnic 365
All for Geraldine 360, **361**, 511
All for the Dough Bag 95-96, 98, 102, 414
All for Uncle 345, **346**, 347, 497-498
All Jazzed Up 103
All Wet 379
Allied Distributing Corporation 226
Alma and Oliver (George McManus comic strip) 286
Alt, Alexander "Al" xx, 66, **208**, 219, **220**, 224-226, **227-228**, 239, 244-245, 247, 256, 264, 269, **270**, **280**
Alt-Howell Comedies 226-227
Ambassador Hotel 170, 384
Ambassador Pictures 382
Ambrosia Film Company 17, 58
American Film Manufacturing Company 192
American Mutoscope and Biograph Company 1
American Society of Cinematographers 343
American Vitagraph Company x-xi, 57, 90, 98, 121, 198, 219, 222, 229, 253, 282
An Account of a No-Account Count 224
An Empire of Their Own (Neal Gabler author) xxii
An Idle Roomer **137**, 433
An Oil Can Romeo 91, **115**, 116, 419
An Oriental Romeo 87, 91-92, 410
And George Did! 310, 312-313, 316, 487
Anderson, Gilbert M. 92
Anderson, Robert **222**
Andy Gump Comedies 180, 183, 244, 283, 332, 344
Anthony, William 287
Apartment Wanted 196, 438
Arbuckle, Roscoe "Fatty" xii, xix, 1, 55, 146-147, 224-225, 337
Archainbaud, George 309
Are Golfers Cuckoo? **350**, 351
Armandi, Pietro (see Gordon, Eddie) 252
Armando, Peter (see Gordon, Eddie) 255
Armstrong, Billy 3, 35, 39, 53, 55, 58, **59**
Around Corners 123, 125, 432

Arrow Comedies 133, 137, 264
Ash, Jerry 191, 194-195
Asher, Max xiii, xxii, 192, **251**
Asher, Roland 324, 333, 335, 342
Atkinson, Dr. Donald T. 291
Aubrey, Jimmy 198, 222
Automaniacs 45, **47-48**, 56, 405
A-Z of Silent Film Comedy (Glenn Mitchell author) xxii
Babe the Camel 74
Baby Doll Bandit, A 67, **68**, 110, 413
Baby Peggy xiii, xxi, 72-73, 109, 120, **121-123**, 126, 130,
        132, 135-137, **138**, 139-140, 147, 154, 156, 176-
        177, 180, 182, **186-189**, 190-191, **194**, 198, **199**,
        209-210, **213**, 215, **229**, **239**, **241**, 244-245, 273,
        302, 398, 401
Baby Peggy Special Universal Century Comedies 186
Baby Talks **362**, 380-381
Back to Earth 192, 450
Badmen of Thunder Gap 383
Bakery, The 179, 253
Balboa Feature Film Company 315
Balloon Bandits, The 47, 404
Balloonatics 45, **46**, 47, 56, 404
Balshofer, Fred 1
Bank, The 58
Bankruptcy of Boggs and Schultz, The 40
Banks, Monty **62**, 103, 198
Barbarous Plots 91
Barnett, Ida Ione 235
Barnyard Romance, A **92**, 412
Barry, Eddie **37**, **39**, 55, 58, **134**
Bate, Henry 333
Battle of the Century, The 316, 360
Bawled Out 53, 407
Be My Wife 318, 490
Beach Combers, The 79
Bears and Bad Men 253
Beat At His Own Game 393
Beaudine, Harold 380
Beaudine, William 150, 230
Becker, Frederick G. 273
Behind the Front 54, 119, 408
Behrendt, Sam 2, 4, 294
Belles of Liberty, The 91
Benjamin Franklin 243
Benny, Jack 392
Bergman, Henry 3, 35, 383
Berlin, Irving 128
Berman, Harry M. 161
Bernard, Hyman 216
Bernstein Film Productions 4
Bernstein, Isadore 2-4
Berry, James "Bubbles" 203, 224, **233**, 234-235
Berwilla Film Corp. 264
Better 'Ole, The 128
Betty series 137
Betty Sets the Pace 137
Betty's Green-Eyed Monster 137
Bevan, Billy 3, **10**, 65-66
Big City, The 344, 477
Big Game George 339-340, 373, 507
Big Game, The 221
Big Jim McLain 220
Big Noise, The 355
Big Pie Raid, The 366
Big V Riot Squad 253

Binney, Josh 224
Biograph (see American Mutoscope and Biograph
        Company)
Biron, Lillian (see also Byron, Lillian) 87, 107,
        108, 109, **114**, 116, **123**, **126**, 181, 404
Birth of a Nation, The 264
Birthday Tangle, A 106, 112, 419
Bishop of the Ozarks, The 356
Bison 101 Film Company (see 101 Bison Film
        Company)
Black Diamond Comedies 75
Blackton, J. Stuart 351
Blaisdell, Bill 228
Blind Husbands 168, **169**
Blind Men's Eyes 120
Blondeau Tavern 23
Blondeau, Marie 292
Blow Out, The 233, 462
Blue, Edgar (see Washington, Blue)
Bluebird Photoplays 54-55, 283
Blystone, John "Jack" 3, **7**, **10**, 35-36, **41**, 42-43, 50,
        56, 59, 61
Bokor, Edwin 386
Bokor, Susan Frances 386
Bonner, Joseph Adam 177, 216, **220**, 224, 229,
        240, **341**
Boob McNutt (Rube Goldberg comic strip) 325
Born, Sylvia 170
Bostock, Frank 64
Bouldon, Eddie 75
Bounding Gordons, The 252
Bowers, Charley 325
Bowes, Cliff xiii, 65, 115, 344
Boyhood Days 202, 444
Brand of Courage, The 344
Brandt, Joe 159
Braun, Maurice (see also Engle, Billy) 192
Brave Little Waldo 56
Bray Studios 235, 291, 366
Bray, J.R. 219
Bergerman, Stanley 375
Brenon, Herbert 24
Bretherton, Fred (see also Spencer, Fred) 198, 404
Bride 13 80
Bringing Up Buddy 202, **205**, 218, 451
Bringing Up Father (George McManus comic
        strip) 286
Broadway Beauties 226, 257, 465
Broadwell, Robert 83
Broncho Film Company xxiv, 64
Brother for Sale 381
Brown, Karl 129
Brownie the Dog 92, 95, 106, 109, 113, 116, **118**,
        119-120, **121**, 122, **123**, 124, **125-126**, 128,
        130, 132, **134**, 135, 140, 147, **151**, 154, 156,
        177, 181, **182**, 192, 198, 209, 271, 398
Brownie, the Peacemaker 92, 95, **96**, 119-120, 420
Brownie's Baby Doll 121, 140, 431
Brownie's Busy Day 98, 119, 414
Brownie's Doggone Tricks 95, 119, 411
Brownie's Little Venus 121, 132, 430
Brunette, Fritzi 25
Buckingham, Tom **114**, 127, **128-132**, 133-136,
        153, 179
Budding Youth 203, 231, 461
Buddy at the Bat 202, 449

Bull Thrower, The 95, 415
Bull's Eye Film Corporation 90, 109
Bumpers 253
Burkett, Bartine xvi, **39**, 55, **62**, 87, 95-96, **97**, 98, 140, **142**, 269, **329**
Burning Youth 379
Burns, Harry 70, **71**, 73, 109
Burns, Neal xiii, 53, 55, 57, **58**, 107
Burns, Sammy 43
Burston, Louis 120, 297
Busher, The 196
Busted Honeymoon, A 7, 40
Buster and the Dude 270
Buster Be Good 205, 276, 474
Buster Brown and His Dog Tige in a Series of Very Funny Pranks (Richard F. Outcault comic strip) 270
Buster Brown and the German Band 271
Buster Brown and the Treatment of Goats 271
Buster Brown Causes a Commotion 271
Buster Brown series 244, **271**, **273**, 282-283, **298**, 341, 354, 365, 372, 382, 404
Buster Brown, Tige and Their Creator, R.F. Outcault 271
Buster Brown's Education 271
Buster Minds the Baby 342, 365, 506
Buster Steps Out 342, **354**, 501
Buster, Come On! 342, 344, 496
Buster, Watch Tige 300, 484
Buster's Bust-Up 276, **277-278**, 313, 331, 398, 476
Buster's Dog to the Rescue 270
Buster's Home Life 342, 497
Buster's Initiation 300, 332, 494
Buster's Mix-Up 276, 279, 480
Buster's Narrow Escape 300, 485
Buster's Nose Dive 276-278, 398, 478
Buster's Orphan Party 279, 482
Buster's Skyrocket 276, 278, 331-332, 479
Buster's Sleigh Ride 300, 489
Buster's Spooks 368, **370-371**, 517
Busting Buster 372, 507
By George 310, **313**, 488
Byron, Lillian (see also Biron, Lillian) 109, 117, 404
Cabbage Queen, The 53-54, 95, 407
Cactus Kid, The 107
Cactus Nell 64
Cake Eater, The 98
Cameo Comedies 179-180, 219
Cameo the Dog 149-150
Camisole the Dog (see Cameo the Dog)
Campbell, Sadie **202-203**, 216, 230-231, **234**
Campbell, William S. 69-72
Camping Out 155
Cannibals and Carnivals 103
Canon, Maurice 216
Cantor, Eddie 392
Cap the Dog 176
Cap'n Kidd **173**
Capitol Comedies 120
Captain Suds 263, 269, 281, 476
Carey, Harry 163, **172**, 173-174
Carmen, Jr. 186, **187**, 188, 229, 450
Carr, Trem 382-383
Carver, Louise **226**, **267**

Cary, Diana Serra (see also Baby Peggy) xiii, 72-74, 98, 112, 121, 126, 138, 206, 211, 217-218, 404
Cavender, Glen **180**, 200
CBC Film Sales Corporation 90-91, 111, 159, 178, 227, 230
Century Beauties 177
Century Comedy Kids 203
Century Dogs 176
Century Film Corporation
Incorporation 75
Beginnings with Alice Howell 45-59
Longacre Distributing Company 45-46, 54-55, 61-62
Regrouping post-Howell 61-76
Paired with Rainbow Comedies 87-117
1920-21 Season: Brownie, Baby Peggy 119-134
1921-22 Season: Harry Sweet, Lee Moran 135-157
1922-23 Season: Jack Earle 175-213
1923-24 Season: Century Kids, Wanda Wiley 215-241
1924-25 Season: Star System 243-268
1925-26 Season: Buster Brown 269-295
Rebranding as Stern Brothers Comedies 284
Studio Fire 292-295
Century Follies Girls 207, 215, 237-238, 241, 244-245, 247
"Century Limited, The" (*Universal Weekly* column) 175
Century Lions 63, **100**, **102**, 112-113, 128
Century Week 147, 177
Century Wonder Dog (see Brownie)
Chadwick Pictures Corporation 293, 356
Champion Loser, A 99, 128, 416
Champion, The 112
Chaney, Lon 201
Change in Lovers, A 42
Chaperones 363, 516
Chaplin, Charles x, xii, xix, 1, 58, 61, 92, 112, 120, 150, 239, 309, 383
Chaplin, Syd 128
Charlie Gets a Job 92, 413
Charlie of the Orient (see also Hong, Chai) 91
Charlie the Elephant 73-74
Charlie the Hero 57, 75, 99
Chase, Charley 93, 232, **262**, 263, 382
Chasing Her Future 110, 410
Checking Out 221, 227, 458
Cheerful Charlie (George McManus comic strip) 286
Chester Comedies 69-70, 282
Chickie 309
Chief Cook, The 137
Child Needs a Mother, The 42, 56
Child Stealers of Paris, The 24
Choice Productions 298
Choo Choo Love 53, 58, 406
Christie, Al xix, 58, 133, 137, 309, 351
Christie Film Company 58, 109, 127, 133, 192, 228, 285, 293, 359
Christmas Cheer 381
Chums 121, 433
Cinema-Craft Productions 364
Circus Clowns 121, **122-123**, 124, 240, 432
City After Midnight 390
Clair, Ethlyne 285, 288, **304-306**, **308**, 309, **310-311**, 318, 321, **331**, 336, 343
Clear the Way 263, 468
Clever Comedies 298
Close Shaves 373, 516

Clown Princes and Court Jesters (Kalton Lahue and Sam Gill authors) xxi
Coburn, Dorothy 354, 359-360, **361**
Cochrane, Robert H. 14, **15**, 17, 23, **27**, **29**, 161
Cody, Lew 92
Cohn, Frances 388
Cohn, Harry 159
Cohn, Harvey 388
Cohn, Jack 393-394
Cohn, Irving 208
Cold Hearts and Hot Flames 42
Collegians series 327, **328**
Columbia Broadcasting System 374
Columbia Pictures Corporation 159, 316, 388, 393
Columbia University 180
Colvig, Pinto 205
Colvig, Vance de Bar "Pinto" (see Colvig, Pinto)
Comique Film Corporation 109
Conklin, Chester 107
Conklin, Heinie 107
Conley, Lige 109, **199**, 344
Connelly, Edward 72
Coo-Coo the Dog 50
Cooper, Jack xiii-xix, **191**, 192, 198, 207, 215-216
Corby, Francis 287, 300, 311, 313, 316-317, 320- 321, 324, 335, 342-344, **345**, 346-347, 354-355, 357-358, 363-364, 367
Corman, Roger 218
Country Kid, The 230
Cowboy Holiday 383
Cowboy Sheik, The 98
Cowdin, J. Cheever 377
Crooks and Crocodiles 56
Crosby, Bing 137
Cross Country Bunion Race, The 359, **360**, 373, 510
Crowd, The 365
Crowning the Count **254**, 255, 477
Crusaders Exhibiting Company 25
Cub Comedies 58
Cuckoo Comedies 224
Cullison, Webster 297-298
Cummings and Lee Comedy Co. 350
Cunard, Grace 77, 78
Cupid Trims His Lordship 351
Cupid vs. Art 53, 407
Cupid's Rival 137
Cupid's Uppercut 351
Cupid's Victory **287**, 288, 473
Cured 148-149, 440
Dad's Dollars and Dirty Doings 40, 95
Dainty Damsels and Bogus Counts 90, 410
Daly, Bob 24-25
Dancing Daisies 207, 227, 465
Dancing Fools, The 343, 345, 496
Dangerous Adventure, A 355
Dangerous Peach, A **228**, 467
Daniels, Thelma 288, 309, **311**, 318, **320**, 321, 343, 404
Dante, Joe 218
Dare Devil Daisy 280, 481
Daring Lions and Dizzy Lovers 111-112, 410
Dark Horse, A 115, 196, 436
Darling of New York, The 241
Darling, Constance 263, 265-266, **280**, 281, 316-317, **318**, 319, **331**
Darlington, Beth **253**, 255, **262-263**, 281
Darrell, Joe 363

Davis, H.O. 38-39, 77
Davis, James D. 57, 59, 87-89, **91**, 93, 116, 127, 178, 315
Dawn Express 383
Dawn, Charlotte 343
Dawn, Norman 404
Daytime Wives 356
Delivering the Goods 230, 458-459, 516
Democracy Film Co. 84
Dempsey, Jack 109
Desert's Price, The 280
Detective Dan Cupid 133
Devil's Pass Key, The 168
Dewing, Nathan (see Karr, Hilliard) 224
Dienstag, Minnie 20
Dillon, John Francis 129
Dintenfass, Mark 23, **27**, 224
Disney, Walt 365
Disordered Orderly, The 343, 498
Dixon, Wheeler 204
Dizzy Sights 359-360
Dog's Life, A 120
Dog-Gone Clever 106, 128, 416
Dogville Comedies 150
Don't Fall 137, 464
Don't Get Fresh 202, 448
Don't Scream 200, 451
Donlin, Mike 196
Dooley, Billy 285, 307, 366
Dooley, Ethel 307
Dooley, Jed 285, **304-308**, 309, **331**
Doran, Bob 66
Doree, Jean 343, 346
Dorety, Charles 65-66, 103, **105-106**, 107, **108**, 109-110, **115**, 116, **124**, **126**, 127-128, 135-136, 139, 198, 324, 342-343, **344**, 345, **346**, 348, 351, 354, 364
Double's Trouble, The 40
Douglas, Earle 344
Douglas, Marian 198
Down in Jungle Town **72**, 73, 521
Down to the Sea in Ships 207
Down to the Ship to See 207, 452
Dr. Pyckle and Mr. Pryde 315
Drinkwater, John xxii-xxiii
Dry Agent, The 109-110
DuBois, Lucille 216
Duffy, Jack **155**
Dukes, Addie Oakley (see also McPhail, Addie) 337
Dumb Bell, The 130-131, 433
Dunham, Phil 3, **34**, 35, 38-39, 53, 55, 87, 92, 95, **96**, 98, 103
Dunn, Bobby 244
E and R Jungle Film Company 69
Earl, Frank 216
Earle, Jack (see also Jacob Reuben Erlich) **190-191**, 192, **193**, 194-195, **214**, 215-216, 225, 239
Eaton, Doris **206**, 207, **208**, 343
Éclair Film Company 351
Eddie Lyon Comedies 133
Edison, Thomas A. 18, 270-271
Educating Buster 275-276, 473
Educational Film Exchange xix, 69, 95, 111, 127, 137, 179, 181, 192, 196, 274, 337

Edwards, Gus 187, 192, 202, 224, 226, 256
Edwards, Harry 3, 35, **178**, 202, 218, 221
Edwards, Neely 244
Egan, Jack 317, 337, **338**, **352**, 354-356, **357**, 358
Eldorado Film Company 253
Elmo the Fearless 79, **80**, 139
Elmo the Mighty 78
Elwyn, Marny 343
Emerald Motion Picture Company 59
Enemy, The 365
Engel, Gilbert 386
Engel, Joseph 23
Engel, Judy 386
Engel, Paul 386
Engle, Billy (see also Maurice Braun) 87, **92**, 93,
    94, 99, **113-114**, **182**, 192, **193**, 215-216
Enright, "Brick" 155
Erlich, Andrew 191
Erlich, Jacob Reuben (see Earle, Jack) **190**, 191
Escovar, Louise (see Lorraine, Louise) 138
Essanay Film Manufacturing Company 58, 92,
    112, 150, 271, 314
Evans, Audree 307
Evans, Roy 284
Excuse Maker series 280, 287, 300, 316-317, 321,
    323
F.B.O. (see Film Booking Offices of America)
Fairbanks, Douglas 198, 227
Fairbanks, Douglas, Jr. 237
Fairy Tale series 177, 188-189, 191
Family Secret, The 240-241
Famous Players-Lasky Corporation 282
Fare Enough (Century) 191, 321, 447
Fare Enough (Weiss Brothers) 360
Farley, Dot xix, 65-66
Farm Follies 192, 444
Fashion Follies 207, 452
Fat Little Rascal, The 103
Father Was a Loafer 40
Fatty's Fast Flivver 224
Fatty's Feature Fillum 56
Fatty's Frivolous Fiancee 224
Fealy, E. 24
Fearless Fools 225, 227, 459
Fellow Students 379
Fight and Win series 109
Fighting Seabees, The 220
Fighting Through 79
Film Booking Offices of America 99, 219, 226,
    274, 315, 336, 356
Finishing School 372, 515
Finishing Touch, The 360
Finlayson, Jimmy xiii, xxii, **43**, 52, **129**, **137**
Fireman Save My Child 139
First National Pictures 78, 128
Fish Stories **363**, 510
Fishback, Fred **63**, 64, 66-67, 87, 103, 110-112,
    120-122, 125, 127, 132, 135, 138, 141, 146-
    148, 150, 153, 179, 226, 344, **345**
Fistical Culture Comedies 291
Flaming Disc, The 79
Fleckles, Anna 18, 20, 330
Fleckles, Maurice 18, 20, 85
Flintstones, The 215
Flirt, The 201
Flirtation a La Carte 40

Flivver Vacation, A 207, **270**, 479
Florida Film Corporation 224
Flower Girl, The 239, 458
Flyer in Folly, A 218
Flying A 192
Flying Wheels **249-250**, 478
Foelker, Adam Herman (see Herman, Albert) 150
Foolish Lives 196, **197**, 440
Foolish Questions (Rube Goldberg comic strip) 325
Foolish Wives 166, **167**, 168, 196
Fools First 136
For Ladies Only 316
For the Love of Mike and Rosie **4**, 58
Forbes-Eppler, Susan Wiley xvi
Forbes, Henry 333
Forbidden Valley 351
Ford, Francis 77, **78**, 297
Forseck, Lesandro 236
Fortune, Louise (see Lorraine, Louise) 138, 404
Foul Ball 379
Four Horsemen of the Apocalypse, The 104
Fouret, Georges 245-246
Fowl Play 366
Fox Sunshine Comedies x-xii, 45, 59, 63-65, 93,
    98-99, 103, 105-106, 110, 130, 134, 150-151,
    153, 178-179, 192, 207, 282
Fox, Jessie **96**
Fox, Johnny **89**, 111, 140, 154, 177, 179, **180-181**,
    182, **185**, **188**
Foy, Bryan 243
France, Charles H. 271
Franey, William xii, 93, 115
Frankel, Dave 292, 333
Fred Fishback Productions 112
Fred Hibbard Productions 147, 179
French Leave 379
Fresh from the Farm **130**, 424
Fresh Kid, The 179, **180**, 184, 441
Freshman, The 177, 519
Frisky Lions and Wicked Husbands 65, 105, 408
Frohman Amusement Corp. 129
Full House, A 350, 506
Funny Fatty Filbert Comedies 224
Gabler, Neal xxii, 328
Gallant Gob, A 366
Game Hunter, The 155, 181, 445
Ganly, Raymond 357-359, 361, 370-371, 379, 381
Garcia, Billy 66
Garcia, Esther 237
Garmes, Lee 70
Gay, Charles 63-64, **65**, 82-83, 148
Gay's Lion Farm 217
Gee Whiz, Genevieve 98
Gee, Charles 120
Geezer of Berlin, The **62**, 96, 407-408
General Film Company 75
George Leaves Home 310, 492
George Runs Wild 316, 489
George Steps Out 339, 497
George the Winner 309, **311**, 344, 483
George's False Alarm 339, 373, 502
George's in Love 310, 486
George's Many Loves 316, 493
Gerdes, Emily 117, **191**, 274
Gertie's Gasoline Glide 42
Gertie's Joy Ride 42

Getting Buster's Goat 370, 518
Gibson, Hoot 107
Gill, Sam xvii, xxi
Gillespie, David 291
Gillstrom, Arvid E. **136**, 137, 153, 155-156, 178, 209, 218, 221, 245
Ginger Face 111, 184, 442
Gleason, Jackie 392
Godfrey, Rae **40**
Goldberg, Rube 324, **325**
Golden Bed, The 309
Golden West Photoplay Company 92
Goldstein, Emanuel H. 54, 161-162
Goldstone, Phil 382
Goldwyn Pictures 201
Golfing 121, 429
Golf-mania 192, 452
Good Little Brownie 103, 119, 414
Good Scout Buster 372, 507
Good Ship Rock'n'Rye 67, **69**, 110, 412
Good Skates 364, 518-519
Goodwin, Leslie 219, **220**
Gordon, Eddie **252-254**, 255-257, 263, 269-270, 404
Gordon, Pete (see Gordon, Eddie) 252, 404
Gore, Rosa **39**
Gorham Follies Girls 207, **208**
Gorham, Joseph K. 207
Gould, Charles 333
Goulding, Alf xiii, 75, 135, 139, **140**, 141, 148, 153, 156, 177-178, 186, 188, 194, 204, 218, 240
Grand Asher Pictures 221
Grand National Pictures 383
Grant, Edith Lee 216
Great Radium Mystery, The 83, 85
Great Smash, The 7, 40
Great Western Producing Company 78-79, **80**, 81, **84**, 163
Gregory, Edna 95, **101**, 102, 115, 117, 198
Gregory, Ena **89**, 115, 130, 140, **180**, **185**, **196-198**
Gribbon, Eddie 374
Gribbon, Harry 3
Griffith, D.W. 129, 264
Griffith, Julia **288-289**, **352**
Griffith, Raymond 3
Grimm, Ben H. 47-48
Grocery Clerk, The 253
Gross, Harry 223
Gump Family Comedies 180, 183, 244, 283, 332, 344
Hackett, Lillian 216
Hairbreadth Harry Comedies 219
Half-Back Buster 370, 508-509
Hall Room Boys Comedies 90, 109
Hamberg, Alfred P. 2, 4
Hamilton, Gilbert 129
Hanam, Edna (see Marian, Edna) 256, **258**
Handcuffed 383
Hanford, Ray 62
Hank Mann Company 297
Hannaford, Poodles 360
Hansel and Gretel **188**, 189, 194, 453
Hardwick, Lois 354, **365**, 367-368, 370
Hardy, Oliver 360
Harem Follies 207, **208**, 465
Harman, Eve 333
Harold Teen 355
Hasbrouck, Olive 244

Haunted Heiress, A 280, 480
Haviland, Walter 251
Hayes, Tony 264, **319**
Hazards of Helen, The 314
He Loved Like He Lied 93, **94**, 417
Hearst, William Randolph 272, 286
Hee! Haw! 180, 273, 444
Heerman, Victor 5-6, 35
Hello, Judge! 196, 442
Hello, Mars 140, 184, **185**, 439
Hellzapoppin 218
Helpful Al 228, 269, 477
He-Male Vamp, A 99, 103, 418
Henderson, Jack **131**, 216
Henkel, Charles V. 23
Henley, Consuela "Connie" 87, **107-108**, 404
Henry Lehrman Comedies 95, 105, 109, 151, 195
Henry, Gale xix, xxi, 40, 98, 218
Her Ambition 269, 483
Her Bareback Career 50, 405
Her City Sport 221, 226, 237, 461
Her Daily Dozen 257, 466
Her Lucky Leap 250, **251**, 477
Her Movie Madness 218
Her Naughty Eyes 40
Her Unmarried Life 51, 55, 406
Herbel, H.M. 245, 268-269
Here He Comes (Century) 273, 464
Here He Comes (Sierra Pictures) 344
Herman, Albert 148-151, **152**, 155-156, 178-180, 205, 209, 218, 222, 234, 245-246, 315, 321, 383
Hey Doctor! 53-54, 58, 406
Hibbard, Fred (see also Fishback, Fred) 122, 125, 147-148, 179
Hicks, Tommy 203, **205**, 234, **270**
Hickville's Romeo 151, 440
High Flyin' George **339**, 500
High Kickers 207, 450
High Life 140, 430
High Sign, The 96
Hill, Ouida (see also Daniels, Thelma) 309, **311**, 404
Hill, Robert F. 79, 82, 344
His Bachelor Daddy 381
His Bitter Pill 64
His First Degree **225**, 226, 466
His Girl Friday 280
His Marriage Wow 316
His Musical Sneeze 105
His Nobs the Duke 351
His Temper-Mental Mother-In-Law 40
Hit 'Em Hard **214**, 215-216, 225, 456
Hold 'Er Cowboy 360
Hold On 192, 321, 448, 450
Hold Your Breath 103, **106**, 430
Hold Your Horses 364, 372, 512
Holderness, Fay 117
Holding His Own 360
Holiday Inn 180
Hollywood Boulevard 218
Hollywood Bound 221
Hollywood Photoplay Productions 252
Hollywood's Children (Diana Serra Cary author) 138
Holmes, Leon 279

Home Made Movies 282
Honeymooning with Ma 265, 316, 480
Hong, Chai 57, 65, 75, 87, 91, **92**, 93, 120, 140, **141**
Hoot Toot 53, 407
Horse Sense 148, **149**, 434
Horse Tears 148, **150**, 438
Horsley, David 23, 64, 132
Hotaling, Arthur 62
How Stars Are Made 40
Howard, Marjorie 42
Howe, Jay A. "Kitty" 35, 43, **88**, 95, 98
Howell, Alice xii, xx-xxi, 3, **5**, 6-7, 35, **36**, 40, **41**, 42, **43**, 44, 47-48, **50-54**, 55-59, 61, 63, 98, 119, 208, 244
Howell, Helen 226, **227**
Howell, Yvonne 208
Howl Comedies 43-44
Howling Lions and Circus Queens 65, 409
Howling Success, A 126, 182, 192, 445
Hughes, Donald **202**, **234**
Hula Hula Hughie 57, 91
Hungry Lions in a Hospital 63, 106, 110
Huns and Hyphens 253
Husbands Won't Tell 363, 508
Hutchinson, Craig 4, 35, 43
Hutton, Lucille 3, **10**, 38, **226**
Hyer, William 274
Hyman, Bynunsky **267**, **280**
Hysterical History Comedies 243
I Can't Escape 383
I Do 182
I Never Thought of That (Rube Goldberg comic strip) 325
Illinois Exhibiting Company 25-26
IMP (see Independent Motion Picture Company) xxii, 1, 17, **19**, 20, 21, 23-24, **27**
Imperfect Lover, The 126, 448
In Bad All Around 103, 106
In Dutch 52, **53**, 54, **57-58**, 59, 406
Ince, Thomas 64, 330
Independent Motion Picture Company 19
Indiscreet Corrine 129
Indoor Golf 350, 502
Ingram, Rex 72, 79
Injustice 84
Inslee, Charles **4**, 38, 82
International Crime 383
Inventors, The 351
Irving, William 54-55, **94**, 121, 216
Itala film company 17
Itching for Revenge **254**, 255, 469
Ivanhoe 24
Jack and the Beanstalk 188-189, 191, 194, 460
Jack the Parrot 152
Jackson, Grant 75
Jacobs, Jessie 31, 77, 116, 168-169
Jacobs, Louis 31, 37, 75, 77, 81, 85, 169
Jacobs, Oscar 81, 83
Jacobs, Paul 55
Jail Breaker, The 93, 403, 409
Jameison, Bud (see Jamison, William Edward "Bud") 112
Jamison, William Edward "Bud" xiii, 66, 107, 112, **113-115**, 116, 123, **124**, **126**, 127-128, **130-131**, **137**, **156**, 318-319

Jane's Engagement Party **319**, 321, 486
Jane's Flirtation **320**, 321, 488
Jane's Inheritance 321, 344, 484
Jane's Predicament 321, 487
Jane's Troubles 321, 485
Jazz Monkey, The 69, 520
Jenkins, Herbert 111
Jerry the Dog 343, 354, **365-366**, 367, **369**, 370
Jessel, George 392
Jewel Productions (see Universal-Jewel)
Jiggs the Chimpanzee 73
Jivaro 220
"Joe Martin Soliloquizes" (*Universal Weekly* column) 209
Joe Martin Turns 'Em Loose 66
Joe the Monkey 150
Joker Comedies 42, 95, 192, 394
Joseph, Billy 66
Jossenberger, Laurence Richardson (see Richardson, Larry) 256
Joy Riders, The 95
Judge magazine 282
Julian, Rupert 168
Jungle Gentleman, A 66, 110, 408
Junior Jewel Productions (see Universal-Junior Jewel)
Just an Echo 137
Just Dogs 150, 442
Juvenile Comedies 235
Kaiser, the Beast of Berlin, The 62, 408
Kalem Company 95, 103, 137, 178, 228, 314
Kann, George E. 351
Karno, Fred 58
Karns, Roscoe **200**
Karr, Hilliard Sinclair "Fatty" **193**, **214**, 224, **225-226**, 227, 244-245, **253**, **270**, **280**, **291**
Keaton, Buster xi, xix, 96, 105, 128
Keep Going 192, 454-455
Keeping His Word 280, 316, 318, 492
Keeping in Trim 349, 496
Keeping Up with the Joneses series **324**, 335, 337, 348-349, 351, 355
Keeping Up with the Joneses (Pop Momand comic strip) 324
Keith and Orpheum Circuit 128
Kellar, "Baby" Jimmy 363
Kelley, James T. **142**, **180**
Kelly, Patsy 382
Kerr, Robert 57, 216, 218, **219**
Kerr, Walter xxii
Keystone Film Company xi, xix, xxiv, 1, 3, 7, 41, 45, 64, 103, 128, 137, 178, 192, 394
Kick in High Life, The 95, 151
Kicked About 255, 470
Kickin' Fool, The 130, 180-181, 441
Kid Reporter, The **186**, 240, 447
Kid's Pal, The 122-123, 426
Kinemacolor Company of America 1
King Bee Comedies 137
King, Charles Lafayette, Jr. xiii, 251, 263-264, **265-266**, 269, 274, 280, 287, **289**, **311**, 315, **316-318**, **320**, **324**, 343, **344**, 345, **346**, 348, 354, 381
Kingsbury, Stanley C. 32
Kinney, Martin **357**
Kirk, Phyllis 390
Kirkland, David 4, 35
Klaw and Erlanger 103
Knockout Buster 367-368, 371, 514

Knopp, Robert 235
Kohn, Edith Josephine (see Roberts. Edith) 110
La Gallienne, Eva 291
La Rocque, Rod 209
Laemmle Film Service 16-17
Laemmle, Carl xv, xxii-xxiii, 2-3, **5**, 8-9, 11, **12-13**, 14-16, **17**, 18-19, 21, **22**, 23-26, **27**, 28, **29**, 30, **31**, 32, 45, 61-62, 74, 77, 80-81, 86, 107, 116, 138, 147, 157, 159-164, 166-168, 170, 172-175, 177, 209, 223, 239, 241, **242**, 243, 245, 282, 292, **327**, 328-330, 373, 375-377, 379, 393-394, 398
Laemmle, Carl, Jr. 327-328, 330
Laemmle, Joseph 11
Laemmle, Julius (see Laemmle, Carl Jr.) **327**
Laemmle, Julius Baruch 11
Laemmle, Rebekka 11
Laemmle, Recha 11-12, **13**, 20, **27**, **31**, **33**, 62, 327
Laemmle, Rosabelle **13**, 170, **242**, 243, 330, **375**
Lahue, Kalton C. xxi, 312
Lame Brains and Lunatics (Steve Massa author) xix
Lamont, Charles 218, **221**, 222-223, 245-246, 255, 264, 274, 276, 287, 321, 383
Lamont, Dixie 127, **222**, 223
Lamplighter, The 263
Landis, Cullen 293
Landloper, The 224
Lane, Lupino 180
Langdon, Harry x, xii, xix, 137, 309, 316
Lardner, Ring 196, 374, 383, 389
Larry Rich and His Friends 256
Lascelle, Ward 249
Last Gangster, The 220
Latimer, Villie **291**
Laurel, Stan 4, 90, 103, 315, 360
Laurel and Hardy xix, 382
Law Forbids, The 241
Layman, Gene (see Laymon, Gene "Fatty") **348**, 351
Laymon, Gene "Fatty" **350**, 351
Leather Pushers, The, series 237
Lee, Florence 109
Lee, Joung Hoon 388
Lee, Soon Myoung 388
Leff, Jacob 386
Lehrman Knock-Out (see L-Ko Motion Picture Company) 2
Lerhman, Henry "Pathe" xii, xx, 1, **2**, 3-4, **5**, 7, **8**, 9, 20 26, 31-32, 35, 37, 41, 58-59, 63-64, 75, 95, 98-99, 103, 105, 110, 150-153, 192, 195, 212, 268, 284, 316, 393-394
Let George Do It (George McManus comic strip) 286, 325
Let George Do It series **285**, 287, 300, 309, 313, 326, 339, **340**, 341, 343, 359, **362**, 373
Lewis, George 327, **328**
Liberty Film Company 150, 314
Liberty Pictures 129
Life magazine 282
Life Publishing Company 282
Light Hearts and Leaking Pipes 103, 416
Lilac Time 365
Limburger Cyclone, A 98, 103
Limit, The 344
Lincoln, Elmo 78, **79-80**, 81, 83, **84**
Lion Comedies (Century) 65-66, **67**, 103, 105, 148
Lion Comedies (Fox Sunshine) 63-64
Lion Comedies (Master Pictures) 224

Lion in the House, A 65, 87, 103, 410
Lion Special, A 65, 409
Lion's Alliance, A 112-113, **114**, 416
Lions' Jaws and Kittens' Paws 99, **101-102**, 103, 418
Liquorish Lips 226
Little Billy's School Days 55
Little Bo Peep 188
Little Boy Blue 188
Little Match Girl, The 188
Little Mermaid, The 188
Little Miss Hollywood **229**, 452
Little Miss Mischief 137, 434
Little Napoleon the Chimpanzee 109
Little Rascal, The 123, 136-137, **199**, 437
Little Red Riding Hood (see also *Red Riding Hood*) 177, 188, 190, 475
Litwack, Isidore Irving (see Luddy, Edward I.) 218
Live Wires **89**, 184, **185**, 438
Lizzie's Lingering Love 40
L-Ko Motion Picture Company/L-Ko Komedy Kompany/ L-Ko Comedies xiii, xx-xxi, 1-9, **10**, 26-27, 31-32, **33**, 35-46, 49, 55-59
Lloyd Hamilton Comedies 179
Lloyd, Harold x, xii, xix, 112, 139, 182, 256
Lockwood, Harold 224
Loeb, Edwin 168
Lofty Marriage, A 215, 457
Lois Weber Productions 55
Lonesome Hearts and Loose Lions 65, 99, 409
Lonesome Luke series 112
Long Rifle and the Tomahawk, The 382
Long, Harry **348-349**, 350
Longacre Distributing Company 45-46, 54-55, 61-62
Look Out—Buster! 300, 332, 491
Look Pleasant 373, 509
Looking Down 245, **246**, 250, 466
Looney Lions and Monkey Business 65, 105, 408
Loose Lions and Fast Lovers 99, 100, 415
Loranger, Connie 248
Lorraine of the Lions 274
Lorraine, Harry **37**, 38
Lorraine, Louise 79, 82, **84**, 127, 139, **140**, 195, 404
Lost Control **193**, 215, 460
Love 'Em and Leave 'Em 355
Love and Sour Notes 55
Love and Surgery **3**
Love and the Lottery Ticket 24
Love or a Throne 24
Love Sick 259, 470
Love's Hurdle 317, 484
Low Bridge 231, 462-463
Loyal Hearts 84
Lubin Manufacturing Co. 27
Lucenay, Harry C. 126, 209, **210**
Lucky Rube, The 221
Luddy, Edward I. 218, **219-220**, 228, 245-246, 249, 251, 403-404
Ludwig, Edward (see Luddy, Edward I.) 404
Luley, Gustave Peter Ludwig (see Meins, Gus) 282
Lusk, Norbert 27-28
Lynn, Jewel 216
Lynn, Neva 216
Lyons and Moran Comedies 55, 244

Lyons, Eddie 132, **133**, 141, 244, 263
Lyons, Edgar 333
Lytell, Bert 120
M & A Alexander Productions 383
Ma and Pa Kettle series 223
Mabel and Fatty's Wash Day 192
Mack, Hughie **37**, 40, 52-55, **57**, 62, 91, 218
Mad Hour 355
Madcap Ambrose 64
Madison, Cleo 83
Make It Snappy 379
Mama's Cowpuncher 140, **142**, 431
Man of Letters 373, 501
Man to Man **172**, 174
Man Who Waited, The 219
Mann, Hank xix, 3, **5**, 6, **7**, **9**, 42
Mann, Harry **39**, 115, 228
Man-Woman-Marriage 355
Marcel, Marjorie 202, 216, 288, 321, 343
Marian, Edna (see also Marion, Edna) xx, 205,
    226, 245, 255-256, **257**, 258, **259**, 260, **261**,
    269, 279-280, 344, 404
Marion Morgan Dancers 355
Marion, Edna (see Marian, Edna) 256, 404
Marked Women 226
Married Neighbors 263, 470
Martell, Harry **261**, **316**, **352**, 354, 359, **360-361**
Martin, Al 333, 348
Martin, Joe **39**, 66, **68**, 69, **70-72**, 73, 82, **84**, 165,
    209, 244, 404
Martin, Mrs. Joe 66-67, **68-69**, 73, 110
Mary the Dog 158
Mason, Shirley 263
Massa, Steve xvi-xvii, xix, 281
Master Pictures 224
Mathews, Harriett 351, 354
Maude the Mule 130, 148, 180, **181**
May, Betty **153**, 195
May, Dolores 343
Mayer, Louis B. 166
Mayo, Archie **178**, 200, 207, 218, 221
McCarthy, Earl 288, **290**, **331**
McClure Syndicate 324
McCoy, Harry 192, **193**, **214**, 215-216, 225, 227,
    238, **267**
McCoy, Ruby **299**
McDougall Kids series 366
McGinis vs. Jones 350, 507
McGowan, J.P. 79, 83
McKeen, Lawrence "Sunny", Jr. xxi, 302, **303-306**,
    336, 338, **352**, 380, **381**
McKeen, Merry Mae 342, 343
McKeen, Sunny (see McKeen, Lawrence "Sunny")
    xiii, 302, 326, 342, 353-355, 358, **362**, 379
McKenzie, Ella 202
McKenzie, Eva 50, 55
McKenzie, Ida Mae 50, 202
McKenzie, Robert 38, 50, 55
McManus, George 284-285, **286**, 302, **303**, 309,
    325, 335, 338
McPhail, Addie (see also Dukes, Addie Oakley)
    334, 336, **337**, 348, 351, 354
McRae, Henry 79
McWilliams, George 274
Me and My Mule 180, 443

Meins, Gus 276, **281**, 282, 285, 287, 298, 300, 313, 324,
    335, 339, **348**, 349, 355, 357, 359, 364, 370, 379-
    380, 382
Mermaid Comedies 111, 128, 179-180, 196, 218, 344
Merry-Go-Round 264
Messenger, The 137
Messinger, Gertrude 220
Messinger, Melvin Joseph "Buddy" 137, 198, **201-203**,
    205, 209, 215, 218, **225**, 226, 230, **231**, 232-233,
    234, 244, 404
Metro Pictures 104, 120, 315
Metro-Goldwyn-Mayer 397
M-G-M (see Metro-Goldwyn-Mayer) 150, 235, 351
Mickey McGuire series 366
Mike and Ike (They Look Alike) (Rube Goldberg comic
    strip) 325
Mike and Ike (They Look Alike) series **324**, 342, 372
Mike and Jake Among the Cannibals 192
Mike and Jake series 192
Mike and Jake Go Fishing 192
Mike and Jake Join the Army 192
Miles of Smiles 239, **240**, 452-453
Miller, Rube 3, **5**
Mind the Baby 200, 209, 462
Mirth of a Nation, The 7
Mitchell, Glenn xxii
Mix, Tom 209
Model George 339, 500
Modern Hercules, The 78
Momand, Arthur Ragland "Pop" 324, **347**, 348-349
Monberg, George "Zip" 65, 82, 87, **89**, 90, 93, 95, **101-
    102**, 103, 107, 109, **130**, 153, 195, 227, **247**, 404
Money Talks 64, 192
Monkey Bell Hop, A 71, 521
Monkey Hero, A 70, 521
Monkey Movie Star, A 71, 521
Monkey Schoolmaster, A 71, 521
Monkey Shines 274
Monkey Stuff 69-70, 519-520
Monogram Pictures 383
Monsieur Don't Care 315
Moonshines and Jailbirds 93, 98, 417
Moore, Joe 47-48, **50**, 55, **193**, 216
Moore, Roger (see Young, Joe) 362, 404
Moore, Vin 35, 55, 59, 66-67, 103
Moran, Esther 154-155
Moran, Lee xxii, 132, **133**, 141-142, **144**, 145, **146**, 151,
    153, 154, **155-156**, 177, 179, 195-196, **197-198**
Moran, Polly 64
Moranti Comedies 229
Moranti, Milburn 229
Morgan, Jackie **89**, **124**, **150**, 154, 182, **183**, 199
Morris, Dave 3, 40
Morris, Reggie 3, **7**, 221
Morrison, Pete 148, **150**, 263
Morschauser, Joseph 171
Morse, Waldo G. 22
Motion Picture Distributing and Sales Company, The 21
Motion Picture Patents Company 18
Motion to Adjourn 264
Motor Trouble 265, 316, 481
Movie Hero, A **110**, 138, 420

Movie Madness 218, 344, 480
Movie Star, A 64
Mr. Suicide: Henry "Pathé" Lehrman and the Birth of Silent Comedy (Thomas Reeder author) xx, 76
Mrs. Plum's Pudding 133
Muddy Bride, A 121, 432
Murdock, Henry 224, 228-229
Murnau, F.W. 267
Murphy, Joe **142, 145,** 244
Mush Again 381
Mustang Westerns 280, 283
Mutts 150, **151,** 435
My Baby Doll 257-258, **259,** 467
My Dog Pal 112, **113,** 415
My Pal **200,** 209, 453
My Salomy Lions 105-106, 417
Myers, Carmel 171
Myers, Harry 27, 82
Myers, Zion 150, 171, 191, 202, 207
Nabbing a Noble 98
Nathan Busts Into the Movies 224
National Broadcasting Company 374
National Film Recording Company 382
National Film Recording Studios 382
National Laugh Month 283
National Screen Service 299
National Telepix 388
Necessary Evil, The 309
Neck and Neck 344
Neighbors 381
Neilan, Marshall 139
Neilson, Lois 87, 89, **90**
Nelson, Eva 3, **4-5, 7, 9,** 35
Neptune's Naughty Daughter 45, 48, **49,** 50, **54,** 56, 405
Nero the Lion 64
Nervy Dentist, The 105, 431
Nestor Film Company 23, 42, 58, 61, 95-96, 132-133, 178, 351
Nethersole, Olga 314
Neufeld, Samuel (see Newfield, Samuel) 321
Neufeld, Sigmund 203, **204,** 212-213, 246, 266, 293-295, 297, 321, 333, 340, **352,** 379-380, 382
Newfield, Samuel 287, 300, 319, 321, **322,** 335, 339, 355, 364, 366, 370, 379, 382-383
Newlyweds and Their Baby, The (George McManus comic strip) 286
Newlyweds and Their Baby, The series 284, 287, 300, 302, 325, 335, 355, 371
Newlyweds Build, The 305, **306,** 488-489
Newlyweds in Society, The 356-357, 372, 515
Newlyweds Lose Snookums, The 356, 511
Newlyweds Need Help, The **358,** 372, 511-512
Newlyweds Quarantined, The 305, 484-485
Newlyweds Unwelcome, The 356, 372, 509
Newlyweds' Advice, The 337, 356, 500
Newlyweds' Angel Child, The 356, 358, 517
Newlyweds' Christmas Party, The 336, 499
Newlyweds' False Alarm, The 337, 506
Newlyweds' Happy Day, The 336, 505
Newlyweds' Hard Luck, The 355, 508
Newlyweds' Headache, The 356, 398, 512
Newlyweds' Holiday, The 372, 514
Newlyweds' Neighbors, The **304,** 483
Newlyweds' Servant, The **334,** 336-337, 501
Newlyweds' Surprise, The 335, 497
Newlyweds' Troubles, The 335, 496

Newlyweds' Visit, The 372, 513
Newman, Bobby 354
Nibsy the Newsboy (George McManus comic strip) 286
Night Out, A 112
Nimbo, Charlie 107
Nip the Dog 123
No Blondes Allowed 343, 345-346, 372, 502
No Boy Wanted 381
No Monkey Business 70, 520
Nobody's Darling 239, 451
Nobody's Sweetheart 347, 467
Normand, Mabel 1
Novak, Eva **37,** 38
Numa Pictures Corporation 82-83, **84**
Numa the Lion 83
Nuts in May 4
O'Brien, Jack 79
O'Connor, Bob **142**
O'Connor, L.J. 203
O'Day, Dawn 216
O'Donnell, Walter "Spec" 203, 224, 229, **230-231,** 234, 273
O'Herlihy, Dan 390
O'Neill, Tom 189
Oakland Stock Company 350
Obey the Law 192, 454
Off His Beat 130, **132,** 437
Off His Trolley 93, **94,** 98, **99,** 321, 419
Officer Number Thirteen 269, 473
Oh Nursie! 321, 446
Oh! Buster! 276, 475
Oh! Mabel! 345, 499
Oh! You East Lynn 90, 95, 412
Oh, Baby! 51, **52,** 58, 405
Oh, What a Knight! 64, 192
Old Man Rhythm 220
Olin, Earl 66, 253
On Again, Off Again Finnegan 42
On Deck 339, 343, 499
On Furlough 343, 494-495
On the Trail of the Lonesome Pill 95
On With the Show 315, 426
One Horse Town, A **129,** 130, 435
Orpheum Picture Company 85
Orth, Louise 3, **4-5,** 35
Ostriche, Muriel 137
Our Gang Comedies xiii, 209, 230, 263, 370, 382
Our Pet 239, 458
Out at Home 372, 512
Out of Place 224
Outcault, Richard Felton "R.F." 244, 269, 271, **272,** 275, 283
Outdoor Sports 379
Over the Ocean Wave 92-93, 96, 414
Over the Transom 67, 111, 414
Ovey, George 107, 115
P.D.Q. 141
Pacific Coast Producing Co. 83
Pacific Film Co. 84, 163
Pacific Producing Co. 83-84, **85**
Paging a Wife 264, 472
Paging Money 228, 461
Painless Pain 288, **291,** 479
Paint and Powder 356

Pal the Dog **89**, 126, 150, **200**, 209, **210-211**, 215, 221, 227, 230, 244, 275
Pals 121, 130, 427-428
Panhandle Pete (George McManus comic strip) 286
Paramount Pictures Corporation 75, 137, 220, 223, 236-237, 387, 397
Parrott, Charles 93
Parson, Smiling Billy 120
Parsons, Louella 288, 291
Partners in Crime 3
Passing the Joneses **348**, 350, 498
Payson, Blanche xiii, 136, 142, **143**, 144, **153**, **197**, **199**, 255, 263-265, **270**
Peaceful Riot, A 359
Peaches the Dog 150
Peacock, Capt. Leslie T. 84
Pearce, Peggy 3
Pee Wee Holmes Westerns 332
Peg o' the Mounted **194**, 195, 398, 455
Peg o' the Movies 186, 229, 446
Peg o' the Ring 77
Peggy, Behave! 136-137, 198, 435
Pembroke, Marian Scott 313
Pembroke, Percy Stanley (see also Pembroke, Scott) 82, 109, 313-314
Pembroke, Samuel J. 313
Pembroke, Scott 286-287, 300, 312-314, **315**, 316, 321
Penrod 136
People's Stock Company 350
Perdue, Derelys 317, 337, **338**, 351, 354-355, **356-358**
Perez, Marcel 298
Pete the Dog xii-xiii, 203, 209, **271**, **273-275**, **277**, **301**, 331-332, 342, 354, 365-366, 369-370
Petrova, Olga 355
Phantom Raider, The 78
Philbin, Mary 209
Phillipi, Charles E. 223
Pickford, Mary 198, 274
Picking On George 339, 498
Piedmont Pictures 58
Pie-Eyed 315
Pike Peak Photoplay 256
Pink Pajamas 120
Pinto (see Colvig, Vance de Bar "Pinto") 205
Piping Hot 269, **270**, 474
Pirates of the Air 40, **41**
Pitts, ZaSu 382
Plain Jane 321, 495
Plane Crazy 379
Playgoers Pictures 219
Playing the Swell 288, 480
Playmates 120, **121**, 125, 398, 427
Please 137
Please Don't 316, 495
Please Excuse Me **318**, 319, 486
Please, Teacher! 230, 273, 459
Plenty of Nerve 259, 471
Plus and Minus 344
Pochahontas and John Smith 243
Pollard, Harry 21
Pollard, Snub 139, 256, 292
Polo Kid, The 255, 471
Polo, Eddie 79, **81**, 159-160, 165, **173**, 174

Poor Kid 239, 460
Poppy Comedies 129
Popular Pictures 219
Popular Villain, A 98, 411
Potters, The 355
Powdered Chickens 259, 468
Powell, Russell 38, 55
Powers Picture Plays 95
Powers, Patrick 23, **27**, 75, **161**
Pratt, Gilbert 179, 219
PRC (see Producers Releasing Corporation)
Present Arms 246, 465
Pretty Plungers 207, 457
Price of Youth, The 264
Prince of Pilsen, The 103
Prince the Camel 74
Producers Releasing Corporation 382-383
Professor Lucifer Gorgonzola Butts (Rube Goldberg comic strip) 325
Prohibition Monkey, A 70, 520
Pruning the Movies 133
Pulitzer, Joseph 272, 286
Punch of the Irish 95
Puppy Love 424
Puppy Love Comedies 256, **258**
Pure and Simple 226
Puritan Pictures 382
Purple Mask, The 78
Putting On Airs 259, 468
Putting Pants on Philip **360**
Puzzled By Crosswords **253**, 255, 263, 468
Quality Pictures Corporation 218
Queen of Aces, The **247**, **256**, 398, 469
Queen of Burlesque 383
Queenie the Dog 120
Queenie the Horse 148, **150**, 152, 177, 181, 229
Quick Triggers 356
Quirk, James 218
Quit Kiddin' 200, 205, 455
Racing Kid, The 230, **231**, 232, 457
Radio Hound 182, 440
Radium Mystery, The 83, **85**
Rainbow Comedies xv-xvi, xix-xx, 75, 87-93, 95-96, 98-99, 103-104, 106-107, 109, 116, 128, 140, 198, 321, 397-398
Raisin' Cain **263**, 468
Ramsdell, Major Leland S. 257
Rangers Take Over, The 383
Rappe, Virginia 146-147
Ray, Marjorie **34**, 35, 38, 65, **100**
Rayart Pictures Corporation 228, 293, 361
Raymaker, Herman **178**, 204, 218
Red Hot Finish, A 103, 415
Red Riding Hood (see also *Little Red Riding Hood*) 139, **189**, 190, 239, 273, 475
Reddy, George J. 355, 359, 370
Reelcraft Pictures Corporation 59, 95, 226-227
Reeves, Bob 83
Reid, Laurence 106
Reisner, Charles "Chuck" **127**, 128
Renault Brothers 176
Renfrew of the Mounted (TV series) 388
Renfrew of the Royal Mounted (radio series) 388-389
Republic Pictures 107, 382
Restaurant Riot, A 98, 103, 417
Rich Pup, The 209, 454

Rich, Cheri 256
Rich, Victor 256
Richardson, Hazel (see Lamont, Dixie) 222
Richardson, Larry **228**, **254**, **256**, **288**
Riot, The 198
Rip Van Winkle (1921) 219
Rip Van Winkle (1924) 243
Ripley, Arthur 166
Ritchie, Billie xxi, **3**, **5**, 6, **8-10**, 35, 42
Rittenhouse, Mignon 363
RKO Radio Pictures 130, 219-220, 387, 390
Roach, Bert xiii, **4**, **10**, 38, **43**, 55, 62, 103, 130, **132**, **208**, **244**
Roach, Gladys 38
Roach, Hal 209, 231, 255, 315, 351, 360, 369, 382
Roaring Lions and Wedding Bells 63, 110
Roaring Lions on the Midnight Express 63
Roaring Love Affair, A 93, 107, 415
Robbins, Jess 87-88, 92, **93**, 115, 245-246, 255, 288, 321
Roberts, Edith **63**, 66, 110, **111**
Robertson-Cole Pictures Corporation (R-C) 129, 172-173, 219, 361
Robinson, Edward G. 220
Robinson's Trousseau 141
Rock, Joe 180, 226, 315, 359
Rogers, Gene 3, 35
Rogers, Will 98, 263, 307
Rolf the Dog 176
Rolin Film Company 45, 90, 112, 139
Romance of Tarzan, The 78-79
Romeos and Jolly Juliets 103, 411
Roof Garden Rough House, A 87, 89, 91
Roosevelt, Buddy 223
Roping Her Romeo 64
Rosie the Monkey 148-149, 156
Ross, Tad 216, 404
Ross, William "Kewpie" 226
Rothchild, Dave 333
Rough But Romantic 42
Rough on Husbands 106
Rough Party, A **280**, 281, 471
Round Figures 207, 215, 450-451
Rubber Necks 360, 508
Rubel, Beno 287, 293-295, 297, 299
Run Buster! 342, 500
Russell, Dan **10**, **34**, 35, 38, 42, 65, **100**
Russell, Harry **4**, **9**
Ryckman, Chester 38
Saffarons, Thomas 291
Sahara Blues 239, 463
Sailing Along 234, 467
Sailor George 339, 504-505
Sailor Maids 237, 459
Sailor Suits 360, 512
Sailor, Leo (see Saylor, Sid) 309
Sally the Horse 148
Sandra 309
Sandrich, Mark 180-181
Sanford Productions 298
Santa Rosa, California 253
Santell, Al 70
Sapho 314
Sava Films, Inc. 255, 351
Saving Susie from the Sea 40
Sawmill, The 179
Saxon, Hugh **357**

Say It with Love 344, 479
Say Uncle 360
Saylor, Sid 285-286, 300, **306**, **308**, 309-310, **311**, 312, **313**, 316, 326, **329**, 335, 338, **339-341**, 352, 353-354, 359, **360-362**, 379, 404
Saylor, Syd (see Saylor, Sid) xii-xiii, xxi, 309, **380**, 381, 404
Scared Stiff 228, 461
Schaefer, Albert 342, **354**, 367, 370
Scheurich, Victor 333
Schlank, Morris R. 298
Schmidt, Art 147
School Days 51, 405
Schrock, Raymond 28
Scott, Lois 130
Scott, Sherman 382
Scrapped, a Life Story in Tabloid 363
Seashore Shapes 123, 139, 147, 431
Second Hand Excuse, A 280, 487
Second Hundred Years, The 360
Sedgwick, Eileen 83
Seeing is Believing 315, 426
Selby, Gertrude 3, **5**, **7**, 35, 58, 116
Select Pictures 112, 115
Selig Polyscope Company 192, 350
Semon, Larry 123, 179, 200, 219, 253, 255
Sennett, Mack xix, xxi, 1, 7, 59, 99, 104, 120, 123, 130, 134, 137, 178, 192, 200, 207, 215, 218, 282, 312, 337, 351, 361, 394, 398-399
Seventh Heaven 365
Shadows 201
Shadows of Conscience 224
Shall We Dance 180
Shaved in Mexico 42
Shaw, Brinsley Sheridan 27
She Did Her Bit 50, **51**, 405
She's a He 381, 452
She's a Pippin 363-364, 372, 514
She's My Cousin 318, 491
Shearer, Norma 209
Sherman, Gilbert xv-xvi, 98, 390-391, 401-402
Sherman, Lewis 386
Sherman, Lowell 146
Sherman, Susan Stern 12
"Shins of Society, The" (Hans Henry Sneider play) 213
Shipwrecked Among Animals **148**, 433
Shipwrecked Among Cannibals 148, 433
Shirley, Anne 216
Shooting the Bull 372, 510
Short, Gertrude 315
Should Tailors Trifle? 128-129, 421
Should Waiters Marry? 128, 418
Show Cowpuncher, The 480
Showing Off 350, 499
Sic 'Em Brownie 182, 436-437
Sid's Long Count 379
Sierra Pictures 344
Silk Hose and High Pressure 4
Simpkin, Joe 123
Singer Midgets 176
Singing River 264
Singleton, Jack 264
Sirens of the Suds 103
Sister's Pest 381
Skate at Sea, A 106, 109

Slapstick Divas (Steve Massa author) xix
Sleeper, Martha 202-203, 224, 230, **231-232**
Small Town Derby, A 180, **181**, 184, 315, 443
Smart Alec, The 130, 428
Smarty 202, 445-446
Smith, Chester J. 349
Smith, David 141
Smith, Noel 4, 35, 57, **178**, 218, 221, 227, 245-246, 265
Smith, Sid (comedian) 109, 221
Smith, Sidney (cartoonist) 244
Smoke Eaters, The 293
Snappy Eyes 226, 238, 463
Sneider, Hans Henry 213
Snookums' Buggy Ride 485-486
Snookums Disappears 309, 489-490
Snookums' Merry Christmas **308**, 309, **311**, 326, 487
Snookums' Tooth **305**, 484
Snooky the "Humanzee" 69-70
Snow White 177
Snub Pollard Company 292
Society Breaks 350, 497
Society Stuff 54, 408
Some Family 196, **198-199**, 441
Some More Excuses 316, 318, 490
Some Tomboy 227, 238, 464
Son of a Hun, The 106
Sons-In-Law 215, 455-456
Sophie of the Films 133
Southern Feature Film Association 4
Spare Ribs and Gravy (George McManus comic strip) 286
Speed 'Em Up **184**, 437-438
Speed Boys 234, 273, 464
Speed Bugs 200, 449
Speed Wild 274
Spencer, Fred 136, 181, **197**, 198, **199**, 200, **205**, 216, 228, 404
Spooky Romance, A 192, 445
Spoor, George 92
Spreckels, J.D. 38
Spuds 219
St. Clair, Mal 93
St. John, Al 224
Star Comedies 104, 110, 128, 133, 351
Star System xx, 39, 245
Starr, Jimmy 74
Starving Beauties 207, 237-238, 460
Stealin' Home 140, 430
Steamboat Bill, Jr. 128
Stecker, Carl 73
Stecker, Curley 70, 73-75, 83
Stein, Al 146-147
Steiner, Edith Betty 385
Step Forward 282
Step Lively 139
Step Right Up 379
Stephen Steps Out 237
Stephens, Walter 38
Stepping Some **239**, 459
Sterling Comedies 1, 3
Sterling, Ford 1-2
Sterling, Merta **37**, 38, 65, 92, **101-102**, 103, **113-114**, **145**

Stern Brothers Comedies xv-xv1, xix-xxi, 158, 284, 298-299, 309, 323, 330, 332, 341, 351, 353, 364, 376, 398, 403
  1926-27 Season: Focus on Comic Series 297-333
  1927-28 Season: The Newlyweds 335-352
  1928-29 Season: Wrapping Up 353-378
Stern Brothers Realty Co. 384
Stern Enterprises, Inc. 383
Stern Film Corporation 284, 376
Stern Film Productions, Inc. 383
Stern Pictures and Finance Corporation 383
Stern Pictures and Industrial Corporation 383
Stern, Abraham "Abe" xii-xiii, xv-xvi, xx, xxii, 1-2, **5-6**, 9, 11, **13**, 25, **26**, 31-32, **33**, 35-38, 43, 50, 61-62, 75, 77, 80, 83, 86-87, 98-99, 116, 132, 134-135, 154, 156, 161-162, 164-165, 168-170, 176-177, 195, 204, 207, 211-213, 216-218, 223, 241, **242**, 243, 245, 262, 285, **292**, 294-295, **296**, 297, 312, 324, 330, 332-333, **352**, 373-374, **375**, 376, 382, 384, 387, **388**, 394, 397, 401-402
  Early years 25-26
  L-Ko 2-9, 26, 31-32, 38-43, 55-59
  Century's Origins 42-59
  Marriage to Jessie Jacobs 31-32, 168-169
  As Universal's Treasurer; 3-Man Commission 161-162
  Marriage to Hortense Westheimer 170. 394
Stern, Alfred **242**, 243, 375
Stern, Anna 11-12, 18, 20, **33**, 168-169, 330
Stern, Arnold 387
Stern, Barbara Westheimer 170
Stern, Edith 386, **387**, **389-390**, **392**
Stern, Frieda **242**, 243
Stern, Hannah 242
Stern, Herman **242**, 384
Stern, Irma **242**, 243
Stern, Jesse L. 386
Stern, Joseph 11-12, **13**
Stern, Julius xii-xiii, xv-xvi, xx, xxii, 1, 9, 11-12, **13**, 14-15, **16**, 17-20, 22, **23**, 25, **27**, 28-30, **31**, 32, **33**, 35-40, 43-49, 61-62, 64, 75, 77-82, **83**, 84-87, 92, 98-99, 107, 112, 116, 119, 129, 132, 134-136, 141, 147, 152, 154-157, 159-160, 162-166, 168-171, 174-176, 189, 195, **204**, 206-207, 209-212, **213**, 216-218, **223**, 239, 241, **242**, 243, 245, 264, 266-268, 271, 283-284, **292**, 294, 297, 302, 312, 322-323, 326-327, 329-333, 336, 353, 366, 374, **375**, 376-377, 382-386, **387**, 388, **389-392**, 393-394, **395**, 397-399, 401-402
  Origins; with Laemmle 11-20
  Early Universal 21-31
  L-Ko 38-43, 55-59
  Century's Origins 42-59
  Serials 77-86
  Back with Universal 159-174
  Irving Thalberg 163-166
  Foolish Wives and Erich von Stroheim 166-168
  Marriage to Sylvia Born 170-171
  Marriage to Edith Betty Steiner 385-386, 389-394
  Unaffiliated Independent Exhibitors, Inc. 386-387
  Real Estate Holdings 85, 383-384, 387-388
Stern, Larry 387
Stern, Loeb **242**, 243
Stern, Louis Albert 394
Stern, Malchen Herzberger **242**, 243
Stern, Marie Grace 386
Stern, Recha 11

Stern, Sam 11, 14
Stern, Sylvia (see also Born, Sylvia) 170-171
Sternbach, Bert 333
Sternbros Motion Picture Enterprises, Inc. 388
Sternbros Realty Corporation 388
Stevens, Ted 66
Stevens, Walter 66
Stewart, Peter 382
Still Alarm, The 269, 280
Stonehouse, Ruth 77-78
Stop Snookums 338, 493
Stop That Noise 381
Stop, Look and Listen 128
Stork's Mistake, The 274
Straphanger, The 141-143, **144**, 433
Stuffed Lions 128, 425
Such Is Life 229, 454
Summerville, Slim 103, 244
Sunkist Comedies 219
Sunny Jim series 380, **381**
Sunshine Comedies (see Fox Sunshine)
Swain, Mack xxi, **40**, 64, 98, 129
Swanson, Charles S. 23
Swanson, Gloria 398
Swanson, William H. 22, **27**
Sweet Dreams **236**, **238**, **267**, 464
Sweet Sixteen Comedies 244, 267
Sweet, Harry 87, 99, 101, **130-132**, 137, 139-140, **141-142**, **148-149**, 153, 156, 181, **184**, 185, 221, 227, 273, 404
Sweetie 186, 446
Swett, Harry (see Sweet, Harry) 99, 404
Swiss Family Robinson 220
Taking Orders 186, 448
Taking Things Easy 133
Tale of a Dog, The 128, 417
Tantor the Elephant 82
Trailing Trouble 230, 273, 458
Tarkington, Booth 201
Tarzan of the Apes 78
Tattle Tail, The 182, 443
Tattle-Tale Alice 40
Taurog, Norman 178, **179**, 180
Taxi War, A 269, 475
Taxi! Taxi! 225, 457
Taylor, Kenneth 249
Taylor, Ted 74
Teacher's Pest 342, **343**, 372, 510
Teddy the Dog 120, 123, **124**, 398
Teddy's Goat 123, **124**, 432
Tee Time 58, 315, 424
Telepix 388
Television George xii, 361-362, 513
Tennek Film Corporation 351
Thalberg, Irving 70, 162-163, **164**, 165-166
Thanks for the Boat Ride 321, 489
That Oriental Game 221, 456
That Woman Opposite 390
That's No Excuse **316**, 318, 493
That's Rich 273, 456
The Great Smash 7, 40
The Life and Adventures of Carl Laemmle (John Drinkwater author) xxii-xxiii
The Long Shadows: The Story of Jake Erlich (Andrew Erlich author) 195
The Silent Clowns (Walter Kerr author) xxii

Theby, Rosemary 27
Their Last Haul 42
There's a Will 345, 500
Third Class Male 109, 428-429
Thomas, Olive 355
Those Bitter Sweets 192
Those Wedding Bells 351
Three Bears, The 177
Three Fatties series 226
Three Weeks Off 184, 437
Thrilling Romance, A 288-289, **290**, 398, 481-482
Thrills-in-History 79
Through the Back Door 274
Thunder Over Texas 383
Tiffany Pictures 382
Tige's Girl Friend 369, 514
Tight Fix, A 140, **141**, 411
Tillie's Punctured Romance 7
Tillie's Terrible Tumble 7, 40
Tim the Horse 194
Time is Money 24
Tin Cans 147, 431
Tincher, Fay 244
Tips 186, 209, 449
Tired Business Men 219, 458
Todd, Thelma 382
Tom's Tramping Troupe 98
Ton of Fun Comedies 226
Too Many Babies 264, 316, 479
Too Many Women 379
Too Much Mother-In-Law 363-364, 473
Top Hat 180
Topsy Tree, Miss 67
Touchdown, The 143, **145**, 434
Tourneur, Maurice 73
Tower Pictures 382
Traffic Troubles 379
Tramp, The 112
Treat 'Em Rough 383
Triangle Film Corporation 93, 96, 109, 129, 192, 355
Trifling Women 72
Trimbell, Arthur xii-xiii, 203, 234, **271**, **273**, 274-275, **277-278**, **298**, **301**, 331, 335, **342**, 353, **354**, **365**, 368-370, **371**, 382
Trouble Bubbles 58, 423
Trouble Fixer, The 227, 239, 463
True Blue 151, 181, 229, 442
Trust, The 18
Turner, Doreen xii, **271**, **273**, 274-275, **277**, 278-279, **298**, **301**, **342**, **354**, 365
Turpin, Ben 360
Tuttle, Frank 355
Tweedy Comedies 298
Twilight Baby, A 105
Twin Sisters 265, 481
Two of a Kind 130, **131**, 435
Two Star Comedies 110, 351
Two-Gun Gussie 139
UFA 267, 390
Unaffiliated Independent Exhibitors, Inc. 386
Uncle Tom's Cabin (book) 259
Uncle Tom's Cabin (film) 366
Uncle Tom's Gal **257**, 259, **260-261**, 474
Under Crimson Skies 79

"Under the Spreading Century Plant" (*Universal Weekly* column) 175
Under the Table **7**, 42
Unhand Me, Villain 40
United Features Syndicate 205
United States Motion Picture Corporation 75
Universal City 3, 28, 30, 64, 69, 73, 83, 133, 162, 165-166, 171-172, 237, 282, 328, 330, 376
Universal Film Exchanges, Inc. 55
Universal Film Manufacturing Company 21, 75, 161, 177
Universal Joy Week 177, 282, **283**
Universal Oak Crest Ranch 23
Universal Pictures Corporation 177
Universal-Jewel 55, 62, 69, 133, 141, 174, 201, 241, 245, 298
Universal-Junior Jewel 327, 335, 341, 355, 403
Untamed Ladies 53, 407
Upper and Lower 143, **146**, 435
Valentino, Rudolph 236
Vamped 192, 446
Van Loan, H.H. 7
Varden, Gladys 38
Venice Miniature Railroad 234, 240
Vera, Lillian 75
Verity Film Co. 110, 351
Vernon, Bobby 398
Vernon, Dorothy 274
Victor Film Company 27, 66
Village Blacksmith, The 50, 405
Village Venus, A 87, 110, 409-410
Villain's Broken Heart, A 98, 418
Vitagraph (see American Vitagraph Company) x-xi, 57, 90, 98, 121, 198, 219, 222, 229, 253, 282
Vitaphone 256
Vogue Motion Picture Company 90-91
Von Ronkel, Samuel 244
Von Stroheim, Erich 166, **167**, 168, **169**, 196, 264
Voss, Franklin H. "Fatty" 3, **10**, 35, **47**, 48, 55, **56**, 57
Wade, Thomas 176
Wagner, Blake 150
Wagner, Gaylord 388
Wait a Bit 344, 482
Waiter's Wasted Life, A 110
Waiting at the Church 133
Wake of the Red Witch 220
Wallach, Max 386
Wampas Baby Stars 279
Wanamaker, Marc xvi, 297, 401
Ward, Hap **71**
Warner Bros. 230, 336, 356, 397
Warran, Edna 332
Warwick, Virginia 87, 104
Washington, Blue xiii
Washington, Edgar (see Washington, Blue)
Washington, Hannah "Oatmeal" 354, 366, **367-368**, 370
Watch the Birdie **365**, **369**, 372, 511
Watson, Coy, Jr. 274
Watson, William H. 88, 102-103, **104**, 109, 127, 245-247
Wayne, John 220
Weber, William 333
Wedding Pumps 182, 441

Week Off, A 147, 430
Weiss Brothers-Artclass Pictures **84**, 91, 137, 219, 235, 337, 360-361
Weiss, Adolph 81, **83**
Weiss, Louis 81, **83**
Weiss, Max 81, **83**
Welch, Bessie (see Welsh, Betty) 404
Welch, Marjorie 216
Wells, Mai **40**
Welsh, Bessie (see Welsh, Betty) 404
Welsh, Betty **208**, **225**, 354, **363**, 404
Wenzel, Arthur S. 160
West Brothers 219
West, Billy 137, 229
West, Ford 216
Westheimer, Hortense 170, 394
Wharton, Theodore 271
What An Excuse 318, 494
What Ever Happened to Baby Peggy? (Diana Serra Cary author) 126, 138
What Happened to Jane? Series 284, 287-288, 300, 316, 321, 323
What! No Spinach? 359
What'll You Have? **317**, 318, 488
What's the Matter with Father? 51, 55, 58, 406
What's Your Hurry? 318, 489
Where is My Husband? 40
Where is My Wife? 42
White Peacock, The 355
White Trail, The 356
White Wing Monkey, A **72**, 73, 521
White, Gordon 257
White, Jack xix, **10**, 103, 111, 128, 137, 150, 180, 196, 200, 219, 228, 235, 337, 344
Whose Baby? **220**
Whose Wife 363, 505
Why Dogs Leave Home **182**, 447
Wilcox, Silas **340**
Wild Lions and Loose Bandits 69, 520
Wild Night, A 70, 520
Wild Women and Tame Lions 63
Wiley, James Alexander 235
Wiley, Roberta Prestine (see Wanda Wiley) 235
Wiley, Wanda xvi, xx, 224, 226-227, **235-238**, 239, 241, 244-245, **246-247**, 248, **249-251**, 252, **256**, 264-265, **266-267**, 268-269, 284, **287-291**, **319-320**, 321, 398, 404
William Tell 243
Williams, Albert "Buddy" **188**, 189
Williams, George (see Monberg, George "Zip") 90
Williams, Zack 177
Williamson, Alice Muriel 28
Williamson, Ethlyne Clair (see Clair, Ethlyne) 309
Winnie Winkle Comedies 219
Winninger, Charles 3
Womanless Wedding, The 224
Women Chasers 363, 505
Won By a Nose 107, **108**, 419
Wonder, Tommy 187
Wood, Esther 66, 111
Woodmansee, H.A. 363
Woods, Marie 343
World of Laughter (Kalton Lahue author) xxi
Worshippers of the Cuckoo Clock, The 50, 405
Worth, Lillian 82, 264
Wray, Fay 200

Wright, T. Page 288, 324, 333
Yearning for Love **288-289**, 479
Yellow Kid (Richard Felton Outcault comic strip) 272
Yes, We Have No Bananas (song) 208
Yes, We Have No Pajamas 208
"You Know Me Al" (Ring Lardner stories) 196, 374, 383, 389
You're Next 228, 455
Young Tenderfoot, The 202, 232, 456
Young, Joe 339, **352**, 354, **359**, 361, **362-363**, 364, 404
Young, Katherine 274
Young, Robert 361